DRUGS, SOCIETY, AND BEHAVIOR 96/97

Eleventh Edition

Editor

Hugh T. Wilson
California State University, Sacramento

Hugh Wilson received his Bachelor of Arts Degree from California State University, Sacramento, and his Master of Arts degree in Justice Administration and his Doctorate in Public Administration from Golden Gate University in San Francisco. Dr. Wilson is currently a professor of criminal justice at California State University, Sacramento. He has taught drug abuse recognition, enforcement, and policy to police officers and students of criminal justice for more than 20 years.

Annual Editions
A Library of Information from the Public Press

Cover illustration by Mike Eagle

Dushkin Publishing Group/
Brown & Benchmark Publishers
Sluice Dock, Guilford, Connecticut 06437

The Annual Editions Series

Annual Editions is a series of over 65 volumes designed to provide the reader with convenient, low-cost access to a wide range of current, carefully selected articles from some of the most important magazines, newspapers, and journals published today. Annual Editions are updated on an annual basis through a continuous monitoring of over 300 periodical sources. All Annual Editions have a number of features designed to make them particularly useful, including topic guides, annotated tables of contents, unit overviews, and indexes. For the teacher using Annual Editions in the classroom, an Instructor's Resource Guide with test questions is available for each volume.

VOLUMES AVAILABLE

Abnormal Psychology
Africa
Aging
American Foreign Policy
American Government
American History, Pre-Civil War
American History, Post-Civil War
American Public Policy
Anthropology
Archaeology
Biopsychology
Business Ethics
Child Growth and Development
China
Comparative Politics
Computers in Education
Computers in Society
Criminal Justice
Developing World
Deviant Behavior
Drugs, Society, and Behavior
Dying, Death, and Bereavement
Early Childhood Education
Economics
Educating Exceptional Children
Education
Educational Psychology
Environment
Geography
Global Issues
Health
Human Development
Human Resources
Human Sexuality

India and South Asia
International Business
Japan and the Pacific Rim
Latin America
Life Management
Macroeconomics
Management
Marketing
Marriage and Family
Mass Media
Microeconomics
Middle East and the Islamic World
Multicultural Education
Nutrition
Personal Growth and Behavior
Physical Anthropology
Psychology
Public Administration
Race and Ethnic Relations
Russia, the Eurasian Republics, and Central/Eastern Europe
Social Problems
Sociology
State and Local Government
Urban Society
Western Civilization, Pre-Reformation
Western Civilization, Post-Reformation
Western Europe
World History, Pre-Modern
World History, Modern
World Politics

Cataloging in Publication Data
Main entry under title: Annual Editions: Drugs, Society, and Behavior. 1996/97.
    1. Drugs—Periodicals. 2. Drug abuse—United States—Periodicals. 3. Alcohol—Periodicals.
4. Drunk driving—Periodicals. I. Wilson, Hugh, comp. II. Title: Drugs, Society, and Behavior.
ISBN 0-697-31591-6   362.2'92'0973'05   87-649280

Eleventh Edition

Printed in the United States of America

Printed on Recycled Paper

To the Reader

In publishing ANNUAL EDITIONS we recognize the enormous role played by the magazines, newspapers, and journals of the *public press* in providing current, first-rate educational information in a broad spectrum of interest areas. Within the articles, the best scientists, practitioners, researchers, and commentators draw issues into new perspective as accepted theories and viewpoints are called into account by new events, recent discoveries change old facts, and fresh debate breaks out over important controversies. Many of the articles resulting from this enormous editorial effort are appropriate for students, researchers, and professionals seeking accurate, current material to help bridge the gap between principles and theories and the real world. These articles, however, become more useful for study when those of lasting value are carefully *collected, organized, indexed,* and *reproduced* in a *low-cost format,* which provides easy and permanent access when the material is needed. That is the role played by ANNUAL EDITIONS. Under the direction of each volume's *Editor,* who is an expert in the subject area, and with the guidance of an *Advisory Board,* we seek each year to provide in each ANNUAL EDITION a current, well-balanced, carefully selected collection of the best of the public press for your study and enjoyment. We think you'll find this volume useful, and we hope you'll take a moment to let us know what you think.

Since there is no predictable American expression of ideology on the subject of drugs, it is difficult to define the framework by which we make decisions and develop perspectives on the use of drugs. We do appear united, however, in our lack of ambivalence toward drugs. We all can point quickly to some dimension of American life that has been changed for better or worse by drugs. When one out of three Americans has someone close to them negatively affected because of drugs, the dimension is, more often than not, for the worse. For many, life is a struggle to keep drugs accessible, while for others life is a struggle to keep them away. Our national will toward drugs is defined by a whole range of individual experience.

Subsequently, the prevailing legacies of what we refer to as the drug war, or the drug problem, will continue to evolve and transform and become more or less meaningful as do other social maladies that regularly compete for our attention. Terrorist bombings, war, crime, and an assortment of political crises intervene frequently, sometimes to alter and sometimes to lessen our concern for drug-related problems. Infrequently, however, do they lessen the significance that drugs play in affecting how we live.

The articles contained in *Annual Editions: Drugs, Society, and Behavior 96/97* are a collection of facts, issues, and perspectives designed to provide the reader a framework for examining current drug-related issues, something to think about and something to think with. It is a unique collection of materials of interest to the casual as well as the serious student of drug-related social phenomena.

Unit 1 addresses the historical significance that drugs have played in early as well as contemporary American history. It emphasizes the often overlooked reality that drugs, legal and illegal, have remained a pervasive dimension of past as well as present American history. Unit 2 examines the physiological and psychological basis for what we define as use, abuse, dependence, and addiction. It also provides an overview of how drugs produce such severe physiological and psychological consequences. Unit 3 examines the major drugs of use and abuse along with issues relative to understanding the individual impacts of these drugs on society. It also illustrates the necessity to perceive the differences and similarities produced by the use of legal and illegal drugs. Unit 4 reviews the dynamic nature of drugs as it relates to changing patterns and trends of use. Unit 5 analyzes the linkages between the demand for drugs and crime. Implications from individual criminal behavior as well as organized, syndicated trafficking are discussed. Unit 6 focuses on the social costs of drug abuse and why the consequences overwhelm many American institutions. Unit 7 illustrates the complexity and controversy in creating and implementing drug policy. Unit 8 concludes the reading with discussions of current strategies for preventing and treating drug abuse. Can we deter people from harming themselves with drugs, and can we cure people addicted to drugs? What works and what does not?

We encourage your comments and criticisms on the articles provided and kindly ask for your review on the return postage-paid rating form at the end of the book.

Hugh T. Wilson

Hugh T. Wilson
Editor

Contents

Unit 1

Living with Drugs

Six articles in this unit examine the past and present historical evolution of drugs in the United States.

Unit 2

Understanding How Drugs Work—Use, Dependence, and Addiction

Six articles in this section examine ways drugs act on the mind and body. The relationship of pharmacology with dependence and addiction is described.

The concepts in bold italics are developed in the article. For further expansion please refer to the Topic Guide, the Index, and the Glossary.

Unit 3

The Major Drugs of Use and Abuse

This unit addresses some major drugs of use and abuse. Cocaine, heroin, marijuana, alcohol and tobacco, and methamphetamine are discussed.

The concepts in bold italics are developed in the article. For further expansion please refer to the Topic Guide, the Index, and the Glossary.

Unit 4

Other Trends and Patterns in Drug Use

The eight articles in this unit discuss some developing patterns of drug use along with their subsequent implications for society.

Unit 5

Drugs and Crime

Seven articles review the numbing social malady caused by criminal behavior that is created, sustained, and perpetuated by the use of drugs.

The concepts in bold italics are developed in the article. For further expansion please refer to the Topic Guide, the Index, and the Glossary.

Unit 6

Measuring the Social Costs of Drugs

Ten articles speak to the diverse way in which the impacts of drugs affect and overwhelm numerous public and private American institutions.

The concepts in bold italics are developed in the article. For further expansion please refer to the Topic Guide, the Index, and the Glossary.

Unit 7

Creating and Sustaining Effective Drug Control Policy

The ten essays in this unit illustrate the complexity of creating effective drug-related policy.

Unit 8

Prevention and Treatment

Addressing some tough questions concerning previously
accepted ideas about drug treatment, the seven unit
articles review effectiveness, financial costs, education,
and controversial new treatments.

The concepts in bold italics are developed in the article. For further expansion please refer to the Topic Guide, the Index, and the Glossary.

Topic Guide

This topic guide suggests how the selections in this book relate to topics of traditional concern to students and professionals involved with the study of drugs, society, and behavior. It is useful for locating articles that relate to each other for reading and research. The guide is arranged alphabetically according to topic. Articles may, of course, treat topics that do not appear in the topic guide. In turn, entries in the topic guide do not necessarily constitute a comprehensive listing of all the contents of each selection.

TOPIC AREA	TREATED IN	TOPIC AREA	TREATED IN
Addiction	1. Opium, Cocaine, and Marijuana 4. Global Tobacco Epidemic 7. Is Nicotine Addictive? 8. Addictive Drugs 11. Hooked/Not Hooked 12. Back from the Edge 15. Kicking Butts 16. Heroin, Be the Death of Me 17. Kiss of Meth 26. And Still the Drugs Sit There 31. Drugs, Alcohol and Violence 42. Crack Investigation 49. For Addicts, Alternatives to Prison 50. Teenage Smoking 54. Is Drug Treatment Effective? 55. Back from the Drink 56. 'Harm Reduction' Approach 57. Cost of Living Clean 58. New Drug Approval Approach	**Cocaine**	1. Opium, Cocaine, and Marijuana 3. Worldwide Drug Scourge 11. Hooked/Not Hooked 19. Overview of Key Findings 26. And Still the Drugs Sit There 27. Killer Cowboys 28. Cocaine Money Market 29. Reducing Crime 31. Drugs, Alcohol, and Violence 32. Homicide in New York City 33. Why Good Cops Go Bad 40. It's Drugs, Alcohol and Tobacco, Stupid! 41. Crackpot Ideas 42. Crack Investigation 43. Drug Sentencing Frenzy 45. Why Drugs Keep Flowing
Advertising	4. Global Tobacco Epidemic 13. Selling Pot 15. Kicking Butts 24. One Pill Makes You Larger 36. Alcohol and Kids 37. Should Cigarettes Be Outlawed? 39. Pushing Drugs to Doctors	**Drug Economy**	3. Worldwide Drug Scourge 4. Global Tobacco Epidemic 15. Kicking Butts 17. Kiss of Meth 24. One Pill Makes You Larger 25. Mail-Order Muscles 27. Killer Cowboys 28. Cocaine Money Market 29. Reducing Crime 30. Colombia's Drugs Business 33. Why Good Cops Go Bad 37. Should Cigarettes Be Outlawed? 39. Pushing Drugs to Doctors 45. Why Drugs Keep Flowing 53. Golden Triangle's New King
Alcoholism	2. Alcohol in America 11. Hooked/Not Hooked 14. Alcohol in Perspective 21. Are America's College Students Majoring in Booze? 34. Dealing with Demons 36. Alcohol and Kids 55. Back from the Drink 59. Alcohol, Drug Addiction Recovery Rate	**Epidemiology**	1. Opium, Cocaine, and Marijuana 2. Alcohol in America 4. Global Tobacco Epidemic 8. Addictive Drugs 15. Kicking Butts 16. Heroin, Be the Death of Me 17. Kiss of Meth 19. Overview of Key Findings 20. Pot Surges Back 21. Are America's College Students Majoring in Booze? 22. New View from On High 23. Choose Your Poison 25. Mail-Order Muscles 26. And Still the Drugs Sit There 27. Killer Cowboys 31. Drugs, Alcohol, and Violence 32. Homicide in New York City 36. Alcohol and Kids 40. It's Drugs, Alcohol and Tobacco, Stupid! 41. Crackpot Ideas 50. Teenage Smoking 57. Cost of Living Clean
Amphetamine	11. Hooked/Not Hooked 17. Kiss of Meth 18. Wired in California 19. Overview of Key Findings		
Children/Teenagers	13. Selling Pot 17. Kiss of Meth 18. Wired in California 19. Overview of Key Findings 20. Pot Surges Back 21. Are America's College Students Majoring in Booze? 25. Mail-Order Muscles 27. Killer Cowboys 32. Homicide in New York City 34. Dealing with Demons 36. Alcohol and Kids 40. It's Drugs, Alcohol and Tobacco, Stupid! 41. Crackpot Ideas 43. Drug Sentencing Frenzy 50. Teenage Smoking 60. D.A.R.E. Bedeviled		

TOPIC AREA	TREATED IN	TOPIC AREA	TREATED IN
Etiology	4. Global Tobacco Epidemic 7. Is Nicotine Addictive? 8. Addictive Drugs 9. Brain by Design 11. Hooked/Not Hooked 12. Back from the Edge 15. Kicking Butts 16. Heroin, Be the Death of Me 42. Crack Investigation	**Marijuana**	1. Opium, Cocaine, and Marijuana 7. Is Nicotine Addictive? 9. Brain by Design 11. Hooked/Not Hooked 19. Overview of Key Findings 20. Pot Surges Back 44. Marijuana and the Law
Heroin	1. Opium, Cocaine, and Marijuana 3. Worldwide Drug Scourge 7. Is Nicotine Addictive? 11. Hooked/Not Hooked 12. Back from the Edge 16. Heroin, Be the Death of Me 19. Overview of Key Findings 26. And Still the Drugs Sit There 45. Why Drugs Keep Flowing 47. Toward a Policy on Drugs 49. For Addicts, Alternatives to Prison 53. Golden Triangle's New King 54. Is Drug Abuse Treatment Effective? 58. New Drug Approval Approach	**Nicotine**	4. Global Tobacco Epidemic 7. Is Nicotine Addictive? 8. Addictive Drugs 11. Hooked/Not Hooked 15. Kicking Butts 19. Overview of Key Findings 37. Should Cigarettes Be Outlawed? 50. Teenage Smoking
		Race, and Drug Use	1. Opium, Cocaine, and Marijuana 17. Kiss of Meth 18. Wired in California 19. Overview of Key Findings 27. Killer Cowboys 32. Homicide in New York City 41. Crackpot Ideas 43. Drug Sentencing Frenzy
Law Enforcement	1. Opium, Cocaine, and Marijuana 2. Alcohol in America 3. Worldwide Drug Scourge 17. Kiss of Meth 27. Killer Cowboys 28. Cocaine Money Market 29. Reducing Crime 30. Colombia's Drugs Business 31. Drugs, Alcohol, and Violence 32. Homicide in New York City 33. Why Good Cops Go Bad 35. Society of Suspects 37. Should Cigarettes Be Outlawed? 38. Most Complex Problem 43. Drug Sentencing Frenzy 44. Marijuana and the Law 45. Why Drugs Keep Flowing 47. Toward a Policy on Drugs 48. Military's Counterdrug Policy 53. Golden Triangle's New King	**Research, Drug**	4. Global Tobacco Epidemic 6. Historic Milestones 8. Addictive Drugs 11. Hooked/Not Hooked 15. Kicking Butts 19. Overview of Key Findings 24. One Pill Makes You Larger 42. Crack Investigation 45. Why Drugs Keep Flowing 54. Is Drug Abuse Treatment Effective? 55. Back from the Drink 58. New Drug Approval Approach 59. Alcohol, Drug Addiction Recovery Rate
Legalization	37. Should Cigarettes Be Outlawed? 45. Why Drugs Keep Flowing 47. Toward a Policy on Drugs 52. Will Legalizing Drugs Benefit Public Health? 56. 'Harm Reduction' Approach	**Treatment, Drug**	7. Is Nicotine Addictive? 8. Addictive Drugs 11. Hook/Not Hooked 12. Back from the Edge 15. Kicking Butts 24. One Pill Makes You Larger 31. Drugs, Alcohol, and Violence 34. Dealing with Demons 41. Crackpot Ideas 45. Why Drugs Keep Flowing 49. For Addicts, Alternatives to Prison 54. Is Drug Abuse Treatment Effective? 55. Back from the Drink 56. 'Harm Reduction' Approach 57. Cost of Living Clean 58. New Drug Approval Approach 59. Alcohol, Drug Addiction Recovery Rate

Living with Drugs

When attempting to define the American drug experience, one must examine the past as well as the present. Too often drug use and its associated phenomena are viewed through a contemporary looking glass relative to our personal views, biases, and perspectives. And although today's drug scene is definitely a product of the counterculture of the 1960s and 1970s, the crack trade of the 1980s, and the sophisticated, criminally syndicated, technologically efficient influence of the late 1980s and early 1990s, it is also a product of the past. This past and the lessons it has generated, although largely unknown, forgotten or ignored, provide one important perspective from which to assess our current status and guide our future in terms of optimizing our efforts to manage the benefits and control the harm from drugs.

The American drug experience is often defined in terms of a million individual realities, all meaningful and all different. In fact, these realities often originated as pieces of our national, cultural, racial, religious, and personal past that combine to influence significantly present-day drug-related phenomena.

The contemporary American drug experience is the product of centuries of human attempts to alter or sustain consciousness through the use of mind-altering drugs. Early American history is replete with accounts of the exorbitant use of alcohol, opium, morphine, and cocaine.

Heroin and cocaine "epidemics" of the twentieth century are analogous to opiate and cocaine epidemics of the eighteenth and nineteenth centuries. A review of early American history clearly suggests the precedents by which we continue to pursue stimulant and depressant drugs such as cocaine and heroin. In terms of social costs produced by our historical use of legal and illegal drugs, it is no wonder some describe us as a nation of addicts. Seldom has American history expressed a collective capacity to use an addictive drug responsibly. On what grounds do we justify 10 percent of the American population as alcoholic and over 1,000 tobacco-related deaths each day? On one hand we recoil from the consequences of drug use while on the other we profess our helplessness to change.

Drug use and its concomitant influences are pervasive. We will all be affected and forced to confront a personally, professionally, or socially troublesome or even tragic event instigated by someone's use of drugs. As you read through the remaining pages of this book, the pervasive nature of drug-related influence will become more apparent. Unfortunately, one of the most salient observations one may make is that drug use in our society is a topic about which many Americans have too little knowledge. History suggests that we have continually struggled to respond and react to the influence of drug use in our society. The lessons of our drug legacy are harsh, be the subject public health or public policy. Turning an uninformed mind toward a social condition of such importance will only further our inability to protect ourselves from drug-related ills.

The articles and graphics contained in unit 1 illustrate the multitude of issues influenced by the historical evolution of drug use in America. The historical development of drug-related phenomena is reflected within the character of all issues and controversies addressed by this book. Drug-related events of yesterday provide important meaning for understanding and addressing those of today and tomorrow. Creating public policy and controlling crime surface immediately as examples with long-standing historical influences. As you read this and other literature, the dynamics of drug-related historical linkages will become apparent.

Looking Ahead: Challenge Questions

What are the implications for public health resulting from a historical lack of drug-related educational emphasis, and what will history reflect 20 years from now?

Is there a historical pattern of educational shortcomings that we should change?

Why is history important when attempting to understand contemporary drug-related events?

What historical trends are expressed by the use of legal drugs versus illegal drugs?

What are the historical drug-related landmarks of drug prohibition and control?

How is the evolution of drug-related influence on American society like and unlike that occurring in other countries, and what can we learn from these comparisons?

AMERICAN
CANCER
SOCIETY

Opium, Cocaine and Marijuana in American History

Over the past 200 years, Americans have twice accepted and then vehemently rejected drugs. Understanding these dramatic historical swings provides perspective on our current reaction to drug use

David F. Musto

DAVID F. MUSTO is professor of psychiatry at the Child Study Center and professor of the history of medicine at Yale University. He earned his medical degree at the University of Washington and received his master's in the history of science and medicine from Yale. Musto began studying the history of drug and alcohol use in the U.S. when he worked at the National Institute of Mental Health in the 1960s. He has served as a consultant for several national organizations, including the Presidential Commission on the HIV epidemic. From 1981 until 1990, Musto was a member of the Smithsonian Institution's National Council.

Dramatic shifts in attitude have characterized America's relation to drugs. During the 19th century, certain mood-altering substances, such as opiates and cocaine, were often regarded as compounds helpful in everyday life. Gradually this perception of drugs changed. By the early 1900s, and until the 1940s, the country viewed these and some other psychoactive drugs as dangerous, addictive compounds that needed to be severely controlled. Today, after a resurgence of a tolerant attitude toward drugs during the 1960s and 1970s, we find ourselves, again, in a period of drug intolerance.

America's recurrent enthusiasm for recreational drugs and subsequent campaigns for abstinence present a problem to policymakers and to the public. Since the peaks of these episodes are about a lifetime apart, citizens rarely have an accurate or even a vivid recollection of the last wave of cocaine or opiate use.

Phases of intolerance have been fueled by such fear and anger that the record of times favorable toward drug taking has been either erased from public memory or so distorted that it becomes useless as a point of reference for policy formation. During each attack on drug taking, total denigration of the preceding, contrary mood has seemed necessary for public welfare. Although such vigorous rejection may have value in further reducing demand, the long-term effect is to destroy a realistic perception of the past and of the conflicting attitudes toward mood-altering substances that have characterized our national history.

The absence of knowledge concerning our earlier and formative encounters with drugs unnecessarily impedes the already difficult task of establishing a workable and sustainable drug policy. An examination of the period of drug use that peaked around 1900 and the decline that followed it may enable us to approach the current drug problem with more confidence and reduce the likelihood that we will repeat past errors.

Until the 19th century, drugs had been used for millennia in their natural form. Cocaine and morphine, for example, were available only in coca leaves or poppy plants that were chewed, dissolved in alcoholic beverages or taken in some way that diluted the impact of the active agent. The ad-

vent of organic chemistry in the 1800s changed the available forms of these drugs. Morphine was isolated in the first decade and cocaine by 1860; in 1874 diacetylmorphine was synthesized from morphine (although it became better known as heroin when the Bayer Company introduced it in 1898).

By mid-century the hypodermic syringe was perfected, and by 1870 it had become a familiar instrument to American physicians and patients [see "The Origins of Hypodermic Medication," by Norman Howard-Jones; SCIENTIFIC AMERICAN, January 1971]. At the same time, the astounding growth of the pharmaceutical industry intensified the ramifications of these accomplishments. As the century wore on, manufacturers grew increasingly adept at exploiting a marketable innovation and moving it into mass production, as well as advertising and distributing it throughout the world.

During this time, because of a peculiarity of the U.S. Constitution, the powerful new forms of opium and cocaine were more readily available in America than in most nations. Under the Constitution, individual states assumed responsibility for health issues, such as regulation of medical practice and the availability of pharmacological products. In fact, America had as many laws regarding health professions as it had states. For much of the 19th century, many states chose to have no controls at all; their legislatures reacted to the claims of contradictory health care philosophies by allowing free enterprise for all practitioners. The federal government limited its concern to communicable diseases and the provision of health care to the merchant marine and to government dependents.

Nations with a less restricted central government, such as Britain and Prussia, had a single, preeminent pharmacy law that controlled availability of dangerous drugs. In those countries, physicians had their right to practice similarly granted by a central authority. Therefore, when we consider consumption of opium, opiates, coca and cocaine in 19th-century America, we are looking at an era of wide availability and unrestrained advertising. The initial enthusiasm for the purified substances was only slightly affected by any substantial doubts or fear about safety, long-term health injuries or psychological dependence.

History encouraged such attitudes. Crude opium, alone or dissolved in some liquid such as alcohol, was brought by European explorers and settlers to North America. Colonists regarded opium as a familiar resource for pain relief. Benjamin Franklin regularly took laudanum—opium in alcohol extract—to alleviate the pain of kidney stones during the last few years of his life. The poet Samuel Taylor Coleridge, while a student at Cambridge in 1791, began using laudanum for pain and developed a lifelong addiction to the drug. Opium use in those early decades constituted an "experiment in nature" that has been largely forgotten, even repressed, as a result of the extremely negative reaction that followed.

Americans had recognized, however, the potential danger of continually using opium long before the availability of morphine and the hypodermic's popularity. The American Dispensatory of 1818 noted that the habitual use of opium could lead to "tremors, paralysis, stupidity and general emaciation." Balancing this danger, the text proclaimed the extraordinary value of opium in a multitude of ailments ranging from cholera to asthma. (Considering the treatments then in vogue—blistering, vomiting and bleeding—we can understand why opium was as cherished by patients as by their physicians.)

Opium's rise and fall can be tracked through U.S. import-consumption statistics compiled while importation of the drug and its derivative, morphine, was unrestricted and carried moderate tariffs. The per capita consumption of crude opium rose gradually during the 1800s, reaching a peak in the last decade of the century. It then declined, but after 1915 the data no longer reflect trends in drug use, because that year new federal laws severely restricted legal imports. In contrast, per capita consumption of smoking opium rose until a 1909 act outlawed its importation.

Americans had quickly associated smoking opium with Chinese immigrants who arrived after the Civil War to work on railroad construction. This association was one of the earliest examples of a powerful theme in the American perception of drugs: linkage between a drug and a feared or rejected group within society. Cocaine would be similarly linked with blacks and marijuana with Mexicans in the first third of the 20th century. The association of a drug with a racial group or a political cause, however, is not unique to America. In the 19th century, for instance, the Chinese came to regard opium as a tool and symbol of Western domination. That perception helped to fuel a vigorous antiopium campaign in China early in the 20th century.

During the 1800s, increasing numbers of people fell under the influence of opiates—substances that demanded regular consumption or the penalty of withdrawal, a painful but rarely life-threatening experience. Whatever the cause—overprescribing by physicians, over-the-counter medicines, self-indulgence or "weak will"—opium addiction brought shame. As consumption increased, so did the frequency of addiction.

1. Opium, Cocaine, and Marijuana

At first, neither physicians nor their patients thought that the introduction of the hypodermic syringe or pure morphine contributed to the danger of addiction. On the contrary, because pain could be controlled with less morphine when injected, the presumption was made that the procedure was less likely to foster addiction.

Late in the century some states and localities enacted laws limiting morphine to a physician's prescription, and some laws even forbade refilling these prescriptions. But the absence of any federal control over interstate commerce in habit-forming drugs, of uniformity among the state laws and of effective enforcement meant that the rising tide of legislation directed at opiates—and later cocaine—was more a reflection of changing public attitude toward these drugs than an effective reduction of supplies to users. Indeed, the decline noted after the mid-1890s was probably related mostly to the public's growing fear of addiction and of the casual social use of habit-forming substances rather than to any successful campaign to reduce supplies.

At the same time, health professionals were developing more specific treatments for painful diseases, finding less dangerous analgesics (such as aspirin) and beginning to appreciate the addictive power of the hypodermic syringe. By now the public had learned to fear the careless, and possibly addicted, physician. In *A Long Day's Journey into Night*, Eugene O'Neill dramatized the

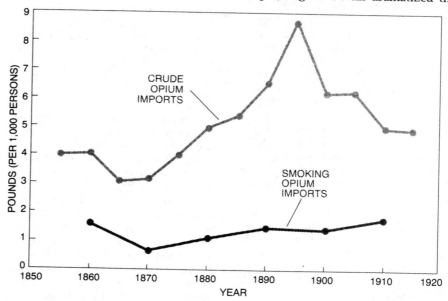

OPIATE CONSUMPTION was documented by the Treasury and the Commerce Departments, starting in the mid-19th century. The importation of smoking opium became illegal in 1909, and crude opium and its derivatives were severely restricted in 1915. After 1915, the data reflected medicinal use.

painful and shameful impact of his mother's physician-induced addiction.

In a spirit not unlike that of our times, Americans in the last decade of the 19th century grew increasingly concerned about the environment, adulterated foods, destruction of the forests and the widespread use of mood-altering drugs. The concern embraced alcohol as well. The Anti-Saloon League, founded in 1893, led a temperance movement toward prohibition, which later was achieved in 1919 and became law in January 1920.

After overcoming years of resistance by over-the-counter, or patent, medicine manufacturers, the federal government enacted the Pure Food and Drug Act in 1906. This act did not prevent sales of addictive drugs like opiates and cocaine, but it did require accurate labeling of contents for all patent remedies sold in interstate commerce. Still, no national restriction existed on the availability of opiates or cocaine. The solution to this problem would emerge from growing concern, legal ingenuity and the unexpected involvement of the federal government with the international trade in narcotics.

Responsibility for the Philippines in 1898 added an international dimension to the growing domestic alarm about drug abuse. It also revealed that Congress, if given the opportunity, would prohibit nonmedicinal uses of opium among its new dependents. Civil Governor William Howard Taft proposed reinstituting an opium monopoly—through which the previous Spanish colonial government had obtained revenue from sales to opium merchants—and using those profits to help pay for a massive public education campaign. President Theodore Roosevelt vetoed this plan, and in 1905 Congress mandated an absolute prohibition of opium for any purpose other than medicinal use.

To deal efficiently with the antidrug policy established for the Philippines, a committee from the Islands visited various territories in the area to see how others dealt with the opium problem. The benefit of controlling narcotics internationally became apparent.

In early 1906 China had instituted a campaign against opium, especially smoking opium, in an attempt to modernize and to make the Empire better

able to cope with continued Western encroachments on its sovereignty. At about the same time, Chinese anger at maltreatment of their nationals in the U.S. seethed into a voluntary boycott of American goods. Partly to appease the Chinese by aiding their antiopium efforts and partly to deal with uncontrollable smuggling within the Philippine Archipelago, the U.S. convened a meeting of regional powers. In this way, the U.S. launched a campaign for worldwide narcotics traffic control that would extend through the years in an unbroken diplomatic sequence from the League of Nations to the present efforts of the United Nations.

The International Opium Commission, a gathering of 13 nations, met in Shanghai in February 1909. The Protestant Episcopal bishop of the Philippines, Charles Henry Brent, who had been instrumental in organizing the meeting, was chosen to preside. Resolutions noting problems with opium and opiates were adopted, but they did not constitute a treaty, and no decisions bound the nations attending the commission. In diplomatic parlance, what was needed now was a conference not a commission. The U.S. began to pursue this goal with determination.

The antinarcotics campaign in America had several motivations. Appeasement of China was certainly one factor for officials of the State Department. The department's opium commissioner, Hamilton Wright, thought the whole matter could be "used as oil to smooth the troubled water of our aggressive commercial policy there." Another reason was the belief, strongly held by the federal government today, that controlling crops and traffic in producing countries could most efficiently stop U.S. nonmedical consumption of drugs.

To restrict opium and coca production required worldwide agreement and, thus, an international conference. After intense diplomatic activity, one was convened in the Hague in December 1911. Brent again presided, and on January 23, 1912, the 12 nations represented signed a convention. Provision was made for the other countries to comply before the treaty was brought into force. After all, no producing or manufacturing nation wanted to leave the market open to nonratifying nations.

The convention required each country to enact domestic legislation controlling narcotics trade. The goal

was a world in which narcotics were restricted to medicinal use. Both the producing and consuming nations would have control over their boundaries.

After his return from Shanghai, Wright labored to craft a comprehensive federal antinarcotics law. In his path loomed the problem of states' rights. The health professions were considered a major cause of patient addiction. Yet how could federal law interfere with the prescribing practices of physicians or require that pharmacists keep records? Wright settled on the federal government's power to tax; the result, after prolonged bargaining with pharmaceutical, import, export and medical interests, was the Harrison Act of December 1914.

Representative Francis Burton Harrison's association with the act was an accidental one, the consequence of his introduction of the administration's bill. If the chief proponent and negotiator were to be given eponymic credit, it should have been called the Wright Act. It could even have been called a second Mann Act, after Representative James Mann, who saw the bill through to passage in the House of Representatives, for by that time Harrison had become governor-general of the Philippines.

The act required a strict accounting of opium and coca and their derivatives from entry into the U.S. to dispensing to a patient. To accomplish this control, a small tax had to be paid at each transfer, and permits had to be obtained by applying to the Treasury Department. Only the patient paid no tax, needed no permit and, in fact, was not allowed to obtain one.

Initially Wright and the Department of Justice argued that the Harrison Act forbade indefinite maintenance of addiction unless there was a specific medical reason such as cancer or tuberculosis. This interpretation was rejected in 1916 by the Supreme Court—even though the Justice Department argued that the Harrison Act was the domestic implementation of the Hague Opium Convention and therefore took precedence over states' rights. Maintenance was to be allowed.

That decision was short-lived. In 1919 the Supreme Court, led by Oliver Wendell Holmes and Louis Brandeis, changed its mind by a 5-4 vote. The court declared that indefinite maintenance for "mere addiction" was outside legitimate medical practice and that, consequently, prohibiting it did not constitute interference with a state's right to regulate physicians. Second, because the person receiving the drugs for maintenance was not a bona fide patient but just a recipient of drugs, the transfer of narcotics defrauded the government of taxes required under the Harrison Act.

During the 1920s and 1930s, the opiate problem, chiefly morphine and heroin, declined in the U.S., until much of the problem was confined to the periphery of society and the outcasts of urban areas. There were exceptions: some health professionals and a few others of middle class or higher status continued to take opiates.

America's international efforts continued. After World War I, the British and U.S. governments proposed adding the Hague Convention to the Versailles Treaty. As a result, ratifying the peace treaty meant ratifying the Hague Convention and enacting a domestic law controlling narcotics. This incorporation led to the British Dangerous Drugs Act of 1920, an act often misattributed to a raging heroin epidemic in Britain. In the 1940s some Americans argued that the British system provided heroin to addicts and, by not relying on law enforcement, had almost eradicated the opiate problem. In fact, Britain had no problem to begin with. This argument serves as an interesting example of how the desperate need to solve the drug problem in the U.S. tends to create misperceptions of a foreign drug situation.

The story of cocaine use in America is somewhat shorter than that of opium, but it follows a similar plot. In 1884 purified cocaine became commercially available in the U.S. At first the wholesale cost was very high—$5 to $10 a gram—but it soon fell to 25 cents a gram and remained there until the price inflation of World War I. Problems with cocaine were evident almost from the **beginning, but popular opinion and the voices of leading medical experts depicted cocaine as a remarkable, harmless stimulant.**

William A. Hammond, one of America's most prominent neurologists, extolled cocaine in print and lectures. By 1887 Hammond was assuring audiences that cocaine was no more habit-forming than coffee or tea. He also told them of the "cocaine wine" he had perfected with the help of a New York druggist: two grains of cocaine to a pint of wine. Hammond claimed that this tonic was far more effective than the popular French coca wine, probably a reference to Vin Mariani, which he complained had only half a grain of cocaine to the pint.

Coca-Cola was also introduced in 1886 as a drink offering the advantages of coca but lacking the danger of alcohol. It amounted to a temperance coca beverage. The cocaine was removed in 1900, a year before the city of Atlanta, Ga., passed an ordinance (and a state statute the following year) prohibiting provision of any cocaine to a consumer without a prescription.

Cocaine is one of the most powerful of the central nervous system euphoriants. This fact underlay cocaine's quickly growing consumption and the ineffectiveness of the early warnings. How could anything that made users so confident and happy be bad? Within a year of cocaine's introduction, the Parke-Davis Company provided coca and cocaine in 15 forms, including coca cigarettes, cocaine for injection and cocaine for sniffing. Parke-Davis and at least one other company also offered consumers a handy cocaine kit. (The Parke-Davis kit contained a hypodermic syringe.) The firm proudly supplied a drug that, it announced, "can supply the place of food, make the coward brave, the silent eloquent and . . . render the sufferer insensitive to pain."

Cocaine spread rapidly throughout the nation. In September 1886 a physician in Puyallup, Washington Territory, reported an adverse reaction to cocaine during an operation. Eventually reports of overdoses and idiosyncratic reactions shifted to accounts of the social and behavioral effects of long-term cocaine use. The ease with which experimenters became regular users and the increasing instances of cocaine being linked with violence and paranoia gradually took hold in popular and medical thought.

In 1907 an attempt was made in New York State to shift the responsibility for cocaine's availability from the open market to medical control. Assemblyman Alfred E. Smith, later the governor of New York and in 1928 the Democratic party's presidential candidate, sponsored such a bill. The cost of cocaine on New York City streets, as revealed by newspaper and police accounts after the law's enactment, was typically 25 cents a packet, or "deck."

Although 25 cents may seem cheap, it was actually slightly higher than the average industrial wage at that time, which was about 20 cents an hour. Packets, commonly glycine envelopes, usually contained one to two grains (65 to 130 milligrams), or about a tenth of a gram. The going rate was roughly 10 times that of the wholesale price, a ratio not unlike recent cocaine street prices, although in the past few years the street price has actually been lower in real value than what it was in 1910.

Several similar reports from the years before the Harrison Act of 1914 suggest that both the profit margin and the street price of cocaine were unaffected by the legal availability of cocaine from a physician. Perhaps the formality of medical consultation and the growing antagonism among physicians and the public toward cocaine helped to sustain the illicit market.

In 1910 William Howard Taft, then president of the U.S., sent to Congress a report that cocaine posed the most serious drug problem America had ever faced. Four years later President Woodrow Wilson signed into law the Harrison Act, which, in addition to its opiate provisions, permitted the sale of cocaine only through prescriptions. It also forbade any trace of cocaine in patent remedies, the most severe restriction on any habit-forming drug to that date. (Opiates, including heroin, could still be present in small amounts in nonprescription remedies, such as cough medicines.)

Although the press continued to reveal Hollywood scandals and underworld cocaine practices during the 1920s, cocaine use gradually declined as a societal problem. The laws probably hastened the trend, and certainly the tremendous public fear reduced demand. By 1930 the New York City Mayor's Committee on Drug Addiction was reporting that "during the last 20 years cocaine as an addiction has ceased to be a problem."

Unlike opiates and cocaine, marijuana was introduced during a period of drug intolerance. Consequently, it was not until the 1960s, 40 years after marijuana cigarettes had arrived in America, that it was widely used. The practice of smoking cannabis leaves came to the U.S. with Mexican immigrants, who had come North during the 1920s to work in agriculture, and it soon extended to white and black jazz musicians.

As the Great Depression of the 1930s settled over America, the immigrants became an unwelcome minority linked with violence and with growing and smoking marijuana. Western states pressured the federal government to control marijuana use. The first official response was to urge adoption of a uniform state antinarcotics law. Then a new approach became feasible in 1937, when the Supreme Court upheld the National Firearms Act. This act prohibited the transfer of machine guns between private citizens without purchase of a transfer tax stamp—and the government would not issue the necessary stamp. Prohibition was implemented through the taxing power of the federal government.

Within a month of the Supreme Court's decision, the Treasury Department testified before Congress for a bill to establish a marijuana transfer tax. The bill became law, and until the Comprehensive Drug Abuse Act of 1970, marijuana was legally controlled through a transfer tax for which no stamps or licenses were available to private citizens. Certainly some people were smoking marijuana in the 1930s, but not until the 1960s was its use widespread.

Around the time of the Marihuana Tax Act of 1937, the federal government released dramatic and exaggerated portrayals of marijuana's effects. Scientific publications during the 1930s also fearfully described marijuana's dangers. Even Walter Bromberg, who thought that marijuana made only a small contribution to major crimes, nevertheless reported the drug was "a primary stimulus to the impulsive life with direct expression in the motor field."

Marijuana's image shifted during the 1960s, when it was said that its use at the gigantic Woodstock gathering kept peace—as opposed to what might have happened if alcohol had been the drug of choice. In the shift to drug toleration in the late 1960s and early 1970s, investigators found it difficult to associate health problems with marijuana use. The 1930s and 1940s had marked the nadir of drug toleration in the U.S., and possibly the mood of both times affected professional perception of this controversial plant.

After the Harrison Act, the severity of federal laws concerning the sale and possession of opiates and cocaine gradually rose. As drug use declined, penalties increased until 1956, when the death penalty was introduced as an option by the federal government for anyone older than 18 providing heroin to anyone younger than 18 (apparently no one was ever executed under this statute). At the same time, mandatory minimum prison sentences were extended to 10 years.

After the youthful counterculture discovered marijuana in the 1960s, demand for the substance grew until about 1978, when the favorable attitude toward it reached a peak. In 1972 the Presidential Commission on Marihuana and Drug Abuse recommended "decriminalization" of marijuana, that is, legal possession of a small amount for personal use. In 1977 the Carter administration formally advocated legalizing marijuana in amounts up to an ounce.

The Gallup Poll on relaxation of laws against marijuana is instructive. In 1980, 53 percent of Americans favored legalization of small amounts of marijuana; by 1986 only 27 percent supported that view. At the same time, those favoring penalties for marijuana use rose from 43 to 67 percent. This reversal parallels the changes in attitude among high school students revealed by the Institute of Social Research at the University of Michigan.

The decline in favorable attitudes toward marijuana that began in the late 1970s continues. In the past few years we have seen penalties rise again against users and dealers. The recriminalization of marijuana possession by popular vote in Alaska in 1990 is one example of such a striking reversal.

In addition to stricter penalties, two other strategies, silence and exaggeration, were implemented in the 1930s to keep drug use low and prevent a recurrence of the decades-long, frustrating and fearful antidrug battle of the late 19th and early 20th centuries. Primary and secondary schools instituted educational programs against drugs. Then policies shifted amid fears that talking about cocaine or heroin to young people, who now had less exposure to drugs, would arouse their curiosity. This concern led to a decline in drug-related information given during school instruction as well as to the censorship of motion pictures.

The Motion Picture Association of America, under strong public and religious pressure, decided in 1934 to refuse a seal of approval for any film that showed narcotics. This prohibition was enforced with one exception—*To the Ends of the Earth,* a 1948 film that lauded the Federal Bureau of Narcotics—until *Man with a Golden Arm* was successfully exhibited in 1956 without a seal.

Associated with a decline in drug information was a second, apparently paradoxical strategy: exaggerating the effects of drugs. The middle ground was abandoned. In 1924 Richmond P. Hobson, a nationally prominent campaigner against drugs, declared that one ounce of heroin could addict 2,000 persons. In 1936 an article in the *American Journal of Nursing* warned that a marijuana user "will suddenly turn with murderous violence upon whomever is nearest to him. He will run amuck with knife, axe, gun, or anything else that is close at hand, and will kill or maim without any reason."

A goal of this well-meaning exaggeration was to describe drugs so repulsively that anyone reading or hearing of them would not be tempted to experiment with the substances. One contributing factor to such a publicity campaign, especially regarding marijuana, was that the Depression permitted little money for any other course of action.

Severe penalties, silence and, if silence was not possible, exaggeration became the basic strategies against drugs after the decline of their first wave of use. But the effect of these tactics was to create ignorance and false images that would present no real obstacle to a renewed enthusiasm for drugs in the 1960s. At the time, enforcing draconian and mandatory penalties would have filled to overflowing all jails and prisons with the users of marijuana alone.

Exaggeration fell in the face of the realities of drug use and led to a loss of credibility regarding any government pronouncement on drugs. The lack of information erased any awareness of the first epidemic, including the gradually obtained and hard-won public insight into the hazards of cocaine and opiates. Public memory, which would have provided some context for the antidrug laws, was a casualty of the antidrug strategies.

The earlier and present waves of drug use have much in common, but there is at least one major difference. During the first wave of drug use, antidrug laws were not enacted until the public demanded them. In contrast, today's most severe antidrug laws were on the books from the outset; this gap between law and public opinion made the controls appear ridiculous and bizarre. Our current frustration over the laws' ineffectiveness has been greater and more lengthy than before because we have lived through many years in which antidrug laws lacked substantial public support. Those laws appeared powerless to curb the rise in drug use during the 1960s and 1970s.

The first wave of drug use involved primarily opiates and cocaine. The nation's full experience with marijuana is now under way (marijuana's tax regulation in 1937 was not the result of any lengthy or broad experience with the plant). The popularity and growth in demand for opiates and cocaine in mainstream society derived from a simple factor: the effect on most people's physiology and emotions was enjoyable. Moreover, Americans have recurrently hoped that the technology of drugs would maximize their personal potential. That opiates could relax and cocaine energize seemed wonderful opportunities for fine-tuning such efforts.

Two other factors allowed a long and substantial rise in consumption during the 1800s. First, casualties accumulate gradually; not everyone taking cocaine or opiates becomes hooked on the drug. In the case of opiates, some users have become addicted for a lifetime and have still been productive.

Yet casualties have mounted as those who could not handle occasional use have succumbed to domination by drugs and by drug-seeking behavior. These addicts become not only miserable themselves but also frightening to their families and friends. Such cases are legion today in our larger cities, but the percentage of those who try a substance and acquire a dependence or get into serious legal trouble is not 100 percent. For cocaine, the estimate varies from 3 to 20 percent, or even higher, and so it is a matter of time before cocaine is recognized as a likely danger.

Early in the cycle, when social tolerance prevails, the explanation for casualties is that those who succumb to addiction are seen as having a physiological idiosyncrasy or "foolish trait." Personal disaster is thus viewed as an exception to the rule. Another factor minimizing the sense of risk is our belief in our own invulnerability—that general warnings do not include us. Such faith reigns in the years of greatest exposure to drug use, ages 15 to 25. Resistance to a drug that makes a user feel confident and exuberant takes many years to permeate a society as large and complex as the U.S.

The interesting question is not why people take drugs, but rather why they stop taking them. We perceive risk differently as we begin to reject drugs. One can perceive a hypothetical 3 percent risk from taking cocaine as an assurance of 97 percent safety, or one can react as if told that 3 percent of New York/Washington shuttle flights crash. Our exposure to drug problems at work, in our neighborhood and within our families shifts our perception, gradually shaking our sense of invulnerability.

Cocaine has caused the most dramatic change in estimating risk. From a grand image as the ideal tonic, cocaine's reputation degenerated into that of the most dangerous of drugs, linked in our minds with stereotypes of mad, violent behavior. Opiates have never fallen so far in esteem, nor were they repressed to the extent cocaine had been between 1930 and 1970.

Today we are experiencing the reverse of recent decades, when the technology of drug use promised an extension of our natural potential. Increasingly we see drug consumption as reducing what we could achieve on our own with healthy food and exercise. Our change of attitude about drugs is connected to our concern over air pollution, food adulteration and fears for the stability of the environment.

Ours is an era not unlike that early in this century, when Americans made similar efforts at self-improvement accompanied by an assault on habit-forming drugs. Americans seem to be the least likely of any people to accept the inevitability of historical cycles. Yet if we do not appreciate our history, we may again become captive to the powerful emotions that led to draconian penalties, exaggeration or silence.

1. Opium, Cocaine, and Marijuana

FURTHER READING

AMERICAN DIPLOMACY AND THE NARCOTICS TRAFFIC, 1900–1939. Arnold H. Taylor. Duke University Press, 1969.

DRUGS IN AMERICA: A SOCIAL HISTORY, 1800–1980. H. Wayne Morgan. Syracuse University Press, 1981.

DARK PARADISE: OPIATE ADDICTION IN AMERICA BEFORE 1940. David T. Courtwright. Harvard University Press, 1982.

THE AMERICAN DISEASE: ORIGINS OF NARCOTIC CONTROL. Expanded Edition. David F. Musto. Oxford University Press, 1987.

AMERICA'S FIRST COCAINE EPIDEMIC. David F. Musto in Wilson Quarterly, pages 59–65; Summer 1989.

ILLICIT PRICE OF COCAINE IN TWO ERAS: 1908–14 AND 1982–89. David F. Musto in Connecticut Medicine, Vol. 54, No. 6, pages 321–326; June 1990.

Alcohol in America

W. J. Rorabaugh

W. J. Rorabaugh is professor of history at the University of Washington in Seattle, and author of The Alcoholic Republic.

F or centuries Europeans have downed large quantities of beer, wine, and hard liquor. When Europeans began to migrate to North America in the early 1600s they brought along their hearty drinking habits. Thus Americans have been heavy users of alcohol for more than three hundred years.

English colonists in Massachusetts and Virginia imported beer, but this was expensive, and for a time they brewed their own. After 1700 the colonists drank fermented peach juice, hard apple cider, and rum, which they imported from the West Indies or distilled from West Indian molasses.

Virginians had a carefree attitude about alcohol. Drinking was an important part of the culture, and people passed around jugs or bowls of liquor at barbecues, on market days, and at elections. Candidates gave away free drinks. A stingy candidate had no chance of winning. Practically everyone drank.

Even restrained New Englanders consumed great quantities of liquor. The Puritans called alcohol the "Good Creature of God," a holy substance to be taken proudly yet cautiously. Though unopposed to the use of alcohol, New England ministers did declare public drunkenness a sin that led to poverty, crime, and violence, especially wife beating.

By 1770 Americans consumed alcohol, mostly in the form of rum and cider, routinely with every meal. Many people began the day with an "eye opener" and closed it with a nightcap. People of all ages drank, including toddlers who finished off

> *By 1770 Americans consumed alcohol routinely with every meal. Many people began the day with an "eye opener" and closed it with a nightcap.*

the heavily sugared portion at the bottom of a parent's mug of rum toddy. Each person consumed about three and a half gallons of alcohol per year. This is about double the present rate of consumption.

The American Revolution drastically changed drinking habits. When the British blockaded the seacoast and thereby cut off molasses and rum imports, Americans looked for a substitute. Scot-Irish immigrants who had settled on the western frontier provided whiskey.

After the revolution whiskey replaced rum, since the British refused to supply it and the new federal government began to tax it in the 1790s. Whiskey also thrived because it was cheap. The settlement of the corn belt in Kentucky and Ohio created a corn glut. Western farmers could make no profit shipping corn overland to eastern markets, so they distilled corn into "liquid assets." By the 1820s whiskey sold for twenty-five cents a gallon, making it cheaper than beer, wine, coffee, tea, or milk. In many places whiskey was also less

dangerous than water, which was frequently contaminated.

By 1830 consumption of alcohol, mostly in the form of whiskey, had reached more than seven gallons a year for every person over age fifteen or three times the current rate.

Liquor tended to be taken in small quantities throughout the day, often with meals. Instead of a morning coffee break, Americans stopped work at 11:00 a.m. to drink. A lot of work went undone but in this slow paced, preindustrial age this was not always a problem. A drunken stage coach driver posed little threat, since the horses knew the route and made their own way home. However, there was growing opposition to alcohol.

The earliest attacks on alcohol came during the late 1700s from Methodists and Quakers. Dr. Benjamin Rush, a prominent Philadelphia physician, led this first temperance movement. Rush believed that overuse of hard liquor was unhealthy, but that small quantities of weak mixed drinks were harmless. Most Americans ignored the doctor's warnings.

Protestant ministers shifted the attack against alcohol from the issue of health to the question of sin. Arguing that any drinking easily led to drunkenness, they demanded teetotalism, or total abstinence from alcohol. Soon churches required members to take a pledge not to drink.

By 1850 the consumption of alcohol had dropped by more than half. This decline did not mean that the average American drank only half as much. Rather, half the population had stopped drinking. Other people continued to drink as they had before the temperance movement.

As early as the 1830s temperance leaders resorted to government power to coerce the remaining drinkers to give up liquor. Temperance became prohibition, and in 1838 Massachusetts passed the first prohibition law. Ignoring beer, cider, and wine, the state legislature banned the sale of hard liquor in any quantity under fifteen gallons. Retailers dodged the law. One enterprising seller sold the right to see his blind pig for six cents. The purchaser also got a free drink. This is the origin of the term "blind pig" to describe an illegal drinking establishment. Two years later the prohibition statute was repealed.

In 1851 Neal Dow, a crusading dry Quaker who had served as mayor of Portland, Maine, persuaded his state to enact a prohibition law. Although several states copied the Maine Law, as it was called, they all found that effective enforcement was impossible and consequently rescinded the legislation.

During the Civil War northern soldiers turned from traditional hard liquor to a preferred new German light lager beer, which enjoyed great popularity after the war. This period saw the emergence of today's largest breweries, including Anheuser-Busch, Schlitz, Pabst, and Miller (originally Mueller).

In 1873-1874 women living in several small towns in Ohio started the Women's Crusade. Lacking the vote and feeling powerless, they turned to direct action. Locally prominent women invaded all-male saloons, dropped to their knees, and said loud prayers. Customers fled, but the crusading women stayed to demand that each saloon be closed. Any retailer who had the women arrested faced public outrage. Many saloons closed. These tactics failed, however, in large cities. Cincinnati saloon-keepers' wives attacked the prohibitionists.

Frances Willard then organized the Woman's Christian Temperance Union, which gained more than a million members and became the world's largest women's organization. The WCTU decided to "do everything." Willard advocated making children take the pledge, banning drinkers from jobs as school teachers, legislating prohibition, and giving women the vote.

After Willard's death in 1898, anti-liquor leadership passed to the Anti-Saloon League. This organization, which included both men and women, operated as a political pressure group. Elected officials who favored prohibition were rewarded with campaign funds and workers while those against prohibition risked defeat. After 1900 the ASL, in cooperation with the WCTU, succeeded in drying up most of the country. National prohibition, however, still looked unlikely.

There was little support in the country's large cities for national prohibition. The cities were run by corrupt political machines that used saloons owned by the brewers as the basis of their power. Prohibitionists attacked the connection between saloons and corrupt politics with only limited success.

Prohibition was finally adopted not because of women's groups, but because of World War I. German-American brewers lost their political effectiveness amid anti-German hysteria, and in 1917 prohibitionists persuaded Congress to pass a temporary war time dry law. Food was in short supply, and anti-liquor forces warned that brewing or distilling grain threatened the war effort. In this milieu the Eighteenth Amendment was proposed and took effect after three-fourths of the states ratified it in January 1920.

The amendment did have its oddities, however. It outlawed the manufacture, sale, or transportation of intoxicating liquors for beverage purposes but did **not** prohibit consumption. Congress also had to define the percentage of alcohol that was intoxicating. Many people hoped that beer and light wine might be kept legal, but the Volstead Act of 1919 banned any beverage that contained over one half of one percent alcohol.

In the 1920s enforcement proceeded in earnest, at least in some areas. In cities such as New York or San Francisco, however, prohibition was not successful. The law did reduce consumption, perhaps by half, and it did change the ways in which people drank. For example, the all-male saloon disappeared and was replaced by the speakeasy, where men and women drank together out of teacups. People also drank in hotel rooms and in private homes where arrest was unlikely.

Liquor was imported illegally, largely from Canada. Soon rum runners' boats outraced the Coast Guard's, and Canadian distillers Hiram Walker and Seagrams—still major forces in the American liquor business—profited mightily.

By the late 1920s, because of corrupt and incompetent Prohibition agents, and because of public opposition, the Eighteenth Amendment was impossible to enforce. In Chicago, where Al Capone was making an estimated $200 million a year, at least 400 policemen were "on the take." Although the "dry" Herbert Hoover called prohibition a noble experiment and defeated the "wet" Al Smith for the presidency in 1928, a sense of exasperation about prohibition was growing.

Public opinion had turned against prohibition, and in 1933 Congress passed and the states ratified the Twenty-first Amendment which ended America's dry years. Newly elected President Franklin D. Roosevelt celebrated in the White House by mixing the first of many nightly martinis.

The end of prohibition did not mean a resurgence of the saloon. Many states, especially in the South and Midwest, prohibited sales of alcohol by the drink, while other states discouraged consumption by creating state liquor stores that restricted advertising, locations, and business hours. Both the federal government and the states imposed high taxes on alcoholic products.

From the 1950s through the 1970s alcohol consumption rose steadily. The post-World War II economic boom stimulated the market, which has always correlated with wealth. The poor drank the least, the rich drank the most. Doctors and lawyers, as befitted their status, were the heartiest topers. Whites drank more than blacks. The young drank more than the old. Alcohol use peaked between ages twenty-five and thirty-five, especially for single males. The large number of baby boomers in the prime drinking age bracket in the 1960s and 1970s accounted for much of the consumption.

Drinking styles changed as well. Not only did more women drink, they drank more. Women preferred sweet drinks like ready-mixed canned cocktails, wine coolers, or white wine. Wine sales, especially of upscale, expensive wines, soared, and white wines marched past red. Hard liquor tastes shifted from American whiskey to Canadian whiskey and Scotch, and by the 1970s to vodka, gin, and white rum.

Imported beers, often darker and more flavorful than American-style lager, gained a market, and regional brewers collapsed under pressure from a half dozen nationally advertised giants. Anheuser-Busch became the industry leader by its early decision to sponsor sporting events on television. Shrewd advertising techniques created a huge market for light beers that appealed to the calorie-conscious.

During the past two decades teenage drinking has become a major issue. In the 1970s, many states reduced the legal drinking age to eighteen, and in some states liquor-related teen auto accidents then grew rapidly. The age of taking a first drink dropped into the early teens. More alarming was evidence of severe alcohol-related problems, including physical addiction among older teens who had been drinking only a few years. Patterns of alcohol abuse that took a decade or more to develop in an adult emerged among teens in far shorter periods. These trends produced a backlash against teen drinking amid charges that the liquor industry's advertising enticed young people to drink.

In the 1980s changing demographics spurred a decline in alcohol consumption. In addition, there were rising health concerns, especially about the effects of alcohol on the health of the unborn children of pregnant mothers. Any woman at a particular early stage of pregnancy who consumed a small number of drinks was at risk for fetal alcohol syndrome.

A major social cost associated with alcohol abuse continued to be drunken driving. Each year intoxicated drivers caused about half of nearly 50,000 automobile accident fatalities. Mothers Against Drunk Driving (MADD) lobbied to raise the drinking age to twenty-one. Eventually, Congress coerced the states to adopt such a policy. State legislatures also imposed stricter definitions of legal drunkenness. Those convicted of driving under the influence found it harder to keep their licenses and were more likely to serve time in jail.

Attitudes toward alcohol in the 1990s are more intolerant than at any time since the early 1930s. Although legal, liquor has not become entirely respectable. The acceptance of alcohol has always depended upon the social context surrounding its use. American attitudes have varied considerably and may be said to express widespread ambivalence. Simultaneously, Americans have accepted alcohol as part of a European heritage, but have rejected it as a destructive substance. When Americans react to the mention of alcohol, they typically respond with an uneasy laugh that is symbolic of both the joy and sorrow of alcohol in American culture.

Worldwide Drug Scourge

The Expanding Trade in Illicit Drugs

This article is the first of a two-part series examining the global drug challenge in the post-Cold War era. The first part outlines how the revolutionary changes in the international system are altering patterns of drug production, trafficking, and consumption. The second part will examine current U.S. drug control strategy and suggest how it might be revised to secure better results both at home and abroad.

Stephen Flynn

Lieutenant Stephen Flynn is a Coast Guard officer who is serving as a guest scholar in the Brookings Foreign Policy Studies program. This article presents the findings of a year-long project that he directed while serving as an adjunct fellow at the Center for Strategic and International Studies and as a Council on Foreign Relations International Affairs fellow. The author gratefully acknowledges the assistance of Rens Lee, Lamond Tullis, Richard Clayton, Bob Nieves, Felix Jimenez, David Long, Bill Taylor, Georges Fauriol, and Greg Grant.

Now that the Cold War is over, calls for a greater emphasis on the American domestic agenda have reached a crescendo. The problem of illicit drugs is invariably mentioned as one of the leading domestic ills deserving the full measure of the federal government's attention. But the drug issue is no more purely a domestic problem than are ozone depletion and disease control. As with greenhouse gas emissions and the AIDS epidemic, the drug scourge is a global phenomenon, and it is expanding at an alarming pace. Further, even the most aggressive domestic response cannot insulate the United States from the political, economic, and social fallout associated with the explosive growth in illicit drugs worldwide.

In the Central Asian republics, for instance, thousands of acres have been given over to the cultivation of opium poppies and cannabis. Over the past year, Hungary and Czechoslovakia have become major transit countries for Asian heroin destined for West Europe. Recently, Polish health officials warned that a dramatic rise in intravenous drug abuse in Warsaw has unleashed an AIDS epidemic. Especially ominous are reports of expanding organized criminal networks engaged in drug trafficking with the former Soviet Union, Central Europe, and Latin America.

The surge in the illicit narcotics trade in Eurasia and elsewhere has been first and foremost fueled by its tremendous profitability. Today drugs are a $100 billion a year transnational industry. The illicit stockholders and operatives come from every continent and include Colombians, Mexicans, Italians, Nigerians, Poles, Turks, Chinese, Lebanese, and Georgians.

Second, the recent unraveling of socialism and the move toward freer trade among industrialized countries has created a fertile environment for international businesses—even illicit ones—as deregulation and integration gather momentum. As commercial banks, investment firms, insurance companies, full-service brokers, and asset managers have all globalized their operations, the menu of financial institutions through which both clean and dirty money can be moved has never been so extensive. With the North American Free Trade Agreement, EC '92, the Asia-Pacific Economic Cooperation effort, and the collapse of the Iron Curtain, torrents of people, goods, and services are pouring across borders. In their midst, drug shipments can move with little risk of detection by customs authorities.

Third, the colossal social and economic dislocations connected with both the implosions of the communist world and the desperate standard of living in much of the third world are creating the ideal climate for widespread drug production and abuse. In the third world, the loss of superpower benefactors, declining rates of per capita GNP, unstable commodity prices, and rising domestic and foreign debt make the hard currency and profits connected with the drug trade almost irresistible. For many of the destitute and disaffected survivors of impoverished third world states and once rigidly controlled communist societies, drugs offer a seductive reprieve from an unpleasant world.

Finally, the recent resurgence of ethnic, religious, and nationalistic conflict slows or precludes altogether the development of new regional and international regulatory regimes to control illicit activities within the global community. It also hampers intelligence sharing and cooperation among neighboring law enforcement agencies, a development of which criminal drug organizations are a direct beneficiary.

The results: the production of heroin, cocaine, cannabis, and synthetic drugs is at a record high and will continue to

From *The Brookings Review*, Winter 1993, pp. 6-11. © 1993 by the Brookings Institution. Reprinted by permission.

1. LIVING WITH DRUGS

rise; narcotics traffickers are moving drugs and money throughout the international economy with virtual impunity; and drug consumption is exploding in many countries that had hitherto escaped the drug scourge.

Global Drug Production

Because drug production is illicit, estimating its worldwide extent can be no more than an exercise in guesswork. But clearly the production of opium poppy, coca, and cannabis is on the rise. According to U.S. government estimates, in 1991 cocaine production in Latin America grew by 85 tons—a 7 percent increase over 1990. Opium production was estimated to be 4,200 tons in 1991, a 33 percent increase since 1988. Hashish production from the four major producing countries grew 65 percent between 1990 and 1991 to 1,244 tons.

More disturbing than the rise in global drug production is the sudden proliferation of producers. Within Peru, the world's leading producer of coca, illicit cultivation has spread out of the Upper Huallaga Valley into the Cuzco, Ayacucho, Pasco, and Puno Departments. New coca cultivation has been reported in remote regions in Brazil, Ecuador, and Venezuela. Cocaine refinement, once restricted to Colombia, now takes place in Peru, Bolivia, Venezuela, Argentina, Ecuador, and Brazil. Brazil's involvement is particularly ominous since it is the only South American country where acetone and ether, the chemicals used to turn coca base into cocaine, are manufactured in industrial quantities. Over the past year, European authorities have even discovered cocaine processing laboratories in Portugal, Spain, and Italy.

Opium cultivation has spilled over from the traditional production regions of Mexico, the Golden Triangle (Burma, Thailand, and Laos), and the Golden Crescent (Pakistan, Afghanistan, and Iran). Guatemala and Colombia are now major source countries in the Western hemisphere. U.S. officials estimate that Colombia may have produced about 4 tons of heroin in 1992—close to Mexico's 6.8 tons in 1990. The Colombians almost certainly have the means to become the chief world heroin suppliers of the 21st century.

In Eurasia, extensive opium poppy cultivation has been reported in Poland, Ukraine, Moldova, the Caucasus, and Central Asia. In January 1992 Sergey Tershchenko, the prime minister of Kazakhstan, legalized the cultivation of the opium poppy. The government of Kyrgzstan toyed with the idea, but backed away. In Central Asia, per capita income is approximately 40 percent below, and unemployment nearly 70 percent above, the average of the other former Soviet states. The economic incentives for poppy production will be even greater when Moscow ends its annual subsidy of billions of rubles to the region. Central Asia could very well become the "Andean region" of Eurasia.

Opium cultivation has also reemerged in China after being virtually eliminated by the communists when they seized power in 1949. Law enforcement authorities have spotted poppies in at least 13 of China's 23 provinces and 5 autonomous regions, with the largest plots in the remote southern province of Yunnan and in the northern province of Inner Mongolia.

Among traditional source countries for cannabis (the United States ranks second), production fell in 1991 because of bad weather and stepped-up eradication efforts. Still, the capacity for large-scale cultivation is spreading quickly. Brazil has become a major producer, with illegal cultivation taking place in at least 20 of its 26 states. In the former Soviet Union cannabis plants grow freely on more than 2.5 million acres, mostly in Kazakhstan, Kyrgzstan, Siberia, and the Far East. Cannabis is being grown throughout Africa. Hashish production soared in 1991, with Lebanon increasing its total production almost sixfold over 1990.

Production of synthetic narcotics also appears to be spreading. Laboratories in Taiwan and South Korea are the chief source of "ice," a high-purity methamphetamine developed during the mid-1980s. Poland has recently become one of the largest producers of amphetamines for the European market. According to police lab analyses, in 1991 some 20 percent of the amphetamines seized in West Europe and 25 percent of those seized in Germany originated in Poland. Underground laboratories for synthetic drugs have been discovered in Moscow, St. Petersburg, Sverdlovsk, and many other large cities in the former Soviet Union. Methaqualone ("mandrax") is produced throughout India, primarily for the large market in Southern Africa.

Spreading Like Weeds

Neither geography nor laboratory technology can constrain the cultivation of illicit drugs. Poppy, coca, and cannabis can be grown almost anywhere, and the ability to refine them or to produce synthetic drugs is widely available. All the coca and opium poppy plants being grown in the world would fill a space not much larger than the Eastern Shore of Maryland. The global capacity for cultivating these drugs is virtually untapped.

Illicit drug production is taking root most quickly in areas with few other meaningful economic options. Sub-Saharan Africa, Inner Mongolia, southern China, Central Asia, Afghanistan, and northeastern Brazil are among the most remote and impoverished places on the planet. Although peasants rarely get rich growing coca, poppies, or cannabis, they can earn up to 10 times what they can by growing traditional farm products. That can mean the difference between providing for the most basic needs of one's family or exposing it to life-threatening poverty.

Throughout much of the developing world, national currencies are nonexchangeable and worthless. Businessmen trying to finance capital improvements, insurgents and terrorists seeking the weapons and resources to fight their causes, and governments struggling to keep their economies afloat are in desperate need of hard currency at a time of global capital shortage. For them, too, the drug trade is almost the only answer.

The temptation to produce drugs may also prove almost irresistible in Eastern Europe and the former Soviet Union.

In Eurasia, extensive opium poppy cultivation has been reported in Poland, Ukraine, Moldova, the Caucasus, and Central Asia.

One-third of the people in Hungary now live below the poverty level. By the end of 1991 unemployment in eastern Germany was 30 percent. In Russia as many as 10–11 million people, or 15 percent of the work force, may be unemployed by the year's end.

Drugs are usually produced where they are most difficult to stop—generally in remote areas safely outside a government's reach, often in territory under the sway of insurgency groups. The criminal organizations that support drug production have the resources to corrupt, intimidate, or bypass the authority of governments that, in addition, often face political problems that are more pressing than drugs or cannot take effective enforcement action because of a lack of political legitimacy.

The "Big Business" of Drug Trafficking

In essence, drug trafficking is a form of commodities trade conducted by transnational consortiums. Acquiring chemicals to produce drugs, transporting the drugs to wholesale distributors, and laundering the profits require interacting with and blending into legitimate markets. The size and complexity of these operations mandate that the drug industry pattern itself after the modern multinational corporation. Yet unlike traders in oil, automobiles, or microchips, traders in illicit drugs must outwit a dynamic enforcement environment designed to defeat them. Consequently, over the past two decades the drug trade has undergone something of a Darwinian evolution, the survivors of which have developed into sophisticated and highly flexible organizations. As one senior American drug enforcement official put it, "Lee Iacocca could learn a heck of a lot from these people!"

For those in the business of moving illicit drugs and money, the post–Cold War era has much to offer: a trend toward privatization and liberalization; an increase in the volume and diversity of world trade; the deregulation of national economies; the integration of global transportation, communications, and financial systems; and increasingly open and unmonitored borders between states. And since trafficking organizations are not bound by the legal constraints of domestic and international commerce regulation, they are particularly well placed to respond rapidly and with considerable ingenuity to these changes in the international economic system.

A prime example of the modern drug trafficking organization is the Cali "cartel." Like its better known counterpart from Medellin, the Cali cartel is a loose conglomeration of Colombian families based in a major Colombian city. But unlike the often violent Medellin cartel, which conjures up images of well-heeled thugs surrounded by private armies, the Cali cartel operates more like the senior management team at Exxon or Coca Cola. Its transportation, distribution, and money-laundering networks cover the globe. Outside the Western hemisphere, Cali operatives work in Japan, Hungary, Czechoslovakia, Poland, Germany, Italy, Spain, Portugal, the Netherlands, France, and Great Britain.

Because the huge U.S. and European markets are so far from coca production areas, transportation is critical to the cocaine business. Contrary to popular belief, most drugs do not cross American borders on low-flying Cessnas or aboard fast-moving "cigarette" boats. Most reach their markets by way of commercial conveyances. Containerized shipments, bulk cargo, false documentation, and front companies conceal the movement of cocaine by water. By land, most co-caine crosses the U.S.-Mexican border in hidden compartments of tractor trailers and other vehicles or in commercial cargo itself. For these border crossings, the Cali cartel relies on Mexican smugglers.

The Cali organization uses international shipping centers in Central and South America, particularly in Brazil, Venezuela, Surinam, and Panama, to ship cocaine by sea to Europe and to the eastern United States. It conceals the drugs in a variety of imaginative ways, one of the most creative of which was to hide 15.7 tons of cocaine in 2,000 concrete cement posts (U.S. authorities seized that shipment in September 1991). Occasionally drugs are shipped to the United States circuitously, passing through Europe or Canada before arriving.

When commercial airliners are used for shipping cocaine, the drug is hidden on the plane itself, or it is carried by human "mules," who swallow condoms containing pellets of cocaine. It is also concealed in luggage with false bottoms, in aerosol cans, and sneakers with hollowed-out soles. Sometimes it is converted to liquid and smuggled in bottles of shampoo, mouthwash, and liquor.

By blending shipments within the growing volume of international trade, the Cali cartel greatly reduces the chance of discovery. Interdicting drugs has always been a "needle-in-a-haystack" exercise for customs authorities, but when those drugs are hidden among general merchandise or on the person of international travelers, the task becomes overwhelming. In 1991, for example, 1.8 million containers arrived in the Port of Newark alone, but U.S. customs inspectors there were able to search thoroughly only 15–18 containers a day.

Getting the Goods to the Wholesalers

Once the drug arrives, it must be distributed. The Cali cartel has set up wholesale distribution networks throughout the country and exercises complete control over the New York and Washington, D.C., markets. If a load of cocaine arrives at Kennedy International Airport or at the Port of Newark, one of the 10 to 12 Cali distribution cells in New York receives it. Each cell, made up of 15–20 Colombian employees who earn monthly salaries ranging from $2,000 to $7,500, conducts an average of $25 million of business a month. Each cell is self-contained, with information tightly

---

The surge in the illicit narcotics trade in Eurasia and elsewhere has been first and foremost fueled by its tremendous profitability.

---

compartmentalized. Only a handful of managers know all the operatives. The cell has a head, bookkeeper, money handler, cocaine handler, motor pool, and 10 to 15 apartments serving as stash houses.

Communications are conducted in code over facsimile machines, cellular phones, and pay phones. To eliminate any risk of interception, cellular phones are purchased and discarded, often two or three times a week. When a wholesale customer wants to make a purchase, a cell member is notified by a pager system. That cell member proceeds to a public phone and arranges a rendezvous site. He then gets, from the motor pool, a rental car that is returned to the rental agency after the transaction. The transaction itself, including any travel receipts, is logged by the bookkeeper, and the money is turned over to the money handler to be shipped to the financial network set up by the cartel to hide and invest it. A favorite way to ship within the United States is the U.S. Postal Service's "Express Mail."

Such tactics stretch traditional law enforcement surveillance to the limit and beyond. Most national police authorities are finding themselves completely "outgunned" by technologies that are relatively cheap for organized crime but financially out of reach for the law enforcement community. The situation in Poland is suggestive. Between 1990 and 1991, Poland's police budget fell 13 percent. The use of patrol cars was limited to 60 kilometers a day, and police abandoned plans to modernize their vehicles or buy new car radios. Throughout the country only 30 police officials were assigned full-time to antidrug operations.

Once the cartel has received the money for its drug sales, it moves it into and through the legal financial system to conceal its origins. If the Cali cell broken up by federal authorities in December 1991 is typical, the Cali financial network must launder up to $300 million each year per cell. Money laundering typically involves three independent phases. First, drug proceeds are "placed," or used to make deposits or to purchase monetary instruments or securities that can be turned into cash elsewhere. Second, the money is "layered," or sent through multiple electronic funds transfers or other transactions to make it difficult to track and blur its illicit origin. Finally, the source of the money disappears as it is "integrated," or invested into seemingly legitimate accounts and enterprises.

The revolution under way in the global financial and banking markets has made all three of these jobs easier. Drug traffickers have a vast new array of possibilities for the placement of funds as national currencies become convertible and new and largely unregulated private banking institutions spring up throughout the former Soviet bloc and the third world. Many of the new banks have primitive accounting practices, no computers, and little or no experience with international banking practices. The integration and increased efficiency of the global banking system allows money launderers to layer money with virtual impunity. The sheer volume of electronic funds transfers makes them almost impossible to track. In 1991, for example, the Clearing House Interbank Payment System handled some 37 billion transactions worth $222 trillion. Finally, the sudden shift away from state to private ownership throughout the former communist world provides launderers with an array of "front" organizations to integrate their money into seemingly legitimate enterprises. The Cali cartel set up a number of such companies in Hungary, Czechoslovakia, and Poland in 1991.

Of course, the Cali cartel is not the only beneficiary of the changing international business environment. Italian, Polish, Turkish, Georgian, Chinese, Vietnamese, Lebanese, Pakistani, Nigerian, and many other transnational trafficking organizations are profiting as well.

Trends in Global Drug Consumption

Predicting with any precision the character and dimension of the global drug market is difficult. Most drug abuse re-

search has been done on population groups within advanced societies, and epidemiologists are understandably hesitant to apply these findings to the developing world. Too, drug epidemics typically refuse to stay within tidy political, cultural, or geographical boundaries. Islamic fundamentalism seems to help explain why drug abuse is uncommon in Saudi Arabia, but not why more than a million Iranians and 1.7 million Pakistanis use drugs.

But although it may not be possible to anticipate precisely which specific locations are likely to suffer from widespread abuse and when, forecasting the overall trend in global drug consumption is less problematic. The prospect for growing drug abuse worldwide can be correlated with the prevalence of its three requisite ingredients: an awareness of drugs, access to them, and the motivation to use them.

The awareness of drugs has become almost universal. In the third world, demographic pressures are forcing millions of people out of their isolation in remote villages and into large cities, where it is impossible not to know about drugs. And the collapse of the communist regimes in the former Soviet bloc has ended the state's monopoly on information and has made it possible for people to travel freely both at home and abroad. Word of a drug that has acquired popularity somewhere can spread quickly almost everywhere.

Access to drugs is also increasing with the projected rise in production and trafficking. Further, if democratization and economic liberalization persist, individuals will have greater personal freedom, mobility, and control over their personal incomes, facilitating contacts with drug distributors and their purchases.

People in most third world societies are also increasingly motivated to use drugs. For one thing, the population of the developing world is growing younger. More than half the people in Nigeria and Kenya, and more than 40 percent in Latin America, are under the age of 20—an age group known for risk-taking behavior and the willingness to challenge social conventions. In addition, rapid population growth rates are causing people, particularly young men, to move to big cities. Separated from their families, often unemployed or underemployed, and with little opportunity for schooling, more and more of these disillusioned young people are at great risk of taking up drugs.

Peer pressure and the mass media can also push vulnerable young people to become drug users. Many European and American movies and television programs—even programs like "Miami Vice" and movies like "Scarface" that presumably show that "drug crimes don't pay"—portray drugs as luxury goods consumed by wealthy Americans. As such, drugs end up serving as status symbols, or as one Nigerian addict recently put it, as a way to "become like an American."

Finally, the dislocations associated with the end of the socialist experiment and the desperate economic plight of much of the third world are increasing the willingness of people, young and old, to violate the law.

Drug Use on the Rise

What evidence is there that global drug consumption is in fact on the rise? Although the data are soft, health officials around the globe are becoming increasingly alarmed. In Poland, 75 percent of all alcoholics are also addicted to either licit or illicit drugs. Most of these drug abusers in Poland are infected with the AIDS virus as a result of sharing intravenous needles. In Yugoslavia there are 300,000–400,000 addicts, with more than 15,000 in Belgrade alone. Estimates of drug abuse in the former Soviet Union range anywhere from 1.5 million to 7.5 million people. In all three areas, the spread of drug abuse is worst among the young. Almost two-thirds of Polish drug abusers are under 21 years of age.

In Eastern and Southern Asia nearly every country is reporting rising drug abuse. As the Burmese heroin trade has spilled increasingly into the subcontinent, Nepal, Bangladesh, and India all confront burgeoning user populations. In Pakistan, heroin users have grown from a few hundred to more than a million in little over a decade. Drug use in Thailand appeared to be stabilizing after an initial surge in large-scale opium poppy production in the 1970s, but new reports indicate that many villagers are shifting from traditional opium consumption to the more debilitating heroin addiction. As noted, opium and heroin are making a comeback in China, where police estimate that 300,000 use drugs, despite a relentless enforcement effort that featured the public execution of 250 drug traffickers in 1991.

In the barrios of Central and South America, cocaine addiction is becoming more prevalent, with the most worrisome trends in Colombia, Peru, Bolivia, Brazil, Ecuador, and Panama. One of every three secondary school students in Peru uses drugs. In Chile, Argentina, and Brazil, drug consumption is rising most dramatically among young people from upper-income families.

Africa represents the greatest unknown in the consumption picture, though it has virtually all the high-risk factors. Nigeria, Kenya, and South Africa, the wealthiest countries on the Sub-Saharan continent, are witnessing a rising incidence of drug abuse. In South Africa the drug of choice is "mandrax," a synthetic drug imported from India. In Nigeria and Kenya cannabis is the most widely abused drug, although there have been a growing number of reports of cocaine and heroin use.

The seductiveness of mood-altering substances is age-old and virtually universal. As the conditions that support widespread abuse become more prevalent within much of the global community, the prospect of expanding drug markets appears almost inevitable.

Needed: An International Response

The profound changes connected with the passing of the Cold War era have transformed the drug trade into a transnational challenge of the first order. As with other such challenges—weapons proliferation, disease control, migration, ozone depletion—states can do little on their own to stand up against the rising tide of drug production, trafficking, and consumption.

Acknowledging that the drug trade has become a transnational activity that is outstripping the traditional tools available to governments to combat it has important implications for current U.S. drug control strategy. In 1992, 93.6 percent of the $11.9 billion national drug control budget was spent on domestic enforcement, demand reduction, and border control. Of the rest, 6.3 percent went to bilateral programs to help governments in source and transit countries fight illicit narcotics. One-tenth of one percent ($15.5 million) of the total budget supported multilateral drug programs.

What these budget allocations tell us is that U.S. policymakers see drugs as essentially a domestic problem that can be resolved with a national response. At home, it is assumed that large doses of law enforcement, prevention, and treatment programs will erode the market for illicit narcotics. Likewise, along the borders, we seem to believe that a full-scale investment in interdiction will keep traffickers at bay. Overseas, selected governments are enlisted in an American effort to disrupt the production and transit of drugs destined for our shores.

Even if a national strategy to combat the scourge of drugs were to succeed at home, Americans would still face the effects of a flourishing drug trade overseas. As recent events in Peru illustrate, large-scale drug production can disrupt national economies and destroy democratic institutions. When drug trafficking can infiltrate with virtual impunity the commercial conveyances, migrant labor forces, banks, and securities markets that service a global economy, it provides fuel for protectionist forces who seek to slow or reverse the global trend toward greater economic liberalization. Finally, the reduced worker productivity and the public health consequences, including the spread of AIDS, associated with widespread drug abuse jeopardize further the limited development prospects of many third world countries, weakening their potential to become strong U.S. trading partners and stable allies.

The surging global drug epidemic requires an international drug control response and sooner rather than later. What this response should look like and what role the United States should play in it will be considered in the second part of this series. [See *The Brookings Review*, Spring 1993, for second part of series. Ed.]

The Global Tobacco Epidemic

*Cigarette smoking has stopped declining in the U.S.
and is rising in other parts of the world. Aggressive marketing
and permissive regulations are largely to blame*

Carl E. Bartecchi, Thomas D. MacKenzie and Robert W. Schrier

CARL E. BARTECCHI, THOMAS D. MacKENZIE and ROBERT W. SCHRIER collaborate at the University of Colorado School of Medicine. Bartecchi, who helped to found the Southern Colorado Clinic in Pueblo, is a clinical professor in the department of medicine at the school. MacKenzie is a general internist with the Denver Department of Health and Hospitals and an assistant professor of medicine at the University of Colorado Health Sciences Center. Schrier is professor and chairman of the department of medicine at the University of Colorado School of Medicine.

Since the early 1960s, medical research, public information campaigns and government assessments have exposed the dangers of tobacco smoke. The result has been a substantial drop in the number of smokers in the U.S.—from a peak of 41 percent to its current level of about 25 percent. Yet despite considerable scientific evidence and continuing exhortations from the medical community, the trend has now mostly ceased: the number of adult smokers has remained static since 1990. Similarly, the proportion of adolescents who smoke has changed little in the past 10 years. Perhaps even more disconcerting is that in the global picture, cigarette production during the past two decades has increased an average of 2.2 percent each year, outpacing the annual world population growth of 1.7 percent. Because of growing cigarette consumption in developing nations, worldwide cigarette production is projected to escalate by 2.9 percent a year in the 1990s, with China leading the way with jumps near 11 percent a year.

To understand the driving forces behind modern directions in tobacco consumption and to formulate strategies to combat its pervasiveness, the medical community has had to extend observations beyond the individual smoker and the addictive power of nicotine. The focus of some recent work has been on the tobacco industry itself. In this context, changes in smoking behavior depend in large part on cigarette pricing, advertising, promotion and exportation. Researchers in preventive medicine and public health agree that education campaigns must be supplemented. The new strategies should aim to regulate the marketing of cigarettes, to raise taxes on tobacco and to rethink current trade practices.

A 1,000-Year-Old Habit

Although humans probably began sampling tobacco during the first millennium, based on Mayan stone carvings dated at about A.D. 600 to 900, physicians did not begin to suspect in earnest that the plant could produce ill effects until around the 19th century. The renowned colonial physician Benjamin Rush condemned tobacco in his writings as early as 1798. By the mid- to late 1800s, many prominent physicians were expressing concern about the development of certain medical problems connected with tobacco. They suggested a relation between smoking and coronary artery disease, even recognizing the potential association between passive smoking (inhaling smoke from the air) and heart problems. They also noted a correlation with lip and nasal cancer.

Although tobacco use was relatively common in that century, it did not produce the widespread illnesses it does today. Individuals of the time consumed only small amounts, mostly in the form of pipe tobacco, cigars, chewing tobacco or snuff. Cigarette smoking was rare. Then, in 1881, came the invention of the cigarette-rolling machine, followed by the development of safety matches. Both significantly encouraged smoking, and by 1945 cigarettes had largely replaced other forms of tobacco consumption. Smokers increased their average of 40 cigarettes a year in 1880 to an average of 12,854 cigarettes in 1977, the peak of American consumption per individual smoker.

The rise in tobacco use made the adverse effects of smoking more apparent. Medical reports in the 1920s strengthened the suspected links between tobacco and cancers. The connection to life span was first noted in 1938, when an article in the journal *Science* suggested that heavy smokers had a shorter life expectancy than did nonsmokers.

In 1964 U.S. Surgeon General Luther Terry released a truly landmark public health document. The work of an independent body of scientists, it was the country's first widely publicized official recognition that smoking causes cancer and other diseases. In many subsequent reports by the surgeon general's office, cigarette smoking has been identified as the leading source of preventable morbidity and premature mortality in the U.S. These statements enumerate many experimental studies in which animals have been exposed to tars, gases and other constituents in tobacco and tobacco smoke.

A review of mortality statistics underscores the tobacco epidemic. Of the more than two million U.S. deaths in 1990, smoking-related illnesses accounted for about 400,000 of them and for more than one quarter of all deaths among those 35 to 64 years of age. When deaths from passive smoking are included, estimates near 500,000. A recent British study suggests that one half of all regular smokers will die from their habit. Statistically, each cigarette robs a regular smoker of 5.5 minutes of life.

Tobacco also drains society economically. The University of California and the Centers for Disease Control and Prevention (CDC) have calculated that the total health care cost to society of smoking-related diseases in 1993 was at least $50 billion, or $2.06 per pack of cigarettes—about the actual price of a pack in the U.S. That price figure greatly exceeds the average total tax on a pack of cigarettes in the U.S., now currently about 56 cents. Although a 1989 study suggested that smokers "pay their

own way" at the current level of excise taxes (because they live long enough to contribute to their pensions and to Social Security but die before they enjoy the benefits), more recent estimates show otherwise. These newer calculations, which incorporate the effects of passive smoking, indicate that smokers take from society much more than they pay in tobacco taxes.

Moreover, because tobacco kills so many people between the ages of 35 and 64, the cost of lost productivity

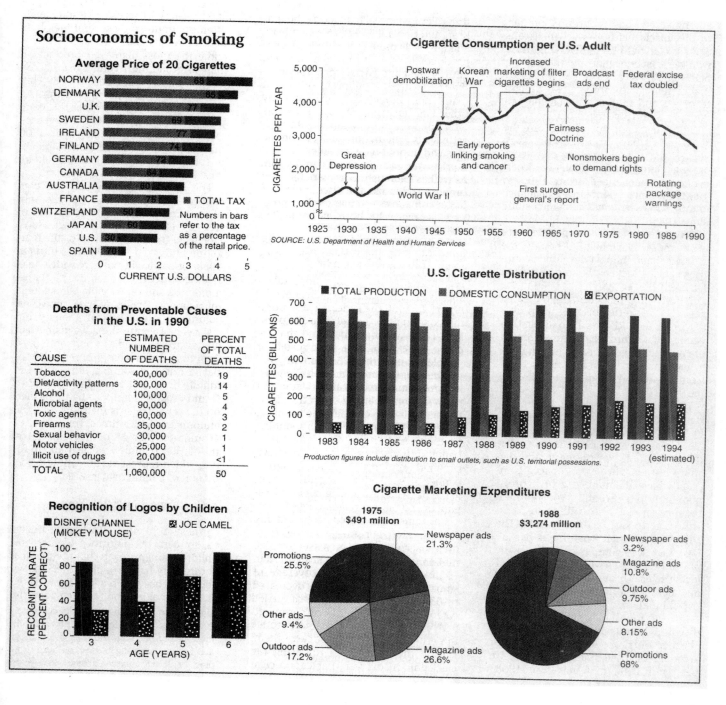

Socioeconomics of Smoking

Average Price of 20 Cigarettes

NORWAY 68
DENMARK 85
U.K. 77
SWEDEN 69
IRELAND 77
FINLAND 74
GERMANY 72
CANADA 64
AUSTRALIA 60
FRANCE 75
SWITZERLAND 50
JAPAN 60
U.S. 30
SPAIN 70

■ TOTAL TAX

Numbers in bars refer to the tax as a percentage of the retail price.

CURRENT U.S. DOLLARS

Deaths from Preventable Causes in the U.S. in 1990

CAUSE	ESTIMATED NUMBER OF DEATHS	PERCENT OF TOTAL DEATHS
Tobacco	400,000	19
Diet/activity patterns	300,000	14
Alcohol	100,000	5
Microbial agents	90,000	4
Toxic agents	60,000	3
Firearms	35,000	2
Sexual behavior	30,000	1
Motor vehicles	25,000	1
Illicit use of drugs	20,000	<1
TOTAL	1,060,000	50

Recognition of Logos by Children

■ DISNEY CHANNEL (MICKEY MOUSE)   ▨ JOE CAMEL

RECOGNITION RATE (PERCENT CORRECT)

AGE (YEARS)

Cigarette Consumption per U.S. Adult

CIGARETTES PER YEAR

Postwar demobilization
Korean War
Increased marketing of filter cigarettes begins
Broadcast ads end
Federal excise tax doubled
Great Depression
Early reports linking smoking and cancer
Fairness Doctrine
Nonsmokers begin to demand rights
World War II
First surgeon general's report
Rotating package warnings

SOURCE: U.S. Department of Health and Human Services

U.S. Cigarette Distribution

■ TOTAL PRODUCTION   ▨ DOMESTIC CONSUMPTION   ▨ EXPORTATION

CIGARETTES (BILLIONS)

1983 1984 1985 1986 1987 1988 1989 1990 1991 1992 1993 1994 (estimated)

Production figures include distribution to small outlets, such as U.S. territorial possessions.

Cigarette Marketing Expenditures

1975
$491 million

Promotions 25.5%
Newspaper ads 21.3%
Other ads 9.4%
Outdoor ads 17.2%
Magazine ads 26.6%

1988
$3,274 million

Newspaper ads 3.2%
Magazine ads 10.8%
Outdoor ads 9.75%
Other ads 8.15%
Promotions 68%

must be accounted for in the analysis. With this factor in mind, the average annual expense to an employer for a worker who smokes has been pegged at $960 a year. The total toll of tobacco consumption for the country may exceed $100 billion annually.

Staying Addicted

Expanding public awareness of tobacco's dangers is probably the reason for the decline of smoking in the U.S. Based on a 1993 count, an estimated 46 million adults (25 percent) in the U.S. smoke—24 million men and 22 million women. Smoking prevalence is highest among some minority groups—in particular, black males, Native Americans and Alaskan natives—and among those with the least education and those living below the poverty level. Perhaps most disheartening, an estimated six million teenagers and another 100,000 children younger than 13 years smoke.

Of greatest concern, however, are the most recent data from the CDC. They suggest that overall smoking prevalence among adults, at approximately 25 percent, was unchanged from 1990 to 1993. Moreover, smoking prevalence among adolescents has remained static since 1985.

On a global scale, the patterns are even more alarming. Although the smoking habit in most developed countries is being kicked, the rate of decline has been slower than it has been in the U.S. In developing countries, data suggest that cigarette smoking is up by 3 percent a year. Richard Peto of the University of Oxford has estimated that the total number of deaths attributable to smoking worldwide will increase from 2.5 million today to 12 million by the year 2050.

There are several reasons for the current pattern of cigarette consumption. In the U.S. the flattened decline since 1990 may have resulted from recent price wars between premium and discount brands. For years, tobacco companies have maintained a high profit margin despite dwindling consumption because smokers are willing to pay a stiff price to satisfy their craving. The addiction of their customers has allowed tobacco companies to boost the price of cigarettes with minimal fear of losing sales. Throughout the 1980s, for instance, the price of cigarettes outpaced inflation.

But the rapidly rising popularity of discount brands has made cigarettes cheaper and more accessible. The market share of these brands rose from 10 percent in 1987 to 36 percent in 1993.

They earn about five cents per pack in profit, compared with 55 cents for a brand-name pack. This trend forced a series of price cuts by the major brands in 1993. If the cuts are sustained, smoking prevalence in the U.S., especially among young and poor populations (for whom price is often important), may actually increase.

Despite the recent price deductions, cigarette companies are likely to remain financially and politically potent entities. The two biggest corporations—Philip Morris and R. J. Reynolds—expanded their presence appreciably in the consumer market during the 1980s by acquiring many big, nontobacco-related firms. For instance, Philip Morris bought Kraft and General Foods, among others, and now sells more than 3,000 different products. In 1992 it ranked as the seventh largest industrial corporation in the U.S., with $50 billion in sales, and made more money that year than any other U.S. business. Almost half of its $4.9 billion in profits came from cigarette sales. The major tobacco companies will undoubtedly be able to afford a price war with discount competitors as well as establish their own discount brands. And unlike the discounters, the larger companies can market their products aggressively, both at home and abroad.

There has been little government restriction on the marketing of cigarettes in recent decades. The bulk of today's regulations stems from actions taken shortly after the 1964 surgeon general's report. In 1966 the Federal Trade Commission required that all cigarette packages carry warning labels and that tobacco advertising not be directed at people younger than 25 years. In 1967 the Federal Communications Commission mandated that local television and radio stations that ran cigarette advertisements had to compensate by airing public service announcements about the product's bad effects. Cigarette advertising shifted completely from television and radio in 1971, when Congress banned all such advertising on electronic media. As a result, magazines, newspapers and billboards took over.

Magazines benefited substantially from the shift. For some, revenues from the tobacco industry increased by $5.5 million per magazine a year (figured in 1983 dollars). Moreover, coverage of smoking-related health issues decreased by 65 percent in magazines that carried cigarette advertisements, as compared with a 29 percent drop in similar stories in periodicals that did not carry them. During the three years following the electronic media ban, per capita ciga-

rette consumption actually rose slightly before resuming its drop. Many analysts attribute the brief surge to the cessation of public service announcements that coincided with the electronic ban.

Several major health organizations, including the American Medical Association, have recommended barring tobacco advertising completely. In other developed countries, such antitobacco legislation is common. By mid-1986, 55 countries had enacted legislation to control advertising: 20 with total bans, 15 with strong partial bans and 20 with moderate ones.

In comparison, the U.S. has been lax. Since 1971 it has passed nothing to restrict cigarette advertising, despite many attempts to do so by several members of Congress. Instead tobacco has become the most displayed product on billboards and the second most marketed product in magazines. In 1989 Philip Morris spent $2 billion on advertisements—more than any other U.S. company. The industry as a whole increased expenditures on advertising from $500 million in 1975 to more than $5 billion in 1992, which represents a fourfold increase in constant 1975 dollars.

The tobacco industry has also concentrated on promotion. Sponsorship of sporting events, the distribution of free cigarettes and other strategies have increased from one quarter of the marketing budget in 1975 to two thirds in 1988. Of particular note are widely televised competitions such as the Camel motocross and the Virginia Slims tennis tournament (Philip Morris, however, voluntarily pulled out of sponsorship last year). Despite the advertising ban on electronic media, sponsorship of such tournaments has granted substantial airtime. For example, during the 93-minute broadcast of the 1989 Marlboro Grand Prix, the Marlboro name flashed on the screen or was mentioned by the announcers 5,933 times, for a total of 46 minutes. For 18 of those minutes, the Marlboro name was clear and in focus, which represents an estimated $1 million of commercial airtime.

Appealing to the Young

These marketing efforts have begun to focus on minorities, women and children, an approach that the medical community has strongly criticized. Recent work has found a link between the start of smoking and targeted advertising [see box "Looking for a Market among Adolescents"]. Children are probably the most vulnerable segment. The average age that habitual smoking begins has been dropping for decades and is currently 14.5 years.

Approximately 90 percent of regular smokers start before the age of 21.

Data suggest that the tobacco industry recognizes these figures and develops advertisements to appeal to children and teenagers. For example, in 1988 R. J. Reynolds fashioned "Old Joe Camel," a cartoon character who shoots pool, rides motorcycles and associates with attractive women as he smokes cigarettes. Three years after the campaign began, several studies clearly demonstrated that children and teenagers easily recognized Joe Camel. One study showed that six-year-olds knew the character as often as they picked out Mickey Mouse. Teenagers were likewise influenced. Surveys done in 1988 and 1990 show that the proportion of teenage smokers who bought the Camel brand increased from 0.5 to 32 percent. In this same period, it is estimated that Camel cigarette sales to minors soared from $6 million to $476 million.

How can minors purchase cigarettes so easily? Although 46 states have laws prohibiting the sale of cigarettes to minors, compliance has been consistently poor in many communities. Furthermore, only nine states have stopped the sale of cigarettes in vending machines, and just 22 states prohibit the free distribution of cigarettes to underage individuals. Many legislators and health officials have suggested that the sale of cigarettes should require licensing similar to that for the sale of alcohol.

The tobacco industry may be relying on a more insidious strategy to gain new customers—that is, through smokeless tobacco. It is estimated that 7.5 million people in the U.S. use tobacco in this way, with snuff (shredded tobacco that is sucked but not chewed) being the most popular. A 1994 *Wall Street Journal* article reported that tobacco companies doctor their snuff products to increase the nicotine that the mouth can absorb—an alarming assertion, given that the average age for first-time snuff users is nine years. The article argued that these companies try to appeal to young people with pleasant-tasting, milder forms that are lower in free nicotine (that is, in a form immediately available for absorption) and then to graduate these consumers to very potent, very addictive brands high in free nicotine. Although the tobacco companies admit they can control the amount of nicotine in the product, they deny that they do so to addict individuals.

Despite the toxic effects of tobacco, the agencies primarily responsible for protecting the consumer—the Food and Drug Administration and the Consumer Product Safety Commission—have never subjected tobacco products to health and safety regulations commonly used for hazardous compounds. Their permissiveness very likely stems from the lobbying efforts by the tobacco industry, which is considered one of the most powerful at all levels of government today. In 1992 the tobacco industry donated more than $4.7 million to the leading political parties, representing three times the amount given in 1988. Few government representatives refuse these contributions. In 1989 it was reported that over a two-year period, 420 of 535 congressional representatives and 87 of 100 senators accepted tobacco campaign contributions, making the tobacco lobby one of the most influential forces in government.

Tobacco companies have also formed industry organizations to channel contributions and to give them a central voice. One such group, the Tobacco Institute, has consistently created a public smoke screen by questioning the association between smoking and human disease. As late as 1986, a Tobacco Institute publication stated that "eminent scientists believe that questions relating to smoking and health are unresolved."

The regulation of tobacco products may change because of allegations that the industry has knowingly manipulated the nicotine content of cigarettes to maximize addiction and has suppressed evidence pointing out the hazards. To many, the congressional testimony of tobacco executives last year—who stated their belief that nicotine was not addictive and that cigarettes were not proved to cause cancer—was designed to avoid any potential liability. The FDA is now considering regulating cigarettes as drug-delivery systems for nicotine (which can act as a stimulant or as a tranquilizer, depending on the amount used). Although the new Congress is much less enthusiastic about such regulations, the health care community regards the FDA's case to be strong enough to force passage of some kind of legislation. How new laws will alter the control of tobacco is unclear. But given current standards of consumer product safety, the introduction and sale of a similar product today would assuredly be denied.

Taxing Tobacco

The political might of the tobacco industry has prevented significant rises in cigarette excise taxes, thus keeping the cost of the habit afford-able. The federal tax has risen from eight cents a pack of 20 cigarettes in 1951 to only 24 cents today, a climb far less than inflation. (Adjusted for inflation, the 1951 tax would be approximately 40 cents today, meaning that the tax has actually declined.) With the addition of state and local taxes, the average total tax on a pack of cigarettes in the U.S. is 56 cents, or 30 percent of the average retail price. This amount is substantially lower than those in many other industrial nations.

The tobacco companies have employed a strategy of identifying themselves as "citizens against tax abuse" and spend millions of dollars to fight against tax increases. The industry probably feels that such large expenditures are necessary to fend off the perceived threat to profits. A 10 percent increase in cigarette prices reduces consumption by 4 percent, mostly by keeping new smokers away. The drop would probably be much larger in populations that are highly sensitive to price hikes, such as teenagers. Because the vast majority of smokers begin in their teens, a major drop in teenage smoking would seriously threaten the future of the tobacco industry.

The American Heart Association, the American Cancer Society and the American Lung Association have recommended a $2 increase in federal tax per pack of cigarettes. Their counsel is based in part on data from Canada and California, where cigarette tax hikes have significantly reduced consumption. The potential benefits of high tobacco taxes are many. Several states have earmarked the revenue for public health education campaigns, antitobacco advertising and health care for the poor. With the recent fall in average cigarette prices, tax increases have become particularly important to counteract a possible acceleration in consumption among teenagers. Many bills were introduced in Congress during the past two years to up the federal tax by $1 or less, both as independent proposals and as part of health care reform packages. None received sufficient support to pass.

Exports to Hook New Customers

Even if tighter marketing restrictions and higher excise taxes prove successful in decreasing tobacco smoking in the U.S., the industry has a means to counteract loss of revenue: exportation. Indeed, although total cigarette consumption in the U.S. has been declining for over a decade, domestic production has been buoyed by steadily increasing shipments overseas. Cigarette exporta-

The Medical Effects of Tobacco Consumption

Discovered in the early 1800s and named nicotianine, the oily essence now called nicotine is the main active ingredient of tobacco. Indeed, researchers recognized in 1942 that smoking dried tobacco leaves was basically a means of administering nicotine, just as smoking opium was a means of obtaining morphine. Nicotine, however, is but a small component of cigarette smoke, which contains more than 4,700 chemical compounds, including 43 cancer-causing substances. Condensates of tobacco smoke suspended in acetone and applied to the skin of mice for long periods cause papillomas or carcinomas at the site. Toxins in cigarette smoke cause breaks in the DNA of cultured human lung cells. In some cases, these carcinogens greatly accelerate the mutation rate in dividing cells, which in turn can lead to tumor formation.

Unfortunately for the smoker, no threshold level of exposure to the toxins has been found. What is clear is that years of cigarette smoking vastly increase the risk of developing several fatal conditions. In addition to being responsible for more than 85 percent of lung cancers, smoking is associated with cancers of the mouth, pharynx, larynx, esophagus, stomach, pancreas, uterine cervix, kidney, ureter, bladder and colon. Cigarette smoking is thought to cause about 14 percent of all leukemias and 30 percent of new cases of cervical cancer in women. All told, cigarette smoking is responsible for 30 percent of all deaths from cancer and clearly represents the most important preventable cause of cancer in the U.S. today.

Smoking also increases the risk of cardiovascular disease, including stroke, sudden death, heart attack, peripheral vascular disease and aortic aneurysm. Cigarettes caused almost 180,000 deaths from cardiovascular disease in the U.S. in 1990. Components of cigarette smoke damage the inner lining of blood vessels, which can lead to the development of atherosclerosis. The toxins can also stimulate occlusive elements in coronary arteries, thus promoting clots to form and triggering spasms that close off the vessels. In this regard, the smoking of a single cigarette can profoundly disturb blood flow to the heart in patients with existing coronary artery disease.

Furthermore, cigarette smoking is the leading cause of pulmonary illness and death in the U.S. In 1990 smoking caused more than 84,000 deaths from pulmonary disease, mainly resulting from such problems as pneumonia, emphysema, bronchitis and influenza.

Passive smoking—the breathing of sidestream smoke (emitted from the burning tobacco between puffs) or of smoke exhaled by the smoker—poses a similar health risk. A 1992 Environmental Protection Agency report emphasized the dangers, especially of sidestream smoke. This type of smoke contains more particles of smaller diameter and is therefore more likely to be deposited deep in the lungs. On the basis of this report, the EPA has classified environmental tobacco smoke as a "group A" carcinogen, to which radon, asbestos, arsenic and benzene belong.

Of the estimated 53,000 annual deaths in the U.S. caused by passive smoking, 37,000 come from associated heart disease. A nonsmoker living with a smoker has a 30 per-

cent higher risk of death from ischemic heart disease or myocardial infarction. Lung cancer risk also skyrockets. Any exposure from a spouse who smokes is associated with at least a 30 percent excess risk of lung cancer. Increasing daily amounts and the number of years of smoking significantly heighten the risk. The figure jumps to 80 percent if the spouse has been smoking four packs a day for 20 years. Another recent study points out that 17 percent of the cases of lung cancer among nonsmokers can be attributed to exposure to high levels of tobacco smoke during childhood and adolescence.

The health consequences of smoking among women are of special concern because of the deleterious effect on reproduction. Unfortunately, the fastest-growing segment of smokers in the U.S. is women younger than 23 years. Smoking reduces fertility, spurs the rate of spontaneous abortions and stillbirths, can cause excessive bleeding during pregnancy and results in lower birth weights in infants. Moreover, children of smokers do not grow as large or attain the same level of educational achievement as unexposed children.

Smoking is a significant cause of cardiovascular diseases and strokes in women, especially if they also use oral contraceptives. Lung cancer has now surpassed breast cancer as the primary cause of death from cancer among women. In 1993 lung cancer claimed an estimated 56,000 deaths, whereas breast cancer took 46,000 lives.

The elderly also face special harm from smoking. Among those older than 65, the rates of total mortality among current smokers are twice those among people who have never smoked. A 1992 *Time* magazine article noted that three life insurers owned by tobacco companies charge smokers nearly double for term insurance.

Smoking is associated with a variety of other ailments: cataracts, delayed healing of broken bones, periodontal maladies, predisposition to ulcer disease, hypertension, brain hemorrhages and skin wrinkles, to name just a few.

Recently some studies have suggested that cigarette smoking ameliorates symptoms of Alzheimer's disease. It is not surprising that with its powerful effect on the central nervous system, nicotine may influence the condition. Yet methodological flaws plague many of these studies. Moreover, other researchers suggest that smoking may increase the risk of Alzheimer's, in that it accelerates the natural consequences of aging. With its many and potent toxins, cigarettes would in any case be an inappropriate vehicle for delivering nicotine should the compound ever prove valuable in treating Alzheimer's.

There is much to be gained by those who kick the habit. After a year, mortality from heart disease drops halfway back to that of a nonsmoker; by five years, it drops to the rate of nonsmokers. A person's risk of lung cancer is cut in half in five years; by 10 years, it drops almost to the rate of nonsmokers. Such gains make sense, however, only if smokers quit in time, before they show any signs of tobacco's lethal effects.

Looking for a Market among Adolescents

In 1992, the most recent year for which data are available, the tobacco industry spent $5 billion on domestic marketing. That figure represents a huge increase from the approximate $250-million budget in 1971, when tobacco advertising was banned from television and radio. The current expenditure translates to about $75 for every adult smoker, or to $4,500 for every adolescent who became a smoker that year. This apparently high cost to attract a new smoker is very likely recouped over the average 25 years that this teen will smoke.

In the first half of this century, leaders of the tobacco companies boasted that innovative mass-marketing strategies built the industry. Recently, however, the tobacco business has maintained that its advertising is geared to draw established smokers to particular brands. But public health advocates insist that such advertising plays a role in generating new demand, with adolescents being the primary target. To explore the issue, we examined several marketing campaigns undertaken over the years and correlated them with the ages smokers say they began their habit. We find that, historically, there is considerable evidence that such campaigns led to an increase in cigarette smoking among adolescents of the targeted group.

National surveys collected the ages at which people started smoking. The 1955 Current Population Survey (CPS) was the first to query respondents for this information, although only summary data survive. Beginning in 1970, however, the National Health Interview Surveys (NHIS) included this question in some polls. Answers from all the surveys were combined to produce a sample of more than 165,000 individuals. Using a respondent's age at the time of the survey and the reported age of initiation, the year the person began smoking could be determined. Dividing the number of adolescents (defined as those 12 to 17 years old) who started smoking during a particular interval by the number who were "eligible" to begin at the start of the interval set the initiation rate for that group.

Mass-marketing campaigns began as early as the 1880s, which boosted tobacco consumption sixfold by 1900. Much of the rise was attributed to a greater number of people smoking cigarettes, as opposed to using cigars, pipes, snuff or chewing tobacco. Marketing strategies included painted billboards and an extensive distribution of coupons, which a recipient could redeem for free cigarettes and a variety of other premiums. Some brands included soft-porn pictures of women in the packages. Such tactics inspired outcry from educational leaders concerned about their corrupting influence on teenage boys. Thirteen percent of the males surveyed in 1955 who reached adolescence between 1890 and 1910 commenced smoking by 18 years of age, compared with almost no females.

The power of targeted advertising is more apparent if one considers the men born between 1890 and 1899. In 1912, when many of these men were teenagers, the R. J. Reynolds company launched the Camel brand of cigarettes with a revolutionary approach. In the months before the Camel debut, every city and hamlet in the country was bombarded with print advertising. According to the 1955 CPS, initiation by age 18 for males in this group jumped to 21.6 percent, a two thirds increase over those born before 1890. The NHIS initiation rate also reflected this change. For adolescent males, it went up from 2.9 percent between 1910 and 1912 to 4.9 percent between 1918 and 1921.

It was not until the mid-1920s that social mores permitted cigarette advertising to focus on women (public clamor forced a 1919 ad aimed at women by Lorillard Company to be withdrawn). In 1926 a poster depicted women imploring smokers of Chesterfield cigarettes to "Blow Some My Way." The most successful crusade, however, was for Lucky Strikes, which urged women to "Reach for a Lucky Instead of a Sweet." The 1955 CPS data showed that 7 percent of the women who were adolescents during the mid-1920s had started smoking by age 18, compared with only 2 percent in the preceding generation of female adolescents. Initiation rates from the NHIS data for adolescent girls were observed to increase threefold, from 0.6 percent between 1922 and 1925 to 1.8 percent between 1930 and 1933. In contrast, rates for males rose only slightly.

The next major boost in smoking initiation in adolescent females occurred in the late 1960s. In 1967 the tobacco industry launched "niche" brands aimed exclusively at women. The most popular was Virginia Slims. The visuals of this campaign emphasized a woman who was strong, independent and very thin. Consequently, and ironically in conjunction with the rise of the women's movement, initiation in female adolescents nearly doubled, from 3.7 percent between 1964 and 1967 to 6.2 percent between 1972 and 1975 (NHIS data). During the same period, rates for adolescent males remained stable.

Thus, in four distinct instances over the past 100 years, innovative and directed tobacco marketing campaigns were associated with marked surges in primary demand from adolescents only in the target group. The first two were directed at males and the second two at females. Of course, other factors helped to entrench smoking in society, such as the provision of free cigarettes during wartime and the romanticization of actors smoking in the movies. Yet it is clear from the data that advertising has been an overwhelming force in attracting new users.

Despite subsequent regulations barring advertisement geared to minors, the tobacco industry nonetheless has retained its targeted approach. In 1988 R.J. Reynolds introduced another novel campaign featuring the ultracool cartoon character "Joe Camel." Recent data from California indicate a rising market share for Camels in youths and a turnaround in adolescent smoking prevalence, which had been declining during the 1980s. Future surveys of adults will most likely show a jump in adolescent smoking initiation rates coincident with the rolling out of this campaign.

—*John P. Pierce and Elizabeth A. Gilpin*

The authors are researchers at the Cancer Prevention and Control Program at the University of California, San Diego.

tion climbed from 8 percent of production in 1984 to 30 percent in 1994. Unmanufactured tobacco leaf exportation now exceeds 34 percent of production. The U.S. currently leads the world in tobacco exports and has capitalized on the markets in underdeveloped countries, which have few if any restrictions on advertising or product labeling.

The six major transnational tobacco companies (three are based in the U.S., and the others in the U.K.) have experienced little resistance to gaining footholds in these developing countries. Often the only competition comes from government-run production companies, for which there is marginal advertising. Many have argued that the introduction of Western advertising in developing countries has done much more than shift the existing market share to the transnational companies. In Hong Kong, for instance, only 1 percent of the women now smoke, but the advertising by transnational companies has heavily targeted women—clearly indicating that the companies are making an effort to carve out a new market. This kind of exploitation equates with the disgraceful export of opium from England to

1. LIVING WITH DRUGS

China in the 1830s.

As assistant secretary of health under President George Bush, James Mason stated in 1990 at the Seventh World Conference on Tobacco and Health in Perth, Australia: "It is unconscionable for the mighty transnational tobacco companies to be peddling their poison abroad, particularly because their main targets are less developed countries. They play our free trade laws and export policies like a Stradivarius violin, pressuring our trade promotion agencies to keep open—and force open in some cases—other nations' markets for their products."

The U.S. government has remained remarkably unresponsive to such claims. One reason for this inaction may be that in 1990 the U.S. realized a $4.2-billion trade surplus from tobacco exports, accounting for 35 percent of the entire agricultural trade surplus. In that same year Vice President Dan Quayle stated during a North Carolina news conference: "I don't think it's news to North Carolina tobacco farmers that the American public as a whole is smoking less. We ought to think about the exports. We ought to think about opening up markets, breaking down the barriers rather than erecting new tariffs, new quotas and things of that sort."

Much of the aggressive trade behavior by the tobacco industry is sanctioned under section 301 of the 1974 Trade Act. Public health officials have repeatedly asked that Congress reevaluate this act and current tobacco trade practices, but the representatives have failed to take action. Moreover, many have questioned the difference in health standards applied to domestically consumed and exported tobacco. For example, there are no U.S.-imposed regulations on the labeling, tar content or advertisement of tobacco products exported to developing nations. It is truly ironic that the U.S. freely exports cigarettes to countries such as Colombia in the face of huge expenditures on both sides to restrict the trade of cocaine, which accounts for many fewer deaths.

The magnitude of tobacco-related diseases and deaths around the world cannot be overstated. Cigarette smoking is the number-one preventable cause of premature death in the U.S. Yet it enjoys remarkable tolerance among Americans. On an international level, trends in smoking prevalence suggest an even more profound rejection or ignorance of the health risks of tobacco use.

For these reasons, the obstacles facing the antitobacco campaign are formidable. From the standpoint of public health, it is clear that a battle plan must emphasize intervention programs that specifically target children and adolescents. These plans include increased government regulation of tobacco advertisements, restrictions on access to cigarettes by minors and higher tobacco taxes. Other possibilities are support for personal-injury litigation against the tobacco industry, government subsidies for the conversion of tobacco crops to other plants and comprehensive restrictions on workplace and public smoking. Concerned citizens, public health officials, government representatives and health care providers must join forces to adopt a multidisciplinary strategy to control this global epidemic.

FURTHER READING

SMOKING AND HEALTH: REPORT OF THE ADVISORY COMMITTEE TO THE SURGEON GENERAL OF THE PUBLIC HEALTH SERVICE. PHS Publication No. 1103, 1964.

THE WORLDWIDE SMOKING EPIDEMIC: TOBACCO TRADE, USE AND CONTROL. William C. Scott et al. in *Journal of the American Medical Association,* Vol. 263, No. 24, pages 3312–3318; June 27, 1990.

TOBACCO, BIOLOGY AND POLITICS. Stanton A. Glantz. Health Edco, Waco, Tex., 1992.

THE HUMAN COSTS OF TOBACCO USE. C. E. Bartecchi, T. D. MacKenzie and R. W. Schrier in *New England Journal of Medicine,* Vol. 330, No. 13, pages 907–912; March 31, 1994, and Vol. 330, No. 14, pages 975–980; April 7, 1994.

The international trade in drugs has become an increasingly important issue in global security. It is a problem, however, that falls outside traditional national security concerns, even though it threatens the political stability of many states.

Global Reach:
The Threat of International Drug Trafficking

RENSSELAER W. LEE III

RENSSELAER W. LEE III, *president of Global Advisory Services in Alexandria, Virginia, and associate scholar at the Foreign Policy Research Institute in Philadelphia, is the author of* The White Labyrinth: Cocaine and Political Power *(New Brunswick, N.J.: Transaction Press, 1989).*

Narcotics industries rank as the world's most successful illegal enterprises, generating annual profits of roughly $200 billion to $300 billion. Major production and trafficking complexes in the Andes, Southwest Asia, and the Golden Triangle of Southeast Asia thrive, impervious to international enforcement programs. Indeed, between 1982 and 1994, worldwide opium production more than doubled, and the global output of coca leaves rose by 300 percent. Opium cultivation is expanding rapidly in several communist or former communist states, primarily China, Vietnam, Uzbekistan, Tajikistan, and Turkmenistan. (In China, the revolutionary government claimed four decades ago that the once pervasive problem of opiate addiction was all but obliterated, but poppy plantings have been reported in at least 17 of the nation's 30 provinces, and drug use is escalating rapidly.)

China currently serves as an important transit country for Burmese heroin, and entrepreneurial North Koreans are entering the heroin business, possibly with the backing of their government. Colombia, which produces an estimated 70 to 80 percent of the world's refined cocaine, is the world's third largest opium producer, with an estimated 20,000 hectares under poppy cultivation. Moreover, the distinctive signature of Colombian-refined heroin is increasingly appearing in United States retail markets. A similar trend toward diversification in the industry is also seen in Peru, the world's largest producer of coca leaf, where low levels of poppy cultivation are being recorded. In addition, several communist or former communist countries—Poland, China, Russia, Azerbaijan, and the Baltic states—are emerging as important producers and exporters of sophisticated amphetamines. And narcotics such as LSD, Ecstasy, and trimethylphentanil (a powerful synthetic opiate) are marketed with increasing frequency in former Soviet states.

Narcotics industries are becoming larger, more powerful, and more entrenched in the global economy and in the economies and societies of individual producing states, although they differ significantly in organizational sophistication and systematic effects. For example, trafficking organizations in China are at a rudimentary stage of development, with small staffs that often disband after one or two deals. Furthermore, the profits generated by smuggling opium or heroin out of China flow primarily to overseas Chinese, not mainlanders. Consequently, Chinese drug organizations exert little influence on China's economic system and are generally not viewed as a threat to state authority. (Virtually no reports of high-level drug corruption in China have surfaced.)

At the other extreme, Colombia's highly developed trafficking enterprises employ hundreds of specialized personnel—pilots, shippers, chemists, accountants, lawyers, financial managers, and assassins—directly or on contract, and earn an estimated $4 billion to $7 billion annually, mainly from cocaine sales in the United States and Europe. These revenues endow the narcotraffickers with a significant capability to bribe or otherwise influence the behavior of key Colombian officials and political leaders. (United States law enforcement officials estimate that the Colombian cartels spend more than $100 million annually on bribes in the country.) Colombia constitutes a model of advanced or mature narcotics enterprises that have the economic and political problems associated with a large criminal sector.

Some worrisome trends have arisen in narcotic industry strategies: widening economic influence, that is, the impact of the illicit drug trade on illegal economic structures and processes in major producing or transit countries; the increasing political corruption in such countries; the growing intrusion of narcocriminal enterprises into the realm of the state and the law, a process that some scholars associate with the delegitimation of government; the successes of narcotics businesses in innovation, avoiding detection, and increasing operating efficiency; and, especially apparent since the late 1980s, the growing transnational cooperation among criminal empires that deal in drugs and other black market items. All these trends suggest that narcotics industries are enhancing their power and reach, developing new and advanced capabilities, and establishing new bases of support. At the same time, the leaders and citizens of some trafficking countries are exhibiting clear signs of drug war fatigue. Much to the dismay of the United States, support is growing for peaceful resolutions of the drug trade issue, ranging from negotiated surrenders that treat drug kingpins leniently to the outright legalization of narcotics.

DRUG ECONOMICS

The economic effects of the drug trade stem mainly from the processes of legitimizing narcotics earnings in the country or countries of origin. Different nations display different patterns. For example, officials in the Chinese Ministry of Public Security believe that opium and heroin smugglers invest few of their earnings in ventures that benefit the Chinese economy. Most drug proceeds are banked in noncommunist Asian countries and the little money that does return to the country tends to be used to buy luxury housing, furniture, electronic equipment, and gold jewelry. In Russia the sales of illicit drugs total an estimated $800 million each year, and law enforcement officials contend that much of the startup capital for small, legitimate businesses, such as stores, restaurants, and fruit stands, is supplied by the narcotics trade. (However, the economic effect of drugs in Russia is difficult to separate from the effect of organized crime groups in general, which operate many profitable illegal enterprises.) Colombia is probably suffering from the most advanced case of narcoeconomic penetration; traffickers annually repatriate an estimated $2 billion to $5 billion from narcotics exports, or approximately 4 to 9 percent of Colombia's GDP of $55 billion. One Colombian economist, Francesco Thoumi, has calculated that accumulated trafficker assets in Colombia and abroad reached anywhere from $39 billion to $66 billion between 1989 and 1990, a scale of narcowealth so immense that it could easily alter Colombia's economic and political status quo.

Indeed, drug money pervades the Colombian economy. For example, according to the Colombian Institute of Agrarian Reform and the Colombian Farmers Association, drug dealers expanded their direct or intermediary ownership of agricultural land from 1 million hectares in the late 1980s to an estimated 4 million hectares in 1994. Today, traffickers own or control between 8 and 11 percent of agriculturally usable land in at least 250 of 1,060 Colombian

municipalities, making them a powerful force in the rural Colombian economy. Technological improvements in cattle raising and commercial agriculture sometimes accompanied narco land investments, strengthening traffickers as rural leaders in some areas. Furthermore, as the so-called Cali cartel gained ascendancy, the infiltration of legitimate businesses by drug dealers reached significant new levels. Earlier generations of traffickers, such as the leaders of the Medellín cartel of the 1980s (then the dominant trafficking group in Colombia), were relatively unsophisticated economic actors who were more concerned with laundering drug earnings than realizing adequate returns on their investments. However, these earlier traffickers clearly spent to enhance their status. Conspicuous examples abound. Jose Gonzalo Rodriguez Gacha accumulated 140 country estates, collectively worth an estimated $100 million; some of these residences were lavishly furnished with items such as pillows stuffed with ostrich feathers, gold-plated bathroom fixtures, and imported Italian toilet paper stamped with likenesses of Botticelli's *The Birth of Venus*.

In contrast, the Cali group cultivated an image of business respectability by investing in a wide range of economic activities. According to a recent report by the Colombian Department of Administrative Security, Cali drug money has "infiltrated the construction industry, drugstore chains, radio stations, automobile dealerships, department stores, factories, banks, sports clubs, and investment firms." Agribusiness enterprises such as cut flowers, tropical fruit production, and poultry farms can be added to this list. "In what sectors of the economy has the Cali cartel not invested?" asked Gabriel de Vega Pinzon, the head of the Colombian National Drug Directorate, in a December 1994 interview with this writer.

DRUG POLITICS

Drug trafficking also has wide-ranging effects on political and administrative systems in developing countries. Narcotics industries in countries such as Myanmar, Afghanistan, and Colombia (especially between 1989 and 1991) are associated with extreme antistate violence or with the disintegration of national authority. However, most drug dealers are not pursuing independent political initiatives, preferring to coexist with and manipulate the state authority. "We don't kill judges or ministers, we buy them," remarked Cali cartel leader Gilberto Rodriguez Orejuela on one occasion. Indeed, corruption has assumed outlandish proportions in Colombia. In 1994 police and judicial investigations detected evidence of trafficker payoffs to: a former president of the Colombian national congress, a former comptroller general, a recently elected congressman, 12 retired army officers (communication and security specialists "decorated for their outstanding service to the army"), more than 150 Cali police officers, almost the entire contingent of Cali airport police, employees of the El Valle telephone system, the Cali regional prosecutor, 6 of 22 Cali city councillors, and the mayors of 4 Colombian cities, among them Medellín.

The pattern of corruption in Latin America also includes attempts by traffickers to purchase influence at the highest political levels. During the 1980s, narcocorruption involving top national leaders or their closest associates was documented in Bolivia, Panama, the Bahamas, and the Turks and Caicos Islands. One drug informant claims that Fidel Castro's brother Raúl personally authorized the shipment of 6 tons of cocaine through Cuba between 1987 and 1989. Traffickers have also indirectly sought political leverage by contributing to presidential election campaigns. Trafficker support of the 1989 Bolivian campaign of President Jaime Paz Zamora prompted Paz in 1991 to appoint a known drug dealer, Faustino Rico Toro, to head the Bolivian Special Narcotics Force, although pressure from the United States subsequently forced Paz to dismiss Rico Toro from that post; in early 1995 the Bolivian Supreme Court authorized the extradition of Rico Toro to the United States on drug charges. In Colombia a major scandal erupted in June 1994 when a taped telephone conversation leaked to the press showed Gilberto Rodriguez Orejuela and his brother discussing a possible donation of $3.8 million to the presidential campaign of Ernesto Samper Pizano. Some Colombian and United States observers—among them Jose Toft, the United States Drug Enforcement Agency (DEA) representative in Colombia at the time—contend that the Samper campaign did in fact receive millions of dollars from the Cali cartel. Toft, who resigned from the DEA last September, summarized a widely held belief about the state of Colombian politics when he commented to a Colombian television news station that, "I cannot think of a single political or judicial institution that has not been penetrated by the narco-traffickers—I know that people don't like to hear the term 'narcodemocracy,' but the truth is it's very real and it's here."

Modern narcotics enterprises have also helped criminal authority grow at the expense of legitimate state authority. In Latin America this encroachment spans issues such as social welfare, counterinsurgency, and (ironically) the maintenance of law and order. For example, in Mexico, Colombia, and Bolivia, traffickers have cultivated a Robin Hood image by devoting vast resources to community development projects such as roads, schools, airport repairs, and housing, or by donating money and gifts to the poor. Such activities cemented political support for the drug capos among marginalized social groups such as Medellín slum dwellers and poor farmers in the Bolivian Beni—populations that governments and legitimate nongovernment organizations cannot serve. In Colombia a weak government presence in the countryside, an ongoing rural insurgency, and the acquisition of landed estates by drug lords in the 1980s created new political opportunities and roles for narcotics dealers. For example, paramilitary organizations financed by trafficking interests emerged, supplanting an impotent Colombian state by furnishing local security against predatory guerrilla groups. Curbed somewhat by the Colombian government's 1990 crackdown on the Medellín cartel, narco-backed paramilitaries nonetheless pursue their mission in the middle Magdalena Valley, Cordoba, Uraba, and other guerrilla-infested regions. (Of course, paramilitary operations to root out and exterminate leftist guerrilla sympathizers pose serious human rights challenges for Colombia.) Legitimate private groups conducting business in the Colombian hinterlands—coffee growers, cattlemen associations, and foreign oil companies, for example—admittedly provide public welfare and security protection functions. However, the assumption of such roles by the narcotraffickers generates particularly ominous overtones for the Colombian political process.

Traffickers tend to support their local police on law and order issues such as the defense of property rights and maintenance of basic community services; police who spearhead government narcotics crackdowns or work for rival trafficking organizations, however, stand a good chance of being murdered. The Cali cartel supported a perverted and socially regressive form of law enforcement, the so-called social cleansing groups, which targeted marginal urban dwellers such as prostitutes, thieves, beggars and drug addicts. In some regions of Latin America and Asia, trafficking interests for all practical purposes are the law, since the government does not exercise real sovereignty in those areas. (Drug trafficker Khun Sa's Shan state enclave in Myanmar represents perhaps the most egregious modern example of narcowarlordism.) Yet, opportunistic traffickers also assist or form alliances with governments that persecute rival criminal organizations. For example, in Myanmar, the Wa insurgent trafficking groups are enlisting government help to fight Khun Sa's Shan United Army—and managing to broaden their territorial base in the process.

In Colombia the Cali cartel found it politically and commercially expedient to furnish "valuable information" to the government for its ultimately successful manhunt for Pablo Escobar and some of his lieutenants, a contribution recently acknowledged by Colombian prosecutor general Alfonso Valdivieso (according to the Cali regional prosecutor's office, the Cali group hired Japanese communication experts to track Escobar's movements in the months before his demise). Moreover, in a June 1994 interview with this writer, Valdivieso's predecessor, Gustavo de Grieff, referred to a report that a special government search force in Medellín received a $10 million payment from Cali traffickers shortly after Escobar was killed last December and allegedly distributed the funds among ranking members of the force. "Apparently, [the force] was an instrument of Escobar's enemies, not of the government," de Grieff commented.

Such scattered examples confirm the ability of traffickers, who command enormous power and resources, to pirate government functions or inherit them by default. In surrender negotiations with the Colombian government, the Cali traffickers surprised no one by wielding their contributions to the anti-Escobar campaign as leverage against the government. In a letter to President Cesar Gaviría in January 1994, Gilberto Rodriguez Orejuela petitioned for house arrest rather than a jail cell, in part on grounds of his "collaboration with the prosecutor general's office and the search group to achieve the well-known results."

Finally, new patterns of domestic and international cooperation have spawned among criminal empires that deal in illicit drugs. Such cooperation connects criminal groups such as the Colombian cartels, Mexican smuggling organizations, Japanese *yakuza,* Hong Kong Chinese syndicates, Sicilian mafia, and Russian organized crime. Central issues of common concern include the organization of markets, trade deals (for example, exchanges of drugs for weapons, drugs for cash, and drugs for drugs), smuggling logistics, and laundering or repatriation of trafficking proceeds.

Cooperation between Colombian traffickers and Italian organized crime groups to sell cocaine in Italy and the rest of Europe apparently stands at a particularly advanced stage. The Cali cartel and the Sicilian mafia are experimenting with franchise arrangements that would allow the mafia to distribute large consignments of Cali cocaine to European buyers outside Italy. The Cali group has also established working relationships with organized crime figures in Poland, the Czech Republic, and Russia. The Cali traffickers' strategic design uses these countries as a back door to deliver cocaine to western Europe. Such relationships are underscored by Russian government seizures of 1.1 tons of cocaine in Vyborg in February 1993, and 400 kilograms of the drug in St. Petersburg in April 1994; both shipments could be traced to Cali trafficking organizations. In general, international narcocooperation opens new markets for narcotics and other illegal products, exploits economies of scale for selling in those markets, enhances organized crime's penetration of legal economic and financial systems, and generally increases the power of criminal formations relative to national governments.

TREATING THE DRUG PROBLEM

Confronting powerful narcotics lobbies and publics weary of drug wars, government commitment to suppress narcotrafficking is waning perceptibly in some source countries. One manifestation of this trend is rising political support to legalize drugs. Bolivia's president, Gonzalo Sanchez de Losada, openly favors this; he declared to a Spanish newspaper in 1993 that "The antidrug fight is the politician's tomb—prohibition has achieved nothing but making vices extremely profitable for traffickers. It is terrible to say it, but some tax on drugs should be created." The Bolivian government promised coca farmers in September 1994 that it would mount an international campaign to decriminalize the coca leaf (but not the products derived from it). Colombian President Ernesto Samper recently canceled plans for a popular referendum to overturn a May 1994 decision by the Colombian constitutional court that legalized personal drug use.

The legalization or selective decriminalization of drugs is gaining ground elsewhere in the world. Poland, Russia, and Italy have lifted criminal penalties for personal drug use, and cannabis products are openly sold to adults in coffeehouses in the Netherlands. In China, where drug dealers are routinely executed with great public fanfare, some local cadres advocate removing restrictions on poppy growing to help isolated mountain areas "get rid of poverty"— possibly a sign of the significant proportions of the private opium trade in that country.

In the Andean countries, governments have not legalized drug production—an action that would spur certain retaliation by the United States—but they have attempted to diminish conflicts with the cocaine industry by negotiating with participants and leaders in the trafficking chain. Colombia's negotiations with Medellín cartel leaders date to May 1984, when former President Alfonso Lopez Michelson and Attorney General Carlos Jimenez Gomez held separate meetings with Pablo Escobar and other kingpins in Panama. Since 1990, Colombia has offered reduced sentences and other legal inducements to traffickers who surrender, confess, and turn state's evidence.

Colombian officials see negotiations as a tool of social policy that can subdue the power of individual trafficking organizations. Negotiations doubtless helped reduce narcoterrorist violence in the 1990s, but produced few successes against cocaine trafficking. Important traffickers negotiated relatively short sentences that ranged from 4 to 8 years, but furnished little information on the workings of cocaine enterprises. Ivan Urdinola, for example, refused to name major accomplices, averring that such disclosures would place him in mortal danger, and liberally laced his confessions with fatuous statements. (At one point, he informed a judge, "Aside from being a drug trafficker, I am an admirable person."). Perhaps the late Pablo Escobar abused the surrender policy most notoriously. After negotiating a deal with the government in mid-1991, Escobar was incarcerated in the La Catedral prison near Medellín, where he continued to manage his cocaine business until his escape 13 months later. (Subsequent revelations indicated that Escobar paid $2 million for construction of the facility, which was equipped with cellular telephones, fax machines, and computers.) In Bolivia, the government's repentance program produced similarly disappointing results. Repenters characterized themselves as simple cattle farmers who only dabbled in cocaine or lent money to traffickers; the three most important traffickers who surrendered under the Bolivian program received sentences of only 4 to 6 years.

Cali cartel leaders recently offered to implement a plan that would reduce cocaine exports from Colombia by 60 percent (their estimate of their share of the business) if they spent little or no time in jail. Of course, such an offer invites skepticism, since the Cali dons might not control or directly influence a sufficiently large percentage of Colombian refining and exporting capacity to fulfill such a commitment. Recent information suggests that the Colombian cocaine industry is more decentralized and balkanized than during the 1980s. Gilberto Rodriguez Orejuela himself noted in a November 1994 letter to *El Tiempo* that "there are many cartels"; moreover, the industry depends on a multitude of subcontractors and freelancers. Of course, drug kingpins possess considerable leverage over lower level operators; they can stop purchasing products and services or simply withhold protection from laboratories, transport companies, distribution cells, laundering operations, and other key trafficking entities. But, in putting forth their offer, the Cali traffickers provided no blueprint or timetable for dismantling their multibillion-dollar enterprises. Also, a number of factors—the size of the illicit drug industry, the prevalence of official corruption, and the weakness of the Colombian criminal justice and judicial institutions—indicate that Colombia could not successfully implement such a deal.

Debates over legalization, democratization, and negotiated accords with traffickers in key source countries have produced consternation in Washington. Yet, disillusionment with overseas narcotics control and with drug prohibition in general is also widespread in the United States. Many Americans favor scrapping supply-side programs altogether, shifting resources to education and prevention programs, or even legalizing the production and use of some drugs. United States international initiatives, including the roughly $1 billion allocated to counternarcotics operations in the Andes since 1989, certainly have had few long-term effects on the availability or purity of drugs in America's major urban markets. Some United States policies are wasteful, counterproductive, or worse. For example, the Bolivian government spent $48.1 million in American aid between 1987 and 1993 to pay farmers to eradicate 26,000 hectares of coca. Farmers, however, planted more than 35,000 new hectares of coca during the same period. The planned compensation for eradication transformed into little more than a coca support program.

At least in the short term, the objective of restricting internationally the suppliers of illegal drugs is probably not attainable. The number of potential drug suppliers is virtually unlimited; few geographical, organizational, or technological barriers obstruct entry into narcotics industries, and crops, laboratories, drug shipments, planes, money, chemicals, and routes can be easily replaced if destroyed. Of course, the value of international drug control does not necessarily lie solely in controlling narcotics. The war on narcotrafficking can be justified as a moral imperative even if it is a practical failure. Furthermore, the United States has staked its prestige and predicated its diplomatic relations with several countries on combating the drug scourge.

More important, however, is the fact that enterprises such as the Colombian cartels and counterpart groups in Europe and Asia dangerously aggregate power that can destabilize governments and facilitate global breakdowns in law and order. (For example, some United States intelligence officials believe that drug-trafficking networks and routes can be easily reconfigured to smuggle chemical weapons, plutonium, or tactical nuclear weapons to terrorist nations and groups.) Demolishing such power can stand alone as a worthwhile objective. Similarly, United States policy expresses legitimate concerns when helping governments curb the political and economic reach of the drug lords, contain narcoterrorist violence, and in general cope with the divisive effects of the drug business. Between 1989 and 1993, the United States supported a crackdown on the Medellín cartel that decimated the group's leadership (all the Medellín founding fathers are either dead or in jail) and removed a lethal threat to the Colombian political order. American pressure or intervention prompted the ouster of narcotics-linked military regimes in Bolivia in 1980 and 1981, and in Panama in 1989, two countries where narcotics trafficking interests had built cozy relationships with the military, giving them de facto control of the national government apparatus for controlling drug crime. In Bolivia, United States pressure on the Paz administration in 1991 prevented the appointment of Bolivians apparently linked to the cocaine trade to head the Ministry of Interior, the National Police, and the Special Narcotics Force.

In a number of countries—such as Bolivia, Thailand, and Laos—United States foreign assistance has fostered positive economic growth, widened income opportunities for farmers who cultivate drugs, and weakened the relative economic clout of narcotics industries. Perhaps international drug policy cannot substantially control entrenched drug trafficking, but supply-side programs can be reconfigured to target criminal organizations, promote stability and growth in drug-torn countries, and enhance positive United States influence.

What Are Some of the Historic Milestones in Early U.S. Drug Control Efforts?

Drugs of abuse have changed since the 1800s—most rapidly over the past quarter century

Problems with opiate addiction date from widespread use of patent medicines in the 1800s. The range of drugs included opium, morphine, laudanum, cocaine, and, by the turn of the century, heroin. The tonics, nostrums, and alleged cures that contained or used such drugs were sold by itinerant peddlers, mail order houses, retail grocers, and pharmacists. There also was unrestricted access to opium in opium-smoking dens and to morphine through retailers.

When morphine was discovered in 1806, it was thought to be a wonder drug. Its use was so extensive during the Civil War that morphine addiction was termed the "army disease." The availability of the hypodermic syringe allowed non-medicinal use of morphine to gain popularity among veterans and other civilians. After 1898, heroin was used to treat respiratory illness and morphine addiction in the belief that it was nonaddicting.

In the 1880s coca became widely available in the U.S. as a health tonic and remedy for many ills. Its use was supported first by the European medical community and later by American medical authorities. In the absence of restrictive national legislation, its use spread. Initially cocaine was offered as a cure for opiate addiction, an asthma remedy (the official remedy of the American Hay Fever Association), and an antidote for toothaches.

By 1900, in the face of an estimated quarter of a million addicts. State laws were enacted to curb drug addiction. The major drugs of abuse at the time were cocaine and morphine.

The first laws controlling drug use were passed in the last quarter of the 19th century

By the late 1870s concern about opiate addiction and the nonmedical use of drugs had intensified. The first recorded antidrug law was a municipal ordinance passed in San Francisco in 1875 that banned smoking opium in opium dens. A series of State and local legislative actions followed. By 1912 nearly every State and many municipalities had regulations controlling the distribution of certain drugs.

The first actions taken at the Federal level prohibited importation of opium by Chinese nationals (1887) and restricted opium smoking in the Philippines (1905). These actions were followed by passage in 1906 of the Pure Food and Drug Act, which required over-the-counter medicines to correctly label the inclusion of certain drugs but did not restrict their use.

Much Federal antinarcotics legislation before the 1930s supported U.S. efforts to reduce international drug traffic

The U.S. launched a series of international conventions designed to stimulate other nations to pass domestic laws on narcotic control. The Shanghai Opium Convention of 1909 strongly supported such controls, but its recommendations generated little actual legislation among the nations involved, including the U.S. Failure to pass the proposed Foster Antinarcotic Bill led to debate at the 1911 International Conference on Opium at The Hague about whether the U.S. Would actually enact such legislation.

Ratification of the convention resulting from this Hague conference by the Senate in 1913 committed the U.S. to enact laws to suppress the abuse of opium, morphine, and cocaine and helped ensure passage of the Harrison Act as the cornerstone of Federal antidrug policy.

The U.S. experienced a cocaine problem for a 35-year period around the turn of the 20th century

The epidemic of cocaine and crack that struck the U.S. in the 1980s was not this Nation's first addictive experience with the "white powder." America's "first cocaine epidemic" extended from around the mid-1880s until the 1920s. Cocaine abuse decreased substantially by the 1920s and then

From *Drugs, Crime, and the Justice System: A National Report from the Bureau of Justice Statistics*, December 1992, pp. 78-81. Reprinted by permission of the Bureau of Justice Statistics, U.S. Department of Justice.

virtually disappeared from the American scene until the 1970s.

The first epidemic had three phases—

- first its introduction to the American public in the 1880s
- a middle period of wide use and initial recognition of the potential for addiction
- a final period of regulation and suppression just prior to World War I.

By the turn of the century the dangers of addiction had become apparent. As early as 1887 some States had begun regulation. Despite the absence of Federal police power, by 1910 the President presented congress with a State Department report stating that cocaine was "more appalling in its effect than any other habit-forming drug used in the U.S."

A year earlier, President Roosevelt had led the effort to ban drugs in the Nation's capital when informed by local police that the use of cocaine predisposes the user to commit criminal acts. When the Harrison Act became law in 1914 the use of cocaine had largely died out (though the consequences of use extended into the 1920s) and the national focus was on the temperance movement which led to the prohibition of alcohol.

Passage of the Harrison Act in 1914 shaped Federal domestic drug policy

The Act was ostensibly a revenue measure that required persons who prescribe or distribute specified drugs to register and buy tax stamps. It also provided that possession of narcotics by an unregistered person is unlawful unless prescribed by a physician in good faith. It was enforced by Treasury agents in the Prohibition Unit of the Narcotics Division.

The Harrison Act was passed amidst controversy on the treatment of drug users

This conflict in the medical community and between physicians and Federal

law enforcement agencies influenced Federal drug law enforcement for the next several years. From the first, the Treasury Department held that medical maintenance of opiate addicts (treatment through declining usage) was not permissible, but physicians opposed this view. Initially, maintenance was upheld by the lower courts, but a series of Supreme Court decisions ended in a 1919 ruling in *Webb v. U.S.* that prescriptions for addicts were illegal. This ruling was handed down on the same day as *U.S. v. Doremus* that upheld the Harrison Act.

Initial enforcement included arrests of physicians, pharmacists, and unregistered users. Private sanitariums that claimed to cure addiction had existed since the mid-1800s, but they were inadequate to serve all the addicts left without treatment when private physicians became wary of prescribing maintenance regimens. In response to this need, 44 cities opened municipal clinics between 1919 and 1921 to provide temporary maintenance for addicts. However, a primary goal of the Narcotics Division was closure of such clinics. The clinics did not receive enough public support to withstand this opposition, and all had closed by 1925.

The 1922 Narcotic Drugs Import and Export Act expanded Treasury Department responsibilities in drug control

The Act restricted opium imports and exports to nations that had ratified The Hague Convention. It also created the Federal Narcotics Control Board composed of the Secretaries of State, Treasury, and Commerce.

Most details for enforcing this law were left to the Narcotics Division, but the act did expand the role of the Customs Department in prohibiting illegal shipments of narcotics into the U.S.

During the 1930s the Treasury Department's focus shifted from heroin to marijuana

In 1930, the Federal Bureau of Narcotics (FBN) was created within the Treasury Department under the direction of Commissioner Harry Anslinger. It officially separated enforcement of alcohol laws from enforcement of other drug laws. The FBN was charged with enforcing the Harrison Act and other related drug laws, but the responsibility for interdiction remained with the Bureau of Customs. Marijuana use had not been included in earlier Federal antidrug legislation, but the FBN did include an optional provision in the Uniform Narcotic Drug Act that it promulgated to the States. However, growing public concerns about marijuana prompted the passage of many State laws prohibiting its use. By the mid-1930s marijuana had been elevated to national awareness and was placed on the FBN agenda. The antimarijuana efforts of the FBN led to the Marijuana-Tax Act of 1937, modeled after the earlier Harrison Act, which required a substantial transfer tax for all marijuana transactions.

Federal involvement in drug treatment began with the opening of hospitals for convicted addicts

In 1929 the Porter Narcotic Farm Act authorized the Public Health Service to open Federal hospitals for the treatment of incarcerated addicts. Two facilities were eventually opened: one in Lexington, Kentucky, in 1935 and one in Fort Worth, Texas, in 1938. These facilities provided medical and psychiatric treatment for inmates, but they were essentially modified prisons. This model for Federal treatment efforts held until the mid-1960s when the focus changed to financial support for community-based treatment.

In 1963, the President's Advisory Commission on Narcotics and Drug Abuse (the Prettyman Commission) called for a larger Federal role in treatment of narcotics addicts, judged the Lexington and Fort Worth facilities to be inadequate and only marginally effective, and prescribed a network of treatment and rehabilitative services.

1. LIVING WITH DRUGS

The Community Mental Health Centers Act of 1963 provided the first Federal assistance to non-Federal entities for treatment. The 1968 amendments to this Act established specialized addict treatment grants which expanded rapidly during the early 1970s. Federal drug control measures were extended to programs to prevent initiation of drug taking by adolescents. By including "narcotic addiction" in the definition of mental illness, Congress brought about a major policy shift that paved the way for Federal support of local drug dependence treatment.

During the 1950s, Federal sanctions for drug violations were increased

In two major laws, the Boggs Act in 1951 and the Narcotic Control Act of 1956—

- the severity of criminal penalties for violations of the import/export and internal revenue laws related to narcotics and marijuana were significantly increased
- penalties included mandatory minimum prison sentences that were later increased and broadened and higher potential fines for violations.

In the early 1960s, concern about the drug problem led to a variety of drug control activities

The United Nations adopted the Single Convention on Narcotic Drugs in 1961. It established regulatory schedules for psychotropic substances and quotas limiting production and export of licit pharmaceuticals. The signatories, which included the U.S., committed themselves to work cooperatively to control these substances.

In 1963, the Prettyman Commission recommended—

- imposition of strict Federal control for nonnarcotic drugs
- transfer of the Treasury Department's enforcement and investigative responsibilities to the Department of Justice (DOJ)
- transfer of responsibilities for the

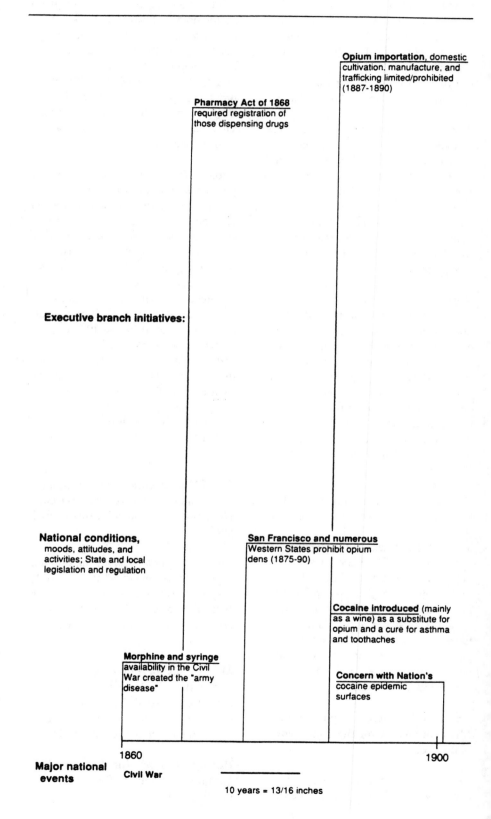

Major Federal legislation and international conventions

Opium importation, domestic cultivation, manufacture, and trafficking limited/prohibited (1887-1890)

Pharmacy Act of 1868 required registration of those dispensing drugs

Executive branch initiatives:

National conditions, moods, attitudes, and activities; State and local legislation and regulation

San Francisco and numerous Western States prohibit opium dens (1875-90)

Cocaine introduced (mainly as a wine) as a substitute for opium and a cure for asthma and toothaches

Concern with Nation's cocaine epidemic surfaces

Morphine and syringe availability in the Civil War created the "army disease"

1860

Major national events

Civil War

10 years = 13/16 inches

1900

regulation of legitimate drug trade from the Treasury Department to the Department of Health, Education and Welfare (HEW).
Key rulings of the Supreme Court

(such as *Robinson v. State of California*, 370 U.S. 660 (1962) and the recommendations of several Presidential Commissions supported a renewed clinical approach to the drug problem.

In 1964 Drs. Vincent Dole and Marie Nyswander launched a pilot program in New York City for methadone maintenance that met with early enthusiasm as a treatment for opiate addiction.

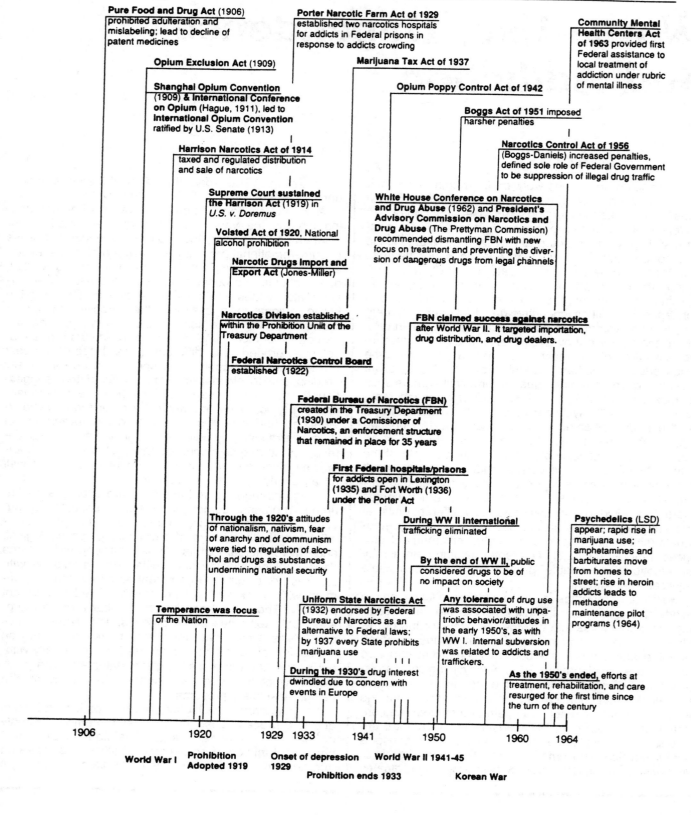

Understanding How Drugs Work—Use, Dependence, and Addiction

Understanding how drugs work on the human mind and body is a critical component to the resolution of questions and issues concerning drug use and abuse. An understanding of basic pharmacology is requisite to informed discussion on practically every drug-related issue and controversy. Unfortunately, one does not have to look far to find misinformed debate, much of which surrounds the basic lack of knowledge of how drugs work.

Different drugs produce different bodily effects and consequences. All psychoactive drugs influence the central nervous system. The central nervous system, in turn, sits at the center of how we physiologically and psychologically interpret and react to the world around us. Some drugs such as methamphetamine and LSD precipitate great influence on the nervous system, while others such as tobacco and marijuana illicit less pronounced reactions. Almost all psychoactive drugs have their effects on the body, mitigated and influenced by the dosage level of the drug taken, the manner in which it is ingested, and the physiological and emotional state of the user. PCP taken in large versus small doses may result in a person's being changed physically and emotionally forever. Cocaine smoked in the form of crack versus snorted as powder produces profoundly different physical and emotional effects on the user. LSD taken by emotionally stable persons in a controlled environment produces a more predictably favorable reaction than use by an emotionally unstable person in an unpredictable physical environment.

Molecular properties of certain drugs allow them to imitate and artificially reproduce certain naturally occurring brain chemicals that provide the basis for the drug's influence. The continued use of certain drugs and their repeated alteration of the body's biochemical structure provide one explanation for the physiological consequences of drug use. For example, heroin use replicates the natural brain chemical endorphin, which supports the body's biochemical defense to pain and stress. The continued use of heroin is believed to deplete natural endorphins, causing the nervous system to produce a painful physical and emotional reaction when heroin is withdrawn. The user's fear of withdrawal perpetuates continued use. Thus, one physiological theory of dependence and addiction is illustrated briefly.

A word of caution is in order, however, when proceeding through the various theories and explanations for what drugs do and why they do it. Many people, because of some emotional proximity to the world of drugs, assert a subjective predisposition when interpreting certain drugs' effects and consequences for the user. One person's alcoholic is another's social drinker. People often argue, rationalize, and explain the perceived benign or insidious nature of drugs' effects based upon an extremely superficial understanding of diverse pharmacological properties of different drugs. If the 10 percent of the American population suspected to be genetically predisposed to alcoholism were aware of that suggestion, then perhaps the age at which the onset to alcoholic drinking typically begins would be older than twelve. A detached and scientifically sophisticated awareness of drug pharmacology could very well prove the best defense to the negative consequences of drug use. Unfortunately, such an awareness is probably a distant as well as an overly comprehensive reality.

Drug dependence and addiction are usually a continuum of a process comprised of experimentation, recreational use, regular use, and abuse. The process is influenced by a plethora of physiological, psychological, and environmental factors. To say that one will become dependent on cocaine after initial experimentation with crack is not possible. To say that someone may experiment with crack and not become addicted is also not possible. The current population of cocaine users represents both extremes of the process. The exhortation of cocaine as a candidate for a safe recreational drug on the basis that certain people do use it recreationally without undue harm is a meaningless statement. The pharmacology of the drug as it pertains to use by human beings absolutely prevents it.

Largely, drugs are highly addictive or less addictive due to a process described as "reinforcement." Simply defined, reinforcement is a physiological and psychological influence on behavior that causes repeated introduction of a drug to the body. Cocaine and the amphetamines are known as drugs with high reinforcement potential. A parent of needy children who spends the last of the family income on crack to the detriment of the children epitomizes the powerful reinforcing nature of the drug. Persons addicted to drugs known to be strongly reinforcing typically report that they care more about getting the drug than anything else.

Reinforcement does not, however, provide the basis for understanding addiction. Addiction is a cloudy term used to describe a multitude of pharmacological and environmental factors that produce a compulsive, non-negotiable need for a drug. A thorough understanding of addiction requires an awareness of these many factors.

The articles in unit 2 illustrate some of the current research and viewpoints on the ways drugs act upon the human body. An understanding of these pharmacological processes is critical to understanding the assorted consequences of drug use and abuse. Furthermore, the articles help reveal that a drug's pharmacological properties and potential for abuse may not determine the drug's legal status. It is inappropriate to attempt to weigh a drug's potential benefits or threat to public health on the basis of its legal status. The two concepts are often interpreted independently of each other.

It is extremely important, however, to understand pharmacologically why different classes of drugs, be they depressants, stimulants, hallucinogens, and so forth, produce different influences upon human behavior and action. A policy debate on cocaine must entertain the basic notions of the drug's powerful psychoactive effects.

Looking Ahead: Challenge Questions

Why are some drugs so reinforcing?

What class of drugs presents the greatest potential for abuse and why?

Why do some people become dependent upon certain drugs far sooner than other people? Is it possible to predict one's personal threshold for becoming drug dependent or addicted? Defend your answer.

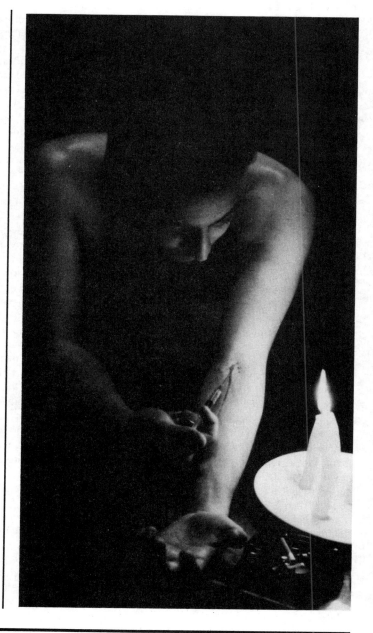

Is Nicotine Addictive? It Depends on Whose Criteria You Use

Experts say the definition of addiction is evolving.

Philip J. Hilts

Special to The New York Times

WASHINGTON, Aug. 1—When heavily dependent users of cocaine are asked to compare the urge to take cocaine with the urge to smoke cigarettes, about 45 percent say the urge to smoke is as strong or stronger than that for cocaine.

Among heroin addicts, about 38 percent rank the urge to smoke as equal to or stronger than the urge to take heroin. Among those addicted to alcohol, about 50 percent say the urge to smoke is at least as strong as the urge to drink.

In April, seven chief executives of tobacco companies testified before a Congressional subcommittee that nicotine was not addictive. Experts in addiction, while disagreeing with that assessment, say that the definition of addiction is evolving, and that they can see how such a statement might be made.

HEARINGS ON SMOKING

This week, the Food and Drug Administration is holding hearings to consider whether cigarettes fit in the array of addictive drugs and whether the Government should regulate them.

The standard definition of addiction comes from the American Psychiatric Association and the World Health Organization, which list nine criteria for determining addiction. The two groups, which prefer the term drug dependence, base their definition on research done since the 1960's, which has determined that multiple traits must be considered in determining whether a substance is addictive.

Thus although cigarettes do not offer as intense an effect as drugs like heroin and cocaine, they rank higher in a number of other factors. They not only create dependence among users but also elicit a high degree of tolerance, the need for more and more of a drug to satisfy a craving. When all the factors are added up, the consensus view among scientists is that nicotine is strongly addictive.

In smoking, it is not the nicotine or addiction that is most harmful, but other toxic chemicals produced by burning tobacco, which cause most of the 400,000 deaths each year that are attributed to smoking.

Dr. Lynn T. Kozlowski, an addiction expert at Pennsylvania State University, said addiction could generally be defined as "the repeated use of a psychoactive drug which is difficult to stop." He added that there might be many explanations for why it was hard to stop, including withdrawal that was too disturbing, or a high that was too enticing.

A diagnosis of mild dependence on a psychoactive drug is determined by meeting three of the nine criteria. Five items show moderate dependence and seven items indicate a strong dependence. (Not all nine items apply to each drug. For example, time and effort spent acquiring a drug are a significant feature of heroine addiction, but have no meaning in nicotine addiction.)

9 ADDICTION CRITERIA

These are the criteria:
- Taking the drug more often or in larger amounts than intended.
- Unsuccessful attempts to quit; persistent desire, craving.
- Excessive time spent in drug seeking.
- Feeling intoxicated at inappropriate times, or feeling withdrawal symptoms from a drug at such times.
- Giving up other things for it.
- Continued use, despite knowledge of harm to oneself and others.
- Marked tolerance in which the amount needed to satisfy increases at first before leveling off.
- Characteristic withdrawal symptoms for particular drugs.
- Taking the drug to relieve or avoid withdrawal.

Before applying a test of the nine criteria, the expert first determines if the symptoms have persisted for at least a month or have occurred repeatedly over a longer period of time.

Asked about the tobacco executives' testimony on addiction, Dr. Kozlowski said: "In a way, I can see how they could say that. It has to do with a mistaken image of what addiction is, and I have many well-educated, intelligent people say something like that to me. People often think of a person taking one injection of heroin and becoming hopelessly addicted for the rest of their lives. That is wrong."

In addition, he said, when people tend to think of the high that heroin produces, one that is about as intense as cocaine and alcohol, they cannot believe cigarettes are in the same category. And they are not. Even though in large doses nicotine can cause a strong high and hallucinations, the doses used in cigarettes produce only a very mild high.

But researchers now know, says Dr. Jack Henningfield, chief of clinical pharmacology at the Addiction Research Center of the Government's National Institute on Drug Abuse, that many qualities are related to a drug's addictiveness, and the level of intoxication it produces may be one of the least important.

If one merely asks how much pleasure the drugs produce, as researchers used to do and tobacco companies still do, then heroin or cocaine and nicotine do not seem to be in the same category. Dr. Kozlowski said, "It's not that cigarettes are without pleasure, but the pleasure is not in the same ball park with heroin."

But now, he said, there are more questions to ask. "If the question is, How hard is it to stop? then nicotine is a very impressive drug," he said. "Its urges are very similar to heroin."

Among the properties of a psychoactive drug—how much craving it can cause, how severe is the withdrawal, how intense a high it brings—each addicting drug has its own profile.

Heroin has a painful, powerful withdrawal, as does alcohol. But cocaine has little or no withdrawal. On the other hand, cocaine is more habit-forming in some respects, it is more reinforcing in the scientific terminology, meaning that animals and humans will seek to use it frequently in short periods of time, even over food and water.

Drugs rank differently on the scale of how difficult they are to quit as well, with nicotine rated by most experts as the most difficult to quit.

Moreover, it is not merely the drug that determines addiction, says Dr. John R. Hughes, an addiction expert at the University of Vermont. It is also the person, and the circumstances in the person's life. A user may be able to resist dependence at one time and not at another.

A central property of addiction is the user's control over the substance. With all drugs, including heroin, many are occasional users. The addictive property of the substance can be measured by how many users maintain a casual habit and how many are persistent, regular users.

According to large Government surveys of alcohol users, only about 15 percent are regular, dependent drinkers. Among cocaine users, about 8 percent become dependent.

For cigarettes, the percentage is reversed. About 90 percent of smokers are persistent daily users, and 55 percent become dependent by official American Psychiatric Association criteria, according to a study by Dr. Naomi Breslau of the Henry Ford Health Sciences Center in

Detroit. Only 10 percent are occasional users.

Surveys also indicate that two-thirds to four-fifths of smokers want to quit but cannot, even after a number of attempts.

Dr. John Robinson, a psychologist who works for the R. J. Reynolds Tocacco Company, contests the consensus view of nicotine as addictive. Using the current standard definition of addiction, he said at a recent meeting on nicotine addiction, he could not distinguish "crack smoking from coffee drinking, glue sniffing from jogging, heroin from carrots and cocaine from colas."

It is not that Dr. Robinson and other scientists supported by tobacco companies disagree with the main points made by mainstream scientists, but that they define addiction differently.

Dr. Robinson says intoxication that is psychologically debilitating is the major defining trait of an addicting substance. It is a feature that was part of standard definitions of the 1950's, and is still linked to popular ideas about addiction, but which experts now say is too simplistic and has been left behind as scientific evidence accumulates.

How Experts Rate Problem Substances

Dr. Jack E. Henningfield of the National Institute on Drug Abuse and Dr. Neal L. Benowitz of the University of California at San Francisco ranked six substances based on five problem areas.

1 = Most serious   **6 = Least serious**

HENNINGFIELD RATINGS

Substance	Withdrawal	Reinforcement	Tolerance	Dependence	Intoxication
Nicotine	3	4	2	1	5
Heroin	2	2	1	2	2
Cocaine	4	1	4	3	3
Alcohol	1	3	3	4	1
Caffeine	5	6	5	5	6
Marijuana	6	5	6	6	4

BENOWITZ RATINGS

Substance	Withdrawal	Reinforcement	Tolerance	Dependence	Intoxication
Nicotine	3*	4	4	1	6
Heroin	2	2	2	2	2
Cocaine	3*	1	1	3	3
Alcohol	1	3	4	4	1
Caffeine	4	5	3	5	5
Marijuana	5	6	5	6	4

*Equal ratings

Withdrawal Presence and severity of characteristic withdrawal symptoms.

Reinforcement A measure of the substance's ability, in human and animal tests, to get users to take it again and again, and in preference to other substances.

Tolerance How much of the substance is needed to satisfy increasing cravings for it, and the level of stable need that is eventually reached.

Dependence How difficult it is for the user to quit, the relapse rate, the percentage of people who eventually become dependent, the rating users give their own need for the substance and the degree to which the substance will be used in the face of evidence that it causes harm.

Intoxication Though not usually counted as a measure of addiction in itself, the level of intoxication is associated with addiction and increases the personal and social damage a substance may do.

Addictive Drugs: The Cigarette Experience

THOMAS C. SCHELLING

The author is in the Department of Economics and the School of Public Affairs, University of Maryland, College Park, MD 20742, and was formerly director of the Institute for the Study of Smoking Behavior and Policy.

Cigarettes are among the most addictive substances of abuse and by far the most deadly. In this country smokers know it and try to stop. Their success has been dramatic but partial and excruciatingly slow, and until recently quite uncoerced by government. Cigarettes and nicotine have characteristics distinct among addictive drugs, and some of these help explain why efforts to quit smoking are so often frustrated. Nicotine itself is the most interesting chemical in the treatment of addiction and, in some forms, can pose a dilemma: compromise by settling for pure nicotine indefinitely, or stay with cigarettes and keep trying to quit. Nicotine is not alone among addictive drugs in becoming increasingly identified with the poorer classes.

HALF THE MEN WHO EVER SMOKED IN THIS COUNTRY have quit, and nearly half the women. At the end of World War II, three-quarters of young men smoked; the fraction is now less than a third and going down. Fifty million people have quit smoking, and another 50 million who would have become smokers since 1945 did not.

This dramatic abandonment of a life-threatening behavior was entirely voluntary. Until recently there was virtually no regulation of smoking by any level of government. The situation changed sharply in the late 1980s after dramatic changes in smoking behavior were well under way.

Surveys documented that the public was aware of the risks (*1*). Ninety percent or more answered yes to whether smoking caused cancer and heart disease. The facts were impressive. In 1982 the Surgeon General estimated 130,000 premature cancer deaths, in 1983 170,000 deaths from heart disease, and in 1984 50,000 deaths from lung disease (*2*). The total was later increased to more than 400,000.

Where do people learn about these dangers? Newspapers reported the annual reports of the surgeons general, but smoking was rarely news and inherently a dull subject. Only recently have city ordi-nances, airline restrictions, liability suits, advertising bans, and excise taxes made cigarettes occasional front-page news. Magazines rarely mention smoking; some of the most popular magazines report more than 25% of their advertising revenues from cigarettes.

The only emphatic repetitive communications about the hazards of smoking are the advertisements on billboards, and in magazines and newspapers. For two decades the central theme has been tar and nicotine. The message sent is that lighter cigarettes are safer but the message received must also be that smoking is dangerous. It is anybody's guess whether the cumulative impact is to entice people into smoking and to keep them smoking, or to drill home the deadly message about tar and nicotine.

No surgeon general has ever publicized the benefits of lower tar and nicotine, but the tar and nicotine have fallen by half. Smokers can infer that the government would not require labeling unless tar and nicotine made a difference.

Thirty years ago smoking was not much associated with social class. It is now. In 1980, a quarter of professional men smoked, a third of white collar men, and almost half of blue collar men (**40%** overall); for women the figures were similar (**30%** overall) (*3*). Among high school seniors in the 1980s, more than 20% of the noncollege bound smoked half a pack or more daily, but less than 10% of the college bound (*4*).

Which is more astounding, that some 50 million people have quit smoking or that nearly 50 million still smoke, most of them knowing that it is potentially fatal? Why don't they try to quit?

The answer is that they do. In 1980, two-fifths of all current smokers said they had made three or more serious attempts to quit. Among the youngest age group, more than half said they had made an attempt within the preceding 12 months. In fact, a third of the men of all ages and two-fifths of the women who smoked in 1980 said that they had attempted to quit within the preceding 12 months (*5*).

Quitting is evidently attractive and, even more evidently, hard. Is it that some can quit and already did and others cannot and never will? Probably not. In 1970, 1975, and 1980, former smokers, both women and men, had smoked as many cigarettes per day as current smokers (*6*). And while two-fifths of the men and women still smoking in 1980 had made three or more attempts to quit unsuccessfully, in 1975—the question was not asked in 1980—more than half the former smokers, men and women, claimed to have made three or more attempts before they succeeded (*7*).

Quitting was hard for those who succeeded and hard for those still trying. Why so hard? I shall turn to that shortly but first bring our history up to date. For those who hope to quit and desire reinforcement through restrictions on their smoking, the situation changed dramatically in the second half of the 1980s. The military services not only took cigarettes out of the field rations but banned smoking in most buildings and vehicles. The General Services Administration imposed controls on smoking in all federal buildings under its jurisdiction. Major cities were imposing tight restrictions on smoking in public places and the workplace. Smoking was eliminated on all domestic airline flights. Only 10 or 12% of the nation's largest corporations had restrictions on smoking in the early 1980s, mostly to avoid the risk of fire and contamination; more than half had restrictions by the late 1980s, and the increase was due to the publicized hazards to health as well as to complaints about the disagreeableness of environmental smoke (8).

The trend toward restriction was given a push by the Surgeon General's Report of 1986, which concluded that secondhand smoke could cause respiratory cancer and could aggravate respiratory difficulties in children. (That the estimate of deaths due to environmental smoke was two orders of magnitude smaller than deaths due to smoking did not weaken the impact of this new report.) Two committees of the National Academy of Sciences expressed concern about the effects on health of environmental tobacco smoke, and especially the contamination of air in passenger airlines.

It remains your choice whether to be more impressed, and heartened, by the massive change in smoking behavior in the United States over the past two or three decades or to be more impressed, and disheartened, by the massive recalcitrance of smoking among 45 million continuing smokers, most of whom have tried unsuccessfully to quit. Both phenomena are impressive. Can we expect the growing unpopularity of smoking to continue and, if so, can we foresee the end in this country of a dangerous and somewhat offensive behavior?

It is too soon to declare victory. Still, fewer are smoking in all occupations and social classes. It is not surprising that those with more favorable life prospects, like those who go to college, should be the most sensitive to information about behaviors that affect mortality late in life, whereas people lower in socioeconomic status with lower life expectations follow a decade or two behind.

Some Pertinent Characteristics

Why is it so hard to quit? How does nicotine compare with other drugs?

Cigarettes are cheap; a pack a day costs less than half an hour's work at the federal minimum wage. Cigarettes are quickly available; smokers are rarely more than a few minutes from the nearest cigarette. Smoking requires no equipment other than a match. Cigarettes are portable and storable; a pack fits in a shirt pocket and requires no refrigeration. Being commercially available and brand named, cigarettes pose no problem of quality control. There is no fear of overdose; nicotine is a poison in large quantities, but a smoker feels the effects before any dangerous quantity can be inhaled.

Until the last few years, when regulations began to restrict smoking, the habit had an almost universal compatibility. People smoked anywhere, indoors and out, at work and at play, alone and with others, on the telephone, on horseback, with coffee or soft drinks or alcohol, at any time of day or night. There is almost no moment in a former smoker's life when a cigarette might not have been appropriate, and the former smoker's day is full of occasions and activities that would once have prompted a cigarette and still may prompt the thought of one.

Cigarettes produce no impairment of any faculty. There is no intoxication, no slurring of speech or loss of balance, no loss of visual acuity. Smoking is the only drug, with the possible exception of caffeine, that my airline pilot may indulge in without my being the least concerned.

Until smoking began to fall into disrepute in the last few years, there were hardly any social norms governing where or when or with whom it was appropriate to smoke. A person would not think of attending an afternoon conference with a bowl of hot soup or a pitcher of martinis—usually not even a sandwich or a candy bar—but smoking was never impolite. Perhaps the most powerful norm governing smoking behavior was that one offered a cigarette to a companion before lighting one's own.

Smoking is a socially facilitating activity. People who want to appear poised get support from the motions of extracting a cigarette, lighting it, exhaling the smoke, and holding the cigarette. This benefit is probably independent of the nicotine. Smoking is something that every smoker is good at.

The damage is slow in arriving. The people who suffer cancer and lung and heart disease from smoking have typically smoked for three decades or more before symptoms appear.

Addiction to Nicotine

Cigarettes are extremely addictive. Most users are addicted; few who have smoked regularly for a year or more find it easy to quit. Relapse rates may not measure the "strength" of an addiction, in the sense of pain, discomfort, and obsession upon withdrawal, but in the balance between desire to quit and desire to stay free, cigarettes are among the hardest to stay away from. Most studies indicate a success rate—at least two years' abstinence—at about one in five per attempt. (That half of all smokers in this country eventually made it is due to repeated attempts.) The Surgeon General devoted his entire annual report for 1988 to the behavioral and chemical criteria according to which nicotine is a highly addictive substance.

Inhaled nicotine in cigarette smoke provides an instant response—10 seconds or less to reach the brain—and a short high. Unlike any other addictive or psychoactive substance, cigarettes have a pleasurable effect that lasts no longer than the lighted cigarette. The recycle time is short, less than an hour on average. With the possible exception of benzedrine inhalers when they were still on the market, there is no drug that has been taken with comparable frequency or in which the user is so practiced; a pack a day is 7,500 cigarettes per year, 75,000 inhaled puffs.

It is generally thought that nicotine is the main chemically addictive substance in cigarette smoke. The Surgeon General's Report treated nicotine exclusively as the addictive agent. There are two additional possible contributors to addiction. One is the taste of tobacco smoke. Without the nicotine one probably would not become addicted, but after smoking tens of thousands of cigarettes the association of nicotine with the flavor may give the flavor itself addictive qualities. The taste of cigarettes gives the addict something tangible to crave; if there were no tobacco it is not clear what a nicotine addict would crave other than relief from withdrawal symptoms.

The other possible dimension of addiction may be in mood control. A person may smoke at one time to calm down and at another time to perk up. (This homeostasis is almost unique to cigarettes; most drugs are stimulants or depressants but not both.) Once a person has smoked several thousand times to reduce tension or to stimulate alertness, lighting a cigarette may be an acquired habit that makes a person keep lighting up after saturation, when all the effect is gone. Many smokers smoke so much that they report getting little pleasure except on those occasions when, unable to smoke for an hour or two, they have gotten rid of the overdose.

From all I have read, users of most drugs, including prescription and over-the-counter drugs, have a good idea of the effect they are seeking, especially of drugs that produce a high or a rush or a "euphoria" of some kind. Most tobacco smokers cannot describe any attractive effect except what they might describe as the "taste" of tobacco smoke in their mouth and lungs and nasal passages. Being addicted to cigarettes is more like being addicted to chocolate than to the hard drugs, more like the flavor of a dinner wine than the perceived alcohol content. True, as mentioned, some rely on a cigarette to calm down; but what a deprived smoker is conscious of wanting is usually not the calming but the taste of the cigarette. I belabor this point because it is an important contrast between nicotine, which is always administered through tobacco smoke that is the object of craving, and drugs that need no such medium. (Possibly people who chew coca and betel leaves have a sense of appetite for the leaves, not just a desire for the medicinal effects.)

Some addictive substances require increasing doses to get a given effect as one cumulatively experiences the drug; most smokers within the first few years stabilize on a steady diet. A narrow range of daily dosage covers most smokers; the preponderance of smokers smoke between 1 dozen and 4 dozen cigarettes per day. There appears to be greater variance among users of coffee, alcohol, marijuana, the hard drugs, and the medicinal drugs.

There is, in contrast, great variability in the time it takes to get over withdrawal symptoms and especially the craving for cigarettes. For some the worst is over in 3 days, for others 3 weeks, for others 3 months, and for some 3 years. How much of that variability is physiological and how much due to environmental stimuli is hard to guess.

Few smokers attempt to reduce the amount they smoke. The two responses to the publicized hazards are trying to quit and switching to lower tar and nicotine.

There is experimental evidence that people who switch to low nicotine compensate by inhaling more deeply, holding the smoke longer in the lungs, smoking more cigarettes or more of each cigarette, and even holding the cigarette in a way that lets less ventilation into the cigarette (reducing the dilution of nicotine). They probably end up with less tar and nicotine than they used to get but nothing like proportionately less unless they smoke extremely low-nicotine cigarettes. (They may get more carbon monoxide.)

In the drug literature there is evidence that many people mature out of their habits. Other interests take over, use of the drug ceases to match a more mature lifestyle; marriage, job or parenthood becomes incompatible with continued use. Hardly anybody "matures out" of cigarettes. Smokers quit, but not through loss of interest; quitting requires determination.

A few medicinal substances have shown an apparent ability to suppress a craving for cigarettes for people undergoing withdrawal. But the interesting drug is nicotine itself. For about 4 years a chewing gum with the trade name Nicorette has been available by prescription. Nicotine is released through controlled chewing and absorbed through the mouth to maintain a steady level of nicotine in the blood. The instructions are to use it with a dosage that tapers off over 90 days. It is reported to reduce the withdrawal discomfort but to provide no pleasure; it reduces the craving for cigarettes but is not itself desired. The principle is like that of methadone, which reduces withdrawal discomfort for heroin addicts but provides little of the pleasure that heroin can provide. There are currently experiments with other less troublesome methods of self-administering nicotine during withdrawal. (Nicorette requires a lot of chewing, enough to fatigue the jaws.) Skin patches and subcutaneous implants are reported to be undergoing testing.

There have been a few reports on the efficacy of Nicorette: the permanent success rate may be as high as one-third or better; that would be about double the usual estimate of successful quitting. If the reports are true, the self-administration of pure nicotine on a tapering-off schedule is the first major advance in quitting technology to be successfully marketed.

Nicotine may not deserve all the credit. Nicorette is available only by prescription; every user is under the supervision of a physician, who may be an important support. And just having something to do at regular intervals through the day, every day, may keep the patient engaged in a constructive quitting regime. We should keep in mind that the users of Nicorette are self-selected, and limited to people who see a physician, either to seek help in quitting or in circumstances that make the subject of smoking pertinent to the visit.

An altogether different approach would be to deliver the nicotine in the quantity a smoker wants and in a form that offers the usual satisfaction but causes less damage. One proposal has been to develop tobacco that is high in nicotine but low in tar. This is not easy to do naturally; nicotine and tar are highly correlated in the tobacco leaf. One method would be to add nicotine to a low tar, low nicotine cigarette. As far as anybody outside the cigarette companies seems to know, that has not been done.

An extreme version has been tried. R. J. Reynolds (RJR) spent nearly $1 billion developing, and tested in three cities, an almost pure nicotine delivery device, a glass tube the size of a cigarette with ignited charcoal that heated the air drawn through it and vaporized nicotine in a controlled way. Some glycerine was added solely to produce "smoke," and a bit of tobacco was included. (Whether the tobacco was for flavor or to permit classifying the device as a "cigarette," and not as a nicotine delivery system, we do not know.) There was an effort to get the Federal Trade Commission to declare jurisdiction over this "nontobacco" device. Organizations concerned about smoking were unanimously opposed to its introduction. The device was withdrawn after a few months of testing; newspapers reported that it had not caught on with smokers. Maybe RJR will tinker with the flavor and try again. Presumably there would be little or no danger of respiratory or oral cancer, and most lung disease might be eliminated. Such a device might be a replacement for regular cigarettes or perhaps only a replacement where cigarette smoking is not allowed. (The Department of Transportation would have had to decide whether the use of that device in an airplane was "smoking.")

Whether the device should be welcomed or deplored is not obvious. It has been almost unanimously deplored, just as cigarettes low in tar and nicotine have been almost invariably disparaged by organizations concerned about smoking and health. If there are smokers who would like to quit but cannot, denying the pure nicotine condemns them to getting what they need only with carcinogenic tar and poison gases. The alleged objection is that the device gives smokers who might otherwise quit an excuse for inhaling pure nicotine instead.

Lessons and Observations

One heartening observation is simply that there can be massive changes of behavior in the direction of abstinence with a highly addictive substance. And they occurred in the absence, until very recently, of any even mildly coercive efforts by government or any other institutions in our society. Eventually changes in behavior on this scale are associated with changes in attitudes, expectations, and norms. When the efforts at abstinence are numerous enough to be unmistakably noticeable, they generate a social environment that is supportive of efforts to abstain. But the change was very, very slow.

A related observation is less heartening. A habit that was widespread among all socioeconomic groups, with only a gender differential that was on the way to disappearing, has become markedly identified with lower education and employment status. The motivation for quitting is probably strongest among people who are in a condition to appreciate longevity and are best positioned to receive and understand health messages from credible sources. Cigarettes are distinctive among addictive drugs in the extreme delay from use to symptoms. This convergence of use, over several decades of intense efforts to publicize the harm, on the least advantaged and least influential social classes may be proving typical of other drugs. The effects on the politics of prohibition could be substantial.

The information about the health effects of smoking came from a source that never lost its credibility. The Surgeon General's reports patiently brought together, year after year, biomedical and other evidence and presented conclusions that were never really challenged from any reputable quarter. And the one Surgeon General whose face became familiar had a style that inspired trust. In contrast, children had little reason to trust the information they used to be given about marijuana and other drugs. Of course, the Surgeon General had a message that did not need exaggeration.

A possible inference from the cigarette experience is that "society" can tolerate addiction to a chemical substance if the behavioral consequences hurt only the addicted consumers. The drugs policy literature reveals a widespread belief that addiction to any drug is morally offensive and socially degrading. Until recently few Americans were morally offended by the widespread smoking of cigarettes or thought it an index of social depravity. The only behavior that smokers engaged in that nonsmokers did not was smoking. The increasingly explicit mention of nicotine as an addictive substance, the increasing objection of nonsmokers to smoking in their presence, and the increasing identification of smoking with lower classes may succeed in making nicotine addiction per se objectionable.

Even among the youngest adults who smoke, both men and women have been persuaded to try to stop. Except for those lowest in socioeconomic status, motivating people to quit is no longer the problem. The problem is relapse. And there are two parts to coping with relapse.

One is to avoid relapse. Few people who quit just come to decide quitting is not worth the hardship and resume smoking. Most people who relapse had no intention, the day before relapse, of resuming smoking.

The second aspect of coping is recovering from the relapse. When somebody does break down and have a cigarette or two, it is usually not a brief interlude in a quitting program but a crash finish.

One reason why relapse is so common is the shortness of time between loss of resolve and having a cigarette in one's lips. Most smokers who have quit are rarely more than 5 minutes from the nearest cigarette, and it takes only the briefest loss of control to consummate the urge to smoke. If one had to wait until the next day to acquire cigarettes there might be plenty of intervening changes in the stimuli, and plenty of opportunity to get one's self under control; one could wake up the next morning relieved at having been rescued by the unavailability of cigarettes the night before.

Furthermore, as mentioned earlier, there is almost no moment in a former smoker's life when a cigarette might not have been appropriate, and the former smoker's day is full of occasions and activities that once would have prompted a cigarette and still may prompt the thought of one.

REFERENCES AND NOTES

1. A 1985 Gallup poll, "Survey of Attitudes Toward Smoking" reported that 94 percent of Americans believed smoking was hazardous to health (American Lung Association, *News*, 5 December 1985).
2. *The Health Consequences of Smoking: Cancer*, a report of the Surgeon General [U.S. Government Printing Office (GPO), Washington, DC, 1982]; *The Health Consequences of Smoking: Cardiovascular Disease*, a report of the Surgeon General (GPO, Washington, DC, 1983); *The Health Consequences of Smoking: Chronic Obstructive Lung Disease*, a report of the Surgeon General (GPO, Washington, DC, 1984).
3. *The Health Consequences of Smoking: Cancer and Chronic Lung Disease in the Workplace*, a report of the Surgeon General (GPO, Washington, DC, 1985), p. 25, table 2.
4. L. D. Johnston *et al.*, *Drugs and American High School Students, 1975* (GPO, Washington, DC, 1984), p. 12.
5. *The Health Consequences of Smoking: Cancer*, a report of the Surgeon General (GPO, Washington, DC, 1982), pp. 372–373, tables 5 and 6.
6. *ibid.* p. 369, table 2.
7. *ibid.* p. 372, table 5.
8. For a review of private and public regulations on smoking, see *Reducing the Health Consequences of Smoking: 25 Years of Progress*, a report of the Surgeon General (GPO, Washington, DC, 1989), chap. 7, pp. 465–644.
9. Condensed from a study for the RAND Drug Policy Research Center with a grant from the Alfred P. Sloan Foundation.

BRAIN BY DESIGN

An Era of Molecular Engineering, Aimed at Refining and Refocusing
the Effects of Marijuana and Other Psychoactive Drugs, May Be at Hand

RICHARD RESTAK

Richard Restak is a neurologist living in Washington, D.C.
This article is adapted from his book, DESIGNER BRAIN,
published by Bantam.

A T A FOURTH OF JULY PARTY I ATTENDED RE-
cently, the hostess proposed an intriguing
game. To begin, she taped a name tag to the
forehead of each guest—on which she had written not the
guest's name but the name of a historical person, place or
event. No one was told his or her designation; the object
of the game was for the guests to discover their own "identity" by asking questions of the others.

Later that night I dreamed I was at a similar gathering,
except that the guests and theme of the party were different. All the world's most distinguished brain scientists were
there, and taped to their foreheads were the names of parts of
the brain. Some of the labels referred to large areas of the
brain, such as the temporal lobe, or to the neuron; others
identified chemical messengers, known as neurotransmitters;
still others signified whole, elaborate processes.

In my dream I was talking to a woman wearing the label
dopamine, the name of a neurotransmitter, on her brow. She
had already learned her own identity; now she was trying to
help me discover mine. But whatever I asked her, and no
matter how skillfully she answered, I could not guess what was
written on my forehead. Finally the woman reached out, put
her arms around me and planted a passionate kiss on my lips.
Then she stepped back, wide-eyed, and asked: "Do you know
who you are now?"

And, of course, I did; I was the receptor for dopamine.
When one neuron sends a message to another one, it does
so by releasing a neurotransmitter across a minuscule gap between the two nerve cells called the synapse. After crossing
the synapse the neurotransmitter makes contact with a specialized receptor—a large molecule, most often a protein—
on the membrane of the target neuron. And so, like two
lovers, dopamine and its receptor, and indeed all the other
brain neurotransmitters and their unique receptors, embrace

across the synaptic threshold. By that process the nerve cells
of the brain communicate, within the brain itself and throughout the body.

My dream intrigues me for several reasons. For one thing,
there is the Felliniesque scene of brain scientists engaging
their brains in the game of guessing the name of the brain
element they have been assigned to represent. For another, all
the players in my fantasy, taken together, represent the brain
with all its parts. Finally, the parts—the players in the game—
are challenged, individually and collectively, to comprehend
not only their own role in the functioning brain but also, by
extension, the operation of the whole. And that raises a central
question for neuroscience: Is such analysis even possible? Can
the understanding of one component—say the neuron, physiologically the most elemental unit of the brain—provide insights into the functioning of the whole? And what of my
seductive interrogator: the brain messenger reaching out and
embracing a specific receptor, in this exciting instance, me?
What part does that intricate interaction play in understanding
the workings of the brain?

INVESTIGATORS HAVE DISCOVERED
both a marijuana receptor in the
brain and a natural brain molecule
that binds to it.

A great deal, I would argue. Scientific insight into the
brain is being advanced remarkably by studies of the relation between neurotransmitters and their receptors. One of
the most productive lines of research has focused on the actions of cannabis, or marijuana, a substance that can bring
about a complicated spectrum of psychological effects in
people. In the past several years investigators have discovered both a marijuana receptor in the brain and a natural

brain molecule that binds to it. The success in dealing at the molecular level with a chemically complex substance that can induce such complex psychoactive effects strongly suggests that an era of "brain modulation" with "designer drugs" may be at hand. Such drugs would mimic certain biological and psychological actions of natural substances while eliminating some of their undesirable effects. For example, in the next decade drugs to treat intractable mental illnesses may become available. Drugs to alter normal mental functions such as memory, intelligence, concentration and emotional well-being may also come on the market. The design of such drugs will be the direct outcome—the practical payoff—of research on brain receptors and the substances to which they naturally bind. Yet as the research and its applications become more sophisticated, patients, physicians, policy makers and ethicists will have to confront a daunting question: What are the manifold implications of a technology that, in effect, enables one to design one's own brain and, perhaps, makes it possible for some people to design the brains of others?

THE UNDERSTANDING OF CHEMICAL COMMU-nication in the brain has brought about a change in the very definition of the brain. In itself such change is nothing new; throughout history metaphors for the brain have been colored by the biases of the contemporary science and technology. The early Greeks, captivated by their own successes in building aqueducts, thought of mental processes in terms of the flow of bodily fluids. In the seventeenth century, when automatons were the rage, the French philosopher René Descartes compared the working brain to the interplay of gears, cogs and cams in a complex machine. In the nineteenth century the emphasis was on the physical connections among brain components, an approach stimulated by the contemporary fascination with railway networks.

Today the brain often is compared to circuitry and its functioning to computations, reflecting the influence of electronics and computers. No doubt those comparisons will continue to be overhauled with each new wave of innovation. But to neuroscientists, at least, it has begun to seem that all technological metaphors, no matter how sophisticated, are doomed to falter when placed alongside the complexity and uniqueness of the human brain. What, then, is the best way to characterize the gray mass within the skull, so close at hand and yet so elusive?

Studies of the brain at the chemical and molecular level suggest that the fundamental underpinnings of thought and emotion are interactions much like the one between the seductive woman and me in my dream. Indeed brain research suggests that we human beings share certain properties and reactions with the micromolecules that make us up—a finding perhaps best summed up by the slogan "Behind every crooked thought there is a crooked molecule." Such a finding is not even surprising, given the marvelous parsimony of nature. As successful principles evolve over millennia, nature employs them again and again at various levels of the organism, and so events at one level mirror what is going on several higher or lower orders away.

WHAT CHARACTERISTICS OF NEUROTRANS-mitters and their receptors shed light on the functioning and organization of the brain? Every neurotransmitter molecule has a unique three-dimensional structure—and so does every receptor molecule; roughly speaking, neurotransmitters fit specific receptors somewhat the way keys fit specific locks. But in contrast to a lock and its key, a neurotransmitter and its receptor are not rigid structures. Like all matter at room temperature protein molecules in the brain vibrate with thermal energy, and in one mode of vibration the molecules alternately expand and contract their enclosed volume. Physicists call the process breathing, and such motions play a major role in the binding of neurotransmitters to their receptors. Furthermore, in transmitter–receptor interactions, the electrons in one molecule exert a force, just as a magnet does, that influences the spatial distribution of the electrons in the other. Thus the interaction derives not from the direct influence of the neurotransmitter on the receptor, or vice versa, but from the mutual influence of their electromagnetic fields.

The upshot of such dynamic and continuously modulating interplay is that a given neurotransmitter may find itself in competition for the same receptor with another neurotransmitter of slightly different configuration. In that case the receptor will adhere to only one of them. Thus, depending on the degree of fit with the receptor, a given neurotransmitter may be taken up by a receptor in one instance but fail to be taken up in another, when an additional molecule is present whose affinity with the receptor is even stronger. As in dating and mating, what is finally settled for is always a function of what is available.

There are other implications of the dynamic nature of the association between neurotransmitter and receptor. Typically no one neurotransmitter is responsible for a particular mental function. Memory, for instance, is modified by the neurotransmitters acetylcholine, adrenaline, noradrenaline and probably serotonin. All of them interact with one another like the instruments in a symphony.

Even individual neurons have been found to respond to several neurotransmitters, rather than to only one, as investigators had long believed to be the case. That discovery, one of the most exciting insights of recent brain research, implies a versatility of response, on the molecular level, that may well form the basis of the rich behavioral complexity of human life. The picture that emerges seems less and less like a digital circuit, in which the neurotransmitters act as switches for the on-or-off firing of neurons. Rather, the neurotransmitters act more as a modulator, functioning in a sense as the lenses and filters of a camera do. Just as a filter modulates the tone and quality of a photograph, a neuromodulatory transmitter modifies a neuron's basic response in some way.

Neuromodulatory functions are not confined to the brain; for the past decade many neurotransmitter chemicals in the brain have also been discovered in various places throughout the body. For example, regulatory hormones such as substance P gastrin and lipotropin occur not only in the brain and spinal cord but also in the gut, adrenals and sexual organs. Such a chemical equivalence suggests, for instance, that "gut" feelings are more than mere metaphor, since some of the same neurotransmitters and peptide modulators occur in both the brain and the gastrointestinal tract. And so an intriguing question arises: Has neuroscience become too rigid in its concept of what is and is not brain and, by implication, what is and is not mind? As the neurosurgeon Richard M. Bergland, now at Beth-Israel Hospital in New York City, writes in *The Fabric of Mind*:

The stuff of thought is not caged in the brain but is scattered all over the body. . . . There is little doubt now that the brain is a gland; it produces hormones, it has hormone receptors, it is bathed in hormones, hormones run up and down the fibers on individual nerves, and every activity that the brain is engaged in involves hormones.

Neuromodulation takes place at every level of brain function. Think back to the last time you took an antihistamine or a sedative, or perhaps had a bit too much to drink. In each such instance a chemical modulated your responsiveness, making you more tired, irritable or inattentive. Or consider the variety of substances people have sought for millennia to distill from plants to achieve new states of consciousness. Some of the substances are exotic and others are illegal, but many are so commonplace that most people scarcely think of them as drugs. Few people complete their day without recourse to coffee, tea, chocolate or some other stimulant. Is there anyone who has never taken an aspirin for a headache? To relax, some of us reach for a drink or a cigarette.

None of that, of course, is news. What is news is the perspective on the effects of such substances afforded by the study of neurotransmitters and their receptors. Neuromodulation at the behavioral level gets mirrored at the molecular level: drug, alcohol, coffee, nicotine—all help alter one or more of the neurotransmitters or their receptors. And so all such substances, licit or illicit, natural or synthesized, have become windows onto the functioning brain.

CONSIDERABLE KNOWLEDGE ABOUT THE POtential for such drug actions—and their potential malfunctions—has been gathered from studies of the effects of marijuana. That substance, derived from the cannabis plant, is extremely complex, containing more than 400 chemicals. Corresponding to its chemical diversity are its many and varied psychological and physiological effects. Depending on the dosage, the individual user, and the part of the plant from which the substance is extracted, the drug can sedate, relieve pain or induce an altered perception of time and space. Moreover, in contrast to many other mind-altering substances, marijuana has legitimate uses, in treating asthma, glaucoma and the nausea and vomiting often brought on by cancer chemotherapy. The drug has also been investigated as a treatment for epilepsy, insomnia, anorexia, loss of appetite and high blood pressure.

On the debit side, however, laboratory experiments suggest that marijuana, contrary to long-held claims by its advocates, has at least the potential to cause dependence. It is also clear that marijuana interferes with many aspects of cog-

nitive processes such as arithmetical reasoning, verbal and non-verbal problem-solving and short-term memory. To explain those effects investigators have concentrated on the drug's effects in the brain, rather than elsewhere in the body. Those effects include alterations of the nerve cell membrane, changes in the turnover of the neurotransmitters dopamine and serotonin, and variations in the synthesis of prostaglandins, a large family of hormone-like chemicals.

HAS NEUROSCIENCE BECOME TOO RIGID *in its concept of what is and is not brain and, by implication, what is and is not mind?*

The current chapter in the study of the biological action of marijuana began in the late 1970s, when the chemists M. Ross Johnson and Lawrence S. Melvin, Jr., both then of Pfizer Central Research in Groton, Connecticut, synthesized a group of cannabinoids—substances whose action is similar to that of cannabis—with varying potencies. One of their creations, levonantradol, was intended for use as a painkiller, but though it relieved pain it also displayed many marijuana-like side effects that prevented its use as a medication: dryness of the mouth, reddening of the eyes, dizziness and mood alterations. But a failure in therapeutics can sometimes be turned into a winner as a tool of basic laboratory research. Such was the case with levonantradol.

Kenner C. Rice, a chemist at the National Institute of Diabetes, Digestive and Kidney Disease in Bethesda, Maryland, created a radioactive compound from levonantradol that made it possible to track the drug and follow its path within the brain. Then, in the late 1980s, workers at the National Institute of Mental Health (NIMH), led by the neurobiologist Miles Herkenham, used the compound to map the distribution of levonantradol receptors in the brain. The distribution corresponded strikingly to the actions of marijuana itself: it was highest in those areas of the brain concerned with mood, memory and movement, namely the cerebellum, the basal ganglia and the hippocampus.

At about the same time as Herkenham was doing his work, the pharmacologist Allyn C. Howlett of the Saint Louis University School of Medicine discovered that cannabis derivatives affect neurological function by inhibiting the action of adenylate cyclase, an enzyme that stimulates a cascade of crucial chemical reactions in the brain. Then, in August 1990, two molecular biologists at NIMH announced an even more exciting advance: they had cloned the marijuana receptor, after discovering the gene that codes for it. Paradoxically, that achievement did not follow directly from the work of either Herkenham or Howlett. It resulted instead from a third area of investigation.

IN 1987 LISA MATSUDA WAS WORKING IN THE laboratory of Tom I. Bonner at NIMH to clone the genes for two substances that transmit pain impulses in the brain: neuromedin and substance P. As a shortcut she and Bonner worked with substance K, which is similar to substance P, and for which the receptor gene had recently been cloned by workers in Japan. Matsuda and Bonner reasoned that since substance K is structurally and functionally similar to substance P, the receptors and the genes for their formation should also be similar.

Their first step was to make a gene probe, a synthetic DNA sequence capable of recognizing and binding to a segment of the substance K gene. The probe worked as planned, pulling out a gene that coded for a protein with the general features of a receptor. But a receptor for what? Tests showed that it was not a receptor for the substances involved in pain. Moreover, its structure provided no clues about what it would bind. Matsuda and Bonner began to map the areas of a rat brain where the mystery gene appeared to be most active. Unknown to them, the brain areas in their map corresponded to areas mapped by Herkenham for the marijuana receptor. The irony is that Herkenham's laboratory is just down the hall from Bonner's. When Matsuda learned of Herkenham's map, she walked down to his office, and the two of them compared maps. In an instant Matsuda had the identity of the receptor gene she and Bonner had cloned. The concentrations of marijuana receptor on Herkenham's map were highest for the same brain sections in which the mystery gene was most active.

The next step was straightforward: to test whether cannabinoids affect cells that have been given the gene that coded the mystery receptor. Matsuda placed cannabinoid drugs of varying potency in a culture of cells containing marijuana receptors and the gene. The drugs reacted with the receptors. Even more intriguing, when the cloned gene was introduced into a culture of cells from the ovary of a test animal, a Chinese hamster, and cannabinoids were then put into the culture, the production of adenylate cyclase was inhibited only in the cells carrying the transferred receptor gene.

Some important questions about marijuana receptors remained, of course. Many people have never tried marijua-

As the potential for developing a wide range of more precisely targeted drugs increases, so do the ethical questions regarding their use by people generally considered "normal."

na, and yet the brain contains receptors for the substance. Does that mean, then, that the body harbors natural chemicals similar to marijuana? And if so, could it be that the euphoriant and medicinal qualities of marijuana are based on that similarity? The answer to one of those questions came last December when the chemists William Devane, Raphael Mechoulam and their colleagues at the Hebrew University in Jerusalem identified a brain molecule that binds to the marijuana receptor. Named anandamide, from the Sanskrit *ananda,* meaning internal bliss, the substance

mimics the action of the most active agent in the cannabis plant—THC (tetrahydrocannabinol).

ANANDAMIDE IS JUST ONE OF PROBABLY MANY internal substances that bind to the marijuana receptor. Once discovered, any of them could be grown in quantity through cloning. But now the real work of drug design can begin in earnest. The basic idea is to design new and more specific synthetic analogues of marijuana, generally with the help of a computer. Why is such a strategy necessary? For one thing, natural marijuana-like substances in the body are apt to exert such powerful effects, on so many parts of the body, that in many cases the substances could not be used therapeutically. A person with low blood pressure, for instance, could not use the substance to treat glaucoma because it would further, and dangerously, lower the blood pressure. What is more, the unaltered drug induces a number of socially unacceptable effects, which might be eliminated by blocking certain marijuana receptors. What is wanted are ways of turning on only those aspects of the chemical that would be useful in treating a specific illness, stimulating marijuana's positive effects while eliminating the harmful ones.

The recent work on manipulating marijuana and its analogues serves as a case study in drug design. Like the couturier who creates a new fashion by taking inspiration from a past success, the neuropharmacologist begins with an effective drug and then tries to improve it. The first step in the so-called drug-design cycle is to identify the structure and chemical properties of both the drug and its receptor. Next, one tries to learn how and why the neurotransmitter recognizes and interacts with that receptor. Finally, one enhances the drug, often by altering the electronic charge of the drug molecule or by changing the relative affinity of its parts for water—so that it better fits the receptor.

As the biochemical understanding of receptors increases, the pharmaceutical industry will inevitably design drugs that modify a wide range of conditions. Depression, for instance, has been traced to abnormalities in the prefrontal cortex, the limbic system and subcortical regions of the brain; targeting receptors in those regions may provide a new and more powerful generation of antidepressants. Memory disorders associated with aging and Alzheimer's disease can be similarly localized. Chemical maps of receptors may lead to treatments of such conditions as introversion, extroversion, obsession or compulsion. Positron emission tomography, or PET, scans of the brains of people with obsessive-compulsive disorder show abnormalities in the basal ganglia, a group of structures under the cortex that integrate motor responses and thought processes. One can treat the disorder with drugs that block the re-uptake, or reabsorption, of the neurotransmitters serotonin or norepinephrine after they are released into the synapse between two neurons. The drugs do not always eliminate the symptoms but usually make them less bothersome.

Perhaps the most interesting—and most troubling—potential application of new psychoactive agents is the modification of character, personality and habit. Drugs are now in development that will help stimulate motivation, increase energy level, repair feelings of chronic low self-esteem—and in short, make many people not suffering from a definable emotional illness feel better about themselves and the quality of their lives. One could argue that such applications may not be proper ones for mind- and brain-altering drugs; we are not always the best judges of how best to improve ourselves. But consider the strategy many philosophical and psychological systems have suggested for enduring and prevailing in an uncertain world: Do not seek to modify the world, but change your own responses to it. Properly and sensibly used, it seems to me that psychoactive drugs can help achieve the goal.

THERE IS A DARKER SIDE TO RECEPTOR RE-search. Brain-altering drugs sometimes cause permanent harm; even worse, they can act like a time bomb that goes off a decade or more after one's exposure to them. Could the milder tranquilizers or antidepressant agents now in use by millions of people lead to similar horrors? And what about medications such as Ritalin, now almost routinely prescribed to control hyperactivity in children? That case is particularly troublesome, since a child's brain is still developing and may thus be at even greater risk than an adult's. Unfortunately, neither neuroscientists nor anyone else can provide absolute assurance about the safety of present or future mind- and brain-altering drugs.

As the potential for developing a wide range of more precisely targeted drugs increases, so do the ethical questions regarding their use by people generally considered "normal." What, for instance, should one say to the seventy-hour-a-week workaholic who wants a brain-altering chemical in order to work even longer and harder? Here legitimate controversy is likely to arise. Some clinicians would argue that such behavior is not "normal" at all but indicates a deep-seated psychopathology. Totally immersed in their careers, workaholics neglect spouses, children and countless other obligations. Should they be encouraged?

Should drugs be made available to help someone drive himself to a level of physical or emotional collapse?

MANY NEW MIND-ALTERING DRUGS WILL surely target other comparatively "minor" problems—the milder forms of panic and social withdrawal—rather than totally disabling behavioral and emotional disturbances for which the ethical questions seem relatively straightforward. Even now Prozac, the most successful and widely employed antidepressant in history, is being increasingly requested by people without any diagnosable emotional illness, who simply feel that "something is missing" from their lives. Many such people report feeling better after starting a regime of Prozac. But obviously there is a danger here. Dependence on easy fixes for easy problems may invite a slide to riskier fixes for harder problems when they arise. It is too easy to forget that everyday problems of adjustment are part of being alive.

The last decade of the twentieth century has been declared the Decade of the Brain. Caveats about drug dependence notwithstanding, the unifying concept in brain investigation and intervention will undoubtedly be the role of the receptor and its binding agent. That concept will likely prove more valuable than ever in advancing the understanding of thoughts, moods and behavior. Just as physicists have long searched for some fundamental organizing principle—a unified field theory—neuroscientists can now hope to unite observable human behavior with the actions of chemicals and molecules, substances that operate at microscopic levels far smaller than the manifest behavior of a human being. Receptors are a bridge between the world of chemicals and the person, who may be crippled by a phobia, depressed to the brink of suicide or simply consumed with compulsive behavior. Thanks to research on neurotransmitters and receptors the brain by design may soon become a personal option as well as a matter for regulation and control.

A Prescription for Trouble: When Medications Don't Mix

Jeff Schein

JEFF SCHEIN, M.P.H., IS AN EPIDEMIOLO-GIST SPECIALIZING IN DRUG INTERACTIONS. HE HAS RECEIVED AWARDS FROM THE NATIONAL INSTITUTES OF HEALTH AND FROM THE NATIONAL PRESS CLUB FOR OUTSTANDING MEDICAL WRITING FOR CONSUMERS.

✔ Medications can be lifesaving. Often, however, someone needs to take more than one medication at a time. When this happens, there is a risk of one drug affecting how the other drug acts. Such reactions can also occur with certain food and drug combinations, or a drug's activity can be hindered by cigarette smoking. Usually these effects are minor—the person taking the drugs might not even notice the changes—but, occasionally, the outcome is more serious. Certain interactions increase a patient's risk of adverse effects.

What Is a Drug Interaction?

A drug interaction is a change in the effect of a drug that occurs when a person is taking another drug at the same time. The change may be desirable, adverse or inconsequential. One example of a desirable drug interaction is in cancer treatment: Patients with cancer often receive combinations of drugs that act in concert to fight the malignancy.

Most drugs can be taken in combination without any problems occurring. Certain combinations of medication should be avoided, however, because an adverse outcome—such as nausea or dizziness—may occur. Most adverse drug interactions result in an increase or decrease in the effect of one of the drugs, but a combination of drugs can, on rare occasions, result in a new reaction—one not seen with either of the drugs when they are taken alone.

Increased effect of a medication. In one of the most common drug interactions, one drug causes an "increased effect" of another medication. This does not mean that the affected drug works better; rather, it indicates an abnormal, exaggerated effect. This exaggerated effect may be associated with various undesirable symptoms, such as sweating, nausea or rapid heartbeat. The type of symptoms that develop, as well as their severity, depends on the specific drugs being taken and on the individual variability of the patient's own body.

If severe undesirable symptoms develop, the increased effect is termed a "toxic" effect. When cimetidine (brand name, Tagamet), a drug used to treat stomach and intestinal ulcers, is taken with theophylline, a medication used to relieve asthma, the result may be an increased amount of theophylline in the blood, possibly resulting in theophylline toxicity. The symptoms of theophylline toxicity can include nausea, vomiting, diarrhea, headache, irritability, restlessness, nervousness, rapid heartbeat, insomnia, tremor and even seizure.

Decreased effect of a medication. Another common drug interaction involves just the converse of the interaction described above: One drug may decrease the effectiveness of another drug. The end result depends on the degree of the decreased effect. If the decrease is small, the affected drug may still retain most of its pharmacologic activity. If the decrease is large, however, the effectiveness of the drug may be greatly diminished—or it may not work at all. If ciprofloxacin (Cipro), an antibiotic used to treat various bacterial infections, is combined with antacids that contain aluminum or magnesium (such as Maalox or Mylanta), the absorption of Cipro is greatly diminished, as is the bacteria-fighting ability of the antibiotic.

Selected drug–drug interactions are listed in Tables 1 and 2. The interactions included were chosen because of the widespread use of some of these medications, and because their effects are deemed "clinically significant"—that is, their effects have been detected in the human body as opposed to being observed only in vitro or in animal studies.

It is very important to note here that anyone taking any of the medications listed in the tables should not alter the dose of his or her medication without the prescribing doctor's consent and supervision. Patients should discuss all medication-related questions with their physicians and pharmacists.

Cigarette Smoking and Drug Interactions

In addition to having numerous adverse health effects associated with it (increased risk for various cancers, heart disease, stroke, ulcer and other conditions), cigarette smoking can also affect the way medications work. Smoking can reduce the efficacy of certain medications and make drug therapy more unpredictable.

TABLE 1: INTERACTIONS WITH DRUGS TAKEN FOR HYPERTENSION
(Brand names of drugs are shown in **boldface** in the table; generic names are in plain type.)

DRUGS	INTERACTS WITH	RESULTS AND PRACTICAL TIPS
diltiazem (**Cardizem**)	lithium (**Cibalith-S, Eskalith, Lithane, Lithobid** and others)	This interaction could lead to neurotoxicity. Possible symptoms include nausea, vomiting, muscular incoordination and ringing in the ears.
nifedipine (**Adalat; Procardia XL**); diltiazem (**Cardizem CD**)	cimetidine (**Tagamet**)	May increase the amount of nifedipine in the blood, thereby increasing the antihypertensive effect. Possible nifedipine toxicity—evidenced by symptoms such as dizziness, flushing and headache—may occur.
nifedipine (**Adalat; Procardia XL**)	barbiturates	Significantly decreases the amount of nifedipine available in the body, possibly leading to a decreased effect of the nifedipine. This effect is particularly likely when nifedipine is taken orally. (Much of the evidence for this interaction comes from studies of phenobarbital, but other barbiturates are expected to interact similarly.)

Table 3 identifies some well-documented effects cigarette smoking has on certain medications. (It's important to note here that—regardless of the effect a patient's smoking may have on a prescribed medication—a patient should never change the dose of a medication he or she is receiving without checking with the prescribing physician.)

Cigarette smoking increases the risk of heart attack and stroke in persons with high blood pressure who are on medication to keep their blood-pressure levels normal. Persons with angina—an often (though not always) painful condition in which the heart is deprived of oxygen or the arteries in the heart are narrowed—fare worse if they smoke.

The relationship between smoking and the development of ulcers has also been studied. Many studies have shown a strong positive association between cigarette smoking and the incidence of ulcers, their recurrence, delayed healing rates and an increased risk of complications. The question of whether (and the extent to which) smoking interferes with the efficacy of anti-ulcer drugs is still controversial.

In general, when smokers are compared with nonsmokers, ulcer healing and recurrence rates are poorer in smokers treated with certain anti-ulcer medications. One group of investigators found that smokers who were given cimetidine (Tagamet) were as likely to have a recurrence as were nonsmokers who received a placebo. The investigators concluded that smoking cessation may be more important than the administration of cimetidine in preventing the recurrence of ulcers.

Women who smoke and take oral contraceptives are at substantially higher risk of developing heart attack, stroke or blood clots than are similar nonsmokers. This finding is important in view of the fact that the number of young women taking up cigarette smoking has not declined over the last decade—as have the numbers taking up smok-

TABLE 2: INTERACTIONS WITH DRUGS TAKEN TO FIGHT INFECTION
(Brand names of drugs are shown in **boldface** in the table; generic names are in plain type.)

DRUGS	INTERACTS WITH	RESULTS AND PRACTICAL TIPS
amoxicillin (**Amoxil, Larotid,** and others); penicillin V (**Ledercillin VK, Pen-Vee K, V-Cillin K, Veetids**)	estrogen-containing oral contraceptives such as **Brevicon, Demulen, Enovid, Lo/Ovral, Norinyl, Ortho Novum, Ovcon, Ovral, Tri-Norinyl, Tri-Phasil** and many others.	Although aminopenicillins (such as amoxicillin) may reduce the efficacy of oral contraceptives, this result is probably rare. Menstrual irregularities, such as spotting or breakthrough bleeding, may be a sign that this interaction is occurring. Other types of penicillins and other oral antibiotics in general may produce similar effects. *Recommendation:* Women wishing to avoid pregnancy would be prudent to institute another form of contraception—in addition to use of their oral contraceptive—while taking amoxicillin or other penicillins in this class (i.e., aminopenicillins).
ciprofloxacin (**Cipro**)	· dairy products · multivitamin supplements · antacids that contain aluminum or magnesium	Greatly diminishes absorption of ciprofloxacin. Cations (e.g., calcium, magnesium, iron, aluminum, etc.) bind with ciprofloxacin and markedly reduce its absorption, possibly leading to decreased antibiotic effect. Do not take ciprofloxacin and cations (such as iron-containing vitamin supplements, dairy products, antacids, etc.) simultaneously. Ciprofloxacin should be taken at least two hours before or six hours after taking dairy products, vitamins or antacids to minimize the occurrence of this interaction.
erythromycin	terfenadine (**Seldane**); astemizole (**Hismanal**)	Erythromycin may cause increased plasma levels of **Seldane** or **Hismanal**, which could lead to cardiac arrhythmias. Changes in the EKG—namely prolonged QT interval—have been observed in patients combining erythromycin with these allergy medications. This interaction is serious. How often this interaction occurs is unknown, yet caution is certainly warranted.

TABLE 2 (CONTINUED): INTERACTIONS WITH DRUGS TAKEN TO FIGHT INFECTION

DRUGS	INTERACTS WITH	RESULTS AND PRACTICAL TIPS
erythromycin	theophylline (**Primatene Tablets, Slo-Bid, Theo-Dur, Theo-24, Uniphyl** and others)	Erythromycin may increase the amount of theophylline in the blood. Although most people do not seem to have much trouble with this interaction, some develop theophylline toxicity. Symptoms of theophylline toxicity include nausea, vomiting, diarrhea, headache, irritability, nervousness, rapid heartbeat, insomnia and tremor. In serious cases, seizure can occur. The effect is usually delayed, so that theophylline concentrations start to rise after 5–7 days of treatment with erythromycin. Furthermore, theophylline may cause reduced blood levels of erythromycin, possibly leading to diminished effect of erythromycin.
erythromycin	triazolam (**Halcion**)	This combination can lead to a substantial increase in the concentration of triazolam in the blood, possibly increasing its sedative effect, which could lead to drowsiness, impaired ability to concentrate and forgetfulness. *Recommendation:* If signs of triazolam toxicity are present, a patient may wish to discuss this with his or her physician; dosage reduction may be necessary.
tetracyclines	calcium · milk · dairy products · calcium supplements · calcium-containing multivitamins	Calcium supplements, calcium-fortified vitamins and foods containing calcium may substantially reduce the absorption of tetracycline, thereby diminishing its effect. The absorption of related compounds (i.e., doxycycline, minocycline) when taken with calcium is also reduced, but to a lesser extent. Foods with moderate to high amounts of calcium include milk, yogurt, cheese, sardines, salmon, soybeans, tofu, broccoli and turnip greens. *Recommendation:* Do not take tetracycline and calcium products simultaneously. In fact, avoid taking any cations (e.g., iron, magnesium, zinc, aluminum) with tetracycline. Take tetracyclines at least two hours before or at least four hours after eating dairy products or calcium-containing vitamins.

TABLE 3: EFFECT OF CIGARETTE SMOKING ON MEDICATIONS

DRUG	EFFECT ON CIGARETTE SMOKERS
theophylline (used to treat asthma)	Smoking may lead to a decrease in the effect of theophylline. Cigarette smoke increases the production of the enzymes in the liver responsible for metabolizing this medication; as a result, less of the medication enters the blood, and a decreased response may ensue.
tacrine (used to help manage Alzheimer's disease)	Smoking may lead to a decrease in the effect of tacrine.
insulin (used to manage diabetes mellitus, a condition that results in excessively high amounts of sugar in the blood and urine)	An insulin-dependent diabetic who smokes heavily may require a 15% to 30% higher dose of insulin than a nonsmoker.
flecainide (used to treat life-threatening arrhythmias—irregularities of the heartbeat and heart rhythm—of the lower chambers of the heart)	Smoking may decrease the amount of flecainide in the body. A doctor may need to prescribe a higher dose of this medication to a smoker than to otherwise similar nonsmokers.

ing in other segments of the population—but has remained relatively unchanged.

Are Drug Interactions Preventable?

Drug interactions are preventable in virtually every case. However, physicians and pharmacists must know what medications a patient is taking in order to head off trouble. Patients should inform physicians and pharmacists about other prescriptions as well as any vitamin or mineral supplements or over-the-counter medications they take routinely.

If a person is receiving (or is about to receive) interacting drugs, there are several ways to head off potential problems. Sometimes the best way to avoid an adverse drug interaction is simply for the doctor not to prescribe the interacting drugs. Several different medicines are available for the treatment of most disorders, and it may be possible to select an alternative to one of the interacting drugs.

If a patient truly needs both interacting drugs, other preventive measures may be called for. Sometimes the dose of one of the drugs can be adjusted to correct for the alteration caused by the drug interaction. Sometimes the physician will need to monitor the patient's response more carefully. Sometimes the interaction can be prevented by spacing the doses of the interacting drugs appropriately, or by giving one of the drugs by a different route of administration.

Using these and other methods, a doctor can typically prevent the adverse effects of drug interactions. But prevention must be a cooperative effort between the patient, the doctor and the pharmacist.

Hooked

Why Isn't Everyone an Addict?

Not Hooked

Deborah Franklin

Deborah Franklin is a staff writer.

In 1974, cocaine was making a splash among the American middle class, and Craig Reinarman was a graduate student in sociology casting about for thesis ideas. Academic journals were rife with papers on the seductive horrors of cocaine; a leading drug researcher writing in the *Journal of the American Medical Association* called cocaine "the highest high of all," and warned that where cocaine went, depraved addiction and rampant violence were sure to follow. But Reinarman noticed that when he shelved the journals and went home to the potlucks and parties of his San Francisco neighborhood, where some of his peers were beginning to dabble in cocaine, he saw a different picture.

"I was an ethnographer, accustomed to looking at a little social world and describing what I saw," says Reinarman, now a sociologist with the University of California at Santa Cruz. "And in this case, what I *didn't* see was moral depravity, decomposing lives, physical ill health, or anything remotely resembling the classic definition of addiction.

"I figured I might be on to something."

What he was on to was moderate, measured use of a drug that most people assumed could never be used in a moderate, measured way. There was a precedent. The late Norman Zinberg, a Harvard University psychiatrist, had described "weekend warriors"—people who restricted their heroin use to a Friday night pop without becoming addicted. They could walk away from heroin, and did every now and then, without undergoing the withdrawal pangs that junkies suffer. They never increased the amounts they used, and they never stole nor otherwise compromised their values to get more heroin. Most were successful, middle-class students and businesspeople who, when they wanted to relax, happened to snort or shoot heroin instead of drinking martinis. To understand why these people didn't become addicted, Zinberg said, it was necessary to look beyond biochemistry, to the motivations and environment of the drug user.

The idea that "hard" drugs can be used moderately is as surprising today as it was two decades ago. The $10-billion-a-year federal drug war has taken wide aim, and in its wartime vernacular, every drug user is an abuser, and every drug abuser a budding addict.

Certainly, the oft-told tales of alcoholics or crack addicts whose lives have crumbled under the weight of a habit are tragic and true. But press a knowledgeable drug warrior, and he or she will agree that there is another side to the story. In every survey and study ever commissioned to gauge the scope of America's drug problem, one result has held constant: Most of the people who use alcohol, heroin, cocaine, or any other recreational drug never develop the life-warping, bottomless craving known as addiction.

How come? At a time when the War Against Drugs is siphoning twice as much from the national coffers as the combined wars against cancer, AIDS, and heart disease, it is prudent to pause, and to ask how so many are able to avoid chemical bondage. It may be impossible to imprison every user and dealer; worse, it may be irrelevant. Better, say many researchers, to tease apart the reasons why some become addicted and others don't.

SURVEYING THE DRUG SCENE in 1974, sociologist Reinarman figured that the conventional line on cocaine was pure bunk. There have been drug scares as long as there have been moralists, he reasoned; before cocaine, it was reefer madness or demon rum that was to blame for society's decline. So Reinarman proposed a small study. He called the San Francisco–based Institute for Scientific Analysis, a nonprofit think tank noted for sponsoring social science studies too small or too controversial to gain mainstream attention, and convinced sociologists Sheigla Murphy and Dan Waldorf to join him in a little cultural spying. As Margaret Mead had hunkered down with a village of Samoans 50 years earlier to learn the daily rituals and values of that culture, Reinarman and his crew would eat, party, and otherwise hang out with a network of cocaine snorters and sellers.

The network consisted of ten members of two extended families—the Joyces and the Austens*— and 22 of their assorted spouses, lovers, friends, and acquaintances. The group was linked by the four Austen and three Joyce sisters, who ranged in age at the start of the study from 19 to 30. Mostly native San Franciscans born to educated, white, middle-class parents, the young women and their friends were taking college classes and working part-time as they mosied toward careers. Nearly all were single and childless, with few responsibilities.

"It was a very social time in all our lives, and drugs were just a part of that," says Dede, the youngest Joyce sister. In 1990, she is the only member of the group willing to discuss her drug use with a reporter, and then only by phone. "Today if college kids hear that you do drugs, they look at you like you're some kind of monster," she says. "But at that time people were still lighting up joints in movie theaters."

The group's emotional heart in 1974, and chief conduit for family gossip as well as drugs, was Dede's eldest sister, 27-year-old graduate student and cocktail waitress Bridget Joyce. She had lived with a couple of small-time drug dealers over the years, and periodically sold cocaine and marijuana herself. Her apartment served as the group's chief meeting place; on weekends members would gather there to study, shoot the bull, work on each other's cars. In the evenings, visitors would be offered beer, wine, or marijuana—"as routinely as any suburbanite would be offered cocktails or mixed drinks," Reinarman says. Drugs were never

*The names and other identifying characteristics of this group have been changed.

the focus, they simply greased the social wheels.

"Most members were seasoned drug users who had experimented with hallucinogens and a variety of other illicit drugs in the late 1960s and early 1970s," Murphy says. About half had experimented with injecting cocaine, but all said they preferred snorting. Injecting or smoking a purified version of cocaine, they said, seemed to produce a rush too intense and fleeting to be safely worked into a well-rounded life.

MOST MADE SNORTING TOO MUCH COKE SOUND LIKE EATING TOO MUCH PIZZA OR WATCHING TOO MANY DOUBLE FEATURES. YOU JUST STOP. NO BIG DEAL.

Cocaine was considered a luxury, restricted to special occasions and close friends. Typically, once every few weeks or so, someone would buy one or two grams for the group—about 50 or 100 lines— to be snorted over the course of a weekend. (For most casual users, one matchstick-sized "line" of snorted cocaine hydrochloride produces a general alertness and sense of well-being that lasts about 20 or 30 minutes.)

Most agreed that there was a downside to using too much cocaine, and they regulated their use to minimize it. A weekend binge could irritate the throat and nasal passages, leaving users with what felt like a bad head cold. The drug also seemed to act as a sensual intensifier, which was great if you were already feeling lively and energetic, but wearing if you were tired or depressed. According to group wisdom, taking cocaine when you had a headache only intensified the pain.

They also discovered that continual cocaine use over a 10- or 12-hour period (snorting every 20 or 30 minutes) led to short-term tolerance, which meant that users stopped feeling as high from the drug. And after that came the inevitable crash, a landing that could be soft or could be hard.

"Instead of going full tilt—sharp, clear, everything all together, incredible thinking power—it starts dwindling away and eventually dissipates into a shitty feeling mentally, a very depressed state and physically run-down," a heavy user told one of the researchers in describing the landings that weren't soft. To help ease the crash, users would sometimes take one or two quaaludes or other sedatives toward the end of a coke binge.

Most had neither the time, money, nor inclination to experience such crashes frequently, any more than they were willing to suffer frequent hangovers. For many, simply the need to be at work early Monday morning kept both cocaine and alcohol binges in check. But a few others, with more flexible schedules, periodically used coke every day for months. After a month or more of such steady use, the snorter would begin to feel chronically tense, restless, and irritable—"coked out"—to a degree as obvious to him or her as to the rest of the group. The few who snorted that much cocaine learned to recognize such symptoms, and alleviated them by abstaining for a week or so, and after that cutting back to less regular use.

The group was concerned about one member in 1974. Nineteen-year-old Lisa Austen, a charming party girl, was admired and valued by friends and family both for her social stamina and her ability to organize "boogies" for herself and everyone else. But her sisters worried that her alcohol-fueled party binges were at times excessive. The Austens' parents had died in an accident in 1971, leaving each daughter with a substantial inheritance. The three older women had used their money to buy houses; Lisa was using hers to finance month-long ski trips and Hawaiian vacations. Still, it was primarily her heavy drinking, not her moderate cocaine habit, that concerned her friends and family.

Even the four or five heaviest users of cocaine, defined by the researchers as anyone who said they used at least two grams a week for six months or more, or who used any amount daily, didn't fit the classic definition of chemical dependency. But all agreed that the drug did sometimes wield considerable power, as a user sought to maintain the high and avoid the crash.

"It's psychologically addicting, I think," one heavy user named Leo told the sociologists. "You continue to use so you don't have to go through the space of coming down, you know, just to keep from coming down."

Most group members made snorting too much coke sound like eating too much pizza or having too much sex or watching too many double features. You spend too much time doing one thing and you feel sick, and need a break. But you can always walk away. No harrowing withdrawals, no life of decrepitude, no confessing to strangers at a Cokenders' meeting. You just stop. No big deal.

At the end of six months, Reinarman, Murphy, and Waldorf put away the notebooks and wound up their study. Cocaine's reputation as a violent seductress was groundless, they decided—a conclusion they would, however, feel compelled to amend 11 years later. In 1975 they confidently reported in a published summary: "Cocaine is much more mild and subtle in its effects than its legal or mythological status would indicate."

IN HIS BASEMENT LABORATORY in San Diego, George Koob is conducting a few drug experiments of his own. A leading neurobiologist at the Research Institute of Scripps Clinic, Koob is studying the ways cocaine and heroin alter the inner work-

Easy to Get Hooked On, Hard to Get Off

TO RANK today's commonly used drugs by their addictiveness, we asked experts to consider two questions: How easy is it to get hooked on these substances and how hard is it to stop using them? Although a person's vulnerability to a drug also depends on individual traits—physiology, psychology, and social and economic pressures—these rankings reflect only the addictive potential inherent in the drug. The numbers below are relative rankings, based on the experts' scores for each substance.

	10	20	30	40	50	60	70	80	90	100

NICOTINE

ICE, GLASS (METHAMPHETAMINE SMOKED)

CRACK

CRYSTAL METH (METHAMPHETAMINE INJECTED)

VALIUM (DIAZEPAM)

QUAALUDE (METHAQUALONE)

SECONAL (SECOBARBITAL)

ALCOHOL

HEROIN

CRANK (AMPHETAMINE TAKEN NASALLY)

COCAINE

CAFFEINE

PCP (PHENCYCLIDINE)

MARIJUANA

ECSTASY (MDMA)

PSILOCYBIN MUSHROOMS

LSD

MESCALINE

Research by John Hastings

ings of brain cells. His laboratory is lined with what look like hotel-room refrigerators. Except that these boxes aren't refrigerated, and instead of cold drinks each houses a rat high on cocaine.

Each rat wears a metal skullcap anchoring an electrode, through which Koob and his colleagues can both stimulate and record the activity of a middling section of the animal's brain. A clear plastic catheter also tethers each rat to its own bottle of cocaine-laced salt water. Every time the rat presses a lever, a drop of the liquid flows down the tube and directly into the upper left chamber of the animal's heart.

There's something funny—funny strange—about these rats. Theirs isn't a druggy contentment; remove the box lid and they want to look around. But neither do they exhibit the feverish darting of an escaped hostage or speed-crazed hysteric. When graduate student Athina Markou picks one up, holding it gently in the crook of her arm as she uses both hands to tweak the catheter, the rat stands as comfortably still as a horse being groomed.

"Our rats are all chippers," Koob says, using the street term coined years ago to describe people who take opiates every now and then. "They can start and stop taking cocaine without any ill effects, as long as they're only exposed to it for a few hours a day."

Brain researchers realized four decades ago that if they electrically stimulated a stirrup-shaped stretch of neurons slightly off center in a rat's brain, the animal seemed enthralled; it would traverse a maze, run a treadmill, or perform any other task the inventive researchers set before it, simply to get more stimulation. That section of the brain came to be called the "reward system." Most drug researchers now believe that the reward system at least partly underlies drug intoxication and, perhaps, addiction.

For instance, when all wired up and left to their own devices, Koob's rats will press a lever to electrically stimulate the reward system at an even, predictable rate of once or twice a second. If he then adds cocaine, putting them on a steady, metered drip, they'll press the electrical lever more often, as though the cocaine enhances the pleasure. Stop the cocaine drip, and they'll immediately return to the slower, steady pressing.

That pattern holds true as long as the rats' access to cocaine is limited to about three hours a day. But if, instead, Koob and Markou give the rats cocaine for 24 hours straight and then take it away, mimicking a cocaine binge, the animals respond quite differently. After a moment of frantic pressing, they'll stop completely, as though somehow the longer-term drug use has damped their ability to feel pleasure. Koob and Markou believe the rats' response mimics the coke-outs experienced by cocaine bingers.

Scientists don't know exactly how cocaine affects the brain's reward circuitry. They do know

that many of the neural "wires" in the circuit rely on the chemical dopamine to transmit messages from cell to cell. The brain cell that's sending a message squirts out its chemical signal—dopamine. The dopamine is detected by the next cell in line, and the message—in this case, pleasure—is passed along. Almost immediately the dopamine molecules floating around between the cells are taken up again by the transmitting cell and repackaged in a neat bit of biological recycling.

Cocaine seems to block the removal of dopamine from between the cells. As a result, or so goes one theory, the receiving cell is overstimulated, producing the cocaine high. The transmitting cell depletes its dopamine stores and temporarily loses its ability to send messages. This dearth of dopamine, say researchers, might be at the root of the cocaine crash: No dopamine, no pleasure.

NINE OF EVERY TEN PEOPLE WHO LIGHT UP A CIGARETTE WILL HAVE TROUBLE QUITTING, COMPARED WITH TWO OF TEN FIRST-TIME COCAINE USERS.

That's a nice, understandable model of how the biology might work, Koob says, but it's a little too pat. There is every indication from behavioral studies that even among lab rats, better known for their overbred sameness than their idiosyncratic flair, individual differences abound.

For example, Koob currently has about a hundred rats in training for his lever-pressing cocaine experiments, and their enthusiasm for the procedure—and the drug—varies widely. "At least thirty to forty percent of the rats will not take cocaine, or at least not readily," he says. "On the other hand, sixty to seventy percent will take it immediately, without training. How come?"

The variation in response is not unique to cocaine. In a test a couple of years ago, Koob came across a rat with an inordinate affection for heroin. The test regimen was similar to the cocaine experiment: three hours of unlimited access to the drug. "I'll never forget it," he says. "Back then, we had to put the levers in and take them out at the beginning and end of each session. Normally that wasn't a problem, you'd just open the cage door, stick the lever in, and the rats wouldn't bother you. But this one particular rat wouldn't let us do that. You'd open the door and he'd grab the lever out of your hand, run to the back of the cage and frenetically gnaw on the lever." Unlike the rest of the rats who merely pressed often enough to keep a steady level of the drug circulating through their blood, this

Is There an Addictive Personality?

IT'S TEMPTING TO THINK you can spot the vulnerable ones—the lonely and needy types or the hyper thrill-seekers—those friends and acquaintances whose behavior makes them most likely to become dependent on drugs. In fact, there's no such thing as an addictive personality. Most researchers now studying drug use believe that it takes a combination of factors—not only psychological influences, but also biological and social forces—to push drug users to addiction. And the particular mix varies from person to person.

Some of the major factors are described below. A single isolated characteristic means nothing; having an alcoholic parent, for instance, doesn't preordain alcoholism in a child any more than snorting a line of coke leads inevitably to cocaine addiction. But the more of these characteristics a person has, and the stronger each trait or condition is, the more vulnerable that person is to addiction.   —D.F.

THE DRUG

A Fast, Big Bang

The more intense the euphoria produced by a substance, and the quicker it's over, the more likely it is that a user will take large amounts of the drug often. That's why crack cocaine is more likely to produce dependency than subtler, slower-acting powder cocaine, and why both drugs are much more likely to lead to addiction than a hallucinogen such as LSD.

▼

A Painful Crash

If a drug creates painful withdrawal symptoms, psychological or physical, a heavy user is more likely to continue using it just to avoid that pain. Withdrawal from alcohol, barbiturates (prescription sedatives), and narcotics is particularly difficult. Many researchers also believe that the sudden depression that follows withdrawal from a cocaine binge helps fuel the addiction.

THE BODY

An Addict in the Family

Having an alcoholic parent increases the risk of having a drinking problem, partly because of inherited body chemistry; abuse of other drugs may also have a genetic component, but that's less well established.

▼

Chronic Pain

Narcotics are often the most effective treatment for the pain of cancer and surgery, and there is a lot of evidence that the drugs *do not* lead to addiction in these patients. But other kinds of chronic pain—back pain, migraines, or the pain of arthritis, for example—don't usually respond to narcotics such as morphine, Percodan, or Demerol, and can foster dependence in people who take increasing doses hoping for relief.

▼

Drug Sensitivities

Some people feel the exhilaration of a drug's high and the pangs of its withdrawal more acutely than others—perhaps because of slight genetic differences that lead to differences in the way their bodies react to or metabolize the drug.

THE MIND

Brash, Lacks Self-Control

Uninhibited people who rarely put the brakes on in their lives are more likely to lack restraint in their drug use as well.

▼

Lacks Values That Constrain Drug Use

Certain religious tenets, a strong health ethic, or any core beliefs that value sobriety can all limit drug use. Without them a person is more vulnerable to addiction.

▼

Has Low Self-Esteem, Feels Powerless

Drugs can grant a feeling of power, so heavy use may be more tempting for people who feel frustrated and defeated.

▼

Depressed

According to one theory, some depressed and anxious people may be susceptible to uncontrolled drug use because they have an underlying neurochemical imbalance that the drugs temporarily correct.

THE SETTING

Barren Environment

War zones, urban slums, and prisons are all more likely to foster heavy drug use than places that offer alternative adventures, pleasures, and opportunities.

▼

No Supportive Social Group

Isolation or alienation from friends and family can encourage uncontrolled drug use.

▼

Drug-Rich Environment

Whether a drug user is rich or poor, if most of his or her friends and mentors are compulsive, out-of-control drug users, he or she is more likely than the average person to use drugs that way, too. Conversely, being surrounded by people who use drugs moderately is a tempering influence. Having easy access to a plentiful, cheap drug supply also tends to increase use.

▼

Few Social Guidelines for Acceptable Use of a Drug

In the United States, it's generally acceptable to drink alcohol in the early evening, but not before noon. As long as the drinker's not driving, most people believe it's okay to get tipsy or even drunk on a Friday night with friends, but not on a Tuesday night alone. Such rules and rituals—different for every culture and every drug—help moderate use. Illegal substances, pushed outside the circle of social respectability, aren't as bound up in social constraints, and may be more likely to be used to excess.

particular animal took more and more heroin each day, at the expense of eating and drinking.

"He effectively became hugely dependent on heroin in just his three-hour sessions until he eventually overdosed and died," Koob says. "Now where did *he* come from?"

Even in animals, let alone people, it's neither easy nor cheap to study variation; just for starters, you need a lot more subjects to turn up subtle differences than you need to hunt for broad similarities. But in the last five years, a few researchers have noticed that if you focus on the trees instead of the forest, you get a different—and in many ways more informative—picture. Some of the most interesting clues so far have emerged from alcohol research.

T. K. Li, for example, a geneticist at Indiana University in Indianapolis, noticed in the mid 1970s that while almost all rats dislike the taste of alcohol, it is easier to get some—about two in a hundred—to drink than others. The characteristic, he learned, seems to be inherited. By breeding about 20 generations, each time mating only those animals that somewhat liked alcohol, he eventually developed a strain in which nearly every member of every litter preferred an unflavored, 10 percent solution of ethanol to water. (That's about the same concentration of alcohol as is found in most wines.) The animals not only found pleasure in alcohol, they also had a high, long-lasting tolerance to its negative effects. Genetically endowed with the two distinct characteristics, Li's rats were much more likely than most to become chemically dependent, he says.

In the last few years, researchers have also selectively bred lines of rats and mice that, because of differences in their genetic makeup, either strongly prefer or strictly avoid opiates, cocaine, and some tranquilizers. Another strain of rats is more sensitive to the stimulant effects of cocaine, still another more sensitive to the drug's tendency to cause seizures at high doses. Some animals metabolize alcohol faster, and so can drink more without getting intoxicated. Others get intoxicated with very low blood levels of alcohol. The point to be taken from all this research, Li says, is that there are a number of distinct ways that individuals can differ in their biological response to drugs.

And if rats can vary, how much more so people, whose neural wiring has a few extra miles of loops and cross-connections. In fact, the animal work dovetails nicely with the findings of researchers studying children of alcoholics. Marc Schuckit, of the University of California at San Diego, found in several studies that sons of alcoholics are less sensitive than men with no family history of alcoholism to the drug's effects: They can drink others under the table, achieve a high level of alcohol in their blood, and still perform mental and physical gymnastics. Because they could drink more alcohol before feeling its effects, Schuckit argues, they might be more likely to drink enough to develop dependency.

Studies of identical twins and adopted children convincingly show that a vulnerability to alcoholism is partly inherited. But the important flip side of such results is that genes don't *determine* alcoholism; the vast majority of the children of alcoholics, and of identical twin siblings of alcoholics, do not develop the disorder.

It's highly unlikely that specific "addiction" genes exist, researchers say. Instead, a few hundred genes may work together to coordinate the metabolism of alcohol or other drugs, and perhaps several dozen others control the release and recycling of a neurotransmitter at a synapse. It probably takes major inherited flaws in several genes to gum up the works of even one such process, and a number of such fractured processes to lay the biological groundwork for addiction.

THE LIKELIHOOD OF ADDICTION IS DETERMINED IN PART BY HOW FAST THE DRUG GETS INTO THE BRAIN, HOW BIG THE BANG IS, AND HOW LONG THE BANG LASTS.

There is also no guarantee that just because you aren't biologically vulnerable, you won't become addicted to a particular drug if you take enough of it. Some drugs, by the nature of their chemistry, seem intrinsically more habit-forming than others.

"There's some abuse potential with marijuana," Koob says. "For example, it's probably at least as dangerous for someone to drive while high on marijuana as to drive while drunk. But on my list of drugs likely to produce dependency—people who are out of control of their use and want to quit, but can't—it's pretty far down the line."

By the same token, LSD may be dangerous if it makes you think you can fly and you dive out a window, but it's unlikely to produce addiction. "It is just not a drug that people take in a compulsive way," Koob says. Some people scoffed when the Surgeon General four years ago called nicotine the most addictive drug known. But survey figures indicate that nine of every ten people who light up a cigarette will one day have trouble quitting, compared with perhaps two of ten first-time cocaine users. It is important to remember, says Koob, that not all dangerous drugs are equally addictive, and not all addictive drugs are equally dangerous.

You can also change a hard drug into a soft one, and vice versa, by changing the way you take it into your body. For example, periodically chewing a wad of lime-treated coca leaves, as many native

Peruvians still do their entire lives, may never produce addiction because the cocaine that reaches the brain that way is released slowly and in small quantities. Alternatively, snorting powder cocaine delivers more of the refined drug to the brain faster, and smoking crack—a concentrated form of cocaine—delivers the drug even more efficiently. From coca leaves to crack, there is a progression in the likelihood of producing addiction that is largely determined, Koob says, by "how fast the drug gets into the brain, how big the bang is, and how long the bang lasts." Even Reinarman, who thinks that at least some of crack's devil-drug rep-

utation is hype, calls smoking crack cocaine "using an already powerful drug in the most dangerous way possible."

"I think the suspicion of many people working in the field," says Koob, "is that if you make the route of administration strong enough, and the access to the drug continuous and unlimited, you could turn any chipper into an addict."

Of course, people are more than the sum of their biological parts, and many drug users choose to limit their own access to a drug. Norman Zinberg was one of the first to point out that while drugs are indeed chemically powerful, that chemistry is

---

Are Teenagers Saying No?

The young are permanently in a state resembling intoxication;
for youth is sweet and they are growing. —ARISTOTLE, *Nicomachean Ethics*

BY THE TIME THEY REACH their teen years, today's young people are looking for something stronger than the sweetness of youth to induce intoxication. Yet for all their wild hair, their nose studs, and their jaded-rebel posturing, teenagers are almost as conventional as adults when it comes to using drugs: They're much more likely to drink or smoke than take illegal substances, and they view drugs in general with increasing disfavor.

"In fact," says Lloyd Johnston of the University of Michigan's Institute for Social Research, "the likelihood of a young person in high school actively using illicit drugs is only about half what it was a decade ago." The institute annually surveys students in 135 high schools across the country, from big-city public schools to small, exclusive academies in ritzy suburbs. According to its findings, in just the past five years marijuana smoking has gone down about 35 percent, the use of stimulants such as amphetamines has fallen off more than 45 percent, and the number of teens who regularly take cocaine has dropped by almost 50 percent.

Johnston says this decline is in part a result of teenagers' growing perception that drugs can be harmful: Eight in ten teenagers concede that regular marijuana use is unhealthy, he says, and six in ten think even trying cocaine is risky. Both of these numbers have been on the rise since before 1986.

Not that your average high schooler isn't curious. According to a recent institute survey, nine out of ten kids try alcohol during their teens, and two out of three experiment with cigarettes. About 60 percent of the drinkers become social users, who drink at least once a month, whereas just 5 percent develop daily habits. A third of those who try cigarettes become daily smokers.

Nor is everyone's curiosity satisfied by booze and cigarettes. For example, 44 percent of teenagers try marijuana, 38 percent of them going on to smoke at least once a month and 7 percent to smoke daily. Twenty percent try stimulants; between 10 and 15 percent sample depressants. But the number of high schoolers who actually go on to use these drugs regularly is minuscule— around one percent for each.

Cocaine appears to attract more hype than it does teenage users. Just 10 percent of teens have tried the drug, according to the institute's figures, and fewer than 5 percent have tried crack— about one-third of each group going on to use the drug at least monthly. Experimenting with more exotic substances—LSD, PCP, heroin—is even less common, and regular use of these drugs during the teen years is almost unheard of.

The University of Michigan surveys don't include high school dropouts, who are more likely than regular students to use drugs, and who are more

numerous in impoverished school districts than in middle-class or affluent regions. "But we're seeing some of the same antidrug attitudes in poorer areas as well," says Johnston, "such as the backlash against crack users recently reported in poor sections of Brooklyn."

Simply experimenting with drugs— sampling, without regular use—causes teenagers no apparent harm, at least while they're still teenagers, according to the most recent evidence. Researchers led by psychologist Jack Block of the University of California at Berkeley followed 101 Oakland-area young people from age 3 through age 18, exhaustively tracking the boys' and girls' psychological development and drug use, among other things. By their senior year in high school, most fell into one of three groups: those who were smoking marijuana at least weekly, some of them sampling stronger drugs; those who smoked pot only occasionally; and those who abstained from drugs altogether.

Both before and after they started taking drugs, the frequent users tended to be impulsive, insecure, and alienated from their peers and families—significantly more so than the young people who didn't develop regular drug habits. But the middle group, the experimenters, were at least as well developed psychologically as youngsters who shunned drugs altogether, even slightly less anxious and socially inhibited.
—*Benedict Carey*

Ice, LSD, Chocolate, TV: Is Everything Addictive?

ACCORDING TO THE STANDARD psychiatric definition, any drug user who passes three of the nine tests below is hooked. We asked several researchers to apply the tests not only to drugs but also to other substances and activities—chocolate, sex, shopping. Their responses show it's possible to become addicted to all sorts of things. For example, serious runners could pass three of the tests by spending more time running than originally intended, covering increasing distances, and experiencing withdrawal symptoms (a devoted runner forced to stop because of an injury, say, might become anxious and irritable.) Of course, that sort of dependency isn't necessarily destructive. Conversely, a drug that fails the addictiveness test—LSD, for instance—may be harmful just the same. That so many things are potentially addictive suggests the addiction's cause is not confined to the substance or activity—our culture may play a large role, too.

	NICOTINE	ALCOHOL	CAFFEINE	COCAINE	CRACK	HEROIN	ICE*	LSD	MARIJUANA	PCP	VALIUM, XANAX, ETC.**	STEROIDS	CHOCOLATE	RUNNING	GAMBLING	SHOPPING	SEX	WORK	DRIVING	TELEVISION	MOUNTAIN CLIMBING
TAKES substance or does activity more than originally intended	✓	✓	✓	✓	✓	✓	✓		✓	✓	✓	✓	✓	✓	✓	✓	✓	✓		✓	✓
WANTS to cut back or has tried to cut back but failed	✓	✓	✓	✓	✓	✓	✓		✓	✓	✓	✓	✓	✓	✓	✓	✓	✓		✓	✓
SPENDS lots of time trying to get substance or set up activity, taking substance or doing activity, or recovering	✓	✓		✓	✓	✓	✓	✓	✓	✓				✓	✓	✓	✓	✓		✓	✓
IS OFTEN intoxicated or suffers withdrawal symptoms when expected to fulfill obligations at work, school, or home		✓		✓	✓	✓	✓		✓	✓	✓										
CURTAILS or gives up important social, occupational, or recreational activities because of substance or activity		✓		✓	✓	✓	✓		✓	✓				✓	✓	✓	✓	✓		✓	✓
USES substance or does activity despite persistent social, psychological, or physical problems caused by substance or activity	✓	✓	✓	✓	✓	✓	✓	✓	✓	✓	✓	✓	✓	✓	✓	✓	✓	✓		✓	✓
NEEDS more and more of substance or activity to achieve the same effect (tolerance)	✓	✓	✓	✓	✓	✓	✓			✓											
SUFFERS characteristic withdrawal symptoms when activity or substance is discontinued (cravings, anxiety, depression, jitters)	✓	✓	✓	✓	✓	✓	✓			✓			✓	✓	✓	✓	✓	✓		✓	✓
TAKES substance or does activity to relieve or avoid withdrawal symptoms	✓	✓	✓	✓	✓	✓	✓			✓											

*Methamphetamine smoked
**Benzodiazepines

Research by Valerie Fahey

played out in a person who has specific values and a wide range of competing motivations. In a refrain that would be picked up by those who came after, Zinberg argued that a stake in the conventional world—a rewarding job, or healthy relationships, or goals and dreams that seem within grasp—are motivators as powerful as any chemical. Many people who might be biologically vulnerable to drug addiction, or who sample a particularly potent form of the drug, escape addiction because they have goals and values that aren't compatible with heavy drug or alcohol use.

Conversely, there are people who may be more vulnerable for social reasons: those at the bottom-most rung of the socioeconomic ladder who can't see their way clear to climb up, for example, or those at the top of the ladder who no longer recognize the possibility that they could fall. Like the caged rats who have nothing to do all day but press a lever for cocaine, such people have few competing motivations to constrain their drug use.

IN 1986, 11 YEARS AFTER they had closed the books on the Joyce and Austen clan, Murphy, Reinarman, and Waldorf looked up the group members again.

"They called me the Rambo of interviewers," Murphy says. "They'd put me off and put me off, and I'd go to their houses and wake them up, and say 'Here are the bagels and the coffee, let's talk.' I'd pound on the door, and yell, 'It's Sunday, I *know* you're still asleep. Come *on*.' "

Dede, now 37 and finishing the last few courses of an undergraduate business degree, explains the reluctance: "It's not like that was a bad part of our lives, but it's behind us now, just not something we want to dwell on. We've moved on."

And so they have. The intervening years have brought seven marriages and five divorces, 12 academic degrees, nine children, and ten houses. Two are artists, and one is a poet, but most are mid-career lawyers, teachers, or businesspeople. The two members who did the most cocaine over the longest period (13 years) are well ensconced in profitable careers as an attorney and the owner of a small art business. "We're talking Middle America here," Dede says, and laughs.

Most members of the group still do some drugs, but in a less concerted way than in 1974. Dede and her husband—she met him at a party in 1973—will still have a beer, or smoke a joint to relax at the end of a long day, but no longer have time for the late-night-bull-session-party-till-you-drop weekends that they both enjoyed ten years ago. "When you're young you do stupid stuff," she says. "I used to routinely take a quaalude and snort a line, and you know that that sort of slowing your heart down and then jolting it can't be good for you." She says the words with the matter-of-fact reluctance of a middle-aged runner who gave up jogging because it was too hard on the knees.

She and her husband save cocaine for birthdays, anniversaries, or other special occasions, and never use more than a quarter gram in a month. "We bought a gram almost a year ago and still have it," she says. "People who use more regularly hear that and say, 'How can you keep from going through the drawers for it?' But who has time? Between going to work and school and keeping a relationship solid, there's very little time left."

If all, instead of merely most, group members had gone on to have a drug career like Dede's, Murphy, Waldorf, and Reinarman might not have felt the need to amend their early report. But there were a few troubling cases that led them to note in their published follow-up in 1986, "From our current perspective we realize that our description [in 1974] probably would have been less sanguine had we studied the group longer."

REINARMAN CALLS THE DRUG WAR AN IDEOLOGICAL FIG LEAF. "UNFORTUNATELY, THESE KIDS CANNOT 'JUST SAY NO' TO POVERTY AND UNEMPLOYMENT."

For example, there's Maria. In 1974, the second eldest Joyce sister was a 24-year-old single college student working part-time as a telephone operator. The most conservative member of a flamboyant family, she was, for the first five years, the most moderate in her cocaine use. As Maria remembers it, she sometimes felt "the urge to do more" even during those first years, and might have acted on the urge if she'd had a bigger budget or a cheaper supply. In 1980, that abundance arrived. Her older sister Bridget and a few friends began selling cocaine to supplement their own incomes and were generous with the family. Daily access to the drug did not increase Bridget's use, but marked the beginning of problems for Maria.

Maria stepped up her daily consumption, staying up late at night to do cocaine by herself long after everyone else had gone to bed. Increasingly worried, her friends and family stopped giving or selling it to her; in reaction, the formerly responsible, straitlaced Maria began to steal the drug from them. "I handled the guilt by just doing more cocaine," she told Murphy. The heavy, uncontrolled use lasted 18 months, including one harrowing night of hallucinations and convulsions, until the day she learned she was pregnant. Immediately, with the support of her family, but without professional help, she quit.

"Everybody comes to a decision point with their drug use," says Dede. "For me it was getting married and buying a house, for Maria it was getting pregnant. When she found something she wanted more than sitting around the house and getting high, she stopped."

But Murphy, Reinarman, and Waldorf aren't so sure that everybody gets an equal chance to decide. Despite the tightly knit safety net of family support, education, and relative wealth, a few members of the group fell through. For example, Bridget and her husband, Sebastian, both blame his escalated cocaine and heroin use for the disintegration of their marriage; it also derailed his career and, despite great desire, he has struggled unsuccessfully to pull away from drugs. Today he is an on-again, off-again methadone maintenance patient work-ing as a limousine driver in New York City.

And then there's Lisa. She continued to live with cocaine dealers, and would often put up the money for large cocaine buys that her lovers would sell. She and five others once snorted an ounce of cocaine in two days—more than 500 liberal lines—and at her peak she regularly used five or six ounces a month. By 1978, she had depleted her inheritance on drugs and travel, and began working as a cocktail waitress and bartender in a San Francisco nightclub. Cocaine was integral to backstage life at the club, and she continued to use more and more, drinking alcohol to counteract

The Rise and Fall of a Street Drug

DURING THE JAZZ AGE, cocaine kept people dancing. A decade later, barbiturates greeted the Great Depression. And when the sixties rolled around, the counterculture got high on LSD. Almost all drugs go in and out of fashion, their popularity riding the ups and downs of economic and social change.

A good recent example is the animal tranquilizer phencyclidine. Like other abused drugs, it was once a promising medicine. But its development as a human anesthetic came to an abrupt halt in 1965 when researchers discovered it provoked nightmares and delusions in many patients.

Phencyclidine made its first illicit appearance in the summer of 1967 at a free rock concert in the Panhandle of San Francisco's Golden Gate Park. The amateur chemists who passed it out called it the PeaCePill, or PCP. In small to moderate doses, PCP can be either a stimulant or a depressant. But because paranoia and frightening hallucinations often accompany large amounts, it quickly earned a reputation as a bummer drug. By 1969, after a brief appearance on the East Coast, PCP had all but vanished from the drug scene.

In 1970, the federal government cracked down on illegal drugs and imposed strict penalties on people caught making or importing them. As a result, speed, quaaludes, and LSD became harder to find. The price of cocaine soared. With the competition under fire, the underdog moved in.

PCP had two of the most important traits a street drug needs. It was easy to make: Even a layman could get his hands on the necessary chemicals, retire to his kitchen, and turn a $100 investment into $100,000 worth of drugs. And it was cheap: A cigarette of mint or parsley leaves laced with PCP cost only a couple of dollars. By the early seventies, PCP's star was rising.

Along with its new popularity came a new type of user—the kind typically attracted to drugs on the fast track. Instead of big-city hippies, they were white, middle-class teenagers, who could get their hands on a PCP joint more easily than they could a six-pack of beer. And by smoking the drug instead of swallowing it, they could control the dose and avoid some of the unpredictable side effects that had frightened users in the sixties. Almost 750,000 kids aged 12 to 17 had tried PCP by 1976. A year later, that figure had nearly doubled.

As PCP spread from the big coastal cities inland, a drug's usual migration, disturbing news reports began to surface, stories of people committing violent crimes while high on the drug. "Sixty Minutes" aired interviews with two PCP users: one who had stabbed a pregnant woman and murdered her child, and another who had shot and killed his parents.

The government reacted; it stiffened jail sentences for individuals convicted of making or selling the drug, kept a watchful eye on people who purchased its key ingredients, and launched anti-PCP programs. California, for example, spent $600,000 teaching educators how to prevent PCP abuse.

More importantly, street experience backed up the media scares and official warnings. Between 1976 and 1979, the number of hospital emergency room visits involving PCP almost quadrupled, totaling an estimated 10,000 in 1979. The government's education efforts, coupled with a public panic, seemed to turn the tide: A year later, the number of PCP emergencies fell by a third, and the figure continued to drop through the early eighties. PCP finally appeared to be falling out of fashion.

But not for everyone. In 1983, PCP abuse was on the upswing again, mainly among the inner-city poor, who often adopt drugs that the middle class deems dangerous and discards. By the mid-eighties, more than half the hospital patients with PCP-related emergencies were black, and almost two-thirds were in their twenties, mostly men. As abuse approached its 1979 levels, a new and cheaper version of another middle-class drug appeared—crack cocaine. Unlike PCP, its high was predictable. As crack's popularity soared, PCP's declined. By 1989, PCP use was concentrated in only a few urban areas, including parts of San Jose, California, and Washington, D.C.

Will PCP just fade away? A recent survey of high school seniors showed a slight increase in its use, but not enough to mark a trend. If the main supplies of imported drugs ever dry up, though, America's homemade high could quite possibly make a comeback.

—Mary Hossfeld

the wired feeling. Today both her drinking and cocaine use are out of control and her family is worried. "She is the one person in the group of thirty-two who has come closest to the stereotypical image of an addict—one who loses it all because of their drug use," Murphy says.

What went wrong? Reinarman is willing to hazard a guess. "She was the youngest—sixteen when her parents died—and losing them was hardest on her. She was least prepared to take that kind of tragedy, and then suddenly, boom—she's handed a big chunk of change. She's moving in circles where drug use is everywhere, so she kind of went off the deep end." She may also have been particularly vulnerable to alcoholism.

"She always drank too much. Before she could drink legally, she was guzzling down beers with the best of the boys," Reinarman says. "Then she started cocaine, and when you titrate cocaine and alcohol, you've got an upper and a downer, which means you can drink more and not feel it—though it's definitely having an effect on your body—and you can snort more cocaine and not feel over-amped. Lisa often did that. It's a nice high, but you don't recognize the toll it's taking." Eventually, like

Why Do People Take Drugs?

THERE ARE WAYS to ask the question that make the answer seem self-evident. What's so seductive about the mellow, golden languor that slides out of a bottle of whiskey? Where's the charm in coffee's edgy omnipotence? Why the allure of psychedelics' existential ecstasy, the meaning of the universe in a warped and vibrating flower?

The quick answer, the obvious one, is that people take drugs because they like what drugs do to them. Right or wrong, that's nothing new. By 2500 B.C., the Sumerians had a symbol for opium that archeologists translate as "joy" or "rejoicing." Nor is drug use unusual. According to addiction expert Andrew Weil, every culture but the ice-dwelling Inuit has fashioned some kind of drug from available plants—and if ice could intoxicate, the Inuit probably would have had themselves a drug as well. It's enough to make some researchers talk about a human "drive" for intoxication.

Nevertheless, the very word intoxication makes it clear that whether casual or compulsive, drug use is a form of self-poisoning. Such loopy human behavior begs for a psychological explanation, and experts, largely focusing on addicts, have come up with many. Self-destructiveness, for instance. Peer pressure. More recently, Harvard psychiatrist Edward Khantzian has suggested that some addicts use drugs to self-medicate—that they're not after a high so much as just trying to reach ground level. When he asked addicts what drugs did for them, he says, they'd tell him, "Well, they made me feel normal."

According to Khantzian, such drug users choose their drug with almost a physician's attention to specific symptoms. For instance, many people who gravitate to cocaine do so because they suffer from depression; typically, the drug energizes and at least temporarily boosts self-esteem. Drug users whose history of family violence has left them with an overwhelming sense of rage may be drawn to a narcotic like heroin, which dampens fear and aggression.

Khantzian's theory segues nicely into another explanation for the drug use of addicts and non-addicts alike: the "Life is nasty, brutish, and short" theory posited by, among others, writer Aldous Huxley. In *The Doors of Perception*, an essay prompted by his experience with mescaline, he predicted that people would always need what he called artificial paradises: "Most men and women lead lives at the worst so painful, at the best so monotonous, poor and limited that the urge to escape, the longing to transcend themselves if only for a few moments, is and has always been one of the principal appetites of the soul."

In other words, drug-taking as escapism. Yet it's evident that Huxley believed he found a different sort of transcendence through mescaline. Elsewhere in his essay, he describes looking at a bouquet of flowers and understanding grace, "the miracle, moment by moment, of naked existence." That's the standard sixties rationale for drug-taking: to rise above normal limits to perception. The idea still has currency.

According to Harvard drug researcher Lester Grinspoon, the desire to take drugs springs from the same roots as creativity and intuition. "There are many people who use cannabis for very serious reasons," Grinspoon says. "They say that alteration of consciousness allows them to see around corners they otherwise can't see around."

Can't—or, more precisely, don't, says Grinspoon. There *are* other doors to this kind of perception. Sensory deprivation, sufi dancing, or long-distance running; breathing exercises, fasting, or religious experiences: All can make you high. In fact, any child who's ever spun round and round into a dizzy stupor knows a drug-free high. So do the children who hold their breath or take turns choking each other into near-unconsciousness for the sheer head-changing thrill of it. Such behavior reflects the human desire for mental as well as physical variety, and it makes Weil put an asterisk next to the universal "human urge to take drugs." Really, he says, it's a more general drive to experience altered states of consciousness.

Ultimately, perhaps, drug-taking reflects *two* basic human characteristics. The desire to alter one's consciousness is the first. The second might be called, for lack of a better term, laziness. "There are many ways to alter consciousness that don't involve a molecule introduced into your body," Grinspoon says. "But many take discipline and training. And Americans are impatient."

—Lisa Davis

Li's two-in-a-hundred rats that enjoy the buzz of alcohol and are also immune to its negative effects, Lisa drank enough booze and snorted enough coke to become physically and psychologically dependent on both drugs.

SHEIGLA MURPHY IS NOW in the midst of another ethnographic study, this time of inner-city women who use powder cocaine and crack. The world she's profiling this time, though only a few miles from where the Joyces and Austens grew up, is bleak. "For impoverished people, life on the streets has gotten very hard and mean in the last decade," she says. She tells of driving to interview one subject in the study, a black woman who lives in a neighborhood of boarded-up buildings and broken glass. In front of one house—a known crack house, Murphy says—an angry man guarded the doorway. Across the face of the building, F . . . THE BITCHES had been spray-painted in foot-high black letters. Behind the locked door of her nearby two-room apartment, the single, working mother struggles to raise two small children. The woman also, every now and then, smokes crack.

Is *she* likely to be a lifelong moderate user, or is she merely in the early stages of addiction? "It's too soon to tell," Murphy says, but the fact that the woman is able to hold together a job, a place to live, and a family life are good indicators that her two-year-old drug habit hasn't overwhelmed her.

There is, as yet, no good way of estimating how typical such "controlled use" of crack is, but in Murphy's study—she's logged about 200 hours of interviews with 63 of the 125 women she eventually hopes to talk to—it seems to be rare. "We see a few," says coworker Jeanette Irwin, "and there are similarities among them. They are the ones who tend to have real conventional ideas about how they should live. They say things like, 'My parents always told me I should stay in school and get a good job.' They place restrictions on their lives, and those restrictions carry over to their drug use." The self-imposed restrictions, Murphy says, are the same sorts of social rules that the Joyces and Austens used to circumscribe their drug use.

For those who would argue that addiction, not controlled use, is a more typical outcome of drug use in the inner city, Murphy whole-heartedly agrees. Recreational drugs clearly do their worst damage among the nation's poor. But by focusing on the chemicals to the exclusion of the powerful social forces that push casual drug use out of control, drug warriors miss the point, Murphy says.

Reinarman goes further, calling the drug war "an ideological fig leaf" that politicians have used to hide the true urban ills that their fiscal policies have aggravated: urban ills that foster addiction.

"For the New Right," he says, "people don't abuse drugs because they are jobless, or poor, or depressed, or alienated; they are jobless, poor, depressed, or alienated because they use drugs."

"It kills me to read in the paper about someone who 'spent all their money on crack,' as though that's a sign of ultimate decadence," Murphy says. "If you're on General Assistance, getting two hundred dollars every two weeks, all your money won't buy you much of a drug or anything else. Crack has come along and made those people's lives worse—but not that much worse."

Still, even if a drug war doesn't solve societal ills, can it hurt? Reinarman says yes, for at least two reasons. First, it diverts resources from other programs that might be more useful in moderating drug use. "The 'Just Say No' administration has just said no to virtually every social program aimed at creating alternatives for inner-city young people," he says. "Unfortunately, these kids cannot 'Just Say No' to poverty and unemployment."

Secondly, and this affects the drug-naive teen as surely as his streetwise counterpart, people who exaggerate the dangers of drugs inadvertently romanticize them as well. Reinarman likes to cite the words, taken down by a colleague, of a 1987 college student who had just read a *Newsweek* editorial likening crack to medieval plagues and the attack on Pearl Harbor.

"I had never heard of it until then," the student said, "but when I read that it was better than sex and that it was cheaper than cocaine and that it was an epidemic, I wondered what I was missing. The next day I asked some friends if they knew where to get some."

"There's no reason to lie to kids," Murphy says. "The truth is bad enough. Cocaine is not a benign drug but then neither is alcohol. As I tell my own kids and their friends, any youngster who takes a drink doesn't know whether they'll be among the twelve percent of people who will become alcoholic. And in the same way, a certain percentage of people may be especially vulnerable to cocaine dependence." Youngsters should also recognize, says Murphy, that illegal drug use is more dangerous today. For example, the risk of arrest is higher than it was 20 years ago, and because drug use is more covert, teens are less likely to learn rules for moderate use. "But ultimately," she says, "parents have only so much influence over their children. Taking drugs is a personal decision."

Craig Reinarman spends much of his time these days giving lectures on the sociology of deviance to college students. His office at UC Santa Cruz carries the flavor of the old days—antiwar posters and labor-union placards wedged between walls lined with books. Over his door, plainly read from his desk, is a bold banner from Nancy Reagan's campaign to warn children away from drugs. JUST SAY NO it screams in bright red letters, except that Reinarman has used a blue ballpoint pen to change the "NO" to a quieter "be careful."

Back from the edge

A Quebec politician's fight against addiction

ANTHONY WILSON-SMITH

Almost eight years after what he calls the "end of my nightmare," Gilles Baril can recall exactly what he did that night and how he felt. Where he was and how he got there, however, is another story. At 5 a.m. on Nov. 13, 1986, he sat naked in a north-end Montreal hotel room, drunk and high after eight hours of drinking scotch and snorting cocaine, wondering what excuse he could give for not showing up in another hour to host his morning radio show. A strip dancer staying next door had just given him his last line of coke. He accepted that, but when she offered him herself, the then-30-year-old Baril was, he said, "too out of it" to comply. It was another too-typical night for the man who had become, after the 1981 provincial election, the youngest member of the National Assembly. Then, he was known alternately as the "rock-and-roll politician" and the Parti Québécois's "young wolf," and regarded by political allies and foes alike as one of Quebec's most promising and charismatic politicians. But on that night in 1986, he recalled later, "I felt like a trapped animal, alone in my lair."

Early this week, Baril will mark what he proudly calls "a most important anniversary": seven years and 10 months of sobriety. For a reformed substance abuser living one day at a time, a month of recovery is cause for celebration. But that Sept. 12 anniversary has other significance for Baril: he was hoping to celebrate—with friends and lots of soda water—his return to the National Assembly as the Parti Québécois MNA for rural Berthier riding in the Quebec election. That would square the circle for a politician and reformed addict whose first snort of cocaine came on the night of his election victory in 1981. Since then, there has been his self-described "descent into hell," and his incarnations—

since he climbed back out—as best-selling author and host of several radio and television programs.

But most important, says Baril, is his emergence as role model to Quebec's troubled youth through his work as director of one of the province's most successful drug and alcohol rehabilitation centres. Baril has been the chief administrator at the privately run Pavillon du Nouveau Point de Vue in his riding for the past 4½ years: at any one time, it holds up to 45 patients who stay there for 28 days. For those who can pay, it is $2,500; similar rehabilitation programs in the United States can cost eight times that. But most of the underprivileged young who make up much of the centre's clientele are admitted free. Ninety per cent of the annual $1.5-million budget is paid for by private donors, while the rest comes from the federal and provincial governments. Sadly, Baril says, there is always a waiting list.

If elected, Baril planned to continue working with the centre on a volunteer basis. Then, his present job will almost certainly be given, with Baril's enthusiastic endorsement, to Yvon Picotte, a retiring provincial Liberal cabinet minister from a neighboring riding who is a recently reformed alcoholic. Although Baril is a fervent sovereigntist, "there are," he says, "no party distinctions when it comes to fighting addiction."

Battling for causes—whether it is against addiction or for other principles—is something that comes naturally to the otherwise-amiable Baril. Quebec writer Pierre Migneault, who wrote the introduction to Baril's book *Tu ne sera plus jamais seul* (You won't be alone any more), called him a "Western Don Quixote" whose struggles "represent those of all of us." The adopted son of a farmer in the tiny town of St-Eugene-de-

Guiges in northern Quebec, Baril became involved in politics in his mid-teens. His nomination by the PQ in 1981 in the riding of Rouyn/Noranda/Témiscamingue came about only because the original candidate became ill shortly before the election. Baril's candidacy was opposed by PQ candidates from neighboring ridings because, they said, at 24 he was too young. In the subsequent election, he beat the favorite, colorful Liberal MNA Camil Samson, by 4,000 votes.

Around the legislature in Quebec City, it was sometimes difficult to tell who was more uncomfortable with each other—Baril, or his PQ caucus mates. He spent his first year in the National Assembly waiting, he said, for "someone to demonstrate that the PQ really was the party that cared about youth." Other than then-minister Bernard Landry—one of the few people to encourage his initial candidacy—no one did.

Baril found his own ways of expressing his interests. He produced and starred on a rap-style record called *Rock 'n' Reve* (Rock and Dreams), with several professional musicians and poet Raoul Duguay. Its lyrics included, memorably, an exhortation to "rock 'n' dream of politics that will be/erotic, free and in music." He gave the profits to various youth groups.

At the same time, Baril seemed intent on cramming almost all those objectives contained in the lyrics into his own life. He went through a string of girlfriends, travelled to California to meet with actress Jane Fonda and futurologist Marylin Ferguson, and founded a group called Conspirators of the Year 2000, aimed at charting an outline for Quebec society. He donated part of his salary to the group.

By the time of the 1985 election, Baril felt, he recalls, "very alone." Increasingly, he turned to scotch and cocaine for solace. By then, the PQ was split between hard-line sovereigntists and more moderate nationalists. When the election came, said Baril, "the PQ was lost. So, to a much greater extent, was I."

He lost his seat. For Baril, the party was almost over, in every sense.

The riding of Berthier, where Baril makes his home, sits on the north side of the St. Lawrence River and begins about an hour's drive from Montreal. The area's income is based primarily on farming, pulp and paper and striking scenery that makes it a tourist mecca for other Quebecers. A large number of full-time residents are elderly, retired ex-Montrealers. Most of the towns are small, and activities close down early.

It is a different choice of lifestyle for Baril, who says he used to "draw energy from the big-city lights." But it is not as vivid a contrast, considering his past, as the position Baril occupies at the Pavillon du Nouveau Point de Vue. "Not so long ago," says Baril, "it was more likely that I would be dead than working in a place like this."

Redemption and recovery did not come easily or quickly. After his loss, Baril took his savings and severance pay of $40,000 and went on a six-month trip through South America. He has photographs of the places he saw, but no real memories: he spent almost all of the money on cocaine. He was freebasing by then—a process that amounts to smoking a highly processed, extra-potent form of cocaine. He was aware that he was out of control, but unwilling to confront that realization.

That did not come until that November night in 1986, when the drunk, stoned and scared Baril decided he had "hit bottom, and could go no further." He phoned a friend, Sylvain Vaugeois, and said simply: "I need help." Vaugeois phoned publishing magnate Pierre Péladeau of Quebecor Inc. and

Péladeau, a reformed alcoholic, arranged Baril's admission the same day to the Pavillon. That, said Baril, "was the beginning of my rebirth."

He emerged 28 days later, clean, broke and jobless: he had been fired by the radio station. Only a few friends knew of his ordeal, although it was rumored in media circles. He kept a low profile over the next 2½ years and ran for the PQ in the Montreal riding of Bourget in 1989. In a Liberal landslide, he lost by 165 votes. After the election, Baril, jobless but feeling increasingly upbeat, decided to tell his story on television to former PQ colleague Claude Charron, whose weekly program was one of the most popular in Quebec.

The response was enormous, and mostly sympathetic. As a result, Baril wrote his book about his experiences. It sold 25,000 copies, and Baril donated the proceeds to youth and anti-drug groups. The book, written in blunt and straightforward style, mixes his memories with advice on how to treat substance addiction. His notoriety led to offers to host Quebec-wide programs on radio and TV in which he continued on the same themes.

There were several notable exceptions to his popularity. His parents, hurt and confused, did not speak to him for almost a year. (Now, he says, "we are closer than ever.") Within the PQ, the fallout was also unpleasant, and longer-lasting. After his revelations, he recalls, "Péquistes in my riding told me I should not have talked about my problems publicly, because it wasn't proper." Furious, he resigned from the local association, telling members in an angry letter that they were "refusing to look reality in the face." At about the same time, he was offered the directorship of the rehabilitation centre, and moved to Lanoraie: one of the directors who recommended him was his former roommate during his treatment.

Some of those objections surfaced again

when Baril decided this year to run for the Berthier nomination. Once again, his friend, PQ vice-president Landry, was supportive, though other senior PQ figures were not. Party Leader Jacques Parizeau, say some of Baril's friends, was initially opposed, but changed his mind because of strong support for Baril among the party's grassroots members.

Today, Baril lives in a small rented flat overlooking the St. Lawrence River. Before the election campaign began, he spent up to 12 hours a day at the centre. Most of his free time comes on weekends when he sees his girlfriend, a television researcher in Montreal. Otherwise, he says, "I live as quietly as most people around here."

But Baril, a compact figure who resembles the actor Jean-Claude Van Damme, remains a rocker at heart. Alongside the stereo system that dominates his living room, there are compact discs by U2 and former Genesis lead singer Peter Gabriel. And one of his new pet projects is to stage a rock concert in support of Quebec independence. But he also now listens to more tranquil music, such as the brooding Celtic-based sounds of Loreena McKennitt. Baril says he discovered different kinds of music, and prayer, on the advice of Péladeau, who told him to "replace the spirits"—meaning alcohol—"in your life with spirituality." Péladeau, in an interview with *Maclean's* last week, recalled his experiences with Baril. "Gilles was a young man who had lost his way, just as so many have," he said. "To see him find himself, and help so many others, is an example we all can draw strength from."

Perhaps more to the point, Baril remains a fighter who has learned through painful experience which battles count the most. "To win as a politician is important to me," he said last week. "But I can never forget that, as a person, I have already won the most important victory of my life, by taking control of it."

The Major Drugs of Use and Abuse

The following articles discuss those drugs that have prevailed historically as drugs of choice. Although pharmacological modifications emerge periodically to enhance or alter the effects of certain drugs or the manner in which various drugs are used, basic pharmacological properties of the drugs remain unchanged. Crack is still cocaine, ice is still methamphetamine, dusters are still PCP, and black tar is still heroin. In addition, tobacco products all supply the drug nicotine, while the plethora of alcoholic beverages all provide the drug ethyl alcohol. These drugs all influence how we act, think, and feel about ourselves. They also produce markedly different effects within the body and within the mind.

To understand why certain drugs remain popular over time, one must be knowledgeable of the effects caused by individual drugs. Why people use drugs is a bigger question than why people use heroin. However, understanding why certain people use heroin, cocaine, or marijuana is one way to construct a framework from which to tackle the larger question of why people use drugs in general.

Misinformation abounds as to what different drugs do and why they do it. People tend to discuss the subject of drugs generically, often referring to all drugs as "narcotics." Narcotics refer to a specific class of drugs, that being opium and its derivatives. Cocaine and LSD, for

Unit 3

example, are not "narcotics." Understanding the differences between various drugs and their properties is significant to understanding how numerous and specific dimensions of drug use are perpetuated. Both the etiological and the epidemiological fields of research identify trends and patterns relative to the use of specific drugs that help us collectively to understand why people turn to drugs. Understanding why people use heroin is pertinent to understanding why people use cocaine. Experts on drug use and abuse understand the specific nuances produced by the use of different drugs, and they seldom speak to those nuances in generalities. Health care professionals, for example, can speak quickly to the behavioral similarities produced by the effects of different drugs, but the basis for their understanding lies in their knowledge of specific drug-related phenomena.

Understanding why people initially turn to drugs is a huge question that is debated and discussed in a voluminous body of literature. Determining why people continue to use a specific drug like cocaine or alcohol may be decided more easily by thinking about the scenarios and events described in these articles. One reason people initially use a specific drug, or class of drugs, is to obtain the desirable effects historically associated with the use of that drug. Heroin and opiate-related drugs produce, in most people, a euphoric, dreamy state of well-being. Cocaine and related stimulant drugs produce euphoria, energy, confidence, and exhilaration. Alcohol produces a loss of inhibitions and a state of well-being, and nicotine typically serves as a relaxant. Although effects and side effects may vary from user to user, a general pattern of effects is predictable from most major drugs of use. Varying the dosage or altering the manner of ingestion is one way to alter the drug's effects. Some drugs, such as phencyclidine, PCP, LSD, and some types of designer drugs, produce effects that are less predictable and more sensitive to variations in dosage level as well as the physical and psychological makeup of the user. For example, it is extremely easy to overdose on PCP, which can act as a stimulant, depressant, hallucinogen, convulsant, and/or anesthetic.

Although all major drugs of use and abuse have specific reinforcing properties perpetuating the drug's continued use, they also produce undesirable side effects that regular drug users attempt to mitigate. Most often, users attempt to do so with the use of other drugs. Cocaine, methamphetamine, heroin, and alcohol have long been used to mitigate one another's side effects. The classic "speedball" of heroin and cocaine is a good example. When combined, cocaine accelerates and intensifies the euphoric state produced by heroin, while the heroin softens the comedown from cocaine. Most abusers of the major drugs are polydrug users.

Lastly, when reviewing literature or discussing the topic of major drugs of use and abuse, one must be cautious with assumptions based on a drug's legal or illegal status. Drug abuse in America spans the spectrum of legality, and the association of only illegal drugs with abuse and criminality is shortsighted. In terms of drug-related social impacts, any discussion of major drugs would arguably begin and end with the topics of alcohol and nicotine. The pursuit of drugs and the effects they produce may be influenced by, but is not bound by, legal status. For the student of drug-related phenomena, an attachment to the concepts of legality or illegality for purposes of comprehensively rationalizing drug-related reality is inappropriate. For example, yearly alcohol-related deaths far outnumber deaths from all illegal drugs combined.

Looking Ahead: Challenge Questions

How is it that specific drugs evolve, develop use patterns, and lose or gain popularity over time?

How have user profiles relative to heroin changed over the last 30 years?

Does the manner in which a drug is ingested help define its respective user population?

How does the manner in which a drug is used influence the severity of consequences related to that drug? Or does it?

Why does the use of certain drugs encourage the use of other drugs?

SELLING POT

THE PITFALLS OF MARIJUANA REFORM

"Whatever the cultural conditions that have made it possible, there is no doubt that the discussion about marihuana has become much more sensible," Harvard psychiatrist Lester Grinspoon wrote in 1977. "If the trend continues, it is likely that within a decade marihuana will be sold in the United States as a legal intoxicant."

Jacob Sullum

Jacob Sullum is associate editor of REASON.

This was not a silly prediction. At the time, there was good reason to believe it would come true. Six years before, the National Commission on Marihuana and Drug Abuse, appointed by Congress and the Nixon administration, had recommended that the federal government and the states legalize both private possession of marijuana for personal use and casual, nonprofit transfers of the drug in small amounts.

In 1973 Oregon became the first state to "decriminalize" marijuana, making possession of less than an ounce a civil offense punishable by a maximum fine of $100. In 1975 Alaska removed all state penalties for private cultivation and possession of up to four ounces. By the end of the decade, 11 states had decriminalized marijuana possession, a policy endorsed by President Carter, the American Bar Association, the American Medical Association, and the National Council of Churches. Every other state had reduced the penalty for simple possession, nearly all of them changing the offense from a felony to a misdemeanor. Most allowed conditional discharge, without a criminal record.

So Grinspoon's optimism was justified. Yet the year after his prediction, things started to turn around: In 1978 the federal government's policy of spraying Mexican marijuana crops with the herbicide paraquat, which can cause lung fibrosis and death when swallowed in small doses, prompted a nationwide panic among pot smokers. That same year, Carter drug adviser Dr. Peter Bourne, who was sympathetic to reform, was forced to resign after press reports that he had used cocaine at a party sponsored by the National Organization for Reform of Marijuana Laws. His replacement, Lee Dogoloff, took a hard line on illegal drugs, including pot. And the percentage of Americans favoring marijuana legalization in the Gallup poll dropped from the first time in a decade, from 28 percent in 1977 to 25 percent in 1978. (By the late '80s, the figure was down to about 16 percent.)

OVERPLAYING THE BENEFITS OF CANNABIS MAY PROVE JUST AS RISKY AS UNDERPLAYING ITS POTENTIAL HARMS.

The '80s and early '90s saw a series of further setbacks:

❖ In 1983, the Drug Enforcement Administration began spraying paraquat on marijuana crops in the United States. Throughout the decade, the federal government pursued an aggressive domestic eradication policy, especially in California.

❖ The Reagan administration announced a "zero tolerance" program, imposing draconian seizure penalties for marijuana possession, even in tiny amounts.

❖ In 1987 Supreme Court nominee Douglas Ginsburg withdrew under pressure from his erstwhile supporters after admitting that he had smoked pot as a law professor.

❖ In 1989 the federal government launched Operation Green Merchant, raiding the homes of people suspected of growing marijuana because they had purchased gardening equipment.

❖ In 1990 Alaska voters passed a referendum, pushed vigorously by Bush administration drug czar William Bennett, that recriminalized marijuana possession.

❖ That same year, Congress approved a transportation appropriations bill that threatens to withhold funding from states that do not suspend the driver's licenses of drug offenders, including marijuana users, for at least six months.

❖ In 1992 the Department of Health and Human Services canceled a federal program that was supposed to supply patients with medical marijuana.

Under the Clinton administration, there's reason to hope that the pendulum may begin to swing in the other direction again. Both President Clinton and Vice President Gore have used marijuana, and both recall more with nostalgia than with hostility the counterculture of the '60s that many older Republicans still associate with the drug. Clinton has slashed the staff of the Office of National Drug Control Policy, and he has sought advice from scholarly critics of the Bush war on drugs, at least one of whom supports marijuana legalization. Perhaps most significantly, the woman Clinton plans to appoint as surgeon general, Dr. Joycelyn Elders, has said patients who can benefit from medical marijuana should be able to receive it.

But before reformers try to take advantage of what promises to be a more tolerant policy environment, they need to understand what went wrong the first time around. Since marijuana is both the most widely used and the least harmful of the major illegal drugs, the lessons of the anti-pot backlash have broad implications. If reformers cannot succeed in the case of marijuana, where the arguments for legalization seem to be strongest, it's not likely they will succeed elsewhere.

Several factors contributed to the reversals that began in the late '70s, but the most important was a persistent misperception: Both opponents of reform and the general public seemed to believe that the argument for legalization was based on the premise that "marijuana is harmless." So far as I can tell, no serious scholar or prominent activist who favored changing the marijuana laws ever made this claim. Rather, the reformers argued that pot was less harmful than other drugs and less harmful than the government had led people to believe. But by the time the policy debate filtered into local newspapers, college campuses, and suburban living rooms, these nuances were lost—partly because, in the experience of most users, marijuana *was* harmless.

This perception established a test that marijuana was bound to fail, since no drug is safe in every dose and circumstance. Consequently, the growing public and official tolerance of marijuana use was vulnerable from the start. Confronted by a powerful counter-reform movement in the late '70s and early '80s, it withered.

Current attempts to revive progress toward legalization run the risk of repeating this pattern. One major approach to reform emphasizes the medical uses of cannabis; another emphasizes the remarkable versatility of the hemp plant, from which marijuana is derived. There is good evidence for these claims. But like the notion that marijuana is completely safe, they tend to establish excessively ambitious criteria for legalization. Overplaying the benefits of cannabis may prove just as risky as underplaying its potential harms.

This is partly a matter of emphasis, but also a matter of style. If you're trying to convince the average American that legalization is a wise policy, it's deadly to come across as a marijuana enthusiast. The most successful reformers have been sober, cautious people far removed from pothead stereotypes—people like Harvard's Grinspoon, author of the 1971 book *Marihuana Reconsidered*.

Grinspoon set out to present credible evidence of marijuana's harms to pot-smoking kids who were ignoring the government's warnings. "I was concerned about all these young people who were using marijuana and destroying themselves," he says. But after examining the research on marijuana's effects, "I realized that I had been brainwashed, like everybody else in the country." In his book, he methodically debunked the many spurious claims about pot, including fears that it causes crime, sexual excess, psychosis, brain damage, physical dependence, and addiction to other drugs.

The following year, the National Commission on Marihuana and Drug Abuse reached broadly similar conclusions: that the dangers of pot had been greatly exaggerated and could not justify punitive treatment of its users. The commission introduced the concept of decriminalization, which the newly formed National Organization for the Reform of Marijuana Laws soon adopted as a goal. At a time when some 600,000 people were being arrested each year on marijuana charges, most for simple possession, the strategy had broad appeal. Liberals were concerned about the injustice of sending college students to jail for carrying a joint or two. Conservatives worried about the mass alienation and disrespect for the law that the policy was breeding.

"There was the beginning of a consensus," says NORML founder Keith Stroup. "It said, 'I don't like marijuana smoking, but I don't think it should be treated as a criminal matter.'" Stroup argues that decriminalization was a necessary first step toward legalization. "Otherwise," he says, "you'd never get beyond the fear that, without criminal penalties, everybody would be stoned all the time, and the whole state would go down the tube."

But, as Grinspoon noted in the 1977 edition of *Marihuana Reconsidered*, decriminalization is inherently unstable. "As long as marihuana use and especially marihuana traffic remain in this peculiar position neither within nor outside the law, demands for a consistent policy would remain strong," he wrote. "We would have to ask ourselves why, if using marihuana is relatively harmless, selling it is a felony; then we would have to decide whether to return to honest prohibition or move on to legalization."

Americans did indeed ask this question, and since the late '70s the trend has been back toward "honest prohibition." An important harbinger of this reaction came in 1974, when

Sen. James Eastland (D-Miss.) convened hearings on the "marijuana-hashish epidemic" with the avowed purpose of countering the "good press" that pot had been receiving. Dr. Gabriel Nahas, author of *Marijuana: Deceptive Weed* and *Keep off the Grass*, led a group of researchers who testified that marijuana may cause lung damage, birth defects, genetic abnormalities, shrinkage of the brain, impairment of the immune system, reduction in testosterone levels, and sterility.

Of these hazards, only lung damage has been well established by subsequent research. All the other claims have been discredited or remain controversial. Much of the research cited in the Eastland hearings was heavily criticized soon after it appeared. Some of it was laughably bad, with skewed samples and no control groups.

Despite the poor quality of these studies, anti-marijuana activists continue to cite them. "Those papers, and the ideas they brought forth, are at the heart of the anti-marijuana movement today," says Dr. John P. Morgan, professor of pharmacology at the City University of New York Medical School. "Nahas generated what was clearly a morally based counter-reform movement, but he did a very efficient job of saying that he was actually conducting a toxicological, scientific assessment."

The Eastland hearings left the impression that Americans had been duped by reformers about the nature of marijuana. The title of a piece in the June 10, 1974, issue of *U.S. News & World Report* is revealing: THE PERILS OF 'POT' START SHOWING UP. The writer was clearly confident that the speculation offered by Nahas and his colleagues was only the tip of the iceberg.

The testimony seemed to have a similar impact on Dr. Robert L. DuPont, then director of the National Institute on Drug Abuse. Although he initially supported reducing the penalties for marijuana possession, DuPont renounced decriminalization in 1979. "I have learned that it is impossible to be pro-decrim and anti-pot," he told an anti-marijuana group, "because no matter how you try to explain it to them, young people interpret decrim as meaning that pot must be okay because the government has legally sanctioned it."

DuPont's remarks reflect one of the main concerns that drove the anti-pot backlash: rising marijuana use among teenagers. According to NIDA's National Household Survey, the percentage of Americans between the ages of 12 and 17 who had ever used marijuana rose from about 14 percent in 1972 to about 31 percent in 1979, after which it declined steadily. NIDA's High School Senior Survey shows a similar trend: About 47 percent of seniors reported having used marijuana in 1975 (when the survey began); this figure rose steadily to a little over 60 percent in 1979, after which it declined. The most alarming and frequently cited NIDA pot statistic is for "daily" use by high-school seniors: It rose from 6 percent in 1975 to a peak of nearly 11 percent in 1978.

These numbers overstate the percentage of seniors who got stoned every day in the late '70s. First of all, they don't represent actual daily use throughout the year—only use on 20 or more of the previous 30 days. Granted, that's still pretty heavy. But the numbers include kids who had recently gone

through a brief period of heavy use. And as Mark Kleiman, associate professor of public policy at Harvard's John F. Kennedy School of Government, notes in *Marijuana: Costs of Abuse, Costs of Control*, the data are probably inflated by error or exaggeration: Experience with marketing surveys indicates that questions about habitual activities like "On how many of the last 30 days did you use marijuana?" tend to elicit systematic overreporting. Furthermore, the 11-percent "daily use" figure appears to be inconsistent with information from NIDA's household survey.

NO ONE HAS EVER DIED FROM A MARIJUANA OVERDOSE. MARIJUANA ITSELF (AS OPPOSED TO THE ACT OF SMOKING) DOESN'T CAUSE ORGAN DAMAGE.

In any event, it seems that teen-age marijuana use, like adult marijuana use, rose dramatically in the '70s, peaking around 1979. Many parents were alarmed at this trend, and there was reason to be concerned. Both supporters and opponents of legalization agree that it's not a good idea for unsupervised minors to use pot. Whatever the health hazards of the drug, they are likely to be more serious for children. Furthermore, frequent marijuana intoxication can interfere with emotional development, and there's no question that stoned kids have trouble absorbing and recalling information.

But the hysterical reaction of what came to be known as the Parent Movement for Drug-Free Youth, which attracted the active support of the federal government, cannot be understood merely as a response to these dangers. After all, the same concerns could be raised about alcohol use, which was also rising markedly among teenagers during this period. These parents focused their wrath on marijuana because it was an illegal, alien presence in their middle-class, suburban lives—a presence that was tolerated, if not condoned, by a large and growing number of Americans.

The police were looking the other way as tens of millions lit up. College professors, doctors, and lawyers were smoking pot. Movies and music glamorized drug use. There were water pipes in the local record store, for heaven's sake. Morgan, the CUNY pharmacologist, says the reform movement was caught off guard by the parental backlash: "We didn't know the revulsion and hatred that middle-class parents felt about marijuana and their kids getting high. We didn't have any idea how strongly they felt." The outraged parents who would eventually form the backbone of the anti-marijuana movement saw the drug as a lurking threat that would turn out to be far more hazardous than everyone seemed to believe.

Those fears were reinforced by a series of articles that appeared in mainstream magazines in the late '70s and early '80s—articles with titles like "All the Evidence on Pot Isn't In!" (*Seventeen*), "How I Got My Daughter to Stop Smoking

Pot" (*Good Housekeeping*), "Marijuana Alert: Enemy of Youth" (*Reader's Digest*), "Marijuana: Now the Fears Are Facts" (*Good Housekeeping*), "Marijuana: The Latest Dope on Its Dangers" (*Mademoiselle*), and "The Perils of Pot" (*Discover*). The articles delivered the same message as the Eastland hearings: You have been deceived. Marijuana is a lot more dangerous than you think.

The most influential anti-marijuana writer was probably the late Peggy Mann, a journalist who started writing about pot in 1978. After attending a conference in France on the dangers of marijuana, organized by Nahas and other anti-pot researchers, she wrote "The Case Against Marijuana Smoking," which appeared on the front page of *The Washington Post*'s Outlook section. During the next few years she wrote many magazine articles on pot, including a four-part series in *Reader's Digest* that prompted a record 6.5 million reprint requests. In 1985 Mann published *Marijuana Alert*, which Nancy Reagan describes in the foreword as "a true story about a drug that is taking America captive."

Marijuana Alert gathers together almost every scrap of research that reflects badly on marijuana, including thoroughly discredited studies, while virtually ignoring anything that would give a different impression, including major surveys of the literature. This is not simply the mirror image of the approach taken by reformers. Scholars such as Grinspoon, John Kaplan, Norman Zinberg, Edward Brecher, and Andrew Weil were forced to deal with speculation about marijuana's harms and the research supporting it. Indeed, their task was precisely to confront those claims.

Mann, on the other hand, deals with the opposition's arguments and evidence mainly by omitting them. While she describes Nahas's studies finding that marijuana impairs cellular immunity, she neglects to mention that other researchers have tried but failed to replicate them. She discusses Harold Kolansky and William T. Moore's 1971 study suggesting that marijuana use causes a host of psychological problems, but not the storm of criticism it prompted. She cites A. M. G. Campbell's 1971 study finding that marijuana causes cerebral atrophy but leaves out the methodological flaws that made it worthless: All 10 subjects were psychiatric patients, and there was no nonpsychiatric control group; the study also failed to control for epilepsy, head injuries, mental retardation, and the use of other drugs, including alcohol. When Mann does mention criticism, it's only to dismiss it.

This approach is quite effective. If you haven't already heard about the studies and surveys she ignores, Mann's book may well convince you that marijuana is a very dangerous drug. Largely because of Mann and other anti-pot propagandists, many Americans have a vague sense that recent scientific findings show marijuana to be considerably more hazardous than people thought it was in the '70s (a notion reinforced by a similar impression about cocaine). Yet the basic picture remains the same: No one has ever died from a marijuana overdose; based on extrapolations from animal studies, the ratio of the drug's lethal dose to its effective dose is something like 40,000 to 1 (compared to between 4 and 10 to 1 for alcohol and between 10 and 20 to 1 for aspirin). Unlike alcohol used to excess, marijuana itself (as opposed to the act of smoking) does not appear to cause organ damage. And virtually all of marijuana's negative effects are associated with heavy use (the equivalent of several joints a day).

In his 1992 book *Against Excess*, Kleiman writes: "Aside from the almost self-evident proposition that smoking anything is probably bad for the lungs, the quarter century since large numbers of Americans began to use marijuana has produced remarkably little laboratory or epidemiological evidence of serious health damage done by the drug."

Anti-marijuana activists commonly claim that today's pot is more dangerous because it is "much more potent" than the pot of the early '70s, with an average THC content 10 times greater. This claim, which was influential in the successful drive for recriminalization in Alaska, is doubly wrong. As Morgan has noted, the assertion that pot is 10 times more powerful than it used to be is based on a spurious comparison of low-grade Mexican marijuana from fewer than 20 seizures tested in the early '70s with high-grade domestic marijuana from more than 200 seizures tested in the early '80s. The average THC content of domestic seizures tested by the federal government has been pretty stable—around 2 percent to 3 percent—since 1979, the first year for which reliable data are available.

But even if average THC content were significantly higher now than in the '70s, this is more likely a health benefit than a hazard. Since marijuana users generally smoke until they achieve a desired effect, higher potency means less inhalation—a positive result, since lung damage is the only well-established physical risk associated with marijuana use by otherwise healthy adults.

Although they talk about the physical effects of smoking pot, anti-marijuana activists seem to worry more about its psychological impact. *Marijuana Alert*, for example, is full of horror stories about sweet, obedient, courteous, hard-working kids transformed by marijuana into rebellious, lazy, moody, insolent, bored, apathetic, sexually promiscuous monsters. The most striking thing about these accounts is the extent to which the symptoms of marijuana use overlap with the symptoms of adolescence. "It was very easy for parents to blame marijuana for all the problems that their children were having, rather than to accept any responsibility," Grinspoon observes. "It became a very convenient way of dealing with and understanding various kinds of problems."

In addition to confusing correlation with causation, anti-marijuana activists blur the distinction between short-term and long-term effects. Under the influence of marijuana, for example, users appear listless; their thinking may seem disordered, and their short-term memories are impaired. But to judge by the anecdotes that Mann offers, these are persistent traits of pot smokers, intoxicated or not. She says the problems may not disappear for months after the last joint, if at all.

For anyone who knew a pothead or two in high school or college, this depiction of marijuana's effects may have the ring of truth. One of my colleagues cites the impact that pot seemed to have on some of his fellow students: They sat around getting stoned all day, skipping classes, accomplishing nothing. But since the vast majority of people who use marijuana don't end up this way, it's clear that heavy pot use is more likely to be the expression of psychological problems or personality traits than the cause of them. Of course, being stoned all the time would exacerbate almost anyone's problems, but that doesn't mean pot can magically transform a straight-A student into a burned-out hippie.

Another frequently cited behavioral result of smoking pot is the so-called gateway effect. In 1985 I covered a pot bust in northeastern Pennsylvania, following a long line of state police cars up winding dirt roads through the woods until we arrived at a modest marijuana farm. Watching the troopers uproot the tall, bright-green plants, I asked the officer in charge what all the fuss was about. He gave the standard response: "Marijuana may not be so bad, but it leads to harder drugs. I've seen it a thousand times."

I've been mulling that over, on and off, for the last eight years. My initial reaction was, "That's not true." I have since arrived at a more sophisticated position: "*What's* not true?" The gateway theory is deliberately ambiguous and therefore impossible to disprove. It's not clear what it means to say that marijuana "leads to" other drugs.

For example, heroin use is usually preceded by marijuana use, but marijuana use is rarely followed by heroin use. Those who use marijuana are statistically more likely to use other drugs (as are users of alcohol and tobacco), but this tells us nothing about causation. In particular, it does not tell us whether eliminating marijuana from the planet would have any impact at all on cocaine or heroin use. And to the extent that a "gateway effect" works by introducing pot users to the black market, prohibition is the real problem. In short, the most useful thing that can be said about the gateway theory is that it's not very useful—as a scientific concept, that is; it's very useful as a rhetorical device.

You could say the same for the entire case against marijuana. From a scientific perspective, it's not very impressive. But it has made a real difference in the hearts and minds of many Americans. The main reason the anti-pot campaign has been so successful is that many people believed they'd been told marijuana should be legalized because it was harmless. Therefore it did not take much evidence to discredit the reform movement. Just as the advocates of decriminalization drew strength from the actual lies the government had been telling about marijuana for decades, the anti-pot movement drew strength from the perceived lies of the reformers.

The "myth of harmlessness" shows up again and again in Mann's writings; it's her favorite foil. It also appears in essays by political commentators. In a 1983 *National Review* article, for example, Richard Vigilante refers to "much rhetoric about marijuana's being 'a harmless recreational drug'" and describes the task of reformers as "having to argue for the drug's legality by proving its harmlessness." News coverage confirms

that many people thought they were hearing the message that pot is harmless during the '70s. In its article on the 1974 Eastland hearings, for example, *U.S. News* reported: "The researchers…agreed that the claim that cannabis is an innocuous drug is ill-founded." In 1980 *Newsweek* could casually refer to "the widely accepted public view today that [pot] is probably harmless."

"This is just bizarre," says Richard Cowan, who became NORML's national director last year. "No one here ever claimed that marijuana is harmless. That's an easy straw man, since nothing is harmless." A charter member of Young Americans for Freedom, Cowan wrote an influential piece for *National Review* in 1972, "American Conservatives Should Revise their Position on Marijuana." In the two decades since then, he has repeatedly encountered the "marijuana is harmless" straw man.

No doubt anti-marijuana propagandists have sometimes deliberately mischaracterized the arguments of their opponents. But there is also an element of genuine misunderstanding here, rooted in the limitations of the English language. There is no convenient, shorthand way to express what the reformers have been trying to say: Marijuana is not so harmful, compared to other (legal and illegal) drugs, compared to a wide range of recreational activities, compared to its image as portrayed by the government, and compared to the laws aimed at suppressing its use. There is no word that means "acceptably risky" or "not all that dangerous," no word that expresses a low relative evaluation of harmfulness in the same way that *inexpensive* expresses a low relative evaluation of cost.

So reformers trying to be pithy have had to make do with

> ## "NO ONE HERE EVER CLAIMED MARIJUANA IS HARMLESS," SAYS NORML'S NATIONAL DIRECTOR. "NOTHING IS HARMLESS."

modified versions of *safe*, *innocuous*, and *harmless*, as in "comparatively safe," "relatively innocuous," or "harmless for most people." When their arguments are summed up by others, the crucial modifiers are often lost.

For today's reformers, then, it's not enough to have the facts straight and to formulate solid arguments. They have to be aware of how their arguments will be perceived. In this connection, there are serious pitfalls for activists pursuing either of the two approaches to reform that are now prominent within the marijuana movement.

The problems with the hemp-as-wonder-plant strategy are pretty obvious. Marijuana activists Jack Herer of California and Gatewood Galbraith of Kentucky are among the leading advocates of this approach, which has also attracted the support of *High Times* and country singer Willie Nelson. In his 1985 book *The Emperor Wears No Clothes*, which *High Times* editor Steve Hager calls "the bible of the hemp movement," Herer explores the history and the many uses of the hemp plant: In addition to medicine, it can be a source of food, oil, fuel, paper, building materials, and fiber for rope and fabric. He argues that hemp derivatives could successfully compete with current products, and he implies that the pharmaceutical, paper, and petroleum industries have conspired to suppress marijuana. He contends that substituting methane, methanol, and charcoal from hemp-based biomass for fossil fuels would halt global warming and thereby "save the world."

There are some good things to be said for Herer's approach. His book demonstrates how our view of hemp, which was once a very important legal crop in the United States and other countries, has been warped by the government's campaign against marijuana. And it is no doubt true that entrepreneurs would rediscover profitable, nonpsychoactive uses for the plant if legal barriers were removed.

Perhaps most important, the hemp movement has attracted interest from a lot of people—mostly young and leftish, but also libertarians, including *Orange County Register* columnist Alan Bock and some readers of this magazine. Herer's organization, HEMP (Help Eradicate Marijuana Prohibition), sets up a stand on weekends in Venice, California, touting the plant's uses and offering passers-by the opportunity to examine hemp rope and clothing. People stop and chat, and some of them sign a petition to get a marijuana legalization initiative on the ballot. Rallies and the sale of hemp products by mail also help to arouse curiosity.

Still, it would be fair to say that the hemp movement has limited appeal. What goes over in Venice does not necessarily go over in Provo—or in Washington, D.C. Kevin Zeese, vice president of the Drug Policy Foundation, praises the Hererites for getting young people involved in the fight against prohibition. But he observes: "That wing [of the movement] presents the marijuana user as a stereotype that frightens society—the long-haired hippie. It scares people."

In addition to the image problem, there's the substance of Herer's arguments. Even leaving aside the idea of a "marijuana conspiracy," Herer asks people to accept a host of claims about hemp—some clearly true, some dubious. And not only about hemp: To believe that this plant can "save the world," you have to buy (at least) the global-warming theory—as if marijuana legalization weren't controversial enough. Regardless of how truthful Herer's claims are, it's just *too much*. As Zeese puts it: "It comes across as, 'This is the wonder drug that can save the world, the environment, the trees, the fuel supply; it can heal the blind and crippled.' It really sounds like a snake-oil salesman, even though there's a lot of truth to it."

The Herer approach also seems like a ploy to distract people from the real issue. After all, hemp's main use in the United States today is not for paper or cloth or fuel. Any mildly skeptical person, upon hearing a guy with a long beard in a tie-dyed shirt talk about the wonderful versatility of the hemp plant, is going to have a pretty good idea what's *really* on his mind. The appearance of deceit only makes getting high seem all the more sinister: If there's nothing wrong with it, what are they trying to hide?

The issue of medical marijuana presents some of the same problems, but it's much harder for people to dismiss. For one thing, there is strong evidence that marijuana can relieve pain, help treat glaucoma, control nausea and vomiting, and stimulate appetite. There's also some indication that it's helpful for controlling seizures and muscle spasms. In 1988, after hearing 13 days of testimony and reviewing 18 volumes of evidence, the DEA's chief administrative law judge, Francis Young, concluded that marijuana has significant potential as a medicine and called it "one of the safest therapeutically active substances known to man." Furthermore, there is a real, potentially huge, and very sympathetic constituency for medical marijuana. Polls find that a large majority of Americans agree the drug should be available to these patients.

Most of the reformers I interviewed for this article predicted that medical marijuana would be legally available soon, perhaps within the first year of the Clinton administration. The change would not require legislation, or even direct presidential action. "I don't expect President Clinton to touch the marijuana issue, after his inhaling comments," Zeese says. But Clinton could instruct people at the DEA, HHS, and the Food and Drug Administration either to resume the federal government's medical marijuana program or to reclassify the drug so it could be available by prescription. Either way, if the new policy is for real, thousands of cancer, glaucoma, and AIDS patients could start receiving legal pot.

That prospect raises the complicated question of what connection, if any, medical marijuana has to broad legalization. Anti-pot activists such as Peggy Mann have long argued that medical marijuana is a red herring, a tactic to make the drug more acceptable and thereby promote legalization. Robert Randall, president of the Alliance for Cannabis Therapeutics, notes that, logically, marijuana could be legally available as a medicine but not as a recreational or social drug.

"We do that with almost every drug on the planet," he says. "It's illegal for you to have Valium if you don't have the scrip. So what's the big difference here?"

The big difference may be that marijuana is a lot more popular. Tens of millions of Americans smoke pot from time to time, and more might if it were easier to get or if it became more socially acceptable. Marijuana is also easier to manufacture than Valium. Still, it's wrong to argue, as Mann and the DEA do, that the drive for medical marijuana is merely a ruse. Many people want marijuana because it can help save their sight or relieve their suffering. There is a humanitarian argument for medical marijuana that is distinct from the argument for broad legalization. Nonetheless, it's clear that medical availability would affect the legalization debate.

The question is, how? Zeese, who ran NORML from 1983 to 1986, suggests medical access could hurt the drive for legalization in the same way decriminalization did: by eliminating sympathetic victims (in that case, the middle-class college kids who were going to jail for marijuana possession). "You'd be taking a lot of the steam out of the legalization movement, because you'd be putting a kinder and gentler face on the drug war," he says. "We wouldn't have those cancer patients and AIDS patients and glaucoma patients at our side as allies. We'd no longer have that compassionate argument."

Cowan offers a more optimistic scenario: Hundreds of thousands of people will be using legal pot, free to speak out about its effects without fear of repercussions. "The cat will be out of the bag," he says. "That is going to totally change the dynamics of the issue....If we get medical access, we're going to get legalization eventually. The narcocracy knows this; it's the reason they fight it so much."

Grinspoon, too, suggests that medical access would be difficult to contain. "The problems connected with that are so vast that it will not work," he says. He estimates that legal pot would retail for about $10 an ounce, much less than current black-market prices, typically $100 to $300 an ounce, depending on quality and availability. "Everybody will be going to the doctor and saying, 'Oh, I've got a backache, I've got this, I've got that.' The doctors are not going to want to be gatekeepers."

Moreover, any preparation of marijuana that was available by prescription would have to receive FDA approval. Grinspoon notes that pharmaceutical companies are not likely to pay for the expensive tests that would be necessary to meet the FDA's strict standards for efficacy, since marijuana could not be patented. In any case, he says, "why should people wait? They're suffering."

If the government didn't reclassify marijuana, Grinspoon says, it would need "an army of bureaucrats" to supervise any workable medical marijuana program. And what the bureaucracy gives, it can take away. A new administration could once again block medical access. Since availability would be based on claims about marijuana's therapeutic value, the government could always decide that new research or the development of "better" alternatives justified cutting off the legal supply. For all these reasons, Grinspoon argues that legalization is the best way to achieve medical availability, rather than the other way around.

If Grinspoon is right, it may be time to plow through the research again and dig up all those arguments from the '70s. In fact, this is what's happening in Alaska, where the challenge to recriminalization will involve rehashing the debate over marijuana's hazards. A Superior Court judge there has concluded that the 1990 anti-pot initiative can be upheld only if the drug's effects have changed significantly since 1975, when the Alaska Supreme Court ruled that the state constitution's privacy clause protects marijuana use in the home.

Putting marijuana on trial is an approach that's designed to favor the prohibitionists. It requires, if not proof of harmlessness, something very close to it. And even if the opponents of recriminalization can meet the burden of proof, the issue can always be raised again in 10 or 15 years. It is never finally settled.

Part of the problem is that most Americans do not view marijuana simply as a drug—a substance with certain benefits and certain hazards, one that can be used moderately or excessively, responsibly or irresponsibly. As a subject of public concern, marijuana has always been fraught with symbolism, and it has always represented something foreign to white, middle-class America: Mexicans, jazz musicians, ghetto blacks, hippies.

Decriminalization succeeded—and, despite the setbacks, it largely remains a success—because reformers were able to take the focus off the drug, with all its potent symbolism, and put the law on trial instead. But once the penalties for possession were reduced, the spotlight shifted back to marijuana's harmfulness. "A poor job was done, from the late '70s on, of framing the arguments," Cowan says. "We stayed on the defensive, allowing the debate to be focused on 'the latest research.' What we needed to do was to start telling people about the effects of the laws." If legalization is to succeed, reformers will have to

THE HEMP MOVEMENT HAS LIMITED APPEAL. IT PRESENTS THE MARIJUANA USER AS A STEREOTYPE THAT FRIGHTENS SOCIETY: THE LONG-HAIRED HIPPIE.

stress the injustice of prohibition—not just for the college kid caught with a few joints or the woman who gives pot brownies to AIDS patients, but for anyone who grows or sells marijuana. Not long ago REASON received a letter from a reader:

"I am a 42 year old male and married to a wonderful woman. We have three children who I love very much. My desperation is derived from the fact that I was taken away from my wife and children by the U.S. government and sent to prison in another state for a conviction of conspiracy to import and distribute marijuana. Although I have never been in trouble before with the law and always have been a productive, taxpaying citizen, the Government sentenced me to 25 years in prison without the possibility of parole. There was no violence or guns involved in this alleged conspiracy, and I can honestly proclaim that I have never broken any of God's Ten Commandments, but the Government has taken the rest of my life away from me. My children are ages 12, 2, and 1. I will never see or feel any of the cherished moments of their childhood, which breaks my heart. More importantly, they will grow up without a father, which hurts me more than anything."

I suspect that the average American would have little sympathy for this man. Unless that changes, marijuana will never be legal again.

Alcohol in perspective

rue or false?

An ounce-and-a-half of 80-proof vodka or whiskey contains ore alcohol than a 12-ounce can of beer.

A woman gets more intoxicated than a man from the same nount of alcohol.

Most Americans drink little or no alcohol.

Fatalities caused by alcohol-impaired driving are declining.

Measured in real dollars, the cost of alcoholic beverages has en steadily during the last 40 years.

nswers

False. They contain the same amount. So does a five-ounce ass of wine.

True. The box on page 78 explains why.

True. Abstainers account for about 35% of the adult popu-tion, and light drinkers another 35%. Light drinkers, in the ficial definition, are those consuming two drinks a week or ss. Moderate drinkers, who average one-half to two drinks a y, account for another 22%. Heavier drinkers—8% of us—nsume more than two drinks a day.

True. The percentage of road crashes involving alcohol clined from 57% to 49% over the past decade. And the greatest cline was among teens and young adults. This is attributed to w laws setting the minimum drinking age at 21 in all states and widespread educational efforts.

False. It cost less (in inflation-adjusted dollars) to drink in 92 than it did in 1951. That's not a good thing—see below.

Double messages

lcohol, a natural product of fermentation, is probably the most idely used of all drugs. It has been a part of human culture since story began and part of American life since Europeans settled this continent. "The good creature of God," colonial Ameri-ns called it—as well as "demon rum." At one time, beer or hiskey may have been safer to drink than well water, but there ive always been many other reasons for drinking: the sociabil-y of drinking, the brief but vivid sense of relaxation alcohol can ing, and the wish to celebrate or participate in religious and mily rituals where alcohol is served. In some cultures, abstention the rule. In others, the occasional use of alcohol is regarded as easurable and necessary—but such use is carefully controlled d intoxication frowned upon. Tradition and attitude play a owerful role in the use of this drug.

Some people, unfortunately, drink because of depression and/or addiction to alcohol. Apart from such needs, powerful social and economic forces encourage people to drink. For starters, alcoholic beverages are everywhere—from planes and trains to restaurants and county fairs. Also, drink is cheap. The relative cost of alcohol has declined in the last decades. Since 1967 the cost of soft drinks and milk has quadrupled, and the cost of all consumer goods has tripled, but the cost of alcohol has not even doubled. This is because the excise tax on alcohol is not indexed to inflation. Congress has raised the federal tax on beer and wine only once in 40 years (in 1990). The tax on hard liquor has been increased only twice—small raises in 1985 and 1990. Opinion polls have shown that the public is in favor of raising federal excise taxes on alcohol, but the alcohol industry success-fully fights increases. Furthermore, about 20% of all alcohol is sold for business entertainment and is thus tax deductible, making it that much less costly to whoever pays the bar bill.

Finally, the alcohol, advertising, and entertainment industries tirelessly promote the idea that it's normal, desirable, smart, sophisticated, and sexy to drink. In print, on television, and at the movies, we see beautiful, healthy people drinking. Beer ads associate the product with sports events, fast cars, camaraderie, and sex. Hollywood's stars have always imbibed plentifully, on and off camera: "Here's looking at you, kid," echoes down the ages. Among modern American male writers, alcoholism has been a badge of the trade: Hemingway, Fitzgerald, and Faulkner were all alcoholics. In *The Thirsty Muse*, literary historian Tom Dardis cites the deadly effect of alcohol on male American writers, many of whom made a credo of heavy drinking.

Considering all these pro-drinking forces, it is amazing that 35% of us over 18 never drink, and another 35% drink lightly and only occasionally. It's equally amazing that our drinking levels have been declining for the past 10 years. But it's estimated that only 8% of us consume more than half of all the alcohol. Still, out-and-out alcoholism is only one factor in the grief caused by drinking, and alcohol problems are not a simple matter of the drunk versus the rest of us.

Alcohol's toll

It's a rare person in our society whose life goes untouched by alcohol. Alcohol causes, or is associated with, over 100,000 deaths every year, often among the young. In 1990, alcohol-

Reprinted with permission from the *University of California at Berkeley Wellness Letter,* February 1993, pp. 4-6. © 1993 by Health Letter Associates.

related traffic crashes killed more than 22,000 people—almost the same number as homicides. Half the pedestrians killed by cars have elevated blood alcohol levels. At some time in their lives, 40% of all Americans will be involved in an alcohol-related traffic crash. Alcoholism creates unhealthy family dynamics, contributing to domestic violence and child abuse. Fetal alcohol syndrome, caused by drinking during pregnancy, is the leading known cause of mental retardation. After tobacco, alcohol is the leading cause of premature death in America. The total cost of alcohol use in America has been estimated at $86 billion annually, a figure so huge as to lose its meaning. But money is a feeble method for measuring the human suffering.

In a free society, banning alcohol is neither desirable nor acceptable. But government, schools, and other institutions could do more than they do to protect the public health, teach the young about the dangers of alcohol, and treat alcoholics. As individuals and as citizens, we could all contribute to reducing the toll alcohol exacts on American life.

Alcohol and the body: short-term effects

Five ounces of wine, 12 ounces of beer, and 1.5 ounces of 80-proof spirits—all average servings—put the same amount of pure alcohol (about 1/2 to 2/3 ounce) into the bloodstream. But how fast it gets into the blood depends on many things. Some alcohol is absorbed through the stomach lining, enabling it to reach the bloodstream very quickly. If the stomach is empty, absorption is even faster: food slows it down. Aspirin in the stomach can hasten alcohol absorption. Since the alcohol in beer and wine is less concentrated, it tends to be absorbed more slowly than straight whiskey (and presumably you drink beer and wine more slowly than a shot of whiskey). But downing two beers in an hour raises blood alcohol concentration (BAC) more than one drink of whisky sipped for an hour. It's the alcohol that counts. A BAC of 0.10 is defined as legal intoxication in most states (0.08 in California, Maine, Oregon, Utah, and Vermont). It's hard to predict BAC accurately, since so many factors affect it. But a 150-pound man typically reaches a BAC of 0.10 if he has two or three beers in an hour. Any BAC impairs driving ability.

It takes the body about two hours to burn half an ounce of pure alcohol (the amount in about one drink) in the bloodstream. Once the alcohol is there, you can't hurry up the process of metabolizing it. You can't run it off, swim it off, or erase the effects with coffee. Leaner, larger people will be less affected by a given amount of alcohol than smaller ones with more fatty tissue—women, for instance. The effects of a given BAC are also greater in older people than in younger.

Every cell in the body can absorb alcohol from the blood. Of the short-term effects, none is more dramatic than those on the central nervous system. At first the drinker gets a feeling of ease and exhilaration, usually short-lived. But as BAC rises, judgment, memory, and sensory perception are all progressively impaired. Thoughts become jumbled; concentration and insight are dulled. Depression usually sets in. Some people get angry or violent. Alcohol induces drowsiness but at the same time disrupts normal patterns of sleeping and dreaming. It also adversely affects sexual performance.

The most unpleasant physical after-effect of too much alcohol is a hangover: dry mouth, sour stomach, headache, depression, and fatigue. Its cause is over-indulgence—not, as some believe, "mixing" drinks or drinking "cheap booze." No remedy has ever been found for hangovers.

The heart effect: worth drinking for?

Much recent research shows that moderate drinkers have a lower risk of developing heart disease. Supposedly, this beneficial effect comes from alcohol's ability to raise HDL cholesterol, the "good" type that protects against atherosclerosis. Some researchers have suggested that only one kind of beverage—for example, red wine—is protective. But it's more likely to be alcohol itself. Still, it's only moderate drinking that's helpful, and some people can't stick to moderation, while others (pregnant women) shouldn't drink at all. Few doctors suggest that nondrinkers begin drinking to protect their hearts.

Different for a woman

The alcohol industry has tried for some time to hitch a ride on women's quest for equality. Liquor ads promote the idea that if a woman can work like a man, she can, and indeed should, drink like a man. Nothing could be further from the truth.

Today 55% of women drink alcoholic beverages, and 3% of all women consume more than two drinks a day. But the ads don't tell a woman that she'll get more intoxicated than a man from the same amount of alcohol. Alcohol is distributed through body water, and is more soluble in water than in fat. Since women tend to be smaller than men and have proportionately more fatty tissue and less body water than men, the blood alcohol concentration resulting from a given intake will be higher for a woman than for a man of the same size. Recent research also shows that the stomach enzyme that breaks down alcohol before it reaches the bloodstream is less active in women than in men.

This may explain why excessive drinking seems to have more serious long-term consequences for women. They develop cirrhosis (liver disease) at lower levels of alcohol intake than men, for instance, and alcohol also puts them at increased risk for osteoporosis.

Finally, pregnant women who drink heavily risk having babies with fetal alcohol syndrome—characterized by mental retardation, structural defects of the face and limbs, hyperactivity, and heart defects. Because no level of alcohol consumption during pregnancy is known to be safe, pregnant women (as well as women planning pregnancy or having unprotected intercourse) are advised not to drink and to continue to abstain while breastfeeding. The amount of alcohol that passes into breast milk is smaller than the amount that crosses the placenta during pregnancy, but recent studies suggest that even a small amount can inhibit motor development in an infant. The idea that drinking beer promotes milk supply and benefits the baby is a myth.

Heavy drinking: long-term effects

Chronic, excessive use of alcohol can seriously damage nearly every organ and function of the body. When alcohol is burned in the body it produces another, even more toxic substance, acetaldehyde, which contributes to the damage. Alcohol is a stomach irritant. It adversely affects the way the small intestine transports and absorbs nutrients, especially vitamins and minerals. Added to the usually poor diet of heavy drinkers, this often results in severe malnutrition. Furthermore, alcohol can produce pancreatic disorders. It causes fatty deposits to accumulate in the liver. Cirrhosis of the liver, an often fatal illness, may be the ultimate result. Though alcohol is not a food, it does have calories and can contribute to obesity.

The effects of heavy drinking on the cardiovascular system are no less horrific. For many years doctors have observed that hypertension and excessive alcohol use go together, and according to a number of recent studies, heavy drinkers are more likely to have high blood pressure than teetotalers. Heavy alcohol consumption damages healthy heart muscle and puts extra strain on already damaged heart muscle. And it can damage other muscles besides the heart.

Some of the worst effects of alcohol are directly on the brain. The most life-threatening is an acute condition leading to psychosis, confusion, or unconsciousness. Heavy drinkers also tend to be heavy smokers and are also more likely to take and abuse other drugs, such as tranquilizers. Excessive drinking, particularly in combination with tobacco, increases the chance of cancers of the mouth, larynx, and throat. Alcohol appears to play a role in stomach, colorectal, and esophageal cancers, as well as possibly liver cancer.

What causes alcoholism?

Alcoholism is a complex disorder: the official definition, recently revised by a 23-member committee of experts, is "a primary, chronic disease with genetic, psychosocial, and environmental factors influencing its development and manifestations. The disease is often progressive and fatal. It is characterized by impaired control over drinking, preoccupation with the drug alcohol, use of alcohol despite adverse consequences, and distortions in thinking, most notably denial."

Alcohol use, by itself, is not sufficient to cause alcoholism. Medical science cannot yet explain why one person abstains or drinks rarely, while another drinks to excess—or why some heavy drinkers are able to stop drinking, while others continue until they die of cirrhosis. One area currently under intensive investigation is heredity. Are children of heavy drinkers more likely to fall victim to alcohol than others?

The answer is yes, but not just because these children were raised in an adverse environment. Studies have shown that, even when raised in nonalcoholic households, a significant number of children of alcoholic parents become alcoholics. This suggests that the ability to handle alcohol may be in part genetically determined. Not long ago, researchers claimed to have located an alcoholism gene, setting off a bitter controversy and raising the possibility of testing children, job applicants, and even fetuses for latent alcoholism. But if there are alcoholism genes, they remain to be identified, and a test for potential alcoholism is a long way off. Researchers point to differences in blood enzymes among alcoholics and non-users—but do not know whether the difference is responsible for the alcoholism or the result of it. Perhaps the chemistry of the body will prove to be the key to whether a person can drink moderately or not. Though most investigators believe that alcoholism has genetic, as well as environmental, causes, this does not mean that any individual is "doomed" to be an alcoholic. Alcoholic parents don't always produce alcoholic children. And many alcoholics come from families where no one ever drank.

Alcoholism is treatable

One problem in treating alcoholism is that it is hard to recognize. A person who is chronically drunk in public is obviously an alcoholic. But not all alcoholics display their problem by falling down in the street, losing their jobs, causing traffic crashes, or getting arrested. Many drink secretly or only on weekends, only in the evening, or even only once a month. Some may drink from depression, while others are sensation-seekers. They may successfully hold down a job or practice a profession. Yet at some point, whatever their drinking patterns, they have lost their ability to control their use of alcohol.

Many of the serious physical and personal consequences of alcoholism can be halted or reversed if drinking is discontinued soon enough. There are many different approaches to alcoholism: Alcoholics Anonymous and similar 12-step programs, individual or group psychotherapy, hospitalization and detoxification, and other methods. No single system will work for everyone. For some people, a combination of methods can help. Others may do as well with individual counseling. Family therapy may help others. The families of alcoholics also need therapy and other forms of social support. Scientific data about treatment are inconclusive. The crucial factor, most experts agree, is for the drinker to recognize that a problem exists and to seek the kind of treatment he or she needs.

KICKING BUTTS

Nicotine is more powerfully addictive than most people realize. It will probably take several tries before you learn enough tricks to stay cigarette-free for good.

Carl Sherman

Carl Sherman writes on health, medicine, and psychology for national magazines and medical newspapers. He lives in New York City. He last wrote for Psychology Today *about sexual abuse in psychotherapy. He is the coauthor of a book on psychological aspects of skin disorders and his writings are anthologized in many collections.*

It may not be a "sin" anymore, but few would dispute that smoking is the devil to give up. Of the 46 million Americans who smoke—26 percent of the adult population—an estimated 80 percent would like to stop and one-third try each year. Two to 3 percent of them succeed. "There's an extraordinarily high rate of relapse among people who want to quit," says Michael Fiore, M.D., M.P.H., director of the Center for Tobacco Research and Intervention at the University of Wisconsin.

The tenacity of its grip can be matched by few other behaviors, most of which, like snorting cocaine and shooting up heroin, are illegal. Since 1988, nicotine dependence and withdrawal have been recognized as disorders by the American Psychiatric Association, legitimizing the experience of the millions who have tried, successfully and otherwise, to put smoking behind them while kibitzers told them to use more willpower.

It's not just a habit, the medical and scientific communities now fully agree, but an addiction, comparable in strength to hard drugs and alcohol.

In fact, the odds of "graduating" from experimentation to true dependence are far worse for cigarettes than for illicit drugs, which testifies to tobacco's one-two punch of addictiveness and availability: Crack and heroin aren't sold in vending machines and hawked from billboards. Alcohol is as legal and available as cigarettes are, and as big a business, but apparently easier to take or leave alone. The majority of people who drink are not dependent on alcohol, while as many as 90 percent of smokers are addicted.

If nothing else, the persistence of smoking in the face of a devastating rogue's gallery of bodily damage, little of which has been kept secret, attests to the fact that this is no rational lifestyle decision. "Take all the deaths in America caused by alcohol, illicit drugs, fires, car accidents, homicide, and suicide. Throw in AIDS. It's still only half the deaths every year from cigarettes," says Fiore.

The news, however, isn't all bad. For the last 20 years, the proportion of Americans who smoke has dropped continuously, for the first time in our history. In America today, there are nearly 45 million ex-smokers, about as many as are still puffing away.

These quitters, perhaps surprisingly, are for the most part the same folk who tried and failed before. The average person who successfully gives up smoking does so after five or six futile attempts, says Fiore. "It appears that many smokers need to go through a process of quitting and relapsing a number of times

TIPS FOR QUITTERS

• Nicotine addiction is powerful. Expect to struggle for a couple of months. It's an up-and down course.

• Don't despair. It may take six tries to learn enough skills to beat this addiction.

• Aim for absolute abstinence—even a single puff leads to relapse.

• Inventory those things that make you feel good and treat yourself to them—exercising, kissing, reading, taking a nap—instead of a smoke.

• Watch your coffee intake. Not only is it a trigger to smoke, your sensitivity to caffeine increases, mimicking nicotine-withdrawal symptoms.

• Change routines associated with smoking. Take a walk before your morning coffee. Drive to work a different way.

• Although most quitters succeed (eventually) on their own, programs that involve counseling improve the odds, especially for the depressed or anxious.

• Don't dismiss nicotine replacement with patch or gum. Gum allows you control over your blood nicotine level.

• Keep your guard up. Most lapses occur three or four weeks out, when you're feeling better.

• In the first weeks, avoid, or severely limit, alcohol.

before he or she can learn enough skills or maintain enough control to overcome this addiction.''

'Evidence has mounted that a substantial number of smokers use cigarettes to regulate emotional states, particularly to reduce anxiety, sadness, or boredom.'

Never underestimate the power of your enemy. Although nicotine may not give the taste of Nirvana that more notorious drugs do, its effects on the nervous system are profound and hard to resist. It increases levels of acetylcholine and nor-epinephrine, brain chemicals that regulate mood, attention, and memory. It also appears to stimulate the release of dopamine in the reward center of the brain, as opiates, cocaine, and alcohol do.

Addiction research has clearly established that drugs with a rapid onset—that hit the brain quickly—have the most potent psychological impact and are the most addictive. "With cigarettes, the smoker gets virtually immediate onset," says Jack Henningfield, Ph.D., chief of clinical pharmacology research for the National Institute on Drug Abuse. "The cigarette is the crack-cocaine of nicotine delivery."

Physiologically, smoking a drug, be it cocaine or nicotine, is the next best thing to injecting it. In fact, it's pretty much the same thing, says Henningfield. "Whether you inhale a drug in 15 seconds, which is pretty slow for an average smoker, or inject it in 15 seconds, the effects are identical in key respects," he says. The blood extracts nicotine from inhaled air just as efficiently as oxygen, and delivers it, within seconds, to the brain.

The cigarette also gives the smoker "something remarkable: the ability to get precise, fingertip dose control," says Henningfield. Achieving just the right blood level is a key to virtually all drug-induced gratification, and the seasoned smoker does this adeptly, by adjusting how rapidly and deeply he or she puffs. "If you get the dose just right after going without cigarettes for an hour or two, there's nothing like it," he says.

The impetus to smoke is indeed, as the tobacco companies put it, for pleasure. "But there's no evidence that smoke in the mouth provides much pleasure," says Henningfield. "We do know that nicotine in the brain does."

For many, nicotine not only gives pleasure, it eases pain. Evidence has mounted that a substantial number of smokers use cigarettes to regulate emotional states, particularly to reduce negative affect like anxiety, sadness, or boredom.

"People expect that having a cigarette will reduce bad feelings," says Thomas Brandon, Ph.D., assistant professor of psychology at the State University of New York at Binghamton. His research found this, in fact, to be one of the principal motivations for daily smokers.

Negative affect runs the gamut from the transitory down times we all have several times a day, to clinical depression.

Smokers are about twice as likely to be depressed as non-smokers, and people with a history of major depression are nearly 50 percent more likely than others to also have a history of smoking, according to Brandon.

Sadly, but not surprisingly, depression appears to cut your chance of quitting by as much as one-half, and the same apparently applies, to a lesser extent, to people who just have symptoms of depression.

According to Alexander Glassman, M.D., professor of psychiatry at the Columbia University College of Physicians and Surgeons, the act of quitting can trigger severe depression in some people. In one study, nine smokers in a group of 300 in a cessation program became so depressed—two were frankly suicidal—that the researchers advised them to give up the effort and try again later. All but one had a history of major depression.

"These weren't average smokers," Glassman points out. All were heavily dependent on nicotine, they smoked at least a pack and a half daily, had their first cigarette within a half hour of awakening, and had tried to quit, on average, five times before. It is possible, he suggests, that nicotine has an antidepressant effect on some.

More generally, suggests Brandon, the very effectiveness of cigarettes in improving affect is one thing that makes it so hard to quit. Not only does a dose of nicotine quell the symptoms of withdrawal (much more on this later), the neurotransmitters it releases in the brain are exactly those most likely to elevate mood.

For a person who often feels sad, anxious, or bored, smoking can easily become a dependable coping mechanism to be given up only with great difficulty. "Once people learn to use nicotine to regulate moods" says Brandon, "if you take it away without providing alternatives, they'll be much more vulnerable to negative affect states. To alleviate them, they'll be tempted to go back to what worked in the past."

In fact, negative affect is what precipitates relapse among would-be quitters 70 percent of the time, according to Saul Shiffman, Ph.D., professor of psychology at the University of Pittsburgh. "We invited people to call a relapse-prevention hot line, to find out what moments of crises were like; what was striking was how often they were in the grip of negative emotions just before relapses, strong temptations, and close calls." A more precise study using palm-top computers to track the state of mind of participants is getting similar results, Shiffman says.

Most relapses occur soon after quitting, some 50 percent within the first two weeks, and the vast majority by six months. But everyone knows of people who had a slip a year, two, or five after quitting, and were soon back to full-time puffing. And for each of them, there are countless others who have had to fight the occasional urge, desire, or outright craving months, even years after the habit has been, for all intents and purposes, left behind.

Acute withdrawal is over within four to six weeks for virtually all smokers. But the addiction is by no means *all* over. Like those who have been addicted to other drugs, ex-smokers apparently remain susceptible to "cues," suggests Brandon: Just as seeing a pile of sugar can arouse craving in the former cocaine user, being at a party or a club, particularly around smokers, can rekindle the lure of nicotine intensely. The same process may include "internal cues," says Brandon. "If you smoked in the past when under stress or depressed, the act of being depressed can serve as a cue to trigger the urge to smoke."

Like users of other drugs, Henningfield points out, addicted smokers don't just consume the offending substance to feel good (or not bad), but to feel "right." "The cigarette smoker's daily function becomes dependent on continued nicotine dosing: Not just mood, but the ability to maintain attention and concentration deteriorates very quickly in nicotine withdrawal."

Henningfield's studies have shown that in an addicted smoker, attention, memory, and reasoning ability start to decline measurably just four hours after the last cigarette. This reflects a real physiological impairment: a change in the electrical activity of the brain. Nine days after quitting, when some withdrawal symptoms, at least, have begun to ease, there has been no recovery in brain function.

How long does the impairment persist? No long-term studies have been done, but cravings and difficulties in cognitive function have been documented for as long as nine years in some ex-smokers. "There are clinical reports of people who have said that they still aren't functioning right, and eventually make the 'rational decision' to go back to smoking," Henningfield says.

The conclusion is inescapable that smoking causes changes in the nervous system that endure long after the physical addiction is history, and in some smokers, may never normalize.

The wealth of recent knowledge about smoking clarifies why it's hard to quit. But can it make it easier? If nothing else, it should help people take it seriously enough to gear up for the effort. "People think of quitting as something

short term, but they should expect to struggle for a couple of months," says Shiffman.

What works? About 90 percent of people who give up smoking do so on their own, says Fiore. But the odds for success can be improved: Programs that involve counseling typically get better rates, and nicotine replacement can be a potent ally in whatever method you use.

In a metaanalysis of 17 placebo-controlled trials involving more than 5,000 people, Fiore found that the patch consistently doubled the success of quit attempts, whether or not antismoking counseling was used. After six months, 22 percent of the people who used the patch remained off cigarettes, compared to 9 percent who had a placebo. Of those who had the patch and a relatively intense counseling or support program, 27 percent were smoke-free.

More than 4 million Americans have tried the patch, which replaces the nicotine on which the smoker has become dependent, to ease such withdrawal symptoms as irritability, insomnia, inability to concentrate, and physical cravings that drive many back to tobacco.

'Smoking causes nervous system changes that endure after the physical addiction is history. Some people may never normalize.'

You're likely to profit from the patch if you have a real physical dependence on nicotine: that is, if you have your first cigarette within 30 minutes of waking up; smoke 20 or more a day; or experienced severe withdrawal symptoms during previous quit attempts.

Standard directions call for using the patches in decreasing doses for two to three months. Some researchers, however,

BORN TO SMOKE

Although the difference between smokers and nonsmokers appears to reflect complex environmental and social factors, genetics apparently plays a role comparable to that observed in alcoholism, responsible for about 30 percent of the propensity.

In particular, shared genetics appears to account for the link between smoking and depression, according to data collected on nearly 1,500 pairs of female twins. "The twin data show that whatever gene puts you at risk for depression, the same gene puts you at risk for smoking," says Alexander Glassman.

Further evidence for this conclusion comes from a prospective epidemiological study, in which 1,200 people in their twenties were surveyed twice, 18 months to two years apart. Nonsmokers who were depressed at the first interview were more likely to be smoking at the time of the second, while nondepressed smokers were more likely to have become depressed by then.

Genetics may even play a role in *how* you smoke. Shiffman studied a group of people who had smoked regularly but lightly, five cigarettes or less, four days or more a week, for several years at least. Says Saul Shiffman: "They had ample opportunity to become addicted—on average, they'd smoked 46,000 cigarettes, but we found not the slightest evidence of dependence: they showed no signs of withdrawal when abstinent. They really could casually take smoking or leave it."

Such nonaddicted users—"chippers," in drug culture parlance—are also seen among consumers of hard drugs. "We didn't delve deeply into what made these smokers different," says Shiffman. "But we did find evidence that they also had relatives who smoked with little dependence, who followed the same pattern. This makes it plausible, although it doesn't prove that these folks are biologically different." With rare exceptions, chippers have always smoked that way, he points out. For a once-addicted smoker to try to become a chipper is "a risky business" that's probably doomed to failure.—C.S.

suggest that for certain smokers, the patch may be necessary for years, or indefinitely.

"It's already happening," says Henningfield. "Some doctors have come to the conclusion that some patients are best able to get on with their life with nicotine maintenance." One such physician is David Peter Sachs, M.D., director of the Palo Alto Center for Pulmonary Disease Prevention. "I realized that with some of my patients, no matter how slowly I tried to taper them off nicotine replacement, they couldn't do it," says Sachs. "They were literally using it for years. Before you start tapering the dose, you should be cigarette-free for at least 30 days."

His clinical experience leads him to believe that 10 to 20 percent of smokers are *so* dependent that they may always need to get nicotine from somewhere. One study of people using the gum found that two years later, 20 percent of those who had successfully remained cigarette-free were still chewing. The idea of indefinite, even lifetime, nicotine maintenance sounds offensive to some. "Clearly, the goal to aim for is to be nicotine-free," says Sachs. "But if that can't be reached, being tobacco-free still represents a substantial gain for the patient, and for society." And getting nicotine via a patch or gum source means a far lower dose than you'd get from a cigarette. Plus, you're getting just nicotine, and not the 42 carcinogens in tobacco smoke.

Although the once-a-day patch has largely supplanted the gum first used in nicotine replacement, Sachs thinks that for some, the most effective treatment could involve one or both. The patch may be easier to use, but the gum is the only product that allows you control over blood nicotine level. Some people know they'll do better if they stay in control. And would-be quitters who do fine on the patch until they run into a stressful business meeting may stifle that urge to bum a cigarette if they boost their nicotine level in advance with a piece of gum, Sachs says.

However, nicotine replacement "is not a magic bullet," says Fiore. "It will take the edge off the tobacco-withdrawal syndrome, but it won't automatically transform any smoker into a nonsmoker." Other requisite needs vary from person to person. A standard approach teaches behavioral "coping skills," simple things like eating, chewing gum, or knitting to keep mouth or hands occupied, or leaving tempting situations. Ways people cope cognitively are as important as what they do, says Shiffman.

He advises would-be quitters at times of temptation to remind themselves just why they're quitting: "My children will be so proud of me," or "I want to live to see my grandchildren," for example. Think of a relaxing scene. Imagine how you'll feel tomorrow if you pass this crisis without smoking. Or simply tell yourself, "NO" or "Smoking is not an option."

Coping skills, however, are conspicuously unsuccessful for people who are high in negative affect. Supportive counseling works better. Depression or anxiety may interfere with the ability to use cognitive skills.

One exercise that Brandon teaches patients asks them to inventory—and treat themselves to—things that make them feel good, a substitute for the mood-elevating effect of a cigarette. These might include exercising, being with friends, going to concerts, reading, or taking a nap. "Positive life-style changes that improve mood level" are particularly useful if you use cigarettes to deal with negative emotional states, he says.

Depression treatment is particularly important for those trying to quit smoking. One study found that cognitive therapy significantly improved quit rates for people with a history of depression. Various antidepressants have been effective in small studies, and a large double-blind trial using the drug Zoloft is underway.

Fiore has found that having just one cigarette in the first two weeks of a cessation program predicted about 80 percent of

NICOTINE IN THE NINETIES

Smoking just doesn't have the cachet it once did. Instead of a mark of worldliness and *joie de vivre,* it's become something of a social disease, banned from airplanes, restaurants, and, in some localities, public parks. Except on billboards and in magazine ads, the smoker him- or herself is less likely to be the object of admiration than of pity and contempt.

The change in smoking's status is no doubt in part responsible for the 40 percent decline in its prevalence since 1964. And it would seem logical that those people who are still smoking in the face of such adversity are an increasingly hard-core, heavily addicted bunch, unable to quit.

Alexander Glassman conjectures that as the social environment grows more hostile to smoking, the genetic component of the behavior will become more evident. And as the number of smokers drops, an increasing percentage will have psychiatric problems, particularly depression.

But the change hasn't yet been documented. "Actually, I don't think the data support the idea that today's smokers are

very different from years back," says Fiore. "The average number of cigarettes they smoke today isn't dramatically different from 20 years ago—about 22 per day."

One thing that has happened is a change in the socio-demographics of smoking. "More and more, it's a behavior predominantly exercised by disadvantaged members of society: 40 percent of high-school dropouts smoke, compared to 14 percent of college grads. Poor people are more likely to smoke than wealthy. It's getting marginalized," he says.

If nothing else, today's antismoking climate has eliminated much denial about the true nature of the cigarette habit. "Smokers are much more aware of being hooked," says Saul Shiffman. "You can't tell how dependent you are if access is easy. If you can smoke at your desk and at a restaurant, you can delude yourself, as people have for decades: 'I like to smoke but I can take it or leave it.' It's hard to say that when the only place you can smoke is outside when it's hailing and 20 degrees."—C.S.

relapses at six months. Even when the withdrawal symptoms are gone, a single lapse can rekindle the urge as much as ever.

In the critical first weeks without cigarettes, a key to relapse prevention is avoiding, or severely limiting, alcohol, which not only blunts inhibitions, but is often powerfully bound to smoking as a habit. Up to one-half of people who try to quit have their first lapse with alcohol on board.

Watch your coffee intake, too. It can trigger the urge to smoke. And nicotine stimulates a liver enzyme that breaks down caffeine, so when you quit, you'll get more bang for each cup, leading to irritability, anxiety, and insomnia—the withdrawal symptoms that undermine quit efforts.

Try to change your routine to break patterns that strengthen addiction: drive to work a different way; don't linger at the table after a meal. And don't try to quit when you're under stress: vacation time might be a good occasion.

And if you do have a lapse? Don't trivialize it, because then you're more likely to have another, says Shiffman. But, "if you make it a catastrophe, you'll reconfirm fears that you'll never be able to quit," a low self-esteem position that could become a self-fulfilling prophecy. "Think of it as a warning, a mistake you'll have to overcome."

Try to learn from the lapse: examine the situation that led up to it, and plan to deal with it better in the future. "And take it as a sign you need to double your efforts," Shiffman says. "Looking back at a lapse, many people find they'd already begun to slack off; early on, they were avoiding situations where they were tempted to smoke, but later got careless."

Don't be discouraged by ups and downs. "It's normal to have it easy for a while, then all of a sudden you're under stress and for 10 minutes you have an intense craving," says Shiffman. "Consider the gain in frequency and duration: the urge to smoke is now coming back for 10 minutes, every two weeks, rather than all the time."

If lapse turns into relapse and you end up smoking regularly, the best antidote to despair is getting ready to try again. "Smoking is a chronic disease, and quitting is a process. Relapse and remission are part of the process," says Fiore. "As long as you're continuing to make progress toward the ultimate goal of being smoke-free, you should feel good about your achievement."

Heroin, Be the Death of Me

South Beach nightlife sophisticates know they can handle it. A little puff now and then won't kill you. No Big Deal.

Elise Ackerman

David has sunk deep into the plush brown cushions on his couch. He looks comfortable, but he's not. Too many hours have passed since his last fix and now he's feeling the pangs of withdrawal—the aching muscles, the overwhelming fatigue. Soon however, his dealer will arrive (a house call, so to speak) to set things right again. But David vows this will be the last time, one final blowout before he quits.

He's tried that several times before, of course, and it hasn't stuck. Tonight, though, will be different. Tonight will be the end of the bad and the beginning of the good. "Your last memory must be your most beautiful," he murmurs, his decorum flawless despite the tortured symptoms of withdrawal. As he speaks, he twirls a clove cigarette in one hand, wielding it with the grace of a conductor's baton.

David is one of South Beach's best-known nightclub party promoters, a creator of alternative realities, fond of decorating clubs with flowers, of sneaking Gregorian chants under the techno rhythms of disco music, of spouting stream-of-consciousness poetry and spontaneously breaking into dance. He has themed this special evening around a particularly bleak reality: his addiction to heroin.

He was clean of heroin for two and a half months, though cocaine had taken its place. Then four days ago he returned to "chasing the dragon"—sucking up the smoky curlicues produced by heating heroin on a bit of aluminum foil. If David continues to smoke, he knows he'll be consumed, fried to a crisp by the dragon's searing but seductive breath. He's not yet 25 years old, but to many people on the Beach who have noted his progressive dissipation, he has already self-destructed. David has heard them whispering behind

his back, has seen them avert their eyes. Sylvester Stallone was the kindest. "Get some new role models, kid," the actor told him.

But tonight will be the end of it. He says he's going to quit once and for all, going to leave town and simply stop. Cold turkey. Ever the publicist, he's even invited a reporter to observe his narcotic version of the Last Supper. But not to reveal his true name. (David is a pseudonym. The names of some other individuals in this article have also been changed.)

During the past few months, six of David's friends and acquaintances have died as a result of heroin overdoses.

"Everyone thinks the heroin high is so incredible, but it's nothing like that," he says. "It's like falling asleep and being dead. You just become numb. You don't feel anything and you just fade away." During the past few months, six of his friends and acquaintances have permanently faded away as a result of heroin overdoses. Among the dead: the owner of a popular nightclub, two young models, and the granddaughter of Victor Posner, one of Florida's richest men.

According to the Dade County Medical Examiner's Office, 30 people died of heroin-related overdoses in 1994, a startling jump over 1990, when only one such death was reported. And in the first two months of this year, at least nine people have died of overdoses involving heroin. During the past four years, the number of emergency room patients reporting personal heroin use increased about 300

percent. Jim Hall, executive director of the Miami-based Up Front Drug Information Center, says those figures, while small in comparison to New York and Los Angeles, reflect heroin's rise in Dade County.

Long known as a reliable marketplace for high-grade cocaine, Miami has never seen much in the way of top-quality heroin. What local smack could be found was usually dirty and weak, its purity levels hovering around four percent. Until recently, that is. According to the Drug Enforcement Administration and other law enforcement agencies, the Colombian cocaine cartels have diversified their product line and are now marketing an extremely potent brand of heroin. They're employing the same recession-proof strategy they used to sell cocaine in the early Eighties: Pitch heroin as a glamour product and target young, sophisticated drug-users. With the right mystique surrounding the substance, the suburban market will sell itself. "This is almost a drug for the cognoscenti," remarks Hall, adding that most young people trying the new, deluxe Colombian heroin have already dabbled with cocaine.

"I'm seeing it all over and I can't believe it," notes Brian Antoni, author of the novel *Paradise Overdose* and a well-known South Beach social host. "It's become part of the scene as far as I'm concerned." Antoni, who does not use heroin, says those who are experimenting with it are generally well read and highly educated. "The people I'm seeing it hit most are people who consider themselves to be living on the edge. They want to go back to the whole Paul Bowles romantic thing, which is really stupid, considering what happened then."

Another nightclub promoter, Sam Zaoui, concurs: "A few years ago heroin was very difficult to get on the Beach, but now

From *New Times* (Miami), April 27–May 3, 1995, pp. 22-32. © 1995 by New Times. Reprinted by permission.

it's all over." While Zaoui himself has never tried the drug, he says he has seen plenty of people chasing the dragon, the telltale flash of a cigarette lighter under foil briefly illuminating a club's dim corner.

For long-time junkies who ridicule the notion of "heroin chic," the increased availability has eased much of the hassle associated with scoring dope. Three Miami Beach friends—Debbie, Mike, and Jack— all shoot heroin rather than smoke or snort it. And they've done so for years. "In the old days, it was really dangerous copping in the city," recalls Jack, an artist. "I've been stabbed like six times. I've been shot at once. Ten years ago, before heroin started hitting the Beach, before it was fashionable like it supposedly is now, I was one of the few people who was getting high. I used to go to Overtown. I used to ride my bicycle to Liberty City. There was no dope in Miami Beach. Now, in the last two years, there has started to be dope. So it has become a lot safer to cop."

Safer and more convenient, too. In fact, Jack and Debbie have just scored some heroin from their dealer at a prearranged spot near Epicure market on Alton Road. Back in the dim South Beach efficiency apartment shared by Mike and Debbie, the trio prepares to shoot up.

Debbie bubbles with excitement as she opens the teak box in which she keeps her needles and then arranges a small bottle of bleach, a dab of cotton, a candle, and a teaspoon. "Hurry up, hurry up," she giggles. As Mike heats the teaspoon— filled with a small mound of heroin and water—above the candle flame, Debbie does some energetic deep knee bends, her sundress billowing. Pretty and petite, with delicate bones and long brown hair, she smiles apologetically, explaining that she doesn't have any veins left in her arms, so she's going to shoot the heroin into her thigh.

Within a matter of minutes, all three have injected, cleaned their needles, and are now blissfully calm. Debbie huddles in a chair, her knees drawn up close to her chest. Asked how she feels, she smiles and languidly drops her head: "Um, nice." Several weeks earlier she and Mike had decided to quit. They even drove down to Key West, rented a hotel room, and waited out the painful, flulike symptoms of withdrawal. But after being back in Miami Beach a few days, they decided to try just a small amount of smack to see if they could get away with it. They couldn't.

Mike admits that he hates being hooked. He used to operate his own business and was making $40,000 a year. Though he had experimented with heroin occasionally, he only began shooting up regularly after he met Debbie. "My lifestyle has dropped a few notches," he says quietly. "I never thought I would live in a place like this. I feel trapped. I feel imprisoned by this drug. And it's not me, it's not in my makeup."

"I'm seeing it all over and I can't believe it. It's become part of the scene as far as I'm concerned."

But if they don't shoot up every day, they immediately feel sick, and Mike will miss work at a local restaurant. Their bills will go unpaid. So now they are doing just a little bit in order to maintain. "It's kind of stupid," Debbie concedes. "But it makes you feel normal." Without the drug, she says she feels exhausted. "After five days, I may not be in pain any more, but I have no energy, and that drives me crazy."

Some users of the new heroin become addicted in a matter of weeks or even days. Others, like David, spend a couple of years as "chippers"—social smokers— until one morning they wake up with a voracious habit. Quitting, they discover, is so painful it only intensifies the longing for heroin's illusion of death.

Tall and lanky, with a full head of straight, dark hair, David would be conventionally handsome were it not for the ravages of unabated drug use. His skin is pale and oily, his shoulders hunched. Obsessed by the continual need to control his attraction to heroin and cut back his intake, his eyes have assumed the beseeching aspect of an animal caught in a trap. His movements are either too fast or too slow, as if powered by an unreliable battery. His drug dependency is so great that even gradual reduction causes physical distress. This past December he spent ten days in an Oklahoma rehabilitation program, part of an unsuccessful attempt to kick heroin. The experience, he says, was like surviving brutal combat: After the initial euphoria of kicking his addiction, he began to experience post-traumatic stress.

"I went for two and a half months with a dead body," David recalls. "I mean *dead,*

like paralyzed. I was sleeping 48 hours a day." He struggled to keep up appearances and continued to plan and promote nightclub parties. But he was so exhausted that he'd sleep through his own events. "I tried everything—antidepressants, wake-up soap, wake-up shampoo, wake-up rosemary, wake-up sea salts. There's an aromatizer by my bed that's supposed to be an energizer, and energizing drinks in the refrigerator. If you look in my bathroom, there are probably 30 products there. Everything energy, energy, energy. I just couldn't find it." He inhales from his cigarette and squints at the ceiling.

"What I fell into was cocaine. It started with one bump lasting for two hours and led to eight grams a night, *just to stay awake.* You can imagine! The whole month of March I did that. Just yesterday I was in the emergency room. My nose went all the way through—the cocaine ate it. My nose has been in pain for a week now and I've been sticking it up there anyway. I tried taking apart an antibiotic and putting the cocaine in the capsule and eating it, and that didn't work. I tried drinking it. I tried everything for energy and it didn't work. The only way it works is through your stupid nose."

And as the pain spread outward from his nose, David sought relief. He found his way back to his heroin dealer.
Heroin. Be the death of me.
Heroin. It's my wife and it's my life.
Because a mainer to my veins leads to a center in my head,
and then I'm better off than dead.

Lou Reed's raspy voice rises from David's stereo. While in rehab, he listened to that notorious 1967 song over and over again in an effort to stifle his urge to get high. But the tune reminded him too much of the early days in his relationship with heroin, when his pharmacological love affair was young and innocent and sweet, and he believed he could walk away if things got too messy or complicated.

David first tried heroin in the early Nineties, hoping it would lead him to an intellectual precipice, to the dark side of Margaritaville. He had experimented with other drugs—marijuana, acid, Ecstasy, cocaine—fervently believing they were opening the doors of perception, intensifying his aesthetics. His was a personal trip, a spiritual journey, an intimate exploration of self, not a textbook progression from stoner to cokehead to junkie, and certainly not some Pavlovian response to a cartel-inspired marketing campaign—

or so he believes and will assert with conviction.

"You start out doing perception-enhancing drugs like acid and Ecstasy," David explains. "But once we've developed our senses and we've created the ability to love at a f___ ___ ___ high range like you can't *imagine,* and we've learned to really, really appreciate detail and beauty, we now also have the ability to unfortunately see the pain and horrors that we never really noticed before. And you fall into a certain amount of pain. And heroin is calling you."

"My lifestyle has dropped a few notches. I feel imprisoned by this drug. And it's not me, it's not in my makeup."

Two friends—young, female, and beautiful—have gathered around David as he speaks. They nod sympathetically. The waterfront apartment, located in one of Miami's most exclusive condominiums, is filled with antiques, paintings, and tapestries. A gilded French candelabra adds an air of decadence. Lou Reed's Velvet Underground gives way to ethereal organ music as two men arrive and head for David's bedroom at the back of the apartment. He continues his story without acknowledging them.

"Do you want to know the real, honest, truthful reason I got into heroin?" he says, hesitating with embarrassment. "The physical reason I got into it was honestly to enhance sex." For a year he would snort a touch of heroin before making love. The act was so subtle that many of his girlfriends didn't realize what he was doing. Just a dozen or so grains spilled into a small silver spoon.

By repressing feelings of self-consciousness, heroin also eased David's anxiety during work. He stopped feeling stupid and gawky. He was no longer worried about what people thought of him. And carelessly, he began to violate the rules he had set for himself to prevent addiction. Instead of once per week, he would use smack three times. He would do it on successive days.

Then it happened. He met a girl on a Friday. He snorted some heroin. They made love. "Saturday you're with the same person, and you know you can't do it [heroin] the next day. But since you're on your down day, you're not only not able to have sex like you normally do. You're even *worse* because you're on your down day. In other words, you probably won't be able to have sex for more than, honestly, ten seconds. She's like, 'What's wrong?' And you humiliate yourself. So you go into the bathroom and you do just one little baby line. Like that." He holds up his fingers, centimeters apart. "It's not going to kill you." That weekend he used heroin every day.

When he woke up on Monday, his eyes were watering, his nose was running, and his hands shook—all classic symptoms he recognized as heroin withdrawal. "I was addicted that day," David admits. He had a business meeting scheduled that morning and he didn't want to arrive doped up, but he decided to bring along an emergency supply just in case. Halfway through the meeting, he began to tremble and his eyes began to tear. "People are looking at me like, 'Are you crazy?' I had to literally excuse myself and go into the bathroom and do a millimeter of heroin just to be normal." Once he realized he was addicted, his habit seemed to take on a life of its own, and expanded until he was spending $8000 each month on heroin.

At this point David pauses, excuses himself, and disappears into his bedroom. Forty-five minutes later he and the two male visitors return to the living room. One of them, Frank, is a nationally known actor also addicted to heroin. The other, though not introduced as such, appears to be the long-awaited dealer. Frank sits down. Like David, he says this will be his last night using the drug. He started snorting six years ago in part to calm nerves badly jangled by cocaine abuse. "I was really in the phase—like the song says—'I want a new drug,'" Frank explains. For years heroin barely interfered with his work. Then last winter he lost control. He began to nod out, to fall asleep in the middle of conversations. Heroin began to affect his ability to act. This past January he left California and entered a drug treatment program "I left under the worse possible circumstances," he says. "No car. Being evicted by the landlord. Me, a guy who's in the movies. A supposedly responsible, dependable person." Tonight is the first time he's lapsed. And, he claims, it will be the last.

Frank squirms when Colombia is mentioned. He doesn't want to talk about the source of tonight's heroin. Who cares where it came from? David avoids the subject of sources as well, except to provide a detailed description of some blood-and-feces-covered condoms he once saw at a dealer's apartment. The condoms, which had arrived from somewhere, were stuffed with heroin.

Users may shrink from discussing their supply, but the federal Drug Enforcement Administration has little doubt about the origins of high-grade Miami heroin. "Most if not all of the heroin we seize at the airport in conjunction with customs is coming from Colombia," asserts Jim Shedd, a spokesman for the DEA's local office. Shedd adds that the powder has been exceptionally potent, 98 to 100 percent pure.

Last year airport agents nabbed 101 people who carried heroin somewhere inside their bodies, "body packers," as they are known. That figure represents a dramatic increase from 1990, when only one body packer was arrested. And body packers account for only a fraction of all airport heroin seizures. "It's like an ant army," Shedd says. "They're swallowing it, bringing it in their shoes, stuffing it into false-bottom suitcases. Every day there's a seizure of heroin that's being made."

While Colombia supplies a relatively small portion of the U.S. heroin market (around fifteen percent, according to a recent narcotics intelligence report produced by the DEA in collaboration with eleven other federal agencies), the nation is the world's fourth-largest source of opium poppies. Because it is far more lucrative to smuggle heroin than cocaine, experts believe that Colombians are simply adding heroin to their existing network of cocaine distributors. According to the intelligence report: "Colombian traffickers used a variety of tactics to establish mid- and retail-level outlets for their heroin. In addition to providing heroin of unusually high purity, Colombian traffickers offered free samples of heroin to potential distributors, offered to front [on credit] ounce and multi-ounce quantities of heroin to first-time buyers, and persuaded their established cocaine distributors to purchase and sell heroin as a condition of doing business." To avoid competition from ethnic Chinese and other established heroin importers in major markets like New York City, the Colombian cartels have expanded into smaller metropolitan areas such as Hartford and Bridgeport, Connecticut; Providence, Rhode Island; as well as Atlanta, New Orleans, and

Miami, the report states. Pressure on Miami's cocaine dealers to recruit new heroin customers may explain a couple of last year's more puzzling overdoses.

On September 26, Marianne Hebrard returned home to find her husband, Paul Flandrak, lying on the bed in their master bedroom, cold to the touch. According to police reports, on the nightstand next to the bed were five plastic bags filled with small amounts of white powder. A line of powder had been traced out on top of the nightstand, as if waiting for the next sniff up the nose. From the white residue caked near Flandrak's nose, there was little doubt for whom that line was intended.

David first tried heroin in the early Nineties, hoping it would lead him to the dark side of Margaritaville.

An autopsy revealed that Flandrak, 42-year-old owner of the popular South Beach nightclub called Dune, had died of a cocaine and heroin overdose. A former owner of the successful Paris club Le Boy, Flandrak had recently moved to South Florida and was renting a home in Bay Harbor Islands while he renovated a Mediterranean-style mansion he had purchased on Pine Tree Drive in Miami Beach. Although Flandrak had admitted an earlier problem with cocaine, he claimed he was now clean. "I never saw Paul doing drugs," recalls promoter Sam Zaoui, "and I saw him many times during the course of an evening." Nevertheless, he concedes it's possible that Flandrak may have occasionally lapsed from his no-drugs pledge. This time his dealer may have talked him into trying some of the new heroin along with his coke.

By the time David learned of Flandrak's death, he says he had already resolved to quit. But heroin's new-found popularity made that difficult; nearly everywhere he went, smack would make an appearance. "There's a very rich man who lives in Palm Beach who has some big parties there sometimes," he remembers. "I was coming down, trying to do less and less heroin every day, so I was very tired, and I felt like shit *all* the time." A man David describes as "one of the richest people in the world—not the owner of the house"—approached him at a party and invited him to get high. Thinking he was being

offered a bump of cocaine, David followed him into a bathroom. "Literally, this guy pulls a piece of aluminum foil out of his pocket and starts smoking *heroin,* and for me to, uh, protect my image I have to say, 'Heroin! Oh my God, are you crazy? That stuff will *kill* you, man.' "

Indeed, David believes heroin *is* killing him. Around one in the morning, after his guests have left the apartment, David heads out as well, hoping to collect on a few outstanding debts so he can pay his bills before leaving town. First stop is Bar None at 411 Washington Avenue, where he mingles briefly before rushing up the street to Risk. He has no luck there either, so he returns to Bar None. At every nightclub it's the same story: The people who owe him money have always left just before he arrives.

David begins to fret. Without the money, he'll have difficulty leaving Miami. Yet he's certain that the longer he stays, the more drugs he'll use and the more difficult it will be to get clean. "I'm at the point where I just built a new business, and I can't walk away from it right now," he says. I have investors waiting for results, and there's money that needs to come in every week. So I really have to keep destroying myself every day, and every day I know it's going to be harder by the time I go to rehab."

But this drug use itself has also been hurting his business. His extended trips to the bathroom, where he struggles to shove cocaine up his damaged nose, have not gone unremarked. If he yields to fatigue in public, snoozing, for example, through mindless chatter in the nightclub VIP room, he's accused of nodding out on heroin. Most offensive, he says, are the frequently repeated stories that he's foisted heroin on young models, rumors he hotly denies. Enough people apparently believed them, however, to alert the Miami Beach police. This past November 20 David was arrested outside Amnesia, the massive nightclub in the South Pointe neighborhood.

Although the ostensible reason for the arrest was an outstanding warrant for driving with a suspended license, one of the police officers later testified he had received information that David was dealing heroin. According to the police report, David quickly incriminated himself by readily admitting he was a heroin addict and was carrying "a small amount" to stave off withdrawal.

David's own account of his arrest does not contradict the police report, though

he adds some details. He was in a nearby parking lot, he says, when a police officer approached him and started asking how much money he was earning. Then the officer suddenly announced that David was going to jail, handcuffed him, and placed him in the back of a squad car. While David sat there, another officer, whom he describes as a friend, opened the door and urged him to hand over any drugs before he was booked. Believing that his friend wanted to do him a favor, David turned over a piece of aluminum foil he kept in his wallet. It was coated with traces of heroin.

"I told him, 'Listen, man, I've been addicted to this shit. I swear to God I'm trying to quit.' I thought this cop was going to throw it away for me," David recalls, shaking his head at his naiveté. He was promptly charged with possession of heroin. Eventually he pleaded guilty to avoid extended probation, which would have restricted his freedom to travel outside Dade County. In return for his plea, a judge sentenced him to time served (the one day he spent in jail), and did not adjudicate him guilty, so his record is clean.

Marianne Hebrard returned home to find her husband, Paul Flandrak, lying on the bed in their master bedroom, cold to the touch.

Almost immediately after his arrest, David entered the rehab program in Oklahoma, and within days of returning to Miami, he learned that another friend had died from an overdose.

In her last fashion show, held at Coconut Grove's Ensign Bitters, Anna Tchernycheva sashayed out on the nightclub floor wearing a lacy white teddy. Prancing between two male models, she added a bit of verve to what was really nothing more than a glorified nightclub act. That December 8 appearance would be the last for the 25-year-old Russian model.

According to friend Lucy Marchany, who also modeled that night, Anna complained of feeling sick after the show, but she insisted on going out anyway. Marchany says she begged off, and Anna left with two male friends. According to a medical examiner's report, sometime during the night she overdosed on opiates and cocaine.

A police investigation revealed that Anna had left Ensign Bitters with a man named Hector Ferrera. Several of Anna's friends say they do not believe she was dating Ferrera, who had been arrested in 1992 for selling cocaine. (He pleaded no contest and was ordered to serve six months probation.)

Around 8:00 p.m. the next night, Ferrera dialed 911 to report that Anna was lying unconscious in his house on NE 77th Street in Miami. The story Ferrera gave the police was succinct, even terse. He said they had gone out drinking after the fashion show and had returned to his place after dawn. They went to sleep, and when he awoke that evening, Anna did not appear to be breathing. She was pronounced dead at North Shore Medical Center. After a brief police investigation, her death was determined to be accidental and the case was closed. (Ferrera could not be reached for comment.)

"I want to find out what the hell happened that night," Marchany angrily says today. She and Anna's other friends say they knew she had been unhappy with her career and that she had admitted snorting cocaine, but as far as they knew she was not using heroin. She had been part of the first group of Russian models to work in the United States following the collapse of the Soviet Union. But after an initial flurry of publicity, including appearances on several television talk shows,

the gimmick grew old and the girls had a hard time finding jobs. Anna ended up marrying a photographer and moving to Miami, where she worked as a runway model. A year later her marriage broke up and she began to seek solace in South Beach nightlife.

Drug use, an inseparable part of the club scene, is also not uncommon in the modeling business. "I had the idea that some of them used cocaine to stay thin. It was almost an occupational hazard," says Gary Khurtorsky, an ex-boyfriend who identified Anna's body for the medical examiner.

Anna's death obviously had little effect on David, despite their friendship. He began using cocaine to the point of physical damage, and then turned back to heroin to ease the pain. "Want to see something scary?" he asks as he sprawls out on the floor of his bedroom. "Listen." He wriggles his nose from side to side with his fingers. The bone and cartilage crackle as they rub together. It's early morning. Since his unsuccessful nightclub foray to collect money, he has compulsively been cutting lines of cocaine. When the pain in his nose becomes too great, he takes a tiny puff of heroin.

"You're probably looking at me thinking, 'Why are you doing all this to come down, just to come back up again?' What if I told you it was two different things," he says in an effort to justify his behavior. Then he gives up. "It's no excuse at all. It's really stupid. Do you realize I literally

snorted an eight ball [one-eighth an ounce] one hour before? See, I am consciously, purposely letting you see what it's really like." He sniffles loudly, the air reverberating inside his scarred nose like a vacuum cleaner. "This *sucks,* man. This *really* sucks."

After this long last night of heavy drug use, David remains remarkably lucid, though his thoughts are scattered. He turns back to the subject of his rehab experience this past December. The most difficult part, he says, was returning to Miami Beach. He was greeted with knowing smiles and insincere comments: "It was like, 'Oh David, I'm so proud of you. You look great. I was so worried about you. I love you.' And a *minute* later, when they thought I wasn't listening: 'So f - - - ing stupid. F - - - ing heroin addict. God, the kid's so f - - - ed up. Just comes out of rehab and he's on the shit a day later.' And I wasn't. I was just so *tired.*"

So tired, and in so much pain, and heroin is calling.

At ten o'clock in the morning he tries to sell some of his antique furniture. Sensing desperation, the potential buyer suggests a paltry $300. Furious, David turns him down.

He is determined to find a way to leave Miami.

Only one more day of maintaining, then he'll quit forever.

But four more days will pass before he finally escapes to Europe. Far from the nightlife crowds. Out of range of his dealer's beeper. Somewhere, he hopes, beyond the call of heroin.

The Kiss of Meth

Once known as 'poor man's cocaine,' methamphetamine is rapidly becoming the drug of choice for affluent suburban teens

Henry K. Lee

Chronical Staff Writer

The wind stirs up dust and pollen as it rustles through the shoulder-high cornfields. The sun reflects off the gray-metal shed. Roosters strut and cackle near the ranch-style house outside Byron in eastern Contra Costa County.

It didn't look like a farm capable of generating a million dollars a week.

But agriculture was at best a secondary pursuit on the six-acre property near Discovery Bay. According to law enforcement authorities, the pastoral setting concealed a major methamphetamine laboratory.

In a raid on the farm last month, state, federal and local authorities found enough flasks, chemicals and funnels in the shed to produce up to 100 pounds of the illicit drug, known on the street as "speed." They seized more than two pounds of methamphetamine with a street value of approximately $9,000 and arrested two suspects allegedly linked to the Hell's Angels motorcycle gang. A third suspect, wounded in a gang-related shooting the day before the raid, remains at large.

Although significant, the raid and arrests won't even put a dent in the illegal methamphetamine trade in California, law enforcement officials say. For every clandestine lab investigators raid, dozens of others remain in operation, especially in rural areas where drug operations are hard to detect.

California has been the nation's leading methamphetamine producer for more than a decade. Authorities raided a record 547 labs last year in California, up nearly 32 percent from the 415 labs shut down in 1993.

Methamphetamine use has increased dramatically in recent years, particularly among teenagers, including many in affluent suburbs.

"It's not just the down and out, lowlife, park bench types who are using methamphetamine," said Russ Reeds, a state Bureau of Narcotic Enforcement agent in Redding. "It seems like more people are doing it than people not doing it. It's just atrocious."

"Methamphetamine is the drug of choice for young people," said Contra Costa County Sheriff's Captain Russ Pitkin. "It's a very prevalent problem, nothing that is minor on any sort of scale."

Known as "poor man's cocaine," methamphetamine is a white crystalline powder that can be smoked, snorted, injected or taken in tablet form.

"The high you get from meth is going to last hours, as compared to minutes with cocaine," said Paul Mountain, a commander with the Contra Costa County narcotics task force.

Also known as "speed" or "crank," methamphetamine is a central nervous system stimulant developed by Japanese chemists in the early 1900s. First used for medical purposes in Germany in the 1930s, it is still used for treatment of narcolepsy, attention deficit disorder and obesity.

A small dose of methamphetamine produces a high that can last up to 14 hours. Many users report an increased sex drive and feel like they can go indefinitely without sleeping or eating.

"They can go for days like this, but then they crash and can get very depressed and suicidal," said David Shragai, a counselor at San Ramon Valley Discovery Center in Danville, where 24 percent of the clients last year were treated for methamphetamine abuse.

Methamphetamine use has reached "epidemic levels," said Bill Ruzzamenti, acting special agent in charge with the Drug Enforcement Agency's office in San Francisco.

In more severe cases, users develop "speed psychosis," characterized by extreme paranoia and agoraphobia, or fear of open spaces, said Wendy Wiehl, a staff pharmacist at the Haight-Ashbury Free Clinic in San Francisco.

Auditory hallucinations are also common. "A lot of times people see shadows or something out of the corner of their eye. Others hear voices, somebody calling their name," Wiehl said.

Methamphetamine abuse became rampant in the 1960s, when outlaw motorcycle gangs in Southern California, particularly the Hell's Angels, began manufacturing the drug by the quart. (The term "crank" comes from the gangs' practice of stashing the drug in motorcycle crank cases.)

Methamphetamine abuse expanded steadily over ensuing decades; users ranged from college students cramming for tests to truck drivers wanting to stay awake for long cross-country hauls to people wanting to lose weight, according to health officials.

Now, authorities say, teenagers are getting methamphetamine from numerous sources—from drug dealers on the street to other youths on high school campuses. Other teenagers are becoming dealers themselves.

"It reaches the point where someone who is maybe addicted to the drug realizes that selling the drug not only keeps them with a steady supply of meth, but also provides money that allows them to buy more," Mountain said.

In recent months, teens from the affluent communities of Blackhawk, Danville and Alamo have gone on crime sprees to support their methamphetamine habits.

Several Danville youths were charged with burglary earlier this year after allegedly stealing golf clubs from open garages in Blackhawk. The teens sold the equipment to a sporting goods store to get money for drugs, according to police.

"It's the drug that gets people in a lot of trouble," said Martin Starr, a counselor at New Connections, a drug program in Concord. "They get aggressive, they get nasty and they stop going to school or get into arguments at home."

Methamphetamine can be made virtually anywhere. Pickup trucks, backpacks and motel bathtubs have all doubled as fully functioning labs.

"The majority of people who manufacture this drug learn just by watching somebody else do it one or two times," said John Coonce, who coordinates the Drug Enforcement Agency's methamphetamine lab task force in Washington. "You don't have to be a rocket scientist or chemist to cook it."

San Bernardino County ranked first in the state in lab busts last year with 154; Los Angeles County ranked second with 115, according to law enforcement statistics compiled by the Western States Information Network.

In the nine-county Bay Area, 15 labs were raided in Santa Clara County, 12 in Contra Costa County and 11 in Alameda County.

Until the mid-1980s, methamphetamine producers commonly used a liquid chemical called phenyl-2-propanone, or P2P, to make the drug. The P2P and other easily obtained ingredients were mixed in ether.

"Whenever law enforcement agents smell ether, they get suspicious," said Henry Rapoport, professor emeritus of chemistry at the University of California at Berkeley. "Why would there be ether, unless you were working at a hospital or doing chemistry?"

To avoid detection, producers in the mid-1980s began making methamphetamine with ephedrine, a drug extracted from the desert shrub ephedra that is used as a decongestant in over-the-counter cold medicines. Anyone who visited the corner drugstore, in essence, could make methamphetamine that was more potent and purer than could be produced using the P2P method.

In 1987, California enacted legislation restricting bulk sales of ephedrine to pharmaceutical companies. But the crackdown failed to halt massive ephedrine shipments to Mexico and, more recently, to neighboring Guatemala. The majority

of shipments—an estimated 170 tons last year—came from China, India, Thailand, the Czech Republic, the United Arab Emirates, Germany and Switzerland.

Fueling the drug's popularity has been a sharp drop in its price. Four years ago, a pound of methamphetamine in San Francisco cost $6,000, compared with $4,500 today.

Much of the decrease in the drug's price is attributed to an increased role in narcotics trafficking by well-organized Mexican drug syndicates, which not only distribute heroin, cocaine and marijuana but also smuggle methamphetamine and chemicals used in the drug-making process.

'The majority of people who manufacture this drug learn just by watching somebody else do it one or two times'
—*D.E.A. AGENT JOHN COONCE*

"The Mexican nationals have brought the price way, way down and they're undercutting just about everyone else," said Berkeley Police Sergeant Dennis Ahearn, who heads the department's undercover narcotics detail.

In addition to ephedrine, Mexican syndicates have begun trafficking in pseudoephedrine, a chemical cousin of ephedrine, which they can obtain legally in tablet form through East Coast mail-order outlets. Drug enforcement officials and the Food and Drug Administration are hastening efforts to have pseudoephedrine declared a controlled chemical.

The chemicals used in methamphetamine labs are extremely volatile. Red phosphorus, for example, can convert to yellow phosphorus and explode. Phosphene gas released during methamphetamine production can cause a person to collapse seconds after inhalation. Concoctions can get too hot and catch on fire.

Hydriodic acid, similar to the acid used in swimming pools, is particularly hazardous. Methamphetamine producers and drug agents alike have suffered collapsed lungs after breathing the fumes.

"It creates a very, very nasty mineral acid burn to the lungs," said Roger Ely, senior forensic chemist at the DEA's lab in San Francisco. "Basically you get

chemical pneumonia, which builds fluid in the lungs until you drown in it."

Like other methamphetamine ingredients, hydriodic acid has been restricted, but producers manager to smuggle it, purchase it or simply make their own.

Drugs agents in Southern California found the bodies of two men five days after an apparent hydriodic acid spill. One of them had stuffed his mouth with dirt to stop the burning in this throat.

Another danger is the toxic waste that results from making methamphetamine. The deadly by-products are often found seeping into the ground or are haphazardly dumped into nearby streams or drains. Drug agents routinely don protective gear and respirators before entering labs. After each raid, private toxic waste contractors are summoned to clear up the chemicals, at a cost of up to $125,000 per lab.

During the July 13 raid in Byron, agents were amazed to find equipment and chemicals—P2P, ephedrine and pseudoephedrine—specific to all three methamphetamine production methods. Methamphetamine producers usually specialize in one procedure, said drug officers.

Agents arrested a resident of the home, Norene Kovach, 30, and Stephen Vanderveer, 32, of Newark, on suspicion of conspiracy to manufacture, possess and intent to distribute methamphetamine.

Inside the shed, investigators found a large cylinder of hydrogen chloride gas and nearly 20 gallons of amber liquid, apparently methamphetamine "oil." The ventilation system consisted of a fan on the east side of the shed. On the ground was a drain where waste was allegedly dumped.

In a garage attached to the house, agents found containers labeled chloroform, acetone and toluol. The latter two solvents are flammable. More hazardous materials, 275 gallons in all, were found in large plastic containers in a truck near the shed. Investigators, who say the cleanup cost $66,000, believe the producers planned to use chemicals in the leftover waste to make more methamphetamine.

The Byron lab was a "throw-back to the past" because it was run by people with ties to the Hell's Angels, said Bill Ruzzamenti of the Drug Enforcement Agency's office in San Francisco.

Police sources said the Byron operation was set up by Blair Gutherie, whom authorities considered one of Northern

California's most notorious methamphetamine manufacturers. Kovach's husband, George, was reportedly trained to run the lab by Guthrie, 50, and has been linked to the Hell's Angels.

But George Kovach and Guthrie had a falling out. In 1993, Kovach was shot three times—once in each shoulder and once in the groin, a technique known in motorcycle-gang parlance as "clipping the wings." Kovach refused to cooperate with authorities and no charges were filed.

On July 3 of this year Guthrie was found dead in a burning Chevrolet Blazer on Twitchell Island in Sacramento County. Guthrie, who had been sought by myriad law enforcement agencies since December, was shot three times in an apparent "wing-clipping" ritual.

On July 12, George Kovach, 43, was shot three times while attending a funeral in Richmond for Guthrie. The assailant, who mingled with 200 mourners at Rolling Hills Memorial Park, fired eight rounds, scattering the crowd.

By the time Richmond police arrived, only 20 people remained—and few were talking. There have been no arrests.

Drug agents, knowing they had to act quickly unless they wanted to jeopardize 18 months of undercover work, converged on the Kovach home the next morning. That same day, George Kovach checked out of John Muir Medical Center in Walnut Creek—against medical advice—and disappeared.

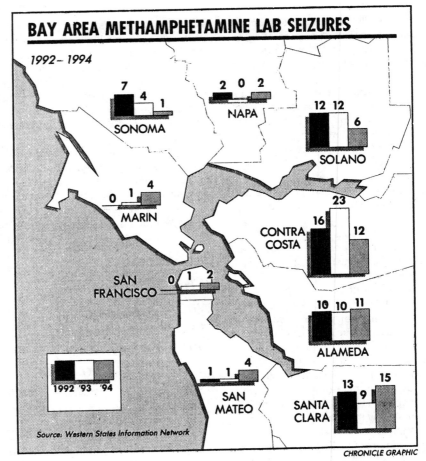

BAY AREA METHAMPHETAMINE LAB SEIZURES

1992–1994

SONOMA 7 4 1

NAPA 2 0 2

SOLANO 12 12 6

MARIN 0 1 4

CONTRA COSTA 16 23 12

ALAMEDA 10 10 11

SAN FRANCISCO 0 1 2

1992 '93 '94

SAN MATEO 1 1 4

SANTA CLARA 13 9 15

Source: Western States Information Network

CHRONICLE GRAPHIC

Wired in California

Meth, the drug that snuffed out the Summer of Love, is back, and California is exporting it all over the nation

Anthony R. Lovett

ANTHONY R. LOVETT *is a free-lance writer based in Los Angeles.*

AN HOUR EAST OF LOS ANgeles is the San Gabriel Valley, a sprawl of tract homes and minimalls where the big attraction is a theme park called Raging Waters. Out here, far from the smog and crime of downtown, the teen-agers do not care about cocaine, ecstasy or other glamorous drugs of the big city. They prefer getting spun, as they call it, on crystal methamphetamine.

And suddenly there's plenty of it around. According to Brenda Heng, an agent with the California Bureau of Narcotics Enforcement (CBNE), amphetamine use is reaching epidemic proportions on the West Coast. "Even crack is not as widespread in this state as methamphetamine," she says. "The market is flooded, so more and more people are doing it."

In 1993, the CBNE seized 360 clandestine meth labs, about 160 more than the federal Drug Enforcement Administration (DEA) seized nationwide. Speed-related emergency-room visits are up; drug counselors are treating a greater number of kids messed up on the drug.

Authorities have attempted to stem this flood of speed not only by imposing tough mandatory-minimum sentences but also by classifying certain "precursors" – chemicals essential in the manufacture of methamphetamine – as Schedule II substances. (Drugs are rated under federal law from Schedule I to V in terms of their effects, medical use and potential for abuse.) Ironically, many amphet-

amines come under the less serious Schedule III.

The federal mandatory minimum sentence for trafficking 10 to 99 grams of meth is five years; for 100 grams or more, it's 10 years. The feds even target the small-time user. The Anti-Drug Abuse Act of 1988 allows the Department of Justice to ask for a civil penalty of up to $10,000 for illegal possession of small amounts of meth for "personal use."

What brought on the new deluge of methamphetamine? According to sources at the FBI and DEA and local law-enforcement agencies, the organized biker gangs that once controlled the production and distribution of speed from San Diego to Sacramento have in recent years been pushed aside. Now, Mexican nationals are producing export-size quantities of high-grade methamphetamine, some of it in factories located south of the border, where the key ingredient, ephedrine, is not a controlled substance. The rest of the supply seems to be coming from huge, environmentally hazardous labs located in remote areas throughout California.

"The Mexican labs we've seized have far greater production capabilities than the bikers ever dreamed of," says Heng. "And the stuff they're producing is 90 percent pure, which is amazing considering the filthiness of these labs. The bikers could never touch that kind of purity level." The purity is partly responsible for the surge in speed-related emergency-room visits in California during the past

year. The other prominent factor is the sheer number of new recruits – especially white, male teen-agers.

Ken, 18, works three jobs. He lives in the heart of the San Gabriel Valley, where not too long ago he spent his days and nights getting spun on "oda" (meth) and "just clucking away." Now, Ken says he has stopped using, but with demand as high as it is, he can't resist dealing a little.

Meth is relatively inexpensive to produce, and the current street price is comparable to cocaine's, so meth offers a greater profit margin without the risks of smuggling. Out in the San Gabriel Valley, small-time dealers can pick up an ounce of meth for $600 to $900. On the street, a gram sells for about $100 for average quality; $150 for "glass," which is extremely pure. The once-popular, less-pure form of speed known as crank is the cheapest of all, but demand has dwindled. "I really don't know anyone who still deals around with that crank shit," says Ken. "Everyone tries for crystal.

"Speed is a really big deal out here, because so many people are making it," Ken continues. "San Dimas, La Verne, Covina, Glendora, are the biggest manufacturers of methamphetamine. There's a lot of cooks around here. They go from hotel to hotel."

And the demand is high, especially for crystal meth, which teen-agers here recently began smoking in glass pipes. The fearless kids of the San Gabriel Valley call it "sucking the glass dick."

Donna Mognett, a licensed psychotherapist in Covina, Calif., works with

AMPHETAMINES ELEVATE mood, heighten endurance and eliminate fatigue, which explains their popularity with the military. American army airmen stationed in Great Britain in WWII took 180 million benzedrine pills.

teens who have run into trouble with drugs. Mognett calls speed "the most frustrating problem" she has dealt with in 20 years of practice. "We've seen some pretty bizarre behavior and done some serious interventions in my time in order to get through to the patient," says Mognett, "but [speed] doesn't compare. These kids have no response. They're flattened, turned off, pathological. Their thought processes are so skewed, they can't think properly."

Mognett thinks the real culprit here is not the dealer or the manufacturer but the user's own low self-esteem. For this, she puts the onus on parents and the school system, both of which Mognett accuses of failing to pose an educational and ethical challenge for young people.

"A lot of these kids are from good families," Mognett says, "and what I see quite often is that they've been given too much freedom. The school day is very short; many students are on the street by 1 in the afternoon."

In his six years of practice at Charter Oak Hospital, in Covina, Dr. Said Jacob has seen a marked increase in white, teenage, male speed freaks who use the drug "to give them more energy for sports and for sex — especially for sex." Jacob has also noted a decrease in the age of his patients, having treated some regular meth users as young as 11.

Dr. Raymond Manning works with depressive disorders at Las Encinas Hospital, in Pasadena. He treats plenty of speed abusers, because "coming off the drug is so bad, and the depression it brings is so severe, that the user tends to do more [speed] rather than go through coming down again." Manning points out that meth tends to be highly addictive for two other reasons: It is very stimulating, and tolerance grows quickly, as does the user's intake.

"Amphetamine is a sympathomimetic drug," says Manning. "It mimics the effects of naturally occurring brain chemicals called catecholamines, which have a profound effect on our central nervous system." Like cocaine, amphetamine alters the brain receptors for dopamine,

norepinephrine and serotonin — all of which affect our perception of pleasure.

While an extended state of euphoria is the intended goal, the side effects of prolonged use can range from mild panic to extreme paranoia accompanied by hallucinations. Jacob is currently treating a number of patients who, despite quitting speed some years ago, still experience aural and visual hallucinations. And addicts tend to be extremely violent.

AMPHETAMINE WAS FIRST SYNthesized in 1887 but didn't become popular until the pharmaceutical giant Smith Kline and French introduced it as Benzedrine, a nasal inhaler, in 1932. The Depression was in full swing, Prohibition was in effect, and the new drug was almost immediately abused by those looking for a new kick. Clever users soon discovered how to remove the inhaler's Benzedrine strip, which was then soaked in coffee — a picker-upper favored by the great jazz saxophonist Charlie "Bird" Parker. Methamphetamine, more potent than amphetamine and easy to make, originated in Japan in 1919. The crystalline powder is freely soluble in water, making it the perfect candidate for intravenous use and abuse. Smoking the drug creates a rush almost as intense as injecting it, a fact that accounts (along with fear of needles) for the number of suburban kids lighting up. Still legally produced in the U.S. and most often prescribed for weight loss, meth is sold under the trade name Desoxyn.

Amphetamines tend to elevate mood, heighten endurance and eliminate fatigue — all of which explain the drug's popularity with the military. Methedrine, a brand of amphetamine in tablet form, was favored by German panzer troops, and according to medical records, Hitler was injected up to eight times a day with meth. Japanese factory workers, soldiers and pilots were given methamphetamine. American Army Air Corps personnel stationed in Great Britain took good ol' Benzedrine — 180 million pills. The practice continued through the Korean War and reached a fever pitch in Vietnam. Between 1966 and 1969, Americans ingested more government-issued speed in

Vietnam than all British and American troops in World War II.

Speed has been characterized as a trailer-park drug for decades. Traditionally, it was the drug of choice for long-distance truckers and college students pulling all-nighters. It has a high potential for abuse, however, and can, when misused over a long time, contribute to psychosis and violent behavior. "Look at some of the most violent crimes making the news," Heng says. "Like the Polly Klaas murder, where they found methamphetamine in the [accused killer's] trailer."

California is not the only state choking on an overabundance of speed. But the glut of product here has forced producers to seek new markets away from the West Coast. "Now, when we talk to other states," says Heng, "they're tying their labs and their big meth seizures back to people in California. And they're not too happy about that, either." The logic of this expansion is obvious, says Heng: "If you can sell it for twice as much in Florida, why not?" According to DEA statistics, only a few states have not reported a surge of this potent speed from California. "It's not something we're terribly proud of," says Heng.

Two other states are currently seeing a different kind of product: designer speed. In Hawaii, it's called ice, a superpure form of meth especially prepared for smoking. The effects of crystal meth, when smoked, can last well over four hours. Ice can keep the user high for up to 24 hours. Five years ago, the media were buzzing with stories of an impending mainland U.S.A. invasion that would make the crack problem pale in comparison. Meth consumption in the continental U.S. may have increased in the interim, but ice has remained most popular in the Japanese, Filipino and Korean communities in Hawaii. Joe Parra of the DEA's Honolulu office thinks the reason is culturally related.

"It goes back to the '30s and '40s, when the use of amphetamine was pushed in Japan to enhance the industrial output of their society," Parra says. "And they trained the Koreans to manufacture amphetamine. That's remained an integral part of their society."

Meanwhile, in Michigan, a drug called cat (short for Methcathinone) has become a problem for users and police alike. "If you're smart enough to fog up a mirror, you're smart enough to make cat," says Jim McGivney, a public affairs officer with the DEA. Also called goob and morning star, cat is an extremely potent analog of amphetamine that can be whipped up from solvents purchased at a hardware store. For this same reason, the stuff is potentially lethal.

Cat seems to have been first produced in Michigan's Upper Peninsula, but it has spread throughout the state and into Wisconsin. Cat users are loyal to their low-rent drug. McGivney says: "Put a pound of coke and a pound of cat on a table and come back in an hour. The coke will still be there."

Talk to any law-enforcement official in just about any state and you'll hear that, yes, speed is indeed a problem to one degree or another. Yet, according to Heng, no one's listening. "If people really knew what was going on out there," she says, "they wouldn't stand for it, but the issue just isn't sexy at this point."

Other Trends and Patterns in Drug Use

Rarely do drug-related patterns and trends lend themselves to precise definition. Identifying, measuring, and predicting the consequences of these trends is an inexact science, to say the least. It is, nevertheless, a very important process.

Some of the most valuable data produced by drug-related trend analysis is the identification of subpopulations whose vulnerability to certain drug phenomena is greater than that of the greater population. These identifications may forewarn of implications for the average population. Trend analysis may produce specific information that may otherwise be lost or obscured by general statistical indications. The percentage of persons smoking tobacco, for example, reflects significant declines over the last decade. Consistent but general indicators reflect the mitigating of a most nefarious public health problem. Overall—good news. But what about the indications for teenage girls? Trends there are not positive, and the implications for further problems with tobacco and other drugs are not good. Recent studies of specific age groups continue to report alarming increases in smoking by adolescent girls. Tobacco is probably the most prominent of gateway drugs, with repeated findings pointing to the correlation between the initial use of tobacco and later usage of other drugs. This increase might easily go unnoticed in a review of general statistics. Subsequently, the analysis of specific trends related to smoking is very important, as it provides a threshold from which educators, health care professionals, parents, and young people may respond to this significant health threat.

Another important example, analogous to the illustration on smoking, is shown by research investigating drug use by females of low socioeconomic status. This research suggests that drug use as a variable has been found to be more strongly correlated with the variable of economic status than of race. Women of African and Caucasian backgrounds and of low economic status express greater similarities in drug use patterns than do African women and Caucasian women of mixed economic levels. One important implication of this finding is that prenatal injuries to babies brought about by the mother's use of drugs may similarly cross racial barriers to a greater degree than previously believed. The often-held stereotype that crack babies are a problem only within African American communities is an excellent example.

Information concerning drug use patterns and trends, obtained from a number of different investigative methods, is available from a variety of sources. On the national level, the more prominent sources are the National Institute on Drug Abuse, the Drug Abuse Warning Network, the National Centers for Disease Control, the Justice Department, the General Accounting Office, and the Surgeon General. On the state level, various justice departments, including the attorney general's office, the courts, state departments of social services, state universities and colleges, and public health offices, maintain data and conduct research. On local levels, criminal justice agencies, social service departments, public hospitals, and health departments provide information. On a private level, various research institutes and universities, professional organizations such as the American Medical

Association, and the American Cancer Society, hospitals, and treatment centers as well as private corporations are tracking drug-related trends. Surveys abound with no apparent lack of available data. Subsequently, there is an obvious need for examination of research methods and findings for reliability and accuracy.

The articles in unit 4 provide information about some drug-related trends occurring within certain subpopulations of Americans. While reading the articles, contemplate whether the trends and patterns described are confined to specific geographical areas.

Looking Ahead: Challenge Questions

How do trends related to drinking by college students in Florida and Indiana compare? Is an increase in LSD use by high school students in California reflected in other states?

Are declines and increases of drug and alcohol use in the 1980s holding steady into the 1990s?

What factors cause drug-related trends and patterns to change?

How are drug-related patterns and trends related to specific subpopulations of Americans?

How significant is socioeconomic class in influencing drug trends?

Overview of Key Findings

Lloyd D. Johnston, Patrick M. O'Malley, and Jerald G. Bachman

TRENDS IN ILLICIT DRUG USE

- In [a] previous volume . . . we noted that there was an increase in 1992 in the use of a number of illicit drugs among the eighth graders and some reversals among the seniors in key attitudes and beliefs. More specifically, the proportions seeing great risk in using drugs began to decline as did the proportions saying they disapproved of use. We stated that these developments were "very important because they could presage an end to the improvements in the drug situation that the nation may be taking for granted". Unfortunately, that is exactly what it presaged: The use of illicit drugs rose sharply in 1993 in all three grade levels as attitudes and beliefs about them eroded further. So, 1993 was a year in which a turnaround in the long decline occurred for a number of drugs among the nation's secondary school students.

- *Marijuana* use rose sharply in all three grade levels. In the case of eighth graders, this was the second year of increase. Among college students and all young adults, however, marijuana use leveled in 1993, following an earlier rise in use. One in forty high school seniors is a daily marijuana user (2.4%, up from 1.9% in 1992). This is still far below the peak rate of 10.7% daily use reached in 1978.

- Among seniors, the proportions using **any illicit drug other than marijuana** in the past year rose from 14.9% to 17.1%, a rate which is still substantially below the 34% peak rate in 1981. There was little further change for college students or young adults, 13% of whom report such use in 1993.

- Since 1989 there has been an increase in the use of **LSD**—a drug of the late 1960s and early 1970s—among college students and young adults. In 1992, all five populations showed an increase in annual prevalence of LSD use though the one-year increase was statistically significant only among eighth graders (from 1.7% to 2.1%). In 1993, the eighth, tenth, and twelfth graders showed further increase, though this time only the twelfth grade change was significant. The 1989–1992 increase for college students (from 3.4% to 5.7%), and for young adults (from 2.7% to 4.3%) ended in 1993.

Just prior to the significant increase in use among seniors, there was a significant 4.3% decline in 1992 and a nonsignificant, but continued decline in 1993 in the proportion seeing great risk associated with trying LSD. In 1992 there was also a two percentage point decline (nonsignificant) in the proportion disapproving it and this trend continued in 1993. Since LSD was one of the earliest drugs popularly used in the overall American drug epidemic, there is a distinct possibility that young people—particularly the youngest cohorts, like the eighth graders—are not as concerned about the risks of use. They have had less opportunity to learn vicariously about the consequences of use by observing others around them, or to learn from intense media coverage of the issue. This type of "generational forgetting" could set the stage for a whole new epidemic of use.

- Prescription-controlled *stimulants*—one of the most widely used classes of drugs taken illicitly (i.e., outside of medical regimen)—also showed evidence of a turnaround in 1993, with annual and 30-day prevalence rates increasing among four of the five populations. (Young adults were the exception.) Annual prevalence had fallen from 20% in 1982 to 7% in 1992 among seniors and from 21% to 4% among college students. The increase in use among seniors in 1993 followed a sharp drop in perceived risk a year earlier. In 1993, perceived risk continued to decline and disapproval of amphetamine use began to decline as well. This pattern is consistent with our theoretical position that perceived risk can drive both use *and* disapproval.

- The *inhalants* constitute another class of abusable substance where we observe a troublesome increase in 1993. This class of drugs is defined by the form of the substance and its mode of administration—fumes or gases which are inhaled to get high. It includes common household substances such as glues, aerosols, butane, solvents, and so on. One class of inhalants, *amyl and butyl nitrites*, became somewhat popular in the late 1970s, but their use has almost been eliminated. For example, annual prevalence among twelfth grade students was 6.5% in 1979 but 0.9% in 1993.

When the nitrites are removed from consideration it appears that all other inhalants taken together have had an upward trend in use, from 3.0% among seniors in 1976 to 7.0% in 1993. It appears from the retrospective usage data supplied by twelfth grade students that the increase in inhalant use (unadjusted to include the nitrites) also increased at lower grade levels, where

From *National Survey Results on Drug Use* from the Monitoring the Future Study (Volume II, 1975-1993), 1994, pp. 11-25.
Reprinted by permission of the National Institute on Drug Abuse, U.S. Department of Health and Human Services.

inhalant use is more common, during the late 1980s. In 1993 all five populations showed some modest increase in inhalant use, though only the increases in eighth and tenth grade (both of which increased last year as well) reached statistical significance. Some 11% of the 1993 eighth graders and 8% of the tenth graders indicated some inhalant use in the prior 12 months, making inhalants the most widely used class of illicitly used drugs for eighth graders and the third most widely used (after marijuana and stimulants) for the tenth graders. The inhalants can and do cause death, and tragically, this often occurs among youngsters in their early teens.

- The use of *crack* cocaine appeared to level in 1987 at relatively low prevalence rates, at least within these populations. (This occurred despite the fact that the crack phenomenon continued a process of diffusion to new communities that year.) In 1993, annual prevalence held steady at 1.5% for seniors (down from 3.9% in 1987). Among young adults one to ten years past high school, annual prevalence was 1.3%, but only 0.6% among college students—both relatively unchanged since 1991. In high school, annual crack prevalence among the college-bound is lower than among those not bound for college (1.2% vs. 2.7%). There is now rather little regional variation in crack use.

We believe that the particularly intense media coverage of the hazards of crack cocaine, which took place quite early in what could have been a considerably more serious epidemic, likely had the effect of "capping" that epidemic early by deterring many would-be users and by motivating many experimenters to desist use. While 2.6% of seniors report ever having tried crack, only 0.7% report use in the past month, indicating noncontinuation by 73% of those who try it. The longer-term downward trend can be explained both in terms of lower initiation rates among students and higher noncontinuation rates.

Unfortunately, while use did not rise in 1993, perceived risk and disapproval dropped in all three grade levels, which could presage an increase in use in 1994.

- *Cocaine* in general began to decline a year earlier than crack; between 1986 and 1987 the annual prevalence rate dropped dramatically by roughly four-tenths in all three populations studied.* As we had predicted earlier, the decline occurred when young people began to see experimental and occasional use—the type of use in which they are most likely to engage—as more dangerous; and this happened by 1987, probably partly because the hazards of cocaine use received extensive media coverage in the preceding year, but almost surely in part because of the cocaine-related deaths in 1986 of sports stars Len Bias and Don Rogers.

In 1992, this broad decline continued, with annual prevalence falling by nonstatistically significant amounts in all populations *except* eighth graders, who actually showed a statistically significant increase in use. Annual prevalence of cocaine use fell

---

*Unless otherwise specified, all references to "cocaine" refer to the use of cocaine in any form, including crack.

by about two-thirds among the three populations for which long-term data are available. In 1993 cocaine use remained stable in all five populations except the young adults, where use continued to decline.

As with crack, the story regarding attitudes and beliefs is more troubling. Having risen substantially since 1986, the perceived risk of using cocaine in general showed no further change in 1991 among seniors and actually showed some (nonsignificant) decline in 1992. In 1993, perceived risk for cocaine other than crack fell sharply in all grades and disapproval began to decline in all grades, though not as sharply as perceived risk. As with crack, these changes in attitudes and beliefs do not auger well for usage rates next year.

Through 1989, there was no decline in perceived availability of cocaine; in fact, it rose steadily after 1984 suggesting that decreased availability played no role in bringing about the substantial downturn in use. After 1989, however, perceived availability has fallen some among seniors; the decline may be explained by the greatly reduced proportions of seniors who say they have any friends who use, because friendship circles are an important part of the supply system. Eighth and tenth graders reported a significant increase in the availability of crack and other cocaine in 1992, but there was no significant change in 1993.

As with all the illicit drugs, lifetime cocaine prevalence climbs with age, exceeding 30% by age 28. Unlike all of the other illicit drugs, active use—i.e., annual prevalence or monthly prevalence—also climbs after high school.

- *PCP* use fell sharply, from an annual prevalence of 7.0% in 1979 to 2.2% in 1982 among high school seniors. It reached a low point of 1.2% in 1988, increased a bit to 2.4% in 1989, and then fell back to 1.4% by 1991, where it has remained through 1993. For the young adults, the annual prevalence rate is now only 0.2%.

- The annual prevalence of *heroin* use has been very steady since 1979 among seniors at 0.4% to 0.6%. (Earlier, it had fallen from 1.0% in 1975.) It stands at 0.5% in 1993. The heroin statistics for young adults and college students have also remained quite stable in recent years at low rates (about 0.1% to 0.2%). Eighth and tenth graders have an annual prevalence about the same as, or slightly higher than twelfth graders (0.7%) which is probably due to the fact that the eventual dropouts are captured in the lower grades but not in twelfth grade. Their rates remained unchanged in 1993.

- The use of *opiates other than heroin* had been fairly level over most of the life of the study. Seniors had an annual prevalence rate of 3% to 6% since 1975. In 1991, however, the first recent significant decline (from 4.5% to 3.5%) was observed, though no further changes occurred in 1992 or 1993. Young adults in their twenties have generally shown a very gradual decline from 3.1% in 1986 to 2.2% in 1993; college students have likewise shown a slow decrease, from 3.8% in 1982–1984 to 2.5% in 1993. Data are not reported for younger grade levels because we believe the students are not accurately discriminating among the drugs which should be included or excluded from this class.

4. OTHER TRENDS AND PATTERNS IN DRUG USE

- A long and substantial decline, which began in 1977, occurred for *tranquilizer* use among high school seniors. By 1992 annual prevalence reached 2.8% compared to 11% in 1977, but there was a significant increase in 1993 to 3.5%. For the young adult sample, annual prevalence has now declined to 3.1% and for the college student sample to 2.4%.

- The long-term gradual decline in *barbiturate* use, which began at least as early as 1975, when the study began, halted in 1988; the annual prevalence among seniors fell to 3.2%, compared to 10.7% in 1975. (It stands at 3.4% in 1993.) Annual prevalence of this class of sedative drugs is even lower among the young adult sample (1.9%), and lower still among college students specifically (1.5%). For these groups there has been little further change since 1988. As with the opiates other than heroin, we do not include data here for lower grades because we believe the younger students have more problems with the proper classification of relevant drugs.

- *Methaqualone*, another sedative drug, has shown quite a different trend pattern than barbiturates. Its use rose steadily among seniors from 1975 to 1981, when annual prevalence reached 8%. It then fell rather sharply to 0.5% by 1991 and stands at 0.2% in 1993. Use also fell among all young adults and among college students, which had annual prevalence rates of only 0.3% and 0.2%, respectively in 1989—the last year in which they were asked about this drug. In recent years, shrinking availability may well have played a role in this drop, as legal manufacture and distribution of the drug ceased. Because of its very low usage rates, only the seniors are now asked about their use of this drug.

- In sum, five classes of illicitly used drugs which have had an impact on appreciable proportions of young Americans in their late teens and twenties are *marijuana, cocaine, stimulants, LSD*, and *inhalants*. In 1993, high school seniors showed annual prevalence rates of 26%, 3%, 8%, 7%, and 7%, respectively. Among college students in 1993, the comparable annual prevalence rates are 28%, 3%, 4%, 5%, and 4%; and for all high school graduates one to ten years past high school (young adults) the rates are 25%, 5%, 4%, 4%, and 2%. It is worth noting that LSD has climbed in the rankings because it either has not declined, or in some cases has increased, during a period in which cocaine, amphetamines, and other drugs have declined appreciably. The *inhalants* have become relatively more important for similar reasons.

Clearly, cocaine is relatively more important in the older age group and inhalants are relatively more important in the younger ones. In fact, inhalants are the most widely used of the illicit drugs in eighth grade.

- The annual prevalence among seniors of over-the-counter *stay-awake pills*, which usually contain caffeine as their active ingredient, nearly doubled between 1982 and 1990, increasing from 12% to 23%. Since 1990 this statistic has fallen back some to 19% in 1993. Increases also occurred among the college-age young adult population (ages 19–22), where annual prevalence had been as high as 26% in 1989, but is now down to 19% in 1993.

The other two classes of nonprescription stimulants—the *look-alikes* and the over-the-counter *diet pills*—have also shown some fall-off among both seniors and young adults in recent years. Still, among seniors some 23% of the females have tried diet pills by the end of senior year, 12% have used them in the past year, and 5% in just the past month.

College-Noncollege Differences

- American college students (defined here as those respondents one to four years past high school who were actively enrolled full-time in a two- or four-year college) show annual usage rates for a number of drugs which are about average for their age group, including *any illicit drug, marijuana* specifically (although their rate of *daily marijuana use* is about two-thirds what it is for the rest of their age group, i.e., 1.9% vs. 2.7%), *hallucinogens, MDMA, heroin, LSD, opiates other than heroin*, and *tranquilizers*. For several categories of drugs, however, college students have rates of use which are below those of their age peers, including *any illicit drug other than marijuana, cocaine, crack* cocaine specifically, and *barbiturates*. They have a slightly higher rate of use for *inhalants* (3.8% vs. 2.7%).

Since college-bound seniors had below average rates of use on all of these illicit drugs while they were in high school, their eventually attaining parity on many of them reflects some closing of the gap. As results from the study published elsewhere have shown, this college effect of "catching up" is largely explainable in terms of differential rates of leaving the parental home and of getting married. College students are more likely to have left the parental home and less likely to have gotten married than their age peers.

- In general, the trends since 1980 in illicit substance use among American college students have been found to parallel those of their age peers not in college. That means that for most drugs there has been a decline in use over the interval. Further, all young adult high school graduates through age 28, as well as college students taken separately, show trends which are highly parallel for the most part to the trends among high school seniors, although declines in the active use of many of the drugs over the decade of the 1980s was proportionately larger in these two older populations than among high school seniors. In 1993, this general parallel in trends was not evident; the upturn seen among the secondary school students was not replicated in the post-high school population.

Male-Female Differences

- Regarding sex differences in the three older populations (seniors, college students, and young adults), males are more likely to use *most illicit drugs*, and the differences tend to be largest at the higher frequency levels. *Daily marijuana use* among high school seniors in 1993, for example, is reported by 3.3% of males vs. 1.5% of females; among all young adults aged 19–32 by 3.5% of males vs. 1.6% of females; and among college students, specifically, by 2.6% of males vs.

1.3% of females. The only significant exception to the rule

1.3% of females. The only significant exception to the rule that males are more frequently users of illicit drugs than females occurs for *stimulant* use in high school, where females are at the same level or slightly higher. The sexes also attain near parity on *stimulant*, *tranquilizer*, *barbiturate*, *heroin*, and *other opiate* use among the college and young adult populations.

- In the eighth and tenth grade samples, however, there are fewer sex differences in the use of drugs—perhaps because the girls tend to date older boys who are in age groups considerably more likely to use drugs. There is little male-female difference in eighth and tenth grades, for example, in the use of *inhalants*, *cocaine*, and *crack*. As with the older age groups, *stimulant* use is slightly higher among females.

TRENDS IN ALCOHOL USE

- Regarding *alcohol* use in these age groups, several findings are noteworthy. First, despite the fact that it is illegal for virtually all high school students and most college students to purchase alcoholic beverages, experience with alcohol is almost universal among them (67% of eighth graders have tried it, 81% of tenth graders, 87% of twelfth graders, and 91% of college students) and active use is widespread. Most important, perhaps, is the widespread occurrence of **occasions of heavy drinking**—measured by the percent reporting five or more drinks in a row at least once in the prior two-week period. Among eighth graders this statistic stands at 14%, among tenth graders at 23%, among twelfth graders at 28%, and among college students at 40%. After the early twenties this behavior recedes somewhat, reflected by the 32% found in the entire young adult sample aged 19-32.

- Regarding trends in alcohol use, during the period of recent decline in the use of marijuana and other illicit drugs there appears not to have been any "displacement effect" in terms of any increase in alcohol use among seniors. (It was not uncommon to hear such a displacement hypothesis asserted.) If anything, the opposite seems to be true. Since 1980, the monthly prevalence of alcohol use among seniors gradually declined, from 72% in 1980 to 51% in 1993. *Daily use* declined from a peak of 6.9% in 1979 to 2.5% in 1993; and the prevalence of drinking *five or more drinks in a row* during the prior two-week interval fell from 41% in 1983 to 28% in 1993—nearly a one-third decline.

In 1993 there were no statistically significant changes in any of the populations in the prevalence of drinking in the prior 30-days, i.e., current prevalence." There was a significant increase in the binge drinking rate for the tenth grade population. Eighth graders showed increases on both measures, though they were not statistically significant.

College-Noncollege Differences in Alcohol Use

- The data from college students show a quite different pattern in relation to alcohol use. They show less drop-off in monthly prevalence since 1980 (82% to 72% in 1993) and slightly less

decline in *daily use* (6.5% in 1980 to 3.2% in 1993). There has also been little change in *occasions of heavy drinking*, which is at 40% in 1993—considerably higher than the 28% among high school seniors. Since both their noncollege-age peers and high school seniors have been showing a net decrease in occasions of heavy drinking since 1980, the college students stand out in having maintained a very high rate of binge or party drinking. Since the college-bound seniors in high school are consistently less likely to report occasions of heavy drinking than the noncollege-bound, this reflects their "catching up and passing" their peers after high school in their rates of binge drinking.

- In most surveys from 1980 onward, college students have had a *daily drinking* rate (3.2% in 1993) which is slightly lower than that of their age peers (4.3% in 1993), suggesting that they are more likely to confine their drinking to weekends, on which occasions they tend to drink a lot. Again, college men have much higher rates of daily drinking than college women: 5.9% vs. 1.1%. The rate of daily drinking has fallen considerably among the noncollege group, from 8.7% in 1981 to 4.3% in 1993.

Male-Female Differences

- There remains a quite substantial sex difference among high school seniors in the prevalence of **occasions of heavy drinking** (21% for females vs. 35% for males in 1993); this difference generally has been diminishing very gradually since the study began over a decade ago.

- There also remain very substantial sex differences in alcohol use among college students and young adults generally, with males drinking more. For example, 49% of college males report having five or more drinks in a row over the previous two weeks vs. 33% of college females. However, there has been little change in the differences between 1980 and 1993.

TRENDS IN CIGARETTE SMOKING

- A number of important findings have emerged from the study concerning *cigarette smoking* among American adolescents and young adults. Of greatest importance is the fact that by late adolescence sizeable proportions of young people still are establishing regular cigarette habits, despite the demonstrated health risks associated with smoking. In fact, since the study began in 1975, cigarettes have consistently comprised the class of substance most frequently used on a daily basis by high school students.

- While the *daily smoking* rate for seniors did drop considerably between 1977 and 1981 (from 29% to 20%), it has dropped very little during the intervening twelve years (by only another 1.0%, to 19% in 1993) despite the appreciable downturn which has occurred in most other forms of drug use (including alcohol) during this period. And, despite all the adverse publicity and restrictive legislation addressed to the subject during the 1980's, the proportion of seniors who perceive "great risk" to the user of suffering physical (or other) harm from pack-a-day smoking has risen only by 5.8% since 1980 (to 70% in 1993). That means that nearly a third of seniors still do not feel there is a great risk associated with smoking.

- The story may be even more troublesome at the lower grade levels. While we do not have long-term trends from eighth and tenth graders, their current smoking rates were up significantly in the past year to 17% and 25%, respectively. Of particular concern, only 53% of the eighth grade students and 61% of the tenth grade students think that a pack-a-day smoker runs a great risk of harm from that behavior. This fact suggests that the health message has not reached American youngsters at the ages when most of the eventual smokers first initiate smoking. Further, there is no indication of any increase in perceived risk (or of disapproval) of smoking in these age groups. Given that cigarette smoking is the greatest preventable cause of death and disease in the country, the need for a more intense and effective prevention effort aimed at younger children is clearly very great.

Age and Cohort-Related Differences

- Initiation of daily smoking most often occurs in grades 6 through 9 (i.e., at modal ages 11–12 to 14–15), with rather little further initiation after high school, although a number of light smokers make the transition to heavy smoking in the first two years after high school. Analyses presented in this volume and elsewhere have shown that cigarette smoking shows a clear "cohort effect." That is, if a class (or birth) cohort establishes an unusually high rate of smoking at an early age relative to other cohorts, it is likely to remain high throughout the life cycle.
- As we reported in the "Other Findings from the Study" chapter in the 1986 volume in this series, some 53% of the half-pack-a-day (or more) smokers in senior year said that they had tried to quit smoking and found they could not. Of those who were daily smokers in high school, nearly three-quarters were daily smokers 7 to 9 years later (based on the 1985 survey), despite the fact that in high school only 5% of them thought they would "definitely" be smoking 5 years hence. Clearly, the smoking habit is established at an early age; it is difficult to break for those young people who have it; and young people greatly overestimate their own ability to quit. And with the addition of eighth and tenth grade students to the study, we now know that younger children are even more likely than older ones to underestimate the dangers of smoking.

College-Noncollege Differences

- A striking difference in smoking rates exists between college-bound and noncollege-bound high school seniors. For example, smoking half-pack or more a day is more than twice as prevalent among the noncollege-bound (19% vs. 8%). Among respondents one to four years past high school, those not in college show the same dramatically higher rate of smoking compared to that found among those who are in college, with half-pack-a-day smoking standing at 20% and 9%, respectively.

Male-Female Difference

- Since 1980, among college students, females have had slightly higher probabilities of being daily smokers. This long-standing sex difference has not been true of their age peers who are not in college.

RACIAL/ETHNIC COMPARISONS

While we have published articles elsewhere on ethnic differences in drug use, this is only the third volume in this series to include prevalence and trend data for the three largest ethnic groupings—whites, blacks, and Hispanics taken as a group. (Sample size limitations simply do not allow finer subgroup breakdowns unless many years are combined). Further, 1991 was the first year in which we had data on eighth and tenth graders, for whom ethnic comparisons would be less likely to be affected by differential dropout rates among the three groups, than would be true for seniors. A number of interesting findings emerge in these comparisons, and the reader is referred to Chapters 4 and 5 for a full discussion of them.

- Black seniors have consistently shown lower usage rates on most drugs, licit and illicit, than white students; and we now know that this also is true at the lower grade levels. In some cases, the differences are quite large.
- Black students have a much lower prevalence of *daily cigarette smoking* than white students (4% vs. 21% in senior year) because their smoking rate continued to decline after 1983, while the rate for whites stabilized.
- In twelfth grade, *binge drinking* is much less likely to be reported by black students (13%) than by white (31%) or Hispanic students (27%).
- In twelfth grade, of the three groups, whites have the highest rates of use on a number of drugs, including *inhalants, hallucinogens, LSD* specifically, *barbiturates, amphetamines, tranquilizers, opiates other than heroin, alcohol* and *cigarettes*. In 1993 *marijuana* usage rates are about equivalent for whites and Hispanics, but whites have previously had the highest rates.
- However, in senior year, Hispanics have the highest usage rate for a number of the most dangerous drugs: *cocaine, crack, other cocaine,* and *heroin*. Further, in eighth grade, Hispanics have the highest rates not only on these drugs, but on many of the others, as well. For example, in eighth grade, the lifetime prevalence for Hispanics, whites, and blacks is 20%, 11%, and 9% for *marijuana*; 7%, 4%, and 1% for *hallucinogens*; 52%, 47%, and 34% for *cigarettes*; 21%, 13%, and 11% for *binge drinking*; etc. In other words, Hispanics have the highest rates of use for nearly all drugs in eighth grade, but not in twelfth, which suggests that their considerably higher dropout rate (compared to whites and blacks) may change their relative ranking by twelfth grade. Hispanics on average also may have a tendency to begin use earlier—a hypothesis yet to be tested.

- With regard to trends, seniors in all three racial/ethnic groups exhibited the recent decline in *cocaine* use, although black seniors did not show as large an increase in use as did whites and Hispanics; therefore, their decline was less steep.
- For virtually *all of the illicit drugs*, the three groups have tended to trend in parallel. Because white seniors had achieved the highest level of use on a number of drugs—including *stimulants, barbiturates, methaqualone*, and *tranquilizers*—they also had the largest declines; blacks have had the lowest rates, and therefore, the smallest declines.
- Important racial/ethnic differences in *cigarette smoking* have emerged among seniors during the life of the study. In the late 70's, the three groups were fairly similar in their smoking rates; all three mirrored the general decline in smoking from 1977–1981. Since 1981, however, a considerable divergence has emerged: Smoking rates have declined very little, if at all, for whites and Hispanics, but the rates for blacks continued to decline steadily. As a result, in 1993 the daily smoking rates for blacks is one-fifth that for whites.

DRUG USE IN EIGHTH GRADE

It may be useful to focus specifically on the youngest age group in the study—the eighth graders—who are about 13 to 14 years old, because the exceptional level of use that they already have attained helps illustrate the urgent need this country has to continue to address the problems of substance abuse among its young.

- By eighth grade 67% of youngsters report having tried *alcohol* and more than a quarter (26%) say they have already been drunk at least once.
- *Cigarettes* have been tried by nearly half of eighth graders (45%) and 17%, or one in six, say they have smoked in the prior month. Only 53% say they think there is great risk associated with being a pack-a-day smoker.
- *Smokeless tobacco* has been tried by 30% of the male eighth graders, is used currently by 11% of them, and is used daily by 2.9%. Rates are far lower among the female eighth graders.
- Among eighth graders, almost one in five (19%) have used *inhalants* and 5% say they have used in the past month. This is the only class of drugs for which use is substantially higher in eighth grade than in tenth or twelfth grade.
- *Marijuana* has been tried by one in every eight eighth graders (13%), and has been used in the prior month by 5.1%.
- A surprisingly large number say they have tried prescription-type *stimulants* (12%); 3.6% say they have used them in the prior 30 days.
- Consistent with the retrospective reports from seniors, which have been included in this series in previous years, relatively few eighth graders say they have tried most of the other illicit drugs yet.

But the proportions having at least some experience with them still is not inconsequential: *tranquilizers* (4.4%), *LSD* (3.5%), *other hallucinogens* (1.7%), *crack* (1.7%), *other co-*caine (2.4%), *heroin* (1.4%), and *steroids* (1.6% overall, and 2.5% among males.)

- The very large numbers who have already begun use of the so-called "gateway drugs" (tobacco, alcohol, inhalants, and marijuana) suggests that a substantial number of eighth grade students are already at risk of proceeding further along the fairly orderly progression of involvement.

SUMMARY AND CONCLUSIONS

To summarize the findings on trends, over the last decade or so there have been appreciable declines in the use of a number of the *illicit drugs* among seniors, and even larger declines in their use among American college students and young adults more generally. However, we have previously warned, the stall in these favorable trends in all three populations in 1985, as well as an increase in active *cocaine* use that year, should serve as a reminder that these improvements are not inevitable and cannot be taken for granted.

While the general decline resumed in 1986 and, most importantly, was joined by the start of a decline in *cocaine* use in 1987 and *crack* use in 1988, in 1992 we heard a number of alarm bells sounding. While the seniors continued to show improvement on a number of measures in 1992, the college students and young adults did not. Further, the attitudes and beliefs of seniors regarding drug use began to soften. Perhaps of greatest importance, the eighth graders exhibited a significant increase in *marijuana, cocaine, LSD*, and *hallucinogens other than LSD*, as well as a not-quite significant increase in *inhalant* use. (In fact, all five populations showed some increase on *LSD*, continuing a longer term trend college students and young adults.)

In 1993 still more alarms went off. The eighth graders continued to show an increase in their use of a number of drugs and (as their prior shifts in attitudes and beliefs foretold) the tenth graders and twelfth graders joined them. Rises are seen in a number of the so-called "gateway drugs"—in this case *marijuana, cigarettes,* and *inhalants*—which may bode ill for the use of later drugs in the usual sequence of involvement. The softening of attitudes about *crack* and other forms of *cocaine* also is a basis for concern.

As this study has demonstrated over the years, changes in perceived risk and disapproval have been important causes of the downturns which have occurred in the use of a number of drugs. These beliefs and attitudes surely are in turn influenced by the amount and nature of the public attention being paid to the drug issue. The fact that this attention has declined so substantially in the past few years may help to explain why the increases in perceived risk and disapproval among students ceased, and some clear backsliding has begun.

Of particular concern here is not only the possibility that there may be an increase in the use of particular drugs like LSD and inhalants, but that we may be seeing the beginning of a turnaround in the drug abuse situation more generally among our youngest cohorts—perhaps because they have not had the same opportunities for vicarious learning from the adverse drug

4. OTHER TRENDS AND PATTERNS IN DRUG USE

experiences of people around them and people they learn about through the media. Clearly there is a danger that, as the drug epidemic has subsided considerably, newer cohorts have far less opportunity to learn through informal means about the dangers of drugs. This may mean that the nation must redouble its efforts to be sure that they learn these lessons through more formal means—from schools, parents, and focused messages in the media, for example—and that this more formalized prevention effort become institutionalized so that it will endure for the long term.

The following facts help to put into perspective the magnitude and variety of substance use problems which remain among American young people:

- By the end of eighth grade, one-third (32%) of American secondary school students have tried an *illicit drug* (if inhalants are included as an illicit drug). Almost two-fifths of tenth graders have done so (39%), and nearly one-half of twelfth graders (47%).
- By their late twenties, 75% to 80% of America's young adults today have tried an *illicit drug*, including over 50% who have tried some *illicit drug other than* (usually in addition to) *marijuana*. Even for high school seniors these proportions are 43% and 31%, respectively.
- By age 28, about one-third of young Americans have tried *cocaine*; and as early as the senior year of high school 6% have done so. Roughly one in every forty seniors (2.6%) have tried the particularly dangerous form of cocaine called *crack*: in the young adult sample one in twenty-five (4.3%) have tried it.
- One in forty (2.4%) of high school seniors in 1993 smoke *marijuana daily*, as is true among young adults aged 19 to 28 (2.4%). Among seniors in 1993, 9.6% had been daily marijuana smokers at some time for at least a month, and among young adults the comparable figure is 12.8%.
- Some 28% of seniors have had *five or more drinks in a row*

at least once in the prior two weeks, and such behavior tends to increase among young adults one to four years past high school. The prevalence of such behavior among male college students reaches 49%.
- Some 30% of seniors are current *cigarette* smokers and 19% already are current daily smokers, and these numbers are *rising*. In addition, many of the lighter smokers will convert to heavy smoking after high school. For example, more than one in every five young adults aged 19 to 28 is a daily smoker (21%).
- Thus, despite the improvements in recent years, it is still true that this nation's secondary school students and young adults show a level of involvement with illicit drugs which is greater than has been documented in any other industrialized nation in the world. Even by longer-term historical standards in this country, these rates remain extremely high. Heavy drinking also remains widespread and troublesome; and certainly the continuing initiation of a large and growing proportion of young people to cigarette smoking is a matter of the greatest public health concern.
- Finally, we note the seemingly unending capacity of pharmacological experts and amateurs to discover new substances with abuse potential that can be used to alter mood and consciousness, as well the potential for our young people to "discover" the abuse potential of existing products, like Robitussin™, and to "rediscover" older drugs, such as LSD. While as a society we have made significant progress on a number of fronts in the fight against drug abuse, we must continually be preparing for, and remaining vigilant against, the opening of new fronts, as well as the re-emergence of trouble on older ones.
- In sum, the drug problem is not an enemy which can be vanquished, as in a war. It is more a recurring and relapsing problem which must be contained to the extent possible on a long term, ongoing basis.

Pot Surges Back, It's Like a Whole New World

Melinda Henneberger

BABY BOOMERS with fond memories of marijuana brownies and bong hits around the lava lamp may not be particularly alarmed by last week's news that pot is making a major comeback among teen-agers. But the culture of cannabis, which currently goes by name like "chocolate tide" and "chronic," has grown considerably more dangerous in the years since the flower children left Haight-Ashbury to the cappuccino merchants.

More efficient agriculture—new methods of harvesting and processing marijuana plants—has made pot about 20 times more potent than the marijuana on the street in the '60s and '70s, drug treatment experts and law enforcement officials say. And the dramatic increase in teen-age violence and the advent of AIDS, these experts say, have made any drug use that lowers inhibition far riskier.

"Some adults, some parents, may be looking back and romanticizing the pot times of the '60s and '70s and saying, 'What's the point of my getting tough with my kid?' " said Dr. Mitchell S. Rosenthal, president of New York-based Phoenix House, the country's largest residential drug treatment organization. "They say, 'I got through O.K. What's the big deal?' But they ignore how much more potent marijuana is today."

The generation that laughed through "Reefer Madness," the hysterically overstated 1930's cautionary film, may also be ignoring new findings about the nature of addiction and the effect of marijuana use on memory, the lungs and the immune system. The data, Dr. Rosenthal said, clearly suggest that pot was never harmless.

But perhaps in part because earlier messages about the dangers of drug use were so overheated and hyperbolic, the serious research of recent years has not gotten a wide hearing.

Bummer, man: Marijuana is getting more popular, more expensive and more dangerous.

Last week, researchers at the University of Michigan reported that the 50,000 junior and senior high school students surveyed were much less concerned about the ill effects of drug use than in earlier years.

The survey registered a sharp rise in teen-agers' use of marijuana and less dramatic increases in the use of LSD and other drugs. Until last year, when pot smoking registered a modest increase, drug use had been declining for more than a decade. But in 1993, marijuana use among eighth graders increased twice as fast as in the previous year.

In a less-than-scientific survey at four New York City high schools, all of the several dozen students interviewed also said that pot-smoking is pervasive, and perceived as a harmless distraction.

"Other drugs are dangerous," said Carl Thomas, a 10th-grader at William H. Taft High School in the Bronx. "Nobody smokes crack. That will destroy you, you get skinny and you're nothing no more. We only smoke weed around here in the '90s."

Drug treatment experts and law enforcement officials, however, say that all drug use is closely linked to teen violence, crime, sex and H.I.V. transmission. And the number of guns in the hands of teen-agers makes today's drug scene less mellow than in the days when the occasional paranoid pot-smoker was merely a wet blanket—not a potential threat.

"Some people can't handle when they smoke, so you've got to have a gun or a person at the door to search everybody," Mr. Thomas said.

The current drug culture has changed in so many other ways that old hippies would hardly know their way around the head shop.

Phillies Blunt T-shirts and black baseball caps emblazoned with a marijuana leaf are the fashion among teens who roll giant joints by slicing open cigars—Blunts, White Owls or Dutch Masters—replacing the tobacco with pot, which in the vocabulary of this generation is not grass but skunk or boom.

Pot is relatively expensive these days: $5 "nickel bags" have shrunk to the size of a postage stamp and usually contain just enough pot for a single joint. But prices vary widely, based not so much on quality as on the neighborhood or area of purchase, with more affluent urban and suburban buyers paying more.

Psychedelic posters that were popular 25 years ago have given way to renderings of cartoon characters like Bugs Bunny smoking pot. Cheech and Chong's comedy albums have been replaced by videos like the one for "Method Man" by Wu Tang Clan, who raps, "I got fat bags of skunk, I got White Owl Blunt and I'm about to go get lifted."

And beyond their preferred accouterments and artists, today's marijuana users are themselves quite different from the pot-smoking predecessors. They're far less political, and their drug use is rarely an expression of social protest or even of rebellion against authority.

"It's definitely not tied to political protest now—You've got *Republicans* smoking pot," said Doug Crowell, a 12th-grader at Trinity School, a private school on the Upper West Side of Manhattan.

"It's different than it was in the '60s because it's not just your obvious stoner types," he said. "It's the jocks and the A-plus students. It's just about everybody."

Jamar Williams, a 17-year-old student at DeWitt Clinton High School in the Bronx, said he feels he is one of a small minority of the teen-agers he knows who do see any danger in the drug.

WORDS ON THE STREET

POT Skunk, boom.
TO GET HIGH To get lifted, booted, red, smoked out or choked out.
$3 BAG OF POT A tray.
$5 BAG OF POT A nick.
$40 BAG A sandwich bag.
KINDS OF MARIJUANA Chronic, chocolate tide, indigo, Hawaiian, Tropicana.
WATER PIPE SIMILAR TO A BONG A shotgun.
JOINTS Replaced by "blunts," after the Phillies Blunt cigars that pot smokers cut open, hollow out and fill with marijuana. Other favorite brands used to roll "blunts" are White Owls and Dutch Masters.

"A lot of people like to do it because you get dizzy and laughing, like you don't want to come home and you don't feel the cold," he said. "But people can't get off of it too easy. It seems like they have to do it."

Some teens who smoke pot are just experimenting, as young people have always done, but drug counselors say that many of today's users have more serious problems than the teens who smoked marijuana a generation ago, and are more likely to be looking for an escape than a thrill.

Because they're smoking at a younger age, the drug counselors say, they're also at greater risk.

"It used to be young adults, the under-30 generation that had already gotten past some of the hurdles of development before they got involved with drugs," said Suzanne M. Murphy, executive director of Canarsie AWARE, a Brooklyn drug treatment center with programs for adolescents. "But 12-year-old kids are literally slowed down because they're not interested in physical activity or in any of the things they need to be doing."

Lee P. Brown, President Clinton's chief drug policy adviser, promises that the new national drug control strategy scheduled to be announced by the President this week will get through to young people with age-specific and "culturally relevant" prevention programs.

But teen-agers—and even their parents—seem hard to convince.

A 17-year-old from Kinnelon, N.J., who is in a residential drug treatment program, said: "For me personally, I didn't care if it was addictive or not. But it's been said that it's not, so most everyone is smoking it. I've been in here for 15 months, but I've been hearing that even the ones who are quiet—the geeks—even they're smoking pot now."

Are America's College Students Majoring in Booze?

The age-old activity of drinking, once considered a rite of passage on college campuses, has fallen under increased scrutiny. Some researchers report that alcohol consumption has reached "epidemic" proportions and are calling for wide-ranging changes on campus. More moderate voices hope to teach students to drink responsibly.

Stephen Goode

To most Americans, alcohol consumption by college students is as natural and expected as graduating in June. But according to the Center on Addiction and Substance Abuse, or CASA, at New York's Columbia University, student drinking is becoming a major problem that educators ignore at their peril.

A May report, *Rethinking Rites of Passage: Substance Abuse on America's Campuses*, uses terms such as "epidemic" and "crisis" to describe alcohol use — and abuse — at colleges and universities. The situation is so serious, the report concludes, that if circumstances don't change, a significant segment of the current generation of American college students will be lost to alcoholism and its aftereffects: wrecked careers, disastrous personal relationships and early death.

But not everyone is buying these claims or the conclusions. Ruth Engs, a professor of applied health science at Indiana University and longtime alcohol researcher, is one such naysayer. "There is no epidemic, there is no crisis," she says. "Students in Western culture have been drinking since the 12th century and will continue to do so."

Engs levels her greatest skepticism at the report's all-encompassing recommendations for change, including the transformation of what Jeffrey Merrill, CASA's vice president for policy and research, calls "the culture on campus."

The old campus culture glorified drinking as macho, natural and glamorous, explains Merrill. The new culture must regard drinking — especially heavy drinking — as "aberrant behavior" and "totally unacceptable."

To that end, the CASA report recommends that every campus undertake efforts to reeducate and retrain the young with the aim of discrediting the act of drinking as a "rite of passage" for students on their way to adulthood. But, says Engs, even if that aim is desirable and human nature so malleable, "it is too grand a scheme ever to work. It is ridiculous to expect colleges and universities to do more than they are already doing."

The report, which produced no new material but compiled data from a variety of recent surveys and publications, recounted that 42 percent of all college students engage in binge drinking (defined as consuming five or more drinks at one sitting). Among those who drink, the report concludes, a higher number are drinking more heavily than ever before. In Merrill's words, "What is startling is that more than one in three students are now drinking for the purpose of getting drunk."

But these are figures and statements that lead Engs to comment that "where they get this information is the really big question." She calls the CASA report "sloppy, with no peer review" and says it contains no careful explanation of how the information was extrapolated.

Engs points to a study she produced with colleague David J. Hanson of the State University of New York, Potsdam, which covers the decade from 1982 through 1991. During that period, Engs notes, the data they collected show that the percentage of student drinkers decreased from 82.4 percent to 78.8 percent, the total number of drinks consumed per week fell from 14.3 to 12.8 and there was no change in the percentage of heavy drinkers — hardly an indication that alcohol consumption has become rampant or dangerous to students. Three-quarters of student drinkers, she says, "were drinking moderately and responsibly."

According to Merrill, however, it's more honest to focus on negative drinking patterns. For example, CASA reports that 35 percent of female students are drinking heavily. That's a dispiriting finding, he says, because women are more prone than men to suffer from alcohol-related illnesses such as cirrhosis. Also of concern is the fact that 60 percent of college women who contract sexually transmitted diseases were drunk at the time, and 90 percent of rapes that occur on campus happen when alcohol is used by the perpetrator, the victim or both parties.

Engs says she doesn't believe that this information is news, because "drinking is a problem and always has been." Her own research shows that several alcohol-related problems are on the rise, including missed classes due to drinking, fights and vandalism. But she wonders if many of the statements about increased problems due to alcohol abuse might be what she calls "artifactual" — statistics that turn up because more researchers are studying the problem more closely than ever before, at a time when more people are willing to talk.

Others see another agenda at work. Jeffrey Becker, vice president for alcohol issues at the Washington-based Beer Institute, wonders if the CASA report is an example of what he calls "claims-making behavior" — an effort to maintain or increase funding levels for on-campus programs that deal with alcohol abuse.

Expense is one reason most campus alcohol programs remain limited in scope. University administrators find their hands tied in other ways as well. Federal funding for any program, for example, requires that a school advocate abstinence for anyone under age 21 (the nationwide legal drinking age) — at a time when many administrators argue that teaching moderate and responsible drinking probably is a more realistic approach to alcohol use among students.

In addition, administrators are concerned that any effort to bolster alcohol programs may render their schools liable for alcohol-related accidents that occur on campus. (Educators are examining closely a recent decision by the Delaware Supreme Court maintaining that colleges are not responsible for controlling student behavior — but that they are obligated "to care" about student behavior. But exactly what "care" means and how far it extends is unclear.)

CASA's Merrill commends colleges and universities that attempt to deal with alcohol abuse (95 percent have programs in gear, however small). Nevertheless, he finds the efforts "too haphazard and uncoordinated," a patchwork of programs that fail to fully address the problem.

The University of Maryland, for example, has allowed students to have a voice in setting policy: Alcohol can be served at parties only on weekends. Rutgers University, with a bow toward therapy, has set up special dorm rooms for students who have drinking (and drug-related) problems. Indiana University is an alcohol-free institution.

The CASA report is vague on what measures can be taken to reduce alcohol abuse, preferring to recommend that schools beef up and expand their programs. It does urge that a test be devised to rate colleges and universities on how well they deal with alcohol abuse on campus, and that the results of the test be published along with other data such as SAT scores. Parents and prospective students then can have a basis for comparison.

Critics wonder if a fair test could be devised, since most colleges don't always determine which crimes and other problems on campus are alcohol-related (or are reluctant to reveal crime statistics at all, although it is a federal requirement). Schools that are scrupulous about their statistics could gain unfair reputations compared with the less honest.

Sometimes CASA's suggestions are too general to offer practical value. The report, for example, attributes a large portion of student drinking to boredom and urges colleges to alleviate student ennui by providing "meaningful activities." In fact, many institutions do, some keeping gymnasiums open after midnight for basketball and other sports, for example. But it is difficult to imagine a university finding viable substitutes for every form of entertainment — countering the lure of bars or discos where alcohol is served — by offering often drab campus locations as alternatives for student get-togethers.

Alcohol advertising is a big issue as well. Abstinence advocates such as William Cullinane, executive director of the Marlboro, Mass.-based Students Against Driving Drunk, argues that alcoholic beverages should not be advertised on American campuses (approximately 35 percent of all college newspaper ads are alcohol-related). Others believe that banning such ads will not affect student alcohol consumption.

Hard data — with either bent — is hard to come by. In the early 1990s, the Bush administration issued two diametrically opposed reports. The first, a Health and Human Services release, said that no relationship between student alcohol consumption and advertising could be traced. The other, a study originating from the Office of the Surgeon General, claimed that alcohol ads glamorizing drinking by linking it to social success leads students to drink.

If the role such advertisements play in alcohol abuse remains questionable, most experts agree strict laws can change behavior. Nancy Schulte, director of the Drug Education Center at George Mason University, credits the tightening of drinking and driving laws during the last decade with sobering students up about the risks of driving drunk. (Schulte notes that at George Mason, a Virginia school in the Washington suburbs, student drinking in general — as well as binge drinking — declined between 1990 and 1992, according to a campuswide study.)

Experts argue that intensive campus programs are the best approach, as long as they're not laden with heavy moralizing. Schulte notes that George Mason's "is not a once-a-year 'awareness week' program" but a year-round project that includes such elements as internships for students who are interested in serving as counselors on alcohol issues. The best development in recent years, Schulte contends, is that alcohol abuse, once a "hush-hush subject" — particularly when it concerned women — now is very much in the open arena. "The stigma that once clung to people who couldn't control their drinking is gone," she says.

But just how much monitoring is realistic? Schulte notes that George Mason students have easy access to nearby Washington, where, she says, there are bars offering "an impressive array of [high-alcohol content] shooters." Engs notes that students at Indiana University's dry campuses drink in small groups at private apartments or other nonpublic places. She comments: "Can we ask school authorities to scour every student ghetto in university towns to uncover what drinking takes place?"

Peer-group counseling sometimes can overcome many of the questions raised by heavy moralizing and Big Brother scrutiny, and in one way or another, it is the approach that most campuses have adopted. According to

The best development in recent years is that alcohol abuse, once a 'hush-hush subject,' now is very much in the open arena.

Schulte, the key to approaching the freshman class, which includes the most active drinkers on campus, is to understand that "they want to be part of a group and hang out with them." Herein lies the solution to the problem: Get someone their own age that they respect to say, "This is what we do to be cool. We don't have a drink, and we certainly don't drink ourselves silly."

Fraternities and sororities — both of which, in most studies, often qualify as centers of abusive drinking — would do well to try the peer approach, says Drew Hunter, executive director of the BACCHUS and GAMMA Peer Education Network. (BACCHUS, the name of the Roman god of wine, is an acronym for Boosting Alcohol Consciousness Concerning the Health of University Students; GAMMA stands for Greeks Advocating Mature Management of Alcohol. The BACCHUS and GAMMA Network is a Denver-based group that addresses alcohol abuse on U.S. and overseas campuses.)

These days, says Hunter, Greek letter parties often are "bring your own booze" events; all alcoholic beverages are checked at the bar and use is monitored (a result of an increase in liability lawsuits in the late 1980s, according to Hunter). And many fraternity and sorority members have thrown themselves into community-related projects, spending evenings with local kids at baseball games and other sports events, for example. Therefore, says Hunter, when drinking occurs, "it starts later and is not likely to take on binge proportions."

Moderation advocate Engs offers a hypothesis. In high school, she says, students get the "'No, no, no' approach, and they're not told about overconsumption." But many students are at the age where rebellion is the norm, "and they don't believe what they're told. They see it as another piece of teacher propaganda, parent propaganda."

The best way to deal with student drinking isn't a "'no' policy," says Engs, but one that defuses the allure of alcohol by saying, "Yes, drink, but do it moderately." She advocates lowering the drinking age to 19 and offering alcohol at campus events as long as nonalcoholic beverages are available and lots of food is on hand. Such occasions can serve as training schools in moderation, she says.

Abstinence advocates such as SADD's Cullinane wonder if we're doing the young a grievous disservice by teaching them that some drinking is okay, when alcohol has proved so dangerous to society. "You're taking a maturing, developing body and saying to it, 'Go ahead, drink, even though it may harm you, or it may lead you to harm someone else,'" he says.

The debate continues. "Substance abuse, alcohol abuse, is a clear and present danger on American campuses. It is a fact we must come to terms with," claims CASA's Merrill.

Engs counters: "Why not emphasize the fact that alcohol can be a pleasurable experience and not only a negative one, as in a glass of good wine with a good meal?" She insists that the news that should be emphasized is that the majority of student drinkers drink moderately and responsibly and will continue to do so throughout their lives. They pace themselves. They know when to stop, and do, and they set an example for others.

The New View From On High

Trends: A wave of drugs floods the clubs

Most Americans reacted to the death of River Phoenix in October with at least a sigh of sympathy. Among a certain set, though, it sparked a grim curiosity. Early press reports of the actor's death by overdose mentioned GHB, an obscure and dangerous steroid substitute occasionally gulped down by West Coast thrill seekers. Never mind that according to a Los Angeles coroner's report GHB was not found in the actor's body. And never mind, too, that it's scarcely available outside a few Los Angeles nightspots. The hunt was on. "I'd never heard of GHB before. No one in New York had," said a Manhattan drug user last week. "This month it's the only drug."

Even drug abuse is subject to the whims of fashion. It's not that the old standards have quit the scene. Phoenix's death was apparently caused by a mixture of morphine, cocaine and other drugs. But members of his generation, mainly middle class and well educated, have turned to other, more exotic highs to fuel their nights. Whether it's Ecstasy at raves or DMT to launch the mind travel of self-styled "psychonauts," there's an alphabet soup of designer drugs to choose from. "It's a different culture of use," says Carlo McCormick, an editor of the New York trendsheet Paper and a student of drug culture. "These drugs are serving the same function that has existed for 20 years. They're just specific to a new generation."

And they're in plentiful supply. Alexander Shulgin, a pharmacologist at the University of California, Berkeley, has researched 179 potential intoxicants in one psychedelic chemical family alone, the phenethylamines. Forced to play a game of catch-up, last week the Drug Enforcement Administration hastily added one of them, 2C-B, to its schedule of controlled substances. But an informal survey last week by Miami club personality Julian Bain found that 2C-B, sold under the name Nexus, has already become the number-three drug of choice in South Beach.

Of all the drugs in the designer pharmacopeia, the most popular nationwide is MDMA, or Ecstasy. It's

Club Pharmacopeia

Special K (ketamine)
Cost $40-$50 per half gram
Effect Apparent weightlessness, disorientation
Who Uses Mainly New York gays

Ecstasy (MDMA)
Cost $20-$30 per pill
Effect Introspection, euphoria
Who Uses Ravers nationwide; British ravers and soccer fans

GHB
Cost $20 per ounce
Effect Alcohol-like drowsiness
Who Uses Body-builders, West Coast clubgoers

DMT
Cost $200 per gram
Effect Extreme perceptual alteration; "out-of-body" hallucination
Who Uses Serious "psychonauts"

Nexus (2C-B)
Cost $25-$35 per capsule
Effect Giddiness, visual effects
Who Uses Denizens of dance clubs in California and Florida

D Meth (methamphetamine)
Cost $60-$120 a gram
Effect Long-lasting manic energy
Who Uses Formerly bikers/blue collar, now West Coast ravers

been 10 years since "X" hit the bars, including some in Dallas where it could be bought with a credit card. Considered by many the ultimate "dance drug," X is often described as less disturbingly "trippy" than LSD and more serene than cocaine, which are considered cruder drugs. The white pills of MDMA give feelings of empathy and togetherness coupled with an up-all-night amphetamine rush. Despite nine MDMA laboratory busts in 1992, the Department of Health and Human Services reported 236 emergency-room visits involving the drug that year.

Designer-drug use tends to follow regional and demographic trends. With all the high-tech choices, getting high can now mean getting fairly specific. The New York City nightclub Bump! isn't named after the goofy disco dance, says staffer Marc Berkley. It's a tongue-in-cheek reference to a dose of ketamine (street name: Special K), a surgical anesthetic snorted by much of the club's mainly gay clientele in an attempt to magnify dance-floor sensations like lights, music and rhythm. The club has a 100-foot twisting slide lined with flashing lights. It's called the "K-Hole," the slang term for the episodes of numbed confusion that ketamine can induce.

Head rush: San Francisco's small but devoted DMT scene is a far more serious set. The orange powder causes a violent head rush that devotee Terence McKenna, author of "True Hallucinations," says can be used as an "epistemological tool" to understand the world. McKenna's trancelike public readings attract hundreds of fans. But if anyone's actually smoking the stuff, he's far from the crowd—anathema to the herd mentality bred by MDMA and ketamine. DMT has a nasty side effect: total physical collapse. "You're supposed to have someone there with you to take the pipe out of your hand," says Lon Clark, 27, a rave lighting designer who's seen it smoked.

In the clubs, advocates of the designer drugs claim psychological benefits including everything from enhanced self-image to emotional insight. Scientists, however, know little about the drugs' effects. Dr. George Ricaurte of Johns Hopkins recently found signs of damage to the nerves that release the neurotransmitter serotonin in former MDMA users. But Rick Doblin, president of the Multidisciplinary Association for Psychedelic Studies, a North Carolina group that promotes MDMA testing worldwide, disputes whether such effects are lasting or significant. Dr. Charles Grob of UC, Irvine, plans to test MDMA for possible medical applications like pain management for the terminally ill. Step one, set to begin at Harbor-UCLA Medical Center in Torrance, Calif., this month, will seek to determine the drug's toxic effects on the body. That's information from which young clubgoers could profit.

PATRICK ROGERS *with* PETER KATEL *in Miami*

CHOOSE YOUR POISON

While the government boasts that drug use has fallen, the range of intoxicants has increased, ensnaring a new generation

JILL SMOLOWE

IN NEW YORK CITY'S SPANISH HAR-lem, the highs come cheap. To create a "blunt," teenagers slice open a cigar and mix the tobacco with marijuana. To enhance the hit, they fashion "B-40s" by dipping the cigar in malt liquor. In Atlanta, police observed 100 teenagers and young adults at a rave party in an abandoned house—the rage among middle-class youths everywhere with money to burn—and their rich assortment of hooch: pot, uppers, downers, heroin, cocaine and Ecstasy, a powerful amphetamine. In Los Angeles, Hispanic gangs chill out by dipping their cigarettes in PCP (phencyclidine, an animal tranquilizer), while black gangs still favor rock cocaine. Some of the city's Iranians go in for smoking heroin, known as "chasing the tiger," while Arabs settled in Detroit prefer khat, which gives an amphetamine-like high and is also the drug of choice in Somalia.

The high times may be a changin', but America's drug scene is as frightening as ever. Last week the University of Michigan released a survey showing a rise in illicit drug use by American college students, with the most significant increase involving hallucinogens like LSD. Meanwhile a canvas of narcotics experts across the country indicated that while drug fashions vary from region to region and class to class, crack use is generally holding steady and heroin and marijuana are on the rise. Junior high and high school students surveyed by the government report a greater availability of most serious drugs. Law officials and treatment specialists on the front lines of the drug war report that the problem transcends both income and racial differences. "When it comes to drugs, there is a complete democracy," says Clark Carr, executive di-

rector of Narconon Professional Center in North Hollywood, California.

The government paints a much brighter picture. According to the 1992 Household Survey on Drug Abuse, released last month by the Department of Health and Human Services, the nationwide pattern of drug abuse is in decline. The study shows an 11% dip in illicit drug use by Americans 12 years or older, from 12.8 million in 1991 to 11.4 million in 1992. The drop is pronounced in all age groups except those 35 and over, who use drugs at a rate comparable to 1979 levels. Yet the number of hard-core abusers remains unchanged. And a smorgasbord of nouvelle intoxicants is being served up to a new generation of users.

The frenetic '80s infatuation with stimulants has become the mellower '90s flirtation with depressants. Heroin, which has a calming effect, is gaining on crack, which produces high agitation. Some drug experts sense a sociological sea change. "It's really relevant that in the '80s the drug of choice was one that the second you did it, you wanted more," says Carlo McCormick, an editor at a culture and fashion monthly who was the host of LSD parties in New York City in the '80s. "At this point with the current crop of drugs, you're set for the night." Others have a wider perspective. "If you look historically at a large population that has been using a stimulant like cocaine," says James Nielsen, a 26-year veteran with the Drug Enforcement Administration, "they will then go on to a depressant like heroin."

Ironically, the heroin surge also reflects a new health consciousness on the part of drug abusers. Youthful offenders, scared off by the devastation of crack, are dabbling in heroin instead, while

chronic crack addicts are changing over to heroin because of its mellower high and cheaper cost. Among both groups, fear of HIV transmission has made snorting, rather than injection, the preferred method of ingestion. "The needle is out, man," says Stephan ("Boobie") Gaston, 40, of East Harlem, a 26-year abuser. "All they're doing is sniffing." Even so, the risks remain high. Heroin-related incidents jumped from 10,300 during a three-month period in 1991 to 13,400 during a comparable period in 1992, according to a Federal Drug Abuse Warning Network survey of hospital emergency rooms. Heroin-treatment admissions have also increased over the past year.

The turn toward heroin is coupled with a sharp recognition among youthful abusers of the dangers of crack. Anthony M., 13, who is detoxifying from a marijuana habit at the Daytop Village Bronx Outreach Center in New York City, estimates that 20 or so of his 200 classmates use heroin or other drugs, but among them, only one goes in for crack. "That kid wanted others to do it too," he says, "but the other kids were like 'Nah,' because some of the kids, their parents had died because of crack."

Other hard-learned lessons seem not to affect young people today. LSD use among high school seniors reached its highest level last year since 1983, according to an annual study by the University of Michigan's Institute for Social Research. In the rave clubs of Los Angeles $2 to $5 buys a teenager a 10-to-12-hour LSD high. "LSD may be a prime example of generational forgetting," says Lloyd Johnston, principal investigator for the study. "Today's youngsters don't hear what an earlier generation heard—that LSD may cause bad trips, flashbacks schizophrenia, brain damage, chromosomal damage and so on.''

Marijuana, usually the first illegal drug sampled by eventual hard-core abusers, is also back in vogue. Of the 11.4 million Americans who admitted to using drugs within a month of the 1992 Household Survey, 55% referred solely to pot; an additional 19% abused marijuana in combination with other drugs. "Cannabis is the drug that teaches our kids what other drugs are all about," says Charlie Stowell, the DEA's cannabis coordinator in California. He says today's marijuana is considerably more potent and expensive than the pot of the '60s because the amount of THC—the ingredient that provides the high—has risen from 2% or 3% to 12%.

The '90s has also ushered in some drug novelties. Since the turn of the decade, gamma hydroxy butyrate, known as GHB, has been used illegally in the body-building community to reduce fat. Recent-

ly, however, youths have begun to abuse the drug to achieve a trancelike state. In New York City kids concoct a "Max" cocktail by dissolving GHB in water, then mixing in amphetamines. A different mix resulted in several overdoses in the Atlanta area in the past few months. Manhattan's hard-core sex community has also turned on to "Special K," or Cat Valium, an anesthetic that numbs the body.

The Administration appears to be pursuing several drug strategies simultaneously. The President has asked for a 7% rise in the budget for law enforcement as well as $13 billion for drug-control programs, an increase of $804 million over the current year. Last month Lee Brown, the Administration's drug czar, told a Senate subcommittee that the drug-control programs would now emphasize "demand-reduction programs" would now emphasize young people. Attorney General Janet Reno has also adopted a high profile on drugs, campaigning for a "national

agenda for children" that would attack the root causes of drug abuse and violence.

Meanwhile the daily challenge of containing the drug epidemic falls largely to local cops and DEA field offices. Ingenuity is the name of the game. In California, where 19% of the state's marijuana is grown indoors to evade detection, the DEA tracks purchases of illicit equipment, such as high-pressure sodium lights, to pick up the trail of growers. Minneapolis police have grown more sophisticated in tracking crack dealers who no longer keep cars, residences or bank accounts in their own names. "We've begun using financial records and become more knowledgeable in accounting and the flow of money," says Lieut. Bernie Bottema, supervisor of the city's narcotics unit. "We've had to rise to the level of our competition." It appears that level is not going to drop off anytime soon. —*Reported by Ann Blackman/ Washington, Massimo Calabresi/New York and Jeanne McDowell/Los Angeles*

One pill makes you larger, And one pill makes you small . . .

BEYOND PROZAC: Scientific insights into the brain are raising the prospect of made-to-order, off-the-shelf personalities

Sharon Begley

. . . That was 1960s pharmacology. In that turned-on, tuned-out decade, the pharmacopeia of mind-altering drugs was about as subtle as a sledgehammer—uppers replaced sleep, downers offered calm, hallucinogens projected visions of marmalade skies into the brain. Many of them were illegal, and all of them threatened to stop the heart, blow out neurons or cause permanent addiction. This is 1990s pharmacology: suffering stage fright before delivering a speech? Pop a little orange pill. Moping around in the winter doldrums? Try a white one. Want to boost your self-esteem, focus better on your work, tame the impulse to shop till you drop, shrug off your spouse's habit of littering the floor with underwear, overcome your shyness or keep yourself from blurting out your deepest secrets to the first stranger who comes along? Science has, or soon will have, just the legal, doctor-prescribed pill for you.

It's gone beyond Prozac. That antidepressant has spawned a culture of pill poppers: people who do not suffer from severe depression (for which the Food and Drug Administration approved Prozac in 1987) but who find that the little green and white capsule makes them more cheerful, more mellow, more self-assured. Now the same scientific insights into the brain that led to the development of Prozac are raising the prospect of nothing less than made-to-order, off-the-shelf personalities. For good or ill, research that once mapped the frontiers of disease—indentifying the brain chemistry involved in depression, paranoia and schizophrenia—is today closing in on the chemistry of normal personality. As a result, researchers are on the verge of "chemical attempts to modify character," writes neuro-psychiatrist Richard Restak in the soon-to-be-published "Receptors." Most of the new drugs will be aimed not so much at 'patients' as at people who are already functioning on a high level . . . enriching [their] memory, enhancing intelligence, heightening concentration, and altering for the good people's internal moods."

That prospect has brought psychopharmacology—the science of drugs that affect the mind—to "the brink of revolution," as

psychiatrist Stuart Yudofsky of Baylor University puts it. It is a revolution propelled by three advances. First came the theory that every memory, every emotion, every aspect of temperament originates in molecules called neurotransmitters. These chemical signals course through specialized circuits in the brain. Research on brain chemistry starting in the 1940s produced lithium, Valium and other psychoactive drugs, which correct chemical imbalances responsible for grave mental illness. Second, "brain mapping" pinpoints which areas of gray matter become active during particular thoughts or mental states. PET (positron emission tomography), for instance, is a sort of sonogram of the brain that can, among other things, trace sad thoughts to parts of the frontal cortex. Finally, researchers are identifying which neurotransmitters travel those circuits. For example, too much of the neurotransmitter dopamine in the brain's emotion centers, and too little in the seat of reason (diagram, "Mapping the Mind"), seems to cause suspiciousness—raving paranoia and maybe even a habit of wondering if the plumber overcharged you.

Major mental illness wasn't always linked to personality disorders. But according to the model of the mind emerging in the 1990s, mental disease differs from endearing quirks only in degree. Personality disorders arise from *subtle* disturbances in the same systems that produce serious mental illnesses, argues Dr. Larry Siever of Mount Sinai School of Medicine in New York. "Someone just barely able to restrain his impulsive actions wouldn't [seem] psychotic," says Siever. "But he could act rashly"—habitually ducking into a movie instead of going to work, or buying unseen property in Florida on a whim.

As neuroscientists learn what chemicals cause which personality traits, the temptation to fool around with nature will be irresistible. The drugs that perform the mental makeovers are supposed to have no serious side effects and not cause addiction. But more than 40 years of psychoactive drugs has proved that nothing is without hazard (at first, Valium, cocaine, and nicotine were not thought to be addictive, either). "If someone takes a drug every day for four years because it makes him feel or work better, something may happen that we don't know about," warns psychiatrist Solomon Snyder of Johns Hopkins University. That caution, however, has a difficult time standing up against the Faustian power of the new drugs. "For the first time in human history," says Restak, "we will be in a position to design our own brain." Some of the targets:

SHYNESS AND HYPERSENSITIVITY

Of all the traits that bedevil humans, shyness may be the most hard-wired into the brain. About 20 percent of people start life with neurochemistry that predisposes them to be shy, concludes Harvard University psychologist Jerome Kagan; the other 80 percent become shy or outgoing because of life's experiences. Now scientists may have figured out how biology becomes destiny. An inhibited child seems to be born with what amounts to a hairtrigger brain circuit: compared with other children, it takes much less to stimulate his amygdala, a small cashew-shaped structure deep in the brain that helps control heart rate and perspiration. No wonder shy infants squirm and cry: even mild stress makes their hearts pound and their palms sweat. In addition, inhibited children may have excessive levels of the neurotransmitter norepinephrine, a cousin of the fight-or-flight chemical adrenaline: just walking into kindergarten for the first time produces as much stress as a gladiator's facing the lions. "I think the time will come when we will know exactly the chemical profile of the temperamentally fearful child," says Kagan. "Then pharmacologists could work on very specific cures."

In some people, shyness is not a primary trait but instead a means of coping. "So much of social interaction is based on unspoken rhythms and pacing," says Mount Sinai's Siever, "that people who don't get those beats often feel left out and alienated"—like the woman who can't tell from body language that the man she's chatting with wants to flee. Society perceives her as slightly strange; she responds by withdrawing. Siever suspects that suspiciousness and an inability to process the information contained in the rhythms and cues of social interactions arise from an oversupply of dopamine in the brain's emotion-control room and a shortage in the more rational cortex.

One jobless, fiftyish man seemed to fit this description perfectly. He lived alone, filled his days with crossword puzzles and TV, and "worried that others were making fun of him,"

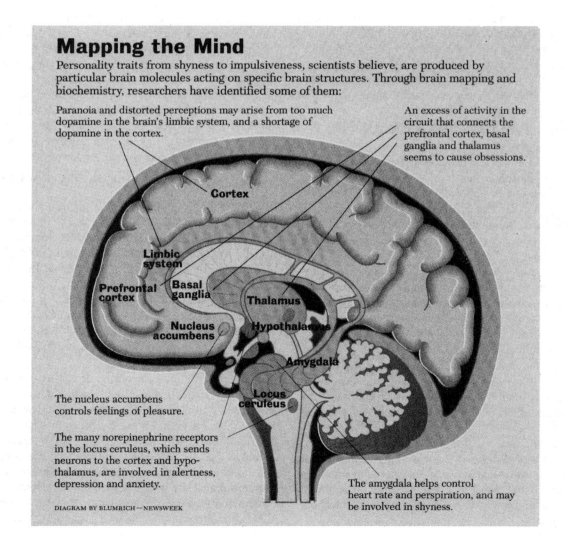

Mapping the Mind

Personality traits from shyness to impulsiveness, scientists believe, are produced by particular brain molecules acting on specific brain structures. Through brain mapping and biochemistry, researchers have identified some of them:

Paranoia and distorted perceptions may arise from too much dopamine in the brain's limbic system, and a shortage of dopamine in the cortex.

An excess of activity in the circuit that connects the prefrontal cortex, basal ganglia and thalamus seems to cause obsessions.

Cortex

Limbic system

Prefrontal cortex

Basal ganglia

Thalamus

Hypothalamus

Nucleus accumbens

Amygdala

Locus ceruleus

The nucleus accumbens controls feelings of pleasure.

The many norepinephrine receptors in the locus ceruleus, which sends neurons to the cortex and hypothalamus, are involved in alertness, depression and anxiety.

The amygdala helps control heart rate and perspiration, and may be involved in shyness.

DIAGRAM BY BLUMRICH—NEWSWEEK

4. OTHER TRENDS AND PATTERNS IN DRUG USE

says Siever. Like all of Siever's patients, he was seriously ill. Siever suspected, based on biochemical tests, that the man's inability to understand social cues stemmed from a dopamine imbalance. The antidepressant Wellbutrin, which stokes the cortex with dopamine, seemed to help: the man felt sharper and "more activated" (though a back disability kept him from working). Still, scientists caution that what works on the seriously ill might have no effect on someone who decides to cure her lack of social grace with a pill when all she needs is a crash course in etiquette.

Shyness can also grow in the shadow of hypersensitivity, the tendency to fall into a deep funk over even an innocuous rejection. For years, psychiatrist Donald Klein of Columbia-Presbyterian Medical Center in New York had noticed something strange about this funk: it closely resembled the reaction of an amphetamine user suffering withdrawal symptoms. That sparked a bold theory. "The brain is normally making its own stimulant," which keeps people on an even keel, and even makes them outgoing, says Klein. Some people who embarrass easily and cower at the very thought of rejection may do so because their brain does not pump out enough stimulants. They become physically pained by rejection just as a speed freak is physically pained by going cold turkey. "Recently we have shown that we can treat this by preserving the balance of stimulants in the brain and so blocking the withdrawal symptoms," says Klein. He and Columbia's Michael Liebowitz give hypersensitive patients Nardil, the trade name for a substance that blocks the destruction of the brain's natural uppers. As a result, it restores a healthy chemical balance in the hypersensitive mind. "With pills twice a day you usually see results in six weeks," says Klein.

IMPULSIVENESS AND OBSESSION

Just about everyone has, at one time or another, succumbed to the impulse to buy those goodies at the supermarket checkout. In more severe forms, such impulsive behavior expresses itself as kleptomania and other mental illnesses whose sufferers act first and think second. But mild or severe, impulsivity may arise from the inability to learn that behaviors have consequences, like punishment, and so must be controlled or modified.

Depending on where the impulsivity comes from, psycho-pharmacologists may soon know how to stifle it. As a teenager, did you repeatedly stay out until dawn despite getting grounded for it every time? Are you prone to doing what gets you fired? The problem may stem from too little serotonin, the chemical whose job it is to censor behavior that previously led to punishment, says Siever. Shortages of serotonin in the frontal lobes and in the brain's limbic system, where emotions come from, also seem to lift the lid off impulses. In this case, the dearth of serotonin seems to have the same effect as a shortage of ink in which to write life's lessons: the person is unable to connect disagreeable consequences with what provoked them. Or the problem may simply be an inept working memory. (*But Mom, I forgot you wanted me home!*) Working memory stores information while the mind considers whether it is worth keeping and how to file it. Working memory falters without enough dopamine.

There's a final suspect in impulsivity. Noticing everything can be as debilitating as noticing nothing. Norepinephrine tells the mind what's important by, in effect, putting a chemical red flag on it to say, "Look at this!" In normal people that system kicks in when, for instance, a lion is charging. But in people with too much norepinephrine *everything* gets pumped up. Every perceived slight from a co-worker demands a response, every twinge of desire becomes an irresistible urge to buy.

If impulsives think about their actions too little, obsessives think about them too much. When Mother double-checks that the sleeping children are indeed breathing, and when she's a stickler about dirt on the carpets or grime in the kitchen, she is being mildly compulsive; when she checks 100 times, vacuums 20 times a day and goes through Fantastik like an alcoholic through rotgut, she is manifesting obsessive-compulsive disorder. Sufferers seem unable to get a sense of completeness from any action, like scrubbing the bathtub a mere once. Brain imaging is now showing such obsession in living color. PETT scans of a patient touched with a dirty rag—cleanliness is a typical obsession—show a response like a broken record. Signals travel between three structures in the brain stem—the prefrontal cortex, the basal ganglia and the thalamus—endlessly. In normal people, the signal stops after one orbit thanks to a new message, screaming, *The floor is clean already!*" "Lots of people have milder variants of this," says neuroscientist Lewis Baxter of the University of California, Los Angeles. "They check the stove two times, though not 102. They say that intellectually they know the stove is OK, but they can't get the *emotional* boost that says, 'Hey, it's working'." Baxter believes that even mild compulsiveness might succumb to drugs that change the brain's regulation of serotonin. In fact, Prozac is about to be approved for use against obsessive-compulsive behavior. The great unknown is whether Prozac and other powerful drugs will work on milder forms of severe disorders.

ANXIETY AND CONCENTRATION

The neural pathways to anxiety exist because early humans who got a little nervous at the sight of, say, a crouching saber tooth had a survival edge over more laid-back tribesmen. Now, in the age of anxiety, many people would just as soon give back this legacy of natural selection. At the National Institute of Mental Health, Philip Gold is figuring out how. He traces stress to the circuit responsible for the fight-or-flight response. In the chronically anxious, he says, "it turns on, but it doesn't turn off." Antidepressants called tricyclics, which throttle back levels of the fight-or-flight norepinephrine, seem to still the perpetual arousal in the circuit.

A *shortage* of norepinephrine seems to rob people of the ability to pay attention to what's important, and only to what's important. Sally Jackson, the fortysomething owner of a Boston public-relations firm, knows the problem well. She had often felt unfocused, so last winter she began taking Ritalin, a stimulant that increases the availability of norepinephrine. Although Ritalin is best known as the controversial medication for children diagnosed with attention-deficit disorder (ADD, alias hyperactivity), adults are now taking the yellow pills to improve their concentration. "Without it, I would sit at my desk for

116

hours and get nothing done," says Jackson, who believes she has ADD. "But once I started Ritalin, every proposal I wrote, we won the account. I'm better on deadline and it keeps me focused on one task at a time." She swallows one pill in the morning and another if she hits a 3 p.m. lull.

I MEDICATE, THEREFORE WHO AM I?

Prozac to cheer you up and Ritalin to focus are merely the most prominent new mind drugs. Anticonvulsants such as Dilantin, prescribed for epileptics, turn out to reduce stress in some people. Beta blockers are heart drugs: they lower blood pressure and heart rate. But doctors figured out an entirely new use for them: combating stage fright. The drugs block receptors for norepinephrine; with less adrenaline igniting their brain circuits, people like oboist Stuart Dunkel, who plays for the Boston Opera, have no trouble calming performance anxiety. Before, complicated solos would make Dunkel's heart beat like a jackhammer and his breathing so shallow he couldn't sustain notes. With beta blockers, "there's a psychological release," he says. The drugs are not addictive, and Dunkel reports no side effects.

Other mind drugs are in the pipeline. One, with the tongue-tying name dexfenfluramine, seems to smooth out mood swings, especially those caused by winter doldrums and premenstrual syndrome. Naturally, it targets neurotransmitters: it keeps brain neurons bathed in serotonin longer than otherwise, explains Judith Wurtman of the Massachusetts Institute of Technology. Already used in Europe and South America as an anti-obesity drug (mood swings often trigger eating binges), dexfenfluramine has been submitted to the FDA for approval. A few weeks ago researchers at UC Irvine announced the discovery of the first drug that seems to improve working memory. The discovery sprang from work on neurotransmitters and their receptors, the shapely molecules that neurotransmitters fit like keys in locks (diagram). Researchers led by Gary Lynch found that in rats, the drug BDP binds to receptors for the neurotransmitter glutamate, which triggers neuronal changes that constitute memory. As a result, it acts like the father who lowers the basketball net for his vertically challenged child, reducing the amount of stimulation neurons require to form memories. If BDP works in people, the history lesson that once took hours to learn would take mere minutes. An Irvine-based start-up, Cortex Pharmaceuticals, Inc., plans to test BDP's safety.

Who could criticize a drug that stamps the rules for long division into your child's head after a single lesson? As psychiatrist Daniel Luchins of the University of Chicago points out, society accepts plastic surgery (albeit with some jokes): "If we have something that made people unshy, are they obliged to stay shy because of some ethical concern? What's the difference between 'I'm unhappy because I don't like my looks' and 'I'm unhappy because I'm shy?' "

For openers, one's core being is defined more by character traits than by the shape of one's nose. Just ask Cyrano. And not everything we feel, let alone everything we are, is shaped by too much or too little of some polysyllabic brain chemical. Yet as society moves ever closer to minds-made-to-order, the pressure on those who cannot, or choose not to, give their brain a makeover becomes intense. Some colleagues, and competitors, of Ritalin-popping executives feel themselves at a disadvantage, like rules-respecting sprinters facing a steroid user. Will guidance counselors urge parents to give their kids memory pills before the SATs? Will supervisors "suggest" workers take a little something to sharpen their concentration? The prospect of pills to make the dour cheery, and the tense mellow, calls into question the very notion of the self—is it truly the "self" in any meaningful sense if it is as easy to change as a bust measurement? "The brain is where our soul and spirit lie," says Harvard's Kagan. "People are very threatened by this."

Perhaps most worrisome is the idea of sandpapering away personality traits that not only make us individuals, but which evolved for a good reason. Anxiety, for instance, "probably evolved in tandem with the evolution of the human brain," writes Restak. Blunting that edge has a price. And just as physical pain keeps us from burning our flesh, perhaps mental pain, like that brought on by the death of a child, serves a purpose—one that is defeated by a pill that soothes when one should instead be raging. Shyness has also served civilization well. Some of history's great thinkers and creators—T. S. Eliot, Emily Dickinson, Anton Bruckner—were shy. "Inhibited children tend to wander off into vocations like music, literature and philosophy," says Kagan. A society that uses drugs to induce conformity does so at its peril.

With DEBRA ROSENBERG in Boston, JOSHUA COOPER RAMO in New York and MARY HAGER in Washington

Mail-Order Muscles

How big is the market for illegal bodybuilding drugs? Huge, says the author, who went on the trail of a steroid-selling scam

Rick Telander

A friend gave me the two-page order form and asked me what I thought of it. I glanced at the sheets and said I thought it was remarkable.

"It is nothing for someone on Steroids to gain 20 . . . 30 . . . or even 40 pounds of muscle in just 12 weeks or less!" the pages screamed. "Isn't it about time that YOU make your bodybuilding dreams a reality!! Make all that hard work pay off! TAKE ACTION NOW!" The form was from a Toronto company called Mass Machine, and it offered most of the anabolic steroids I'd heard of in my sporting and sportswriting careers.

"Can this be real?" my friend asked. I said I didn't know. It is illegal to sell or to use steroids for nonmedical reasons in the U.S. and Canada, but there have long been smuggling pipelines and underground sources for these drugs that are so coveted by bodybuilders and others seeking a shortcut to manliness. I told my friend I would try to find out what was going on.

The most direct way to find out, I reasoned, was to order some drugs from Mass Machine and see what happened. I sat at my kitchen table, and I went down the list: Dianabol, Anadrol 50, Winstrol, Anavar, Halotestin, Testosterone Undecanoate, Deca-durabolin, Testosterone Cypionate, Equipoise. What would the Boz have chosen, or Steve Courson, or the late Lyle Alzado? If I were a 19-year-old weightlifting male with a frail ego—and I decided that was the sort of person most likely to find an order form like this irresistible—what would I tick off the list?

I checked Dianabol, 5-mg tabs, 100 tablets to the bottle. The granddaddy of them all. What the heck, I'd better get

three bottles. At $28 a pop, it seemed like the kind of thing a kid wouldn't pass up. I knew the bodybuilder's cynical credo: Die young, die strong, Dianabol. But does that worry the hundreds of thousands of adolescent males in the U.S. who currently take illicit steroids to try to pump themselves up, or the thousands of other kids who try to get the drugs and can't? Does it worry the professional wrestlers, football players, runners, shot-putters, weightlifters, swimmers, boxers, tennis players—yes, tennis players—who are looking for an immoral edge? Not much, it seems. Die young? I recalled the battle cry of the steroid-abusing players on the University of South Carolina football team a few years back: "Bury me massive!"

But I knew about the potential side effects of steroid use, from the relatively benign—baldness, acne—to the serious: endocrine-system damage, heart and liver problems, tumors, cholesterol buildup, strokes, and shrinkage of certain—ahem—male body parts. And I knew also about 'roid rage, the mental mayhem that often grips users. Every athlete who had ever told me about using steroids had described the edginess, the irritability and the open hostility that rose within him during his cycle.

And so I couldn't believe that a person could simply order all this illegal stuff through the mail the same way you could order a sweater or boxed fruit. My friend had been given the order form by a man who works with him at his real estate office, who had received the form in the mail, unsolicited, at his house. The only thing this original recipient had done that might have made him a candidate for receiving the order form was to subscribe to a couple of running magazines and to *Joe Weider's Muscle & Fitness*

magazine. "That doesn't mean I want steroids," he had said.

My friend thought that perhaps I could get to the bottom of the matter.

I wanted my request to look legit—not so big that it would draw attention and not so small that it would be dismissed by the purveyors as unworthy of their response. I checked off a bottle of Winstrol for $28, a bottle of Halotestin (2-mg tabs, 100 to a bottle, $35), a box of Periactin Appetite Stimulant for $22, four vials of Deca-durabolin for $48, four doses of Sustanon for $48 (though I had no idea what it was) in 1-cc pre-loaded syringes (I was compelled by the "danger" element of the syringe), two 10-cc bottles of Testosterone Cypionate for $50, one bottle of Winstrol-V for $65 (wasn't that the juice of choice for disgraced Canadian sprinter Ben Johnson?) and one bottle of Equipoise for $85.

I added up the numbers, threw in the $6 postage charge and sent a check to Mass Machine for $471, a substantial but not unreasonable amount, I felt (The "$471 for steroid purchase" may be the most unusual item I've ever put on my company expense form, however.) The front page of the mail-order form said that minimum orders were $75; that all new customers would receive a free copy of the 72-page *Steroid Users Guide Book,* a "professional manual" that showed "how to take steroids safely and effectively"; and that the order would arrive in plain packaging marked NUTRITIONAL SUPPLEMENTS. No registered letters would be accepted. All checks had to be filled out with the payee line left blank.

I made arrangements with one of SI's lawyers; I would call him if and when my package arrived; together we would photograph it, open it and document its contents. Then I called an account officer at my local bank and asked her to let me know as soon as my check was cashed. There was nothing else to do except wait. This was in late October 1992.

On Nov. 20 the account officer called to tell me that the check had come through; it had been stamped "All-Star Fitness," and though I had sent the check to a post office box in Toronto, it had been deposited in a Bank of Montreal branch in Montreal. That, I assumed, was a means of skirting the law. Now all I could do was wait for the goods.

I waited and waited. The notion that this was all a scam fixed itself in my mind. That had always seemed the most likely explanation; but then, I wondered, how could anyone expect to get away with it? The trail leading to the culprit or culprits would be thick with canceled checks, ads, deposit slips, bank records, signature cards, the post office box. Police would nail the crooks in a heartbeat. That is, if anyone complained to the police. Complaining to authorities might mean confessing to an attempt to purchase steroids.

I waited some more. No package. In mid-December I visited my bank again, and the officer used numbers on the canceled check to track down the precise location of the bank branch office. She called the bank and talked to an employee there, inquiring about the status of the All-Star Fitness account. The account is active, the bank employee reported. A man comes in regularly to make deposits and withdrawals.

I considered going to Montreal, befriending the bank authorities, sitting in the lobby and waiting for the teller to signal when the bagman arrived. The account officer thought that sounded adventurous. So did I. I pondered the practicality of it. Say I spot the guy. Then what? Do I grab him and demand my steroids? What does he do to me?

Instead I phoned my old pal Anthony Pellicano, private eye, Los Angeles. Actually, calling Pellicano a private eye is like calling Roseanne Arnold a housewife; he is the gumshoe to the stars, having worked for Sylvester Stallone, Ed McMahon, Kevin Costner, James Woods and, yes, even Roseanne herself. These days Pellicano is trying to extricate Michael Jackson from some, uh, unpleasantness. When I called him in early 1993, he sounded like the same old Pellicano I had known when I wrote a newspaper story

about him in '74, when he was a flamboyant, up-and-coming Chicago sleuth.

Now I asked him if he could help me track down the steroid salesmen. Sure, he said. Just fax me your notes. I offered to pay him something for his efforts. Say, $250? There was wild, staccato laughter. "Don't make me laugh," he said.

Time passed. Pellicano was busy with other jobs. Finally, in March, he called. There are three guys in this steroid ring, he told me. They send out mailers to people who buy certain muscle magazines. It's a rip-off of the first degree. The Canadian cops have been on to it for a while and are ready to move. He faxed me the other names the outfit has used on its fliers: Mr. Big, Power Growth, Anabolic Plus, Gym Teck Training, Athletes in Motion. Pellicano said that I should call Marie Drummond in the morality bureau of the Metropolitan Toronto Police for the rest of the info.

I called Detective Drummond, and she told me that three people had been charged with a variety of offenses in the scam, including conspiracy to defraud the public and mail fraud. Two of the men had been arrested; they were brothers, Peter and Paul Fuller, 36 and 32, respectively; the third, Michael Murphy, 28, was on the lam. All of the men were Canadian citizens. They never sent any steroids to anyone, said Drummond. Nothing? I asked. Not even a couple of Dianabol tablets?

"This scam could have been for anything," she replied, "but they saw the market demand for steroids. One of them was a bodybuilder. They've been doing this since 1987."

Who was their market?

"Americans," she said. "Young men. The Fullers and Murphy spent big bucks to get the subscriber lists from bodybuilding magazines and then sent out fliers. They had a rented postal meter that could send out 171 letters a minute. They had spent over $60,000 [Canadian] on postage. These fliers trickled down to high school associations, and in time Canada was perceived as a big steroid deliverer."

How did this go on so long?

"Complaints were minimal," Drummond said, and she added that most victims no doubt didn't want to take their folly public.

And did these guys make much money? Drummond paused, then said, "Let me just say that a very conservative estimate of their take would be a million

dollars." She paused again, and I read in her silence that the figure might be much higher. "However, we don't know where the money has gone. They've hidden it."

I called Toronto attorney Edmund Peterson, the lawyer for the Fuller brothers, and asked him if I could speak to one or both of his clients, who were out on bail. No dice, said Peterson when I called back a few days later. The brothers did not want to talk to me. "This is going to be a lengthy, drawn-out battle," Peterson concluded, speaking of his defense work.

Well, now what? Is there such a demand for dangerous, illegal, muscle-building drugs in this country that people would willingly throw their money down a rathole hoping to get some? Apparently. Arnold Schwarzenegger used steroids at one time. Former University of Oklahoma linebacker Brian Bosworth did too, and in 1987 he signed a 10-year, $11 million contract with the Seattle Seahawks *after* he had been caught using them. What sort of message does that send to kids? According to an article in *U.S. News & World Report,* 57% of teen steroid users said they were influenced to use the drugs by reading muscle magazines; 42% said they decided to use steroids because of the famous athletes they were certain were using the drugs.

In August I flew to Toronto to see if there was anything else to learn. Murphy was still in hiding. The court date for the Fullers would be chosen on Nov. 24.

I looked up a producer who works for CBC-TV in Toronto, a young man named Michael Turschic, who had jumped through some of the same journalistic hoops that I had on this affair. He had received a flier, ordered steroids, sent a check. But nothing had happened. He had gone to the post office where the con artists had a box, and he had staked it out for a while. "I saw one of the guys on the first day I went to the post office," said Turschic. "But I didn't take my car, so I couldn't follow him. He was a big guy."

Like me, Turschic had had no idea what he would do if he had to confront the scammers. He got his flier from a Buffalo physician, who told Turschic that teenage patients of his had sworn they had gotten drugs from Mass Machine.

"I watched the box after that first visit," Turschic continued, "but I never saw the guy come again. They never sent any drugs, and we had other things to do at the station." Turschic shook his head, thinking about the appeal of steroids to young men. "I was a skinny kid on the high school football team," mused Turschic. "I might have been interested in this stuff." I told him I knew what he meant.

My last stop was the office of John Scutt, the government's prosecuting attorney in the case. Scutt was concerned with not divulging any information that might be prejudicial to his case. He was also interested in saving the good taxpayers, as much money as possible. In that regard, I informed him, I was willing to be a witness for the prosecution at my own expense. He pondered this, knowing that a reporter's purposes are

seldom as simple as stated. He said, though, that he would consider using me as a witness.

"I doubt you'll get your money back," he said after a time. "In a sense this is just your standard fraud case. Like purchasing swampland in Florida." He added, though, that most of the victims in this case were "nickeled and dimed," that my order was one of the largest ones. He would call if he needed me, he promised.

On the plane home I realized that what I really wanted was just to see the con men. I wanted to look at them in court

and ask them what they thought they were doing. Did they really think they could get away with this scam? I wanted to ask them if they had realized the world was as twisted and muscle-mad as it is. Were even they surprised by the huge response to their illicit pitch? So many people dying to change their bodies. Think of it. Say the take in this scam was $2 million and the average victim sent in $100, both of which seem reasonable. That means there were 20,000 people who liked what the Fullers and Murphy were offering.

That's massive.

And still the drugs sit there

WASHINGTON, DC

NOT long after a lethal cocktail of heroin and cocaine kills a hip young movie actor, a heroin-addled rock star blows his head off with a shotgun. A top Wall Street economist admits he is addicted to coke. Weeks later, the body of a prominent investment banker is found, naked and lifeless, next to a plate flecked with felonious white powder. Days after that, on May 17th, a teenage ex-tennis-star is arrested for possession of marijuana; her friends are said to be carrying heroin and crack.

Celebrity decadence is nothing new. Yet such a spectacular (and sometimes fatal) litany of drug abuse was bound to cause a bit of a stir. And so it has. For 20 odd years America has been fighting a costly "war on drugs". Until recently there were signs of progress. Consumption was falling; drugs were no longer trendy. But now the press is full of stories about a looming heroin crisis and the surprising persistence of cocaine on Wall Street. Among ordinary folks and the famous alike, say politicians and researchers, drugs are making a splashy resurgence.

This argument is half right: there are indeed a lot of drugs about. But the idea that this is something new—that heroin is making a "comeback", that it is somehow shocking that Wall Street big-shots are still taking cocaine as if it were candy—is misleading. In fact, drug abuse has been remarkably robust over the past 25 years, even at the height of the drug wars. The unwillingness to face up to this awkward fact (plus a profusion of shoddy journalism and opportunist politics) is what makes America's drug debate so hopelessly unconstructive.

If drug consumption is not exactly in resurgence, drug imagery certainly is. Pop culture's tolerance for—or encouragement of—drugs has not been so blatant since the early 1970s. Gone are anti-cocaine television shows such as "Miami Vice". In are a whole range of pro-marijuana totems: from television (the main characters of "Roseanne" lit up this season) to pop music (one multi-million-selling rap record is called "The Chronic", slang for highly potent strains of the weed) to fashion (pot leaves abound on T-shirts). And then there is heroin, newly publicised by bands such as Nirvana and films such as "My Own Private Idaho".

Some think that grunge-laden glamour is having an effect. Since the overdose of River Phoenix, star of "Idaho", and the suicide of Kurt Cobain, Nirvana's singer, the press has been ever more insistently saying that, as one article put it, "smack is back". In the 1970s demand for heroin fell because of its scarcity and impurity. Now, the argument goes, an opium glut has pushed prices down and purity up—from under 10% to as much as 70%—thus making it economical to smoke rather than inject the drug. This in turn has lowered the "needle barrier" (a barrier raised high by fear of AIDS) and tempted a new generation to give heroin a go.

The trouble with all this is that heroin has supposedly been making a comeback for years now. Jack Shafer, the editor of a Washington weekly, the *City Paper*, points out acidly that journalists, bolstered by the claims of government officials and what he calls the "drug-abuse industrial complex", have been reporting dramatic increases in heroin's purity and trendiness since at least 1981. But like the "ice" (smokeable crystal methamphetamine) plague widely predicted in the mid-1980s, the putative heroin revival has remained just that: putative.

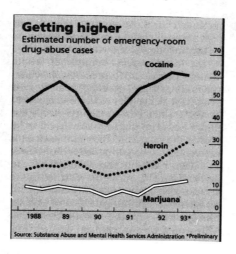

Getting higher
Estimated number of emergency-room drug-abuse cases

Cocaine

Heroin

Marijuana

1988 89 90 91 92 93*

Source: Substance Abuse and Mental Health Services Administration *Preliminary

Worries about heroin are not conjured out of thin air. One of the most reliable indicators of drug abuse—statistics on hospital admissions—showed a 44% rise in heroin-related emergency-room visits in the first half of 1993 compared with the same period in the previous year (see chart). That is disturbing. Yet, as Mr Shafer suggests, the rise may have less to do with an increase in heroin addiction than with a rise in the number of people mixing heroin with other drugs, and with alcohol: a problem, to be sure, but of a different order of magnitude from the heroin "epidemic" some are forecasting.

Such "poly-drug" abuse certainly seems to be the order of the day on Wall Street. First there was the case of Lawrence Kudlow, former chief economist at Bear Stearns, an investment bank, who admitted recently in the *New York Times* that he was a cocaine addict and an alcoholic. Then came the apparent coke-and-vodka overdose of Wardell Lazard, head of one of the biggest black-owned financial firms.

Believing that the days of coke-fuelled wheeling and dealing had gone the way of red braces adorned with dollar signs, laymen were surprised. Bankers and traders were not: they admit there is as much cocaine (plus booze, pot and sometimes heroin) coursing through their firms as ever. Coke may not be served with the canapés at Park Avenue parties, as it once was, but it is still common for messengers to deliver it to users at the office.

Wall Street's hypocrisy about the issue—many firms refuse even to admit that they have drug-treatment programmes—is not unique. Indeed, some experts reckon that much of the fall in middle-class cocaine consumption that was reported to have taken place at the end of the 1980s was a mirage. The emergency-room figures for cocaine are back up again. And drug-use surveys are often unreliable; social pressure may promote fibbing more than pledges of confidentiality promote the opposite.

That is especially true among young people, whose responses to such surveys have been widely interpreted as the most encouraging news that drug use was waning towards the end of the 1980s. Yet even if those responses were truthful, the fact remains that around half of college students still experiment with drugs—a smaller proportion than in the peak year, 1979, but almost precisely the same as when the "war on drugs" was first declared by Richard Nixon in 1971. And though cocaine use is lower than it was in the early 1980s, LSD and other hallucinogens (such as Ecstasy) are on the rise.

The lesson seems a straightforward one. Since 1980 America has spent more than $100 billion in the war on drugs. Despite that, cocaine, heroin and marijuana are as available and as inexpensive as ever. Drug use fluctuates, but it is not going away. Indeed, surveys show that young people now seem increasingly tolerant of drugs and less worried about the health effects of them, if used in moderation.

And yet Bill Clinton, who as candidate talked about more emphasis on drug education and prevention, and about giving addicts "treatment on demand", has proposed a drug-fighting plan that looks almost identical to the ones put forward by his Republican predecessors. Makes you wonder who's really on drugs after all.

Drugs and Crime

Crime is intrinsic to the world of illegal drugs. The types of crimes associated with this world vary according to the types of drugs involved and certain environmental factors associated with them. For example, patterns of violent crime consistently accompany the trafficking of both cocaine and methamphetamine. The lucrative nature of the market, the fierce competition that it generates, and the tendency for street dealers to be users of the product all serve to perpetuate violence. The repeated use of cocaine and methamphetamine produces a loss of judgment, paranoia, and psychosis in the user, promoting aggressive, irrational behavior. This behavior is associated with an increased risk of becoming a victim or perpetrator of crime and being present at a place where crime is occurring. Many illicit drugs fall into similar categories due to their associated black market economy and their pharmacological influence on human behavior.

The use and abuse of legal drugs, although not as publicly sensational, also produce a significant relationship with crime. The most notable is alcohol, which studies repeatedly connect to crimes ranging in severity from shoplifting to rape and homicide. The high percentage of perpetrators as well as victims using alcohol before and during the offense is a long-established criminological phenomenon. One study reported that violence was ten times more likely to occur during the commission of a crime when the offender had been drinking.

With respect to crime, viewing drug use as a simple causal factor is an oversimplification of a complex association. Drug use and crime perpetuate each other, but the relationship is influenced by a wide range of psychological, pharmacological, social, and economic factors. Understanding the drug-crime nexus requires the specific investigation of these different factors.

Ample evidence exists of the strong relationship between drug use and crime. Drug users typically report greater involvement in crime and are more likely than nonusers to have criminal records. Crime increases as drug use increases. Criminal activity is reported to be two to three times higher among frequent users of heroin and cocaine as compared to the criminal activity of irregular users. In most cities surveyed, over 50 percent of arrestees reported having recently used drugs. Three out of four arrestees report drug use in their lifetime. Two out of three state prison inmates reported using drugs once a week or more before their arrest and incarceration. In state-operated juvenile institutions, 40 percent reported being under the influence at the time of their offense.

Additionally, research focusing upon persons in drug treatment has produced further evidence of the drugs-crime relationship. One study by the Drug Abuse Reporting Program (DARP) found that 87 percent had been arrested and 71 percent had been in jail before entering treatment. The Treatment Outcome Prospective Study (TOPS) found that about 60 percent of those entering publicly funded residential treatment programs said that they had committed one or more crimes for economic gain in the year before treatment. Other studies have reflected higher rates. Interestingly, follow-up to these studies shows that the proportion of those who committed crime for financial gain fell dramatically during treatment and that the decrease in crime occurred along with the substantial decrease in drug use.

Consequently, the best evidence suggests that the relationship between drugs and crime is developmental rather than causal and varies by the nature and intensity of drug use. Most evidence highly correlates the two behaviors in a perpetuating relationship.

Further emphasis should be given to the relationship between drug use, drug trafficking, and violent crime. Certain legal and illegal drugs such as alcohol, cocaine, and the amphetamines produce profound physiological and psychological influences in the user. These influences—often visible in the form of aggressive, irrational, paranoid, and psychotic behavior—have long been associated with an increased potential for violence. Whether or not the pharmacological properties of the drug caused the behavior or merely unleashed a latent potential enabling it has been a topic of much debate. Ask any police officer or emergency medical technician, however, and you will probably be treated to bizarre tales of violent scenarios precipitated by the influence of certain drugs on human behavior.

Violence also has a systemic aspect engrained within the apparatus of drug distribution and use, seen not only as a consequence but as a useful tool of the trade. Violence is used to establish reputations, discourage competitors, ensure quality control, enforce contracts, and as punishment for a myriad of rule infractions intrinsic to the trade. Sellers and users are often preyed upon and attacked and have, in essence, created a huge new category of crime victims.

The articles in unit 5 help illustrate the wide range of criminal activity associated with the manufacture, trafficking, and use of some illicit drugs. Discussion of crime related to alcohol is also included. As you read, consider the significance of drugs as they relate to the most pervasive fear in this country—the fear of crime.

Looking Ahead: Challenge Questions

What role does the media play in influencing drug-related crime?

Do you believe drug-related crime is overrepresented or underrepresented?

Is drug-related crime getting worse, or is it getting better? Defend your answer.

Survey your class to determine what percentage has been a victim of crime, and determine what percentage of those were victims of drug-related crime.

Discuss the costs of drug-related crime on the criminal justice, health care, and educational systems in your community.

How is the fear of crime continuing to change the way we live?

Killer Cowboys

The violent saga of the city's deadliest drug gang

Michael Stone

Nine days before Christmas 1991, the people of Mott Haven were doing what people everywhere do this time of year—visiting friends and relatives, putting up decorations, trying to make the paycheck stretch far enough to buy presents for their kids. But along Beekman Avenue—a two-block stretch of crumbling tenements in the heart of that Bronx neighborhood—there were hardly any signs of the holidays, unless you count the special low price Amp Green was running on his crack sales. The reed-thin dealer, a foolish 17-year-old who thought nothing in the world could stop his fun, saw no danger in selling crack vials in the middle of another gang's turf. Amp Green had been warned to clear out—shots had even been fired over his head—but he just kept at it.

A mother of three was shot in the head by a cowboy and died on the pavement still clutching her crack vial.

Green's stubbornness would cost him his life—an all too common occurrence in the city's drug wars. It was what came next that made his execution seem extraordinary. On a cold night in December, two sedans—one white, one black—rolled up to the narrow alleyway where Green did business. Sales were brisk; a dozen people clogged the cement corridor as gunmen surrounded the spot. Two men pinned Green to a wall near the entrance to the alley and pumped six bullets into his legs and stomach. Then, as Green crumpled to the ground, as many as eight gunmen trained their weapons on his workers and customers

and opened fire. For 30 seconds or more, there was chaos as people clambered away from the lit-up guns, the building walls ringing with the stammer of automatic weapons.

Some were able to escape through a tear in the chain-link fence at the rear. But one customer got cut down as he tried to scramble up a fire escape. Another, Cynthia Casado—a mother of three—was headed back to the street when she ran into a man who shot her in the head. She died in the mouth of the alley, still clutching the yellow-capped vial of crack she had bought only moments before.

A slim, fortyish woman named Clarice Jones* was on her way to visit her son and was passing the alley as the bullets started flying. She had known the man who shot Amp Green for years, but that didn't stop him from whirling and firing at her as she fled the scene. She hadn't run more than a few steps when she felt the bullet slam into her back and then her face hit the pavement. Critically wounded, she managed to roll under a parked car.

Manuel Vera was not as lucky. The gunmen chased him 60 feet to the doorway of an adjoining building as he ran from the scene. Police found him there in a pool of blood, a string of crêpe-paper Christmas decorations visible through the lobby doors. He'd been shot fourteen times. "They just walked down the block guns blazing," says one man who witnessed the shooting from across the street. "I've lived here for 30 years, and I've never seen anything like that."

W
ho were these butchers? Neighborhood people thought the killers belonged to a local crack crew that operated on Beekman

---

*Some of the names in this story have been changed to protect the privacy of those involved.

Avenue, and that was true as far as it went. But after a two-year citywide investigation, prosecutors have concluded that the crew was merely one part of a 41-member Washington Heights gang that sold more than $16-million worth of crack each year. That's high on the list of crack crews—but what really set this organization apart was its unfathomable brutality. It was not just ruthless but seemed to revel in the most vicious acts of bloodshed. Although the gang was known on the street as Red Top, its Dominican hierarchy used another name left over from rowdy days at George Washington High School. They called themselves the Wild Cowboys.

With its echoes of frontier lawlessness and shoot-'em-up machismo, the name seemed apt. Wherever the Cowboys ranged over the course of their ten-year association—from upper Broadway to Brighton Beach—lawmen charge they made up their own rules and left a trail of the bodies of those who took exception. But analogies to the Old West do not adequately describe the violent ethos of this organization. The Cowboys moved onto Beekman Avenue like an occupying army. They exterminated local dealers, bullied tenants, and brutalized their own workers. In a dispute over stolen drugs, they drove one family of eight from their rent-subsidized apartment, then tracked them down to another borough and shot one of the sons—just 15 at the time—in the head, according to Bronx prosecutor Donald Hill.

The violence was not always related to drugs. Six months before the alleyway massacre, David Cargill, a Westchester college student, was cut down by a burst of automatic gunfire while driving his pickup on the West Side Highway. Investigators didn't know why Cargill was killed, much less who killed him. But FBI agents eventually got a tip that the

Cowboys were behind the shooting—a chillingly random act.

On September 15, lawmen filed a 66-count indictment against the Cowboys and their leaders, charging them with conspiracy, witness intimidation, and ten murders. But the gang's legacy of mayhem may include more than 30 homicides, according to Manhattan district attorney Robert Morgenthau. "They're the most violent group I've come across," says police captain John Regan, who headed the narcotics end of the investigation.

In the past decade, drug-trafficking gangs have become New York's No. 1 crime problem—the main contributor to its homicide rate and a blight on its quality of life. Armed with automatic weapons, these brutal organizations commandeer chunks of the city's real estate—buildings, blocks, parks, entire neighborhoods—preying on the poor, co-opting the young, and killing the defiant. They are also one of law enforcement's thorniest problems. Their layered conspiracies are virtually immune to the beat cop and the squad detective. Special tactical units (TNTs) are good at busting street sellers and the low-level managers sometimes called Dixie Cups because they're easily replaceable. But penetrating the top levels of these gangs entails a dedicated, long-term investigation—and with the shift toward community policing, only a few task forces in the city still have the savvy and the resources to mount that kind of campaign.

In many ways, the Cowboys are emblematic of a new generation of gangs. They were shaped by today's huge drug profits, deregulated markets, and the easy availability of ultralethal weapons. And much of their violence was part of doing business on the street. But that violence began to feed on itself and spiraled out of control. "The Cowboys thought they were untouchable," says senior Manhattan prosecutor Walter Arsenault. "So we took them down."

Lenin Sepulveda's face jumps out at you from a wall full of mug shots. The leader of the Cowboys, he has eyebrows that knit together, forming a single dark line over penetrating eyes and rugged features. Sepulveda, 25, and his brother Nelson, 26, were born in New York shortly after their parents emigrated from the Dominican Republic. Their father, Roberto, the son of a San-tiago blacksmith, repaired radios and televisions. Their mother found factory work. But neither parent assimilated well. Roberto drank heavily and bickered constantly with his wife, according to a family friend.

Named after the Russian revolutionary—his parents belonged to a generation of Dominicans that believed in sweeping social reform—Lenin was bright and uncontrollable almost from the start. He was constantly in trouble as a youngster—cutting school, jumping turnstiles, getting into gang fights. Nelson, the family friend says, was more reserved at first. But he apparently changed in his teens. He was transferred from Martin Luther King for punching out a teacher, and he became known in the street as "The Wack" for his violent actions.

At George Washington High School, police say, the brothers were the center of a group of truant students that included three of the men charged in the Bronx alleyway shooting almost ten years later: "Fat Danny" Rincon, the Sepulvedas' 300-pound neighbor; "Shorty" Gonzalez, a bright student whose sister was president of her senior class; and Wilfredo De Los Angeles, known as Platano, a former altar boy who, street legend has it, killed a man for using the same street name. A gym teacher is said to have told them, "You're nothing but a bunch of wild cowboys." The name stuck.

While still in school, they began stealing cars. Each week a bunch of them would ride out to the suburban malls of northern New Jersey, corral five or six luxury cars, then drive them back across the bridge to the chop shops in the Heights.

Next, they sold marijuana. Starting small, they dealt ounces from a spot on 183rd Street and Audubon Avenue, but were soon transporting 125 pounds weekly from suppliers in West Texas. The group disbanded its operation after Texas police collared one of its associates with two suitcases full of pot.

Around 1985, they reunited to deal cocaine, buying kilos of the drug on consignment and selling them in smaller quantities. Then crack hit the streets, turning the lower levels of the cocaine trade into a freewheeling, wildly profitable business. Anyone with a few hundred dollars and a hot plate could go into business and triple his money overnight. Thousands did, creating fierce competition for prime selling sites.

That competition triggered the formation of violent drug-trafficking gangs. As their profits grew, street crews armed themselves with automatic weapons and hired teams of enforcers to protect their turf and ease their expansion into less organized neighborhoods. One of the first and most successful of these organizations—Baseballs—sprung up in 1985 just a few blocks from Lenny and Nelson's home at 640 West 171st Street.

Lenny joined Baseballs late in 1986 as a member of one of its most violent crews and helped spearhead its expansion into the Bronx. He managed a location on Boston Road for a while and was developing a new spot at 603 Beech Terrace, a partly abandoned building just off Beekman Avenue, when Drug Enforcement Administration (DEA) agents took down the gang and drove its leader, Santiago Polanco, into exile in the Dominican Republic. His departure left an open field for the Cowboys.

The five-story tenement at 348 Beekman Avenue might have been designed with the Cowboys in mind. Rising like a fortress at the north end of the street, it had high floors that offered the gang a clear view for blocks around; a covered walkway spanning the side alley provided an ideal selling location. The Cowboys stationed lookouts with walkie-talkies on the roof and planted their sellers on the walkway, which they called the Hole.

Bribing and bullying the residents, the Cowboys quickly gained control over the inside of the building as well. Prosecutors say they picked up tenants' rent and used their apartments to stash drugs and guns. They also hired them as low-level workers. Many of these tenants were poor, some of them had drug habits, and nearly all were grateful at first for the infusion of cash and jobs. But the relationship soured once the Cowboys moved in—and then it became impossible to move the gang out.

When Alice Carver* tried to sever her "sublet" plan with the Cowboys—they had slapped her niece and treated her place as their own—Lenny, Nelson, Platano, and Ulysses Mena, a Cowboy enforcer, paid her a visit. Platano tossed a bag of crack onto the living-room table, aimed a gun at her, and mouthed the words "Pow-pow-pow." Then he placed the gun on the table, and Mena picked it up and shot her in the head.

Sales skyrocketed. Many clients came from the neighborhood. Still others poured down from bedroom communities in New Jersey, the North Bronx, and Westchester. At times there were so many buyers that the Cowboys had to herd them into a vacant lot across the street. The Hole became a cash machine operating 24 hours a day, seven days a week. During its peak years, between 1988 and 1991, the organization grossed $45,000 per day.

Like any merchant trying to stand out in a crowded market, Lenny kept an eye on quality control. He manufactured a high-grade product and dealt ruthlessly with anyone who tampered with it. In early 1990, when Nelson caught Anna Velarde* selling "dummies—skimming crack from the vials and replacing it with an inexpensive placebo like soap—he shot her in the leg. The bullet crashed through both legs, fracturing her thighbone. She was four months pregnant at the time.

By the end of 1990, Cowboy justice was becoming not only vicious but capricious—a kind of impulsive mayhem that couldn't be explained by any street code. Merely shooting someone no longer seemed to satisfy the gang. They started seeking new and unorthodox weapons—sometimes primitive ones. In November, for example, just nine months after shooting Velarde, Nelson sent another employee to the roof of 348 Beekman for a similar offense. There, Platano grabbed the worker from behind, and Stanley Tukes, a local arm-breaker, gouged his face with a four-inch construction nail, ripping open a gash from the corner of his eye to his mouth.

The randomness of Cargill's killing triggered alarms in law-enforcement offices.

Then in May 1991, Oscar Alvarez, a Cowboy seller, was shot dead after he was nabbed smoking company crack, even though he had offered to work off his debt. Six months later, the Cowboys caught another worker, Eddie Maldonaldo, stealing from them, and Platano, Stanley Tukes, and Ulysses Mena surrounded him in nearby St. Mary's Park one afternoon. Although the park was crowded with students, they pulled out machetes and a serrated Rambo-style knife and hacked Maldonaldo to death.

David Cargill's spirits were high in the early morning hours of May 19, 1991. Just back from his sophomore year at aeronautical college in Florida, he was happy to see his Tarrytown friends again. He had gone to a party in nearby Elmsford, then driven his red Nissan pickup into Manhattan at about 2 A.M. with John Riguzzi and another friend named Kevin. Cargill had installed a new amplifier in the cab of his truck that afternoon, and he was eager to try it out on the open road.

The amp was still blasting a couple of hours later as they drove back to Tarrytown on the West Side Highway. It was a cold, clear night, there was hardly any traffic on the road, and Cargill had his foot down. So Riguzzi, perched on the speaker in the back of the cab, was surprised when he saw the bright lights gaining on them in the rearview mirror. At first he thought it was the police pulling them over, but when he looked over at the passing lane and saw a beat-up blue sedan pull alongside—its passenger-side window wide open—he felt a chill through his body, a premonition that something bad was about to happen.

That's when he heard the popping noises and felt his eyes fill up with liquid—Cargill's blood, as it turned out. "I went down for about fifteen seconds," he recalls. "I thought they'd thrown firecrackers at us." Riguzzi felt the truck fishtail across the road and heard Kevin say, "Dave, stop . . . around." Then he got his eyes cleared and saw Cargill slumped over on Kevin's shoulder, and Kevin trying to get at the brake with his hand. Riguzzi grabbed the wheel, and together they managed to pull the truck onto the off-ramp at 158th Street. Then, while Kevin ran for help, Riguzzi tried to lift Cargill out of the driver's seat.

Riguzzi hadn't noticed the shattered windows, the blood and flesh smeared on almost every surface of the car. He had seen only the small hole where a bullet had entered the left side of Cargill's neck. But when he reached behind his friend's head and felt the gaping exit wound, he realized what had happened. "I'd never seen anyone dead," he says. "But I knew when I flipped him over, that was it."

The randomness of David Cargill's murder—no one could explain who killed him or why—triggered alarms in law-enforcement offices around town. But no new information surfaced, and the investigation foundered for almost six months. Then in December, just days before the quadruple murder in the Bronx, FBI agents working on an unrelated case got a tip that the Cowboys were responsible for Cargill's death, which is still being investigated.

The gang took steps to counter surveillance by changing the color of its crack vials and shifting sales sites.

The night of the shooting, officials say, several gang members, including Lenny and Platano, went nightclubbing with the Cowboys' Brooklyn-based gun supplier. (Platano told police that Lenny and the dealer were drinking $150 champagne at the Limelight.) At some point during the evening, the dealer returned an automatic Uzi pistol that he had repaired for the Cowboys. While getting onto the highway at about 4:30 A.M., Cargill's pickup swerved across the 57th Street on-ramp, cutting off one of two Cowboy cars. The Cowboys then chased Cargill to about 135th Street and shot him with the Uzi. Platano told police that afterward Lenny boasted, "It was a good time to test the new gun."

News of the Cowboys' involvement sparked an investigation by the Manhattan D.A.'s Homicide Investigation Unit (HIU), a task force of lawyers and detectives that has smashed some of the city's most vicious drug-trafficking gangs. Meanwhile, investigators in the Bronx went after the shooters in the "quad"—the quadruple alleyway murder. The brunt of that task fell to Mark Tebbens, a precinct detective with informants up and down Beekman Avenue.

By January 1992, Tebbens had enough witnesses to arrest two of the shooters: Stanley Tukes, the man who shot Amp Green, and Shorty Gonzalez. But the big fish still eluded him. For years he'd been hearing the name of Platano. Now he had a bead on him. He knew from his sources that Platano had been one of the shooters in the quad, and he had an eyewitness—a former associate of Amp Green's known as Carlos*—willing to testify against him. But by the time Tebbens located Platano—in an Englewood, New Jersey, jail on a drug charge—Carlos was refusing to talk.

A few days before, several Cowboys had driven him to City Island, supposedly for dinner. But when they got there, they took out a 9-mm. pistol from a "clavo," or secret compartment in the car, put the gun in his mouth and dry-fired it. Within days, Carlos went to a lawyer and recanted his testimony.

So began a campaign of terror against virtually all of the witnesses to the murders. One was threatened at gunpoint a few weeks later. Another was told, "Snitches get stitches," and slashed. This was enough to silence most potential witnesses, but one family turned out to be harder to scare.

Ｏne of the few stable families at 348 Beekman, the Cowboys' fortress, was the eight-member Martinez* clan. They'd lived there for more than ten years. Maria Martinez, the mother, had survived a turbulent Bronx adolescence and settled down to become the kind of anchor that's a rare and precious resource in any community. She worked in a nursing home and studied computer programming at night. Her common-law husband held down a job in the meat market at Hunt's Point. Her five children—including Rafael, then 12; Tony, 14; and Jesus, 16—were in school.

The Cowboys hung out in the Martinez apartment, as they did in the apartments of most of the tenants. But they seemed to respect Maria Martinez. They called her *la vieja,* the old woman, and they never abused or stored drugs in her place. Occasionally, Martinez cooked for the gang leaders, and Lenny dated one of her daughters. Maria Martinez even worked briefly as a lookout for the gang. But when it came to her sons, she drew the line. She didn't want them dealing drugs.

With their fancy cars and ruthless reputations, the Cowboys were romantic figures among neighborhood youngsters, whom they recruited because their age shielded them from prosecution under New York's tough drug laws. Platano used to tip Rafael $50 to carry a book bag full of drugs from his car to the Cowboys' stash apartments. Tony and Jesus started as lookouts and became part-time managers. When they began cutting school, Maria complained to Lenny and Platano, but to no avail.

Then, on March 20, 1992, a Cowboy manager was shot to death in the hallway of 348 Beekman while transporting drugs and cash worth thousands of dollars. He lived long enough to make it back to the apartment that he shared in the building with his common-law wife, Rosie Sanchez*. Still clutching some or all of the crack and cash, he begged Sanchez to get it out of the apartment before the police arrived. Sanchez gave the cache to her neighbor—Tony Martinez.

Martinez and his brothers went on a spending spree. Within 24 hours, the Cowboys had tracked the missing drugs and money to the brothers and were threatening to kill their entire family unless they returned them. Later that day, they pistol-whipped Jesus. Maria Martinez got her children to return a portion of the loot, but on March 22, after receiving repeated death threats, they fled into the shelter system and then, to the police.

The Bronx D.A.'s office relocated the Martinez family in a series of shelters, hotels, and safe houses. But it was impossible for the family, who had lived their entire lives within a four-block area, to sever all their connections to the old neighborhood. The Cowboys eventually traced them to the Brownsville section of Brooklyn, where they had moved; and on August 14 at about 10 P.M., Lenny and Jose Llaca, a vicious Cowboy enforcer known as Paqualito, drove alongside Tony Martinez, and shot him in the face, the bullet entering his left cheek and exiting behind his right ear.

The gang was squeezed from the top down through the arrests of its hierarchy.

Remarkably, Martinez survived and moved upstate with his family. But even there, the Cowboys hounded them. On November 9, two Dominican men grabbed Maria Martinez at a supermarket, put a knife to her throat, showed her a photo of her family that the Cowboys had taken from her old apartment, and told her that they would kill them all if she continued talking to the police. Once again the family relocated, continuing the rootless, precarious existence they had begun six months before.

In the interim, though, they helped alter the course of Tebbens's investiga-

tion. The Martinezes knew all the Cowboys and the smallest details of their operation. Maria had stashed the gun Lenny used in a 1989 murder. Rafael had witnessed eight homicides by the time he was 14. Tony, on orders from Platano, had closed down the Cowboys' main crack site a half-hour before the quad. He'd seen Fat Danny handing out weapons to the shooters in the hallway of 348 Beekman. More important, he'd witnessed the entire incident from the street. He was ready to testify that Platano was one of the shooters.

The Martinezes' statements enabled Tebbens to arrest Platano and Fat Danny Rincon. They also helped him see clearly the scope of the Cowboys' conspiracy. The question was what to do with all this information. Since arresting Stanley Tukes in mid-January, Tebbens had been under pressure to wrap up his investigation. He was using every spare minute away from his normal caseload—as well as his own time—just to continue working on the quad.

Then HIU reached out to the Bronx. They were both after the same guys: Why not work together? Manhattan had the resources needed to take out the whole gang. Bronx had the crimes: the murders, extortions, and illegal drug sales—the substantive acts on which a conspiracy case is based. The two offices agreed to pool their efforts.

By the summer of 1992, the Cowboys were under strong attack. Franklyn Cuevas, an old Baseballs associate of Lenny's, had begun muscling in on the Cowboys' crack sites, sparking a gang war. At the same time, a joint NYPD-DEA task force had joined the investigation and were rooting out the Cowboys' crack operations. But instead of retrenching, the Cowboys lashed out. Twice in June, Cowboy gunmen mounted drive-by attacks on a Cuevas outlet in the Bronx, leaving two dead and eleven wounded. The gang also took steps to counter surveillance—changing the color of its vials and shifting sales from the Hole to other sites in the neighborhood. The gang even attempted to expand sales. In June, the Cowboys opened a new site in the Brighton Beach section of Brooklyn, killing a local dealer who opposed them. "It was like a horror movie," Bronx prosecutor Donald Hill recalls. "You drive a stake into the monster's heart and it still rises up and comes after you."

But the Cowboys' new offensive was a death rattle. Throughout the fall the narcotics team stepped up its campaign against the gang, raiding their stash apartments and pulling their dealers off the street. Meanwhile, Tebbens and HIU investigators Terry Quinn and Garry Dugan were resuscitating old cases, linking them into a pattern of conspiracy, squeezing the organization from the top down. In February, Tebbens arrested Lenny for a 1989 murder. In May, with most of the gang's hierarchy already locked up, prosecutors convened a grand jury in the city's Special Narcotics court. Then on September 15, lawmen swept the city, arresting twelve more Cowboys. There are now 38 gang members in custody.

Meanwhile, two and a half years after the shooting, Cargill's parents are still grappling with what happened to their only son. "We can't make sense of it, the mentality that if you don't like someone, you just kill them," David Cargill Sr. says. "I'm not sure I accept totally what happened to David to this day. There are times I have to steel myself and say, "He's never coming home again.""

Neither are some other players in the Cowboys' story. Franklyn Cuevas was ambushed shortly after midnight on July 20 as he stood talking with a friend on West 177th Street. The gunman fired nine slugs into him, hitting every vital organ except his brain and kidneys. Then he shot Cuevas's friend and trotted away. The friend later identified the assassin as Paqualito, who is still at large. Authorities think he's in the Dominican Republic, which has no extradition agreement with the U.S.

Nelson Sepulveda is also believed to be living in the Dominican Republic and hanging out with former Basedballs chief Santiago Polanco, the man who got the Cowboys started in the business.

Prosecutors have told the court they are still tracking down the Sepulvedas' assets: a fleet of cars and motorcycles (several of them registered to a 14-year-old boy); a supermarket in Washington Heights; luxury homes in Teaneck and Rockland County; safes, shoe boxes, and dresser drawers stuffed with money; and substantial properties in the Dominican Republic that may include a Mercedes dealership owned jointly with Polanco.

"Some things never change," says Mark Tebbens.

But Beekman Avenue has changed. The alleyway where four men and women died in a hail of Cowboy bullets is vacant now. So is the one adjoining No. 348, where tens of thousands of dollars' worth of drugs changed hands every day. Only a blister of rock poking through the cement and a red paint stain evoke the carnage that once pervaded this neighborhood.

A hundred yards south, the dealers still hawk their goods in the doorways along 141st Street. But on Beekman Avenue on a recent sunny afternoon, the only sounds come from a group of youngsters tossing a football in the street. It's a heartening image—children running pass patterns on the street that for years has seen only crack vials and bullets. And it's a change not lost on the people of Mott Haven. A local man, a super who serviced several Cowboy strongholds, watches them for a moment, then says, "That's the first time I've seen children playing here in five years."

The Cocaine Money Market

Colombia's sophisticated laundering system has stymied the authorities

Douglas Farah and Steve Coll
Washington Post Foreign Service

Farah reported from Colombia and Panama, Coll from Panama and Washington.

CALI, Colombia

The international dollar trade here has no exchange floor or electronic tickers or pontificating analysts. Yet the market's huge size, sophisticated structure and competitive daily bidding operations would be familiar to any Chicago futures broker. There's just one twist: In Cali, cocaine trafficking capital of the Western Hemisphere, most dollar traders operate in the illegal black market, and they are well-advised never to lose money for their clients. "If you lose drugs, people get upset," one narcotics specialist says. "You lose money and people die."

During the 1980s, Colombia's drug cartels brought home only an estimated 10 percent to 20 percent of the billions of dollars in cash proceeds from their sales of cocaine in the United States. But over the past two years, because of tougher U.S. banking law enforcement and other factors, they have been sending about half of their cash back to Colombia—an estimated $5 billion to $7 billion annually, according to investigators.

This change in the movement of cocaine money has presented U.S. and regional law enforcement agents with a formidable—some say unmanageable—challenge as they seek to disrupt the financial empires of Colombia's largest cocaine traffickers.

Over the past year, Colombian cocaine traffickers have refined and expanded a unique illicit money trading market. Independent Colombian money brokers allied with the cocaine cartels—at least several dozen brokers, and perhaps more, investigators say—have been allowed to bid competitively for the right to transport large blocks of illicit cash to Colombia. The blocks of cash are typically $1 million or more, and come from cocaine sales in U.S. cities.

Cali operatives call the system *bajando el dolar*, or "bringing down the dollar." For the money brokers at its center, the profit potential is huge: the payoff for buying piles of cash in the United States and getting them to Colombia can be as high as 25 percent of the amount transported, or $250,000 for every $1 million. But the risks of trading can be formidable.

For example, a Colombian broker wishing to purchase a cash block in the United States must first show to his cocaine exporting client that he is "bonded"—that is, that he can reimburse the trafficker even if the cash he purchases is lost, stolen or seized by police. This bonding is done either through cash, land or urban properties, according to law enforcement and Cali cartel sources.

Lacking market police equivalent to the Securities and Exchange Commission, which oversees Wall Street, the cocaine cartel often enforces fair trading by sending a few people to stay with the family of a money broker during the period of a trading contract, a cartel source says. When the money broker or his employees call home, these "friends" remind him that completion of the deal is anxiously awaited, the source says.

■

FOR U.S. AND COLOMBIAN LAW ENFORCEMENT officials, disrupting this burgeoning money market has become a major, if daunting, priority. Because of weak Colombian financial laws and the complex expansion of the Cali-based money brokerage system, law enforcement officers have yet to make a major case against the key Colombian brokers, officials say. Some vow this will change very soon; others are skeptical that a major success can ever be achieved.

The trouble in breaking up the money market comes as many law enforcement officials are acknowledging the failure of a long U.S. campaign to choke off production of cocaine in South America and to eradicate the coca leaf, the

MONEY TRAIL TO COLOMBIA

IN THE U.S.

■ Cocaine users buy drug on streets

■ Cash held at safe house

■ Broker buys cash held in United States at discount from cartel family, uses various means to get it into Colombia

ON THE TRAIL

■ "Smurfs" — small-time contractors — smuggle cash in modest amounts for the Colombia brokers, or deposit in banks

■ Cash moves in bulk in shipping containers and cocaine-smuggling planes returning empty

BACK TO THE SOURCE

■ "Tourists" change bulk money into pesos

■ Banks change drug money to stocks or bonds

■ Broker receives cash, sells to legitimate Colombian businessman for pesos at discount. Broker pays off contract with cartel in pesos, keeps profit.

THE WASHINGTON POST

raw product from which cocaine is derived. This setback has prompted the development of the "kingpin strategy," which focuses more time and resources on disrupting the astonishingly sophisticated, multi-billion-dollar financial networks of Colombia's biggest cocaine traffickers.

Since the decline of the cocaine cartel based in Medellin, the Colombian organizations based in Cali now manage about 80 percent of the world's cocaine trade, according to the U.S. Drug Enforcement Administration and other sources. Cali's main kingpins include brothers Miguel and Gilberto Rodriguez Orejuela, and their close friend and longtime associate Jose Santacruz Londono. Sources say the Rodriguez Orejuelas have a remarkably sophisticated operation, relying on a system of computerized bookkeeping, wire transfers and cellular phones to monitor business and keep the money flowing.

The trouble, as with past tactics in the U.S.-led drug war, is that it is one thing to talk about disrupting the financial operations of the Colombian cocaine cartels, and another to succeed.

"We celebrate our hollow little victories that don't mean anything because of the magnitude of the problem," says one weary anti-narcotics agent. "The truth is that every day the traffickers are stronger economically and politically."

Statistics make the point. The DEA estimates annual cash seizures from Colombia-based cocaine trafficking organiza-

tions at about $200 million. That's in a cocaine money industry generating an overall estimated $20 billion in illegal cash profits each year, a senior DEA official says.

"If we get 1 in 4 shipments, it's okay with [the traffickers], and we are getting 1 in 100," says one official. "It is going to take more manpower, resources and intestinal fortitude to get serious about this, and I have not seen that yet by any country."

In financial terms, Colombia's cocaine barons can be seen as ordinary commodity exporters faced with two unique business challenges. One problem is that all their customers pay in cash. The other is that this cash must be converted into forms of wealth that the cocaine exporters can use in Colombia.

During the 1980s, investigators say, the cartels generally solved these problems by depositing directly into U.S. banks the cash they received from retailing large loads of cocaine to smaller organizations that handle U.S. street sales. Then the cartels shifted their wholesale profits through front companies and international accounts until they could be safely invested or held for the benefit of cartel leaders.

■

TO A DEGREE, THAT SYSTEM IS STILL AVAILABLE, according to investigators. But tougher U.S. and European banking regulations, increased law enforcement efforts, economic liberalization in Colombia and high interest rates in Colombian banks have made direct deposits into U.S. banks less attractive and riskier than before, investigators and cartel sources say. Among other measures, U.S. authorities now require banks to keep a record of any deposit over $10,000, preventing traffickers from making large deposits without detection. So increasingly, Colombian cocaine exporters—of whom the largest and most powerful are based in Cali—are attempting to smuggle cash dollars out of the United States and to slip them into the legitimate international financial system elsewhere. The doorways for such cash deposits or other "money laundering" transactions are many, but the preferred points of entry into the banking system these days include Panama, Mexico, Brazil, Venezuela and Colombia itself, investigative and cartel sources say.

Specialists, investigators and cartel sources say that increasingly, the Colombian cartels have large amounts of cash backed up in the United States, waiting to be transferred outside U.S. borders.

In response to this problem, the Colombia-based illicit dollar trading market has expanded and evolved. An account of the way the market works was provided by Greg Passic, who directs money laundering investigations for the DEA; Fernando Brito, director of the Department of Administrative Security, Colombia's equivalent of the FBI; Colombian Attorney General Gustavo de Greiff; other law enforcement sources, and a source who has worked with the Cali cartel in its laundering operations.

◼

WHEREAS THE COCAINE CARTELS FORMERLY INSISTED on receiving every dollar earned in the United States, they have lately decided to pay a share of their dollars to middlemen to make it easier to bring their profits back to Colombia, investigators say. The middlemen, who are Colombian money brokers, are now able, for example, to pay just $4 million to the cocaine traffickers in Cali for the right to take possession of $5 million in cash sitting in a safe house in Houston, according to investigators. The broker pockets the difference, in exchange for transporting the money to Colombia.

The size of the payoff to the middleman or broker varies, partly depending on location. Cash that is stashed in some cities is priced more attractively than in others, investigators say. After agreeing to buy a block of cash stored somewhere in the United States, a money broker guarantees to deliver the total amount—minus his commission—to the cocaine cartel family within 15 days of making the deal. He also pledges to deliver the money in Colombian pesos, rather than in dollars.

The broker's profit rests on his ability to smuggle or otherwise transfer the block of cash he has bought in the United States into a bank. He then sells the dollars to a legitimate Colombian businessman, who pays pesos for them and gets the dollars at a better exchange rate than normal. The broker's "spread," or profit, is the portion of the original dollar stash he gets to keep, minus his expenses and the money he loses by allowing a businessman to buy the rest of the dollars from him at a discount. The broker typically tries to reduce his risk in the market by subcontracting the cross-border smuggling aspect of his work to Mexican, Colombian or other gangs adept at finding low-level runners willing to take physical risks with cash, investigators say.

"What you have with the Colombians—it's not organized crime, it's modular crime," says the DEA's Passic. "They have fragmented each function and assigned that responsibility to an individual."

Typically, law enforcement officers in the United States can catch only the small-time subcontracted smugglers as they attempt to move relatively small blocks of cash out of the United States or deposit the money into banks in small amounts to evade the $10,000 bank reporting requirement.

These smugglers are referred to as "smurfs," a nickname based on television cartoon characters that reflects the runners' relative unimportance in the Colombian-based cocaine industry. For example, when police in Cali were sent in May to round up illegal aliens, they found long lines of tourists outside money exchange houses at the downtown Plaza de Caicedo, all with documents in order and all seeking to change $25,000, the legal limit for tourists under Colombian law, according to Brito.

Further investigation determined that the tourists were receiving their dollars from the Cali cocaine cartel and exchanging them in a vast operation involving more than $400,000 a day, Brito says.

Money is "smurfed" by operatives who buy thousands of small postal money orders in the United States and transfer them to virtually unregulated money exchange houses around Colombia. Brito says an investigation into 15 exchange houses in Colombia and 12 in the United States showed the orders were made out in the names of real people, with correct Colombian national identification numbers, obtained from newspaper announcements of deaths or lottery winners. False identifications are produced for smurfs allied with the cartels.

Cartel families stamp symbols on the backs of money orders—a shield, a swan in a circle, an eagle, a smiling moon face—to make clear which money orders are which, according to U.S. Postal Inspection Service investigators.

On the U.S. end, the preponderance of such cash smuggling has led to a relatively large number of cash seizures this summer at airports, other export terminals and safe houses, according to the DEA. In one case this summer, a man was arrested at New York's Kennedy airport after loading about $120,000 in cash into a number of condoms and swallowing them before boarding a flight to Bogota, a DEA official says. The official called this swallowing feat "a record."

Law enforcement officials in Colombia says bulk shipments of dollars, either by airplane or in shipping containers out of Miami to Panama or a Colombian port, are growing.

◼

WITH THE ONCE HIGHLY PROTECTED ECONOMY OF Colombia opening rapidly to foreign imports and with dollar exchange restrictions easing, Colombian and law enforcement officials fear the problem will only grow.

"This whole process of [economic] liberalization has had a dark side," says University of Miami money laundering specialist Bruce Bagley. Adds Colombian Attorney General de Greiff, "What this means is that we have a $5 billion problem. . . . The criminals have an immense power to buy the things they want."

They are also hurting legitimate Colombian business. One popular dollar repatriation technique of late is use of "San Andresitos," sprawling retail markets in most Colombian cities that thrive on contraband consumer goods, says Salomon Kalmanovitz, an academic and banking director who has studied the practice. Cocaine traffickers launder an estimated minimum of $700 million annually through these markets, according to Kalmanovitz and others, by buying television sets, video recorders, liquor, cameras, cosmetics and other luxury goods for cash in Panama and the United States, then smuggling them into Colombia and selling them to consumers at a discount. The huge influx of drug-financed consumer goods is at least partly responsible for Colombia's wildly warped trade statistics, with the government recently reporting a 78 percent increase over 1992 in imports in the first half of this year. Meanwhile, the constant influx of dollars has revalued the Colombian peso internally, making the dollar worth less on the black market than in official exchanges. That hurts legitimate Colombian exporters, who can buy ever less with their dollars earned abroad.

With so much money washing back to the region, and with such a sophisticated cash flow market to be managed, another rising concern is that the Colombian cocaine cartels are moving aggressively into Latin American banking.

"They buy into stock instruments, government debt redemption certificates. There are increasingly sophisticated schemes that we're seeing in most parts of the world," says Rayburn Hesse, senior policy adviser in the U.S. State Department's Bureau of Narcotics, Terrorism and Crime. "There is literally no horizon."

Cocaine Central: How the Invasion Didn't Stop Panama

Steve Coll and Douglas Farah
Washington Post Foreign Service

Coll reported from Panama and Washington, Farah from Panama and Colombia. Washington Post special correspondent Berta Thayer contributed to this report.

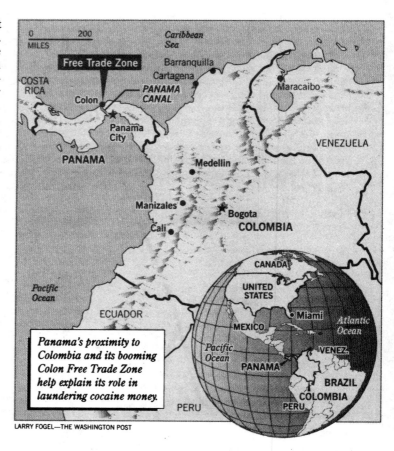

Panama's proximity to Colombia and its booming Colon Free Trade Zone help explain its role in laundering cocaine money.

LARRY FOGEL—THE WASHINGTON POST

COLON, Panama

"Pure Coffee" reads the freshly painted sign on a tin warehouse in this tropical free trade port. But on Sept. 1, federal agents in Miami opened 318 coffee boxes routed from the warehouse and discovered an unusual blend: Panamanian-labeled coffee mixed with 5.2 metric tons of Colombian cocaine.

That large seizure, achieved after Drug Enforcement Administration and U.S. Customs agents penetrated a tangle of front companies and financial records in the United States, Panama, Colombia and elsewhere, is the latest of many signs that Panama remains a major center for cocaine trafficking and the handling of huge cocaine cash profits nearly four years after U.S. forces invaded the country.

The Dec. 20, 1989, invasion was aimed partly at clamping down on Panama's role in the Colombia-based cocaine trade. U.S. troops overthrew Panama's military leader, Gen. Manuel Antonio Noriega, who has been convicted and imprisoned in the United States on cocaine trafficking charges. Yet the State Department acknowledges today that aside from the United States itself, newly democratic Panama is the most active center for cocaine "money laundering" in the Western Hemisphere. Money laundering is the process by which Colombian-based cocaine producers and distributors transfer their illegal cash profits into legitimate bank accounts or other financial assets.

The major cocaine traffickers have begun transferring more and more of their cash profits back to Colombia, creating a vast new illegal market in the transport and exchange of cash dollars. Destabilizing the increasingly sophisticated financial networks of cocaine kingpins has become a priority for U.S. law enforcement and anti-narcotics foreign policy programs. As a result, officials and other experts see freewheeling, post-invasion Panama as one of the major obstacles in the multibillion-dollar U.S. effort to stem the flow of drugs from South America to the United States. Given Panama's proximity to Colombia, its longtime liberal banking rules and its use of the U.S. dollar as its national currency, enforcement officials say some cocaine trafficking and money laundering through the isthmus is inevitable.

But the more pressing issue is whether in democratic Panama the Colombia-based cocaine export industry and its illicit financial services system are just as embedded in major banking, business and government structures as they were under Noriega, when the United States routinely criticized the government.

"What the United States did, you see, was chop off the head but leave the whole rest of the structure intact," a U.S. investigator who concentrates on money laundering says. "The bottom line is that nothing has really changed."

The evidence accumulated so far suggests that Colombian cocaine traffickers today see Panama as a door through which they can move illegal cash profits back to Colombia or into legitimate assets such as bank deposits, real estate and luxury consumer goods.

In part, Panama is a popular gateway because there are no restrictions on the amount of cash that can be imported. There are requirements that large cash deposits to banks be recorded, but records are not analyzed or monitored effectively by the government, U.S. officials say.

PANAMA'S PERVASIVE BUSINESS SECRECY LAWS, which apply to banks and corporations, also make it relatively easy for drug traffickers to build networks of front companies—or businesses that exist only on paper—to disguise, store and siphon cocaine profits into legitimate enterprises, investigators say.

Moreover, a trade in cash is booming in the Panamanian port city of Colon, where the government has set up a "free trade zone" in which items may be imported and sold duty-free. Some traffickers have set up businesses in the zone that are used to smuggle cocaine dollars into the country and deposit them in the Panamanian banking system; others buy luxury consumer goods such as televisions and cosmetics there with cocaine cash, then ship them to Colombia, where they can be sold for Colombian pesos that are "clean" of any taint of trafficking. The State Department recently called Colon a "money-laundering mecca for drug traffickers."

Investigators suspicious of how the Colon zone was being used by Colombian cocaine exporters recently received an education while poring over documents seized in July 1992 from a company called Celeste International. U.S. officials identify Celeste as a major front company that laundered cash for Cali, Colombia, cocaine kingpins Miguel and Gilberto Rodriguez Orejuela. Five tons of cocaine were seized on Celeste's Colon premises.

Situated on the Caribbean mouth of the Panama Canal, the Colon free zone is a teeming trade center for luxury and consumer goods flowing from Western and Asian manufacturers to Central and South American countries. About $9 billion changes hands here every year, roughly 20 percent of it in cash, according to zone officials. Showrooms along its narrow streets display $30,000 watches and glistening Chinese vases as well as duty-free blue jeans, electronics, perfumes and liquor.

Celeste exploited this milieu for the Rodriguez Orejuela trafficking organization by issuing false invoices showing that it received cash for consumer items it never delivered, U.S. officials say. Using these invoices as cover, millions of dollars in cocaine profits allegedly were moved to Celeste's Panamanian bank accounts. From there, they could be routed to wherever the Rodriguez Orejuela group wished—without raising the suspicions of law enforcement officials looking for drug money.

NO ONE KNOWS HOW MUCH OF NEARLY $2 BILLION in annual cash turnover in the Colon free zone is cocaine money washing into the international banking system. But some law enforcement officials are frustrated by what they see as Panama's lack of political will to attack the problem.

The zone's deputy administrator, Gerardo E. Harris, asked about Celeste and other cases of false invoice-based money laundering, replies: "It's not our responsibility. We have no ways or means to determine whether it's occurring or not."

With about 13,000 jobs in the zone at stake, Panamanian officials are reluctant to impose rules that would make Colon less attractive to regional traders. Some Panamanian officials argue that any illicit cash flowing through Colon's free zone most often reflects efforts by traders in a liberalized regional economy to evade tariffs and taxes rather than to launder cocaine profits.

Yet inside and outside the Colon zone, evidence and allegations of cocaine-related money-laundering schemes in post-invasion Panama—or questionable activities by senior officials in the Panamanian government—are plentiful and varied:

■ Panama's suspended attorney general, Rogelio Cruz Rios, has been charged with exceeding his authority when he released in August 1992 about $25 million in alleged Colombian cocaine profits that had been frozen in Panamanian bank accounts at U.S. urging at the time of the 1989 invasion.

Earlier charges that Cruz Rios personally profited by releasing the money have been dropped for lack of evidence. But Panamanian officials say others profited when Cruz Rios unfroze the accounts last year. After the move, a "substantial amount"—millions of dollars—was paid to Panamanian lawyers, according to Carlos Lucas Lopez, president of Panama's Supreme Court. Millions more were transferred out of Panama, he says.

The Panamanian lawyers who benefited say the money they received was for legal fees. "That's the excuse they have given," Lopez says. "But they are very big fees." Investigations are continuing, Lopez says.

■ Panama's Supreme Court recently authorized a more aggressive investigation into accusations that the former head of Panama's customs service, Rodrigo Arosemena, removed and placed in his car trunk $1.8 million in cash from a seized shipment of $7.2 million of suspected cocaine profits smuggled by boat into Panama. The cash was stuffed in cardboard boxes inside a shipping container. Arosemena, who resigned his post to run for the National Assembly, denied taking the cash and called the allegations politically motivated.

■ Last year, after seizing 1.5 metric tons of cocaine, Mexican officials alerted Panama's government that a company in the Colon free trade zone was involved in the shipment, according to sources familiar with the case. A Panamanian businessman was arrested, confessed and was imprisoned. But the U.S. government has learned the businessman has been inexplicably released from jail and has disappeared.

■ An investigation of Panama's booming construction industry has found evidence that many of the luxury towers going up on Panama City's Pacific shoreline have few of the proper permits, raising concerns that the buildings are being constructed to launder large-scale cocaine profits, as is common in Colombia, sources say. By paying cash to buy a piece of property and construct an office tower, investigators say, cocaine traffickers convert illegal cash profits from cocaine into a legal asset—real estate. Panamanian officials counter that such allegations are irresponsible without specific evidence of wrongdoing.

■ A New York judge this year froze millions of dollars held in New York bank accounts by the Hong Kong Bank of Panama on grounds the money represented cocaine profits smuggled into the banking system, consolidated in Panama, then shipped back to the United States, according to an affidavit filed by a U.S. postal inspector.

■ In Miami, two accused cocaine traffickers, Augusto Falcon and Salvador Magluta, are to stand trial on charges that, until 1991, they earned more than $2 billion importing illegal drugs. To disguise their alleged trafficking, the pair employed at least two dozen Panamanian front companies, according to U.S. investigators.

Some of those companies were established more than a decade ago by the law firm of Panamanian President Guillermo Endara. University of Miami money-laundering specialist Bruce Bagley has accused Endara of "willful ignorance" in this and other cases, a view echoed by other critics.

Endara vigorously denies the charge, saying he never

knew that Falcon and Magluta were clients of his large firm. Moreover, Endara's firm withdrew from the matter in 1987 following private warnings that the two clients were unsavory, the president has said.

Whether Endara's involvement will become an issue at the Miami trial is uncertain.

■ The 5.2 tons of cocaine seized in Miami on Sept. 1, routed through a Colon coffee warehouse, has exposed an international network of Panama-based companies and business deals reaching to Europe, the Middle East, the former Soviet Union, South America and the United States, according to sources familiar with that case. Whether investigators will be able to untangle the network fully is another matter.

Indeed, some law enforcement authorities and other critics argue that the cocaine economy has fundamentally poisoned Panama's embryonic democracy. These critics argue that the U.S. government is playing down the extent of cocaine-related organized crime burgeoning in Panama because Washington wants to promote the longevity of Panama's democratic leaders.

"The guys who are supposed to defend the system aren't doing it," says one investigator. "How serious are we? How much can we expect from the local Panamanian officials? . . . The problem is that DEA has nobody to trust here."

■

SENIOR U.S. AND PANAMANIAN OFFICIALS ARGUE that such criticism exaggerates Panama's problem and fails to give its fledgling government credit for what it has accomplished since Noriega's ouster. They say the problem is not as great as it was in Noriega's time, that enforcement efforts are improving and that some difficulties are inevitable in a transition from authoritarian to democratic rule.

"Panamanian authorities are making a good faith and increasingly effective effort to stem the flow of narcotics into and out of Panama," U.S. drug policy director Lee P. Brown declared in an Aug. 11 speech. "But there is more to the problem than trafficking . . . . Panama's financial and business sectors should be at the forefront of [an] effort to help deprive the narco-traffickers of their profits. At stake is not only the reputation of banks and businesses, but the image of Panama."

Yet Panama continues to resist unlocking its bank and corporate secrecy laws or to improve oversight of illicit transactions. Moreover, some Panamanian officials argue that U.S. efforts in this area are hypocritical. From the 1930s, when Washington secretly used Panamanian companies to ship weapons to Britain, to the Iran-contra affair, when the Reagan administration secretly funded the Nicaraguan anti-Communist rebels, Western governments have long exploited Panama's rules for their own ends, Panamanians say.

"It happens now that they're all excited about drugs," Panama's controller general, Ruben D. Carles, says. "But for years, the [U.S.] government used it [the financial system]. Why should we change?"

Reducing Crime Through Street-Level Drug Enforcement

Lieutenant Michael A. Cushing
Narcotics Section, Chicago Police Department, Illinois

Numerous studies confirm that a relationship exists between drugs and crime. A survey of jailed inmates conducted by the U.S. Department of Justice, Bureau of Justice Statistics, found that "three out of four jail inmates surveyed in 1989 reported some drug use in their lifetime. More than 40 percent had used drugs in the month before their offense, with 27 percent under the influence of drugs at the time of their offense. In addition, 13 percent committed their offense to get money to buy drugs. About two out of three state prison inmates reported they had used drugs as frequently as once a week or more for a period of at least a month at some time."[1]

Juveniles and young adults in state-operated institutions have similar backgrounds. More than 60 percent of those surveyed reported using drugs once a week or more for at least a month some time in the past. Almost 40 percent reported being under the influence of drugs at the time of their offense.[2]

Cocaine, the predominant drug found at street level in many major urban areas, has a particularly high correlation with crime. The same survey found that "[c]ocaine or crack users were three times more likely than other drug users to have committed their current offense to obtain money for drugs—39 percent said they were trying to get money for drugs when they committed their crime."[3]

The Drug Use Forecasting (DUF) survey tests the urine of persons in custody who voluntarily submit to testing. In the fourth quarter of 1992, male arrestees in 23 major American cities were tested for drugs. The rate of positive findings for the presence of drugs ranged from 48 percent in Omaha, Nebraska, to 79 percent in Philadelphia, Pennsylvania. The most prevalent drug used by these arrestees was cocaine.[4]

The most frequent distribution of drugs in urban areas occurs at the street level. Generally, the areas where street-level drug dealing occurs are also the areas that have the highest incidence of street crime. It is this form of narcotics distribution that is most troubling to a community. The crack cocaine dealers who stand on the street corners, in the hallways of buildings and outside small convenience stores most negatively affect the perceived quality of life in the neighborhood. The presence of these individuals also brings into the community strangers who either become crime victims or criminal offenders.

Street-Level Operations

Street-level drug dealers are heavily involved in all forms of criminality. Examining the criminal history records of individuals arrested for street-level drug dealing shows that for most, an arrest for street drug dealing is not their first encounter with the criminal justice system. Besides prior narcotics arrests, many of these individuals have been arrested in the past for burglary, robbery, sex offenses, auto theft and/or murder. By targeting street-level drug dealers for enforcement activity, a department is legally removing from the street not only drug dealers, but street criminals who, while free in society, are committing a number of other crimes.

The Narcotics Section of the Chicago Police Department conducts daily operations directed at the street-level distribution of narcotics. Although various methods are employed, the most frequently used is a buy-bust technique, in which controlled purchases of narcotics are made by undercover officers under the watchful eye of surveillance officers. Once the buy officer safely leaves the scene, enforcement officers are directed to the offender by the surveillance officers. The offender is stopped and interviewed by enforcement officers and, after being positively identified by the buy officer, is arrested.

In some operations, the offenders are not immediately arrested. A positive identification is made, and the offender is arrested at a later date with an arrest warrant as part of a larger operation.

Although all forms of illegal drugs are targeted, cocaine is the most frequently purchased drug in these operations, which are conducted city-wide in response to complaints received from citizens, district commanders, community groups and calls to an anonymous drug hotline.

Offenders' Criminal Backgrounds

The criminal histories of offenders in seven street-level enforcement operations were examined. Six of the seven were operations that occurred within the past year; in the seventh, the controlled purchases of narcotics were made within the past two years as part of a larger, long-term investigation that began at the street level. Criminal histories from this seventh operation were included to increase the number of criminal histories examined.

In these seven operations, a total of 291 adult offenders (17 years of age or older) were identified, and arrest warrants were obtained. Any drug dealers who were not positively identified at the time of the controlled purchase were immediately arrested. This prevented the issuance of a warrant on an innocent or non-existent party. Juveniles were also arrested on the scene.

An examination of the criminal backgrounds of these offenders reveals that the individuals selling street-level narcotics are, for the most part, career criminals. As the table below shows, individuals who sold street drugs to undercover police in these operations had had serious contacts with the criminal justice system.

Background of Identified Offenders
(N = 291)

Prior Felony Arrests	Prior Narcotics Arrests	Prior Felony Probation	Prior Prison
129 (44.3%)	176 (60.4%)	103 (35%)	64 (21.9%)

A prior felony arrest includes only those instances in which the individual was charged. In order to be charged for these felony offenses, the case first had to be reviewed and the charges approved by an assistant state attorney from the Felony Review Unit of the Cook County State's Attorney's Office. These felony offenses range from theft to serious violent offenses such as armed robbery, sexual assault, aggravated battery and murder. Felony narcotics offenses were not included in this category.

Prior narcotics arrests were for all violations of Illinois Narcotics Laws. This category includes all narcotics offenses involving the possession, manufacture and delivery of marijuana and controlled substances. These offenses ranged from possession of small amounts of marijuana and hypodermic needles to the manufac-

ture and delivery of controlled substances.

Prior felony probation includes all felony offenses. Violations of the Illinois statutes of criminal offenses and narcotics violations were considered here. Also included in this category were several cases in which the arrestees had received federal felony probation.

Prison time was the result of any felony conviction mandating imprisonment in either a state penitentiary or federal correctional institution. This includes both narcotics and non-narcotics felony convictions.

Court Disposition of Arrestees

Court data for the first 11 months of 1993 involving arrestees charged by narcotics officers with delivery of a controlled substance (i.e., crack, cocaine, heroin, PCP) were also examined. With few exceptions, these deliveries were of street amounts of narcotics, typically under one gram. During these 11 months, 85 percent of the delivery cases initiated by the Narcotics Section resulted in either a finding of guilty or a plea of guilty. Not one case that went to a jury escaped a guilty verdict. In several of the cases that resulted in the judges' acquitting the defendants, the judges stated that they *believed* the defendants to be guilty, but for a variety of reasons did not actually find them guilty.

This conviction rate is higher than the rate for other felony arrests. One must also consider that only a small percentage of other crimes are even cleared by arrest, let alone lead to a felony conviction.

Of the cases that resulted in a guilty verdict for delivery of controlled substances, 40 percent of those convicted were sentenced to one or more years in a state penitentiary. The most common sentence is two to five years.

With crowded penal institutions, it would be extremely rare for someone from a major urban area with no prior criminal record to be sentenced to prison for selling one small bag of narcotics. What sends this 40 percent to the penitentiary is the fact that they are on felony probation for burglary or parole for armed

robbery, or were previously incarcerated for murder. While the holding charge on this trip to the penitentiary may be narcotics, the previous criminal histories reveal that these are career criminals who are being taken off the streets and kept from victimizing the community for a period of time.

Impact on the Community

Vigorous day-to-day enforcement targeting street-level drug dealing offers the community several benefits. Besides removing a criminal element from the street, this strategy responds legally to the community's concerns of individuals openly selling drugs. An effective street drug enforcement program makes the purchase of drugs more difficult for the casual drug user who generally goes outside of his own neighborhood to purchase drugs. The casual drug user in search of drugs and the opportunistic victimizer are both unwelcome in any community.

Conclusion

Often, drug enforcement programs are evaluated solely on their effect on drug distribution networks. However, examining the criminal backgrounds of participants at the street level of drug dealing reveals that many career criminals are involved in street-level drug trafficking. Those selling drugs at the street level are typically the type of criminals that incapacitation programs target. Given the demonstrated pattern of criminal involvement with varied crimes, these individuals are not just street drug dealers; they are armed robbers, burglars, auto thieves and violent offenders. A vigorous street narcotics enforcement program is an effective way to remove them from the street and prevent additional crimes.

[1] Bureau of Justice Statistics, "Drugs, Crime, and the Justice System, A National Report" (Washington, D.C.: U.S. Department of Justice, Office of Justice Programs, Bureau of Justice Statistics, Dec. 1992), p. 3.

[2] *Ibid.*

[3] *Ibid.*

[4] National Institute of Justice, "DUF Quarterly Report," *Research in Brief,* (Washington, D.C.: U.S. Department of Justice, Office of Justice Programs, National Institute of Justice, Fourth Quarter, 1992).

COLOMBIA'S DRUGS BUSINESS

The wages of prohibition

Economic logic and textbook business methods have brought victory in the drug war to the illegal entrepreneurs of Colombia, and those of the city of Cali in particular. The implications are depressing for Colombia, for the inner cities of rich countries, and for prohibitionists everywhere

IT IS more than five years since President Bush declared war on Latin America's illegal cocaine industry. By increasing America's anti-drug budget, involving its armed forces in repression of the drug trade, and by offering hundreds of millions of dollars in aid to the governments and security forces of the Andean cocaine-producing countries, Mr Bush planned to reduce the amount of cocaine reaching the United States from Latin America by 10% within two years, and by 50% in ten years. Half-way through that decade—and after the United States has spent more than $50 billion on its anti-drug fight—Latin America's illegal drug industry is still booming.

Although the issue of illegal drugs is becoming more prominent in many European countries, it no longer commands headlines or the top slot on the political agenda in America. As Europe's politicians may quickly discover, this is mainly because their counterparts in America found that there were few electoral rewards in engaging with such an intractable problem.

Firm figures are few and far between but, such as they are, they give little comfort to anti-drug policemen anywhere. True, American officials reckon that production of cocaine may have fallen recently. (The National Narcotics Intelligence Consumers Committee estimated Latin America's "potential" output of cocaine at 770-805 tonnes in 1993, down from 955-1,000 tonnes in 1992.) But, as the officials admit, the cause has more to do with a fungus that attacked Peru's coca crop than with successful law enforcement. Other analysts believe the com-

mittee may have under-estimated yields. Though much more cocaine is intercepted by the authorities around the world than a decade ago, that positive trend has stopped: total seizures lately seem to have stabilised at between 275 and 350 tonnes a year. In any case, the earlier increase in seizures may reflect higher production as much as tighter prohibition.

The United States remains much the largest market for cocaine. Despite the efforts of a dozen government agencies and all those Bush dollars, repression has not threatened supply. The drug's price is low and stable. For the past five years, wholesale prices have fluctuated around an average of $16,000-20,000 a kilo (down from $50,000-60,000 in the early 1980s). Meanwhile, new markets for cocaine have opened up across the world, especially in Europe. America's State Department notes that all major European capitals have reported a growing influx of cocaine. Last year Russian police seized more than a tonne of Colombian cocaine in St Petersburg.

On the demand side, use of cocaine and crack has spread to Europe's inner cities. In America, government figures suggest that the casual use of cocaine declined sharply after 1985, but is now increasing again. Some analysts doubt the value of this figure: it relies on consumers telling the truth. The figures also show that consumption by regular users is going up. Hospital emergencies involving cocaine—probably the most reliable indicator of consumption—have increased by 25% since 1991 (see chart). In addition, the use of heroin is rising sharply in America.

This bleak picture is not due to lack of effort by the drug fighters. Indeed, they have some notable successes to their credit, thanks partly to unprecedented cross-border co-operation. One such success was "Green Ice", an international operation in 1992 against the money-laundering system of traffickers from Cali, Colombia. Co-ordinated by America's Drug Enforcement Administration (DEA), it led to 200 arrests in seven countries and the seizure of $40m in cash.

A year ago security forces finally caught and killed Pablo Escobar, Colombia's most notorious and most violent drug gangster. The chase, assisted by America's most sophisticated intelligence technology, had taken 17 months. Escobar's death completed the dismantling of the "Medellin cartel", which American officials claimed had been responsible for 80% of the cocaine reaching the United States during the 1980s. Escobar and his cronies were also behind a bloody campaign of bombings, including the blowing up of a civil airliner in mid-flight with more than 100 passengers aboard, as well as the murder of some of Colombia's leading politicians, judges and journalists.

Yet neither operation had a discernible impact on the flow of cocaine. Individual traffickers have come and gone, but taken as a whole the Andean drug industry, whose centre of operations has long been in Colombia, appears stronger than ever. Colombia has also emerged as an important producer of heroin—perhaps the second largest, after Myanmar (Burma). The Colombian trafficking businesses appear to have stepped up both the repatriation of drug profits and their investment in legal businesses. Less than two decades after large-scale exports of cocaine from Colombia began, the country's drug business now seems too big, too diversified and too clever for law-enforcement efforts to have more than a marginal effect on its viability.

Risk and reward

Why has this happened? The answer starts with the peculiar economics of an illegal trade. Prices at each stage in the long chain that turns a coca leaf on an Andean hillside into a gram of cocaine on the streets of the Bronx are determined principally by the risks that stem from the trade's illegal status. That is why the price of a kilo of pure cocaine (measured in relation to its equivalent in coca leaf) rises by a factor of roughly 200 times between the coca farm and the street. Most of that increase occurs once the drug has entered the United States—because law enforcement is tighter in most of America's cities than in, say, the wilder parts of Peru's Amazon basin.

Peter Reuter, an economist at the University of Maryland who has made a detailed study of cocaine economics, argues that even much tougher enforcement in the producer countries would fail to eliminate the supply of cocaine. There are just too many coca farmers, processors, exporters and smugglers. Rather, by adding to the pro-

ducers' risks, the effect of stronger enforcement would be to increase the price at each stage in the chain of supply. But since prices at the manufacturing stages represent a tiny part of the final price, action against coca

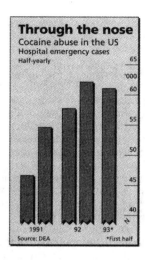

and cocaine producers in the Andes (of the kind championed by Mr Bush) has little effect on the street price in the United States.

Mr Reuter reckons that a tripling of the price of coca leaves would increase the street price of cocaine in the United States by less than 2%. Or to look at it another way: the cost of smuggling a kilo of cocaine to an American port could triple and still leave the smugglers in profit, even if the price they received remained the same.

Aside from economic difficulties, attempts to repress the drug trade in the Andean countries have also been dogged by corruption and lack of political will. Peru's armed forces have made progress against the Shining Path guerrillas in the Upper Huallaga valley (a coca-producing area), but have been less than zealous in pursuing the drug trade itself. Some officers appear to have joined it. In Colombia, despite the honourable record of many politicians, judges and police chiefs, the security forces have taken little action against the Cali traffickers—who collaborated in the pursuit of Escobar. But to repeat Mr Reuter's point, it would make little difference if the institutions of the drug-producing countries were entirely uncorrupt.

Repression has not merely failed. By fragmenting the industry and encouraging innovation it has actually made the drug trade harder to fight. Both effects are apparent in the changing shape of the Andean cocaine industry.

A decade ago, most of the coca used to make cocaine was grown in just two areas: Peru's Upper Huallaga valley, and the Chapare region in Bolivia. After initial processing on site, cocaine paste was flown in light planes to Colombia for refining. Exports to the United States were controlled by a handful of illegal entrepreneurs, based mainly in Medellin and Cali. Now, the industry is much more complicated.

Cultivation of coca has declined in the Upper Huallaga valley since 1992, partly because a leaf-eating fungus hit the most densely planted areas. It has risen only slightly in the Chapare thanks mainly to a programme financed by America, under which coca farmers are paid to withdraw fields from production. But coca has spread elsewhere across north-western Latin America, pushing into increasingly remote areas. Today coca is grown not only in new parts of Peru and Bolivia but also in Venezuela and Panama. And production has surged in Colombia: the area under cultivation may have doubled in the past two years, to 80,000 hectares—bigger than the area under coca in Bolivia, and enough to nullify the effect of the Peruvian fungus.

Drug processing and exporting have also become fragmented. Peruvian traffickers have begun to export cocaine direct, instead of selling semi-processed paste to Colombians. One theory links both this and the growth of the coca crop in Colombia to the installation of American radars on the border between Peru and Colombia and to the Peruvian government's decision to shoot planes down that do not have flight plans registered in advance.

In Colombia, the DEA says that Cali has replaced Medellin as the centre of the industry and supplies roughly three-quarters of the cocaine reaching the United States. But several other important trafficking organisations have emerged. As well as re-organised remnants of the Medellin organisation, they include outfits based on Colombia's north coast, in other areas of the Cauca valley near Cali, in the eastern plains and in Bogota, the capital.

Anything but a cartel

One of the things that makes analysing Colombia's drug industry difficult is that America's policy-makers and journalists are too fond of the term "cartel". The DEA coined it, applying it first to the Medellin traffickers and now to their counterparts in Cali. Economics, evidently, is not among the DEA's strengths.

A cartel is a coalition of producers acting together to restrict supply and drive up the price of their product. Yet, as Francisco Thoumi of Bogota's University of the Andes argues, the cocaine "cartels" have increased production probably threefold over the past 15 years, allowing the average wholesale price in the United States to fall by 75%. Moreover, behind that average, prices vary a great deal from city to city (see chart).

So although there is evidence of co-ordination among different cocaine producers, and of control by certain specialists over aspects of the business such as transport and smuggling, there is little evidence that certain traffickers (such as Escobar and Jorge Luis Ochoa) ever tried to restrict supply, and none that they succeeded. Mr Thoumi suggests the terms "exporters' association" or "co-operative" to describe the Cali organisation. Others talk of "syndicates" or of a commodities-style "cocaine exchange".

There is more to this than semantics. Though everyone agrees that the Cali traffickers currently dominate the business, it is unclear how tightly they control the market—and it is harder to defeat an enemy that you do not understand. A senior DEA official says their organisation is like "the board of directors of a large corporation, which has a number of vice-presidents each in charge of a different branch". But another experienced DEA official, who dislikes the term "cartel", says that Cali is "a consortium [whose members] work together when it suits them, otherwise not. They co-operate on some deals but not on others."

The DEA identified some of Cali's most powerful drug entrepreneurs long ago. They include the Rodriguez Orejuela brothers (Gilberto and Miguel), whose specialities are transporting cocaine to America and money-laundering; Jose Santacruz Londono, who controls wholesale distribution in New York; and three other family clans—the Grajales, whom the DEA believes are important exporters of cocaine to Europe, the Herreras, and the Urdinolas. But Alvaro Camacho, a sociologist at Bogota's National University, says that each town in the Cauca valley now has one or two important drug entrepreneurs operating more or less independently. He says a kind of class structure has developed: at the bottom is a group of young and murderous former gunmen, who have become small-scale cocaine entrepreneurs in their own right.

Politics and commerce

Some Colombians argue that the success of the senior Cali traffickers is due mainly to their political strategy. Whereas Escobar attempted to enter politics openly—and, when thwarted, threw down a military challenge that the state could not ignore—the Cali entrepreneurs quietly cultivated political influence through corruption (though their ways of dealing with traitors have been no less brutal for that). And while Escobar reacted violently to rebuffs by Colombia's traditional elite, his Cali rivals bided their time, investing in a parallel, and legal, business empire.

Other analysts claim that Cali's emergence as the leader of the cocaine industry is due not just to political skills, but also to the sophisticated business methods that the traffickers have used to contain risk and maintain or expand their profits. In certain respects, Colombia's drug entrepreneurs have done this with all the acumen and professionalism of, say, the big international tobacco companies. In developing these methods, Cali's entrepreneurs have been in the forefront:

• **Reducing risk.** Mr Thoumi argues that this aim has determined the opaque structure of the industry—with its mixture of compartmentalised businesses (to increase secrecy) and various forms of association (to make sharing information, especially about the authorities, easier). It has also meant that the family business, where ties of loyalty are strong, has been the typical form of enterprise.

Risks can be reduced in other ways. Cali has extended its reach to the first level of distribution in America; exploiting this greater degree of control, the town's traffickers can demand payment up-front before any cocaine is shipped. Wholesale distributors are required to offer collateral in Colombia—normally a property but sometimes also the names and addresses of family members in the United States.

• **Achieving economies of scale.** Although Escobar and his associates developed large-scale production facilities (in the form of big cocaine-processing labs in Colombia's eastern plains), these involved greater losses when detected. For the past ten years, labs have tended to be dispersed over a wider area, including neighbouring countries such as Venezuela, Ecuador and Brazil. Economies of scale have been sought not in production but in transport.

The pioneer was Carlos Lehder (currently serving a life sentence in the United States). In 1978 Mr Lehder bought a small island in the Bahamas, and began using it as a base for regular flights to small airstrips in the south-eastern United States. This service, for which he charged a fee to cocaine producers in Colombia, accepted loads of 250 kilos or more. Previously, loads had been limited to what could be concealed by individual smugglers ("mules") passing through airports.

The next step was to use commercial aircraft. In 1982 customs agents discovered 2 tonnes of cocaine in a shipment of jeans at Miami International Airport. The DEA reckoned the drugs came from 15 different trafficking organisations.

In addition, Cali's entrepreneurs rely heavily on merchant shipping, using ever more elaborate methods of concealment. (Recent seizures have found cocaine hidden in concrete fence-posts, in cans of fruit juice and stuffed inside frozen fish.) This has permitted shipments of up to 20 tonnes. Since 10m containers pass through America's ports each year (of which customs agents search only 4%), this method further reduces the risk of detection. In the same way, the newest thing in transport—the use of semi-submersible craft and home-made submarines to ferry drugs from Colombia's north coast to Puerto Rico—lessens risk at the same time as providing opportunities for shipping in bulk.

• **Just-in-time supply.** Since most value in an illegal business is added in the final market, competitive advantage derives from an ability to provide continuous supply, which in turn ensures control over distribution networks. Stocks must be maintained at all points along the smuggling pipeline to minimise the effect of lost shipments. The success of the Cali traffickers in this respect may have been a decisive factor in their gaining control of distribution networks in America after 1989-90, when the Medellin traffickers were distracted by a Colombian government crackdown. Such is their confidence in the system that the Cali shippers offer insurance against lost supplies.

• **Developing new products and markets.** The DEA blames Dominican drug dealers in New York for the introduction of crack, a form of cocaine which has a more powerful effect in smaller, cheaper quantities—and which therefore created a new and wider market. Other forms of innovation have paid off too. As the price of cocaine tumbled in the late 1980s, when the American market became saturated, the Colombian industry turned to Europe; the Cali traffickers may have made a distribution deal with the Italian mafia.

Colombia's traffickers also began producing heroin. Although there is some evidence that Colombia's move into heroin production may have been pioneered by smaller trafficking organisations (including leftist guerrillas), Cali is now involved as

United States cocaine prices				
$ per kilogram				
Area	1991	1992	1993	1994*
National range	11,000-40,000	11,000-42,000	10,500-40,000	10,500-40,000
Chicago	18,000-30,000	17,500-37,000	20,000-30,000	21,000-25,000
Los Angeles	12,000-28,000	11,000-20,000	14,000-20,000	15,000-20,000
Miami	14,000-25,000	13,500-25,000	16,000-24,000	16,000-22,000
New York	14,000-29,000	12,500-35,000	17,000-25,000	17,000-22,000
Source: DEA				*Jan-Jun

well. The DEA reports that distributors working for Cali are requiring customers to buy heroin along with cocaine.

• **Developing new production technology.** Colombia's coca crop was traditionally of poor quality. This is changing. Sergio Uribe, a consultant to the United Nations and author of Colombia's forthcoming national anti-drug plan, says that growers have introduced new higher-yielding Peruvian varieties. And using new methods (involving gasoline and powdered cement), it is possible to extract more usable material during the first stage of processing.

Drug capital

This modernisation of the cocaine industry has an important consequence. It means that even if Colombia succeeds in eliminating the senior Cali traffickers, or in persuading them to surrender, the effect on the industry would almost certainly be short-lived. There is no reason to suppose that the accumulated knowledge of business techniques is held exclusively by the top families. The industry is too diversified for that. Anyway, many key tasks (money laundering, record keeping, information processing) are carried out by hired professionals—accountants, lawyers, systems engineers. Lines of succession have in many cases already been devised. The DEA believes that the Rodriguez Orejuela brothers and their colleagues, for instance, are grooming lieutenants to take over their businesses.

The implications of this are only half-recognised by many American officials. President Clinton has shifted the focus of anti-drug rhetoric towards education and treatment. But the administration clings to an "integrated" drug strategy—albeit hampered by budget cuts—with interdiction efforts overseas focused on "source" rather than "transit" countries. Britain is also trying to emphasise education and treatment. Other European countries such as Holland have always followed this approach.

Colombia faces an equally difficult, but different, problem. Apart from the violence and corruption spread by an illegal industry, it must cope with a growing economic problem: the misallocation of resources caused by financial dependence on exports of drugs.

Although most of the profits of the drug industry are made in the retail markets of America and Europe, Colombian economists believe that the drug entrepreneurs have repatriated at least $1½ billion-2½ billion a year for the past decade. The figure may have risen in 1990-92, when the government removed barriers to capital flows in an effort to encourage foreign investment. (Mr Thoumi notes that these figures also exclude investments in Colombia by drug distributors resident in the United States.) This compares with gross investment by the legal private sector averaging $2.8 billion a year during the 1980s. In other words, drug capital now finances a significant fraction of the country's accumulation of capital.

Though Colombia has a diversified and relatively fast-growing legal economy (thanks partly to sound macroeconomic policies), its hopes of becoming a Latin American jaguar are now threatened by the distortions induced by drug money. Much of this cash is invested to bestow social legitimacy on the drug entrepreneurs. Traffickers have built clinics and cinemas in their home towns in the Cauca valley, for example. Colombian analysts estimate that drug entrepreneurs own roughly a third of the country's agricultural land. But where the main purpose of investment is to launder drug money, the effect is often to crowd out legal businesses. Loss-making firms from fruit canning plants to furniture stores may have caused legal rivals to fail.

A lot, and perhaps most, of the drug entrepreneurs' investment is made in the quest for further (not necessarily legal) profits. Two activities stand out: importing electrical appliances, and building. Markets for contraband electrical appliances have boomed. The main one in Bogota now occupies eight blocks, and three others have arisen in the south of the city. These benefit consumers by undercutting conventional retailers, but they encourage tax evasion. The biggest risk to the economy, however, may lie in a property boom.

Cranes tower over Cali. Many are being used to build shopping centres, hotels and luxury flats financed by drug money. Construction is likely to grow by 9% in 1994. (In 1993 it grew even faster, by 12%; the economy as a whole expanded by 4½%.) Salomon Kalmanovitz, of Colombia's central bank, fears that the property boom could eventually trigger a collapse in asset values.

He notes that since 1991 the value of urban property has appreciated by 50-60% a year, compared with an average inflation rate of 22% a year. The immediate headache for the authorities, however, is the rise in the value of the Colombian peso. The influx of drug money coincided with a sharp increase in export earnings from coffee (thanks to record prices) and oil (because of new fields). As a result, the peso has appreciated by 30% so far this year in real terms against the dollar, threatening the competitiveness of Colombia's legal exports.

Hitherto Colombia's policy towards the drug trade has been dictated by political and foreign-policy considerations. As a result, it has oscillated between repression of traffickers who challenge the state, and negotiating the surrender of those who do not. By now, the limits of this approach are clear. If Colombia is to break its own debilitating dependence on drugs, the world's rich countries must understand the economics that drives the drugs trade. Demand creates supply, prohibition notwithstanding.

Drugs, Alcohol and Violence: Joined at the Hip

Joseph A. Califano, Jr.

Drugs, alcohol and violence are joined at the hip, three marauding musketeers, marching in lock step through the streets of American cities, towns and villages, leaving in their wake a grisly kaleidoscope of crime, terrified citizens, overcrowded prisons, overwhelmed court systems, and property damage and security systems that raise the price of everything we do from going to the movies to depositing money in the bank and buying groceries at the supermarket.

Murder. Date rape. Vandalism. Child abuse. Wild-west shootouts in urban streets. Devastated neighborhoods. Metal detectors at school entrances and teachers locked in classrooms for their own safety. Forty thousand highway deaths. Hospital emergency rooms chock-a-block with injuries from knife and gunshot wounds, domestic violence and household accidents. City dwellers on an afternoon walk accosted by angry homeless people. Parks shut down at night because they're too dangerous for anyone to walk. Destroyed neighborhood basketball courts and playgrounds.

Look behind any of these symptoms of savagery in our society and more than likely you will find lurking in the shadows alcohol and drug abuse and addiction.

Watch a local television newscast, read a daily newspaper or walk a city street and the anecdotal evidence of the ravages of drug and alcohol abuse is splattered all over it.

► **Twelve-year-old Polly Klaas** was kidnapped at knifepoint during a slumber party and found strangled to death not far from her home in the small, sleepy town of Petaluma, California. The murderer was 39-year-old Richard Allen Davis, an ex-con with a history of alcohol and drug abuse and run-ins with the law since age 12. On parole following a previous kidnapping, Davis was taking a "potpourri" of drugs that night and "still doesn't know why he did it." Raised by an alcoholic father, Davis was first arrested for being drunk and disorderly at age 19. *People Magazine,* December 20, 1993.

► **Thirteen-year-old Joseph Chaney,** held without bail for trial as an adult for robbing a man at gunpoint, was six years old at the time of his first of more than 15 arrests. His home life was

in shambles due to his mother's drug addiction. "Life wasn't like I wanted it to be," says Joseph about those days. He dreamed of living in "a rich house" where the refrigerator was always full. Last year, Joseph missed 120 days of school. *The Wall Street Journal,* November 30, 1993.

► **Ten-year-old Sheriff S. Byrd,** eulogized as a "bright little star" by the firefighter who tried to save him, was playing with friends near his home on a crack-infested block in the Bronx when he was killed by a stray shot from a .357 Magnum during a shootout among four drug dealers. Four years later, 32-year-old Amado Pichardo was charged with second-degree murder and criminal possession of a weapon. A bullet from his gun, police said, hit Sheriff in the back that afternoon when Pichardo shot at three other drug dealers.

► **Two children—a son, 12, and a daughter, 6—**bade their mother a tearful goodbye as she was led away to serve a minimum five-year sentence for killing the man accused of molesting her son. Ellie Nesler shot Mark Driver, 35, five times in the head and neck while he sat in a courtroom during a hearing to determine if he should stand trial. She admitted using methamphetamine on the day of the shooting. *The New York Times,* January 9, 1994.

► **A 28-year-old legal secretary,** Lisa Bongiorno, sits in a cell at Rikers Island facing the possibility of life in prison. Charged with killing two high-ranking Greek Orthodox priests in Queens, New York, she was smoking her weekly ritual—$10 worth of PCP—when her car plowed into theirs. Every weekday morning, Ms. Bongiorno went to her job at a Manhattan law firm; every Sunday morning, she took her 7-year-old daughter to church, and every payday for the last 10 years she "had to get high." The arresting officer reported: "She said she drove into upper Manhattan to purchase two dime bags of PCP. She stated that while driving back she smoked one of the bags of PCP in a pipe and she remembered being in the accident." *New York Newsday,* March 19 and March 26, 1994.

► **A couple living in a shelter** for the homeless in Westchester County, New York, were charged with accidentally smothering their baby to death in a crack-induced stupor. The couple have lengthy criminal records, including drug possession. The

From the *Center on Addiction and Substance Abuse at Columbia University, Annual Report 1993,* pp. 6-10. Reprinted by permission.

mother had fallen asleep and rolled over on her two-month-old infant. She was on probation after conviction of possessing drug paraphernalia. *The New York Times,* December 31, 1993.

► **In Austin, Texas, in CASA's Children at Risk** program for 6th, 7th and 8th graders, parents asked the police to protect safe houses that the parents were willing to establish on each block of a seven-block corridor their children had to walk to school. The parents wanted to give their children a place for escape when drug dealers accosted them or hopped-up teens tried to rape or rob them.

At least two of the three million individuals on probation or parole in the United States have drug or alcohol abuse or addiction problems.

The statistical evidence is overwhelming:

► Alcohol and/or drug abuse is implicated in some three-fourths of all murders, rapes, child molestations and deaths of babies and children from parental neglect.

► In Boston, alcohol and/or drug abuse was involved in 89 percent of the cases of infant abuse.

► In 1993, American taxpayers forked over more than $6 billion in federal, state and local taxes just to incarcerate individuals sentenced for drug offenses.

► At least two of the three million individuals on probation or parole in the United States have drug or alcohol abuse or addiction problems.

► In Arkansas, 95 percent of the children in juvenile court are charged with drug- or alcohol-related crimes.

► The average prisoner downs eight drinks a day during the year before the crime for which he is convicted.

THE COLLAPSE OF THE AMERICAN SYSTEM OF JUSTICE

The pandemic of drug and alcohol abuse is destroying our legal system.

From 1980 until 1993, the number of drug cases prosecuted has tripled. But that is only the tip of the iceberg. Most rape, assault, criminal child abuse and robbery cases involve defendants who were high on alcohol or drugs at the time they committed the offenses for which they are charged.

Prosecutors accept pleas just to get rid of cases. In most cities each prosecutor is handling caseloads more than double the American Bar Association-recommended number of 150 felonies a year.

Judges are demoralized. Corporate lawyers who gave up their practices to become federal judges looked forward to trying high-visibility anti-trust and securities cases. They now find themselves sentencing one drug offender after another, often seeing the same prisoner return two or three times for the same offenses.

The federal and state civil court systems are suffering from the pressure of criminal cases prompted by drug and alcohol abuse. In 1991, the civil jury system was closed down in eight states for at least part of the year to free up judges and other resources to meet the speedy trial requirements of criminal cases.

The collapse of the judicial system poses a threat to our democracy. America is an increasingly bureaucratic society where the individual can easily become a number before big governments, big banks and big private institutions. The courts are the one branch of government where a citizen can go to be treated as an individual. If someone is angry enough to sue, feels abused enough by some action to hire a lawyer and file an action in a civil court and then cannot have his grievance heard on a timely basis, society is clamping a lid on a head of steam that may eventually burst out in a destructive way.

The most vulnerable victims of the overcrowded judicial system are those caught up in the juvenile and family courts. Originally designed to save the children who went astray and repair shattered families, they, too, have been overwhelmed by cases involving alcohol and drug abuse.

The most vulnerable victims of the overcrowded judicial system are those caught up in the juvenile and family courts. Originally designed to save the children who went astray and repair shattered families, they, too, have been overwhelmed by cases involving alcohol and drug abuse.

Eighty percent of juveniles arrested admit to use of illegal drugs, more than half of them before reaching age 13. The murder arrest rate among 10- to 17-year-olds has risen so rapidly—tripling from 1983 to 1993—that states are rushing to treat these youngsters as adult criminals, denying them otherwise available rehabilitation services.

Family courts are awash with the ravages of alcohol and drug abuse. Child abuse and neglect reports have tripled in the past decade, reaching three million in 1993. The National Council of Juvenile and Family Court Judges estimates that substance abuse is a significant factor in up to 90 percent of the cases that get to family court. Most of the battering of some four million women that occurs each year involves drug and alcohol abuse.

THE PRISONS

The United States of America has more prisoners per capita than any other nation in the industrialized world—455 per 100,000, compared to 311 for South Africa, 111 for Canada and 42 for Japan. In 1993, American prisons bulged with more than 900,000 inmates.

Some 80 percent of those incarcerated in state prisons are there for drug- or alcohol-related crimes; more than 60 percent of those in federal prisons are there for violation of federal drug laws.

For the first time in 1990—and in every year since then—the number of individuals sent to prison for drug crimes exceeded the number sent there for property crimes. And most of those convicted of property crimes were under the influence of alcohol or drugs at the time of commission of their offense.

If we do not act across society to attack substance abuse on all fronts—research, prevention and treatment—we will bear witness to the collapse of our individualized system of equal justice for all.

Most prisoners are Dickensian warehouses, crowded with the mentally ill and substance abusers and addicts, with drugs freely available (often sold by guards), and AIDS and tuberculosis rampant. The incidence of AIDS in federal and state prisons was 362 cases per 100,000 inmates in 1992, 20 times the 18 cases per 100,000 in the total U.S. population. More than three-fourths of prisoners are addicted to cigarettes.

PROBATION AND PAROLE

The time when probation and parole officers could handle their caseloads and help their wards is long past. In Los Angeles, a probation officer can have 1,000 cases assigned at any one time. In other large cities, the situation is similar. Since most individuals on probation and parole have drug and alcohol addiction and abuse problems, their need is far greater than the probationer or parolee of 50 years ago.

WHAT WE CAN DO

The sorry state of the entire criminal justice and court system in America has led CASA to embark on a meticulous analysis of the facts. Who is in American prisons? Who sits on the federal and state benches? How are parole and probation officers trained? What happens in prisons? Are treatment programs available—and if so, how effective are they?

It is our intention over 1994 and 1995 to set out before the American people the cost of all substance abuse to our legal system—including criminal, civil, juvenile and family courts; prisons and juvenile homes; probation and parole; health care; quality of judges and lawyers; and taxpayer dollars. No such analysis has been attempted. It is CASA's belief that once presented with the facts and costs, the American people can be moved to take action.

Many of the problems in the legal system lie outside it. Just as American health care is too important to be left to the doctors, and war too important for the generals, so the legal system is too important to our democratic way of life to be left to the lawyers.

One thing is clear: if we do not act across society to attack substance abuse on all fronts—research, prevention and treatment—we will bear witness to the collapse of one of the four pillars of our democracy, an individualized system of equal justice for all. And if the judicial branches cannot function effectively, at the federal level and in the states, the other three pillars—the executive branches, the legislatures and the free press—will lose an essential source of nourishment and protection.

Homicide in New York City

Cocaine Use and Firearms

Kenneth Tardiff, MD, MPH; Peter M. Marzuk, MD; Andrew C. Leon, PhD; Charles S. Hirsch, MD;
Marina Stajic, PhD; Laura Portera; Nancy Hartwell

Objective.—To determine differences between racial/ethnic groups in overall rates of death by homicide, proportion of firearm homicides, and the use of cocaine prior to death.

Design.—Descriptive epidemiologic survey of a complete 2-year sample of homicides.

Setting.—New York City, NY (population 7 322 564).

Subjects.—All residents (N=4298) of New York City who were victims of homicide during 1990 and 1991.

Main Outcome Measures.—Using medical examiner data, age- and gender-specific rates of homicide were calculated for African Americans, Latinos, and whites. Separate logistic regression analyses were conducted to examine the association between demographic variables and both recent cocaine use and firearm-related homicides.

Results.—Young African-American and Latino men were more likely to be victims of homicide than all other demographic groups. Approximately three fourths of all homicides involved firearms. In the subset of homicide victims dying within 48 hours (n=3890), 31.0% were positive for cocaine metabolites. African Americans (odds ratio [OR], 1.6; 95% confidence interval [CI], 1.2 to 2.1), Latinos (OR, 1.4; 95% CI, 1.1 to 1.9), and victims 25 through 34 years of age (OR, 2.9; 95% CI, 2.5 to 3.5) and 35 through 44 years of age (OR, 2.7; 95% CI, 2.2 to 3.4) were more likely to be positive for cocaine metabolites than other groups. Young males and females were equally likely to have used cocaine before death. Victims 15 through 24 years of age were more likely than other age groups to be killed by a firearm. African Americans (OR, 1.7; 95% CI, 1.3 to 2.3), Latinos (OR, 1.5; 95% CI, 1.2 to 2.0), and Asians (OR, 2.2; 95% CI, 1.4 to 3.6) were more likely than whites to be killed by a firearm. Men (OR, 4.8; 95% CI, 4.0 to 5.9) were more likely than women to be killed by a firearm. There was no association between having used cocaine before death and being killed by a firearm.

Conclusions.—The high rates of death by homicide among young African Americans and Latinos may be due to the increased involvement with both cocaine use and firearms. New efforts must be made to decrease cocaine use and firearm availability.

(JAMA. 1994;272:43-46)

From the Section of Epidemiology, Department of Psychiatry (Drs Tardiff, Marzuk, and Leon and Mss Portera and Hartwell) and Department of Public Health (Dr Tardiff), Cornell University Medical College, New York, NY; and the Office of the Chief Medical Examiner, City of New York, and Department of Forensic Medicine (Drs Hirsch and Stajic), New York (NY) University School of Medicine (Drs Hirsch and Stajic).

Address correspondence to Department of Psychiatry, Cornell University Medical College, 525 E 68th St, Box 147, New York, NY 10021 (Dr Tardiff).

THE UNITED States is the undisputed leader among developed countries in rates of homicide.[1] Of particular concern is the very high rate of death by homicide among African-American males 15 through 24 years of age.[2,3] Little has been said about the high rate of homicide among Latinos in the United States. Yet homicide rates for Latinos are al-most as high as rates for African Americans in all gender groups.[4] Studies of homicide and race and homicide in relation to poverty and other adverse social conditions have used data prior to the mid 1980s.[5-8]

More recently, two other factors may have become important in the increase of homicides among African Americans and Latinos. The first is the increased availability and abuse of crack cocaine, which is reported in household surveys to be more commonly used by African Americans.[9,10] Studies of homicide and cocaine using medical examiner data from the mid 1980s were small and did not adequately evaluate race or ethnicity.[11-16] The second new factor is the increased availability and lethality of firearms. Since 1985, the rate of firearm homicide has increased among young African Americans.[2,3] In 1990, a national survey found that 20% of students reported carrying a gun in high school in the month preceding the survey and that African-American (39%) and Latino (41%) students were more likely than other students to do so.[17]

The current study examined all homicides in New York City, which is under the jurisdiction of one chief medical examiner, during 1990 and 1991. This provides a large number of cases in a short period of time with uniform classification of the variables studied. It sought to determine the following: (1) the demographic characteristics of the homicide victims, (2) the demographic differences in victims of firearm homicide, (3) the demographic differences in the recent use of cocaine by victims prior to the homicide, and (4) the relationship between recent cocaine use and being killed by a firearm.

METHODS

All deaths (N=4298) of residents in New York City in 1990 and 1991 that

Table 1.—Characteristics of Homicide Victims Killed in 1990 and 1991 in New York City (Residents Only)

Characteristic	No. of Cases	% of All Homicides
Age, y		
<1	46	1.1
1-14	93	2.2
15-24	1442	33.7
25-34	1457	34.0
35-44	693	16.2
45-54	289	6.8
55-64	126	2.9
≥65	132	3.1
Total	**4278***	**100.0**
Gender		
Male	3682	85.7
Female	614	14.3
Total	**4296***	**100.0**
Race		
White	402	9.4
African American	2069	48.2
Latino	1648	38,4
Asian/other	171	4.0
Total	**4290***	**100.0**
Cause of death		
Firearms	3131	72.8
All other methods	1167	27.2
Total	**4298**	**100.0**

*Numbers are less than 4298 because of unknowns for age, gender, and race.

were certified as homicides (*Manual of the International Statistical Classification of Diseases, Injuries, and Causes of Death, Based on the Recommendations of the Ninth Revision Conference, 1975*, E960 through E975) by the medical examiner were eligible for the study. Data concerning demographics, cause of death, and toxicology were collected from the files of the medical examiner. The race or ethnicity of the homicide victims was classified on the basis of information supplied by the family or other persons identifying the body, not merely by the last name or the victim's skin color. For further details on data collection and the toxicological measurement of benzoylecgonine (BE), a metabolite of cocaine, the reader is referred to one of our previous studies.[18]

A smaller subset of cases (n=3890) was used to determine the prevalence of recent cocaine use as measured by the presence of BE. A total of 408 cases (7.6%) from the total sample were excluded from the study either because cocaine toxicology was unavailable or because survival times were unknown or so prolonged as to prohibit inferences about cocaine use by victims at the time of their injury. The survival time of 48 hours was used as a cutoff because little metabolite is detectable in urine beyond 48 hours from the last typical cocaine dose.[19-23]

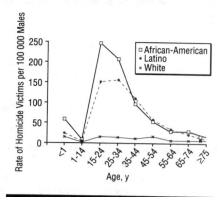

Fig 1.—Race-specific annual rates of homicide (1990 and 1991) for male residents of New York City stratified by age.

Two-tailed χ^2 tests (α=.05) were used to compare the ethnicity and age distribution of the samples that were included and excluded from subsequent analyses. Annual gender-specific homicide rates for residents of New York City were calculated by decennial age groups, separately for three racial/ethnic groups: African Americans, Latinos, and whites. Asians and others were not included in age-, gender-, or race-specific rates because of the small number of cases. Homicide rates are expressed per 100 000 person-years and are based on population denominators obtained from the 1990 US Census (US Department of Commerce, Bureau of the Census. 1990 Census of Population and Housing Summary Tape 1A, New York State). Two separate logistic regression analyses were conducted to examine demographic variables that were associated with firearm homicides and BE-positive homicides. Odds ratios (ORs) and corresponding 95% confidence intervals (CIs) were calculated for each independent variable in the logistic regression model.

RESULTS

There were 4298 homicides among New York City residents during 1990 and 1991. Two thirds of the victims were between the ages of 15 and 34 years, 86% were male, and 87% were African-American or Latino (Table 1). Age- and race-specific rates of homicide are shown by gender in Figs 1 and 2. The rate of homicide was highest for African-American males aged 15 through 24 years (247/100 000), followed by African-American males aged 25 through 34 years (209/100 000). Young Latino males had the next highest rates (157/100 000 and 153/100 000 for males aged 25 through 34 years and 15 through 24 years, respectively). After 34 years of age, rates for African-American and Latino men de-

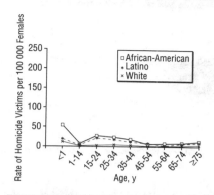

Fig 2.—Race-specific annual rates of homicide (1990 and 1991) for female residents of New York City stratified by age.

clined but were still higher than those of their white counterparts in each age group. White males had lower rates (16/100 000 for those aged 15 through 24 years and 14/100 000 for those aged 25 through 34 years).

African-American women and Latino women had much lower rates of death by homicide than their male counterparts. However, their rates were slightly higher than those of white males, particularly in the 15- through 34-year age groups. White females had the lowest rates of any demographic group, with rates averaging four per 100 000 in the age groups from 15 through 44 years. With the exception of African-American infants less than 1 year of age (males 58/100 000 and females 54/100 000), the very young and the old had the lowest rates of death by homicide in the three racial groups.

Almost three fourths of all homicide victims were killed by firearms (Table 1). The percentage of homicides caused by firearms was higher for males than females in each age group and racial group. African-American, Latino, and Asian males aged 15 through 34 years had the greatest proportion of firearm homicides of all demographic groups. Asian males also had high percentages of firearm homicides in the 45- through 54-year age group. The small number of Asian female homicide victims precluded comparison.

The rest of the analysis used the subset of cases with a survival time of 48 hours or less. These 3890 cases represented 90.5% of all homicide victims among residents of New York City in 1990 and 1991. Comparison of cases included and excluded found Latinos (93%) were slightly more likely than whites (88%) or African Americans (90%) to be included (χ^2=15.41, *df*=3, *P*=.002). Homicide victims in the 15- through 24-year and 25- through 34-year age groups

Table 2.—Percentage of Homicide Victims Positive for Benzoylecgonine in Each Age Group Stratified by Gender and Race*

Age, y	White		African-American		Latino		Asian/Other		Total (N=3890)
	Male (n=272)	Female (n=74)	Male (n=1583)	Female (n=276)	Male (n=1344)	Female (n=184)	Male (n=138)	Female (n=19)	
≤14	0	25.0	2.4	0	3.7	0	0	0	4.1
15-24	18.4	16.7	18.9	35.6	23.7	28.1	8.6	0	21.5
25-34	37.5	59.1	44.4	71.8	43.4	36.1	4.9	0	43.9
35-44	34.0	26.7	49.3	40.8	42.0	31.0	12.1	0	40.9
45-54	12.2	0	27.8	20.0	26.4	14.3	0	0	20.7
≥55	2.3	0	14.0	0	16.3	0	0	0	7.2
Total	22.4	25.7	31.6	39.5	39.9	27.7	6.5	0	31.0

*Denominators include only cases in which there were toxicologic analyses for benzoylecgonine and in which the interval between injury and death was 48 hours or less.

(93% and 92%, respectively) also were more likely to be included in the analysis (χ^2=57.58, df=8, P=.00001). There were no statistically significant gender differences between those included and excluded.

There were 1205 cases (31.0%) among 3890 homicide victims in whom toxicology was positive for BE. The percentage of homicide victims in whom toxicology was positive for BE for each age group, stratified by gender and race, is shown in Table 2. The greatest proportion of BE-positive victims were in the 25- through 44-year age groups. The percentages of white and African-American female victims 25 through 34 years of age who were using cocaine before being murdered exceed the percentages of BE-positive male victims. Few male Asian victims and no female Asian victims were positive for BE.

A logistic regression analysis was performed to determine which demographic factors were related to being BE positive. Young adults were more likely to be BE positive. There were elevated risks of being BE positive at ages 25 through 34 years (OR, 2.9; 95% CI, 2.5 to 3.5) and 35 through 44 years (OR, 2.7; 95% CI, 2.2 to 3.4) relative to ages 15 through 24 years (the standard). The risk of being BE positive was decreased at ages 1 through 14 years (OR, 0.09; 95% CI, 0.03 to 0.29) and age 55 years and over (OR, 0.3; 95% CI, 0.2 to 0.5), but not different at ages 45 through 54 years (OR, 1.1; 95% CI, 0.8 to 1.5). When age and gender were controlled for, African Americans were 1.6 times (OR, 1.6; 95% CI, 1.2 to 2.1) and Latinos were 1.4 times (OR, 1.4; 95% CI, 1.1 to 1.9) more likely than whites to be BE positive. Asians were 20% as likely as whites to be BE positive (OR, 0.2; 95% CI, 0.1 to 0.3). When race and age were controlled for, gender was not related to being BE positive.

A separate logistic regression analysis was conducted to evaluate demographic risk factors for being killed by a firearm and whether being BE positive was associated with being killed by a firearm. Relative to ages 15 through 24 years (the standard), there was a decreased risk of being killed by a firearm at ages 25 through 34 years (OR, 0.7; 95% CI, 0.6 to 0.9), ages 35 through 44 years (OR, 0.6; 95% CI, 0.4 to 0.7), ages 45 through 54 years (OR, 0.4; 95% CI, 0.3 to 0.6), age 55 years and over (OR, 0.15; 95% CI, 0.1 to 0.2), and ages 1 through 14 years (OR, 0.1; 95% CI, 0.01 to 0.2). When age and gender were controlled for, African Americans were 1.7 times (OR, 1.7; 95% CI, 1.3 to 2.3), Latinos 1.5 times (OR, 1.5; 95% CI, 1.2 to 2.0), and Asians 2.2 times (OR, 2.2; 95% CI, 1.4 to 3.6) more likely to be killed by firearms than were whites. When age and race were controlled for, males were 4.8 times more likely than females to be killed by firearms (OR, 4.8; 95% CI, 4.0 to 5.9). When age, gender, and race were controlled for, there was no significant relationship between being killed by firearms and being positive for BE.

COMMENT

Our study confirms that homicide is an important public health problem for both Latino and African-American youths and young adults. Moreover, the rates of homicide of African-American and Latino males aged 15 through 34 years in New York City were roughly twice those of these age groups nationally,[4] although the rates of all other age-, gender-, and race-specific groups approximated the national rates for 1990. It is possible that poverty and other social factors rather than race per se are responsible for the high rates of homicide among African Americans and Latinos as victims as well as perpetrators.[8,24] Our data did not contain information about the socioeconomic status of homicide victims.

It is likely that cocaine use was related to the high rates of homicide, particularly among African Americans and Latinos. Finding out whether cocaine use is more prevalent among homicide victims than the general population is problematic since there are no suitable control groups. The National Household Survey for 1991 may be used as a proxy for the general population.[9] Using those data, it would appear that the proportion of victims using cocaine in the 2 days prior to injury is not merely a reflection of cocaine use in the general population, since use by homicide victims was 10 to 50 times that reported in the past month by respondents in the 1991 survey. Homicide victims may have provoked violence through irritability, paranoid thinking, or verbal or physical aggression, which are known to be pharmacologic effects of cocaine.[25-29] In addition, homicide may have been part of the business of dealing cocaine.[30,31] Violence is often used for the control of sales territory, in retaliation against dealers who may be using cocaine themselves, or in other violent crimes.[32-36]

The use of cocaine was highest among victims 25 through 44 years of age and not the very young. This is not surprising since the onset of cocaine use is likely to be at a later age than alcohol and other drugs.[37] The high proportion of white and African-American female homicide victims who had used cocaine is inconsistent with surveys reporting that women in general are less likely to be drug users.[9] It is possible that female users of cocaine are more likely than nonusers to be victims of violence from spouses, boyfriends, or, in the case of prostitutes, their clients.[38,39]

There is no clear answer as to how we can decrease the heavy use of cocaine, particularly in our cities. There is a major need for public treatment programs, but these will be very expensive, and treatment for cocaine addiction has no methadone analogue yet.[40] Prevention programs aimed at schools require adequate evaluation.[41]

Firearms also constitute a major public health problem, as they account for three fourths of all homicides and for an even greater proportion among young Latinos and African Americans. The young, those aged 15 through 24 years, were particularly likely to be firearm victims. This may be due to increased availability of firearms among high school students.[17,42,43] However, low socioeconomic status rather than race per se may account for access to firearms.[44]

The medical profession has called for the control of firearms.[45-47] However, there is controversy about whether such controls would be effective.[48-50] For instance, New York City has a strict gun law, but guns are brought illegally from neighboring states that have less restrictive regulations. Strict legislation must be implemented at the national level. Others suggest that it would be impossible to regulate the nation's immense firearm arsenal and that bullets should be controlled instead.[51]

To our surprise, the use of cocaine prior to being killed was not statistically related to being killed by a firearm rather than by other methods. The relation between cocaine use and firearms as a means of homicide does not appear as tight as we originally had thought. It is likely that many cocaine dealers are armed and may shoot other dealers and buyers who are using cocaine. Yet cocaine users are killed by means other than firearms in disputes and other situations not related to drug dealing. Thus, policies and interventions must operate on two separate tracks: both to decrease cocaine use and to control firearms (or bullets) in society.

This study was supported by grant DA-06534 from the National Institute on Drug Abuse.

References

1. Fingerhut LA, Kleinman JC. International and interstate comparisons of homicide among young males. *JAMA.* 1990;263:3292-3295.
2. Centers for Disease Control. Homicide among young black males–United States, 1978-1987. *JAMA.* 1991;265:183-184. Originally published in: *MMWR Morb Mortal Wkly Rep.* 1990;39:869-873.
3. Ropp L, Visintainer P, Uman J, Treloar D. Death in the city: an American childhood tragedy. *JAMA.* 1992;267:2905-2910.
4. National Center for Health Statistics. Mortality, part A. *Vital Health Stat 11.* 1990.
5. Griffith EEH, Bell CC. Recent trends in suicide and homicide among blacks. *JAMA.* 1989;262:2265-2269.
6. Wolfgang ME, Ferracuti F. *The Subculture of Violence: Towards an Integrated Theory in Criminology.* New York, NY: Methuen Inc; 1967.
7. Centerwall BS. Race, socioeconomic status and domestic homicide: Atlanta, 1971-72. *Am J Public Health.* 1984;74:813-815.
8. Messner SF, Tardiff K. Economic inequality and levels of homicide: an analysis of urban neighborhoods. *Criminology.* 1986;24:297-317.
9. *National Household Survey on Drug Abuse: Main Findings 1991.* Washington, DC: National Institute on Drug Abuse; 1993. US Dept of Mental Health and Human Service publication SMA 93-1980.
10. Lillie-Blanton M, Anthony JC, Schuster CR. Probing the meaning of racial/ethnic group comparisons in crack cocaine smoking. *JAMA.* 1993; 269:993-997.
11. Harruff RC, Francisco JT, Elkins SK, Phillips AM, Fernandez GS. Cocaine and homicide in Memphis and Shelby County: an epidemic of violence. *J Forensic Sci.* 1988;33:1231-1237.
12. Bailey DN, Shaw RF. Cocaine and methamphetamine-related deaths in San Diego County 1987: homicides and accidental overdoses. *J Forensic Sci.* 1989;34:407-422.
13. Lowry PW, Hassig SE, Gunn RA, Mathison JB. Homicide victims in New Orleans: recent trends. *Am J Epidemiol.* 1988;128:1130-1136.
14. Rogers JN, Henry TE, Jones AM, Froede RC, Byers JM. Cocaine-related deaths in Pima County, Arizona, 1982-1984. *J Forensic Sci.* 1986;31:1404-1408.
15. Hanzlick R, Gowitt GT. Cocaine metabolite detection in homicide victims. *JAMA.* 1991;265:760-761.
16. Tardiff K, Gross E, Wu J, Stajic M, Millman R. Analysis of cocaine-positive fatalities. *J Forensic Sci.* 1989;34:53-63.
17. Centers for Disease Control. Weapon-carrying among high school students—United States, 1990. *MMWR Morb Mortal Wkly Rep.* 1991;40:681-684.
18. Marzuk PM, Tardiff K, Smyth D, Stajic M, Leon AC. Cocaine use, risk taking, and fatal Russian roulette. *JAMA.* 1992;267:2635-2637.
19. Ambre J, Fischman M, Ruo T. Urinary excretion of cocaine, benzoylecgonine, ecgonine methyl ester in human. *J Anal Toxicol.* 1988;12:301-306.
20. Ambre J. The urinary excretion of cocaine and metabolites in humans: a kinetic analysis of published data. *J Anal Toxicol.* 1985;9:241-245.
21. Baselt R. *Disposition of Toxic Drugs and Chemicals in Man.* 2nd ed. Davis, Calif: Biomedical Publications; 1974.
22. Wallace JE, Hamilton HE, Christenson JG, Shimek EL, Land P, Harris SC. An evaluation of selected methods for determining cocaine and benzoylecgonine in urine. *J Anal Toxicol.* 1977;1:20-26.
23. Jatlow PI. Drug of abuse profile: cocaine. *Clin Chem.* 1987;33(October suppl):66B-71B.
24. National Research Council. *Understanding and Preventing Violence.* Washington, DC: National Academy Press; 1993.
25. Cregler LL, Mark H. Medical complications of cocaine abuse. *N Engl J Med.* 1986;315:1495-1499.
26. Lowenstein DH, Massa SM, Rowbotham MC, Collins SD, McKinney HE, Simon RP. Acute neurologic and psychiatric complications associated with cocaine abuse. *Am J Med.* 1987;83:841-846.
27. Wetli CV, Fishbain DA. Cocaine-induced psychosis and sudden death in recreational cocaine users. *J Forensic Sci.* 1985;30:873-880.
28. Mendoza R, Miller BL. Neuropsychiatric disorders associated with cocaine abuse. *Hosp Community Psychiatry.* 1992;43:677-680.
29. Budd RD. Cocaine abuse and violent death. *Am J Drug Alcohol Abuse.* 1989;15:375-382.
30. Zahn M, ed. *Homicide in the Twentieth Century: Trends, Types and Causes in Violence in America.* In Gurr TR, ed. *The History of Crime.* Newbury Park, Calif: Sage Publications; 1989;1.
31. Goldstein RJ. The drugs-violence nexus: a tripartite framework. *J Drug Issues.* 1985;15:493-506.
32. Goldstein PJ, Brownstein HH, Ryan PJ, Bellucci PA. Crack and homicide in New York City: a conceptually based event analysis. *Contemp Drug Probl.* 1989;16:651-687.
33. Collins JJ, Hubbard RL, Rachel JV. Expensive drug use and illegal outcome: a test of explanatory hypotheses. *Criminology.* 1985;23:743-763.
34. Hamid A. The political economy of crack-related violence. *Contemp Drug Probl.* 1990;17:31-78.
35. Fagan J, Chin K. Violence as regulation and social control in the distribution of crack. In: De La Rosa M, Lambert EY, Gropper B, eds. *Drugs and Violence: Causes, Correlates, and Consequences.* Washington, DC: US Government Printing Office; 1990:8-43. National Institute of Drug Abuse research monograph 103.
36. Inciardi JA. The crack-violence connection within a population of hard-core adolescent offenders. In: De La Rosa M, Lambert EY, Gropper B, eds. *Drugs and Violence: Causes, Correlates and Consequences.* Washington, DC: US Government Printing Office; 1990. National Institute of Drug Abuse research monograph 103.
37. Kandel D, Logan JA. Patterns of drug use from adolescence to young adulthood: periods of risk for initiation, continued use and discontinuation. *Am J Public Health.* 1984;74:660-666.
38. Goldstein PJ. Volume of cocaine use and violence: a comparison between men and women. *J Drug Issues.* 1991;21:345-362.
39. Goldstein PJ. *Prostitution and Drugs.* Lexington, Mass: Lexington Books, DC Heath & Co; 1979.
40. Institute of Medicine. *Treating Drug Problems.* Washington, DC: National Academy Press; 1990; 1:220-272.
41. Gerstein DR, Green LW. *Preventing Drug Abuse: What Do We Know?* Washington, DC: National Academy Press; 1993.
42. Fingerhut LA, Ingram DD, Feldman JJ. Firearm and nonfirearm homicide among persons 15 through 19 years of age: differences by level of urbanization, United States, 1979 through 1989. *JAMA.* 1992;267:3048-3053.
43. Webster DW, Gainer PS, Champion HR. Weapon carrying among inner-city junior high school students: defensive behavior vs aggressive delinquency. *Am J Public Health.* 1993;83:1604-1608.
44. Callahan CM, Rivera FP. Urban high school youth and handguns: a school-based survey. *JAMA.* 1992;267:3038-3042.
45. Trent B. The medical profession sets its sights on the gun-control issue. *Can Med Assoc J.* 1991; 145:1332-1336.
46. Kassirer JP. Firearms and the killing threshold. *N Engl J Med.* 1991;325:1647-1650.
47. Houser HB. Common wisdom and plain truth. *Am J Epidemiol.* 1991;134:1261-1263.
48. Loftin C, McDowall D, Wiersema B, Cottey TJ. Effects of restrictive licensing of handguns on homicide and suicide in the District of Columbia. *N Engl J Med.* 1991;325:1615-1620.
49. Centerwall BS. Homicide and the prevalence of handguns: Canada and the United States, 1976 to 1980. *Am J Epidemiol.* 1991;134:1245-1260.
50. O'Carroll PW, Loftin C, Waller JB, et al. Preventing homicide: an evaluation of the efficacy of a Detroit gun ordinance. *Am J Public Health.* 1991; 81:576-581.
51. Moynihan D. *Impact of Bullet-Related Violence on Family and Federal Entitlements: Hearing Before the Subcommittee on Social Security and Family Police, Committee on Finance, US Senate—*Hearing 102-1061, 102nd Cong, 2nd Sess (1993).

Why Good Cops Go Bad

Corruption: A new breed of renegade police officers can be as dangerous as the gangs and drug dealers they are supposed to control

BY MOST ACCOUNTS, FONDA Cecilia Moore was a model cop. Gung-ho, popular with her colleagues on the District of Columbia's tough Anacostia beat, she enjoyed the grit and grime of police work—night patrols in some of Washington's most crime-ridden neighborhoods, undercover investigations against drug dealers and prostitutes, the adrenalin rush of chasing and catching bad guys. "Fonda loved police work," a friend says. "It was her pride and joy." But prosecutors charge that Moore, the mother of two young boys, moonlighted as a confederate of one of Washington's biggest cocaine dealers. Acquitted of murder and other charges in her first trial, she is awaiting trial on charges of conspiring to commit murder and distribute crack.

The charges against her highlight one of the deepest dilemmas facing the U.S. criminal-justice system—the rise of aggressive criminality among cops. There is nothing new about police corruption, and it is probably true that precinct-level graft from bookies, pimps and other underworld types is less prevalent today than it was 50 or 100 years ago. But the crack trade and its gusher of illicit cash are testing the integrity of American law enforcement as never before. Recent scandals in cities like New York and Los Angeles suggest the emergence of a new breed of renegade cops who have gone well beyond taking bribes. Though few in number, these cops actively collaborate—and sometimes compete—with the drug dealers they are supposed to be pursuing. They are criminals behind the badge.

That is the meaning of what is known in New York City as the "Dirty 30" scandal—an internal-affairs sweep that has now led to the arrest of 29 cops in Harlem's 30th Precinct on charges ranging from drug conspiracy to perjury. It is the theme of an unpublished book ("Code of Silence: The Explosive Inside Story of the Largest Police Corruption Scandal in History") by Robert Sobel, a former narcotics detective who has testified in 11 separate trials against former colleagues in the Los Angeles County Sheriff's Department. Other cit-

ies have similar problems: the District of Columbia has its "Dirty Dozen," Miami had "the Miami River case." Last week federal authorities in New Orleans announced the arrest of nine officers in a drug-related sting operation. "I would describe corruption in the New Orleans Police Department to be . . . rampant and systematic," U.S. Attorney Eddie Jordan said.

If the prosecutors in Washington are right, Fonda Moore's case illustrates many of the temptations big-city cops now face. Moore was arrested at Washington's Seventh District precinct house shortly after she showed up for the late shift on June 26, 1992. Her arrest, as shocking to her as it was to her station-house buddies, was the unexpected byproduct of an investigation into the murder of a 19-year-old drug dealer a year and a half earlier. The victim, Billy Ray Tolbert, had been savagely beaten, shot numerous times and stuffed upside down in the seat of his brand-new Acura Legend. That suggested a turf war among crack dealers—and investigators eventually found several druggies who knew all about it.

One informer said Tolbert had been killed in retaliation for the very similar murder of Jimmy Murray, a star salesman for a crack dealer named Javier Card. The informer also said that Murray had a girlfriend who was a District of Columbia police officer—and that the girlfriend had taken up with Card himself after Murray's death. Card was arrested first, followed by other members of his gang. And at the end of an 18-month investigation, Fonda Moore was busted, too.

They videotaped Moore's statement, which was something less than a full confession. She did not admit taking part in Tolbert's murder and denied knowing that Card and his gang were moving drugs out of a Washington sandwich shop that was a focus of the investigation. But she admitted knowing that Card and Jimmy Murray were drug dealers and admitted driving some of Card's gang on a fruitless attempt to find and "take care of" one of Jimmy Murray's murderers. She admitted she used her access to police files to spy on the investigation to help Card. She also said Card himself told her he killed Billy Ray Tolbert—and all that, investigators thought, would put her away.

It didn't, because the video-taped statement was ruled inadmissible. Javier Card and several members of his gang were convicted and went to prison. But the jurors, presented with an unsigned, heavily edited version of the transcript of Moore's statement, balked. They acquitted her of murder and several other charges and failed to agree whether she was guilty of conspiracy to murder. Prosecutor G. Paul Howes will try her again for conspiracy to commit murder early next year; the case against her for conspiracy to distribute cocaine will be tried separately. Moore was suspended without pay from the police department. Neither she nor her attorney will discuss the case, and there is no way to say how the trials will turn out.

Guilty or not, Moore's admitted involvement with Murray and Card poses disturbing questions for police departments everywhere. How could a good cop wind up consorting with men she knew to be big-time drug dealers? "Sex and money," a source says. "She wasn't as pure as freshly fallen snow—or if she was, she drifted a great deal." Moore drove a Saab and former colleagues say she liked to play cards for high stakes. But her salary was only $31,500 a year, she had just been separated and the bills were mounting up. Sources quote Card saying "that cop" was always pushing him for money. Give her the benefit of the doubt—she was struggling financially, and Murray was probably a charming devil.

But it gets worse. Police scandals in New York and other cities clearly show cops go wrong *in groups*—so there is reason to worry about the "corporate culture" of typical big-city police departments. Cops have a nearly impossible job—maintaining order in a disorderly society with a complex legal code. That sometimes means they must go beyond the law to do their jobs but risk harsh discipline when they do. Front-line cops suffer high levels of stress. If they make mistakes in the line of duty, the mistakes can have life-or-death consequences. All of this is why, in many departments, cops are clannish, secretive and likely to have an us-against-them mentality.

Now add huge temptation—cocaine

money. Throw the cops into daily combat with violent perps, and ask them to operate through a legal system that often seems to frustrate elementary justice. That, in a nutshell, is what the Mollen Commission was investigating in New York City. Harlem's Dirty 30 is only the latest precinct to be engulfed in scandal. In 1987, it was the 77th Precinct in Brooklyn; in 1992, it was the 73d, also in Brooklyn.

The 73d was where Officer Kevin Hembury worked. The precinct covers Brooklyn's Brownsville section, saturated with drug-related crime. Cops in the 73d fought unsuccessfully against the anarchy on the streets, and they played by their own rules: brutality was commonplace, illegal searches and seizures were routine and a "good cop" was one who didn't rat. Hembury, assigned to the 73d in 1987, fit in quickly. He went along on "drug raids," which was cop slang for illegal searches mostly intended to show the crack dealers who was boss. The raids were timed to avoid supervision, and usually, no one was arrested: that would create a paper trail. Before long, Hembury and his partner were stealing money from suspects and crack dens.

It was small-time corruption, but it was systematic. By his own testimony, Hembury and his buddies staged about 100 "drug raids" over a two-year-period and the brass never caught on. Then Hembury got greedy—and was nailed in an unrelated drug investigation on suburban Long Island. Hembury was part of a clique of young white officers who commuted to Brooklyn from Suffolk County. He and two of his fellow commuters got involved in a coke ring run by Michael Dowd, the 94th Precinct officer who became famous as "New York's dirtiest cop." Suffolk County authorities arrested Dowd, Hembury and nearly 50 other suspects in May 1992. Hembury was fired from the force and served two and a half years in prison. He now regrets what he did. Being a cop "is a good job," he says. "You should do what you're paid for."

Robert Sobel loved police work, too. Sobel, now 49, was a member of an elite narcotics unit in the L. A. Sheriff's Department from 1987 to 1989, when federal prosecutors nabbed him and some of his fellow detectives in a $30,000 sting. Since then, 27 former deputies have been convicted on various charges and dozens of others have been forced to retire. Sobel says his unit "contained 124 people, and this case knocked down about 45. If there's two or three guys, that's corruption. But when a third of the unit goes down . . . we're talking about *institutional* corruption."

If Sobel's account is accurate—and there is no reason to think that it isn't—he and his fellow narcs worked in a law-enforcement world gone mad. This takes a bit of background. Southern California is a major transshipment point for incoming Colombian

When Cops Betray Their Communities

The chief of New York's 30th Precinct had good news for the Harlem residents gathered in a church basement one recent evening: murders and rapes were down, and his officers had arrested 18 suspected drug dealers in the last five weeks. But several members of the neighborhood association rolled their eyes and heckled. When Deputy Inspector Thomas Sweeney boasted that narcotics arrests had gone up 53 percent, one woman called out, "Not on my block!" The community lost faith in its police when scandal broke last April; 29 cops in the "Dirty 30" have been arrested for allegedly stealing drugs and cash from local dealers. "Residents of the 30th Precinct have been victimized by the police!" another woman shouted angrily.

Community policing is the hot crime-fighting tool of the 1990s. President Clinton's crime law is putting 100,000 more cops on the beat—and even Republicans applaud that idea. But the success of community policing depends on a fragile bond of trust between police and residents—and a corruption case can sunder that quickly. Five of the "Dirty 30" officers were assigned to a community-policing unit that took tips on drug locations and dealers from residents. But instead of making busts, they allegedly made profits. "It was a deep betrayal," says pastor Lenton Gunn Jr. of the St. James Presbyterian Church. "It will be a long time before the policemen in the 30th will be trusted."

No betrayal was more heinous than that of Kevin Nannery. Residents like the 33-year-old sergeant, who used to show up at block parties, and arranged police vans to take kids to the circus or the park. "That boy had a hell of a kinship with everybody in the neighborhood," says Charles, a retired school-teacher who is now too frightened to give his last name.

In the summer of 1993, Charles says, he gave Nannery the names of some local drug dealers. The next day, one of them approached him and said it "ain't cool" to talk to the cops. According to investigators, the sergeant ran an eight-man gang known as Nannery's Raiders, which, among other things, faked calls to 911 to give themselves a pretext for breaking into dealers' apartments and stealing their money and drugs. "Until the bitter end, you thought, Oh naw, man, not Nannery," says Charles. "He's with us."

Being wary: Most Harlem residents are still ardent fans of community policing. Sandra Carter, principal of a private school, wants more cops like Officer Norman Peterson, who stands outside as kids come and go, keeping dealers away by his very presence. "Nobody wants to be mad at the police," says local activist Raymond Curtis. But with cops like Nannery around, they have also learned to be wary.

CARROLL BOGERT *and* GREGORY BEALS
in New York

cocaine and outgoing cocaine money. The FBI, the IRS and the U.S. Customs Service were attempting to track the Colombian cartel by running money-laundering operations that served the smugglers. Local cops routinely used secret information gleaned from these money-laundering operations to bust major dealers. Under federal asset-forfeiture laws, local departments get a share of all drug money seized in such investigations. Sobel says the L. A. Sheriff's Department got $60 million from asset forfeitures in 1988–89—a major source of revenue for the department and the reason command supervision was so lax.

He also says that he and his comrades skimmed huge amounts of cash for themselves from this avalanche of illicit money. "If you look the other way, I can make you a rich man," a fellow deputy told Sobel when he joined the team. "We're taking the whole effing bag . . . the entire [narcotics] bureau is rocking and rolling." Sobel says the narcs bought houses, cars and businesses with their shares of the skim: he himself got

$140,000 over two years. "We were basically doing street robberies," he says. "It was informal taxation of the Colombian cartels . . . We lied in the reports [and] in court."

It had to end, and it did. Sobel and his buddies were trapped in a sting set up by the Feds. Faced with years in prison, he became the government's star witness in a serial prosecution of corrupt deputies that will continue well into 1995. The Sheriff's Department is probably cleaner now, but Sobel says it is only a matter of time before the cycle of corruption begins all over again. He may be right. Cocaine is still plentiful in most major cities in America—and the money is still there for the taking.

TOM MORGANTHAU *with* SUSAN MILLER *in Washington,* PATRICK ROGERS *and* WARD PINCUS *in New York and* JEANNE GORDON *in Los Angeles*

Measuring the Social Costs of Drugs

The most devastating effect of drug use in America is the magnitude with which it effects and impacts the way we live. Much of its influence is unmeasurable. What is the cost of a son or daughter lost, a parent imprisoned, a life lived in a constant state of fear? The emotional costs alone are incomprehensible.

The social legacy of this country's drug crisis could easily be the subject for this entire book. The purpose here, however, can only be the cursory portrayal and outline of drugs' tremendous costs. More than one American president has stated that drug use threatens our national security and personal well-being. Financial costs for maintaining the federal apparatus devoted to drug interdiction, enforcement, and treatment are staggering. Although yearly expenditures vary due to changes in political influence, strategy, and tactics, examples of the tremendous effects of drugs on government and the economy abound. The federal budget for drug control exceeds 10 billion dollars. The Department of Justice devotes 50 percent of its budget to antidrug efforts, the Department of Health and Human Services almost two billion dollars, and the Department of Defense one billion dollars. The per capita cost of the federal drug control budget in 1981 was $6.38, and in 1991 it was $42.78. At the state level, costs are proportionately comparable with federal costs relative to enforcing drug laws and incarcerating offenders.

In addition to the highly visible criminal justice–related costs, numerous other institutions are affected. Housing, welfare, education, and health care provide excellent examples of critical institutions struggling to overcome the strain of drug-related impacts. In addition, annual loss of productivity in the workplace can be measured in billions of dollars, as can demographic shifts caused by people fleeing drug-impacted neighborhoods, schools, and businesses. Housing and welfare departments struggle to distinguish between drug-related and nondrug-related assistance requests. Educational systems struggle to counter the availability of drugs and its associated victimization and fear. Teachers struggle to overcome the time sacrificed to students' drug-related disruptive behavior. Health care systems struggle to respond to annual estimates of between 375,000 to 739,000 drug-exposed newborns in addition to a growing population of drug-related medically indigent. Add injured, drug-related accident and crime victims, along with demands of a growing population of intravenous drug users infected with AIDS, and a failing health care system frighteningly appears. A universally affordable health care plan capable of addressing drug-related impacts of such vast medical consequences may not be possible. Health care costs from drug-related ills are overwhelming.

It should be emphasized that the social costs exacted from drug use infiltrate every aspect of public and private life. The implications of thousands of families struggling from the adverse effects of drug-related woes may prove the greatest and most tragic of social costs. Children who lack emotional support, self-esteem, role models, a safe and secure environment, economic opportunity, and an education because of a parent on drugs suggest a cost we cannot measure.

As you read the following articles, consider the costs associated with legal and illegal drugs. However, before enjoining the debate on which is the greater harbinger of pain and suffering, consider the diversity of impacts to which legal and illegal drugs contribute. Combining pharmacological, environmental, legal, and the multitude of other factors influencing drug-related impacts and cause-and-effect propositions soon produces a quagmire of unextractable proportions. An incremental approach may produce a greater understanding of how to measure social costs than attempting to make a case for a combination of impacts generated because of the legal status of a drug. For example, annual alcohol-related deaths far exceed those related to cocaine, but to say that the reason for alcohol's disproportionate toll stems solely from alcohol's legal status is shortsighted. Certainly, the legality of a drug will enter the process of assessing drug-related impacts and their causes, but it is still just one component within an equation of many.

Looking Ahead: Challenge Questions

What do you believe is the greatest drug-related threat facing our nation?

How do drug-related threats and impacts differ from city to city and state to state? Why?

It is often argued that Americans overreact and over-emphasize the harm from illegal drugs while ignoring or underrepresenting the harm from legal drugs, namely alcohol and nicotine. Do you believe this to be the case?

Has there been a significant shift in public concern over the abuse of legal drugs? Why or why not?

Are the harmful impacts from the abuse of drugs greater today than a decade ago?

BRUARY 20 1983

MADD

Dealing with Demons of a New Generation

Tom Dunkel

Summary: A decade ago society was awakened to what were seen as unique problems facing grown-up children of alcoholics. But now research shows that these problems plague offspring of all sorts of dysfunctional families. As the pool of subjects grows, answers are harder to find.

On the kind of sweltering summer afternoon that's guaranteed to fill empty stools in air-conditioned bars, 15 men and women gather inside the second-floor conference room of a nondescript office building in suburban Washington. They've come to talk about inner demons that, if they didn't know better, might very well drive them to drink.

Robert, a middle-aged recovering alcoholic, takes the floor and tells how he "was forced into the role of becoming an adult at 7 or 8 years old" because his father was a problem drinker. "As things are," he adds with a sad smile that covers the scar tissue of memory, "I survived and came out the other end of the sausage maker."

John, a burly, 51-year-old ex-Marine who describes himself as "an adult child of an alcoholic and a crazy person," is still sorting through the pieces of his fractured upbringing. "Thirty years ago I needed combat," he says. "It was a great therapeutic release to blow something up."

It is nothing new for members of a mutual support group to reveal intimate details about themselves to sympathetic listeners who have traveled the same emotional road. What is new is that Robert and John aren't unburdening themselves just to fellow children of alcoholics. Their group includes participants whose youths were misshapen by sexual abuse, physical abuse and a variety of other homegrown dysfunctions. In fact, three years ago the group stopped identifying itself as Adult Children of Alcoholics and adopted the more generic name Adult Children Anonymous. A few old hands initially resented widening the focus.

"I felt that way for about three meetings; you know, let them go start their own group," John recalls after the hour-long session. "But then the sharing was such a contribution. Anybody that's got a story to tell is a help."

John's less restrictive attitude reflects changes taking place on the professional level. Advocates for the estimated 29 million Americans who can be classified as "children of alcoholics" are backtracking from prior claims that these are people plagued by unique backgrounds and challenges.

A decade ago, when the abbreviation ACOA first came into use, ACOAs were granted almost de facto syndrome status. Telltale symptoms — ranging from low self-esteem and fear of intimacy to depression and poor job performance — were quickly identified. Umbrella organizations such as the National Association for Children of Alcoholics, or NACOA, came into being. A "co-dependency" movement evolved, championing the notion that innocent family members often are damaged by the psychological ripple effects that come from trying to cope with an alcoholic parent or spouse.

But now winds of revisionism are blowing as a body of contrary research — which includes recent studies done under the auspices of Duke University and the University of Missouri — piles high. Maybe being the child of an alcoholic isn't the psychological equivalent of having a new strain of virus, after all.

"Up until now there's been an assumption sometimes that all alcoholic families are similar," notes Deborah Wright, a psychologist at the University of Missouri who, along with colleague Paul Heppner, recently completed an analysis of 80 campus freshmen. "There's an assumption that kids raised in these types of environments will all have similar outcomes and be experiencing similar things. I didn't find that necessarily [true]."

A battery of personality and aptitude tests was given to the Missouri students. Wright and Heppner found just one distinction between those who came from alcoholic families and those who did not: The former were more likely to be abusers of alcohol or drugs. Any additional emotional or behavioral problems were ascribed to other factors, such as parental divorce or the family having had to relocate multiple times.

"I actually think that that writing was helpful at the time," says Wright, referring to the early, largely nonprofessional fieldwork done on COAs, "because we didn't know anything about alcoholic homes. But I think now we need to step back and say this is not necessarily true for everybody, and what is it in particular in those homes that will lead some [children] to struggle as adults, whereas others seem to get by."

A similar caution flag is raised by Shelly F. Greenfield, a psychologist at McLean Hospital in Belmont, Mass. She and a group of researchers at Duke recently went back and pored over statistics culled during an intensive mental health study of 3,000 North Carolina residents conducted in the early 1980s. After screening out potential influences such as divorce and poverty, they isolated some effects of familial alcoholism. Their conclusions were published in the *American Journal of Psychiatry* in April.

"There's so many contradictions in the literature and the field," says Greenfield. "What we were trying to get at in a broad, population-based way is: What are these people really at risk for? Because there is this sort of notion about these people as being an entity unto themselves. ... What we found out is they're at risk for some things and not for other things."

Greenfield found that children of alcoholics show a strong predisposition toward having "psychiatric symptoms" as adults, as well as a "moderately significant" pattern of marital trouble. However, they are no more likely than the general population to have difficulties on the job or in their other personal relationships.

On the surface, those findings would seem to at least partially bolster the assertions of COA proponents. Not so. Greenfield is now involved in a second phase of number crunching on the North Carolina survey that will compare children of alcoholics with children of other dysfunctional parents. Preliminary results indicate that those who suf-

fered sexual or physical abuse also have high rates of psychosis.

"My impression," explains Greenfield, "is that people who have had these very negative experiences early on, many of the things they wind up being at risk for — in terms of psychiatric symptoms and disorders — are similar. There's a lot of overlap."

But still there is conflicting clinical and anecdotal evidence fueling the debate, adds Greenfield. For example, a University of Cincinnati study compared 3-year-old sons of alcoholic and nonalcoholic fathers: The

> "When people begin getting clearer about this — that you can't grow up in an alcoholic home without it affecting you and creating some pain — then they'll look at alcoholism a little more seriously."

children of the alcoholics displayed more impulsive behavior and were not as advanced in language development, fine motor coordination and sociability. Similarly, Ralph Tarter, a professor of psychiatry and neurology at the University of Pittsburgh Medical School, remains a skeptic of COA theory even though he can cite several studies in which infants were removed from alcoholic families and placed in more stable, adopted homes — yet didn't emerge unscathed. "You still see a higher incidence of cognitive disorders," says Tarter, adding that such second-generation effects indicate how much still needs to be learned about the interplay of heredity and environment in alcoholism.

Nonetheless, the tide is running against COA purists who cling to unique-syndrome beliefs. Timmen Cermak is clinical director of Genesis Psychotherapy and Training Center in San Francisco and serves on the advisory board of NACOA. He has argued in the past that schoolteachers should be trained to identify COAs and that school health workers should be allowed to intercede without the consent of parents. But today Cermak, who himself was raised in an alcoholic family, downplays how

different COAs are: "I've never felt it was an exclusive [syndrome]."

Cermak points out that peculiar, egg-before-the-chicken circumstances may have caused some pioneering therapists to be overzealous.

"What happened with adult children of alcoholics is that we've come about looking at people from a different direction than what normally happens," Cermak says. "Oftentimes we discover a disease and then go out to look for the population that has that disease. This is opposite. We've identified a population and then are looking at that population to see what special needs that population might have."

Claudia Black, a cofounder and former chairwoman of the NACOA, agrees with Cermak's assessment and even takes it a step further: There may be adult child syndromes more debilitating than COA. "I think that most professionals — and those of us specifically in the adult children of alcoholics movement — in all fairness recognize that what's true for people in alcoholic homes is very generalizable, particularly to other strongly dysfunctional family systems.... I believe there's probably more aspects of uniqueness when you're dealing with a home where there's physical and sexual abuse, where one's body is violated, versus when we're talking about ... psychologically and emotionally greater dysfunctions."

Even those who think the COA syndrome has been overstated concede that the movement has made positive contributions. Most important, it brought secondary problems of addiction out of the closet and let the forgotten victims of alcoholism know they were not alone. That in itself was therapeutic for many people. Then, too, the attention paid to COAs brought to light the devastating toll exacted by addictions of every stripe.

Cermak hopes that the end result will be a sea change of opinion akin to the public outcry against secondhand smoke. "When people begin getting clearer about this — that you can't grow up in an alcoholic home without it affecting you and creating some pain — then they'll look at alcoholism a little more seriously," he predicts. "It's not something people do by themselves. I think that [message] has not been received by the population at large."

The downside of the COA movement, detractors say, has been the emergence of a remedial cottage industry in which pop psychology masquerades as serious psychotherapy.

"There are economic benefits to treating people and giving labels," notes Pittsburgh's Tarter.

There's also a danger in creating a cult of victimhood in which COAs not only use the syndrome as a crutch to evade personal responsibility (the "it's-all-my-parents'-fault" rationalization), but also accuse fellow COAs of being in a stage of acute denial if they, too, don't feel weighed down by baggage from childhood. Thus, Atlanta psychiatrist Frank Pittman wrote last year in the *Family Therapy Networker* that "the adult child movement . . . has trivialized real suffering and made psychic invalids of those who once had a bad day."

Even if one assumes that the scientific underpinnings are specious, it's uncertain whether the COA movement has had a benign or deleterious effect. "That's the $64,000 question," says Tarter. "Nobody knows."

To date, most research studies have been short-term and have focused on a skewed subset of people who are being clinically treated for one alcohol-related problem or another. That leaves unanswered a host of questions besides the $64,000 vari-

ety. Among them: Are there distinctions between children of male alcoholics and children of female alcoholics? Do children of alcoholics experience different problems at different stages of their lives?

Finding answers will require a comprehensive, decades-long effort analogous to the Framingham, Mass., study of heart disease. No one yet has been willing to devote that amount of money and time to understanding alcoholism.

The University of Pittsburgh Medical School, however, is taking a step in that direction. In 1989, Tarter selected a group of 10-year-old children from 1,000 families. Data will be collected from them until they reach age 30. One statistical curiosity discovered so far indicates that a disproportionate number of children born to alcoholic or drug-addicted parents have abnormal brain wave patterns.

"Those brain wave differences correlate very strongly with certain types of behavioral characteristics, such as impulsivity and social deviance and lower IQ," explains Tarter.

Again, Tarter is not sure how those brain wave patterns might compare with those of children from other

types of dysfunctional families. The phenomenon harks back to those hereditary and environmental factors waiting to be untangled. Nonetheless, Tarter thinks science-minded researchers and children of alcoholics are "coming to some common ground," though there is still a lot of distance between the two camps.

"My own position on this," he says, "is that being a COA in and of itself is not pathognomonic. That's where the scientific community departs from the movement. . . . Even if there's a genetic propensity, it's not necessarily going to be manifest unless a number of key environmental conditions are met. Unfortunately, we haven't studied that part of it very much."

The University of Missouri's Wright is less optimistic about the possibility of ever attaining that elusive common ground: "I don't think we'll ever come to a definitive answer because we can't say all COAs are COAs. It isn't that simplistic, unfortunately. I don't think we'll ever get to a place where we can make definitive statements about this large, large group. Because this large, large group is very heterogeneous. It's just a type of dysfunctional family."

A Society of Suspects:
THE WAR ON DRUGS AND CIVIL LIBERTIES

Property seized in drug raids, including large amounts of money, may be forfeited to the government without proof of the owner's guilt.

A decade after Pres. Reagan launched the War on Drugs, all we have to show for it are city streets ruled by gangs, a doubled prison population, and a substantial erosion of constitutional protections.

Steven Wisotsky

Mr. Wisotsky, professor of law, Nova University, Ft. Lauderdale, Fla., is a member of the advisory board of the Drug Policy Foundation, Washington, D.C., and author of Beyond the War on Drugs. *This article is based on a Cato Institute Policy Analysis.*

ON DEC. 15, 1991, America celebrated the 200th anniversary of the Bill of Rights. On Oct. 2, 1992, it marked the 10th anniversary of an antithetical undertaking—the War on Drugs, declared by Pres. Ronald Reagan in 1982 and aggressively escalated by Pres. George Bush in 1989. The nation's Founders would be disappointed with what has been done to their legacy of liberty. The War on Drugs, by its very nature, is a war on the Bill of Rights.

In their shortsighted zeal to create a drug-free America, political leaders—state and Federal, elected and appointed—have acted as though the end justifies the means. They have repudiated the heritage of limited government and individual freedoms while endowing the bureaucratic state with unprecedented powers.

That the danger to freedom is real and not just a case of crying wolf is confirmed by the warnings of a few judges, liberals and conservatives alike, who, insulated from elective politics, have the independence to be critical. Supreme Court Justice Antonin Scalia, for example, denounced compulsory urinalysis of Customs Service employees "in the front line" of the War on Drugs as an "invasion of their privacy and an affront to their dignity." In another case, Justice John Paul Stevens lamented that "this Court has become a loyal foot soldier" in the War on Drugs. The late Justice Thur-good Marshall was moved to remind the Court that there is "no drug exception" to the Constitution.

In 1991, the Court of Appeals for the Ninth Circuit declared that "The drug crisis does not license the aggrandizement of governmental power in lieu of civil liberties. Despite the devastation wrought by drug trafficking in communities nationwide, we cannot suspend the precious rights guaranteed by the Constitution in an effort to fight the 'War on Drugs.'" In that observation, the court echoed a 1990 ringing dissent by the chief justice of the Florida Supreme Court: "If the zeal to eliminate drugs leads this state and nation to forsake its ancient heritage of constitutional liberty, then we will have suffered a far greater injury than drugs ever inflict upon us. Drugs injure some of us. The loss of liberty injures us all."

Those warnings are cries in the wilderness, however, unable to stop the relentless buildup of law enforcement authority at every level of government. In fact, the trend toward greater police powers has accelerated. One summary of the Supreme Court's 1990-91 term observed that its criminal law decisions "mark the beginning of significant change in the relationship between the citizens of this country and its police."

Despite such warnings, most Americans have yet to appreciate that the War on Drugs is a war on the rights of all of us. It could not be otherwise, for it is directed not against inanimate drugs, but against people—those who are suspected of using, dealing in, or otherwise being involved with illegal substances. Because the drug industry arises from the voluntary transactions of tens of millions of individuals— all of whom try to keep their actions secret—the aggressive law enforcement schemes that constitute the war must aim at penetrating their private lives. Because nearly anyone may be a drug user or seller of drugs or an aider and abettor of the drug industry, virtually everyone has become a suspect. All must be observed, checked, screened, tested, and admonished—the guilty and innocent alike.

The tragic irony is that, while the War on Drugs has failed completely to halt the influx of cocaine and heroin—which are cheaper, purer, and more abundant than ever—the one success it can claim is in curtailing the liberty and privacy of the American people. In little over a decade, Americans have suffered a marked reduction in their freedoms in ways both obvious and subtle.

Among the grossest of indicators is that the war leads to the arrest of an estimated 1,200,000 suspected drug offenders each year, most for simple possession or petty sale. Because arrest and incarceration rates rose for drug offenders throughout the 1980s, the war has succeeded dramatically in increasing the full-time prison population. That has doubled since 1982 to more than 800,000, giving the U.S. the highest rate of incarceration in the industrialized world.

It has been established that law enforcement officials—joined by U.S. military forces—have the power, with few limits, to snoop, sniff, survey, and detain, without warrant or probable cause, in the war against drug trafficking. Property may be seized on slight evidence and forfeited to the state or Federal government without proof of the personal guilt of the owner.

Finally, to leverage its power, an increasingly imperial Federal government has applied intimidating pressures to shop owners and others in the private sector to help implement its drug policy.

Ironically, just as the winds of freedom are blowing throughout central and eastern Europe, most Americans and the nation's politicians maintain that the solution to the drug problem is more repression—and the Bill of Rights be damned. As Peter Rodino, former chairman of the House Judiciary Committee, said in expressing his anger at the excesses of the Anti-Drug Abuse Act of 1986, "We have been fighting the war on drugs, but now it seems to me the attack is on the Constitution of the United States."

In the beginning, the War on Drugs focused primarily on supplies and suppliers. Control at the source was the first thrust of anti-drug policy—destruction of coca and marijuana plants in South America, crop substitution programs, and aid to law enforcement agencies in Colombia, Peru, Bolivia, and Mexico.

Because this had no discernible, lasting success, a second initiative aimed to improve the efficiency of border interdiction of drug shipments that had escaped control at the source. There, too, success was elusive. Record numbers of drug seizures—up to 22 tons of cocaine in a single raid on a Los Angeles warehouse, for instance—seemed only to mirror a record volume of shipments to the U.S. By 1991, the amount of cocaine seized by Federal authorities had risen to 134 metric tons, with an additional amount estimated at between 263 and 443 tons escaping into the American market per year.

A reasonable search and seizure in the War on Drugs is interpreted very broadly and favors local police and Federal drug agents.

As source control and border interdiction proved futile, a third prong of the attack was undertaken: long-term, proactive conspiracy investigations targeted at suspected high-level drug traffickers and their adjuncts in the professional and financial worlds—lawyers, accountants, bankers, and currency exchange operators. This has involved repeated and systematic attacks by the Federal government on the criminal defense bar, raising dark implications for the integrity of the adversarial system of justice. Defense lawyers have been subjected to grand jury subpoenas, under threat of criminal contempt, to compel disclosures about their clients. Informants have been placed in the defense camp to obtain confidential information. In each instance, the effect has been to undermine the protections traditionally afforded by the attorney/client relationship. This demonstrates the anything-goes-in-the-War-on-Drugs attitude of the Department of Justice, which publicly defended using lawyers as informants as "a perfectly valid" law enforcement tool.

As these expanding efforts yielded only marginal results, the war was widened to the general populace. In effect, the government opened up a domestic front in the War on Drugs, invading the privacy of people through the use of investigative techniques such as urine testing, roadblocks, bus boardings, and helicopter overflights. Those are dragnet methods; to catch the guilty, everyone has to be watched and screened.

Invading privacy

Drug testing in the workplace. Perhaps the most widespread intrusion on privacy arises from pre- or post-employment drug screening, practiced by 80% of Fortune 500 companies and 43% of firms employing 1,000 people or more. Strictly speaking, drug testing by a private employer does not violate the Fourth Amendment, which protects only against government action. Nevertheless, much of the private drug testing has come about through government example and pressure. The 1988 Anti-Drug Abuse Act, for instance, prohibits the award of a Federal grant or contract to an employer who does not take specified steps to provide a drug-free workplace. As a result of these and other pressures, tens of millions of job applicants and employees are subjected to the indignities of urinating into a bottle, sometimes under the eyes of a monitor watching to ensure that clean urine is not smuggled surreptitiously into the toilet.

In the arena of public employment, where Fourth Amendment protections apply, the courts largely have rejected constitutional challenges to drug testing programs. In two cases to reach the U.S. Supreme Court, the testing programs substantially were upheld despite, as Justice Scalia wrote in dissent in one of them, a complete absence of "real evidence of a real problem that will be solved by urine testing of customs service employees." In that case, the Customs Service had implemented a drug testing program to screen all job applicants and employees engaged in drug interdiction activities, carrying firearms, or handling classified material. The Court held that the testing of such applicants and employees is "reasonable" even without probable cause or individualized suspicion against any particular person, the Fourth Amendment standard.

For Scalia, the testing of Customs Service employees was quite different from that of railroad employees involved in train accidents, which had been found constitutional. In that case, there was substantial evidence over the course of many years that the use of alcohol had been implicated in causing railroad accidents, including a 197? study finding that 23% of the operating personnel were problem drinkers. Commenting on the Customs case, Scalia maintained that "What is absent in the government's justifications—notably absent, revealingly absent, and as far as I am concerned dispositively absent—is the recitation of even a single instance in which any of the speculated horribles actually occurred: an instance, that is, in which the cause of bribe-taking, or of poor aim, or of unsympathetic law enforcement, or of compromise of classified information, was drug use."

Searches and seizures. Other dragnet techniques that invade the privacy of the innocent as well as the guilty have been upheld by the Supreme Court. In the tug-of-war between the government's search and seizure powers and the privacy rights of individuals, the Court throughout the 1980? almost always upheld the government's assertion of the right of drug agents to use the airport drug courier profile to stop, detain, and question people without warrant or probable cause; subject a traveler's luggage to a sniffing examination by a drug-detecting dog without warrant or probable cause; search without warrant or probable cause the purse of a public school student and search at will ships in inland waterways.

The right of privacy in the home seriously was curtailed in decisions permitting police to obtain a search warrant of a home based on an anonymous informant's tip; use illegally seized evidence under a "good faith exception" to the exclusionary rule (for searches of a home made pursuant to a defective warrant issued without probable cause); make a trespassory search, without a warrant, in "open fields" surrounded by fences and no trespassing signs and of a barn adjacent to a residence; and conduct a warrantless search of a motor home occupied as a residence, a home on the consent of an occasional visitor lacking legal authority over the premises, and the foreign residence of a person held for trial in the U.S. The Court also validated warrantless aerial surveillance over private property—by fixed-wing aircraft at an altitude of 1,000 feet and by helicopter at 400 feet.

Similarly, it significantly enlarged the powers of police to stop, question, and detain drivers of vehicles on the highways on suspicion with less than probable cause or with no suspicion at all at fixed checkpoints or roadblocks; make warrantless searches of automobiles and of closed containers therein; and conduct surveillance of suspects by placing transmitters or beepers on vehicles or in containers therein.

The foregoing list is by no means comprehensive, but it does indicate the sweeping expansions the Court has permitted in the investigative powers of government. Indeed, from 1982 through the end of the 1991 term, the Supreme Court upheld government search and seizure authority in approximately 90% of the cases. The message is unmistakable—the Fourth Amendment prohibits only "unreasonable" searches and seizures, and what is reasonable in the milieu of a War on Drugs is construed very broadly in favor of local police and Federal drug agents.

Surveillance of U.S. mail. Another casualty of the War on Drugs is the privacy of the mail. With the Anti-Drug Abuse Act of 1988, the Postal Service was given broad law enforcement authority. Using a profile, investigators identify what they deem to be suspicious packages and place them before drug-sniffing dogs. A dog alert is deemed probable cause to apply for a Federal search warrant. If an opened package does not contain drugs, it is resealed and sent to its destination with a copy of the search warrant. Since January, 1990, using this technique, the Postal Service has arrested more than 2,500 persons for sending drugs through the mail. The number of innocent packages opened has not been reported.

Wiretapping. As a result of the War on Drugs, Americans increasingly are being overheard. Although human monitors are supposed to minimize the interception of calls unrelated to the purpose of their investigation by listening only long enough to determine the relevance of the conversation, wiretaps open all conversations on the wiretapped line to scrutiny.

Court-authorized wiretaps doubtless are necessary in some criminal cases. In drug cases, though, they are made necessary because the "crimes" arise from voluntary transactions, in which there are no complainants to assist detection. The potential is great, therefore, for abuse and illegal overuse.

Stopping cars on public highways. It is commonplace for police patrols to stop "suspicious" vehicles on the highway in the hope that interrogation of the driver or passengers will turn up enough to escalate the initial detention into a full-blown search. Because the required "articulable suspicion" rarely can be achieved by observation on the road, police often rely on a minor traffic violation—a burned-out taillight, a tire touching the white line—to supply a pretext for the initial stop. In the Alice-in-Wonderland world of roving drug patrols, however, even lawful behavior can be used to justify a stop. The Florida Highway Patrol Drug Courier Profile, for example, cautioned troopers to be suspicious of "scrupulous obedience to traffic laws."

Another tactic sometimes used is the roadblock. Police set up a barrier, stop every vehicle at a given location, and check each driver's license and registration. While one checks the paperwork, another walks around the car with a trained drug-detector dog. The law does not regard the dog's sniffing as the equivalent of a search on the theory that there is no legitimate expectation of privacy in the odor of contraband, an exterior olfactory clue in the public domain. As a result, no right of privacy is invaded by the sniff, so the police do not need a search warrant or even probable cause to use the dog on a citizen. Moreover, if the dog "alerts," that supplies the cause requirement for further investigation of the driver or vehicle for drugs.

Monitoring and stigmatizing. In the world of anti-drug investigations, a large role is played by rumors, tips, and suspicions. The Drug Enforcement Administration (DEA) keeps computer files on U.S. Congressmen, entertainers, clergymen, industry leaders, and foreign dignitaries. Many persons named in the computerized Narcotics and Dangerous Drug Information System (NADDIS) are the subject of "unsubstantiated allegations of illegal activity." Of the 1,500,000 persons whose names have been added to NADDIS since 1974, less than five percent, or 7,500, are under investigation by DEA as suspected narcotic traffickers. Nevertheless, NADDIS maintains data from all such informants, surveillance, and intelligence reports compiled by DEA and other agencies.

The information on NADDIS is available to Federal drug enforcement officials in other agencies, such as the Federal Bureau of Investigation, the Customs Service, and the Internal Revenue Service. State law enforcement officials probably also can gain access on request. Obviously, this method of oversight has troubling implications for privacy and good reputation, especially for the 95% named who are not under active investigation.

Another creative enforcement tactic sought to bring about public embarrassment by publishing a list of people caught bringing small amounts of drugs into the U.S. The punish-by-publishing list, supplied to news organizations, included only small-scale smugglers who neither were arrested nor prosecuted for their alleged crimes.

Military surveillance. Further surveillance of the citizenry comes from the increasing militarization of drug law enforcement. The process began in 1981, when Congress relaxed the Civil War-era restrictions of the Posse Comitatus Act on the use of the armed forces as a police agency. The military "support" role for the Coast Guard, Customs Service, and other anti-drug agencies created by the 1981 amendments expanded throughout the 1980s to the point that the U.S. Navy was using large military vessels—including, in one case, a nuclear-powered aircraft carrier—to interdict suspected drug smuggling ships on the high seas.

By 1989, Congress designated the Department of Defense (DOD) as the single lead agency of the Federal government for the detection and monitoring of aerial and maritime smuggling into the U.S. DOD employs its vast radar network in an attempt to identify drug smugglers among the 300,000,000 people who enter the country each year in 94,000,000 vehicles and 600,000 aircraft. Joint task forces of military and civilian personnel were established and equipped with high-tech computer systems that provide instantaneous communication among all Federal agencies tracking or apprehending drug traffickers.

The enlarged anti-drug mission of the military sets a dangerous precedent. The point of the Posse Comitatus Act was to make clear that the military and police are very different institutions with distinct roles to play. The purpose of the military is to prevent or defend against attack by a foreign power and to wage war where necessary. The Constitution makes the president commander-in-chief, thus centralizing control of all the armed forces in one person. Police, by contrast, are supposed to enforce the law, primarily against domestic threats at the city, county, and state levels. They thus are subject to local control by the tens of thousands of communities throughout the nation.

Since the 1987 enactment of the Uniform Sentencing Guidelines, the penalties for drug crimes have become extreme and mandatory.

To the extent that the drug enforcement role of the armed forces is expanded, there is a direct increase in the concentration of political power in the president who commands them and the Congress that authorizes and funds their police activities. This arrangement is a severe injury to the Federal structure of our democratic institutions. Indeed, the deployment of national military forces as domestic police embarrasses the U.S. in the international arena by likening it to a Third World country, whose soldiers stand guard in city streets, rifles at the ready, for ordinary security purposes.

6. MEASURING THE SOCIAL COSTS OF DRUGS

The dual military/policing role also is a danger to the liberties of all citizens. A likely military approach to the drug problem would be to set up roadblocks, checkpoints, and roving patrols on the highways, railroads, and coastal waters, and to carry out search-and-destroy missions of domestic drug agriculture or laboratory production. What could be more destructive to the people's sense of personal privacy and mobility than to see such deployments by Big Brother?

Excessive punishment

These are some of the many ways the War on Drugs has cut deeply—and threatens to cut deeper still—into Americans' privacy, eroding what Justice Louis D. Brandeis described as "the right to be let alone—the most comprehensive of rights and the right most valued by civilized men." Working hand-in-hand with the political branches, the courts have diminished constitutional restraints on the exercise of law enforcement power. In addition to expanded powers of surveillance, investigation, and prosecution, punishment has been loosed with a vengeance, against enemy and bystander alike.

Punishments have become draconian in part because of permission conferred by Justice William Rehnquist's 1981 circular dictum: "the question of what punishments are constitutionally permissible is not different from the question of what punishments the Legislative Branch intended to be imposed." The penalties have become so extreme, especially since the 1987 enactment of the Uniform Sentencing Guidelines, that many Federal judges have begun to recoil. U.S. district court Judge J. Lawrence Irving of San Diego, a Reagan appointee, announced his resignation in protest over the excessive mandatory penalties he was required to mete out to low-level offenders, most of them poor young minorities. Complaining of "unconscionable" sentences, the judge said that "Congress has dehumanized the sentencing process. I can't in good conscience sit on the bench and mete out sentences that are unfair."

Judge Harold Greene of the District of Columbia went so far as to refuse to impose the minimum guideline sentence of 17.5 years on a defendant convicted of the street sale of a single Dilaudid tablet, pointing to the "enormous disparity" between the crime and the penalty. In the judge's view, the minimum was "cruel and unusual" and "barbaric." Fourth circuit Judge William W. Wilkins objected to mandatory penalties because "they do not permit consideration of an offender's possibly limited peripheral role in the offense." Agreeing with that thinking, the judicial conferences of the District of Columbia, Second, Third, Seventh, Eighth, Ninth, and Tenth circuits have adopted resolutions opposing mandatory minimums.

As drug control policymakers came to realize that the drug dealers were, in an economic sense, merely entrepreneurs responding to market opportunities, they learned that attacks on dealers and their supplies never could succeed as long as there was demand for the products. Thus, they would have to focus on consumers as well as on suppliers. Pres. Reagan's 1986 Executive Order encouraging or requiring widespread urine testing marked a step in that direction. By 1988, Administration policy was being conducted under the rubric of "zero tolerance." In that spirit, Attorney General Edwin Meese sent a memorandum to all U.S. Attorneys on March 30, 1988, encouraging the selective prosecution of "middle and upper class users" in order to "send the message that there is no such thing as 'recreational' drug use. . . . "

Because of the volume of more serious trafficking cases, however, it was not remotely realistic, as the Attorney General must have known, to implement such a policy. Indeed, in the offices of many U.S. Attorneys, there were minimum weight or money-volume standards for prosecution, and the possession and small-scale drug cases routinely were shunted off to state authorities. In fact, in many districts, the crush of drug cases was so great that the adjudication of ordinary civil cases virtually had ceased. The courthouse doors were all but closed to civil litigants.

In the name of zero tolerance, Congress purposely began enacting legislation that did not have to meet the constitutional standard of proof beyond a reasonable doubt in criminal proceedings. In 1988, it authorized a system of fines of up to $10,000, imposed administratively under the authority of the Attorney General, without the necessity of a trial, although the individual may request an administrative hearing. To soften the blow to due process, judicial review of an adverse administrative finding is permitted, but the individual bears the burden of retaining counsel and paying court filing fees. For those unable to finance a court challenge, this system will amount to punishment without trial. Moreover, it has been augmented by a provision in the Anti-Drug Abuse Act of 1988 that may suspend for one year an offender's Federal benefits, contracts, grants, student loans, mortgage guarantees, and licenses upon conviction for a first offense.

Both sanctions are a form of legal piling on. The legislative intent is to punish the minor offender more severely than is authorized by the criminal law alone. Thus, the maximum penalty under Federal criminal law for a first offense of simple possession of a controlled substance is one year in prison and a $5,000 fine, with a minimum fine of $1,000. Fines up to $10,000 plus loss of Federal benefits obviously exceed those guidelines.

The most recent innovation of this kind is a form of greenmail, a law that cuts off highway funds to states that do not suspend the driver's licenses of those convicted of possession of illegal drugs. The potential loss of work for those so punished and the adverse consequences on their families are not considered. The suspension is mandatory.

Seizure and forfeiture

The War on Drugs not only punishes drug users, it also penalizes those who are innocent and others who are on the periphery of wrongdoing. The most notable example is the widespread and accelerating practice, Federal and state, of seizing and forfeiting cars, planes, boats, houses, money, or property of any other kind carrying even minute amounts of illegal drugs, used to facilitate a transaction in narcotics, or representing the proceeds of drugs. Forfeiture is authorized, and enforced, without regard to the personal guilt of the owner. It matters not whether a person is tried and acquitted; the owner need not even be arrested. The property nonetheless is forfeitable because of a centuries-old legal fiction that says the property itself is "guilty." Relying on it, in March, 1988, the Federal government initiated highly publicized zero tolerance seizures of property that included the following:

● On April 30, 1988, the Coast Guard boarded and seized the motor yacht *Ark Royal,* valued at $2,500,000, because 10 marijuana seeds and two stems were found on board. Public criticism prompted a return of the boat, but not before payment of $1,600 in fines and fees by the owner.
● The 52-foot *Mindy* was impounded for a week because cocaine dust in a rolled up dollar bill was found on board.
● The $80,000,000 oceanographic research ship *Atlantis II* was seized in San Diego when the Coast Guard found 0.01 ounce of marijuana in a crewman's shaving kit. The vessel eventually was returned.
● A Michigan couple returning from a Canadian vacation lost a 1987 Mercury Cougar when customs agents found two marijuana cigarettes in one of their pockets. No criminal charges were filed, but the car was kept by the government.
● In Key West, Fla., a shrimp fisherman lost his boat to the Coast Guard, which found three grams of cannabis seeds and stems on board. Under the law, the craft was forfeitable whether or not he had any responsibility for the drugs.

Not surprisingly, cases like the foregoing generated a public backlash—perhaps the only significant one since the War on Drugs was declared in 1982. It pressured Congress into creating what is known as the "innocent owner defense" to such *in rem* forfeitures, but even that gesture of reasonableness is largely illusory.

First, the defense does not redress the gross imbalance between the value of property forfeited and the personal culpability of the owner. For example, a Vermont man was found guilty of growing six marijuana plants. He received a suspended sentence, but he and his family lost their 49-acre farm. Similarly, a New York man forfeited his $145,000 condominium because he sold cocaine to an informant for $250. The law provides no limit to the value of property subject to forfeiture, even for very minor drug offenses.

Second, the innocent owner defense places the burden on the property claimant to demonstrate that he or she acted or failed to act without "knowledge, consent or willful blindness" of the drug activities of the offender. Thus, the Federal government instituted forfeiture proceedings in the Delray Beach, Fla., area against numerous properties containing convenience stores or other businesses where drug transactions took place, claiming that the owners "made insufficient efforts to prevent drug dealings."

Placing the burden on the claimant imposes expense and inconvenience because the claimant must hire a lawyer to mount a challenge to the seizure. Moreover, many cases involve the family house or car, and it often is difficult to prove that one family member had no knowledge of or did not consent to the illegal activities of another. For instance, a Florida court held that a claimant did not use reasonable care to prevent her husband from using her automobile in criminal activity; thus, she was not entitled to the innocent owner defense.

A particularly cruel application of this kind of vicarious responsibility for the wrongs of another is seen in the government's policy of evicting impoverished families from public housing because of the drug activities of one unruly child. The Anti-Drug Abuse Act of 1988 specifically states that a tenant's lease is a forfeitable property interest and that public housing agencies have the authority to hire investigators to determine whether drug laws are being broken. The act authorizes eviction if a tenant, member of his or her household, guest, or other person under his or her control is engaged in drug-related activity on or near public housing premises.

To carry out these provisions, the act funded a pilot enforcement program. In 1990, the Departments of Justice and Housing and Urban Development announced a Public Housing Asset Forfeiture Demonstration Project in 23 states. The project pursued lease forfeitures and generated considerable publicity.

In passing this law, it must have been obvious to Congress that many innocent family members would suffer along with the guilty. Perhaps it was thought vital, nonetheless, as a way of protecting other families from drugs in public housing projects. As experience proves, however, even evicted dealers continue to deal in and around the projects. It is hard to take public housing lease forfeitures very seriously, therefore, other than as a symbolic statement of the government's tough stand against illegal drugs.

Destructive consequences

A policy that destroys families, takes property from the innocent, and tramples the basic criminal law principles of personal responsibility, proportionality, and fairness has spillover effects into other public policy domains. One area in which the fanaticism of the drug warriors perhaps is most evident is public health. Drugs such as marijuana and heroin have well-known medical applications. Yet, so zealous are the anti-drug forces that even these therapeutic uses effectively have been banned.

Marijuana, for instance, has many applications as a safe and effective therapeutic agent. Among them are relief of the intraocular pressure caused by glaucoma and alleviating the nausea caused by chemotherapy. Some AIDS patients also have obtained relief from using cannabis.

Yet, marijuana is classified by the Attorney General of the U.S., not the Surgeon General, as a Schedule I drug—one having a high potential for abuse, no currently accepted medicinal use, and lack of accepted safety for utilization. It thereby is deemed beyond the scope of legitimate medical practice and thus is not generally available to medical practitioners.

The only exception was an extremely limited program of compassionate treatment of the terminally or seriously ill, but even that has been eliminated for political

---

The intensive pursuit of drug offenders has generated an enormous population of convicts held in prison for very long mandatory periods of time; so much so that violent criminals (murders, robbers, and rapists) often serve less time than the drug offenders.

---

reasons. Assistant Secretary James O. Mason of the Department of Health and Human Services announced in 1991 that the Public Health Service's provision of marijuana to patients seriously ill with AIDS would be discontinued because it would create a public perception that "this stuff can't be so bad." After a review caused by protests from AIDS activists, the Public Health Service decided in March, 1992, to stop supplying marijuana to any patients save the 13 then receiving it.

There also are beneficial uses for heroin. Terminal cancer patients suffering from intractable pain generally obtain quicker analgesic relief from heroin than from morphine. Many doctors believe that heroin should be an option in the pharmacopeia. Accordingly, in 1981, the American Medical Association House of Delegates adopted a resolution stating that "the management of pain relief in terminal cancer patients should be a medical decision and should take priority over concerns about drug dependence." Various bills to accomplish that goal were introduced in the 96th, 97th, and 98th Congresses. The Compassionate Pain Relief Act was brought to the House floor for a vote on Sept. 19, 1984, but was defeated by 355 to 55. Although there were some concerns voiced about thefts from hospital pharmacies, the overwhelming concern was political and symbolic—a heroin legalization bill could not be passed in an election year and, in any event, would send the public the "wrong message."

The final and perhaps most outrageous example in this catalog of wrongs against public health care is the nearly universal American refusal to permit established addicts to exchange used needles for sterile ones in order to prevent AIDS transmission among intravenous drug users. In 1991, the National Commission on AIDS recommended the removal of legal barriers to the purchase and possession of intravenous drug injection equipment. It found that 32% of all adult and adolescent AIDS cases were related to intravenous drug use and that 70% of mother-to-child AIDS infections resulted from intravenous drug use by the mother or her sexual partner. Moreover, the commission found no evidence that denial of access to sterile needles reduced drug abuse, but concluded that it did encourage the sharing of contaminated needles and the spread of the AIDS virus. Notwithstanding the commission's criticism of the government's "myopic criminal justice approach" to the drug situation, the prevailing view is that needle exchange programs encourage drug abuse by sending the wrong message.

Public safety is sacrificed when, nationwide, more than 18,000 local, sheriff's, and state police officers, in addition to thousands of Federal agents, are devoted full time to special drug units. As a result, countless hours and dollars are diverted from detecting and preventing more serious violent crimes. Thirty percent of an estimated 1,100,000 drug-related arrests made during 1990 were marijuana offenses, nearly four out of five for mere possession. Tax dollars would be spent better if the resources it took to make approximately 264,000 arrests for possession of marijuana were dedicated to protecting the general public from violent crime.

The intensive pursuit of drug offenders has generated an enormous population of convicts held in prison for very long periods of time as a result of excessive and / or mandatory jail terms. It is estimated that the operating cost of maintaining a prisoner ranges from $20,000 to $40,000 per year, depending upon the location and level of security at a particular prison. With more than 800,000 men and women in American correctional facilities today, the nationwide cost approaches $30,000,000,000 per year. This is a major diversion of scarce resources.

These financial burdens are only part of the price incurred as a result of the relentless drive to achieve higher and higher arrest records. More frightening and damaging are the injuries and losses caused by the early release of violent criminals owing to prison overcrowding. Commonly, court orders impose population caps, so prison authorities accelerate release of violent felons serving non-mandatory sentences in order to free up beds for non-violent drug offenders serving mandatory, non-parolable terms.

For example, to stay abreast of its rapidly growing inmate population, Florida launched one of the nation's most ambitious early release programs. However, prisoners serving mandatory terms—most of them drug offenders, who now comprise 36% of the total prison population—are ineligible. As a result, the average length of sentence declined dramatically for violent criminals, while it rose for drug offenders. Murderers, robbers, and rapists often serve less time than a "cocaine mule" carrying a kilo on a bus, who gets a mandatory 15-year term.

A Department of Justice survey showed that 43% of state felons on probation were rearrested for a crime within three years of sentencing. In short, violent criminals are released early to commit more crimes so that their beds can be occupied by non-violent drug offenders. Civil libertarians are not heard often defending a societal right to be secure from violent criminals, much less a right of victims to see just punishment meted out to offenders. In this they are as shortsighted as their law-and-order counterparts. The War on Drugs is a public safety disaster, making victims of us all.

However uncomfortable it may be to admit, the undeniable reality is that drugs always have been and always will be a presence in society. Americans have been paying too high a price for the government's War on Drugs. As Federal judge William Schwarzer has said, "It behooves us to think that it may profit us very little to win the war on drugs if in the process we lose our soul."

Alcohol and Kids: It's Time for Candor

A series of recent government studies shows that alcohol abuse is by far the biggest drug problem facing America's youth, and existing laws do little to address it

Antonia C. Novello

One pressure young people face makes my job, and our hopes for the future, inherently more difficult: the pressure to drink alcohol.

Alcohol is truly the mainstream drug-abuse issue plaguing most communities and families in America today.

We must realize how confusing the mixed messages are that we send to our children about alcohol. We've made progress in the war against illicit drugs because our youth have gotten consistent messages from their families, their schools, their churches, their communities, their nation—and their media.

We're losing the war against underage use of alcohol, however, because our youth receive some very mixed messages. Advertisements and other media images tell them, "Drink me and you will be cool, drink me and you will be glamorous, drink me and you will have fun!" Or even worse, "Drink me and there will be no consequences."

Our health message is clear—"use of alcohol by young people can lead to serious health consequences—not to mention absenteeism, vandalism, date rape, random violence, and even death." But how can that be expected to compete with the Swedish bikini team or the Bud Man?

In June 1991, I released "Youth and Alcohol: Drinking Habits, Access, Attitudes and Knowledge, and Do They Know What They Are Drinking?"

This collection of studies showed that:

■ At least 8 million American teenagers use alcohol every week, and almost half a million go on a weekly binge (or 5 drinks in a row)—confirming earlier surveys by the National Institute on Drug Abuse.

■ Junior and senior high school students drink 35 percent of all wine coolers sold in the United States (31 million gallons) and consume 1.1 billion cans of beer (102 million gallons) each year.

■ Many teenagers who drink are using alcohol to handle stress and boredom. And many of them drink alone, breaking the old stereotype of party drinking.

■ Labeling is a big problem. Two out of three teenagers cannot distinguish alcoholic from nonalcoholic beverages because they appear similar on store shelves.

■ Teenagers lack essential knowledge about alcohol. Very few are getting clear and reliable information about alcohol and its effects. Some million, to be exact, learn the facts from their peers; close to 2 million do not even know a law exists pertaining to illegal underage drinking.

In September 1991, we released a second set of reports, this one on enforcement of underage drinking laws. It was called, "Laws and Enforcement: Is the 21-year-old Drinking Age a Myth?"

These reports showed that:

■ The National Minimum Drinking Age Act of 1984 started out with five exemptions that in some states have become loopholes.

■ The federally mandated 21-year-old minimum drinking law is largely a myth; it is riddled with loopholes. Two-thirds of teens who drink, almost 7 million kids, simply walk into a store and buy booze.

Police point out that parents do not like their children arrested for "doing what everyone else does." One official described enforcement of alcohol laws as "a no-win" situation. And another commented, "Local police have another priority—[illicit] drugs. They ignore alcohol."

And by and large, there are only nominal penalties against vendors and minors when they violate these laws. While vendors may have fines or their licenses suspended, license revocations are rare.

The penalties against the youth who violate the laws are often not deterrents. Even when strict penalties exist, courts are lenient and do not apply them.

6. MEASURING THE SOCIAL COSTS OF DRUGS

We are seeing over and over again the potential for the kind of tragedy that occurred last year on Maryland's eastern shore where Brian Ball, 15 years old, drank 26 shots of vodka at an "all you can drink" party and died two days later—parties where underage drinking gets out of hand, and no adult is held liable. Only 10 states have adopted so-called "social host" laws that hold the host adult or parent liable for the consequences of underage drinking on their property.

Finally, last Nov. 4, we released a final report titled, "Youth and Alcohol: Controlling Alcohol Advertising That Appeals to Youth."

■ Much alcohol advertising goes beyond describing the specific qualities of the beverage. It creates a glamorous, pleasurable image that may mislead youth about alcohol and the possible consequences of its use.

■ A 1991 poll done by the Wirthlin Group said 73 percent of respondents agreed that alcohol advertising is a major contributor to underage drinking.

Additionally, the majority of Americans think that alcohol industry ads "target the young."

Most recently, as honorary chair of Alcohol Awareness Month, I released a fourth report which deals with usually unreported consequences of teen drinking.

Drinking and driving certainly puts many lives at risk, but an alcohol-impaired person doesn't need to get behind the wheel of a car to do harm to himself and to others. Depression, suicides, random violence, and criminal acts—such as date rape, battery, and homicide—all have strong links to alcohol use. So do the unintentional alcohol-related injuries that result from falls, drownings, shootings, residential fires, and the like.

Crime is a major consequence of alcohol consumption. Approximately one-third of our young people who commit serious crimes have consumed alcohol just prior to these illegal actions.

According to the Department of Justice, alcohol consumption is associated with almost 27 percent of all murders, almost 33 percent of all property offenses, and more than 37 percent of robberies committed by young people. In fact, nearly 40 percent of the young people in adult correctional facilities reported drinking before committing a crime.

Alcohol has also shown itself to be a factor in being a victim of crime. Intoxicated minors were found to provoke assailants, to act vulnerably, and to fail to take normal, common-sense precautions.

Among college student crime victims, for example, 50 percent admitted using drugs and/or alcohol.

Rape and sexual assault are also closely associated with alcohol misuse by our youth. Among college age students, 55 percent of perpetrators were under the influence of alcohol, and so were 53 percent of the victims. Administrators at one US university found that 100 percent of sexual assault cases during a specific year were alcohol-related.

Who can honestly tell me that alcohol is not adversely affecting the future of these young people?

I want to share with you another finding I find particularly shocking and revolting: Among high school females, 18 percent—nearly 1 in 5—said it was okay to force sex if the girl was drunk, and among high school males, almost 40 percent—2 out of every 5—said the same thing.

We found other startling links, such as:

■ 70 percent of attempted suicides involved the frequent use of drugs and/or alcohol.

■ Water activities—of special interest and concern in summer—often result in alcohol use and danger. Forty to 50 percent of young males who drown had used alcohol before drowning. Forty to 50 percent of all diving injury victims had consumed alcoholic beverages.

Clearly, something must be done about this pervasive problem confronting our youth. Two things are clear: First, we all have a role to play in solving this problem; second, by working together we can solve it.

I have urged the alcohol industry to come to the table, to work with us, to become part of the solution. I have also urged schools to make alcohol education a central part of the health curriculum from the earliest grades on. This curriculum must include teaching resistance and risk-avoidance techniques.

And, finally, I have urged families—parents and children—to talk to each other about alcohol, about distinguishing truth from fiction.

This article is adapted from a . . . speech given by [former] US Surgeon General Antonia C. Novello before the Town Hall of California in Los Angeles.

SHOULD CIGARETTES BE OUTLAWED?

A bold new campaign has begun to treat tobacco like a dangerous drug and smokers like pariahs. The industry has tools to fight back, but tough antismoking restrictions are inevitable

For 400 years, tobacco has been a pillar of American enterprise. But now it faces the most sustained assault since the surgeon general in 1964 first declared smoking a health hazard. The dangers attributed to cigarettes moved to a menacing new plane recently when the Environmental Protection Agency declared secondhand smoke responsible for as many as 9,000 deaths annually. Efforts to ban smoking have expanded exponentially: The Labor Department has proposed a broad ban on smoking that would affect 70 million workers; sweeping new no-smoking edicts are being enforced at military installations and in giant fast-food chains like McDonald's, and many more cities and states are thinking about piling additional restrictions on those that already apply to enclosed public spaces in 46 states. Surgeon General Jocelyn Elders has lashed out at cigarette marketing aimed at youth. And a House subcommittee has voted to finance its health care plan with a $1.25-per-pack excise tax on cigarettes, up from the 75-cent hike proposed by the Clinton administration. "We're certainly getting slammed," groused Thomas Lauria, spokesman for the Tobacco Institute.

But the biggest slam of all is being delivered by Dr. David Kessler, commissioner of the Food and Drug Administration (FDA). He has warned that he may use his power to ban cigarettes if Congress does not give his agency the green light to regulate tobacco. Kessler, a zealous antismoker, backed his threat with new evidence that nicotine is addictive and that the tobacco industry manipulates levels of the substance to keep smokers hooked.
Kessler's goal. The FDA boss's aim, *U.S. News* has learned, is to join with allies in Congress to give his agency the

power to control tobacco in much the same way the government now controls drugs. Rep. Mike Synar says Kessler was instrumental in helping craft a bill the Oklahoma Democrat has introduced. Synar's bill would:
■ Require manufacturers to disclose the 700 or so chemical additives—five of which have been declared hazardous substances—in tobacco products;
■ Reduce or prohibit the level of harmful additives (among them, according to a report by National Public Radio, are ammonia and ethyl furoid, which causes liver damage);
■ Require tobacco companies to warn of the addictive nature of nicotine;
■ Restrict tobacco advertising* and promotion, particularly ads aimed at minors;
■ Control the level of nicotine that cigarettes contain.

Kessler's disclosures have unleashed action both on Capitol Hill and in the courts. A landmark class-action suit was filed last month in New Orleans charging the tobacco industry with concealing information about the dangers of smoking. The industry will get knocked around more this week when California Rep. Henry Waxman grills top tobacco executives about their firms' practices.

Still, Kessler and Synar recognize they face a formidable foe in the tobacco industry. It has friends in key places in the congressional subcommittee structure, doles out millions of dollars in campaign

contributions, mounts impressive grass-roots lobbying campaigns and can mount legal challenges to virtually every antismoking step being contemplated. Even so, the politics of smoking and tobacco is changing dramatically. Here's why:
Rights of others. A growing body of evidence has bolstered the argument that even nonsmokers are harmed by the effects of secondhand smoke, making it increasingly difficult for the industry to contend that smoking is an individual choice that doesn't impinge on the rights of others.
A different administration. There is no grand Clinton strategy against cigarettes. But it has helped antismoking forces that Bill and Hillary Clinton openly embrace their ideas. The president has taken a typically two-sided approach to smoking: banning it in the White House, while continuing to

THE REACH AND THE TOLL OF TOBACCO

■ Total annual number of tobacco-related deaths	419,000
■ Of those, cardiovascular-disease deaths	180,000
■ Lung-cancer deaths	120,000
■ Annual number of deaths from secondhand smoke	9,000
■ Male smokers, 1965	28.9 mil.
■ Male smokers, now	24 mil.
■ Female smokers, 1965	21.1 mil.
■ Female smokers, now	22.3 mil.

*U.S. News does accept cigarette advertising. It is the company's policy that, to date, such paid advertising—for a product that is still fully legal—falls under the free-speech protection of the First Amendment.

From *U.S. News & World Report*, April 18, 1994, pp. 32-36, 38, 43. © 1994 by U.S. News & World Report. Reprinted by permission.

chomp unlit cigars. Yet he supports higher tobacco taxes, and the administration is closely examining U.S. tobacco exports, which total $6.2 billion and have been rising more than 6 percent a year. U.S. Trade Ambassador Mickey Kantor declared last year that his office would no longer challenge health-related measures in foreign countries as a violation of U.S. trade laws. Such actions have spurred the antismoking forces in Congress. "I think there's been a real shift in the last year," says Rep. Ron Wyden, an Oregon Democrat and a leading foe of tobacco. "Clearly, the White House is now committed to supporting changes."

Revenues need. Tobacco taxes hold seductive appeal as a revenue source for governments at all levels that cannot get public support for other tax increases. Michigan recently approved a 300 percent increase in cigarette taxes to help pay for public schools, in spite of a $3.3 million campaign by the tobacco industry to squelch it. Rep. Charles Rangel of New York, long a tobacco-industry supporter, has shifted his position and now backs a federal cigarette-tax increase: "We need the money."

Public opinion. The mounting scientific evidence against smoking has helped produce a shift in an increasingly health-conscious electorate. In one recent poll, 73 percent of those surveyed expressed an unfavorable view of the tobacco industry; in another, 68 percent said the government should regulate tobacco like any other drug.

Congressional politics. The choke hold of Southern barons who once controlled key committees and defended tobacco is gradually being loosened. The recent death of Rep. William Natcher of Kentucky, chairman of the House Appropriations Committee, deprived the tobacco industry of a critical ally. "Tobacco has been king of the mountain," says law Prof. Richard Daynard of Northeastern University. "Now, everyone is rushing the mountain at once, and tobacco doesn't look so big anymore."

This new climate has emboldened critics. The House recently approved a ban on smoking in public schools, and after the lawmakers return this week, a fight is expected over Waxman's proposal to ban smoking in all public buildings. But the most critical legislative fight will come over Synar's plan to give the FDA jurisdiction over tobacco. If that happens, the FDA would be able to control the way tobacco products are made, promoted and sold.

The industry has dodged regulation over the years at least in part because no agency has a clear mandate to regulate it. Every piece of consumer-protection legislation, from the Consumer Product Safety Act to the Hazardous Substances Act, specifically exempts tobacco. Even the Federal Trade Commission, which governs tobacco advertising and labels, has ceded responsibility for measuring the tar and nicotine levels that are posted on cigarette packages. Since 1987, those measurements have been performed by the Tobacco Institute, the industry's lobbying arm.

That is why Kessler wants to take control of the issue. The wedge he hopes to use is the evidence that cigarettes could be treated like a drug. FDA statutes say the agency can regulate a substance only if it meets one of two narrow criteria: The product must be "intended" by its manufacturer to be used either to affect the "structure and function of the body" or in the "mitigation, treatment or prevention" of disease.

The key word is "intent." In two hours of congressional testimony last month, Kessler cited a raft of new information that has emerged from antismoking groups and from lawsuits against the industry, attempting to show that tobacco companies knowingly alter the levels of nicotine in cigarettes to satisfy the cravings of smokers. In a February letter to the antismoking Coalition for Smoking OR Health, Kessler said: "It is our understanding that manufacturers commonly add nicotine to cigarettes to deliver specific amounts of nicotine."

Kessler buttressed his assertion by citing a 1972 internal memo by a Philip Morris scientist who wrote: "Think of the cigarette as a dispenser for a dose unit of nicotine." Kessler also pointed to 33 patent filings by the tobacco industry suggesting manufacturers can precisely control nicotine levels in cigarettes. One stated: "It is a further object of this invention to provide a cigarette which delivers a larger amount of nicotine in the first few puffs of the cigarette than in the last few puffs."

A critical piece of evidence, in the FDA's view, comes from agency tests. These dispute the assertions of some manufacturers that tar and nicotine levels are both reduced in "low-yield" cigarettes, which many consumers believe are safer than other brands. According to the industry, tar and nicotine levels fall in tandem. But during his testimony, Kessler said the new FDA tests show that the proportion of nicotine in some brands actually goes up as the level of tar goes down. This raises a question about where the high levels of nicotine come from. "We really need to understand how nicotine levels are being controlled," Kessler told *U.S. News.* Sources say he is gunning for evidence that will allow the FDA to show that manufacturers leave nicotine in cigarettes to hook customers — and that would give him a clear mandate to regulate tobacco.

Nicotine taste. In the industry's defense, spokesman Lauria argues that no nicotine is added to cigarettes. He recalls that a nicotine-free cigarette flopped when it was marketed a few years ago. And he notes that cigarettes now contain 66 percent less nicotine than they did 30 years ago. He also disputes the notion that nicotine is addictive. "Nobody has checked into the Betty Ford Clinic to get off cigarettes," he says. Besides, he notes, nicotine shouldn't be removed because it is part of the taste and the "feel" of tobacco smoke in the mouth and throat.

Two weeks ago, Rep. Waxman released a study suggesting the industry has known for years that nicotine is precisely what keeps smokers hooked. In 1983, Waxman asserts, a Philip Morris researcher team demonstrated that nicotine induces addictive behavior in rats. Their paper was accepted for publication by a scientific journal, but the company forced them to withdraw it.

Since then, dozens of studies have revealed nicotine to be at least as addictive as illegal drugs like cocaine and heroin. Kessler points to the fact that 17 million adults try to quit smoking each year, but only 1 in 10 succeeds. Three out of 4 smokers say that they are addicted, and 80 percent say they wish they had never stated smoking. In more scientific measures, smokers show all the physiological marks of the addict. Before the morning's first cigarette, the smoker has all the signs of withdrawal, including hair-trigger reflexes, a lack of concentration and altered brain waves.

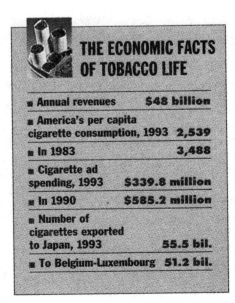

THE ECONOMIC FACTS OF TOBACCO LIFE

▪ Annual revenues	$48 billion
▪ America's per capita cigarette consumption, 1993	2,539
▪ In 1983	3,488
▪ Cigarette ad spending, 1993	$339.8 million
▪ In 1990	$585.2 million
▪ Number of cigarettes exported to Japan, 1993	55.5 bil.
▪ To Belgium-Luxembourg	51.2 bil.

Kessler has flinched from asserting his authority over tobacco before now for two reasons. One, he feared he would be immobilized by litigation from the tobacco industry—a concern highlighted by Philip Morris's recent libel suit against ABC-TV's "Day One," which accused the industry of adding nicotine to cigarettes. Two, he feared that if he seized the initiative over tobacco, he would be left with no alternative but to ban cigarettes outright as unsafe and unhealthy. And even the most ardent tobacco foes do not want that. "We would have a black market in cigarettes that would make the current black market in cocaine and heroine look like a Sunday-school picnic," says Arnold Trebech, director of the Washington-based Drug Policy Foundation. A ban would also find little support even among nonsmokers, according to a recent Gallup poll.

Political compromise. Synar and Kessler have been meeting privately for more than a year to craft a bill that would solve both problems: shield the FDA from lawsuits, while providing the flexibility to regulate tobacco without banning it. "We came up with a new cut," says Synar. "We wanted to get the jurisdiction over tobacco into the FDA. It was simple politics. Once we got the product in there, we wouldn't have to do anything legislatively again."

Even if Synar's bill fails, Kessler will press on in his fight to gain control over tobacco, says a former FDA official. "When [Kessler] believes something is right, he will use whatever moral, legal and regulatory persuasion he has." The most likely scenario if Congress does not act is that Kessler will declare cigarettes unsafe and demand that they be phased out before banning them outright. That would give Congress time to take another run at legislation.

For all the changes in scientific evidence and public opinion, the tobacco lobby still has many friends on key committees. Rep. Tom Bliley, a genial Virginian who is the ranking Republican on the Energy and Commerce Committee, has a tight hold over the committee's GOP votes. In the Senate, tobacco's prime agent is Wendell Ford of Kentucky, the Democratic whip. One sign of his power: Smoking is banned on the House side of the Capitol, but not on the Senate side.

But tobacco's power extends far beyond natural allies like Bliley and Ford, who represent tobacco-growing areas. The industry's $1.6 million in campaign contributions last year is only a fraction of its political largess, which includes contributions to pet charities favored by key lawmakers and their spouses. For example, tobacco companies head the list of contributors to Ohio Democratic Rep. Tony Hall's hunger institute. It is a crafty move on the part of the tobacco lobby because Hall is a swing vote on the House Rules Committee, which decides whether anti-smoking amendments will ever get to the floor. Tobacco money also helps finance the Congressional Black Caucus, and for years it underwrote the annual retreat of House Democrats at the fancy Greenbrier resort.

Barter system. Tobacco's other source of power is votes. Pro-tobacco legislators are among the most tight-knit blocs in Congress and will trade their votes in exchange for support on tobacco. Sources say the House Whip, David Bonior, an outspoken liberal from Michigan, often votes with the tobacco forces as a way of repaying them for their support for bailing out Chrysler when the auto maker was foundering in the late 1970s.

Even so, the days when tobacco was king are over. There are now as many ex-smokers in the United States as there are smokers, and for the first time, smoking foes are optimistic. "Smoking is not going to go away overnight," says Scott Ballin, head lobbyist for the Coalition on Smoking OR Health, "The prospects are better than they have been in 30 years." Surgeon General Elders talked with *U.S. News* about the possibility of seeing tobacco eliminated: "I think that that will come, maybe not in my lifetime but it will come." Maybe. But not without many more very big fights.

BY SHANNON BROWNLEE AND STEVEN V. ROBERTS WITH MATTHEW COOPER, ERICA GOODE, KATIA HETTER AND ANDREA WRIGHT

KICKING THE HABIT: HOW THE ECONOMY WOULD FARE

A nationwide ban on producing, manufacturing, using and exporting tobacco products would have a profound impact on America's economy. Here are the costs and benefits:

BENEFITS	COSTS
LONGER LIVES. Many scientists believe there is a link between smoking and a shortened life span. A ban could increase productivity.	**JOB LOSSES.** Nearly 47,000 workers are employed by the nation's tobacco companies. Many of these jobs could be at risk.
HEALTH CARE SAVINGS. Many studies suggest that billions of dollars now spent on smoking-related diseases could be saved.	**REDUCED FEDERAL AND STATE REVENUES.** Cigarette taxes generated $11.9 billion last year. This revenue could vanish.
LESS ILLNESS. Smoking-related absenteeism could dip. The government says companies could garner an added $8.4 billion.	**EXPORT CUTS.** Tobacco produces a $4 billion trade surplus. A ban could add to trade woes.
WORK GAINS. Without cigarette breaks, smokers could gain a month's work each year.	**INCREASED ENTITLEMENT SPENDING.** Ex-smokers could live longer and receive greater Social Security and Medicare payments.
FEWER FIRES. Accidental fires from smoking cause millions of dollars in damage.	**FARM FEARS.** Tobacco farmers could suffer. Their crop earned about $3 billion last year.

(continued)

TEENS ON TOBACCO

Kids smoke for reasons all their own

Teenagers are the prime target in the tobacco wars. About 1 million start smoking each year—3,000 a day—even though most are too young to buy cigarettes legally. For the tobacco industry, these youngsters are an essential source of new customers. And while cigarette makers deny it, advertising and promotion clearly help attract the attention of teens. The rate of youthful smoking dropped steadily from 1976 until 1984, then leveled off—just as cigarette companies boosted promotional budgets.

The antismoking forces know that an outright ban on cigarettes is impractical and that most of the 46 million Americans who already smoke will not break the habit. So their focus, too, is on teenagers: to keep them from smoking in the first place. Paul Keye, a Los Angeles ad executive who makes antismoking commercials, calls the issue "a war about children." Adds Rep. Richard Durbin of Illinois, a leading antitobacco voice: "If we can reduce the number of young smokers, the tobacco companies will be in trouble and they know it."

Reach out—and rebel. As both sides struggle to shape the attitudes and habits of young people, *U.S. News* discussed the smoking issue with 20 teenagers from suburban Baltimore. Half were boys, half

girls, and all were between 15 and 17. Over more than four hours of conversation, it became clear that most teens start smoking for two seemingly contradictory reasons: They want to be part of a peer group, while rejecting society and its norms. They want to reach out and to rebel at the same time.

The teens estimate that when they party, 75 to 90 percent of the kids are smoking. "It makes you look like you belong," says Davon Harris, a senior at Woodlawn High. "For people who are insecure, it's something they have in common with other people," adds a 10th-grade girl. For these youngsters, smoking, drinking and parties go together—a sign that peer pressure is an enormous factor. Most say teens usually smoke in groups, seldom alone. "If you're drinking, you've just got to have a smoke," says Trey Fitzpatrick, a senior at Gilman Academy.

Teenagers also relish smoking as a sign of independence, even impudence. The more authority figures tell them not to smoke, the more psychic rewards they get from the habit. "A lot of people smoke to give the finger to the world," says Trey Fitzpatrick. Adds Joe Katzenberger, a ninth grader at Glen Burnie High: "I think there's some people who want to be bad but without being a criminal."

The young women add that smoking is something to do when they're bored but don't want to eat. And then they get trapped. "People don't stop, because if they do, they're afraid they'll gain weight," says a freshman girl.

The big woo. There is no doubt in the minds of these young people that they are being wooed by cigarette advertising. And they say it works—at least some of the time. One brand, Camels, has an appealing youthful pitch and is now running a magazine ad featuring "Joe's Place," a swinging nightspot populated by cartoon characters, all smoking and having a great time. Asked her response to the ad, Julia Beavers, a freshman at Dundalk High, said: "Join the party! Everybody's doing it!" Researchers at the Medical College of Georgia report that almost as many 6-year-olds recognize Joe Camel, the brand's standard bearer, as know Mickey Mouse. Scientists at the

University of Massachusetts Medical School say 43 percent of the teens they surveyed thought Joe was "cool," but only 1 in 4 adults agreed.

If Camels appeal to a teenager's desire for acceptance, Marlboros tap his or her impulse to be defiant. Stefanie Albersheim, a junior at Pikesville High, called the Marlboro Man "sexy." Davon Harris looked at a Marlboro ad and interpreted the message: "When you're smoking, you're unstoppable." Michael Eriksen, who heads the Office on Smoking and Health at the Centers for Disease Control and Prevention, says the Marlboro Man "does whatever he wants to do. That appeals to the adolescent who's trying to break away from the rules."

Both brands enhance their appeal by providing coupons in each pack that can be redeemed for hats, jackets and other prizes. Ian Varette, a sophomore at North County High, says one boy he knows is so eager for the merchandise "he'll smoke a couple of packs a day" and steal extra coupons from stores.

These attitudes reinforce the argument of lawmakers who say that one way to curb teenage smoking is to ban cigarette advertising and promotions. But teens are highly skeptical of proposals to raise the legal age for purchasing cigarettes or to increase the price of a pack through higher taxes. "Anyone can get

A HABIT THAT BECOMES HARD TO BREAK

■ Number of teens who smoke	3.1 million
■ Proportion of adult smokers who began before age 20	80%
■ Proportion of teen smokers who said in a survey they had tried to stop	57%
■ Average age when smokers begin	14.5

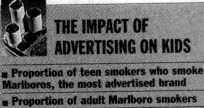

THE IMPACT OF ADVERTISING ON KIDS

■ Proportion of teen smokers who smoke Marlboros, the most advertised brand	69%
■ Proportion of adult Marlboro smokers	24%
■ Proportion of 6-year-olds who know Joe Camel	91%
■ Proportion who know Mickey Mouse	96%

cigarettes now," says Julia Beavers. "It won't change anything." In fact, some teens say, this strategy could backfire: If cigarettes are harder to get, they might become even more desirable.

Another approach that shows little promise: parents and teachers preaching the evils of smoking. Julia Beavers says: "My mother gave me this big old speech—blah, blah, blah—but she smokes." Even the president, the ultimate authority figure, carries little weight. Most of the kids are cynical about the government, and they think politicians are not really serious about reducing smoking, because tobacco taxes bring in so much revenue.

However, these youngsters have been impressed by stark images of the damage caused by smoking. One girl's father, a hospital administrator, gave her photos to take to school comparing the lungs of a smoker and a nonsmoker. The smoker's lungs were "Diet Coke brown" in color and definitely a turnoff. Her conclusion: "Cigarettes kill you inside." A junior boy suggested introducing teens to an older person suffering from smoking-induced cancer: "See this sad sucker; this is what you're going to look like."

But the most effective way to keep kids from smoking is to convince them that it is not cool. The most ardent foes of tobacco in this group find it "disgusting" or "gross," words describing yellowing teeth, foul breath and smoke-stained clothes. One sophomore recalls her first smoke this way: "I remember sitting there and thinking—I was cool, I'm a rebel. Now, I look back, and I was such a dork."

BY STEVEN V. ROBERTS WITH
TRACI WATSON

A MOST COMPLEX PROBLEM

Theodore Vallance

Theodore Vallance is professor emeritus of human development at Pennsylvania State University. He is the author of Prohibition's Second Failure: The Quest for a Rational and Humane Drug Policy *(Praeger, 1993).*

Nothing is as simple as it first appears. This aphorism applies in spades to the way we try to cope with drugs in the United States. The extreme complexity of the drug problem must be recognized before one can come to a workable idea of what can be done to reduce the harms that illicit drugs and their surrounding set of rules and policies inflict on the American public.

What is your perspective? As a parent, you may feel concern lest your children choose alcohol or an illegal drug over other, more wholesome forms of recreation. If you are an economist, you might worry about the dollars that are committed to dealing with the drug problem and therefore not available for other uses. If you are a politician, you might worry about your career should you publicly say something that suggests being "soft on drugs and crime," whatever your personal views might be.

As a social worker, you will anguish over the number of families damaged by drugs and by the drug trade's enticement to high income and high risk for young people. Policemen may wish for duty that is safe from the turf wars of drug-dealing gangs. If you are in the drug-testing business, you will expect profit from the spreading practice of testing workers for drug use. As a teacher or principal in an inner-city high school, you will hope the day ends without police having to disrupt the school while tracking a youthful drug dealer.

As a defense attorney, you will make a good living defending people against charges of serious or trivial offenses against myriad drug laws. If you are a prosecuting attorney, you can make political hay by seeking heavy sentences for major drug dealers or even first offenders carrying three ounces of marijuana for personal use. As a building contractor, you may love the prospect of creating more prisons in which to house people convicted of drug-law violations. As an urban mayor, you will worry about the decline of the inner-city tax base as drug dealing and violent competition for market shares reduce property values and cause people to seek suburban asylum.

If you are a civil libertarian, you will chafe at news of warrantless searches or arrests of people committing what you see as relatively harmless crimes of mutual consent like trading money for cocaine. A member of a drug-law enforcement agency can rejoice in the prospect of career advancement in the pursuit of a worthy cause as prosecution becomes ever more vigorous. A mafioso or lesser practitioner of organized crime will enjoy the likelihood of continuing prosperity so long as certain drugs are illegal. And if you are just a plain old taxpayer (aren't you?), you will wish for the most efficient use of tax dollars toward whatever you define as the public good.

The list of perspectives could go on, illustrating in greater detail the complexity of the drug problem and the inescapable fact that there are winners and losers throughout society no matter what is done, or not done, about it. There are thousands of law-abiding citizens who make legitimate livings on the drug problem, as well as many more lawbreakers. There are no simple solutions to this most complicated problem, and it is important to recognize that any proposed solution will have to contend with a big set of trade-offs. Some aspects of the problem might be driven away, but there will be consequences to any solution that will evoke cries of alarm from some quarter.

So what is "the" drug problem? Clearly, it is many things, and searching for a solution requires knowing "its" parts.

THE 'DRUG PROBLEM' IS A CRIME PROBLEM

Literally millions of lawbreakings occur daily. Most are committed by the estimated 20 million users of illegal drugs who generate more than a million arrests annually. More newsworthy are crimes to obtain money for buying drugs. The average heroin addict needs $10,000 a year to sustain the habit, and nearly all heroin addicts commit predatory crimes: muggings, burglaries, and occasional associated killings. In Miami, 356 heroin users admitted committing nearly 120,000 criminal acts in a single year—an average of 332 crimes per person, which looks much like full-time employment. Studies of heroin users in other cities produce similar results.

Users of cocaine and other nonnarcotic drugs contribute their share of predatory crimes, plus bank and credit card fraud and forgery. Interviews of 500 cocaine hot-line callers showed 45 percent of them reporting that they had stolen to support their cocaine habits. The data on predatory crime are nearly endless. The subsidy for drug prices that prohibition provides too often requires that money be gotten from activities beyond one's regular employment, especially if that employment is erratic or poorly paid. Still more dramatic are the shoot-outs between drug merchants as they try to sustain or expand market share. Because disagreements about drug-selling turf can't be appealed to the courts of law like violations of other business agreements, resort to the court of the gun is common.

Organized crime has always been important in illicit drug trafficking. Managers of any profitable business organization seek to expand their range and increase control over their operations. The illicit drug trade is no exception. Although racketeers had been busy in cocaine and heroin commerce before these drugs became illegal, the government's invitation to organized crime came in 1914 by way of the Harrison Act, which imposed levies on imported heroin and other drugs and was later interpreted by the courts to prohibit the private use of opiates and coca and its derivatives. Well before the Eighteenth Amendment's prohibition of alcohol in 1919, Irving "Waxey Gordon" Wexler, for one example, had become prominent in the Jewish underworld and was a major partner in several cocaine trafficking organizations in New York and Philadelphia.

But then came the Volstead Act, implementing the Eighteenth Amendment's prohibition of the manufacture and sale of alcoholic beverages. This denial of centuries-old traditions involving wine, beer, and hard liquor was rejected by millions of ordinarily law-abiding Americans, whose needs were soon met by purveyors of potable and sometimes lethal alcohol. So lucrative a field led naturally to expansionist and protective reactions of people in the recreational alcohol trade.

Americans of Italian, Sicilian, Jew-ish, and Irish underworld gangs were soon effective in organizing the manufacture and importation of alcoholic drinks, and they made excellent, if hazardous, livings for themselves and for cooperative law-enforcement people until the repeal of Prohibition in 1933. Knowing sound business practices, these people, with the Italians and Sicilians most popularly known as the Mafia, sought and found a replacement profit center in the trade in illicit drugs, customers for which had been slowly increasing and whose sinister attractiveness had been given wide appreciation through the efforts of Harry Anslinger, head of the Federal Bureau of Narcotics.

Salvatore Lucania, better known as "Lucky" Luciano, was a Sicilian American gangster who devised a way to make the world's oldest profession more efficient: Abandoning the traditional Mafia ban on dealing in narcotics and prostitution, he helped prostitutes into narcotics addiction and secured their loyalty through control of the drugs they needed, thus eliminating surplus sales managers (pimps) and cutting overhead costs. Today we call this "downsizing." Luciano was eventually convicted on prostitution charges; he served part of a long sentence before being released and deported to Italy in a deal in which he agreed to use his connections with corrupt labor leaders and importers to maintain the orderly functioning of East Coast dockyards during World War II.

The war produced a major hiatus in international drug trading, but shortly thereafter Luciano and other mafiosi began to rebuild a smuggling operation that helped revive heroin use in the United States. The number of addicts increased threefold by 1952 from the estimated 20,000 that existed at the end of the war. Drug use continued to grow, and by the mid-1960s the market had expanded beyond the traditional urban poor to the suburban middle class and the "baby boom" generation.

Marijuana and various synthetics competed strongly against the more traditional drugs, diversifying both supply and demand in such a way that the control of production and distribution by organized criminals began to decline. This is not to say that large organized criminal syndicates play an insignificant part in the drug problem of today, but only that their role is most prominent in the production of imported drugs. A recent television documentary asserts that the organized international drug trade grosses about $500 billion annually, second only to armaments.

However, the strong hand of "mature" organized criminals, such as the Mafia and its corrupting influence on law-enforcement personnel, has declined along with the management discipline of earlier years. In its place we now have the market competition of various ethnically and racially based upstart and fully armed gangs, still organized criminals, which has turned too many inner-city areas into war zones.

THE DRUG PROBLEM IS AN ECONOMIC PROBLEM

Several recent studies of the economic costs of the drug problem show annual totals ranging from -$44 billion to $76 billion, with differences due mainly to methods of analysis and time period. The most comprehensive analysis was conducted by a group headed by Dorothy Rice at the University of California at San Francisco. Their estimate of total annual cost, as of 1985, was a little over $44 billion. Here are two simple tables compiled from the mass of statistics in their report. Both include costs of the alcohol problem because of the interesting comparisons they afford.

Under the heading "Core Costs," those called direct costs refer to treatment of people who are sick, or just trying to kick the habit, and to the supporting costs of research on the problem and the training of treatment givers and researchers. Indirect costs result from people being sick and unable to earn income or pay taxes and from people dying ahead of schedule and so forgoing opportunities to earn money and pay taxes. In all these categories, legal alcohol costs far exceed those for illegal drugs. This is due largely to the fact that there are at least four times as many alcohol abusers as there are people who abuse illicit drugs; this very fact may be used to underscore the risks of making illicit drugs licit.

In the next category, other related costs, the picture reverses and becomes more interesting, with the cost of illegal drugs being more than three times that of alcohol, the excess arising almost

Economic costs of alcohol and drug use, 1985 data		
	Amount (in millions of dollars)	
Type of cost	Alcohol	Drugs
Total	70,388	44,052
Core costs	58,151	10,624
Direct costs	6,810	2,082
Treatment	6,315	1,881
Support	495	201
Indirect costs	51,371	8,542
Sickness	27,388	5,979
Early death	23,983	2,563
Other related costs	10,546	32,461
Direct costs	7,830	13,209
Indirect costs	3,116	19,252
Special disease groups		
AIDS	——	967
Fetal alcohol syndrome	1,611	——

Table 1

entirely from the fact that illegal drugs are illegal. The second table breaks out these costs.

Here, the direct cost categories for illegal drugs far outstrip those for alcohol under the major heading of crime. Drug users and dealers are far more likely to be candidates for arrest, trial, jailing, and other services of the criminal justice system than are their legal counterparts in the alcohol trade. You can become a criminal justice client simply by getting caught owning, selling, or using an illegal drug. Shooting someone in a trade-association dispute (commonly called drug-gang wars) and robbing or burgling for funds to pay for drugs also qualify. In relation to alcohol, you must become a public nuisance, beat up somebody, get into an auto accident, smash a few windows, or otherwise break some law not uniquely related to possessing alcohol in order to become a criminal justice client. This comparison is clearer in the other direct cost categories of motor vehicle crashes, fire destruction, and social welfare; the costs of the drug prob-

lem are exceedingly modest here in comparison with those of the alcohol problem. Opponents of drug legalization will warn of increases in these costs were legalization to occur.

Look also at the class called indirect costs, where drug-law violations generate six times the cost of alcohol offenses. Black-market drug buyers more often victimize people to support their tastes; they and their suppliers spend a lot more time being involuntarily housed, fed, and given health care at public expense while they are neither earning money nor paying taxes on it. They also engage in careers that do not produce valuable goods and services, and they do not earn or pay taxes on legitimate income.

Additional cost figures are reflected in the president's fiscal-year 1995 budget request: some $1.6 billion for the Federal Bureau of Prisons, $1.2 billion to keep illegal drugs from entering the United States from other places, $232 million for the State Department's international programs, plus other items only in the tens-of-millions range.

Among other nonbudgeted costs, a Small Business Administration report, though criticized by numerous drug-policy analysts, claims that on-the-job alcohol and other substance-abuse problems result in more than $100 billion in lost productivity through absenteeism, accidents, and interrupted work. Finally, consider that the underground economy in illicit drugs generates an annual flow of about $90 billion in sales and profits and assume that this number would decline by three-quarters were the drug business open and legitimate. A total tax on income and sales at, say, 40 percent would generate revenues of about $9 billion. This missing benefit also counts as a cost of the drug problem.

So what does the total economic cost of illicit drugs come to? It is reasonable to add at least 30 percent to Rice's 1985 figures to account for inflation and the fact that high levels of cocaine use did not occur until later in the decade and to include interdiction and other drug-war costs that she didn't; the total then reaches at least $60 billion annually. If

Other related costs of alcohol and drug use, 1985 data

Type of cost	Amount (in millions of dollars)	
	Alcohol	**Drugs**
Total	*10,546*	*32,461*
Direct costs	*7,380*	*13,209*
Crime	*4,251*	*13,203*
Public expenditures	*3,734*	*11,063*
Criminal justice system	*3,734*	*9,508*
Drug traffic control	——	*1,555*
Private legal defense	*324*	*1,381*
Property destruction	*175*	*759*
Other direct expenditures	*3,129*	*6*
Motor vehicle crashes	*2,584*	——
Fire destruction	*457*	——
Social welfare administration	*88*	*6*
Indirect costs	*3,166*	*19,152*
Victims of crime	*465*	*842*
Incarceration	*2,701*	*4,434*
Crime careers	——	*13,976*

Table 2

you then add the lost opportunity to tax drug transactions and even half of the estimated time lost from work, the yearly grand total approaches $135 billion.

As former Sen. Everett Dirksen put it, "A billion here, a billion there—before long it adds up to real money." The unfunny part of this is that most of the money actually spent on the drug problem has to be spent *only* because there is no legal way to obtain mood-altering drugs (other than alcohol, nicotine, and caffeine) for recreational use.

THE DRUG PROBLEM IS A HEALTH PROBLEM

Yes, people do get sick from taking drugs. Some die. A 1979 report cites 900 deaths associated with 57 million Valium prescriptions to help people live with stress and 700 deaths connected with 9 million prescriptions for Elavil to help people feel better. In 1985, nearly 95,000 deaths related to alcohol were reported, with about 17,600 having alcohol as the main cause (cirrhosis of the liver was the predominant diagnosis); nearly 35,000 deaths came from injuries and accidents, including 23,000 from auto accidents. We shouldn't overlook the 430,000 annual deaths associated with nicotine and the by-products of burning tobacco. Nicotine itself is an excellent pesticide; the amount in one good cigar (if extracted and not burned) is twice the human lethal dose.

And yes, lots of people do die from using drugs that are not approved for therapeutic or recreational use. In 1985, according to Rice's report, slightly over 6,000 deaths were connected with illegal drug use; a more recent estimate is 7,600. Well over half were probably accidental: poisonings by drug impurities and contaminated injection needles. We may expect an increase in overdoses of heroin with its recently increased availability in concentrated form, for heroin is the most physiologically addictive illegal drug and most hazardous when taken in large doses. The exchange of contaminated needles among drug users with the HIV virus accounts for a significant increase in AIDS in recent years. A 1991 report of the National Commission on AIDS found that a third of adult and adolescent AIDS cases were related to intravenous drug use. Interestingly, marijuana, the illegal drug that is most popular and most widely discussed in popular literature, has yet to claim a recorded death from overdose.

THE DRUG PROBLEM IS AN INTERNATIONAL PROBLEM

There are drug problems worldwide, of course, and elaborate and handsomely financed organizations to make sure that global

Since cocaine use became popular in the 1970s and exploded in the late 1980s, the economics and politics of Colombia have undergone major changes.

markets are supplied, but here I call attention to the effect of America's drug problem on other countries. Making a product illegal raises its price so long as demand is strong: Drug merchants must cover higher shipping costs and losses through seizures, pay bribes to people who would interfere with their trade, and be compensated for the risk of being arrested, jailed, or killed by competitors. The difference between production costs and street prices of illegal drugs has stimulated a grossly rich drug industry in many otherwise poor countries.

American drug policy has had tremendous impacts in dozens of countries. Notable among them are the Andean nations of South America. To take just one major example, since cocaine use became popular in the 1970s and exploded in the late 1980s, the economics and politics of Colombia have undergone major changes. Coca cultivation is centuries old in the Andean countries, where indigenous Indians found that chewing the leaves killed hunger pangs and made it possible to sustain hard work under difficult conditions. As American interdiction of cocaine shipments increased in the 1970s, prices soared and the coca industry grew rapidly to keep up with demand under the energetic entrepreneurship of Pablo Escobar and others making up a cartel based in the city of Medellín. Revenues from this illegal trade reached about $3 billion in 1988, bringing enormous power to its controllers in a country with a gross legal domestic product of only $35 billion. In 1977, Colombian President Alfonso López Michelsen, urged and backed by the Carter administration, expanded the government's campaign against cocaine traffic. His successor, Julio Cesar Turbay Ayala, extended this crackdown and even agreed to a controversial treaty with the United States that would allow Colombian drug traffickers accused of crimes in the United States to be extradited and tried in U.S. courts. In exchange, the United States tripled its foreign aid to Colombia. Drug traffickers countered effectively, buying tips from police about prospective drug raids and, from judges, dismissals of charges against drug traders or light sentences if convicted. In a despairing comment, Turbay said, "Colombians are not corrupting Americans. You are corrupting us. If you abandon illegal drugs, the traffic will disappear."

A new president, Belisario Betancur Cuartas, renounced the 1979 extradition treaty, preferring to try Colombian traffickers in Colombian courts. Reacting to outrage from Washington, Betancur instructed his new minister of justice, Rodrigo Lara Bonilla, to press the drug war more vigorously in cooperation with the U.S. Drug Enforcement Administration (DEA). The Medellín drug cartel did not take kindly to this and assassinated Lara in April 1984. Police officials and prosecutors were repeatedly threatened and assaulted. A dozen members of Colombia's Supreme Court were murdered. To avoid retribution from friends of accused traffickers, judges adopted the practice of screening themselves from the sight of the accused and using voice scramblers to hide their identities. Life as a Colombian judge has become unattractive.

Colombia continues to enforce its laws against drug traffickers. The Medellín cartel was finally smashed but has been replaced by another one based in the city of Cali. Pablo Escobar, earlier imprisoned, escaped and was killed in a 1994 shoot-out with police. But problems continue. Colombia's prosecutor general, Gustavo de Greiff, has apparently concluded that the "war on drugs" as currently waged cannot be won. He is proposing the adoption of a plea-bargaining process in his country to make the prospect of convictions less threatening to traffickers. In a March 1994 *Washington Post* column, he argued that in the long run some form of legalization and regulation of the drug trade is the most reasonable solution to the international problem that American drug policy has wrought.

A less dramatic sign of pressure on other countries to help solve America's drug problem comes via a 1986 law allowing the U.S. representative to the International Monetary Fund to vote against grants to countries that the American president finds are not doing adequate jobs of helping the United States with its drug problem, that is, are not pursuing traffickers with sufficient vigor or not stamping out cocaine refineries in sufficient numbers. An implicit if unintended message: If you, country X, don't try to stamp out drugs, we will make you more dependent on the drug trade by denying you other funds you need for development.

THE DRUG PROBLEM IS A PROBLEM IN COLLECTIVE-CULTURAL MORALITY

If you were offered an opportunity to make in one month your expected total lifetime earnings just by doing a few unlikely-to-be-discovered but illegal acts, would you be tempted? Of course not! But many people would—and do pick up the opportunity. When the business at hand is illegal and thus puts its practitioners at risk of arrest and imprisonment, one obvious defense is to persuade those who would enforce the law to be less than thorough in their duties. Some policemen in every large American city earn extra income from drug dealers by tipping them off to impending raids or reporting the presence of outside competitors in their turf. A New York study estimated that 40 percent of the price of cocaine in one neighborhood represented the cost of paying cops to direct their vision away from drug transactions.

Cash seized in drug raids offers heavy temptation to the arresting officers; eighteen Los Angeles County sheriff's deputies were suspended in 1989 for yielding to temptation.

Cash seized in drug raids offers heavy temptation to the arresting officers; eighteen Los Angeles County sheriff's deputies were suspended in 1989 for yielding to temptation. More recently, several New York policemen were charged with operating their own business of distributing cocaine seized in raids. Temptations for this kind of behavior are strengthened by the demoralizing conviction that the street-level drug war accomplishes little, that a heavy crackdown in one neighborhood simply moves the drug trade, alive and well, to another. And it's not just police who are corrupted. An assistant U.S. attorney in New York State stole drugs and money from government supplies and was duly convicted, and a federal judge was convicted recently of bribery in a drug case.

Regrettably, we have come to accept bribery and other corruptions as a normal part of politics and law enforcement, undermining public faith in the criminal justice system (Why should I obey the law when thousands are getting away with murder? Should I bother to report the bribe that I know about when I know there won't be any prosecution?) and encouraging the rise of vigilantism. Another moral conflict with which we continue to live is the hypocrisy in our current policy: Alcohol, nicotine, and caffeine are okay, kind of like apple pie. But those other drugs are morally bad, as are the people who use them—and not just because it is wrong to break laws. Somehow, they differ morally from the rest of us (booze drinking) law-abiders.

THE DRUG PROBLEM IS A PROBLEM OF INDIVIDUAL FREEDOM AND CIVIL LIBERTIES

Without question, some drug-law violators restrict the freedom of many people who now fear to venture into their neighborhood streets. But less dramatically and with growing frequency, civil liberties are being eroded in the name of the war on drugs. One scholar claims that all of the first ten amendments that make up the Bill of Rights have been violated in the effort to solve the drug problem. The Fourth Amendment has been most severely battered. It reads in full:

> The right of the people to be secure in their persons, houses, papers, and effects, against unreasonable search and seizure, shall not be violated, and no warrants shall issue, but upon probable cause, supported by oath or affirmation, and particularly describing the place to be searched, and the persons or things to be seized.

In 1989, a New Hampshire man would have been surprised to be told that this statement would protect him from police entering his home with a battering ram at 5:00 A.M. carrying a search warrant based partly on an informant's two-year-old tip. As he rose from his bed to resist, one of the intruders shot him dead. A single marijuana cigarette was found. In recent years, legislative acts and court decisions have watered down Fourth Amendment protections. Drug-enforcement police can now use "profiles" to define who they think might be drug-law violators. Some examples drawn from a recent review: deplaning first; deplaning last; walking rapidly through the airport; walking slowly through the airport; behaving nervously; behaving calmly. A federal circuit judge comments that the DEA's profiles have a "chameleon-like way of adapting to any particular set of observations." The DEA does not reveal records of the numbers of people detained, arrested, or searched on the basis of profiles but claims that profiles have helped catch 3,000 drug-law violators. The few numbers available indicate that well under 10 percent of people searched were actually arrested. Hint: Don't pay cash for an expensive airline ticket; the clerk may put you in touch with a nearby DEA agent.

Among the most imaginative offenses against Fourth Amendment rights is the increasing use of civil forfeiture laws to seize property suspected of involvement in criminal acts. Passed by the First Congress to authorize seizures of ships smuggling goods into the United States, the laws have been amended specifically for use in the war on drugs. Abuses of these laws derive from the fiction that inanimate things can experience guilt and from the financial incentives offered to prosecutors and police.

If you lend your car to someone who leaves a marijuana cigarette in the ashtray, the car may be seized as "guilty" of participating in an illegal act. If your car is in your garage, the garage could also be seized, possibly with your attached house; prosecuting attorneys have lots of discretion. Does the prosecutor have to prove your guilt? No, because you are not being charged, just the car, or the garage, or the house. But, because cars and garages can't appear in court to defend themselves, to get them back you have to prove that you had no connection with the violation. If you can't—and proving a negative is virtually impossible—the police can sell your property and use the proceeds to find more law-breaking property to seize. If this seems bizarre, note these case registries: *United States v. RD 1, Box 1, Thompsontown, Juniata County, Pennsylvania* or *Commonwealth of Pennsylvania v. one 1958 Plymouth Sedan.*

THE TOUGH TRADE-OFFS

Now comes the hard part. Somewhere between the extremes of instant free-market unregulated legalization of all currently illegal drugs and redoubling law-enforcement efforts over and over again must lie a policy that would enlarge some of the good features in our present prac-

Among the most imaginative offenses against Fourth Amendment rights is the increasing use of civil forfeiture laws to seize property suspected of involvement in criminal acts.

tices and reduce many of the bad ones. The aim of such a policy can be termed "harm reduction," recognizing that drugs will always be with us, like them or not. Such a policy would have to placate moralists who insist that "drugs in themselves are bad," as well as libertarians who argue for the individual's right to do to himself what he will. It should appear reasonable to politicians facing voters convinced that there is nothing good about drug-law reform and unconcerned about what costs must be borne to stamp out illegal drugs. In a peaceful and rational world, we should like to have a drug policy that minimizes harms of many kinds: economic, social, and moral. It should be politically tenable, and its rules should be acceptable to most people. But let's go from this comforting abstraction to prospects in the real world.

So large and complex an industry as illegal drugs and other, dependent industries will not readily relinquish economic, political, or moral turf. Thousands of people make legitimate livings from illegal drugs: The DEA alone employs more than 5,000 people, and the individual states have their own DEAs. Many more thousands are to varying degrees prohibition-dependent: prosecuting and defense attorneys, prison builders, guards and administrators, employees and owners of the billion-dollar drug-testing business. One could even list tobacco and alcohol merchants, whose business might suffer competition from quality producers of less-dangerous recreational drugs. (Take note that after the Twenty-first Amendment turned over control of alcohol to the states, bootleggers worked hard in several states to keep alcohol illegal.)

It cannot be refuted that most of the crime associated with drugs derives from their illegality. Making all drugs legal would, of course, define most of these offenses out of existence. But more significant is the fact that drug-related crime would lose its motivational base: the violent crime associated with defend-

ing turf and getting money to support habits, plus the corruption of police, courts, and other public officials.

The many proposals for alleviating the drug problem are far too complex for detailed review here, but a commentary on some major ideas is offered. My own review of the facts and principles convinces me that some form of regulated legalization must come, preceded and accompanied by extensive education about the risks of extensive drug use—reflecting the success of recent efforts in educating people to the hazards of smoking tobacco and drinking alcohol. But before adopting a new policy, here are some of the contingent questions whose answers must be broadly understood. How would legalization affect drug use? Which drugs should be legalized and on what time schedule? How should the drug market be regulated? Can juvenile access and subsequent addiction be prevented? Would drug use be permitted everywhere, or should some restrictions be adopted? How can advertising be controlled? What procedures for regulating drug use in the workplace should be adopted? Legislation that would establish a special commission to examine these and other questions and make recommendations on drug policy has been introduced in Congress.

Here is preliminary commentary on the questions. Further discussion of these and related issues can be found in *America's Longest War* (1994) by Steven Duke and Albert Gross.

Drug use might go up, though experience in the Netherlands and in the ten American states that decriminalized the personal use of marijuana in the 1970s suggests otherwise. Treatment for abuse would be more readily sought were abusers not at risk of arrest. Drug use would not disappear; attaining a drug-free society is as feasible as attaining a sex-free society; drug use and sex are aspects of human life to be appreciated and enjoyed with restraint, not stamped out.

Early regulated legalization of marijuana, including especially its use for medicinal purposes, would test legalization's feasibility and anticipate possible problems in legalizing other drugs.

On market regulation, unfettered distribution could attract children unaware of the risks of drug use. Having the federal government as sole distributor would avoid First Amendment issues about advertising and preclude inconsistencies among state-operated systems.

Restricting juvenile access would be as difficult as it is now for nicotine and alcohol, but serious enforcement of existing laws and practices could become effective. Banning vending machines selling tobacco and other drugs (can you imagine the flap such a proposal would raise?) could defeat today's easy access by juveniles to tobacco as well. Licensing of both sellers and buyers could help enforce age rules and limit volume of sales.

Restricting advertising raises constitutional free-speech issues that the courts have yet to resolve. Truth-in-labeling rules, including wording akin to the surgeon general's warning on cigarette packages, could counteract some promotions, but the best defense will probably be a solid educational offense.

Problems of drug use in the workplace can easily be incorporated in established employee-assistance programs. Smart firms know that helping employees deal with problems like alcoholism, compulsive gambling, family strife, and personal financial management can produce major savings in the form of reduced absenteeism, reduced turnover, and generally happier employees. If drugs were legal and the user largely free from stigma and the risk of being arrested or fired, employees would be more willing to use the assistance programs already available to them.

The tough issues and the necessity for making distasteful trade-offs remain. I leave the reader to ponder: What do *you* think we should do about this problem?

PUSHING DRUGS TO DOCTORS

A young doctor listened intently to a panel of distinguished physicians discuss advances in hypertension treatment at the annual meeting of the American Academy of Family Physicians. By the end of the three-hour presentation, he was thinking seriously about switching some of his hypertensive patients to a drug called a calcium channel blocker, which was much discussed at the presentation. The seminar was sponsored by the pharmaceutical company G.D. Searle and Co., as the young physician knew. But he didn't realize that Searle—which was then running a promotional campaign for *Calan,* one of several calcium channel blockers—had carefully picked speakers who were well-known advocates for this class of drugs.

☐ On one recent Sunday, physicians who tuned in to the Lifetime Cable Network, which runs special medical programming for doctors, saw a 30-minute presentation called "Physician's Guide to Gallstone Disease." The program urged doctors to use medication instead of surgery to treat gallstones. It omitted the fact that gallbladder surgery remains the preferred treatment for almost all patients. The video was produced and paid for by CIBA-Geigy, maker of *Actigall,* the medication being recommended. After the U.S. Food and Drug Administration declared the program false and misleading, the company agreed to clear future *Actigall* promotions with the FDA in advance.

☐ At the American Psychiatric Association's annual meeting in 1991 psychiatrists attended a symposium on new research in the treatment of manic-depression. Despite the broad topic, the session mainly focused on the use of anticonvulsant drugs, even though the FDA has never approved them for this use. The symposium was sponsored by Abbott Laboratories, maker of *Depakote* — an anticonvulsant that speakers at the session discussed as a manic-depression treatment.

☐ Two years ago, cancer specialists around the country were sent several issues of a serious-looking publication called "Oncology Commentary '90," which summarized symposia that dealt with unapproved uses of several anticancer drugs. The publication was produced by the maker of those drugs, Bristol-Myers Squibb, which did not disclose its

The way that drug companies sell their wares is a prescription for inefficient medicine— and a major contributor to soaring health-care costs.

involvement anywhere on the publication. After months of regulatory wrangling, the FDA forced the company to send a letter to every doctor who received the mailing, confessing its behind-the-scenes influence.

Over the past 15 years or so, the $63-billion-a-year pharmaceutical industry has made physicians the targets—sometimes willing, sometimes unwitting—of sophisticated, subtle, and highly effective marketing techniques that permeate nearly every aspect of medical practice. Drug companies organize "educational symposia" that are actually disguised promotional efforts for their products. They pay for sober-looking "supplements" to respected medical journals and fill those supplements with articles selected and edited to make their products look good. They pay doctors to use drugs in "clinical trials" organized not by drug researchers but by drug marketers. And they offer doctors all sorts of gifts and perks, from ballpoint pens to lavish banquets and concerts.

Sometimes the drugs being marketed really are more effective, less costly, or safer than their competitors. But others are unoriginal products seeking to take market share away from established, and frequently less expensive, formulations. Of the 20 or so new drugs the FDA approves in a typical year, the agency usually rates no more than four as truly meaningful therapeutic advances. That leaves the rest to slug it out in the arena of image, promotion, and marketing.

The industry carefully avoids adding up its annual promotional tab, but independent sources place it conservatively at around $5-billion. It must be money well spent; the pharmaceutical industry has long been the nation's most profitable. The top 10 U.S. drug companies averaged 16 percent profit on sales in 1990, more than triple that of the average Fortune 500 company.

But what's good for Searle and CIBA-Geigy may not be good for the rest of us. Between 1980 and 1990, while general inflation was 58 percent, overall health-care costs rose 117 percent—and the cost of drugs rose 152 percent. Every unnecessary prescription, and every unnecessary choice of an expensive, brand-name drug over a cheaper alternative, contributes to these excessive costs.

Besides the money spent directly on drug-company promotion, current marketing practices have a high indirect cost as well. Companies have

the greatest incentive to promote costly drugs, even if they're no more effective than cheaper ones.

High drug prices are a special burden for elderly people, who make up 12 percent of the population but consume 34 percent of prescription drugs. Surveys by the American Association of Retired Persons have found that prescription drugs are the single largest out-of-pocket medical expense for three out of four Americans over 5, and that four out of ten have no prescription drug insurance coverage whatever. One in

seven say they have failed to take prescribed medicine because it was too expensive.

The new age of marketing

For many years, pharmaceutical companies sold their wares the way any business-to-business company does. They sent representatives out to call on doctors with samples and sales patter and placed ads in medical journals—methods that are still the core of their marketing efforts. But then, in 1977, came *Tagamet*. In addition to being a genuine break-

SELF-PROTECTION FOR PATIENTS

ARE YOU GETTING THE RIGHT DRUG?

If you visit the doctor for a lingering cough and cold and come away with a $90 prescription for a brand-name antibiotic, are you getting state-of-the-art treatment or an inappropriate, overpromoted drug? Unfortunately, it's hard to tell. As a patient, you hold very few of the cards in the prescribing game; in the end, only a doctor can write a prescription. That said, however, patients can still improve their chances of getting an effective prescription at a reasonable price. Here are some strategies to keep in mind.

Look for red flags. Brand-name drugs for arthritis, high blood pressure, ulcers, high cholesterol, and respiratory infections are among the most heavily promoted and thus the most likely to be prescribed. If your doctor prescribes one of these drugs, question him or her closely: Why choose this particular drug? Are there other, possibly cheaper, choices? If so, why not prescribe one of them? You may also want to look the drug up in one of the consumer drug guides now available.

Ask about nondrug therapies. You don't have to take a pill for everything that ails you. For example, using a vaporizer, salt-water gargles, plenty of fluids, and acetaminophen may work about as well as a prescription combination product in treating a viral respiratory infection, without causing such side effects as drowsiness. Exercise, salt restriction, and weight loss can successfully treat some people who have cases of mild hypertension.

Don't demand the latest drug. The latest, most expensive drug isn't necessarily the best, despite what you may have read or heard. The oldest antibiotic of all, penicillin,

remains the drug of choice for treating strep throat. Diuretics have a long record of safety, if you can tolerate their mild side effects, and can successfully treat many cases of high blood pressure at a much lower cost than newer agents. Old drugs that are still widely used have generally stayed around for a reason—they're effective and their side effects are well known. Newer drugs are more likely to have unpleasant surprises in store.

Ask about generic or over-the-counter alternatives. Prescription-strength *Motrin*, a brand-name version of the antiarthritis drug ibuprofen, costs $31 for a 30-day supply. The same amount of generic prescription-strength ibuprofen costs about $17. Although specific procedures vary from state to state, pharmacists are now allowed to substitute generics for brand-name drugs. If you don't mind taking three or four tablets at a time, you can also buy ibuprofen over the counter in pills of lower dosage, and simply take more pills to raise the dosage level. That would cost you even less—about $13 a month for a therapeutically equivalent dose.

If you've taken a drug for a long time, remind your doctor occasionally. It may be time to stop. For example, many patients continue to take *Tagamet* or *Zantac*, two ulcer medications, long after their ulcers have healed. They may no longer need the drug at all: Their doctors may simply have neglected to review the need for renewing the prescription.

through in the treatment of ulcers, it was a breakthrough in marketing.

"This was the first prescription drug to open the nightly news," David Jones, a former industry marketing and public relations executive, recalled in a recent speech. "People were asking for it before it was available. . . . The industry quickly realized that . . . if this kind of publicity, generating this kind of demand, could happen naturally with one drug, it could be made to happen with others."

Nowadays, company marketing departments, frequently with the help of outside consultants, draw up elaborate plans to launch and position new products, defend proven sellers against new competition, or increase the market share of existing products. More and more, pharmaceutical companies are promoting their drugs directly to consumers—an ominous trend we'll cover in an upcoming issue. But their major efforts have been directed at doctors. Drug companies use advanced market-research techniques to probe the psyches of unsuspecting physicians, and use the results to fine-tune their pitches. "Basically, industry has been almost in a feeding frenzy, competing to win the attention of physicians by various promotional efforts," says Dr. Stephen Goldfinger, faculty dean for medical education at Harvard Medical School.

Though doctors insist their scientific training, high intelligence, and sophistication enable them to resist manipulation, the truth is that skillful marketers can influence M.D.s just as easily as they can sway the rest of us. A landmark 1982 study by Dr. Jerry Avorn of Harvard showed that doctors' opinions of two popular, heavily advertised drugs came straight from the ads and sales pitches. The doctors believed they'd gotten their information from objective scientific sources, but those sources, in fact, had said all along that the drugs were not effective for their advertised uses.

Even a thorough medical-education campaign may be no match for a drug company's marketing efforts, as Avorn and his colleague Stephen B. Soumerai have shown in analyzing the case of *Darvon*. Between 1978 and 1980, the FDA organized a nationwide effort to reduce the prescribing of this heavily marketed painkiller: The drug had proven to be addictive and was very easy to use as a means of suicide. *Darvon's* manufacturer, Eli Lilly, was supposed to support the FDA's effort, but an FDA

audit found that the company had in fact continued to promote the drug to doctors. During this period, sales of the drug hardly budged. What finally knocked *Darvon* off the sales charts was the expiration of its patent, which made further marketing efforts uneconomical. Lilly then turned to marketing *Darvocet-N*, a combination of *Darvon* and acetaminophen then still under patent; it swiftly rose to become the 10th-most prescribed drug in the U.S.

Ethics and evasions

During the Reagan era, the FDA, which regulates the advertising and promotion of prescription drugs, suffered from both budget cuts and the Administration's anti-regulatory philosophy. The agency took a hands-off attitude toward the new promotional techniques. Its understaffed Division of Drug Marketing, Advertising, and Communications tried valiantly to police the more flagrant abuses, but was no match for the industry in size or resources. "We wrote letters, we wrote letters, and we wrote more letters," the agency's new commissioner, Dr. David Kessler, said in a press conference shortly after taking office last year.

Things began to change somewhat in late 1990. Senator Edward M. Kennedy's Committee on Labor and Human Resources held hearings that spotlighted the most extravagant promotional practices, such as CIBA-

Geigy's sending doctors and their spouses to all-expenses-paid "symposia" at Caribbean resorts to hear about *Estraderm*, an estrogen-dispensing skin patch, or Wyeth-Ayerst's offering physicians frequent-flyer mileage for prescribing *Inderal LA*, a hypertension drug. Not coincidentally, in the weeks before the hearing, the American Medical Association and the drug industry's trade group, the Pharmaceutical Manufacturers Association, hastily adopted new codes of ethics that prohibited such lavish incentives. "The promotional practices of some companies had plainly crossed the line of ethical behavior and had to be stopped," says Kirk B. Johnson, the AMA's general counsel.

The FDA also began to awaken from its decade-long slumber. Last year, Dr. Kessler, the new, activist commissioner, gave the marketing office new staff and authority. Kessler also personally put the profession on notice with a stern, much-quoted article in the New England Journal of Medicine.

The new, more ethical climate is having some effect. "Drug companies are no longer flying physicians around the country or exchanging cash," says the AMA's Johnson. Doctors we interviewed agreed that invitations to resort junkets and offers of cash "honoraria" for merely attending meetings have dried up.

But if consumers can now feel somewhat more confident that a drug prescribed for them did not gain its pride of place through a thinly disguised bribe, they still cannot be sure that a medication's efficacy and price are the only considerations driving the doctor's prescribing habits. The pharmaceutical trade press is now filled with articles about techniques that can keep companies in technical compliance with the new guidelines even if they seem to go against their spirit.

Consider, for instance, the rapid evolution of the dinner meeting. A widely used innovation of the late 1980s, dinner meetings worked like this: A company would invite selected physicians to dinner at an expensive local restaurant. Before eating, they would listen to a product presentation and afterwards would be handed a $100 "honorarium" for their time and attention. According to industry market studies, 80 percent of dinner meetings produce increased sales of the target drug among doctors who attend.

Under the new guidelines, the

dinner meetings are continuing. Except now, instead of a $100 cash "honorarium," attendees get to pick a $100 gift, such as a medical textbook or office equipment, out of a catalog. Consulting firms who design and run campaigns for drug companies are even placing ads in trade publications bragging of their ability to put on sales-boosting dinner meetings that comply with the AMA rules.

The gift obligation

The gifts handed out at dinners are hardly the only ones doctors receive. A staple of the pharmaceutical salesperson's trade is something called "reminder items."

Allen F. Shaughnessy, a pharmacist at the Medical University of South Carolina, actually counted the promotional items in his school's family medicine center. Its 24 examination rooms, waiting room and nursing stations contained 5 pens, 36 notepads, 55 pamphlets and posters, and 43 trinkets such as pushpins, key rings, cups, and tote bags bearing company names or product logos. And this was a clinic at an academic institution; private doctors' offices have many more such items.

Another category of gift is the "hospitality" that drug companies dispense—everything from pizza for hospital residents and interns to banquets and performances by famous entertainers at medical conventions. The money spent is substantial. For its 1991 convention, the American College of Rheumatology responded to the new ethical climate by turning down pharmaceutical money for evening dinners and receptions and paying for those events itself. The College's meeting planner estimates the decision cost $200,000.

Many doctors believe that trivial gifts and entertainments can't possibly influence them. But others contend that the very act of receiving a gift, no matter how small, sets up a culturally conditioned obligation to reciprocate. It's worth noting that the Pharmaceutical Manufacturers Association of Canada, in its ethics code, has banned "reminder items." And in the U.S., the Veterans Administration prohibits its physicians from accepting gifts from companies.

"I learned a lot about gift-giving from my father, who was a very ethical businessman," says Dr. David Schiedermayer, an internist and associate director of the Center for the Study of Bioethics at the Medical College of Wisconsin. "He would never accept a gift without returning it in kind. A gift has strings attached; we all know that. That's why gift-giving is important in our culture."

Evidence that this is so comes from the industry itself. One trade publication, Medical Marketing & Media, recently ran an admiring account of a campaign on behalf of *Anaprox,* one of a number of anti-arthritic drugs jostling for position in a lucrative market. Physicians received direct-mail invitations to send away for a series of exercise-related gifts bearing the drug's logo: a Walkman-type stereo; a jumprope; hand and ankle weights; a fanny pack; an exercise log. Presumably, most physicians could easily afford these items. Yet the promotion appeared to work; after one year, *Anaprox*'s share of prescriptions for exercise-related injuries increased from 33 to 43 percent. The trade journal didn't seem troubled by the fact that *Anaprox* offers no demonstrable benefits over generic ibuprofen, a similar drug which costs much less.

"The costs of gifts to physicians are ultimately passed on to the public," says a report from the AMA's Council on Ethical and Judicial Affairs. "In effect, then, patients may be paying for a benefit that in some cases is captured primarily by their physicians."

Undercover messages

Ambiguous as the gift obligation may be, another pharmaceutical practice concerns industry critics even more: the use of money and marketing expertise to subvert the medical profession's elaborate system of scientific exchange. Since it's an insidious, subtle means of influence, it's also difficult to police.

From medical school on, physicians are taught to regard medical school faculty, medical journals, and professional meetings as sources of unbiased information. Pharmaceutical companies have found ingenious ways to influence all three. In the process, the distinction between promotion and true scientific exchange has been blurred and, in some cases, totally erased.

The confusion is no accident; it serves drug companies well. "From a propagandist's perspective, the less the audience knows it's being manipulated, the greater the opportunity, because its defenses are down," says David Jones, who worked as a public relations executive for several major drug companies before resigning in 1986. He resigned, he says, because he decided that marketing manipulation had gotten out of control.

Promotion disguised as scientific exchange has another very important advantage for drug companies. "Regular" promotions, such as advertisements, direct mail, and sales presentations, must comply with strict FDA rules. Among other things, the regulations prohibit discussion of non-approved uses—uses of a drug that have not been officially sanctioned by the FDA—and require disclosure of a drug's drawbacks and side effects. Truly independent scientific exchange is under no such restrictions. Researchers speaking at scientific meetings can, for example, talk at length about unapproved uses that are still experimental. By appropriating these means of exchange,

Medical Convention Notes
SYMPOSIA, SUPPERS, AND STUFF

Family doctors treat chronic conditions that may require drug therapy for months or years: asthma, high blood pressure, heart disease, depression, menopause. They also prescribe lots of antibiotics for sore throats, ear infections, and respiratory ailments. So the annual meeting of their specialty society, the American Academy of Family Physicians, represents a not-to-be-missed marketing opportunity for drug companies.

One of our reporters spent three days at the AAFP's most recent annual meeting, held last September in Washington, D.C., and found the drug companies' presence there ubiquitous. Most visible were the commercial exhibits that covered two immense floors of the Washington convention Center.

Critics often write of the "carnival" atmosphere of these exhibits, and the comparison is apt: Companies, especially larger ones, had put up bright, fanciful pavilions and staffed them with barkers and magicians. At one point, 14 people were clustered in Wyeth's booth watching a pitchman demonstrate a wooden puzzle as he interwove a sales message for *Premarin,* a drug commonly prescribed for menopausal women. Ortho showed sales messages on a Sony high-definition television. Well-groomed salespeople handed out prizes—stuffed animals, T-shirts, umbrellas, sports bags, and the like—to M.D.s who filled out cards agreeing to see a sales rep when they got back home.

As a non-M.D., our reporter wasn't offered these more valuable gifts. Still, she wound up carrying four tote bags sagging with items laid out for the taking: pens, rulers, notepads, posters, luggage tags, clipboards, over-the-counter product samples, refrigerator magnets, and more, all with company names and logos. In the lobby, a vendor called "Sack Sitters" was doing a huge business packing cartons of freebies for shipment home.

During companies picked up the tab for many of the convention's social programs, including two private performances by Mstislav Rostropovich and the National Symphony Orchestra (Ortho Pharmaceutical, McNeil Pharmaceutical, Janssen Pharmaceutica) and a reception and dance (Eli Lilly). Meeting-goers also received invitations to other social events that weren't part of the official program: a cooking demonstration and four-course meal with a noted cardiologist (Pfizer); an "All Things Chocolate" late-night reception featuring chocolate goodies (Syntex); a concert by Frankie Valli and the Four Seasons (McNeil). Until the new AMA guidelines were released last year, the AAFP also allowed companies to hand out "family travel grants" to member physicians.

Of 35 continuing-education courses given for credit at the convention, 22 had industry sponsors. In most cases, the commercial tie-ins were easy to discern: Ortho, a major manufacturer of birth-control pills, sponsored a session on oral contraceptives; Bristol-Myers Squibb, which

makes a cholesterol-lowering drug, funded a course on treating high cholesterol; Marion Merrell Dow, maker of drugs for asthma and allergies, paid for a course on asthma and allergy treatment. Upjohn sponsored a "Doctor's Lounge," featuring case histories of patients with various conditions. The opening vignette concerned a patient with panic disorder, a condition for which *Xanax,* an Upjohn product, had just received approval from the FDA. Videotapes and viewing stations were also commercially sponsored.

For this convention, as for previous conventions, pharmaceutical companies and their hired consultants were allowed to submit entire courses for inclusion on the educational program. The AAFP's staff and program committee would accept or veto the programs. But the content and faculty were otherwise left up to the sponsors, who paid the faculty directly and frequently supplied slick portfolios and syllabuses for course attendees.

The pharmaceutical industry's presence is likely to diminish noticeably at the next convention: Delegates to the Washington meeting adopted a new, much stricter code of ethics. The new code prohibits commercial sponsors from picking faculty and subjects for educational seminars. From now on, the AAFP will accept industry money for educational programs only if it comes in the form of unrestricted grants—though by following this policy, the AAFP believes it "may risk some reduction in funding in the short-term."

then, drug companies have managed to free themselves from the FDA's restraints.

"We haven't regulated it, even though we have the authority, because it's been hidden from us and, I think it's fair to say, hidden from some of the audiences," says Ann Witt, the newly appointed acting director of the FDA's Division of Marketing, Advertising and Communications. Now, however, the FDA is preparing to draw a clear boundary between scientific and promotional activities—starting with continuing medical education.

Education or promotion?

For most physicians, medical education doesn't stop with the completion of their formal training. If they want to retain hospital privileges, keep their specialty certifications, and, in some states, even keep their medical licenses, they must obtain a certain number of hours a year of continuing medical education credits. Approval of CME programs is granted by institutions—mainly hospitals, medical schools, and medical societies—that meet the standards set by the independent Accreditation

Council for Continuing Medical Education.

Despite its professed reverence for continuing education, the medical establishment hasn't fully supported it with hard cash. One typical medical school, Albert Einstein College of Medicine in New York, provides less than 5 percent of the annual budget for its busy CME department; the rest comes through tuition charges and grants, in roughly equal amounts. The drug industry has been only too happy to help out. Dr. Martin Schickman, a cardiologist and assistant dean for CME at the

University of California at Los Angeles, estimates that 50 percent of CME courses get some sort of commercial support.

The drug industry's public position is that it supports medical education out of concern for the safe and appropriate use of its products and for the professional advancement of its customers, physicians. Indeed, even the industry's most vocal critics concede that some industry-supported education is genuinely impartial and useful. But all too often, it has been turned into a deliberate vehicle for product promotion.

Industry support for CME can take many forms, ranging from subsidies for travel money and speakers' fees to the creation of entire courses, complete with faculty, syllabus, slides, and handouts. The sponsoring drug company may exercise considerable control over the choice of speakers for a CME session—often recruiting nationally recognized experts, who are paid well for their demonstrated ability to attract large audiences.

"It can be a major supplemental source of income for a physician to make 10 to 15 presentations a year to conventions, grand rounds, and so on," says David Jones. "The fee can be $1000 to $5000 per presentation for an important physician, plus the perks of first-class travel."

Drug companies insist they have little if any control over the content of such experts' presentations, and physicians who participate say the same thing. But critics point out that the drug companies needn't influence physician speakers outright in order to meet their marketing objectives. Doctors who frequent the lecture circuit generally have well-known opinions on medical issues; a drug company need only select the speaker whose opinion matches its marketing needs. Dr. Marvin Moser, a hypertension specialist and clinical professor of medicine at Yale University, was able to identify the type of drug being promoted through the hypertension panel described above merely by hearing the speakers' names.

In a revealing article on public relations that appeared in Pharmaceutical Executive, a trade magazine, medical publicist Julie C. Wang advised that "third-party endorsement by opinion leaders" is better than ordinary advertising because "experts . . . without a direct material interest in a product make apparently spontaneous and objective observa-tions about products." And, of course, some doctors seem to be all too willing to follow the company line. "We had a speaker for grand rounds last month, talking about patients who come into the emergency room with severe headache," recalls John Mitchell, the director of pharmacy at Garden City Hospital, a small community teaching hospital near Detroit. "Roche sponsored his presentation. The speaker mentioned only three drugs by trade name during his lecture, all of which were made by Roche. I was absolutely in awe that he was able to work all of them in."

Drug companies, understandably, don't publicize whatever evidence they have that CME sponsorship increases sales. But, in a provocative series of studies, Dr. Marjorie Bowman of the Bowman Gray School of Medicine in South Carolina found clear evidence of that.

Bowman and her colleagues analyzed the content of two industry-supported, university-accredited CME courses. Both were on calcium channel-blocker drugs for high blood pressure, but one was sponsored by Pfizer, which makes *Procardia,* and the other by Marion Merrell Dow, maker of *Cardizem.* In each case, speakers mentioned positive effects more often in connection with the sponsoring company's drug, and negative effects more often with competitors' drugs. Bowman followed up by monitoring the prescribing practices of doctors who attended the courses. In each case, the doctors began prescribing more of the drugs made by the company that sponsored the course they took.

CME sponsorship has proven so cost-effective that an entire category of consulting firms has come into being to organize educational programs on behalf of pharmaceutical companies. A big part of the consultants' job is to shop around for accredited CME providers who will put on such a canned presentation. According to Dr. Goldfinger of Harvard and others, several medical schools and professional societies are well known as willing to accept such programs.

Conversely, CME providers also shop around for drug companies to help pay for their educational programs. The chairman of Wyeth-Ayerst Laboratories said that in a single year, 1989, his company received more than 6000 requests for CME funding.

The CME system has become so intertwined with pharmaceutical companies that some form of regulation now seems all but inevitable. As things now stand, "the whole academic-scientific process runs a significant risk of taint," says Dr. Kessler of the FDA. "We've got to make sure true scientific exchange doesn't lose its value."

Unfortunately, the same can now also be said of drug research itself.

Research: Science for sale?

Research is, of course, vital to the development of new drugs. The law requires that drugs be tested before approval to make sure they have the desired therapeutic result, are safe, and don't produce unacceptable side effects. Much of this research is conducted by doctors at academic medical centers and paid for by pharmaceutical companies.

For many, industry support is a major source of research funds. In a 1990 survey, the American Federation for Clinical Research found that 34 percent of its members received corporate research grants; the average grant was for $31,000 a year. While such grants may play a legitimate role in research funding, a University of Arizona study found that industry research projects at the University were actually a profit center for the scientists who conducted them. They took in far more money—$2000 to $5000 per enrolled patient—than they actually spent on the research.

Traditionally, premarket testing has been overseen by drug companies' research-and-development divisions, which are staffed by scientists trained in the rigors of the scientific

method. But the new pharmaceutical marketing experts have inexorably invaded this area. Writing in the New England Journal of Medicine, Dr. Alan Hillman and colleagues from the University of Pennsylvania, who perform cost-benefit analyses for pharmaceutical firms, outlined some of the ways that companies influence research:

"They fund projects with a high likelihood of producing favorable results. . . . They exclude products that may compare favorably with the sponsor's own. Sometimes, only favorable clinical data are released to investigators. . . . Negative studies may be terminated before they are ready for publication. . . . Corporate personnel may seek to control the content and use of the final report, including the decision to publish."

These manipulations do have a measurable effect. In a review of 107 published studies comparing a new drug against traditional therapy, Dr. Richard Davidson of the University of Florida found that drug company-supported studies of new drugs were far more likely to favor those drugs than were studies supported by noncommercial entities.

Other types of clinical research are even more easily used for commercial purposes. So-called "Phase IV" studies, conducted *after* a drug reaches the market to detect any unexpected side effects, involve large numbers of doctors, and have proven useful for drug-company promotion.

In 1989, Pharmaceutical Executive ran a detailed description of how to design Phase IV studies to "support promotional efforts" while "defusing the critics." As the article in the trade journal stated, "Some companies have implemented very simple studies . . . to directly increase product sales by involving large numbers of investigators who increase their own prescribing as a result of participating in the study. . . . Such studies usually are not intended to yield publishable information."

The physicians shouldn't be given easy-to-criticize incentives like travel junkets, the writer helpfully noted. Instead, the company can make a donation to the physicians' favorite school or research organization, or list them as "authors in papers prepared by company writers and placed in single-sponsor journals."

The publication ploy

Doctors consistently name medical journals as one of their main sources of unbiased information. Especially valued are peer-reviewed journals, journals whose articles are reviewed by experts in the field before being accepted for publication.

Drug companies have found an effective way to use these journals' credibility for their own purposes by subsidizing the publication of "supplements." Piggybacked onto regular issues of the journal, supplements use the same sober-looking design and typography as the regular articles. Frequently, the supplements are based on symposia sponsored by the same companies that pay for the publication.

"Repeatedly, we have found these publications not to be balanced, objective sources of information regarding current drug research or drug treatment," David Banks, an FDA enforcement officer, said in a speech last year.

Select supplements virtually at random from the shelves of a medical library, and it's clear that objectivity is not their goal.

▨ A March 1990 supplement to the American Journal of Medicine carried a write-up of a Squibb symposium focusing on the "continuing efficacy and safety" of *Azactam*, an injectable antibiotic made by Squibb, for a wide variety of patients and conditions. Squibb's marketing department apparently found this supplement so helpful it handed out reprints as a promotion, with prescribing information bound in. By contrast, the Medical Letter, an independent, noncommercial publication that reviews drugs and medical devices, does not cite *Azactam* as the drug of first choice for a single category of infection. (The drug that is the preferred alternative to *Azactam*, Hoechst-Roussel's *Claforan*, costs slightly less.)

▨ A September 1991 supplement to the Journal of Clinical Psychiatry, sponsored by Wallace Laboratories, dealt with "selecting appropriate benzodiazepine hypnotic therapy." The benzodiazepines are a widely prescribed class of tranquilizer that includes a number of drugs, such as *Valium* and *Xanax*. But virtually every article in the supplement focuses on favorable information about *Doral*, Wallace's entry into the furiously competitive sleeping-pill market.

▨ A supplement to the journal Hospital Formulary, entitled "Issues in Reperfusion for the '90s," was sponsored by Genentech. Based on a symposium and "coordinated for publication" by a CME consulting firm, the supplement repeatedly attacked a widely publicized European study showing that Genentech's $2000-a-dose drug *Activase* is no more effective in breaking up heart attack-causing blood clots than its $200-a-dose generic competitor streptokinase. Nowhere in the supplement was the European study defended, even though many experts have done so in professional meetings and the national media.

Many journals actively market their willingness to publish supplements. The American Society of Hospital Pharmacists bought an advertisement in the trade journal Medical Marketing & Media, offering "sole sponsor opportunities." Those opportunities included supplements to its two professional magazines as well as educational symposia and other publications.

Even the American Medical Association, putative guardian of medical ethics and publisher of the Journal of the AMA, found it difficult to resist the lure of such easy money. It planned to charge $25,000 to $150,000 per issue to publish single-topic, industry-sponsored collections of articles. An outcry from consumer advocates and a warning from the FDA eventually persuaded the AMA to drop the plan.

The FDA cracks down

Under Commissioner Kessler, the FDA is now looking for ways to restore balance to a system of research, publication, and education that has clearly been compromised.

Last fall, the agency circulated a "draft concept paper" that, for the first time, proposed general rules and principles governing drug company-supported continuing education. The paper proposed that a company-supported CME program would be considered promotional, and regulated as such, unless it was truly independent—meaning that the sponsoring company had virtually no role in the selection of speakers and that the content was unbiased and scientifically rigorous. Speakers would have to disclose any potential conflicts of interest, such as being on a company's speakers' bureau or accepting company research grants.

The paper specifically stated that the FDA had no intention of meddling in true scientific exchange, which was, in any event, far outside the agency's jurisdiction. But Kessler and his staff also pointed out that the FDA has the clear legal responsibility to regulate drug advertising and promotion, whether those marketing efforts take place in a traditional or a nontraditional guise.

Predictably, the Pharmaceutical Manufacturers Association, the industry's influential trade group, denounced the proposal on sight. If such guidelines were adopted, the PMA said, then drug companies would simply stop funding continuing education programs.

Organized opposition also came from something called the "Coalition of Healthcare Communicators." Operating out of a post-office box in Connecticut, the coalition was made up of nine trade groups that represented medical advertising, public-relations, and marketing interests. In a "Dear Doctor" letter that was circulated widely, the coalition painted the FDA proposals as a threat to free speech and academic freedom. "We must work together to protect scientific independence and integrity from bureaucratic interference," the five-page letter concluded. Whether coincidentally or not, protests from academic physicians soon began descending on the FDA regulators as well.

We support the FDA's efforts to disentangle marketing from scientific exchange, and hope Kessler and his colleagues will be able to resist the pressure to back off. The very source and intensity of the opposition—the mightily profitable drug companies and the well-paid consultants and academicians they employ—itself suggests the degree to which science and commerce have become interdependent.

A careful inspection of the FDA proposal reveals that, far from threatening scientific independence and integrity, it aims to rescue them from commercial influences. The rules wouldn't affect drug companies who practice what they preach and subsidize CME programs that are truly balanced and scientifically rigorous. But the rules would seriously limit the behind-the-scenes manipulation of superficially "independent" scientific presentations.

The FDA, however, does not bear sole responsibility for policing the drug industry's activities. The medical-academic establishment also

needs to continue its efforts to create a more ethical environment for the profession:

■ The medical profession should adequately fund its own continuing education instead of depending on pharmaceutical companies for the bulk of funding.

■ Physicians who accept honoraria, research grants, or placement on industry speakers' bureaus should be required to disclose all such connections whenever they speak at symposia or scientific meetings on subjects related to the companies' products. Those disclosures should also be printed on any brochures announcing their speaking engagements or CME courses, so that doctors could weigh the speakers' objectivity before they decide to attend.

■ Medical-journal editors should design their single-sponsor supplements to distinguish them clearly from regular editorial matter—by means of prominently displayed notices, different typography, different page layout, or, preferably, all

three—just the way newsmagazines already do.

■ Medical schools and residency programs should train students to recognize and evaluate drug-marketing messages, since those messages will surround them for the rest of their working lives.

■ Professional medical associations should consider setting specific limits for the amounts their members can accept as honoraria for speaking engagements. In addition, all physicians should continually ask themselves whether accepting industrial largesse—whether a takeout lunch for the office staff, an expensive textbook, a speaker's fee, or a research grant—has compromised their intellectual and their clinical judgment.

The relationship between physicians and drug companies needs to change dramatically. We believe that can be done quickly. And we believe that effective changes will make the medical marketplace a safer, more honorable one for doctors and patients alike.

[Ed. Note: This is Part 1 of a 2-part series. See Part 2, *Consumer Reports,* March 1992.]

It's Drugs, Alcohol and Tobacco, Stupid!

As the new generation of political leaders in Washington, state capitals and city halls grapples with America's collapsing judicial systems, rising medical costs, persistent poverty amid plenty and the defiant federal budget deficit that looms over future generations, they confront the same 800-pound gorilla: drug, alcohol and tobacco abuse and addiction. The sooner these leaders see how substance abuse has fundamentally changed the nature of the pressing social and economic problems they face, the sooner they'll deal with them effectively.

For 30 years, we've tried to curb crime and renew our ailing court system with tougher punishments,

bigger prisons, and more cops and judges; rein in health costs by manipulating payments to doctors and hospitals for delivering sick care; wage war on poverty with a welfare system that encourages dependence and drives families apart; and reduce the deficit by cooking the federal books. Trying to reform our court and criminal justice systems, restrain health care spending, reduce welfare rolls, trim the deficit and nourish the American family without confronting, front and center, substance abuse and addiction is like trying to clean coastal waters without stopping the flow of oil from the ruptured offshore well. It can't be done.

Criminals and Courts

Congress and state legislatures have been passing laws designed for celluloid gangsters and inmates played in classic 1930s movies by James Cagney and Humphrey Bogart. But today's prisons are wall to wall with drug dealers, addicts, alcohol abusers and the mentally ill (often related to drug and alcohol abuse).

In 1960, less than 30,000 Americans were arrested for drug offenses; by 1991, the number had soared to more than a million. Since 1989, more individuals have been incarcerated for drug offenses than for all violent crimes—and most violent crime is committed by drug and alcohol abusers. Alcohol and drug abuse are implicated in

From the Center on Addiction and Substance Abuse at Columbia University, *1994 Annual Report*, pp. 6-11. Reprinted by permission.

three-quarters of all spouse abuse, rapes, child molestations, suicides and homicides.

In 1994, the number of Americans in prison broke the one million barrier and, on its current trajectory, will double soon after the turn of the century. The United States is second only to Russia in the rate of citizens it imprisons: 519 per 100,000, compared to 558 in Russia, 368 in third-place South Africa, 116 in Canada and 36 in Japan.

Probation and parole are sick jokes in most American cities. With so many parolees needing drug treatment and aftercare as essential first steps to rehabilitation, they demand far more monitoring than their drug-free predecessors of a generation ago. Yet in Los Angeles, for example, probation officers must handle as many as 1,000 cases at a time. With most offenders committing drug- or alcohol-related crimes, it's no wonder so many of them go right back to jail: 80 percent of prisoners have prior convictions and more than 60 percent have served time before.

Drugs have turned the private security industry from a less than four-billion-dollar weakling in 1970 into a 70-billion-dollar behemoth in 1994, as office

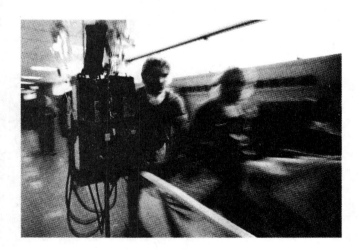

buildings and homes install sophisticated protection systems and commercial properties post guards around the clock.

Judges and prosecutors are demoralized as they juggle caseloads more than double the recommended maximums. The rush of drug-related criminal cases has created intolerable delays for civil litigants: four years in Newark, five in Philadelphia, up to ten in Cook County, Illinois. In many jurisdictions, divorce and separation cases languish for years, as splitting parents and their children struggle to survive in a limbo of nasty uncertainty.

The safety and civility of urban life have been shattered by alcohol- and drug-related crimes. Children kill children and innocents are downed by random gunfire from warring drug gangs. Elementary and high school students are required to pass through metal detectors in order to check for weapons, the deadly companions of the drug trade, and teachers are locked in classrooms for their own protection.

City dwellers can no longer buy out of the mess. Individuals walking Wisconsin Avenue in Washington D.C.'s Georgetown, Madison Avenue in New York, Newbury Street in Boston and the Miracle Mile in Chicago are accosted by angry, aggressive panhandlers, many seeking money for their next fix. The ugly scrawls of graffiti on city buildings mark not only the arrival of spray paint, but also the widespread abuse of drugs and alcohol.

Substance abuse is an equal opportunity killer, snaring addicts in every social and economic class. Store owners lock their doors during daytime business hours in fear of robbery by alcohol- and drug-crazed criminals. Office managers bolt computers to desks to prevent theft. Customers and employees warily read headlines about murders and assaults, often committed under the influence of alcohol and drugs, that have torn apart the comfortable routines where America works, eats and shops— post offices, fast-food restaurants, banks and supermarkets. Two-thirds of illegal drug users are employed, adding an element of Russian roulette to going to work each day.

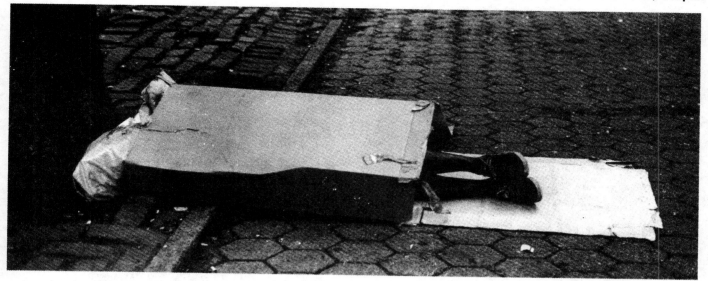

Health care Costs

In 1995, drugs, alcohol and tobacco will trigger some $200 billion in health care costs.

Hospital emergency rooms are piled high with the debris of drug use on city streets. From Boston to Baton Rouge, hospitals teem with the victims of gunshot wounds and other violence caused by alcohol abusers, drug addicts and dealers, and of a variety of medical conditions, such as cancer, emphysema and cardiac arrest, caused by alcohol, tobacco, cocaine and other drugs.

AIDS and tuberculosis spread rapidly and not just among intravenous drug users and crack addicts. Beyond sharing dirty needles and trading sex for drugs, individuals high on beer, other alcohol and pot are far more likely to have sex and to have it without a condom.

The more than 500,000 newborns exposed each year to drugs and/or alcohol during pregnancy is a slaughter of innocents of biblical proportions. Crack babies, a rarity a decade ago, crowd $2,000-a-day neonatal wards. Many die. Each survivor can cost one million dollars to bring to adulthood. Fetal alcohol syndrome is a top cause of birth defects.

Even where prenatal care is available, women on drugs and alcohol are not likely to take advantage of it. Those who do seek help must often wait in line for scarce treatment slots. Mothers abusing drugs during pregnancy account for most of the $3 billion that Medicaid spent in 1994 on inpatient hospital care for illness and injury due to drug abuse.

Poverty in History's Most Affluent Society

Drugs have changed the nature of poverty in America. Nowhere is this more striking than in the persistent problem of welfare dependency.

At least 20 percent of Chicago and Maryland's Montgomery County adults on welfare have drug problems. And that may be low compared to other urban areas. Many of the million teenagers who get pregnant each year are high on alcohol or drugs at the time they conceive, and one of the surest ways to get locked in poverty is to become an unwed mother before graduating from high school. At least half the homeless men and women—some say 80 to 90 percent—are alcohol and drug abusers.

The American electorate is hell-bent on putting welfare mothers to work. But all the financial sticks and carrots and all the job training in the world will do precious little to make employable the hundreds of thousands of welfare recipients who are drug and alcohol abusers. For too long, reformers have had their heads in the sand about this unpleasant reality. Liberals fear that acknowledging the extent of alcohol and drug use among welfare recipients will incite even more punitive reactions than those currently in fashion. Conservatives don't want to face up to the cost of treatment.

This political denial ensures failure. Any reform that will move individuals from welfare to work must provide funds to treat drug and alcohol abuse.

Supplemental Security Income, the welfare program that provides monthly checks to blind, disabled and poor adults, reveals the grim and expensive consequence of the alternative. Of 90,000 individuals receiving SSI primarily because of substance abuse, fewer than ten percent are in treatment. Not surprisingly, the U.S. Department of Health and Human Services found that thousands of these addicts and alcoholics receive benefits until they die.

Illegal drugs have added a vicious strain of intractability to urban poverty. Drugs are the greatest threat to family stability, decent housing, public schools and even minimal social amenities. Widespread drug use derails the emotional, social and intellectual development not only of the children who abuse them, but also of their peers and neighbors who must grapple with the violent consequences of rampant drugs in housing projects and schools. It becomes difficult—sometimes

impossible—for children in this sordid environment to acquire the basic educational and social skills they need to get out of poverty.

The Federal Budget Deficit

In fiscal 1995, tobacco, alcohol and drug abuse will account for at least $77.6 billion in entitlement expenditures, an amount equivalent to 40 percent of the 1995 federal budget deficit.

Of that amount, $66.4 billion are costs to health and disability programs, such as Medicare, Medicaid and veterans' health and disability. Cigarette smoking is by far the biggest culprit. Two-thirds of the $66.4 billion—$44 billion—is attributable to tobacco. Alcohol accounts for 18 percent and drugs for 16 percent.

Substance abuse takes its biggest slice from the veterans' health care program. Nearly 30 percent of the dollars spent on veterans' health is due to substance abuse, more than half of that as a result of alcohol and drug abuse. Welfare payments to illegal drug addicts and alcoholics draw the rhetorical fire of legislators. But American taxpayers fork over $4.6 billion a year to individuals on Social Security disability as a result of smoking cigarettes.

Of the $77.6 billion, the remaining $11.2 billion is spent on welfare, food stamp and Supplemental Security Income recipients who regularly use alcohol and drugs and are unlikely to get off the rolls without treatment and aftercare.

Any honest attack by the President and the Congress on entitlement programs—from Medicare and veterans' health and disability to Medicaid and welfare—has to confront substance abuse and addiction. That means a significant investment in prevention and treatment of all abuse. Simply removing individuals who abuse alcohol and drugs from disability, welfare and health care programs will only shift costs to the states, cities and counties, which will then have to deal with the resulting illness, hunger, homelessness and crime. Indeed, a wholesale denial of benefits to alcoholics and drug addicts without providing treatment and aftercare will push up the crime rate and scatter thousands more homeless individuals on America's streets.

Is There Anything We Can Do?

We can begin by ending our national and personal denial of the tough truth that the common denominator of the nation's hot buttons—crime and violence, health care costs, welfare reform and the budget deficit—is substance abuse. Our denial keeps our sights on the wrong targets. Indeed, 92 percent of federal health entitlement program costs attributable to substance abuse is spent to treat the *consequences* of tobacco, alco-

hol and drugs; only eight percent is spent to treat the tobacco, alcohol or drug dependence itself.

Our leaders and citizens focus on the top killers: heart disease (720,000 deaths in 1990), cancer (505,000), stroke (144,000), accidents (92,000), emphysema (87,000), pneumonia and influenza (80,000), diabetes (48,000), suicide (31,000), chronic liver disease and cirrhosis (26,000), and AIDS (25,000). But they give scant attention to the *causes* of these killers, which, according to a 1993 *Journal of the American Medical Association* study, include tobacco (435,000 deaths), alcohol (100,000) and illicit drug use (20,000).

Our obsession with the consequences and neglect of the causes is not limited to health care. We pump billions into combatting crime—cops, courts, prisons and punishment—and pennies into preventing the drug and alcohol abuse and addiction that spawn so much criminal activity. We pour resources into shoveling up city slums—rebuilding gutted housing, putting more cops on unsafe streets and barbed wire around housing projects—and little into curbing drug and alcohol abuse. And we often use our hefty budget-cutting axes to chop down prevention and treatment programs, which are most likely to reduce the deficit over the long run.

Dealing effectively with the causes requires up-front investments—the kind that corporations make every day to produce long-term results for their stockholders, the kind that parents make to give their children the best education they can get. It also requires that we scrub the stigma off drug and alcohol abuse and devote the kind of energy and resources to research on addiction and its prevention that we have committed to cancer and heart disease. And it requires common sense.

Here are a few starter suggestions:

• Provide federal funds to state and federal prison systems only if they provide drug and alcohol treatment and aftercare for all inmates who need such care.

• Instead of across-the-board mandatory sentences, keep inmates in jails, boot camps or halfway houses until they demonstrate at least one year of sobriety after treatment.

• Require drug and alcohol addicts to go regularly to treatment and aftercare, like Alcoholics Anonymous, while on parole or probation.

• Provide federal funds for police only to cities that agree to enforce drug laws throughout their jurisdictions. End acceptance of drug bazaars in Harlem, southeast Washington, D.C., and south-central Los Angeles, which would not be tolerated on the streets of New York's Upper East Side, Georgetown or Beverly Hills.

• Encourage judges with lots of drug cases to employ public health professionals, just as they hire economists to assist with anti-trust cases. Drug cases

present far more complex human and medical problems than the economic issues posed by commercial litigation.

• Charge higher Medicare premiums to individuals who smoke.

• Cut off welfare payments to drug addicts and alcoholics who refuse to seek treatment and pursue aftercare. As employers and health professionals know, addicts from CEOs to chambermaids need lots of carrots and sticks, including the threat of losing their jobs and incomes, to get the monkey off their backs.

• Subject inmates, parolees and welfare recipients with a history of drug or alcohol abuse to random tests and fund the treatment they need. Conservatives who preach an end to recidivism and welfare dependency must recognize that reincarceration and removal from the welfare rolls for those who test positive is a cruel catch-22 unless treatment is available. Liberals must recognize that getting off drugs is the only chance these individuals (and their babies) have to enjoy their civil rights.

• Identify parents who abuse their children by their own drug and alcohol abuse and place those children in decent orphanages and foster care until the parents go into treatment and shape up.

These are only a few suggestions. The overriding point is that addiction and abuse—involving heroin, cocaine, hallucinogens, amphetamines, inhalants, marijuana, alcohol and tobacco—have fundamentally changed the nature of America's pressing social and economic challenges, and we must rethink how we address them. If a mainstream disease like diabetes or cancer affected as many individuals and families as drug, alcohol and tobacco abuse and addiction do, this nation would mount an effort on the scale of the Manhattan Project to deal with it.

Joseph A. Califano Jr.

THE "CRACK-BABY" SCARE FILLED
THE CONSERVATIVES' NEED FOR
SCAPEGOATS, THE LIBERALS' NEED
FOR PROGRAM FUNDING, AND THE
MEDIA'S NEED FOR HEADLINES.
SO WHAT IF IT WASN'T TRUE?

crackpot ideas

Katharine Greider

Katharine Greider is a freelance writer based in New York.

DURING THE LATE '80s, AMERICANS SHOOK THEIR HEADS IN DISGUST AT reports that poor black mothers were sacrificing the little ones resting in their wombs for the pleasures of crack cocaine, callously dooming a new generation to "a life of certain suffering, of probable deviance, of permanent inferiority," to quote columnist Charles Krauthammer.

Seizing on early studies that raised alarm over fetal damage from cocaine, scientists cited the same inconclusive data again and again. Local news organs spun their own versions of the crack-baby story, taking for granted the accuracy of its premise. Social workers, foster parents, doctors, teachers, and journalists put forward unsettling anecdotes about the "crack babies" they had seen, all participating in a slight of hand so elegant in its simplicity that they fooled even themselves. They talked of babies shrieking like cast and refusing to bond, of children unable to focus on a task—and then they slipped in the part they should have tested, attributing these problems to prenatal cocaine use. Reporters went into hospital nurseries and special schools and borrowed the images of premature babies or bawling African-American preschoolers to illustrate their crack-baby stories. Carol Cole, who taught at the Salvin Special Education School in Los Angeles, remembers reporters asking if they could get pictures of the children trembling.

The crack baby quickly became a symbol for the biological determinism recently promulgated in its rawest form by Charles Murray and Richard Herrnstein in *The Bell Curve:* These (mostly black) bug-eyed morons weren't quite human— and no amount of attention could make them so. In the late '80s, some commentators predicted they would become America's "biologic underclass." By 1991, John Silber, president of Boston University, went so far as to lament the expenditure of so many health care dollars on "crack babies who won't ever achieve the intellectual development to have consciousness of God."

EARLY DISSENT

EVEN AS NEWS OF THE "EPIDEMIC" SWEPT ACROSS AMERICA, A FEW OF the country's most knowledgeable research scientists were beginning to doubt the phenomenon. In Atlanta, Claire Coles, a developmental psychologist at Emory University School of Medicine, has graduate students watching infants for hours at a time: "You could not distinguish the cocaine-exposed babies from the other babies," she says. Nancy Day, an epidemiologist at the University of Pittsburgh School of Medicine, stood up at a conference six years ago and admitted she thought the impairments researchers were observing were not caused by cocaine. "People," she recalls, "were just aghast." At North Central Bronx Hospital, pediatrician and researcher Daniel Neuspiel looked at his own data on newborn behavior and concluded that the alarm over crack babies was misguided.

"It really got out of control," says Donald E. Hutchings, a research psychologist and editor of the journal *Neurotoxicology and Teratology*, "because these jerks who didn't know what they were talking about were giving press conferences. I'd be sitting at home watching TV, and suddenly there'd be the intensive care unit in Miami or San Francisco, and what you see is this really sick kid who looks like he's about to die and the staff is saying, 'Here's a crack baby.'"

But what a few cautious scientists had to say did little to weaken the momentum of the crack-baby myth. In fact, researchers who found no or minimal effects from cocaine had a hard time getting their results before the public. In a 1989 study published in the *Lancet*, Canadian researcher Gideon Koren showed that papers reporting a cocaine effect in child behavior were likely to be accepted over those showing no effect, for presentation at an annual meeting of the Society for Pediatric Research—even when the no-effect studies were of sounder design. "I'd never experienced anything like this," says Emory's

Claire Coles. "I've never had people accuse me of making up data or being an incompetent scientist or believing in drug abuse. When that started happening, I started thinking, *This is crazy.*"

MYTH IN THE MAKING

THE EARLIEST AND MOST INFLUENTIAL REPORTS OF COCAINE damage in babies came from the Chicago drug treatment clinic of pediatrician Ira Chasnoff. His first study, published in 1985 in *The New England Journal of Medicine*, found that the newborns of 23 cocaine-using women were less interactive and moodier than non-cocaine-exposed babies. In the years that followed, Chasnoff was widely quoted and fawned over in the press ("positively zenlike," according to *Rolling Stone*) and became known as the rather pessimistic authority on what happens to babies whose mothers use cocaine.

Of course, Chasnoff wasn't the only researcher to report serious effects. They were legion, some publishing simple case reports that took a few cocaine-exposed kids and racked up their problems. Judy Howard, a pediatrician at the University of California, Los Angeles, piped up regularly, once telling *Newsweek* that in crack babies, the part of their brains that "makes us human beings, capable of discussion or reflection" had been "wiped out."

Some claims of severe effects—that cocaine causes a sharp increase in sudden infant death syndrome, for example—were recklessly extrapolated from small samples. But the fundamental problem in interpreting the data was a failure to tease apart the effects of prenatal cocaine use from the effects of an array of other social and biological burdens that often come as a package deal.

THE REAL SCIENCE

AS A GROUP, WOMEN WHO USE COCAINE WHILE PREGNANT— especially those who are likely to get noticed as addicts or be tested for drugs in the hospital—tend also to drink more booze, smoke more cigarettes, and dip into a greater variety of illicit drugs than other women. They generally have poorer nutrition and overall health, bear and rear their kids in conditions of more profound deprivation, and are more persistently exposed to violence than other women. Such burdens impact not only their pregnancies, but also the daily lives of their children. Cocaine or no cocaine, these kids are more likely than others to have medical, educational, and social difficulties.

No one suggests using cocaine in pregnancy is harmless. But unlike alcohol, which in heavy doses can cause a set of birth defects known as fetal alcohol syndrome, cocaine is not associated with any pattern of defects. Nor does it produce infantile withdrawal, like opiates. Today there is something approaching scientific consensus that cocaine increases the risk of low birthweight and perhaps premature delivery.

According to pediatrician Neuspiel, the birthweight decrement attributable to cocaine is roughly equivalent to that caused by cigarette smoking. Being premature or underweight is serious business for an infant, but the effects are by no means immutable; it's a truism in medicine that preemies of rich parents do better than those of poor parents.

While some studies have found abnormalities in behavior among cocaine-exposed newborns, others have contradicted them; it appears that neurobehavioral effects are subtle if they occur at all. In any case, newborn behavior does not predict what a child will be like at age 3 or 6 or 12. A 1992 commentary in the *Journal of the American Medical Association* decried a "rush to judgment" about long-term effects of cocaine, concluding that the evidence was "far too slim and fragmented to allow any clear predictions about the effects of intrauterine exposure to cocaine on the course and outcome of child growth and development."

Even pediatrician Chasnoff began to temper his message as he saw his work used to fan public outrage against the very women and children for whom he considered himself an advocate—and as a large group of cocaine-exposed children whom he was following reached their third birthdays without apparent cocaine-related intellectual deficits. Now that these children are 6 or so, Chasnoff says, they appear normal in the smarts department, but display a "significant increase in rates of impulsive behavior, distractibility, [and] aggressive behavior." Is this deviance the result of biological damage? The prenatally drug-exposed kids live in the same neighborhoods and go to the same schools as the non-drug exposed controls. But their environments differ in this important respect: All the mothers of the drug-exposed children have relapsed at least once since delivering, and 60 percent are still using.

The Maternal Lifestyles Project, a major study enrolling thousands of women and their infants, will likely offer a deeper understanding of cocaine effects within a few years. But to date, no researcher, taking into account a child's life experiences, has ever demonstrated that cocaine-exposed children are more unruly or any less intelligent than other children.

PROVIDE OR PUNISH?

THE CRACK-BABY MYTH WAS SO POWERFUL IN PART BECAUSE IT HAD something for everyone, whether one's ideological learnings called for enhancing public programs to meet the crisis, or for punishing the drug-addicted mothers seen as responsible for it.

For some, the assertion that crack babies were in dire trouble became a way of begging funds for substance-abusing mothers and their infants. In the late '80s both federal and state governments launched expensive projects to study the consequences of prenatal abuse and try out treatment strategies for mother and child. When, in 1992, *Boston Globe* columnist Ellen Goodman wrote a piece questioning the basis of the crack-baby scare, Chasnoff got calls from alarmed program directors who worried they would lose funding. The public initiative had emphasized the need to help substance-abusing women only while pregnant—as "vessels," as Chasnoff put it. Perhaps it was feared that if those vessels no longer threatened to produce a

t O DATE, NO RESEARCHER, AFTER TAKING INTO ACCOUNT A CHILD'S LIFE EXPERIENCES, HAS EVER DEMONSTRATED THAT COCAINE-EXPOSED CHILDREN ARE MORE UNRULY OR ANY LESS INTELLIGENT THAN OTHER CHILDREN.

damaged and burdensome generation, public interest would falter.

At any rate, it soon became clear that the major thrust of policymaking would be to punish mothers who smoked crack. In the late '80s, local prosecutors began busting women who used drugs while pregnant or whose newborns tested positive. Between 200 and 300 such women have been prosecuted, often under existing child abuse and neglect statutes, and mostly for cocaine. Attorney Lynn Paltrow of the Center for Reproductive Law & Policy in New York City points out the slippery slope: If you call it child abuse when pregnant women use cocaine, then you have to call it abuse when they smoke or drink or engage in any of a host of behaviors that are potentially just as dangerous.

Criminal convictions for prenatal drug use, when challenged, have generally failed to stick. Not so with actions by the civil child welfare system. Thirteen states require doctors to report drug use in pregnancy or positive drug tests in newborns. Nine states specifically define drug use during pregnancy as child abuse or neglect, triggering a range of responses from treatment and other services to an investigation and the possible removal of the child. The bulk of these policies were put in place between 1988 and 1991, as the crack-baby scare peaked.

Some of the policies ostensibly designed to protect cocaine-exposed babies ended up isolating them instead. In the late '80s, the practice of automatically keeping newborns in the hospital if they tested positive for cocaine, now largely but not universally abandoned, contributed to an unmanageable population of boarder babies at some urban hospitals. In New York City, most of these babies eventually went home to their families—after languishing in a crowded hospital nursery for the dawning weeks or even months of their lives. Of those who stayed in the system, according to a study of one six-month period in the mid-'80s, 30 percent still didn't have a permanent home by the time they were 3 years old.

SELF-FULFILLING PROPHECIES

QUITE FREQUENTLY, PEOPLE PRESENT DEVELOPMENTAL PSYCHOLOGIST Dan Griffith with a little person they call a crack kid. "Based on that," says Griffith, a private consultant in Park Ridge, Ill., who once worked with Chasnoff's group, "I have no idea of what I'm going to see. It tells me nothing about the child."

Developmental psychologist Claire Coles, who is also a clinician, has seen "crack babies" who were in fact colicky babies. Often, she says, the anti-social behavior attributed to crack-induced brain damage is a classic sign of neglect. In her work, for example, she has encountered children who ate from the garbage—not because of brain injury, but because they were not accustomed to being fed.

During the height of the crack-baby crisis, experts counseled caretakers to swaddle cocaine-exposed infants, keep them in a quiet, dark place, and avoid gazing into their eyes. This makes sense for any baby with a raw, easily overstimulated nervous system. But to apply these practices to babies who have no symptoms is, in Coles' words, "utter, utter folly."

Griffith, who has seen hundreds of cocaine-exposed children, believes only a few were developmentally delayed because their caretakers had deliberately understimulated

HALE'S CHILDREN

AT A FAMOUS TREATMENT HOUSE, THE ANTIDOTE IS HUGS AND KISSES AND WARM BOTTLES.

Ronald Reagan made Hale House famous in 1985 when he called its founder, Clara Hale, an angel. It is one of the places that produced poster children for the crack-baby crisis. A 1990 *New York Post* series entitled "Children of the Damned" shows a little brown face peering from between the slats of his crib, captioned "A 2 1/2-year-old crack child at Hale House," and quotes Mother Hale as grieving "a lost generation." Today, literature sent to potential contributors claims most of the children were born "craving crack."

Inside it's a different story. It was 25 years ago, long before crack, when Mother Hale took in the baby of a nodding heroin junkie and within two months found herself caring for 22 infants in her modest Harlem apartment. In considering this history, one begins to understand that Mother Hale's "lost generation" may not have referred to brain damage, but to a bewildering social disjuncture.

Since Clara Hale's death in 1992, her daughter Dr. Lorraine Hale, who helped found Hale House, has continued to run it. Dr. Hale thinks the crack-exposed kids are moodier than heroin-exposed kids. But she's not much interested in the cause of their problems, and the program here isn't heavy on complex child evaluations. It is privately supported and tries simply to give as much basic care and hugging and kissing as possible and to promote contact between children and parents, who leave their kids there voluntarily.

This winter day, six infants are upstairs at Hale House. Three lie in their cribs; one sits in a tiny chair, a strap across his belly; another two are cradled in the arms of staff giving them their bottles. Dr. Hale approaches the middle crib and tickles its occupant, who laughs delightedly. In the next crib an infant is hollering, arching his back, his cheeks flushing red; when Hale picks him up, he quiets instantly. The fact these babies might have been subtly damaged by their mothers' cocaine use seems to recede in significance next to the gaping hole in their lives—the lack of a single passionate adult who could coo and chat and laugh and cradle for as long as the two of them liked.—K.G.

THE PUBLICITY BLITZ that spread the crack-baby myth has not been matched by an attempt to unmake the myth—and many people still believe it.

them from infancy. Still one has to wonder, what can a child become when everyone around him braces for the worst? Being identified as drug-exposed sometimes gets a child special state-sponsored services, but it also carries the potential for stigmatization and self-fulfilling prophecy.

If a child was exposed to drugs in the womb, people now assume the worst. A June 1990 federal report explained that would-be adoptive parents were reluctant to take on "crack babies" because of their potential long-term problems. Teachers, too, were aghast to learn, as the '90s began, that they could soon expect the "crack babies" in kindergarten. "The arrival of those first afflicted youngsters will mark the beginning of a struggle that will leave your resources depleted and your compassion tested," warned an article in *The American School Board Journal.*

THE MYTH'S LEGACY

IN RECENT YEARS, THE HEADLINES ABOUT CRACK BABIES HAVE trumpeted the good news: They've beaten the odds! There's new hope! But the odds should never have been laid so early, and those headlines should read, "Oh God, what have we done?" The publicity blitz that spread the crack-baby myth has not been matched by an attempt to unmake the myth—and many, many people still believe in it.

Leake and Watts, a large foster care agency in New York City, still refers drug-exposed babies and their foster parents to a special program where, even if a child seems just fine, he is closely watched. Last year, in a segment about an ongoing legal challenge to a South Carolina hospital that had newly delivered mothers hauled off to jail if their infants tested positive for cocaine, "60 Minutes" showed sick babies, implying that their problems were cocaine-related (while claiming legal considerations precluded identifying exactly *which* babies were cocaine-exposed). Only a few months ago in a *New York Times Magazine* piece entitled "It's Drugs, Stupid," Joseph Califano Jr., a former secretary of Health, Education, and Welfare, wrote that "crack babies" can cost $1 million apiece to bring to adulthood, and suggested that the children of addicted welfare mothers who "refuse" treatment be put in orphanages or foster care.

In some professional circles, the term "crack baby" has given way to "drug-exposed baby." But even layered over with euphemism, however gently its promulgators protest their good intentions, the meaning of the crack-baby epithet is clear. It means we can blame the problems of the least privileged children on the unnatural conduct of their mothers. It means we can all rest easy in the futility of giving our time and money to feed, house, educate, and love these children, whose failings are inborn and past remedy.

DANIEL IN THE LION'S DEN

"THE SCHOOL REPORTS WERE ABSOLUTELY HORRIFYING. I MEAN, IT WASN'T THE SAME CHILD."

Daniel was—is—what some would call a "crack baby." When Janine, a 42-year-old African-American volunteer at a Manhattan public hospital, first laid eyes on him in the boarder-baby nursery, he was tiny and asymmetrical; at 4 months, he looked like a newborn. Janine started visiting Daniel every day, and when he reached 10 months, brought him home with her and set about formally adopting him. Today, greeting a visitor at the door of his mother's comfortable home in an unassuming neighborhood in southern Westchester, he is a fine boy of 4, slender but of average height, with shining eyes.

Although Janine learned not to look for failure in Daniel, others dwelled on his drug exposure. The first school she took him to for enrollment saw a black adopted child and asked, "Is he

drug-exposed?" Janine claimed she didn't know. The second, a preschool special education program, proved more problematic. "This school knew, and it was written up in all the evaluations," says Janine, her voice rising angrily at the recollection. "Everything was related to his history.

"At 2, he could count up to 20. He was beginning to learn how to count in Spanish by the time he was 3. He knew his alphabet. But the school reports were absolutely horrifying. I mean, it wasn't the same child. According to them, he couldn't repeat two numbers consecutively, he couldn't turn the pages of a book, he couldn't hold a pair of scissors.

"I mean, there was nothing this child could do. And that's because they *knew*." —K.G.

Crack Investigation

A new study of rats gives hope that the ravages of cocaine in babies could one day be reversed

EFRAIN C. AZMITIA AND JANET Williamson work in worlds apart, yet they have similar concerns: how best to nurture crack babies—infants whose mothers abused crack cocaine during pregnancy. Azmitia, a biologist at New York University, spends his time in a laboratory studying the effects of cocaine in rat pups; Williamson, a social worker, passes her days on 122nd Street in West Harlem, New York, where she works at Hale House Center. She is one of thirty in the organization who care for children while their mothers try to kick drugs.

According to Azmitia, out of every ten babies now born in the United States, two get exposed to cocaine in utero. Because one effect of cocaine is to induce labor, many of the infants are born dangerously early—after only twenty-six weeks—and die. The ones surviving such a premature birth, and even the ones carried to full term, are often smaller, less coordinated and more prone to hyperactivity and severe learning disabilities than normal babies are. Their features are similar to those of babies born with fetal alcohol syndrome: physical deformities such as a smaller head; skin folds at the corners of the eyes, which are often smaller than average; a thin upper lip; and a low nasal bridge.

Williamson and her colleagues at Hale House think thoughtful care, a balanced diet and lots of attention can give those children a fighting chance. But certain realities are inescapable. Some children behave erratically and cannot control their moods, needs or emotions. Infants arrive at Hale House in the throes of withdrawal from their mothers' drug addictions; vomiting, diarrhea and uncontrollable trembling are their symptoms for the first few days of life.

UNTIL RECENTLY THE HEALTH PROBLEMS of such infants were thought to arise simply out of prenatal neglect: crack, heroin, alcohol—or a combination of the three—were assumed to contribute to the malnutrition of the mother and, thus, the infant. But that thinking has changed. Azmitia says cocaine directly affects the development of the entire embryo, including the growth and differentiation of cells in the brain. The principal target of the drug—surprisingly—is serotonin, the neurotransmitter that has achieved recent fame for its role in the antidepressant Prozac.

But the effects of serotonin extend far beyond alleviating depression. It is an ancient chemical that occurs in all animals and plants and that acts as a growth hormone during development. When serotonin binds to its receptors on the cells of a human embryo, it stimulates growth and differentiation of cells in the brain. But cocaine, as well as alcohol, can interfere with the normal uptake of serotonin by its carrier, thereby preventing the extension of serotonin neurons into the cortex, the layer of gray matter covering most of the brain's surface, which is responsible for sensory perception, muscle control, language and memory. If that takes place, the infant remains smaller and less developed mentally than an infant not exposed to cocaine.

Azmitia and two colleagues, the biologists Patricia M. Whitaker-Azmitia of the State University of New York at Stony Brook and Homayoon M. Akbari of New York University, have been studying the effects of cocaine on pregnant rats. Rats injected with cocaine bear pups whose brains are 20 percent lighter and whose bodies are 25 percent lighter than those of rats in a control group injected with harmless saline solution.

Azmitia injected some newborn rat pups exposed to cocaine with a substance called ipsapirone, which stimulates the same receptor as serotonin does. A control group of rat pups born of cocaine-exposed mothers were injected with saline solution. The body and brain weights of the pups injected with ipsapirone for one week increased to the weights of the pups not exposed to cocaine in utero; the pups not treated with ipsapirone remained underweight and developmentally stunted.

The work seems hopeful, but Azmitia warns that his findings are far from any potential application in human infants. There is no way even to estimate how long it will take, if ever, for his procedures to translate into clinical trials. The Food and Drug Administration is notoriously—perhaps rightfully—skittish about approving drugs that must be injected into newborns.

—WENDY MARSTON

Drug Sentencing Frenzy

JENNIFER ELDEN
Jennifer Elden lives in Olympia, Washington and writes frequently on legal issues.

Two months after his eighteenth birthday, Edward Clary visited friends in California. While he was there, one of them persuaded him to take some drugs back home to St. Louis. Clary didn't even make it past the St. Louis airport. Identified as someone who looked like a drug courier, he was arrested upon arrival and charged with possessing crack. Clary had never attempted to deal drugs before, and he had no criminal record. He was so inexperienced that the crack he bought was only about 20 percent pure, and so adulterated it melted in the evidence room.

According to Clary's lawyer, assistant federal public defender Andrea Smith, Clary is "a nice kid who didn't know what he was doing." Clary grew up in a troubled home, raised by aunts and other family members who took the place of his absent parents. He dropped out of high school and had no skills, and he got caught doing something stupid. Now approaching his twenty-second birthday, Clary has spent forty months in jail.

"He's still a nice kid, even after all this time in jail," says Smith. "I think he's learned his lesson."

Clary was convicted and sentenced under federal guidelines that punish crack offenses 100 times more severely than those involving powder cocaine: a crime involving one gram of crack is penalized the same as a crime involving 100 grams of powder cocaine.

Clary, like defendants in other cases, has challenged the constitutionality of the 100-to-1 ratio. These defendants claim the law is arbitrary and irrational because it assigns such disproportionate penalties to two forms of the same substance. Clary and others also argue that the law discriminates against African-Americans, since the majority of those charged with crimes involving crack are black (92.6 percent of those convicted in 1992 for violations involving crack were black, 4.7 percent were white), whereas powder cocaine users are predominantly white.

Federal courts, however, have consistently rejected the argument that the 100-to-1 ratio violates the equal-protection clause of the Constitution. Several judges have upheld the ratio, finding that Congress had a rational basis for imposing more severe penalties for crack than for powder cocaine, and that there was no evidence of a discriminatory purpose in passing the guidelines. Congress, according to these judges, believed that crack was more dangerous to society because of its potency, its affordability, its highly addictive nature, and its increasing prevalence. When considering the differences between crack and powder cocaine, Congress heard the testimony of drug-abuse experts and police officers.

Still, some courts have questioned the legitimacy of the sentencing guidelines. As it happened, Edward Clary's case came before one such court. Federal District Judge Clyde Cahill of Missouri heard Clary's plea of guilty to possession with intent to distribute almost sixty-eight grams of cocaine base. He also heard Clary's motion challenging the sentencing statute and claiming that the ratio has a disproportionate impact on blacks.

Cahill found that the sentencing ratio deprives blacks of equal protection under the law. In his ruling, he discussed the history of crime in the United States. Fear, he said, has led to a lynch-mob mentality and a desire to control crime at any cost, and Congress has become frenzied in its attempts to deal with crime. Cahill blames the media for making this fear worse, with its lurid reports of the most horrifying violence. This crime scare, according to the judge, led to the unfair sentencing ratio.

Furthermore, the ratio was approved, Cahill said, because the nation and Congress were gripped with what he calls "unconscious racism." People may believe that they are not motivated by discriminatory attitudes, he argued, but they have internalized their fear of young black men, reinforced by a media that has helped create a national image of the young black male as a criminal. "The presumption of innocence is now a legal myth," Cahill said.

"The 100-to-one ratio, coupled with mandatory minimum sentencing provided by federal statute, has created a situation that reeks with inhumanity and injustice," Cahill said. "If young white males were being incarcerated at the same rate as young black males, the statute would have been amended long ago."

Judge Cahill held the ratio invalid and sentenced Clary to four years in prison. With his decision, he hoped to end what he viewed as a dual system of punishment for drug crimes, one for whites and another for blacks.

On September 12, 1994, the Eighth Circuit Court of Appeals reversed Judge Cahill's decision. Disparate impact, said Judge John Gibson, is not enough to invalidate the statute. Clary's lawyer, Andrea Smith, recently applied to the Supreme Court to hear Clary's case. For now, Clary is on supervised release, pending a final determination of his sentence.

The 100-to-1 ratio stands unchanged, and unless the Supreme Court makes his case a landmark, Clary could face a decade in jail.

Creating and Sustaining Effective Drug Control Policy

Formulating and implementing effective drug control policy are troublesome tasks. The path to good drug policy is not clearly defined. Some would argue that the consequences of policy failures have been worse than the problem they were attempting to address. Others would argue that although the world of shaping drug policy is an imperfect one, the process has worked generally as well as could be expected, often in the face of great obstacles. The majority American view has generally been that failures and breakdowns in the fight against drug abuse have occurred mostly in spite of various drug policies, not because of them. Costs and benefits, means and ends, are always arguable. Perceived successes and failures in the fight against drug abuse are often just a blip on the screen, providing, at best, confusing evidence for directing policy. The resurgence of LSD use among high school students in Sacramento may have little meaning for policy debate in New York. Yet the observation bears investigation. Drug policy is an intensely politicized public issue. It is seldom debated from a detached perspective and instead is often the forum that some persons use to expound upon nothing more than their own political agendas. The parameters of reality for policy debate often elude even the most enlightened.

Nevertheless, policy formulation is not a process of aimless wandering. Some explanation of the basic forces at work is in order. Various levels of government have responsibility for responding to problems of drug abuse. At the center of most policy debate is the premise that the manufacture, possession, use, and distribution of psychoactive drugs are illegal. This premise is targeted frequently as misguided, due to the consequences that it is felt to perpetuate, such as syndicated crime and violent competition among criminal organizations and individuals alike. The media is replete with clashing viewpoints about legalizing, decriminalizing, and enforcement. The fact remains, however, that present-day drug control policy evolves around the majority consensus of prohibition. Surveys typically report that 80 percent of Americans think that legalizing dangerous drugs is a bad idea. The fear of increased crime, increased drug use, and the potential threat to children are the most stated reasons. Citing the devastating consequences of alcohol and tobacco, most Americans question a national ability to use any addictive, mind-altering drug responsibly—let alone one like cocaine. The drug problem consistently competes with all major public policy issues, including the economy, poverty, and homelessness.

Currently, the public favors both supply reduction and demand reduction as effective strategies in combating the drug problem. Concomitantly, policy analysts struggle with objectives, citing Americans' insatiable appetite for drugs and 10 percent interdiction rates. Reducing supply or demand in a spirit of apathetic public consciousness is certainly not possible. Saying one thing, doing another, and looking to government before looking to ourselves complicate attempts at viable policy formulation. Nonetheless, shaping public policy is a critical function that greatly relies upon public input. Policy-making apparatus is influenced by public opinion, and vice versa. When the president of the United States holds up a bag of crack and relates its threat to national security, the impact on public opinion is tremendous. In many ways opinion and policy influence each other.

The prevailing character of today's drug policy reflects a punitive, "get tough" approach to control. This character, shaped during the Reagan and Bush years, has caused strategies of treatment, prevention, and education to be less emphasized in the competition for political and economic influence. The consistent decline in drug abuse by middle-class America contributes significantly to the "get tough–stay tough" status quo. Public concerns over the drugs-crime nexus may virtually ensure the continuation of such policy. However, survey research does reflect increasing public support for demand reduction programs of education, prevention, and treatment, perhaps signaling a potential shift in costly, enforcement-oriented federal policy. The degree to which Americans are willing to do this remains to be seen. Additionally, there is much concern that even with such a shift in policy, an intense, enforcement-oriented perspective will remain focused on the nation's poor, inner-urban, largely minority subpopulations. Holding people accountable according to majority perspective is a historical American attribute

Looking Ahead: Challenge Questions

As you read the unit articles, identify additional questions and issues that mold public opinion and shape public policy on drugs. Some examples worthy of discussion are: How serious is the drug problem perceived to be? Is it getting worse?

What are the impacts of drugs on children and schools? How do drugs drive crime, and what are the impacts on policing, the courts, and corrections?

How are public opinion and policy affected by public events, drug education campaigns, announced government policies, and media coverage?

MARIJUANA AND THE LAW

*The vigorous enforcement of marijuana laws has
resulted in four million arrests since the early 1980s. Owing to
mandatory-minimum sentences, many of those convicted are receiving
stiff prison terms, even as violent criminals are released for lack
of space. The second part of a two-part article*

ERIC SCHLOSSER

Eric Schlosser *is a novelist and playwright who lives in New
York City.*

During the 1980s criminal penalties for marijuana offenses
were made much tougher, at both the state and federal levels.
More resources were devoted to their enforcement. And
punishments more severe than those administered during the
"reefer madness" of the 1930s became routine. As a result
there may be more people in prison today for violating
marijuana laws than at any other time in the nation's history.

Mark Young is one of those prisoners. In May of 1991
Young was arrested at his Indianapolis home for brokering
the sale of 700 pounds of marijuana grown on a farm in
nearby Morgan County. He had never before been charged
with drug trafficking. He had no history of violent crime. His
two prior felony convictions—one for attempting to fill a
false prescription, the other for possession of a few
Quaaludes and amphetamines—were more than a decade
old. For each of these convictions he had received a suspended sentence and a one-dollar fine. Young's role in the
marijuana transaction had been that of a middleman. He
never handled either the marijuana or the money. He had
simply introduced two partners in a marijuana farm, Claude
Atkinson and Ernest Montgomery, to a couple of men from
Florida who were acting on behalf of a New York buyer.
Under federal law Young was charged with "conspiracy to
manufacture" marijuana and was held liable for the cultivation of all 12,500 marijuana plants grown on the Morgan
County farm. The U.S. attorney now had the option of filing
for an "enhancement," owing to Young's prior drug
felonies; this would trigger a mandatory-minimum sentence
upon conviction. After being denied bail, Mark Young
learned that his marijuana offense could lead to a mandatory
sentence of life imprisonment without the chance of parole.

His case helps shed light not only on a quiet revolution in the
realm of marijuana laws but also on the often perverse consequences of mandatory-minimum sentences.

THE NEW RULES

THERE have been mandatory-minimum sentences in
the United States since the days of the first Congress,
most of them adopted to punish narrowly defined
crimes. A number of the old mandatory minimums are still
on the books, for offenses such as "robbery by pirates"
(1790) and "practice of pharmacy and sale of poisons in China" (1915). The overwhelming majority of criminal laws
passed by Congress specify only a maximum sentence. It has
historically been the role of a federal judge to determine
whether a convicted offender deserves that maximum, a
lesser sentence, or no prison sentence at all. Until seven
years ago a federal judge had great leeway in choosing sentences: Congress set only the upper limits, thereby protecting
citizens from excessive punishment. Parole boards served as
another brake on unduly harsh sentences, deciding when
prisoners merited early release.

The first broadly defined mandatory minimums were contained in the Boggs Act, which was passed at the height of
the McCarthy era, amid the tensions of the Korean War and
domestic fears of Communist subversion. There seemed to
be an increase in narcotics use among the young, and lenient
judges were thought to be partly to blame. Members of Congress vied to appear tough on drug offenders. Senator
Everett Dirksen favored legislation that allowed the death
penalty for selling narcotics to minors. Congressman Edwin
Arthur Hall advocated giving drug dealers mandatory-minimum sentences of a hundred years. Congressman L. Gary
Clemente introduced a bill recommending the death penalty
for any violation of the Narcotic Drugs Import and Export

Act. The commissioner of the Federal Bureau of Narcotics, Harry J. Anslinger, seemed almost moderate in calling for a mandatory minimum of five years for second offenders, which he assured Congress "would just about dry up the [drug] traffic." Congress followed his advice and then lengthened the anti-drug mandatory sentences, in 1956. One vocal critic of the new sentencing regime was James V. Bennett, the director of the U.S. Bureau of Prisons, who attributed the passage of such laws to "hysteria." Thereafter Bennett was followed by FBN agents, who submitted reports on his movements and speeches.

By the late 1960s a widespread consensus had emerged in both political parties that the anti-drug mandatory-minimum sentences were a failure. Members of Congress, federal judges, and even prosecutors found them too severe, unjust, and, worst of all, ineffective at preventing narcotics use. The spread of the 1960s drug culture had hardly been impeded by the existence of mandatory-minimum sentences. In 1970 Congress repealed almost all the mandatory penalties for drug offenders, an act celebrated by, among others, Congressman George Bush, who predicted that these "penal reforms" would "result in better justice and more appropriate sentences." A movement arose seeking a new means of determining federal sentences. Allowing too little judicial discretion had proved to be unfair, but too much could also lead to inequities: a bank robber in Florida might be given twenty years by a federal judge, whereas a bank robber in California received probation for exactly the same crime. Marvin Frankel, a federal district judge in New York, imagined a system in which a commission of legal experts would set guidelines on how to determine sentences for various crimes, taking into account details of the offender's criminal history and the nature of the offense.

After long and careful deliberation, the Sentencing Reform Act of 1984 was passed by Congress with overwhelming bipartisan support, creating the United States Sentencing Commission. It seemed a triumph of rational jurisprudence over demagoguery, an experiment in social planning that evoked shades of the Progressive Era, when panels of appointed experts were hailed as the ideal form of government. Judge William W. Wilkins Jr., a former protégé of Senator Strom Thurmond and Ronald Reagan's first appointee to the federal bench, was made chairman of the new commission. In only eighteen months Wilkins and his fellow commissioners devised sentences of varying severity for about 2,000 different federal crimes. These sentencing guidelines took effect in 1987. Under the new rules each federal offense was assigned a numerical value; the judge added or subtracted points in a given case, according to various criteria; and punishment was determined by matching an offender's total points with a range of applicable sentences listed on a chart. A judge could depart from the guidelines at sentencing, but had to offer an explanation for doing so.

The sentence could later be appealed by the defendant—or the prosecutor.

The same Congress that passed the Sentencing Reform Act also included in that very bill mandatory-minimum sentences for drug offenses committed near schools. Two years later the Anti-drug Abuse Act of 1986 moved away from the deliberate calibrations of the sentencing guidelines by endorsing the blunt instrument of mandatory-minimum sentences for a wide variety of drug offenses. The University of Maryland basketball star Len Bias had just been killed by crack cocaine, and anti-drug sentiment had reached new heights; lawmakers decided once again to send a tough message. Mandatory-minimum sentences, based on the amount of drugs involved in an offense, were set at five years, ten years, and twenty years. Additional mandatory minimums were added later, including what is now known as a "three strikes, you're out" provision that specified life sentences for repeat drug offenders. During the congressional debates on these mandatory sentences there was little mention of the precedent of failure set by the Boggs Act, or of how the new laws would undermine the sentencing guidelines, or of what the wider effects might be on various aspects of the criminal-justice system, from the initial filing of charges to the ultimate rates of imprisonment. According to one survey, the most commonly cited justification for the harsh new punishments was a desire for retribution, a legal theory nicknamed "just desserts."

For most of the nation's first 200 years a convicted man or woman could ask a federal judge for mercy. On the basis of extenuating circumstances, a judge could reduce a prison sentence or waive it altogether. The new mandatory-minimum laws took that power away from the judge and handed it to the prosecutor. A U.S. attorney now has the sole authority to decide whether a mandatory minimum applies in a particular case—that is, whether to frame a charge under such a statute or not. The only way a defendant can be sure of avoiding a mandatory-minimum sentence is to plead guilty and give "substantial assistance" in the prosecution of someone else. The U.S. attorney, not the judge, decides whether the defendant's cooperation is sufficient to warrant a reduction in sentence. A defendant might cooperate and still not receive a shorter sentence, if the information supplied falls short of expectations. Long mandatory prison terms provide a strong incentive to talk. From the government's point of view, guilty pleas, accompanied by cooperation, avoid expensive trials and supply valuable evidence. From the defendant's point of view, the pressure to name others is enormous.

Some federal judges believe that the quality of much testimony in court has diminished; desperate people will say anything to save themselves. An appeal for compassion is now pointless; all that matters is the demand for cooperation. Under such a system the dilemmas often have an elemental quality. This past January in Kansas City, Tora S. Brown—a nineteen-year-old first offender with an eight-month-old daughter—cooperated with the government in a drug case involving PCP but refused to implicate her own mother. Brown was given a ten-year prison sentence without the chance of parole.

"A SAD DAY FOR EVERYBODY"

ASSISTANT U.S. Attorney Donna Eide, in the Southern District of Indiana, offered Mark Young a reduced sentence in return for a guilty plea and his cooperation: forty years without the chance of parole. Kevin McShane, Young's attorney, thought the offer ridiculous; he wouldn't accept forty years as a plea bargain in a first-degree-murder case. That remained the government's only offer from May to September of 1991. Meanwhile, one by one, the other defendants in the conspiracy case "flipped," agreeing to cooperate.

Claude Atkinson had been facing a mandatory life sentence, the others sentences of ten years to life. By offering cooperation each had received a "cap" on his sentence, an upper limit, of anywhere from eight to thirty-five years. But each could also conceivably walk free, without any prison time. Their sentences would depend on their performances in court, among other things. Young and Ernest Montgomery and his wife, Cindy, were the only remaining defendants who would not plead guilty.

Under the U.S. sentencing guidelines, Mark Young's marijuana offense warranted a prison term of roughly twenty-two to twenty-seven years. The guidelines would apply in his case unless the U.S. attorney decided to file an enhancement, reflecting Young's criminal history and requiring the mandatory life sentence. Donna Eide made one last offer: eighteen years, pending cooperation. Young refused it. The government filed its enhancement on the Friday before the trial was to begin. The wheels had been set in motion, and Mark Young had a long weekend in which to make his choice: agree to cooperate or risk spending the rest of his life in prison.

Kevin McShane does not believe that the government really wanted to give his client a life sentence; that sort of threat is now common in the give-and-take of the plea-bargaining process. He does not believe that the government really wanted any information from Mark Young. Claude Atkinson, who knew more than anyone else about the marijuana farm, was talking up a storm. The identities of the New York and Florida buyers would have been of interest to federal authorities in other districts, but it was not clear that Young even knew their real names. On the eve of the trial it seemed that the government simply wanted to avoid a trial. McShane strongly advised Young to accept the offer of eighteen years; with so many potentially hostile witnesses, his chances in court were uncertain—a roll of the dice. Young's family, which to this point had remained silent on the issue, also urged him to cooperate.

His mother visited him in jail and begged. "At the end, when we saw how bad it was, I just really got on him," she recalls. "'Please, Mark, do it, do like the rest of them are, don't do this, don't end up, you know, with a life sentence, don't do it. Tell whatever you have to tell, like the rest of them are doing, to save yourself.' But no way would he do it. No way."

The day before Mark Young's trial began, Cindy Montgomery agreed to a plea bargain. The trial was notable for the details it revealed about the marijuana-growing operation, but the outcome never seemed in doubt. McShane thinks that Young's case was hurt by being tried alongside that of Ernest Montgomery, who had organized the operation. Jerry Montgomery testified against his brother and proved unable, owing to illiteracy, to read his own plea agreement for the jury. Cindy Montgomery testified against her husband. And Claude Atkinson spoke at length about everybody's criminal activities. The atmosphere at the trial was enlivened by jailhouse rumors that Mark Young not only had threatened the lives of Cindy Montgomery and Claude Atkinson and their families but also had slept with one of the jurors, who was going to thwart any guilty verdict. Young called no witnesses in his own defense. There was no physical evidence linking him to the crime, only testimony by Atkinson and Cindy Montgomery. The jury took just two and a quarter hours to render guilty verdicts on all counts. It had not been informed that a life sentence might apply.

Claude Atkinson was angry to receive a twenty-five-year sentence despite his cooperation. One of the prosecutors later described Atkinson as a "dreamer"; he may have expected to serve only a few years. For a sixty-two-year-old man, a twenty-five-year sentence was tantamount to life in prison. Ernest Montgomery, whose only previous conviction was for disorderly conduct, got thirty-four years without the chance of parole—also, in effect, a life sentence. His brother received eight years, his wife six, and the other defendants sentences ranging from three to ten years in prison. On February 8, 1992, Judge Sarah Evans Barker gave Mark Young a life sentence, as mandated. She also fined him $100, but did not order any of his assets forfeited; he had none, having paid his lawyer with a used car. "Mr. Young, it's a sad day for everybody in the courtroom," she said. "That concludes the matter."

A FEW years ago a federal judge in Utah, Thomas Green, refused to give two young drug offenders mandatory-minimum sentences of ten years each, ruling that their due-process rights had been violated by the decision to prosecute them under federal law. The same charges under state law probably would have brought prison terms of about two years. Congress, Judge Green observed, had severely curtailed the discretion of federal judges at sentencing, but had placed no similar restrictions on the behavior of law-enforcement officers and U.S. attorneys. As a result, the nation now faced "*de facto* sentencing by police and prosecutors." During the Bush Administration, Attorney General Richard

Thornburgh did try to limit the freedom of federal prosecutors. He told them to seek the maximum penalty in every drug case, regardless of mitigating circumstances. The so-called Thornburgh Memorandum, still included in the handbooks issued to all U.S. attorneys, instructs them always to pursue conviction on the most serious "readily provable" charge. U.S. attorneys, however, are not obliged to follow that advice. In some parts of the country they have faithfully adhered to the Thornburgh Memorandum. In other parts individual exceptions have been allowed when a sentence seemed particularly cruel. In a few districts U.S. attorneys who oppose mandatory minimums have been collaborating with sympathetic judges, finding ways to help low-level drug offenders avoid long prison terms.

The Supreme Court has upheld federal mandatory minimums whenever they have been challenged on constitutional grounds, consolidating the increase in prosecutorial power. A U.S. attorney wields enormous influence in drug cases by deciding how to frame a charge, what quantity of the drug to include in the charge—and even whether to press federal charges at all. A different prosecutor might have charged Mark Young only with drug trafficking, likely bringing him a sentence of about seven years. Young's conviction for "conspiracy to manufacture" all 12,500 plants shows how broadly that crime is now being interpreted. The owners of garden-supply stores have been held legally responsible for marijuana grown by their customers—an application of conspiracy theory similar to that which once imprisoned people for selling sugar to moonshiners. Often the most important factor in determining a sentence is the amount of marijuana involved. Mandatory minimums ignore the defendant's role in the crime: a "mule" driving a truckload of marijuana can be subject to the same penalty as the person financing the shipment. In fact, defendants with the smallest role in conspiracies often serve the longest sentences, because they have so little information to trade. According to Judge Wilkins, of the U.S. Sentencing Commission, prosecutors do not pursue mandatory minimums in about two thirds of the applicable cases. Their reasoning is not made public. Unlike sentences administered by judges, those derived through plea bargains are settled behind closed doors.

Drug offenses differ from most crimes in being subject to three jurisdictions: local, state, and federal. A U.S. attorney, simply by deciding to enter a particular case, may greatly skew the range of potential punishments. A person may even be tried twice for the same drug crime: found innocent by a state jury, marijuana growers can be—and have been—subsequently convicted in federal court. There are no established criteria for when a U.S. attorney will enter a marijuana case. The federal government could prosecute any and every marijuana offender in America if it so desired, but in a typical year it charges less than two percent of those arrested. In some districts there is a policy that the U.S. attorney will enter cases involving more than a hundred plants or a hundred pounds. In others a federal prosecutor may simply take a special interest in a case. Two years ago Edward Czuprynski, a liberal activist who had long irritated public officials in Bay City, Michigan, was convicted in federal court of possession of 1.6 grams of marijuana: the amount found in a large joint. Under Michigan law he most likely would have received a $100 fine. But in federal court Czuprynski was sentenced to fourteen months in prison. His license to practice law was suspended. His successful law firm closed down. "They busted me completely," he says, "and that's what they wanted to do." After spending almost eight months in prison, Czuprynski was released by order of the Sixth Circuit Court of Appeals, a decision that the U.S. attorney is now seeking to overturn. Considering his legal fees of $40,000, his lost income of ten times that amount, and the untold thousands of dollars the federal government has already spent on his case, Czuprynski says, "That may be the most expensive joint in the nation's history."

Four years ago Julie Stewart founded Families Against Mandatory Minimums, a grassroots organization with the motto "Let the Punishment Fit the Crime." She had not given much thought to America's drug laws until her older brother was convicted for having grown 375 marijuana seedlings. His sentence was five years. FAMM now has more than 20,000 members, most of them politically active for the first time in their lives. After Mark Young was arrested, his older sister, Andrea Strong, lost three housecleaning jobs in suburban Indianapolis—a sign of the great stigma that marijuana still carries in many parts of the country. Strong is now FAMM's Midwest coordinator, a self-taught expert on federal criminal law and a tireless campaigner for the repeal of mandatory minimums. FAMM lobbies Congress for sentencing reform and compiles case histories of inmates imprisoned under mandatory-minimum laws. Among them are Michael T. Irish, a first offender sentenced to twelve years in federal prison for helping to unload hashish from a boat; Charles Dunlap, a first offender sentenced to eight years in federal prison for renting a truck used by a friend to import marijuana; and Zodenta McCarter, a sixty-six-year-old woman, a first offender, poor and illiterate, suffering from diabetes, described as "naive, trusting, and childlike in comprehension," sentenced to eight years in federal prison for conspiring to sell ditchweed (a strain of wild marijuana that is rarely psychoactive). Since being incarcerated McCarter has had a heart attack, been infected with tuberculosis, and endured three operations.

VISITING HOURS

LEAVENWORTH Penitentiary is the oldest prison in the federal system. It may also be the most dangerous. One hundred years ago there were no federal prisons.

The roughly 2,500 convicts with federal sentences longer than a year served their time in state facilities scattered across the country. In 1896 Congress appropriated funds for construction of the first federal penitentiary, to be located on more than 1,500 acres in rural Kansas, a few miles from the Army base at Fort Leavenworth. The new prison was built by the convicts who would soon occupy it. In the eighty-eight years since it opened, only one prisoner has ever escaped from Leavenworth and eluded recapture. The red-brick walls, with a gun tower at each corner, are thirty-five feet high and extend an equal distance beneath the ground. The main building is massive, ominous, and redolent of power. It was designed to resemble the U.S. Capitol, converting a symbol of freedom into one of punishment and obedience. On a bleak winter morning, when the grayness of the sky and that of the neighboring fields seem to merge, Leavenworth looks exactly as an inmate described it more than six decades ago: like a "giant mausoleum adrift in a great sea of nothingness."

To reach the visiting room, you must state your name and purpose to a corrections officer in a small gun tower and then climb stairs to the front entrance. After passing through two electric doors reinforced with steel bars you are photographed; stamped with invisible ink; asked to sign a pledge that you are not bearing firearms, explosives, or narcotics; led through a metal detector; and then escorted through another large door with steel bars. The visiting room looks like a Knights of Columbus meeting hall, with blond-wood paneling, a row of vending machines, and comfortable chairs separated by small tables. There is no glass between inmates and their guests. Visits are supervised by corrections officers who sit on a platform at one end of the room; surveillance cameras are hidden in the ceiling. As I waited to meet Mark Young, a small boy ran up and down the length of the room playing with his father, a bearded inmate in khaki work clothes.

Jonathan Turley, a professor at George Washington University Law School, regards Leavenworth as a perfect microcosm of the federal prison system today: antiquated, often overcrowded, and extremely dangerous both for inmates and for corrections officers. Leavenworth's rated capacity is about 1,100 prisoners, but at times in the past year it has housed more than 1,600. Overcrowding vastly increases the risk of violence; prison riots become virtually inevitable. The federal system as a whole is operating at about 40 percent above capacity. Some facilities now house two to three times the number of people they were designed to hold, even as the federal prison population increases at a rate of about 10,000 inmates a year.

Tough federal drug laws, strictly enforced, have fueled this unprecedented growth in the federal prison system. The Boggs Act of the 1950s did not have the same effect, because drug offenses were less common and less vigorously pros-

ecuted. As late as 1967 the Federal Bureau of Narcotics had only 300 agents. Its successor, the Drug Enforcement Administration, now has 3,400. During the 1980s annual federal spending to incarcerate drug offenders rose more than 1,300 percent, from $88 million to $1.3 billion. Anti-drug mandatory-minimum sentences and the guideline sentences formulated to mesh neatly with them have transformed the inmate population. In 1970, 16.3 percent of all federal prisoners were drug offenders; today the proportion of federal prisoners who are drug offenders has reached 62 percent. Within three years it should reach 72 percent. Many are first offenders, without so much as a previous arrest, who have been imprisoned for low-level drug violations. Of the 4,244 people convicted last year of violating federal marijuana laws, 56 percent had no criminal record deemed relevant at sentencing. State correctional facilities are also being overwhelmed by drug offenders. The prison systems in forty states are now operating under court order to reduce over-crowding. Violent criminals are sometimes being released early to provide cell space for nonviolent drug offenders whose mandatory sentences do not permit parole. The number of drug offenders imprisoned in America today—about 200,000—is the same as the number of people imprisoned for *all* crimes in 1970. Since the latest war on drugs began, in 1982, the nation's prison population has more than doubled. The United States now has the highest rate of incarceration in the world. No society in history has ever imprisoned so many of its own citizens for purposes of crime control.

Mark Young is big—about six foot five, with the build one would expect of an old biker. He has long hair tied in a ponytail. He seems like a hippie version of the country-and-western star Hank Williams Jr., with a gravelly drawl and a deadpan sense of humor. Before being sent to Leavenworth, Young married his longtime girlfriend, Patricia Rowland, in a Native American ceremony at the local jail. Patricia visits him as often as she can, but it is a nine- or ten-hour drive from Indianapolis to Leavenworth, Kansas. She brings him photographs of changes in their neighborhood: new houses, new stores opening at the mall. They discuss how furniture should be rearranged at their rented home; she later moves things around accordingly, and sends him pictures. She does not want him to forget that a familiar world still exists outside the brutal one he now inhabits.

Young had never been in prison before being sentenced to Leavenworth. A marijuana offense usually leads to incarceration at a minimum-security prison or prison camp. But Young's life sentence labels him as a high risk for attempted escape, requiring that he serve his sentence at a maximum-security penitentiary. Young now finds himself living among some of the most violent repeat offenders in the federal system: murderers, rapists, armed robbers, international terrorists. His two-man cell is eight feet by ten feet, with a solid-metal sliding door and no view of the outdoors, just a window facing the catwalk. A few months after his arrival Young sat in a prison auditorium, packed with inmates, watching *Silence of the Lambs*. A riot suddenly erupted in the darkness. Prisoners divided by race and tore furniture apart to make weapons. Corrections officers were taken hostage. Amid the chaos Young grabbed a piece of a chair and huddled against the theater wall, terrified. When officers finally quelled the riot, hours later, Young was teargassed, handcuffed, and dragged along the floor through a pool of blood. Because of Young's size, other inmates have so far left him alone. "But anything can happen here to anyone, at any time," he told me, snapping his fingers. "Just like that." Inmates with life sentences and no chance of parole have nothing to lose. Last year a good friend of Young's, Clyde Harrison, was stabbed to death in the dining room, before hundreds of other people, over a $50 debt. The killer politely handed the knife to a corrections officer, handle first. Young had never witnessed anything like it. His friend died instantly, and then "people were stepping over him to get to the salad bar."

Young's trial was such a strange experience that he finds it difficult to describe. One would have to be very stoned, he thinks, to appreciate how absurd it felt. He hardly knew Ernest Montgomery and had met Claude Atkinson only twice, spending a total of less than an hour with him. He had never visited the farm where the marijuana was grown, and to this day does not know its location. Most of the people who testified in court were people whom Young had never laid eyes on before. It makes no sense to him that the law should give him a life sentence for conspiring to cultivate marijuana. Young is quite candid about a lot of socially unacceptable things he has done, and he admits to finding a buyer for the Indiana group, but he ridicules Atkinson's efforts during the trial to depict him as a major broker, a Paine Webber of pot. The truth, according to Young, is much less dramatic. He was in Florida, fishing with a buddy and sharing a joint. His friend praised the marijuana, which Montgomery had given to Young as a free sample. A few days later the friend called Young and asked if there was any more of "that good stuff." Young thought there was. His friend then called a friend, who called another friend: a buyer in New York. Young claims that he actually received only a fraction of the $70,000 fee alleged in court. He did not really know either the buyer or the seller. Once the two got together, they did the natural thing—eliminated the middleman. "They cheated me!" Young said, laughing hard.

Although he has always loved to smoke marijuana, Young never thought much about it until coming to prison. Now he is an authority on the subject, a fan of the authors Jack Herer and Chris Conrad, who believe that growing hemp can help protect the environment. The use of its fibers for paper, Young thinks, could save millions of trees, and its distilla-

tion into alcohol-based fuels could end the world's energy shortage. Young is busy in prison designing a Harley Davidson that will run entirely on marijuana—"the Hempster." Much to his family's distress, Young was recently sent to "the Hole," Leavenworth's disciplinary building, for smoking marijuana in prison. The marijuana at Leavenworth is quite good, though expensive, he says. Most illegal drugs are easily obtained in Leavenworth, including hashish, a rarity elsewhere in the Midwest.

I asked Young the question that had been on my mind for weeks: Why didn't he cooperate with the prosecutors, when refusing to talk seemed to guarantee a life sentence? "It crossed through my mind a lot, trying to decide," he said. "But there's two ways I look at it. I feel kind of proud to have principles. And I'm glad I never lost that. But on the other hand, I can't really brag too much, because I didn't have anybody to give them. Who was I going to give them?" I suggested that they just wanted a name, some token of cooperation. The only name Young could provide was that of his fishing buddy; and in the end, he could not do it. "This guy has nothing," he said. "This guy couldn't buy half an ounce of marijuana, okay?" Young understands why the other defendants behaved as they did: "When you're talking the kind of time that they were passing out, you expect anybody to do what they can to fend for themselves." As for him, "No, I wouldn't do it any other way."

The worst thing about Leavenworth, for Young, is the noise, "the constant roar of hundreds of people talking." His cell offers no escape from it, from voices echoing off the steel and concrete, day and night. Should Young ever be released, the first thing he plans to do is go fishing—"I'm sure now that I'm locked up, the bass have come out." He feels great bitterness toward his prosecutors. "Someone who'd do what they're doing is capable of doing anything. . . . They've only proved I'm capable of smoking a joint, or of introducing a guy to another guy who needs some pounds. That's the most they've proved me capable of. What they're doing, they're destroying these families and passing out life sentences, taking people's lives, putting children on the street— I mean horrendous acts." He laughed. "I don't know of anyone that would do anything that malicious for a salary." He has no complaints about the corrections officers—men with families, working toward a pension, who daily walk unarmed amid scores of violent inmates. "I wouldn't take their job for nothing in the world," he said. "Sometimes I wonder if they realize how bad a situation they're in—you know, really." Despite it all, Young expressed a touching faith in the Constitution: "We're just going through a bad period . . . but I believe the Constitution can whip that."

When our time was up, a prison official gave Young a friendly tap on the shoulder and said, "Come on, buddy." Moments later a heavy door closed, and Mark Young was gone.

DISSENSION IN
THE SYSTEM

TOM Dawson has a folksy, small-town manner and a cluttered, unpretentious office, both of which disguise the fact that he is a very successful criminal attorney who has been admitted to the bar in every federal circuit. Dawson grew up in the town of Leavenworth, and is arguing Young's appeal. The issue before the court concerns how much marijuana Young could reasonably have foreseen would be produced by the conspiracy. Dawson and Assistant U.S. Attorney Donna Eide have been sparring over plants and pounds and the proper equation for turning one into the other; at times even the judges on the court of appeals get confused. The dispute might seem worthy of an Abbott and Costello routine if its outcome were not going to determine a man's fate. The gray-haired Dawson is a lifelong Republican who earns a living representing drug offenders, among others. But he has become profoundly disillusioned with the war on drugs. "It is corrupting everything it touches," he told me. At sentencing the degree of a defendant's guilt often seems less important than his willingness to hand over assets and name others. "I've had kingpins walk free," Dawson admitted. In a case handled by another lawyer, a major cocaine dealer with a fleet of Learjets testified against "everybody he ever met," Dawson said, and served less than four years in prison, despite being caught with 20,000 kilos of cocaine. "It's just the guy who doesn't cooperate who then gets everybody else's time. It's just the way it works. And they finally will run into some poor guy who says, just like Mark, 'I'm not going to do it. I've got principles.' Well, then, fine. You take all their time. And that's really about the way it works." Guilty pleas are what keep a legal system that is overwhelmed with drug cases functioning. In certain situations, Dawson believes, an innocent person is better off pleading guilty: "If you don't plead and you bet wrong, the sentences are just too high to serve."

Anti-drug mandatory-minimum sentences have created dissension in the federal legal system, prompting many judges to seek early retirement. Judge William Schwarzer, the head of the Federal Judicial Center, believes that the nation risks losing some of its best judges. In his view, a lack of respect for the profession, a sentencing process that often reduces judges to the status of adding machines, a staggering backlog of drug cases, and a widespread sentiment that judges are not to be trusted in choosing sentences may all combine to persuade highly qualified people to avoid the bench. Judges were meant to be impartial arbiters; too often now they are merely bystanders, as U.S. attorneys administer punishments chosen by Congress. Perhaps a hundred senior federal judges are currently refusing to hear low-level drug cases prosecuted under mandatory-minimum laws. One of them, Jack B. Weinstein, of New York's Eastern District, announced his decision with regret, aware that he might be passing the "dirty work" to his colleagues. "I need a rest from the oppressive sense of futility that these drug cases leave," he wrote in his announcement. "I simply cannot sentence another impoverished person whose destruction has no discernible effect on the drug trade." Weinstein believes that imprisonment can serve as a deterrent; in court I watched him rebuke corrupt taxi inspectors and insist that their plea bargains include prison terms. It is a question of proportion. In refusing to apply a ten-year mandatory minimum to a poor woman caught smuggling heroin, Weinstein quoted the utilitarian philosopher Jeremy Bentham. "Every particle of real punishment that is produced, more than what is necessary," Bentham wrote, "is just so much misery run to waste."

Deborah Daniels was the U.S. attorney in the Southern District of Indiana from 1988 to 1993. She not only supervised Mark Young's prosecution but also helped set the Justice Department's sentencing policy during the Bush Administration. "My position as a prosecutor," she says, "was not to make the laws." Congress had passed legislation to remove judicial discretion through mandatory minimums and guidelines. The Justice Department decided that it would be wrong for prosecutors "to take over that role as judges." The laws were to be fully enforced as written. Daniels acknowledges that in some districts assistant U.S. attorneys would "work a case backward," deciding what punishment a defendant ought to receive and then finding a way to charge for it. "I don't agree with that. That's cheating. And we didn't cheat in the Southern District of Indiana. We played it straight. And that's how Mark Young got his sentence." She denies that the threat of long sentences was used mainly to induce plea bargains: "We didn't do things like that." The policy of her office was to seek conviction on the most serious readily provable charge—in every case, without exception. "The minute you start saying, Well, gee, that's kind of severe for this guy and what he did," she argues, "then you're deciding what the case is worth." Daniels believes that Young's sentence is what Congress mandated for that offense. Many people think it is wrong to give a life sentence when "only marijuana" is involved. Daniels disagrees. The United States cannot discourage other countries from exporting cocaine if it is unwilling to fight an illegal drug produced domestically. "Yes, prisons are expensive," she admits, "but if we are going to crack down on a serious problem . . . we are going to have to bear the brunt of that." She does not think the pressure to cooperate has diminished the quality of testimony in court. And what most people don't realize about U.S. attorneys, she says, is that they spend a good deal of their time getting innocent people out of trouble, by declining to file charges. In Mark Young's case, all things considered, the system worked exactly as intended.

Last year Attorney General Janet Reno amended the Thornburgh Memorandum, allowing U.S. attorneys to take into account the circumstances in a particular case—a tacit acknowledgment of prosecutorial power. Seeking the maximum sentence is still the policy of the Justice Department, but exceptions can be made. Judith Stewart, the new U.S. attorney in Indiana's Southern District, has vowed to seek "consistency without mathematical regimentation." The Clinton Administration, however, does not plan any changes in how the war on drugs is being waged against marijuana. Lee P. Brown, the head of the White House Office of National Drug Control Policy, recently summarized the Administration's view this way: "Marijuana, as you know, is a controlled substance. Our position is that it should remain a controlled substance. We feel that way because it is a potentially dangerous psychoactive drug, with strong links to medical problems and negative, or at least high-risk, behavior among its users." Enforcement policies adopted by the two previous Administrations will continue. The crime bills recently passed by both houses of Congress include weak "safety-valve" provisions that will allow judges to waive mandatory-minimum sentences for some low-level first-time drug offenders, who in return must offer full cooperation. The crime bills also specify the death penalty for any marijuana offender caught with 60,000 plants or more.

One of the great ironies of American drug policy is that anti-drug laws over the past century have tended to become most punitive long after the use of a drug has peaked. David Musto, a professor at Yale Medical School and the pre-eminent historian of American narcotics policy, explains that when drug use is at its height, so is tolerance; but as drugs re-

cede from middle-class homes, their users are marginalized, scapegoated, and more readily punished. The price that society pays for harsh sanctions becomes invisible to most people. Musto thinks that our nation's drug laws reflect cultural changes after the fact; though extreme punishments may help to limit a drug epidemic, the principal causes of its rise and fall lie elsewhere. This theory is supported by recent history. Marijuana use among the young peaked in 1979; strict federal laws were passed seven years later, when use had already fallen by 43 percent; and the explanation most young people gave for quitting marijuana was a concern about the perceived health risks, not fear of imprisonment. A drug culture is once again emerging on college campuses, despite the existence of draconian mandatory minimums. Twelve years after the current war on drugs was declared, some rough numbers may hint at its cost: $30 billion spent so far at the state, federal, and local levels to fight marijuana; two billion dollars' worth of assets seized in marijuana cases; four million Americans arrested for marijuana offenses; a quarter of a million people convicted of marijuana felonies and sent to prison for at least a year. Statistics can only suggest a portion of the truth. As I learned from the families of inmates, the human costs are not so easily measured.

> **Editors note:** The first part of the two-part article may be found in *The Atlantic Monthly,* August 1994.

Why drugs keep flowing: too little emphasis on treating heavy users

Rand study on cocaine finds law enforcement not as effective

David Rohde

Staff writer of The Christian Science Monitor

A major new study indicates that the United States is emphasizing the wrong tactics in its multibillion-dollar, worldwide effort to slow a heavy cocaine-use "epidemic" that is ravaging its inner-city neighborhoods and suburban homes.

Dollar for dollar, spending on treatment of cocaine users is far more effective than the high-profile police and military action the US mounted throughout the 1980s to curb the flow of cocaine, suggests the California-based Rand Drug Policy Research Center in twin reports last month.

The studies are the first ever to compare the effectiveness of various domestic and international anti-cocaine tactics. The results are seen as applicable to other drugs, such as heroin.

Rand researchers were able to show that even if only 13 percent of cocaine users stayed off the drug after counseling, treatment is still twice as effective as reducing overall cocaine consumption as domestic and international law enforcement efforts.

Clinton administration officials say they are following the reports' recommendations and trying to shift more of the $12 billion US antidrug effort toward treating hard-core drug users.

But critics say budget short-falls and partisan bickering are freezing expensive, ineffective antidrug policies in place. Dr. Herbert Kleber, medical director of the Columbia University Center on Addiction and Substance Abuse, says President Clinton needs to fight harder for a treatment increase: "I see good intentions, but no follow-through."

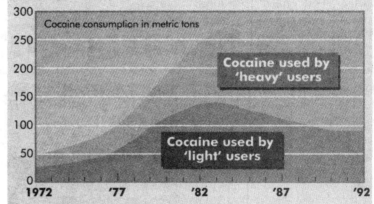

Heavy Cocaine Use: a US Epidemic

While the number of cocaine users has dropped since the early 1980s, increased demand from heavy users has kept total consumption constant.

Cocaine consumption in metric tons

Cocaine used by 'heavy' users

Cocaine used by 'light' users

Note: Crack cocaine is included in all figures. Heavy user is defined as someone who uses cocaine at least weekly. Light user is defined as someone who uses cocaine at least once a year, but not weekly.

Source: Rand Drug Policy Research Center

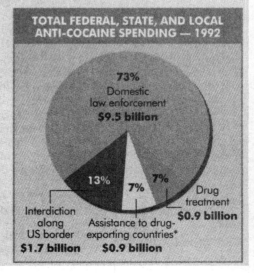

How Government Spends Money To Curb Cocaine's Spread

Treatment or Interdiction?

Critics of US drug policy say less money should go to stopping illegal drugs, including cocaine, from entering the country and more to treatment of users.

TOTAL FEDERAL, STATE, AND LOCAL ANTI-COCAINE SPENDING — 1992

73% Domestic law enforcement $9.5 billion

13% Interdiction along US border $1.7 billion

7% Assistance to drug-exporting countries* $0.9 billion

7% Drug treatment $0.9 billion

What if More Money Went to Treatment?

If $250 million dollars were added to four different ways of fighting cocaine, the one that would reduce cocaine use the most is treatment of drug users.

| 1992 | 1995 | 1998 | 2001 | 2004 | 2007 |

Projected drop in annual cocaine consumption (metric tons), if more money was put into four different efforts.

- ☐ Assistance to drug-exporting countries*
- ■ Interdiction along US border
- ▨ Domestic law enforcement
- ▨ Drug treatment

* Aid to drug-exporting countries refers to police training, crop eradication, asset seizures, and other anti-trafficking programs.

Source: Rand Drug Policy Research Center

But a House appropriations subcommittee has cut the increase to $60 million and Clinton's health care proposal is stalled, essentially leaving US antidrug spending where it was in the 1980s—65 percent to law enforcement and 35 percent to treatment and education.

Kleber, who was a drug policy official in the Bush administration, says a shift in policy is long overdue. "The funding for treatment has been a bipartisan failure," he says. "The Republican administrations did not ask for enough for treatment, and Congress gave us a third of what we asked for."

C. Peter Rydell, principal author of the study says, the "real loser" in the study was US programs to seize trafficker assets, destroy coca crops, and aid local law enforcement in cocaine-producing countries such as Colombia, Bolivia, and Peru.

Latin American governments have long questioned US drug policies, arguing that the problem is the US demand for drugs that fuels drug production in their countries. An accompanying Rand

Dr. Kleber is referring to Clinton's campaign pledge to provide drug treatment "on demand," and the administration's request for $355 million in its fiscal 1995 budget for new heavy drug-user treatment programs.

"We're focusing our efforts on the hard-core drug user," says Lee Brown, director of the Office of National Drug Control Policy. Mr. Brown adds that the Clinton health-care proposal, if enacted, would cover 30 days of drug treatment.

OFFICIAL US COAST GUARD PHOTOGRAPH

DRUG BUST: *Coast Guard agents seize a cocaine shipment. Sixty-five percent of the US government's $12 billion antidrug budget is spent on law enforcement.*

Cocaine Facts

- ■ The US consumes about two-thirds of the world's cocaine.
- ■ The number of US heavy cocaine users nearly doubled from about 1 million in 1980 to 1.7 million in 1992.
- ■ Heavy cocaine users make up only 20 percent of all US users, but consume 80 percent of cocaine in US.
- ■ The number of US cocaine users peaked at 9 million in the early 1980s and has dropped to 7 million today.
- ■ It takes an estimated 10 to 14 days for traffickers to establish a new supply line after a major drug shipment is seized.
- ■ As much as one-third of the cocaine shipped to the US from 1989 to 1992 was seized by authorities, but prices continued to drop.

Source: Rand Drug Policy Research Center, Office of National Drug Control Policy, Department of Justice

study found that despite a drop in total cocaine users from a peak of 9 million in the early 1980s to just over 7 million today, a sharp increase in heavy cocaine users has kept total US cocaine consumption constant.

The number of heavy cocaine users jumped sharply, from approximately a million in 1980 to 1.7 million in 1992. The rise was due in part to the advent of a new, highly-addictive, more purified form of cocaine known as "crack" in the 1980s. Drug policy experts say that US has gotten mixed results from the over $100 billion it has spent on antidrug efforts since 1980. The total number of drug users has been declining, according to the National Household Survey on Drug Abuse, but last year's survey found that reported drug use among high school students increased for the first time since 1979.

The author of the Rand study and drug policy experts warn that aggressive domestic law-enforcement efforts must be maintained to discourage casual drug use, and treatment for heavy users must be increased.

Peter Reuter, a government professor at the University of Maryland, says that, politically, treatment for heavy users is very unpopular.

"It's a population that is in and out of programs, commits a lot of crimes, and does a lot of harm to society," he says, "but that's the reason to treat them."

The Drug War and Clinton's Policy Shift

Robert Bruce Charles

Robert B. Charles is an attorney in the Litigation Department at Weil, Gotshal & Manges, Washington, D.C., and a former Deputy Associate Director of Policy Development in the Bush White House.

Like a commercial jet rising steeply on take–off, then suddenly dipping without explanation, America's assault on illegal drug use, the so-called "Drug War," is in trouble. Reputable studies, including several released earlier this year, indicate that illegal drug use is up, along with drug-related medical emergencies, drug-related crime and aggregate drug-related economic costs. After significant gains in the Drug War between 1986 and 1992, why the slippage?

Reviewing the President's 1993 spending priorities and FY95 Budget, experts agree that the Clinton White House may be behind the slippage. By either consciously de-emphasizing drug enforcement in favor of drug treatment, or turning the Drug War into a low-budget rhetorical flourish, Clinton already seems to have rolled back gains made during the late Reagan and early Bush years.

More than twenty hours of interviews with members of the Administration, Congress, and non-partisan private experts reveal that the drug problem is deepening, and the Clinton Administration's response has people worried.

GAINS MADE IN THE DRUG WAR

Despite the nightly barrage of drug-related stories flowing into our living rooms, significant gains were made in curbing illegal drug use between 1986 and the start of 1992.

Between 1985 and 1990, for example, the public perception of risks associated with drug use changed markedly. Fueled by a new emphasis on drug-related harms by Presidents Reagan and Bush, as well as former First Lady Nancy Reagan's "just say no" campaign, some significant gains included the drop in monthly cocaine use from 2.9 million users in 1988 to 1.3 million users in 1990, and a drop in overall monthly drug abuse from 14.5 million users in 1991 to 11.4 million in 1992. But the story didn't end in 1992.

NEW DATA

Since then, drug abuse has again surged, along with violent and non-violent crime, drug-related AIDS cases, and record-breaking national economic costs. In early 1994, a reputable University of Southern California study estimated that the total economic costs of drug abuse now exceed $76 billion dollars (including medical and AIDS costs, criminal activity and lost economic productivity). The same study projected that this figure will climb to $150 billion by 1997.

Try as we might to forget it, new data is rolling in— and it packs a punch. Nationwide emergency room data collected by the Drug Abuse Warning Network ("DAWN") for example, reveal that medical emergencies from cocaine and heroin reached 119,800 and 48,000 in 1992, *the highest levels ever recorded.* Meanwhile ONDCP reports that injection drug use accounted for 33 percent of reported AIDS cases in 1992, and other studies indicate that student attitudes, reinforced against drug use throughout the 1980's, are shifting. For example, the highly respected Monitoring the Future Study, an annual survey of 51,000 high school students and eighth graders by the National Institute on Drug Abuse at Michigan University, found in 1993 that the use of cocaine, hallucinogens, stimulants and marijuana is up among eighth graders. In 1994, MTF discovered that the use of LSD, hallucinogens, inhalants, stimulants and marijuana are *all* up, and at nearly *all* grade levels. MTF researcher Lloyd Johnston says "the underlying attitudes and beliefs . . . [are] continuing to shift in a direction favorable to drug use. . . . The perceived dangers of nearly

From the Eighth International Conference on Drug Policy Reform, *The Crucial Next Stage: Health Care & Human Rights,* Policy Track Manual 1994, pp. B1-B17. Reprinted by permission of the Drug Policy Foundation.

all the illicit drugs declined in 1993 at *all* grade levels." Now, why?

CLINTON'S POLICY SHIFT

Against the backdrop of this arresting new data, Clinton's White House has seemed oddly ambivalent. Not surprisingly, interviews for this article turned up bipartisan concern. Clinton's 1993 White House decisions on drug policy and February 1994 National Drug Control Strategy are both giving long-time observers pause.

Clinton's policy shift starts with the official White House response to statutory duties imposed upon it by the Anti-Drug Abuse Act of 1988. The Act requires every White House to release an *annual* National Drug Control Strategy. Responsibility for that strategy lies, initially, with the Director of the White House Office of National Drug Control Policy (ONDCP)—the so-called White House Drug Czar—presently Dr. Lee Brown. Final clearance, of course, comes from the Oval Office.

In September 1993, arguing that the President was pressed for time, the White House presented an "interim strategy" to Congress. Drug Czar Brown argued that the White House would eventually offer a "full blown" strategy. The "interim strategy" struck most as a bad joke, not least Democrat co-sponsors and supporters of the 1988 Anti-Drug Abuse Act. It was short, devoid of "quantifiable goals" (a statutory requirement), and lacking in any resource projections. The White House offered no changes.

Representative Charles B. Rangel (D-NY) feels that the President, while "intelligent and compassionate," simply did not show a serious commitment to solving the drug problem. Offering thoughts for this article, Rangel describes the devastation that drug abuse has wreaked on his New York City congressional district, then offers an unexpected admission. "Let me tell you something," he says, "The other day, I got a call from Nancy Reagan, and she was saying she was glad to hear I missed her. Well, I do miss her, and I welcomed that call. Her 'just say no' campaign *was* a policy. . . . At least, it was a policy!" Unexpected praise from a former critic of Reagan's White House.

Rangel's frustration echoed around the Capitol. Senator Joseph R. Biden, Jr. (D-DE), who originally lauded Clinton's condemnation of "hard-core" drug use, also admitted that the administration has not "paid enough attention to the problem." Representative E. Clay Shaw, Jr. (R-FL) called the White House "in full retreat in the war against drugs," and Senator Don Nickles (R-OK), described what he saw as a "pattern of surrender." Representative Benjamin A. Gilman (R-NY), former Vice Chair of the House Select Committee on Narcotics—abolished with Clinton's consent in 1993—explained the foreign damage done by Clinton's neglect of drug policy. At a time when the Caribbean nations are struggling to follow our early lead, Gilman noted that, "regrettably . . . [the White House is) sending the wrong signals to our Latin and Caribbean allies." Senator Orin G. Hatch (R-UT) was more blunt. "The White House offered us an interim list of platitudes . . . . sending out the message that this administration is just not serious about drug programs and drug policy."

If that *was* the message, it got new fuel in December 1993. Clinton's Surgeon General, Joyceln Elders, that month advocated a study of drug legalization. The White House disclaimed her position, but she stood firm, saying: "I feel that we would markedly reduce our crime rate if drugs were legalized." Since then, the White House has steadfastly defended her right to hold this public position. Independent thinking is, of course, laudable. But when it undercuts a fundamental premise of the president's stated policy, what does that say about the policy? On reflection, how could a high ranking administration official not be aware that Clinton opposed legalization, unless the opposition was, itself, weak or little known? Enough said.

People close to the issue for years began to talk. Why is Clinton unwilling to speak out on the drug issue, some asked. In response, defenders noted that Clinton *did* speak out against cocaine use during the '92 campaign (briefly alluding to his brother's former habit in a presidential debate), and was present when the 1994 Drug Strategy was announced. Still, former Federal Judge and DEA Chief Robert Bonner, who served *both* Presidents Clinton and Bush and is now with Gibson, Dunn and Crutcher in L.A., expresses a commonly heard concern. "I have great respect for Dr. Brown, but the *President* has to get out in front on this issue. The message has to come from the top. The President has to stand up and send a strong message of social disapproval. The reason is simple—we are backsliding."

Others wonder aloud why the President gored his own White House office on drug policy. To meet a self-imposed October 1, 1993 deadline for reducing White House Staff by 25 percent, Clinton chopped the drug policy staff from 146 to 25—an 85 percent cut! Underscoring its low priority his FY94 Budget cut ONDCP appropriations from $101.2 million to $5.8 million. In one fell swoop, Clinton left ONDCP—the anti-drug arm of the White House—at one-twentieth its prior strength. These cuts are not restored in the FY95 Budget. If White House staff needed reducing, why target that office? If Clinton felt Republicans had to be removed, why not replace them? After fifteen months in office, Clinton has neither replaced nor restored ONDCP's lost resources. The ONDCP cut still raises eyebrows across the Federal Government. Judge Bonner explains that the "deep cut in ONDCP has symbolic significance not only in Washington . . . but around the world. Our foreign allies read it as a signal that the Clinton Administration is backing away from a strong commitment to drug control policy." Senator Hatch punctuates the point. "With that staff cut, the Administration ham-strung Director Brown. They have given him a paper promotion to the cabinet, while slashing his staff to the bone. . . . He can't lead the War on Drugs with a staff of only 25 people, I mean give me a break."

Clinton's other 1993 decisions are no less troubling. A $200 million reduction in Caribbean drug interdiction activities in October 1993 went largely unmentioned by the national media. The cut's impact is amplified by newly proposed cuts in drug interdiction. Clinton's FY95 Budget proposes to cut $94.3 million more from Federal interdiction efforts, a rollback of 7.3 percent.

In response, Dr. Brown directs public attention to the FY94 anti-drug request for "nearly $13 billion," but neglects a critical fact. The same Clinton White House proposed deep *cuts* in its 1993 anti-drug budget, including cuts in treatment programs it now champions. Reflecting on last year's budget debate, Senator Hatch says, "When you talk about President Clinton and his treatment emphasis, you know, he may emphasize treatment and rehabilitation as his primary weapons in the Drug War . . . but the Administration repeatedly sought cuts in treatment funding [during 1993]." Hatch is specific. "In July, for instance, the Clinton Administration suggested that House lawmakers make a total of $231 million in cuts for drug *treatment* and *education*. They suggested it." So, say the circumspect, why not expect the same in 1994?

DEA sources confirm other fears. One: Clinton's 33 percent reduction in foreign counter-narcotics assistance during the current fiscal year. As a direct result of this Clinton cut, U.S. drug control assistance to Columbia, a major source of cocaine, has been reduced by 50 percent. Similar assistance to Peru, the producer of two-thirds of the world's cocaine, has fallen by 60 percent.

DEA sources note, in addition, that Clinton's January 1993 Executive Order of across-the-board cuts will reduce the total 3700 DEA special agents by 500, resulting in a 14 percent drop, by 1996. One high level DEA source, seeking anonymity, adds: "The disruption will be unbelievable. . . . It will further restrict our ability to pay informants, collect and analyze intelligence and perform current [DEA] functions." Is this how the Drug War will be won?

The State Department's Bureau of International Narcotics will be hit too, suffering a one-third cut between 1993 and 1994. The bureau's budget will fall from $150 million to $100 million, and no other bureau directly handles State's international anti-narcotics efforts.

CLINTON'S 1994 STRATEGY

At last, in February 1994, the President released a National Drug Control Strategy. That strategy raises new questions. Is the White House intentionally tipping the balance of FY95 Federal resources toward drug treatment, and away from international interdiction, intelligence gathering, and enforcement? Does the White House really believe that drug treatment will carry the day against the Columbia cocaine cartels and Golden Triangle heroin dealers? Does the 1994 strategy compensate in any way for the deep 1993 cuts? And what anti-drug programs can Americans expect Clinton to throw out, in the name of budget reduction? Answers to these questions are elusive, but most experts agree that Clinton has so far displayed little leadership, and only a tepid interest, in pursuing the Drug War.

High ranking administration officials, such as Attorney General Reno, who was questioned for this article in February, claim that "no shift [in the Drug War] is occurring." Others, however, disagree. In a December interview with the White House Drug Czar, Brown admitted that the White House has plans for a "new emphasis" in the Drug War, favoring "prevention and treatment." Explained Brown: "The major difference between what you will see coming from this administration, as compared to past policies is we'll place a much greater emphasis on the [drug) demand [reduction] side. . . . When I talk about drug control, I'm not talking about a line item on the budget that says narcotics. I see drug control as health reform, community policing, an enterprise zone program, educational programs, [and] more jobs . . ." The numbers and rhetoric in Clinton's FY95 Budget and 1994 Strategy support Brown's description. But does this amount to a National Drug Control Strategy? Longtime observers are highly skeptical.

Six of nine funding priorities in the Strategy are for "treatment" or "prevention" of "hardcore addicts," with a 14.3 percent increase in resources for "drug treatment," 28 percent for "education and community action," and 5.3 percent for "research." By contrast, the Strategy seeks to *reduce* both drug interdiction and intelligence funding. Attorney General Reno's view notwithstanding, the Strategy states: "This reflects a dramatic shift in program emphasis in favor of treatment and prevention programs." And indeed, it does.

Demand reduction is important, but a "dramatic shift in program emphasis" to untested treatment programs and reduced international enforcement may not be the winning combination. How does Clinton's 1994 Strategy, directed as it is to "hardcore addicts," address the 1992 and 1993 jump in *casual* drug use? After all, "hardcore" addicts start as casual users. How does Clinton's 1994 Strategy compensate for 1993 cuts in supply reduction efforts, ONDCP, international assistance, and interdiction? And where, after all this hype about treatment, does one *find* successful treatment programs? Even if the "dramatic shift" were advisable, note some, what are the odds that Clinton's FY95 request will remain firm? Doubts abound. Here is why.

First, like ships in the dark, the President's 1994 Strategy blithely passes the 1992 and 1993 data evidencing widespread increases in casual use by America's youth. "Hardcore" addiction is, of course, important. But rising casual use is a genuine threat. Second, Clinton's idea of drug "prevention" is not what most Americans would expect. Consistent with Dr. Brown's interview, Clinton's Strategy urges—and defines as "drug prevention"—a shift of $568 million in drug-fighting resources to "Community Policing", or more police "back on the beat." While intriguing, many note that describing "community policing" as "drug prevention" places Community Policing at the mercy of the drug budget *and* misleads the public as to the Strategy's "prevention" component. Prevention, after all, has traditionally meant public education initiatives, not pennies on the dollar for broad police functions. Brown offers no elaboration.

Consistent again with Dr. Brown's interview, the 1994 Strategy places great emphasis on making voluntary treatment available, through "substance abuse provisions" of the President's (unpassed) national health care plan (the Health Security Act). The White House reasoning is as follows. "Although most people who need treatment do not actively seek it, if everyone who needs . . . treatment were to seek it this year, the treatment system could only serve about 60 percent." Thus, continues the Strategy, "the [President's national health] Act uses 30 days of inpatient coverage as the annual coverage base," and adds new outpatient availability with co-payments. Putting aside the merits of the health plan, will increased "availability" of treatment solve the nation's drug problem?

Private experts surveyed for this article say the best voluntary drug treatment programs boast a 25 or 30 percent success rate. While that could improve, the success of voluntary treatment presently rests on the discipline and perseverance of a reluctant addict. Dr. Herbert Kleber of the Center on Addiction and Substance Abuse at Columbia University, now partners with President Carter's former Secretary of H.H.S. Joseph Califano, says this is the Clinton strategy's real weakness. "The treatment offered under the President's Health Security Plan is totally inadequate, even for the kind of 'hardcore' addict that the President says he wants to reach. What is needed by the hard-core addict is just that type of treatment the President's Health Security Plan does not offer. . . . You cannot have just 30 inpatient days a year and 'x' number of out-patient days for which an addict must pay substantial co-payments, and expect results. You cannot do this and say, 'by the way, if you need any additional treat-

ment for mental illness, that will be taken away from your substance abuse allotment.' "

The 1994 Strategy's reliance on treatment is troubling for another reason. Kleber says: "The Health Plan cuts out the existing safety net, eliminates block grants that cover current drug treatment programs." In sum, the President's 1994 Strategy, which relies heavily on the substance abuse provisions, is empty. "The President talks a good game on treatment," says Kleber "but the health care reform proposal is a stupendous disappointment on substance abuse."

Where does this leave us? Dr. Kleber also Deputy ONDCP Director from 1989 to 1991, says that the President *has* an alternative. Even now, he could respond to the new data by refocusing the nation on the Drug War. "I would beg President Clinton, in the name of all of the millions of people who are suffering from this problem, please speak out to say firmly that this is a national scourge, to say clearly to our adolescents that he thinks this is a major problem, that he doesn't want them to use drugs, and that legalization would be a disaster." Judge Bonner agrees, adding that "treatment *must* not be oversold."

But even in the realm of "treatment," there are alternatives to the "increased availability" gambit. "Availability," if dependent on co-payments, is unlikely to reduce nationwide addiction. But the Treatment Outcome Prospective Study (TOPS) found, in 1988, that "legal pressure tends to keep people in treatment for longer periods, and this coercion does not interfere with treatment goals." More recently, the Bureau of Justice Statistics concluded that, "the criminal justice system has been shown to effectively influence individuals with drug problems to commit themselves to treatment." On the treatment side, the answer may therefore lie closer to legally coerced, instead of strictly voluntary, treatment. Toward this end, the Crime Bill considered by Congress contains experimental "drug courts" and "boot camps" for youth offenders, both initiatives that are promising and underfunded.

If the Drug War is to be won, this President *must* lead. He must arrest the slippage, and get the Federal effort back on course. New data on increased drug abuse foreshadows turbulence ahead. Even Clinton's U.S. Attorney for Washington, D.C., Eric Holder, who views Clinton's "shift in emphasis" with promise, nevertheless admits that "the biggest deficiency [in the Drug War] . . . is just the lack of resources." Gains made under Reagan and Bush are being lost. Our nation's flight path now depends on where this president takes us, and there is no time left for dosing at the controls.

TOWARD A POLICY ON DRUGS

Decriminalization? Legalization?

Elliott Currie

Elliott Currie is the author of the award-winning
Confronting Crime: An American Challenge.

One of the strongest implications of what we now know about the causes of endemic drug abuse is that the criminal-justice system's effect on the drug crisis will inevitably be limited. That shouldn't surprise us in the 1990s; it has, after all, been a central argument of drug research since the 1950s. Today, as the drug problem has worsened, the limits of the law are if anything even clearer. But that does not mean that the justice system has no role to play in a more effective strategy against drugs. Drugs will always be a "law-enforcement problem" in part, and the real job is to define what we want the police and the courts to accomplish.

We will never, for reasons that will shortly become clear, punish our way out of the drug crisis. We can, however, use the criminal-justice system, in small but significant ways, to improve the prospects of drug users who are now caught in an endless loop of court, jail, and street. And we can use law enforcement, in small but significant ways, to help strengthen the ability of drug-ridden communities to defend themselves against violence, fear, and demoralization. Today the criminal-justice system does very little of the first and not enough of the second. But doing these things well will require far-reaching changes in our priorities.

Above all, we will have to shift from an approach in which discouraging drug use through punishment and fear takes central place to one that emphasizes three very different principles: the reintegration of drug abusers into productive life, the reduction of harm, and the promotion of community safety.

This is a tall order, but, as we shall see, something similar is being practiced in many countries that suffer far less convulsing drug problems than we do. Their experience suggests that a different and more humane criminal-justice response to drugs is both possible and practical. Today, there is much debate about the role of the justice system in a rational drug policy—but for the most part, the debate is between those who would intensify the effort to control drugs through the courts and prisons and those who want to take drugs out of the orbit of the justice system altogether. I do not think that either approach takes sufficient account of the social realities of drug abuse; and both, consequently, exaggerate the role of regulatory policies in determining the shape and seriousness of the problem. But those are not the only alternatives. In between, there is a range of more promising strategies— what some Europeans call a "third way"—that is more attuned to those realities and more compatible with our democratic values.

One response to the failure of the drug war has been to call for more of what we've already done—even harsher sentences, still more money for jails and prisons—on the grounds that we have simply not provided enough resources to fight the war effectively. That position is shared by the Bush administration and many Democrats in Congress as well. But the strategy of upping the ante cannot work;

From *Dissent*, Winter 1993, pp. 65-71. Excerpted from "Rethinking Criminal Justice" from *Reckoning: Drugs, the Cities, and the American Future* by Elliott Currie. © 1993 by Elliott Currie. Reprinted by permission of Hill and Wang, a division of Farrar, Straus & Giroux, Inc.

and even to attempt it on a large scale would dramatically increase the social costs that an overreliance on punishment has already brought. We've seen that the effort to contain the drug problem through force and fear has already distorted our justice system in fundamental ways and caused a rippling of secondary costs throughout the society as a whole. Much more of this would alter the character of American society beyond recognition. And it would not solve the drug problem.

Why wouldn't more of the same do the job?

To understand why escalating the war on drugs would be unlikely to make much difference—short of efforts on a scale that would cause unprecedented social damage—we need to consider how the criminal-justice system is, in theory, *supposed* to work to reduce drug abuse and drug-related crime. Criminologists distinguish between two mechanisms by which punishment may decrease illegal behavior. One is "incapacitation," an unlovely term that simply means that locking people up will keep them—as long as they are behind bars—from engaging in the behavior we wish to suppress. The other is "deterrence," by which we mean either that people tempted to engage in the behavior will be persuaded otherwise by the threat of punishment ("general deterrence"), or that individuals, once punished, will be less likely to engage in the behavior again ("specific deterrence"). What makes the drug problem so resistant to even very heavy doses of criminalization is that neither mechanism works effectively for most drug offenders—particularly those most heavily involved in the drug subcultures of the street.

The main reason why incapacitation is unworkable as a strategy against drug offenders is that there are so many of them that a serious attempt to put them all—or even just the "hard core"—behind bars is unrealistic, even in the barest fiscal terms. This is obvious if we pause to recall the sheer number of people who use hard drugs in the United States. Consider the estimates of the number of people who have used drugs during the previous year provided annually by the NIDA (National Institute on Drug Abuse) Household Survey—which substantially *understates* the extent of hard-drug use. Even if we exclude the more than 20 million people who used marijuana in the past year, the number of hard-drug users is enormous: the survey estimates over six million cocaine users in 1991 (including over a million who used crack), about 700,000 heroin users,

and 5.7 million users of hallucinogens and inhalants. Even if we abandon the aim of imprisoning less serious hard-drug users, thus allowing the most conservative accounting of the costs of incapacitation, the problem remains staggering: by the lowest estimates, there are no fewer than two million hard-core abusers of cocaine and heroin alone.

If we take as a rough approximation that about 25 percent of America's prisoners are behind bars for drug offenses, that gives us roughly 300,000 drug offenders in prison at any given point—and this after several years of a hugely implemented war mainly directed at lower-level dealers and street drug users. We have seen what this flood of offenders has done to the nation's courts and prisons, but what is utterly sobering is that even this massive effort at repression has barely scratched the surface: according to the most optimistic estimate, we may at any point be incarcerating on drug-related charges about one-eighth of the country's hard-core cocaine and heroin abusers. And where drug addiction is truly endemic, the disparity is greater. By 1989 there were roughly 20,000 drug offenders on any given day in New York State's prisons, but there were an estimated 200,000 to 250,000 *heroin* addicts in New York City alone. To be sure, these figures obscure the fact that many prisoners behind bars for *non*drug offenses are also hard-core drug users; but the figures are skewed in the other direction by the large (if unknown) number of active drug dealers who are not themselves addicted.

Thus, though we cannot quantify these proportions with any precision, the basic point should be clear: the pool of *serious* addicts and active dealers is far, far larger than the numbers we now hold in prison—even in the midst of an unprecedented incarceration binge that has made us far and away the world's leader in imprisonment rates.

What would it mean to expand our prison capacity enough to put the *majority* of hard-core users and dealers behind bars for long terms? To triple the number of users and low-level dealers behind bars, even putting two drug offenders to a cell, would require about 300,000 new cells. At a conservative estimate of about $100,000 per cell, that means a $30 billion investment in construction alone. If we then assume an equally conservative estimate of about $25,000 in yearly operating costs per inmate, we add roughly $15 billion a year to our current costs. Yet this would leave the majority of drug dealers and hard-core addicts still on the streets and, of course, would do nothing to prevent new ones from emerging in otherwise unchanged communities to take the place of those behind bars.

It is not entirely clear, moreover, what that huge expenditure would, in fact, accomplish. For if the goal is to prevent the drug dealing and other crimes that addicts commit, the remedy may literally cost more than the disease. Although drug addicts do commit a great deal of crime, most of them are very minor ones, mainly petty theft and small-time drug dealing. This pattern has been best illuminated in the study of Harlem heroin addicts by Bruce Johnson and his co-workers. Most of the street addicts in this study were "primarily thieves and small-scale drug distributors who avoided serious crimes, like robbery, burglary, assault." The average income per nondrug crime among these addicts was $35. Even among the most criminally active group—what these researchers called "robber-dealers"—the annual income from crime amounted on average to only about $21,000, and for the great majority—about 70 percent—of less active addict-criminals, it ranged from $5,000 to $13,000. At the same time, the researchers estimated that the average cost per day of confining one addict in a New York City jail cell was roughly $100, or $37,000 a year. Putting these numbers together, Johnson and his co-workers came to the startling conclusion that it would cost considerably more to lock up all of Harlem's street addicts than to simply let them continue to "take care of business" on the street.

If we cannot expect much from intensified criminalization, would the legalization of hard drugs solve the drug crisis?

No: it would not. To understand why, we need to consider the claims for legalization's effects in the light of what we know about the roots and meanings of endemic drug abuse. First, however, we need to step back in order to sort out exactly what we *mean* by "legalization"—a frustratingly vague and often confused term that means very different things to different interpreters. Many, indeed, who argue most vehemently one way or the other about the merits of legalization are not really clear just what it is they are arguing *about*.

At one end of the spectrum are those who mean by legalization the total deregulation of the production, sale, and use of all drugs—hard and soft. Advocates of this position run the gamut from right-wing economists to some staunch liberals, united behind the principle that government has no business interfering in individuals' choice to ingest whatever substances they desire. Most who subscribe to that general view would add several qualifiers: for example, that drugs (like alcohol) should not be sold to minors, or that drug advertising should be regulated or prohibited, or (less often) that drugs should be sold only in government-run stores, as alcohol is in some states. But these are seen as necessary, if sometimes grudging, exceptions to the general rule that private drug transactions should not be the province of government intervention. For present purposes, I will call this the "free-market" approach to drug control, and describe its central aim as the "deregulation" of the drug market.

Another approach would not go so far as to deregulate the drug trade, but would opt for the controlled dispensation of drugs to addicts who have been certified by a physician, under strict guidelines as to amounts and conditions of use. Something like this "medical model," in varying forms, guided British policy toward heroin after the 1920s. Under the so-called British system, addicts could receive heroin from physicians or clinics—but the private production and distribution of heroin was always subject to strong penalties, as was the use of the drug except in its medical or "pharmaceutical" form. (A small-scale experiment in cocaine prescription is presently being tried in the city of Liverpool.) Since the seventies, the British have largely abandoned prescribing heroin in favor of methadone—a synthetic opiate that blocks the body's craving for heroin but, among other things, produces less of a pleasurable "high" and lasts considerably longer. The practice of dispensing methadone to heroin addicts came into wide use in the United States in the 1960s and remains a major form of treatment. Methadone prescription, of course, does not "legalize" heroin, and the possession or sale of methadone itself is highly illegal outside of the strictly controlled medical relationship.

Still another meaning sometimes given to legalization is what is more accurately called the "decriminalization" of drug *use*. We may continue to define the production and sale of certain drugs as crimes and subject them to heavy penalties, but not punish those who only *use* the drugs (or have small amounts in their possession), or punish them very lightly—with small fines, for example, rather than jail. Something close to this is the practice in Holland, which is often wrongly perceived as a country that has legalized drugs. Though drug use remains technically illegal, Dutch policy is to focus most law-enforcement resources on sales, especially on larger traffickers, while dealing with users mainly through treatment programs and other social services, rather than the police and courts.

Another aspect of Dutch policy illustrates a further possible meaning of legalization: we may selectively decriminalize *some* drugs, in some amounts, and not others. The Dutch, in practice—though not in law—have tolerated both sale and use of small amounts of marijuana and hashish, but not heroin or cocaine. A German court has recently ruled that possession of small amounts of hashish and marijuana is not a crime, and, indeed, marijuana possession has largely been decriminalized in some American states, though usually as a matter of practical policy rather than legislation.

Let me make my own view clear. I think much would be gained if we followed the example of some European countries and moved toward decriminalization of the drug user. I also think there is a strong argument for treating marijuana differently from the harder drugs, and that there is room for careful experiment with strictly controlled medical prescription for some addicts. For reasons that will become clear, decriminalization is not a panacea; it will not end the drug crisis, but it could substantially decrease the irrationality and inhumanity of our present punitive war on drugs.

The free-market approach, on the other hand, is another matter entirely. Some variant of that approach is more prominent in drug-policy debates in the United States than in other developed societies, probably because it meshes with a strongly individualistic and antigovernment political culture. Indeed, the degree to which the debate over drug policy has been dominated by the clash between fervent drug "warriors" and equally ardent free-market advocates is a peculiarly American phenomenon. Much of that clash is about philosophical principles, and addressing those issues in detail would take more space than we have. My aim here is simply to examine the empirical claims of the free-market perspective

in the light of what we know about the social context of drug abuse. Here the free-market view fails to convince. It greatly exaggerates the benefits of deregulation while simultaneously underestimating the potential costs.

There is no question that the criminalization of drugs produces negative secondary consequences—especially in the unusually punitive form that criminalization has taken in the United States. Nor is there much question that this argues for a root-and-branch rethinking of our current punitive strategy—to which we'll return later in this essay—especially our approach to drug *users*.

But proponents of full-scale deregulation of hard drugs also tend to gloss over the very real primary costs of drug abuse—particularly on the American level—and to exaggerate the degree to which the multiple pathologies surrounding drug use in America are simply an unintended result of a "prohibitionist" regulatory policy. No country now legalizes the sale of hard drugs. Yet no other country has anything resembling the American drug problem. That alone should tell us that more than prohibition is involved in shaping the magnitude and severity of our drug crisis. But there is more technical evidence as well. It confirms that much (though, of course, not all) of the harm caused by endemic drug abuse is intrinsic to the impact of hard drugs themselves (and the street cultures in which drug abuse is embedded) within the context of a glaringly unequal, depriving, and deteriorating society. And it affirms that we will not substantially reduce that harm without attacking the social roots of the extraordinary demand for hard drugs in the United States. Just as we cannot punish our way out of the drug crisis, neither will we escape its grim toll by deregulating the drug market.

The most important argument for a free-market approach has traditionally been that it would reduce or eliminate the crime and violence now inextricably entwined with addiction to drugs and with the drug trade. In this view it is precisely the illegality of drug use that is responsible for drug-related crime—which, in turn, is seen as by far the largest part of the overall problem of urban violence. Criminal sanctions against drugs, as one observer insists, "cause the bulk of murders and property crime in major urban areas." Because criminalization makes drugs far more costly than they would otherwise be, addicts are forced to commit crimes in order to gain enough income to afford their habits. Moreover, they are forced to seek out actively criminal people in order to obtain their drugs, which exposes them to even more destructive criminal influences. At the same time, the fact that the drug trade is illegal means both that it is hugely profitable and that the inevitable conflicts and disputes over "turf" or between dealers and users cannot be resolved or moderated by legal mechanisms, and hence are usually resolved by violence.

For all of these reasons, it is argued, outlawing drugs has the unintended, but inevitable, effect of causing a flood of crime and urban violence that would not exist otherwise and sucking young people, especially, into a bloody drug trade. If we legalize the sale and use of hard drugs, the roots of drug-related violence would be severed, and much of the larger crisis of criminal violence in the cities would disappear.

But the evidence suggests that although this view contains an element of truth, it is far too simplistic—and that it relies on stereotypical assumptions about the relationship between drugs and crime that have been called into serious question since the classic drug research of the 1950s. In particular, the widely held notion that most of the crime committed by addicts can be explained by their need for money to buy illegal drugs does not fit well with the evidence.

In its popular form, the drugs-cause-crime argument is implicitly based on the assumption that addict crime is caused by pharmacological compulsion—as a recent British study puts it, on a kind of "enslavement" model in which the uncontrollable craving for drugs forces an otherwise law-abiding citizen to engage in crime for gain. As we've seen, however, a key finding of most of the research into the meaning of drug use and the growth of drug subcultures since the 1950s has been that the purely pharmacological craving for drugs is by no means the most important motive for drug use. Nor is it clear that those cravings are typically so uncontrollable that addicts are in any meaningful sense "driven" to crime to satisfy them.

On the surface, there is much to suggest a strong link between crime and the imperatives of addiction. The studies of addict crime by John Ball and Douglas Anglin and their colleagues show not only that the most heavily addicted commit huge numbers of crimes, but also that

their crime rates seem to increase when their heroin use increases and to fall when it declines. Thus, for example, heroin addicts in Ball's study in Baltimore had an average of 255 "crime days" per year when they were actively addicted, versus about 65 when they were not. In general, the level of property crime appears in these studies to go up simultaneously with increasing intensity of drug use. One explanation, and perhaps the most common one, is that the increased need for money to buy drugs drives addicts into more crime.

But a closer look shows that things are considerably more complicated. To begin with, it is a recurrent finding that most people who both abuse drugs and commit crimes began committing the crimes *before* they began using drugs—meaning that their need for drugs cannot have caused their initial criminal involvement (though it may have accelerated it later). George Vaillant's follow-up study of addicts and alcoholics found, for example, that, unlike alcoholics, heroin addicts had typically been involved in delinquency and crime well before they began their career of substance abuse. While alcoholics seemed to become involved in crime as a *result* of their abuse of alcohol, more than half of the heroin addicts (versus just 5 percent of the alcoholics) "were known to have been delinquent *before* drug abuse." A federal survey of drug use among prison inmates in 1986, similarly, found that three-fifths of those who had ever used a "major drug" regularly—that is, heroin, cocaine, methadone, PCP, or LSD—had not done so until after their first arrest.

Other studies have found that for many addicts, drug use and crime seem to have begun more or less *independently* without one clearly causing the other. This was the finding, for example, in Charles Faupel and Carl Klockars's study of hard-core heroin addicts in Wilmington, Delaware. "All of our respondents," they note, "reported some criminal activity prior to their first use of heroin." Moreover, "perhaps most importantly, virtually all of our respondents reported that they believed that their criminal and drug careers began independently of one another, although both careers became intimately interconnected as each evolved."

More recent research shows that the drugs-crime relationship may be even more complex than this suggests. It is not only that crime may precede drug use, especially heavy or addictive use, or that both may emerge more or less independently; it is also likely that there are several *different* kinds of drugs-crime connections among different types of drug users. David Nurco of the University of Maryland and his colleagues, for example, studying heroin addicts in Baltimore and New York City, found that nine different kinds of addicts could be distinguished by the type and severity of their crimes. Like earlier researchers, they found that most addicts committed large numbers of crimes—mainly drug dealing and small-scale property crime, notably shoplifting, burglary, and fencing. Others were involved in illegal gambling and what the researchers called "deception crimes"—including forgery and con games—and a relatively small percentage had engaged in violent crime. On the whole, addicts heavily involved in one type of crime were not likely to be involved in others; as the researchers put it, they tended to be either "dealers or stealers," but rarely both. About 6 percent of the addicts, moreover, were "uninvolved"—they did not commit crimes either while addicted or before, or during periods of nonaddiction interspersed in the course of their longer addiction careers.

The most troubling group of addicts—what the researchers called "violent generalists"—were only about 7 percent of the total sample, but they were extremely active—and very dangerous; they accounted for over half of all the violent crimes committed by the entire sample. Moreover, revealingly, the violent generalists were very active in serious crime *before* they became addicted to narcotics as well as during periods of nonaddiction thereafter—again demonstrating that the violence was not dependent on their addiction itself. Nurco and his colleagues measured the addicts' criminal activity by what they called "crime days" per year. Addicts were asked how many days they had committed each of several types of crime; since on any given day they might have committed more than one type of crime, the resulting figure could add up to more than the number of days in the year. The violent generalists averaged an astonishing 900 crime days a year over the course of their careers. The rates were highest during periods when they were heavily addicted to drugs. But even *before* they were addicted, they averaged 573 crime days, and 491 after their addiction had ended. Indeed, the most active group of violent generalists engaged in more crime *prior* to addiction than any other group did *while* addicted. And they continued to commit crimes—often violent ones—long after they had ceased to be addicted to narcotics.

None of this is to deny that serious addiction to heroin or other illegal drugs can accelerate the level of crime among participants in the drug culture, or stimulate crime even in some users who are otherwise not criminal. Higher levels of drug use *do* go hand in hand with increased crime, especially property crime. Certainly, many addicts mug, steal, or sell their bodies for drugs. The point is that—as the early drug researchers discovered in the 1950s—both crime and drug abuse tend to be spawned by the same set of unfavorable social circumstances, and they interact with one another in much more complex ways than the simple addiction-leads-to-crime view proposes. Simply providing drugs more easily to people enmeshed in the drug cultures of the cities is not likely to cut the deep social roots of addict crime.

If we take the harms of drug abuse seriously, and I think we must, we cannot avoid being deeply concerned about anything that would significantly increase the availability of hard drugs within the American social context; and no one seriously doubts that legalization would indeed increase availability, and probably lower prices for many drugs. In turn, increased availability—as we know from the experience with alcohol—typically leads to increased consumption, and with it increased social and public-health costs. A growing body of research, for example, shows that most alcohol-related health problems, including deaths from cirrhosis and other diseases, were far lower during Prohibition than afterward, when per capita alcohol consumption rose dramatically (by about 75 percent, for example, between 1950 and 1980). It is difficult to imagine why a similar rise in consumption—and in the associated public-health problems—would not follow the full-scale legalization of cocaine, heroin, methamphetamine, and PCP (not to mention the array of as yet undiscovered "designer" drugs that a legalized corporate drug industry would be certain to develop).

If consumption increased, it would almost certainly increase most among the strata already most vulnerable to hard-drug use—thus exacerbating the social stratification of the drug crisis. It is among the poor and near-poor that offsetting measures like education and drug treatment are least effective and where the countervailing social supports and opportunities are least strong. We would expect, therefore, that a free-market policy applied to hard drugs would produce the same results it has created with the *legal* killer drugs, tobacco and alcohol—namely, a widening disparity in use between the better-off and the disadvantaged. And that disparity is already stunning. According to a recent study by Colin McCord and Howard Freeman of Harlem Hospital, between 1979 and 1981—that is, *before* the crack epidemic of the eighties—Harlem blacks were 283 times as likely to die of drug dependency as whites in the general population. Drug deaths, combined with deaths from cirrhosis, alcoholism, cardiovascular disease, and homicide, helped to give black men in Harlem a shorter life expectancy than men in Bangladesh. That is the social reality that the rather abstract calls for the legalization of hard-drug sales tend to ignore.

Military's Counterdrug Policy Restructured

Phil Gunby

DEFENSE DEPARTMENT officials are making changes in the military's 5-year war on drugs.

For one thing, there probably will be fewer mentions of its being a war.

Brian E. Sheridan, deputy assistant secretary of defense for drug enforcement policy and support, says the term *drug war* (since the Department of Defense was drafted into the counterdrug effort in 1989) has implied misleadingly that battle lines are clearly drawn and a day of victory can be predicted.

His first year in this assignment, he says, has taught him the importance of recognizing that illicit drug use is a deepseated social problem to be addressed by many agencies in a variety of ways and over the long term.

Supporting Role Suggested

In that regard, the Clinton administration has announced a 1994 National Drug Control Strategy, indicating that numerous agencies should cooperate to attack the drug problem simultaneously in various ways. Sheridan says the Department of Defense has a supporting role to play in that effort.

In response to the administration's strategy and the findings of an internal Pentagon review, Sheridan says, the Department of Defense has been refocusing its policy in the 1994 federal bookkeeping year. Its five "strategic elements," he says, include the following:

• Increased support to nations demonstrating the political will to combat "narcotrafficking."

• Bringing military intelligence capabilities to antidrug efforts, including those of the Drug Enforcement Agency, against the cartels.

• Detecting and monitoring illegal drug transport.

• Supporting domestic law-enforcement agencies, particularly in high-intensity drug-trafficking areas.

• Continuing the military's drug testing and education programs (*JAMA*. 1989;261:2784-2785, 2788) and initiating programs using military people as role models for at-risk youth.

Reduced Budget

When the Department of Defense moved into the counterdrug arena in 1989, its budget for the effort was $380 million. By last year, this had risen to $1.14 billion.

This year, the department's counterdrug budget was reduced to $868 million, putting an end to 24 of its 170 projects. The budget proposed for the 1995 fiscal year would be slightly more, that is, around $874 million (7% of the proposed federal counterdrug budget), and the department plans to conduct ongoing effectiveness reviews of its programs.

In the past year, the department says, its efforts resulted in seizure of more than 100 metric tons of cocaine. Still, it's estimated, more than three times as much coca is being produced as is needed to meet the demands of up to 2.7 million US long-term users, and no significant reduction is foreseen in the near future.

Since 1989, the Department of Defense—while not directly making arrests or directly seizing illegal drugs—has had the lead role in detecting and monitoring aerial and maritime transportation of drugs; has integrated communications, tactical intelligence, and other efforts of federal agencies; and has approved and funded National Guard antidrug support efforts in the states and territories. Still, it's conceded, the department considers the current flow of illegal drugs into the United States to be a national security threat, with cocaine representing the greatest problem, and the increasing supply and purity of heroin becoming an increasingly serious concern.

The department now is consulting with other federal agencies on the heroin situation. The resulting recommendations are expected to be submitted to the president later this year.

The Five Strategic Elements

The source-nation support aspect of the Department of Defense's five strategic elements is focusing its supporting efforts through planned antidrug training of national police and military units in Bolivia, Peru, and Colombia (where the Constitutional Court in Bogotá decided last month that personal use of small amounts of cocaine, hashish, and marijuana is protected by Colombia's constitution). Human rights will be emphasized, the department says.

The second element, dismantling the cartels, involves expanded intelligence gathering and sharing, while the third (detecting and monitoring) will see replacement of some of the more expensive use of US military aircraft and ships to find, track, and intercept drug smugglers with such approaches as relocatable over-the-horizon radar surveillance. A recent newspaper report alleges that some pilots smuggling drugs from Colombia avoided detection by the sophisticated radars of AWACS (Airborne Warning and Control System) aircraft—a US military version of the Boeing 707 jetliner—by, among other approaches, purchasing the AWACS planes' flight schedules from a nonmilitary US government employee (*Wall Street J.* May 9, 1994:A1, A6).

Support of domestic law enforcement, the fourth element, emphasizes efforts in such critical areas as the nation's southwestern border, including possible cargo-container inspection systems using new imaging techniques, providing excess equipment to state police, and funding state or territorial National Guard efforts.

The fifth element, drug demand reduction, involves community outreach. Recommendations are expected to reach Congress this fall.

While the Department of Defense has no means of ending the illegal drug problem quickly, Sheridan says, it does have unique talents and assets to bring to the interagency counterdrug effort. Moreover, he suggests, strategic planning and increased dialogue with other federal agencies and Congress can result in "reasonable expectations" for the department's varied counterdrug programs.

From *JAMA: The Journal of the American Medical Association*, June 1, 1994, pp. 1639-1641. © 1994 by the American Medical Association. Reprinted by permission.

For Addicts, Alternatives to Prison

Some Hail Treatment Approach; Others Think It's Too Soft

James Dao

For Eduardo Rufino, jail was less a place to do penance than to learn from experts about the tawdry urban science of peddling drugs.

So when he emerged from Rikers Island eight years ago after serving time for a purse snatching, he started to sell, then use, crack and heroin, developing addictions so fierce that he lost tract of time, people and money.

In 1992, struggling to feed both habits, he sold heroin to an undercover police officer in Borough Park, Brooklyn, then served 45 days in jail, later returned to the same corner and was arrested by the same officer just months later.

Mr. Rufino might seem one among the minions of low-level drug dealers swept up annually by "buy and bust" operations in New York City. But his case stands out for one reason: after the second arrest, the Brooklyn District Attorney's office told him that instead of serving two to four years in prison, he could enroll in a two-year drug-treatment program. And if he completed it, they would dismiss his charges.

Whether the deal offered Mr. Rufino represents the state penal system at its best or a society gone hopelessly soft has become central to a debate in state capitals around the country over how to cope with a flood of nonviolent, drug-addicted criminals who are crowding prisons.

Opposite Direction

At a time when the Federal Government and many state legislatures are considering measures to keep repeat offenders in prison longer, the Brooklyn program represents a small but firm tug in the opposite direction: toward keeping them outside prison's wire-laced walls altogether.

Proponents, including many prosecutors and advocates for sentencing reform, say the program, known as Drug Treatment Alternatives to Prison, keeps scarce prison cells available for the most violent criminals, saves money by diverting nonviolent criminals into less costly treatment programs, and cuts crime rates in the long run by reducing addictions.

But what has caught the eye of Federal criminal-justice officials and prosecutors in New York and other states has been the program's ability to get recalcitrant drug abusers to stay longer in rigorous drug treatment, which according to many experts is central to ending their addictions. By some statistics, addicts in Drug Treatment Alternatives are two to three times more likely to stay in treatment than noncriminal drug users in similar treatment programs, though the prospect of more prison time is a strong incentive to stay in the program.

"There's no question that D.T.A.P.'s retention rate is extraordinary," said Douglas Young, a senior research as-

sociate with the Vera Institute of Justice in New York City, who is studying the Brooklyn program on a grant from the Federal Department of Justice.

Built on a Paradox

Just why is not entirely clear. But prosecutors who run the programs say they are built on a paradox. Intended to circumvent mandatory sentencing laws for repeat offenders, Drug Treatment Alternatives programs use the threat of prison to cajole addicts into treatment they might never have sought by themselves.

And once in treatment, they are pressured to stay because quitters will be returned to court—tracked down by special teams if necessary—where they will face prison sentences.

"The longer an individual stays in a program, the better their chances of remaining drug-free," said Richard H. Girgenti, the state's Director of Criminal Justice, who has monitored the New York programs. "We have the advantage of being able to use the coercive power of the criminal-justice system to get people to stay."

The Brooklyn program was started by District Attorney Charles J. Hynes in 1990. Similar programs have since been initiated by the New York City Office of Special Narcotics and the district attorneys of Manhattan and

Onondaga Counties. A Queens program has been suspended because of a court ruling saying that it lacked authority to defer sentences; legislation has been proposed to give it that authority. The ruling did not affect the other programs.

Though the programs differ slightly, all are geared toward drug addicts with no records of violent crime who face mandatory prison sentences for second felony offenses. Most are low-level drug dealers who peddle their wares to feed their own habits.

New York's repeat-offender laws, considered among the least flexible in the country are viewed as a major reason why the state's prison system which now houses 64,000 inmates, is 29 percent over capacity. Last year, more than a third of the state's 24,834 new prisoners were nonviolent criminals sentenced under those laws, according to the Correctional Association of New York.

'I may have been arrested, but I was really rescued,' an ex-inmate says.

For Mr. Rufino, 26, the program initially seemed like another way to beat the system. "I thought, I'm going to a country club," recalled Mr. Rufino, his teeth glistening with gold caps initialed with the letter K for his nickname, Kiki.

Thoughts of Quitting

But the first months of treatment at a Samaritan Village residential center in upstate New York were grueling, he said, and made him think repeatedly of quitting. He did not, fearing a return to prison; today he is two months from graduating from the program and is training to become a drug counselor.

"Now I think I may have been arrested, but I was really rescued," he said.

Alfred Issacs of Brooklyn, a college graduate, never gave serious thought to enrolling himself in a drug treatment program, even after he lost two jobs and descended into street-level dealing to finance a $100-a-day crack habit. But when a prosecutor offered him the choice of four years in prison or two years at a Daytop treatment center, the choice was obvious.

"I figured they'd be at my door, ready to put me into prison, and that was motivation enough to stay with it," Mr. Issacs, 36, said.

Of the 396 people who have entered the Brooklyn program since 1990, 144 are still in treatment, 82 have completed treatment and had their charges dismissed and 170 have dropped out, Mr. Hynes's office reported. Of the last group, all but about five have been returned to court.

Comparable statistics are not yet available for the other programs because of their newness. But the prosecutors who run those programs called them successful and said they could place more defendants in treatment if the beds were available. It is also not known how many people in the Brooklyn program stay drug-free over the long term.

Last year, the state paid for 300 treatment beds for criminals referred by those prosecutors. Last week, the State Legislature voted to create 450 new treatment beds, some of which will go to Drug Treatment Alternatives programs.

For elected officials, the program's most enticing aspect is its promise to save tax dollars in two ways. First treatment programs cost less than incarceration: $16,000 per year for one treatment bed, compared with $25,000 a year to maintain one prison bed. And second, by reducing prison crowding, the programs allow the state to avoid new prison construction, which costs $100,000 per cell.

'Turning Around'

"If you send them to prison for three or four years, they come out more

hard-bitten and less trainable for jobs," said William F. Dowling, an assistant district attorney in Onondaga County, which includes Syracuse. "Here you're turning around this vicious cycle of crime and addiction."

But at a time when crime is high on many voters' lists, the idea of releasing repeat drug offenders into treatment makes many lawmakers squeamish, particularly when it seems to involve weakening tough sentencing laws.

"These are not the innocent drug addicts they are made to seem," said John A. McArdle, a spokesman for State Senate majority leader, Ralph J. Marino, an Oyster Bay Republican. "If you're going to sink new spending into this area, we ought to deal with additional prison bed space."

Critics also say the program sends two drastically wrong messages: that scarce treatment beds will be made available to criminals while law-abiding addicts languish on waiting lists and that the state rewards instead of punishes repeat offenders.

A Second Chance

But for Raymond Nelson, 39, the program provided a second chance. When he was arrested on drug charges in East New York, Brooklyn, in 1992, he was facing 7 1/2 to 15 years in prison and the likelihood he would not see his four daughters grow up.

Now he is two months from graduating from a treatment program at Samaritan Village, has earned his high school equivalency diploma and is in training to become a counselor. He sees his four children almost every weekend.

"If I had spent 10 years in prison, it would have been more reason to come out and try to sell enough drugs to get a Lexus," he said. "You come out of jail thinking only about catching up. Now I've got my family. I'm not an outcast."

Teenage Smoking: Fact and Fiction

J. Howard Beales

J. Howard Beales is an associate professor of strategic management and public policy at George Washington University. The statistical analysis reflected in this article was largely conducted in connection with a consulting project for R. J. Reynolds Tobacco Company to analyze several articles, concerning the relationship between Camel advertising and teenage smoking, that originally appeared in the Journal of the American Medical Association. *This article was drafted independently and was not reviewed by Reynolds.*

Teenage smoking provokes controversy and continuing policy proposals to "do something" about a phenomenon that all would prefer did not exist. From the rhetoric surrounding the issue, a casual observer would likely conclude that teen smoking was either a recent problem or a rapidly increasing one. Neither perception is correct, despite recent reports of an increase in smoking among high school students. Although teenage smoking remains a concern, the facts suggest that the long-standing policy of educating teens as well as adults about the risks of smoking is working and is resulting in significant declines in smoking.

The Extent of Teenage Smoking

The most recent large-scale national study of teenage smoking available is the Teenage Attitudes and Practices Survey (TAPS), conducted by the Centers for Disease Control in 1989. The survey reveals that just over two-thirds of 11- to 17-year-old teens—who cannot legally smoke in most states—have not smoked even one whole cigarette. Even among 17-year-olds, a majority have not yet smoked a cigarette.

Teens who have experimented with cigarettes are considered smokers by the standard government definition if they have smoked one cigarette in the previous 30 days. By that definition, 13 percent of 11- to 17-year-olds were smokers. As shown in Figure 1, there are significant differences between younger and older teens. Although only 1 percent of 11-year-olds have smoked in the previous 30 days, 24 percent of 17-year-olds have done so, as have 31 percent of 18- and 19-year-olds. Thus, most teenage smokers are older teens. Fur-

thermore, most teenage smokers are social smokers, who smoke only occasionally, rather than daily smokers. Although some 60 percent of young adult (18- to 24-year-old) smokers are daily smokers, only about a third of teenage smokers smoke daily.

The standard definition of a teenage smoker as someone who has smoked one cigarette in the previous 30 days lumps together teens who are serious smokers and those who are recent experimenters. In fact, 27 percent of the teens defined as smokers used cigarettes on 4 or fewer days during the previous month. Obviously, some teens that researchers classify as smokers do not consider themselves smokers and do not smoke to any significant extent.

Among adults, researchers generally avoid the problem by asking whether respondents consider themselves smokers. The effect of the difference in definitions is to overstate teenage smoking relative to adult smoking. Indeed, about 22 percent of young adults in California (where such a comparison was made) who would be considered smokers under the definition used for teens are not smokers under the standard adult definition.

Appreciating the difference between having tried a cigarette and being a smoker is necessary in order to understand the age at which teens begin to smoke. Among 11- to 17-year-old teens who have smoked a cigarette, the median age of the first cigarette was 13. This median age is undoubtedly lower than it would have been if all teenagers had been questioned. Moreover, most teens have never smoked a cigarette. Thus, only about 18 percent of 11- to 17-year-olds have tried a cigarette by age 13. Additionally, many, and perhaps most, of those who try a cigarette will never become regular smokers. A California study found that among young adults (ages 18–24), a majority of those who have tried cigarettes have *never* smoked regularly. Even among those who have at one time been regular smokers, the median age at which they first smoked regularly was 16.

Trends

Few reliable statistics are available to track the incidence of teen smoking over time. Government studies of teens as a group have been sporadic. The most consistent data available are from an annual survey of high school seniors conducted by researchers at the University of Michigan since 1975.

As Figure 2 shows, cigarette use among high school seniors peaked in 1976. Whether measured as smoking in the past 30 days, daily smoking, or smoking half a pack a day, smoking had declined 20 to 25 percent from that peak by 1980. Since then, the decline in smoking has been less rapid. Moreover, all three measures show an increase in 1993.

If one examines the incidence of smoking in the previous 30 days, teenage smoking since 1980 has been roughly constant, with a slight downward drift through 1992. Counting those who have smoked in the previous 30 days, however, measures both real smokers and teens who have recently experimented with cigarettes, perhaps for the first time. Indeed, success in encouraging younger teens to delay experimenting with cigarettes could actually increase the incidence of recent smoking among high school seniors. Measures of the incidence of daily smoking and smoking half a pack a day are less prone to this problem. These measures, which fell about 25 percent between 1976 and 1980, showed continued declines throughout the 1980s. By 1993, daily smoking was down 11 percent from 1980, and smoking half a pack a day was down 24 percent. Thus, measures of significant cigarette use show continued declines, albeit at a less rapid rate than during the later 1970s. The fraction of high school seniors who have ever smoked even one cigarette, which declined only 6 percent by 1980, also continued to decline, falling an additional 13 percent by 1992.

Some have argued that the apparent increases in smoking in 1993 mark the beginning of a new and worrisome trend. Although definitive answers must await additional surveys in the next few years, it seems more likely that the 1993 results simply reflect chance variations from year to year. The increases, after all, were from the lowest levels of smoking that the survey had ever recorded. The fraction of high school seniors who have ever smoked a cigarette was virtually unchanged, increasing by only a tenth of a percentage point. Moreover, preliminary data from a 1993 follow-up of the earlier TAPS study indicate that smoking by 15- to 17-year-old teens had declined. Certainly, the 1993 uptick provides no basis for aggressive new policies aimed at teenage smoking.

To the extent that the smoking increases are real, they appear to reflect an increased willingness of teens to engage in a variety of risky behaviors. Indeed, the survey found substantially larger increases in the use of illegal drugs, particularly marijuana (up 30 percent based on use in the past 30 days) and hallucinogens (up 28 percent), than in the use of cigarettes (up 7.6 percent).

Why Do Teens Smoke?

Many discussions of public policy toward teenage smoking presume that teenage smoking decisions are fundamentally irrational. Implicitly or explicitly, teenage smokers are treated as the passive victims of social forces compelling them to smoke, forces that are utterly beyond their control. In sharp contrast, careful statistical analysis of actual smoking behavior indicates that teenagers' decisions are, in an economic sense, rational: teens assess the expected benefits and costs of smoking and make their decisions accordingly.

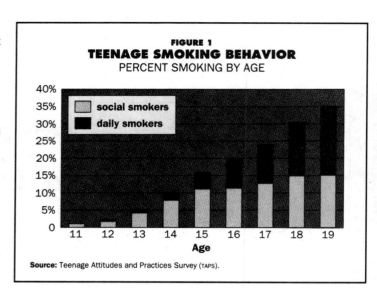

FIGURE 1
TEENAGE SMOKING BEHAVIOR
PERCENT SMOKING BY AGE

Source: Teenage Attitudes and Practices Survey (TAPS).

Using data on the characteristics of teens who smoke at different levels of intensity (for example, daily smokers versus occasional smokers versus those who have tried cigarettes but are not current smokers), statistical analysis can disentangle the various influences on teenage smoking decisions. Essentially, the statistical analysis determines which factors best account for the observed smoking behavior of teens.

Three sets of factors are important influences on teenage smoking. Most important is the behavior of their peers. Teens whose friends are smokers are significantly more likely to be smokers themselves. Second, teen perceptions of the risks of smoking, along with perceptions of benefits such as helping to relax or combat stress, are important determinants of behavior. Finally, the presence of smokers in teen households influences smoking decisions.

One way to compare the relative importance of different influences on the smoking decision is to determine the likelihood that a teen with a particular set of characteristics will have smoked in the previous 30 days. As a base case, consider a 15-year-old from a family of average income who is white,

non-Hispanic, and goes out two or three nights per week for recreation. Like most teens, this baseline teen has uniformly negative attitudes about smoking—he or she thinks that even an occasional cigarette is harmful, that smoking for a year or two is dangerous, and that smoking offers no benefits. None of his or her family members or friends are smokers. For this hypothetical teen, the likelihood of smoking is 1.85 percent. That is, just under 2 percent of teens with these characteristics should be smokers. (For comparison, about 16 percent of 15-year-olds in the sample actually were smokers.) We can then assess the importance of changing any of these factors by determining the change in the likelihood of smoking compared to this baseline teen. If, for example, a particular factor doubles the base probability of smoking to 3.7 percent, the relative odds for that factor would be 2.

The influence of different aspects of peer behavior is depicted in Figure 3. The single most important factor in a teen's decision to smoke is the behavior of his or her best friends of the same sex. A female teen whose best female friends all smoke is nearly six times as likely to smoke as

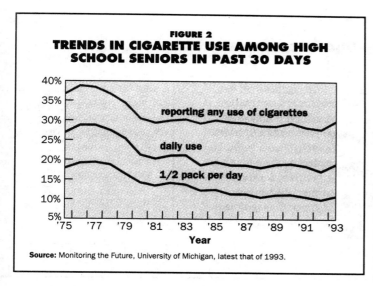

FIGURE 2
TRENDS IN CIGARETTE USE AMONG HIGH SCHOOL SENIORS IN PAST 30 DAYS

reporting any use of cigarettes

daily use

1/2 pack per day

Year

Source: Monitoring the Future, University of Michigan, latest that of 1993.

our baseline teen with no smoking friends. The effect is even greater for boys than for girls: a male teen whose best friends all smoke is nearly eight times as likely to smoke. Indeed, the influence of same-sex peers is greater than the combined influence of having all best friends of the opposite sex smoke and having a steady boyfriend or girlfriend who smokes. Smoking by best friends of the opposite sex also matters, but it is less influential than the behavior of same-sex peers. A teen whose best friends of the opposite sex all smoke (but with no smoking best friends of the same sex) is only about 70 percent more likely to smoke. A teen with a steady boyfriend or girlfriend who is a smoker is just over twice as likely to smoke. Finally, a teen who says that most of his or her acquaintances (as opposed to best friends) smoke is about 80 percent more likely to smoke.

There are at least three possible explanations for the significance of peer behavior in determining teenage smoking decisions. First, teens may benefit socially from behavior that is similar to the behavior of their friends. Teens may per-

ceive being part of a group as a benefit of smoking. Second, smoking is to some extent a social habit; it may simply be more pleasurable to smoke with others than to smoke alone. Finally, smoking among friends may effectively reduce the cost of smoking, because cigarettes are more readily available than they are to teens with no friends who smoke.

The second set of factors influencing teenage smoking decisions is the individual teen's perceptions of the benefits and risks of smoking, as depicted in Figure 4. It is these factors that provide some of the strongest evidence that teenage smoking decisions are rational. Rational teens would be more likely to smoke if they thought the benefits of smoking were greater, and less likely to smoke if they thought the risks were higher. Moreover, rational teens who dislike risk would be less likely to smoke. Actual teens behave in this fashion.

Teens were asked whether smoking helps when bored, whether it helps to relax, whether it helps deal with stress, and whether it helps to feel better in social situations. Teens who agree with all four measures are three times more likely to smoke than teens who do not. The only perceived

benefit that is not individually important is the social benefit of smoking. Apparently, actual behavior of friends is a better measure of the social benefit of smoking than survey questions.

Teens' opinions about the hazards of smoking also influence smoking decisions. Researchers, however, have seldom tried to determine teens' opinions of the actual magnitude of the risk of smoking. Surveys that try to do so have found that teens substantially overestimate the risk of smoking. More commonly, researchers ask teens whether an occasional cigarette is safe, and whether it is safe to smoke for a year or two. Although the "correct" answer to both questions is probably yes, two-thirds of teens think that even an occasional cigarette is harmful, and only 7 percent think that smoking for a year or two is safe.

Those who think it is safe to smoke an occasional cigarette are about 60 percent more likely to smoke. Teens who also think it is safe to smoke for a year or two are just over three times more likely to smoke. For teens who think that smoking is dangerous, attitudes about the ease of quitting are important. Teens who say they could quit any time they want to are almost twice as likely to smoke as teens who think they could not quit. Thus teens consider both risk and the difficulty of quitting in making decisions about smoking.

As one would expect, general attitudes toward risk are also important factors in predicting smoking behavior. Teens who report that they enjoy risky activities are 28 percent more likely to smoke than teens who are neutral about risk, and 63 percent more likely to smoke than teens who dislike risky activities.

The third set of influences on teenage smoking decisions encompasses the smoking be-

havior of other family members. As depicted in Figure 5, the most influential family members are older siblings. As with friends, same-sex siblings are more important than siblings of the opposite sex. An older, same-sex sibling who smokes more than doubles the likelihood of smoking, while opposite-sex siblings are less influential. Younger siblings who smoke have no significant influence on smoking decisions.

The presence of adult smokers in the household also increases the likelihood that a teen will choose to smoke. Interestingly, however, the most influential adults are not parents. Instead, other adults— parents' partners or adult relatives—are more influential. Indeed, to the extent that teenage smoking reflects imitation of an adult role model, it appears that teens look to someone other than their parents as the model. If both parents are smokers, teens are slightly more likely to smoke, but the effect is not large enough to distinguish from simple chance. Indeed, the presence or absence of parents is more influential than their smoking behavior. Teens from households where one parent is not present are significantly more likely to smoke.

Advertising's Effect

Undoubtedly, the potential influence on teenage smoking that has most concerned policymakers is the role of advertising. Antismoking activists, congressmen, and the surgeon general have all argued for restrictions of one sort or another on the ability of the cigarette industry to tell consumers about its product, in the belief that the imagery accompanying such communications will lead vulnerable teens to take up smoking. From an economic perspective, however, the critical question is

7. EFFECTIVE DRUG CONTROL POLICY

FIGURES 3, 4 & 5
THE EFFECTS OF VARIOUS INFLUENCES ON THE LIKELIHOOD OF SMOKING
(11- TO 19-YEAR-OLDS)

The figures show the odds that a teenager with a particular characteristic is a current smoker. The odds are based on a comparison to a hypothetical 15-year-old white non-Hispanic teen with no family members or friends who smoke, who thinks an occasional cigarette is dangerous and that smoking offers no benefits. The likelihood of smoking for this hypothetical teen is 1.85 percent. The first box shows that a female teen whose best friends smoke is nearly 6 times as likely as our baseline teen to smoke.

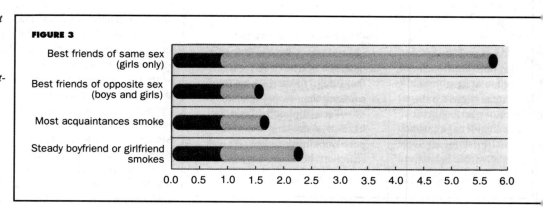

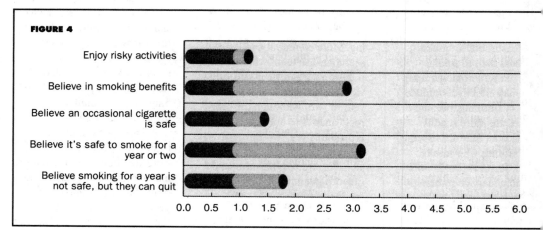

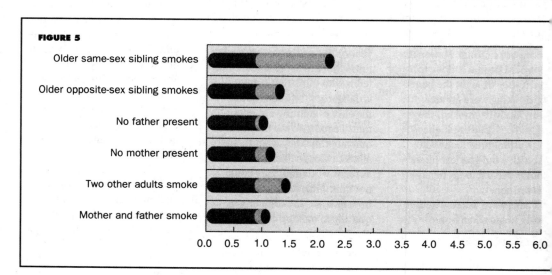

Source: Author tabulations based on Teenage Attitudes and Practices Survey (TAPS) data.

the kind of information conveyed by the cigarette advertisement. If the information is about brand-specific factors such as flavor (mild or strong, menthol or nonmenthol) or tar and nicotine content, there is no reason to expect any appreciable effect on teenage smoking decisions. The important factors motivating teenage smoking decisions are their perceptions of the benefits and risks of smoking, rather than the characteristics of particular brands. On the other hand, if advertising affects teens' perceptions of the benefits or risks of smoking, it could have some influence on smoking decisions. The question is ultimately an empirical one that can only be answered by examining whether a teen's exposure to advertising messages influences his or her smoking decisions.

A 1990 survey of some 5,000 California teens commissioned by the State Department of Health makes possible just such an analysis. Because cigarette advertising varied in different California cities, and because it changed over time, there was substantial variation in the amount of cigarette advertising that individual teens might have seen. Indeed, the teens who were most exposed to advertising could have seen almost 2.5 times as much as the teens who were least exposed. If advertising influences teen decisions to smoke, teens in cities with more advertising or

teens who were interviewed at times when advertising intensity was higher should have been more likely to be smokers.

In fact, they were not. Adding total cigarette advertising expenditures to the factors discussed above—peer behavior, perceptions of the risks and benefits of smoking, family influences—adds nothing to our ability to predict whether individual teens choose to smoke or not to smoke. Teens exposed to the most advertising are just as unlikely to smoke as teens exposed to the least advertising, once their other influences are taken into account.

Of course, different cigarette brands have different appeal to teens and adults. In California in 1990, the dominant brands among teens were Marlboro, with 63 percent of the teenage market, and Camel, with 22 percent. (Nationally, in 1989 Marlboro had 68 percent of the under-age market, while Camel had 8 percent.) Perhaps it is only the advertising for these brands that influences teens' decisions about whether to smoke.

Again, however, there is no evidence of any such relationship. Teens who are most exposed to the advertising of either brand are no more likely to smoke than those who are least exposed. Once other factors that influence smoking decisions are considered, there is no detectable effect of the amount of advertising expendi-

tures by the leading brands among teens.

In short, regardless of the measures of advertising or the definitions of smoking employed, any influence of advertising is not detectable. Whether smoking is defined as daily smoking, smoking in the previous 30 days, or ever having smoked a single cigarette, the advertising expenditures of the industry or the inherent qualities of leading teenage brands have no influence on teens' decisions. Whether advertising expenditures are measured over the previous three months or the previous three years, there is no detectable influence. Whether measures of the perceived benefits of smoking that might be attributable to advertising are included or excluded, advertising expenditures have no detectable effect. There is, in short, no reason to think that restrictions on advertising would have any influence on teenage smoking.

There is one policy alternative that has been shown to reduce teenage smoking. Although virtually every state prohibits sales of cigarettes to teens under a certain age (usually 18), these laws are often only weakly enforced. Studies of communities that have launched enforcement campaigns, however, have found significant declines in teenage smoking. But calls for stricter enforcement of local ordinances simply lack the

political appeal and potential for publicity available from attacks on cigarette advertising, hence their relative scarcity.

Conclusion

Teenage smoking has been declining and continues to do so. Efforts to educate teens about the hazards of smoking have been quite successful, with virtually all teens recognizing that smoking poses risks. Rather than acknowledging this substantial progress, however, some argue for ever more draconian steps to control teenage smoking. While any teenage smoking is regrettable and should surely be discouraged, policymakers have little control over most factors influencing teen smoking. Despite its visibility, there is no discernible influence of cigarette advertising on decisions about smoking. Teens' decisions about smoking are fundamentally rational, determined by the balance between the perceived benefits and risks of smoking. Like other forms of youthful experimentation with adult behaviors, ranging from illegal drugs to sex and alcohol use, some teenage smoking will undoubtedly continue. So too will calls from activists of various stripes and the politicians who seek their support to "do something," regardless of whether it will actually work.

ALCOHOL AND OTHER DRUGS — TOWARD A MORE RATIONAL AND CONSISTENT POLICY

Marcia Angell, M.D.
Jerome P. Kassirer, M.D.

Mind-altering drugs of one type or another have been with us for thousands of years, and in every society some people become dependent on these drugs, perhaps because they find life without them too harsh or are otherwise susceptible. Societies have dealt with such drugs in different ways, but very few have tried to ban them altogether. In the United States, cocaine and heroin were banned in 1914, alcohol in 1920, and marijuana in 1937.[1] The ban on alcohol was lifted in 1933, although alcohol has since been regulated. Caffeine and cigarettes, which have relatively mild short-term psychoactive effects despite their addictive properties, are virtually ubiquitous, and although cigarettes are loosely regulated, caffeine is totally unregulated. The extent of the damage from mind-altering drugs is controversial, but one incontrovertible harm — the deadly effect of driving while under the influence of alcohol or other psychoactive drugs — is illustrated by two Special Articles in this issue of the *Journal*. Brewer et al. present data on alcohol-intoxicated drivers,[2] and Brookoff et al. report on drivers intoxicated with marijuana or cocaine.[3] Before returning to this subject, we here present a brief overview of what is known about the use of mind-altering drugs in the United States.

Aside from caffeine, by far the most commonly used mind-altering drug is alcohol. About 100 million Americans — that is, nearly half the population over 12 years old — drink alcohol regularly.[4] Most are social drinkers, but about 10 percent of those who drink alcohol can be considered alcoholics. Alcoholics drink compulsively, even when it greatly interferes with other aspects of life, and they may also be physically dependent on alcohol. Acute alcohol intoxication, which is common in both social drinkers and alcoholics, profoundly impairs cognitive function and motor skills, often while paradoxically enhancing the drinker's sense of mastery.

The damage alcohol does to society is great. For example, nearly half of the roughly 35,000 fatal automobile accidents in the United States each year are alcohol-related, meaning that someone in the accident, usually a driver, is intoxicated.[5] Drunkenness is also an important factor in other types of fatal accidents, including fires, falls, and drowning. In addition, alcohol is implicated in most homicides,[6] many suicides, and much of the current epidemics of domestic violence and homelessness. The long-term harmful effects of alcohol abuse on the body are also great. Chronic liver disease, about half of which is caused by alcohol abuse, is now the 11th leading cause of death in the United States.[7,8] Alcohol is also associated with many other diseases, including pancreatitis, cardiomyopathy, peripheral neuropathy, dementia and other central nervous system disorders, cancer, and the fetal alcohol syndrome. All told, this drug causes about 100,000 deaths yearly in the United States,[8] about half from trauma, and when all expenses are included, it costs society $100 billion to $130 billion a year[1] (and Rice DP, Institute for Health and Aging, University of California, San Francisco: personal communication).

Other mind-altering drugs — including marijuana, cocaine, and heroin — are used much less commonly. Although it is difficult to be certain of the prevalence of an illicit activity, it is estimated that 9 million Americans use marijuana regularly, and 1.6 million use cocaine or "crack" cocaine. Probably fewer than a million use heroin. Slightly more use LSD (lysergic acid diethylamide) or other hallucinogens, psychoactive inhalants, or other drugs.[4] The psychological effects of these drugs vary, but like alcohol they all alter mood and impair judgment. Their long-term physical effects, particularly those of cocaine, are controversial, but most experts agree that marijuana and heroin are less damaging in their direct biologic effects than alcohol.[9,10] However, the circumstances under which illicit drugs are used carry great medical risks. Shared needles and prostitution to pay for drugs account for a growing percentage of human immunodeficiency virus (HIV) and hepatitis infections. Nationwide, illicit-drug use now accounts for more than a third of all AIDS-related deaths.[11] The resurgence of tuberculosis is also centered on illicit-drug users, especially those infected with HIV.[12]

Despite the fact that all mind-altering drugs impair judgment, society treats alcohol very differently from the others. Drinking alcohol is legal for adults, tolerated among adolescents, and encouraged in many of our social and business interactions. Drunks are generally regarded as ill or even comic, not depraved, and alcohol is sold by average folks in average stores, not by criminals. Alcoholic beverages are reasonably priced and are taxed by the state, yielding $14 billion in government revenues yearly.[13] In contrast, the use, possession, and sale of other psychoactive drugs are illegal, and the penalties severe. These drugs are therefore distributed and sold by criminals, at hugely inflated prices, in an illicit market. Society derives no benefit in the form of taxes. On the contrary, each year illicit drug use costs us from $70 billion to $150 billion[1] (and Rice DP: personal communication) — including the $13-billion federal drug-control budget,[14] the costs of law enforcement, incarceration, and property loss from drug-related crime, and the enormous incomes of drug dealers. Unlike expenditures arising from alcohol use, expenditures on illicit drugs, although similar in total amount, consist overwhelmingly of the costs of the criminal activities that accompany the ban on these drugs[6] — that is, attempts to buy and sell the drugs despite their illegality, as well as law-enforcement efforts. Alcohol-related crime, in contrast, stems primarily from the direct effects of alcohol.

Whatever the effectiveness of the war on drugs, there is no doubt that the burden is extremely high. In addition to the economic costs, there is incalculable human loss. Over half the inmates in our crowded federal prison system are there because of drug offenses,[15] many of which were nonviolent. Local jails also are used increasingly for drug offenders. To make room for these inmates, violent prisoners are sometimes released. Our inner cities have themselves become prisons for their inhabitants, many of whose lives are in thrall to drug-related crime. To pay for drugs, users need to become thieves or dealers themselves. Small children, as well as adolescents drawn by the promise of easy money, are enlisted as pushers or couriers. Dealers fighting for turf murder innocent bystanders as well as one another. Homicide, much of it drug-related, is the most common cause of death among young black men, and about one in four can expect to be in prison at some time in their lives.[16] In this terrifying setting, education and productive work become impossible or irrelevant.

By comparison with society's all-out war on illicit drugs, the prevailing attitude toward alcohol is far more lenient. This disparity is most evident in our tolerance of drunk drivers. Despite the carnage caused by alcohol-intoxicated drivers, they often go unpunished, and there is great reluctance to deprive them of their license to drive. Most cases of drunk driving are resolved before trial, with mandatory attendance at an alcohol-education program as a condition of probation.[17] Among those who come to trial, there are relatively few convictions. In Massachusetts, for example, only 50 percent are convicted, as compared with 70 percent of the accused in all criminal cases and over 80 percent of those tried for offenses involving other drugs. Recently, many states have toughened their laws somewhat, but by and large they remain remarkably weak. A driver's license can be suspended in Massachusetts for a maximum of one year after a first offense, although it rarely is, and not until the fifth offense can it be revoked altogether.[18] Under these circumstances, it is not surprising that Brewer et al. found that 26 percent of a sample of alcohol-intoxicated drivers who were killed in automobile accidents had been arrested at least once for drunk driving.[2] It is perhaps more surprising that 3 percent of the nonintoxicated drivers in the study had also previously been arrested for drunk driving. This is a measure of the

frequency of the offense. Furthermore, it is estimated that for every arrest, 1000 episodes of drunk driving are not discovered.[19]

A more rational and consistent approach to mind-altering drugs is needed. This society will almost certainly not be the first civilization in history to eliminate the use of mind-altering drugs altogether, and in the case of alcohol we admitted the futility of trying 60 years ago. All we can do is try to keep the number of drug-dependent people to a minimum without destroying the fabric of society in our efforts to do so. Many believe that the only reasonable course is to continue our war on the currently illegal drugs,[20] even if this means continuing to accept the inconsistencies, such as the very different status assigned to marijuana and alcohol. Others, emphasizing the violence and destruction of the war on drugs, believe that the same resources would be better spent on education and social programs in the inner cities, which might also be more effective in reducing the demand for drugs.[21] Whatever the answer, this issue, like any other important problem, benefits from open discussion, as the surgeon general recently suggested.[22]

The alternative to criminalization is not necessarily to permit the free use of all mind-altering drugs. Some elements of the approach to alcohol might provide a model for other drugs. Alcohol is not legal for children and adolescents, the content and distribution of alcoholic beverages are regulated, and alcohol use is not permitted in certain settings or under certain circumstances — for example, when people are driving (despite the lax enforcement). But if adults choose to use or even abuse alcohol without harming others, they are usually not stopped, and there has been no appreciable criminal activity surrounding the use of alcohol since the repeal of Prohibition in 1933. Even with regulation, however, many experts believe that the number of people using other psychoactive drugs would increase if the efforts to ban them were relaxed, but some view even this prospect as preferable to the current situation.

One conclusion is inescapable. No mind-altering drug should be permitted to cause the destruction of innocent people that alcohol causes on our roads and highways. It is time we became serious about getting drug-impaired drivers out of their cars — whether the drug is alcohol or, less commonly, marijuana or cocaine, as in the report by Brookoff et al.[3] Enrolling impaired drivers in educational programs or sending them for counseling is only part of the solution, especially in view of the fact that this approach is by no means predictably successful. Fines and jail terms may be appropriate in some cases, but the most important remedy is to be ready to suspend or revoke the driver's license of anyone driving while intoxicated. Suspension for a least a year for the first offense does not seem too severe, given the hazards posed to others, and revocation is warranted on the second offense. Because 5 percent of drunk drivers killed in automobile accidents have already had their licenses suspended or revoked (Brewer RD, Centers for Disease Control and Prevention, Atlanta: personal communication), it may be necessary also to revoke car registrations or even to impound the cars of repeat offenders. The use of mind-altering drugs, even if it is to be condemned, is arguably a private matter, but harming others while under the influence of these drugs must be prevented.

REFERENCES

1. Duke SB, Gross AC. America's longest war: rethinking our tragic crusade against drugs. New York: G.P. Putnam, 1993.
2. Brewer RD, Morris PD, Cole TB, Watkins S, Patetta MJ, Popkin C. The risk of dying in alcohol-related automobile crashes among habitual drunk drivers. N Engl J Med 1994;331:513-7.
3. Brookoff D, Cook CS, Williams C, Mann CS. Testing reckless drivers for cocaine and marijuana. N Engl J Med 1994;331:518-22.
4. Substance Abuse and Mental Health Services Administration, Office of Applied Studies. Preliminary estimates from the 1993 National Household Survey on Drug Abuse. Advance report no. 7. Rockville, Md.: Department of Health and Human Services, 1994.
5. Department of Transportation, National Highway Traffic Safety Administration. Alcohol involvement in fatal traffic crashes — 1991. Springfield, Va.: National Technical Information Service, 1993.
6. Institute for Health Policy, Brandeis University. Substance abuse: the nation's number one health problem: key indicators for policy. Princeton, N.J.: Robert Wood Johnson Foundation, 1993.
7. Centers for Disease Control and Prevention, National Center for Health Statistics. Monthly Vital Statistics Report. Vol. 42. No. 2. Suppl. Advance report of final mortality statistics, 1991. Hyattsville, Md.: Public Health Service, 1993:1-64.
8. McGinnis JM, Foege WH. Actual causes of death in the United States. JAMA 1993;270:2207-12.
9. Marijuana and health: report of a study by a Committee of the Institute of Medicine, Division of Health Sciences Policy. Washington, D.C.: National Academy Press, 1982.
10. Jaffe JH. Drug addiction and drug abuse. In: Gilman AG, Rall TW, Nies AS, Taylor P, eds. Goodman and Gilman's the pharmacological basis of therapeutics. 8th ed. New York: Pergamon Press, 1990:522-73.
11. National Institute on Drug Abuse. AIDS and intravenous drug use: future directions for community-based prevention research. Research monograph series no. 93. Washington, D.C.: Government Printing Office, 1990.
12. Frieden TR, Sterling T, Pablos-Mendez A, Kilburn JO, Cauthen GM, Dooley SW. The emergence of drug-resistant tuberculosis in New York City. N Engl J Med 1993;328:521-6.
13. National Institute on Alcohol Abuse and Alcoholism. Eighth special report to the U.S. Congress on alcohol and health. Washington, D.C.: Department of Health and Human Services, 1993.
14. Treaster JB. President plans to raise drug treatment budget. New York Times. February 9, 1994:B9.
15. Department of Justice. Drugs and crime facts, 1991. Rockville, Md.: Drugs and Crime Data Center and Clearinghouse, 1992.
16. Savage DG. One in four young blacks in jail or in court control, study says. Los Angeles Times. February 27, 1990:A1.
17. Murphy SP. Juries are called soft on drunken driving. Boston Globe. February 3, 1994:A1.
18. An act for increasing the penalty for operating a motor vehicle while under the influence of alcohol. Commonwealth of Massachusetts, 1994 Mass. H.B. 4693.
19. Ayres BD. Big gains are seen in battle to stem drunken driving. New York Times. May 22, 1994:A1.
20. Kleber HD. Our current approach to drug abuse — progress, problems, proposals. N Engl J Med 1994;330:361-5.
21. Grinspoon L, Bakalar JB. The war on drugs — a peace proposal. N Engl J Med 1994;330:357-60.
22. Labaton S. Surgeon general suggests study of legalizing drugs. New York Times. December 8, 1993:A23.

Will Legalizing Drugs Benefit Public Health?

YES
Dr. William London

William M. London, Ed.D. is an associate professor of health education at Kent State University and an M.P.H. student in health administration at Loma Linda University. For the past four years he has directed drug-abuse-prevention training projects funded by the U.S. Department of Education.

The "War on Drugs" has never been a carefully planned public health protection initiative. Government officials did not enact current drug prohibition laws and enforcement policies because of any dispassionate, comprehensive review of drug hazards. Rather, hysterical fear-mongering has always been the real basis for the "War on Drugs."

The association between drugs and crime was firmly established through acts of legislation and enforcement, not through the pharmacological actions of the drugs themselves.

Wars require propaganda to maintain them, and the drug war is no exception. The names of propaganda groups such as Partnership for a Drug-Free America and the U.S. Department of Education (DOE)'s Drug-Free Schools and Communities Program imply that nothing short of a utopian outcome will suffice. Efforts to achieve a drug-free society through war have had less than utopian consequences, however; and those consequences are exemplified by the war's casualties—the victims of infection, violence and criminal injustice.

A HISTORY OF FAILED PROHIBITION EFFORTS

Federal drug prohibition began in the United States in 1914, when Congress passed a law to ensure the orderly marketing of

(YES continued on next page)

NO
Dr. Robert L. DuPont

Robert L. DuPont, M.D., is a former director of the National Institute on Drug Abuse and the second White House "DRUG CZAR." He currently serves as president of the Institute for Behavior and Health, Inc., a nonprofit research and policy organization, and is clinical professor of psychiatry at the Georgetown University School of Medicine.

Proposals for drug legalization are rooted in the belief that drug prohibition does not work. Legalization advocates point out that the prohibition of alcohol failed in the United States two generations ago. They argue that the use of illicit drugs is widespread despite prohibition and that the high costs and negative consequences of that prohibition—ranging from costs for police and prisons to the loss of privacy caused by drug testing in many settings, notably the workplace—are unreasonably high prices to pay for an ineffective policy. But while prohibition has not been the perfect solution to the drug problem, legalization will likely lead to increases in drug use, addiction and drug-related death.

While prohibition has not been the perfect solution to the drug problem, legalization will likely lead to increases in drug use, addiction and drug-related death.

The range of available options within both general categories, drug legalization and drug prohibition, is wide. It is useful to look at the big picture to examine (and question) the whole spectrum of options. In general, we can ask: Is prohibition working? Is it cost effective? Does legalization offer a reasonable alternative to prohibition?

There are three models for legalization that can help us sketch an answer to these fundamental questions. The first is a look back at life in the United States a hundred years ago, when

(NO continued on page 234)

YES (continued) _____

narcotics: the Harrison Narcotic Act. The law responded to concerns about the cut-rate marketing of British opium in China and its effect on China's purchasing power for American products. The congressional debates on the act were concerned with international obligations, not with issues of public health.

To the surprise of many, law-enforcement officers and the courts interpreted the Harrison Act as highly restrictive. Physicians who prescribed opiates to addicts were arrested, convicted and imprisoned. Desperate for drugs, addicts found them available only through illegal channels. Thus, the association between drugs and crime was firmly established through acts of legislation and enforcement, not through the pharmacological actions of the drugs themselves.

The ratification of the 18th Amendment to the Constitution brought about the national prohibition of alcohol in 1920. Prohibition failed to live up to the widespread expectation of its producing an alcohol-free, slum-free, prison-emptied society. Instead, it encouraged the spread of organized crime and the corruption of public officials, overburdened the court and prison systems, made alcoholic beverages more dangerous to consume (black markets tend to lack appropriate manufacturing standards), removed a significant source of tax revenue and increased government spending.

Public health activists should guard against promoting "cures" whose consequences are worse than the "diseases" they address.

The "noble experiment" of national alcohol prohibition ended with the ratification of the 21st Amendment in 1933. However, a new experiment was initiated a scant four years later. Largely due to Harry Anslinger, Commissioner of the Bureau of Narcotics, who had shamelessly been promoting distorted horror stories of marijuana use, Congress passed the Marijuana Tax Act. The law banned the nonmedicinal, untaxed sale or possession of marijuana. At the congressional hearings on the act, there was no medical testimony favoring its passage; the only physician to testify opposed the bill.

By 1988, in the spirit of "zero tolerance," federal law permitted, without even a semblance of due process, drug-enforcement agents to seize boats, cars and planes that contained even traces of marijuana.

PRINCIPLES OF SOUND PUBLIC HEALTH POLICY

Only rarely can we (or should we) try to eliminate health threats the way we have eliminated smallpox. The American Council on Science and Health has documented the folly of numerous public health laws, most notably the Delaney Clause of the Food, Drug, and Cosmetic Act, which tolerates zero risk from food additives regardless of their benefits. ACSH has appropriately promoted the reduction of harm from significant, high-priority, public health hazards, not the elimination of all purported hazards regardless of their public health significance.

Public health activists should guard against promoting "cures" whose consequences are worse than the "diseases" they address. In developing rational policies toward nonmedicinal use of drugs, Charles Murray's "Law of Net Harm" should be considered: "The less likely it is that the unwanted behavior will change voluntarily, the more likely it is that a program to induce change will cause net harm."

In the interest of promoting the greatest good for the greatest number of people, public health interventions may on some occasions limit personal autonomy. In these cases, however, there should always be compelling reasons for the intrusive interventions: and the degree of intrusion should be kept to a minimum.

Sometimes it may be prudent to have public policies that attempt to protect people from making the sort of unwise decisions that can cause harm to themselves. Seat-belt laws are possible examples. It is more important, however, to protect people from the dangerous behavior of others. The gunfire and societal mayhem resulting from drug prohibition endangers people who would never consider taking the prohibited drugs.

DRUG HAZARDS IN PERSPECTIVE

You (yes, you!) have almost certainly self-administered drugs some time in your life. Strictly speaking, drugs are substances that, when administered, act chemically to produce behavioral or biological effects. Drugs are readily and legally available to Americans in over-the-counter products and by prescription.

Although legally sold to adults, one bundle of drugs, tobacco, kills more Americans (over 400,000 annually) than do alcohol and all other drugs combined. Excluding tobacco, alcohol kills more Americans (over 100,000 each year) than do these other drugs combined. American deaths from all other drugs are frequently estimated at about 10,000 per year, with over half of those deaths attributable to cocaine or heroin and none attributable to marijuana.

The gunfire and societal mayhem resulting from drug prohibition endangers people who would never consider taking the prohibited drugs.

There may be no better example of distorted perspective than that of the parents who find out their children are drinkers and exclaim, "Thank God it isn't drugs!" It is unlikely that Partnership for a Drug-Free America—which is funded in part by tobacco, alcohol and pharmaceutical companies and their advertising agencies—would welcome a _truly_ drug-free America.

Far more Americans die from the use of tobacco and the abuse of alcohol than die from abuse of other drugs—largely because far more Americans abuse tobacco and alcohol than abuse other drugs. About 25 percent of American adults, college students and high school students are current smokers. The *National Household Survey* on *Drug Abuse: Population Estimates 1992* showed, for the previous 30 days, 48 percent alcohol use, about four percent marijuana use and less than one percent use of cocaine, crack and heroin.

Defenders of drug prohibition may be tempted to argue that prohibition keeps the prevalence of drug use low and thereby limits drug-related morbidity and mortality. It is possible that the repeal of drug prohibition would lead to increased drug use, but I'm aware of no evidence that a large number of Americans are hoping that drugs will be legalized so that they can *finally* indulge in psychoactive recreations.

Prohibitionists' platitudes about "sending the wrong message" through legalization ignore, first, the dramatic decline in tobacco smoking since the 1960s—without our having instituted tobacco prohibition; second, the very small increase in the use of marijuana, a drug feared far less than cocaine and heroin, following decriminalization in Oregon in 1973; and, third, the expansion of cocaine use during the 1980s, even with no change in cocaine's legal status.

Increases (or decreases) in drug use do not in and of themselves have public health significance—because drug use in and of itself does not imply harmful consequences. The consequences of drug taking are determined by four factors: (1) the pharmacological actions at various doses, (2) the method of administration, (3) set and (4) setting.

(1) Pharmacological actions. "The dose makes the poison" may be the most important concept in pharmacology. Protecting people from small amounts of drugs can have no more than a small impact on public health. Most use of small amounts of drugs—with the notable exception of tobacco—does not lead to disease or addiction.

By introducing standards of identity, purity, sterility and dosage, legalization can reduce the harmful potential of heroin and the other drugs currently sold on the black market.

---

(2) Method of administration. Some methods of drug taking are more dangerous than others. Administration through injection, especially with shared needles, is potentially more dangerous than the drugs being injected.

(3) Set and *(4) Setting.* "Set" refers to the psychological and physical characteristics of the drug user. "Setting" refers to the social and physical environment in which drugs are used. The rarity of addiction to prescribed narcotics for postoperative pain illustrates the importance of both set and setting. Focusing on

the drugs themselves to the exclusion of all else ignores potential opportunities for reducing harm by addressing these "host" and "environmental" factors.

Unlike readily available legal pharmaceuticals, the illegal drugs sold on the street are typically adulterated. By introducing standards of identity, purity, sterility and dosage, legalization can reduce the harmful potential of heroin and the other drugs currently sold on the black market.

If the prohibition of drugs is as necessary as its defenders claim to protect public health, why do so few people promote the prohibition of tobacco and alcohol, the major causes of behaviorally induced mortality in the United States? Perhaps the prohibitionists secretly recognize that expanding the "War on Drugs" to include tobacco and alcohol would expand the number of war casualties.

CASUALTIES OF THE "DRUG WAR"

The number of casualties resulting from the "war" on drugs exceeds the number of casualties resulting from drug use. Because of the legal restrictions placed on the distribution and possession of certain drugs, infection, violence and criminal injustice leave death and destruction in their wake.

A significant number of the 809 juveniles who were victims of gang slayings in the United States in 1992 were undoubtedly child casualties of the drug war.

---

(1) Infection. Inflated drug prices resulting from the lack of a free market provide an incentive to buyers to use the efficient, yet dangerous, injection method to administer drugs. Through many years of syringe and needle prohibition, a culture of sharing the "works" has developed. But the sharing of needles and syringes speeds the spread of infectious diseases such as tetanus, hepatitis and AIDS. According to the CDC, through December 1994 in the United States, there were 109,393 AIDS cases traceable to injecting drug use; 28,521 cases among men who have sex with men and inject drugs; 15,758 cases traceable to heterosexual contact with injecting drug users; and 3,376 pediatric AIDS cases for which the mother was at risk of infection through either injecting drug use or sex with an injecting drug user.

(2) Violence. Major drug dealers have more to lose than anyone from the legalization of drugs. Operating as they do outside free markets and without the burden of the taxes that legitimate business people pay, black-market drug traffickers have opportunities for extraordinary profits.

A common business problem among dealers is the processing of enormous amounts of cash. As a consequence, dealers are usually well armed, both to protect themselves from those law enforcement officers who are not on their payrolls and to blow away anyone else who crosses them. In countries such as Brazil, Peru, Mexico, Panama and Colombia, drug cartels, gangs and death-and-torture squads have murdered countless opponents of the illegal drug trade—including judges, journalists, political candidates and other citizens.

In any forceful response to drug terrorists, additional people—including innocent bystanders—inevitably die. For example, the American military's pursuit and capture of the former drug-trafficking tyrant of Panama, Manuel Noriega, killed over 200 civilians and over 300 soldiers. Hundreds of millions of U.S. dollars were spent on the invasion of Panama and Noriega's trial.

The ties between the drug trade and gangs are close ones. A significant number of the 809 juveniles who were victims of gang slayings in the United States in 1992 were undoubtedly child casualties of the drug war. The U.S. Department of Justice conservatively estimated that 1,284 drug-related homicides occurred in the United States in 1992. Many of those victims were—and continue to be—people who never used drugs or associated with the drug trade but who happened to wind up in the line of fire, some of it from police.

In 1988, drug scams or disputes over drugs accounted for 18 percent of the defendants in murder cases in the nation's 75 most populous counties. It is unrealistic to expect armed drug dealers to handle their most difficult conflicts through legal channels.

(3) Criminal Injustice. Nevertheless, drug dealers and users of illegal drugs often do wind up in the criminal justice system. According to the U.S. Department of Justice, in 1992 there were about 980,700 adult arrests for drug offenses, up from 471,200 in 1980. That 1992 figure was larger than the same year's combined total of arrests for murder, rape, robbery, aggravated assault and burglary. In 1992 there were about 102,000 new court commitments for drug offenses, representing an estimated 30.5 percent of all new court commitments. That figure was up from 6.8 percent in 1980.

Clogged courts mean plea bargaining and reduced sentences for violent offenders—who are the real menaces to society. Overcrowded prisons expose nonviolent offenders convicted on drug charges to prison violence, epidemics of drug-resistant tuberculosis and other infectious diseases and the socialization influences of hardened criminals.

Prematurely releasing violent criminals to make room for nonviolent drug offenders sentenced to draconian mandatory minimum sentences is an outrageous assault on public health. Those who advocate imprisoning drug users (at a cost of about $20,000 per year per offender) are often strongly pro-family, but few events disrupt the functioning of a family—and thereby increase the risk for juvenile drug abuse—as much as a family member going to prison.

The term "War on Drugs" is a misnomer. It is not a war on inanimate objects, but a war on people. Its casualties of epidemic infection, corruption, torture, murder and incarceration far exceed the speculated casualties from drug abuse under any plausible, pessimistic, post-legalization scenario. The failure to heed the Hippocratic dictum "first, do no harm" in formulating drug policy has given us the longest, most destructive war in American history. It's time for peace.

NO (continued from page 231)

addicting drugs were sold like toothpaste and candy. The second is derived from observing the recent trends in the rates of the use of both legal and illegal drugs in the United States and comparing the costs generated by the drugs that now are legal for adults—tobacco and alcohol—and those that are not—marijuana, cocaine, heroin and others. The third is a look at the experiences of other countries that have experimented with legalization. Examining these models gives us valuable perspective as we consider the possibility of lifting prohibition and replacing it with one of the many options for drug legalization.

A LOOK AT THE AMERICAN EXPERIENCE

The American experience with drugs at the end of the 19th century demonstrated the serious problems that can be caused by the general use of a wide range of legally available drugs. These problems were, finally, judged unacceptable by Americans of that day. Prohibition was the result of a nonpartisan public outcry over the negative effects of unrestricted drug use. Thus, the prohibition of heroin and cocaine did not cause widespread drug use; widespread drug use caused prohibition.

Furthermore, the prohibition of drugs has been almost universally supported politically in the United States and throughout the world for more than half a century. The single exception was, of course, the prohibition of alcohol.

A COMPARISON OF COSTS

The goal of a drug policy is to reduce harm. Alcohol and tobacco cause far more harm in the U.S. than all illegal drugs combined. Deaths in the United States from alcohol are estimated at about 125,000 per year. Tobacco use causes about 420,000 deaths a year. Deaths resulting from all illicit drugs combined are fewer than 10,000 per year.

Similarly, the costs to society of alcohol use in the United States in 1990 were estimated at $98.6 billion a year; the costs of tobacco smoking were estimated to be $72 billion; and the 1990 estimated costs of all illicit drugs—including the costs of prohibition—were $66.9 billion.

To put these statistics another way: Whether the standard is drug-caused deaths or drug-related economic costs, the drugs that are legal for adults (alcohol and tobacco) cause far more harm than do all currently illegal drugs combined (see Table 1).

Table 2 shows figures for 1985 and 1993 of the number of people in the United States who said they had used legal and/or illegal drugs in the previous 30 days. The table also shows the decline in the rates of use of all these substances in the years from 1985 to 1993. The prohibited drugs were used at lower levels and showed greater reductions in use over that time span than either cigarettes or alcohol.

Note, in Table 1, that the economic cost of illicit drugs is primarily related to crime: Almost 70 percent of the $66.9 billion total cost of illicit drugs in 1990 was the cost of prohibition. At the same time, crime produced only 16 percent of the cost to society of alcohol and zero percent of the cost generated by tobacco use.

Prohibition is currently reducing the total costs generated by drugs such as marijuana, cocaine and heroin. But human suffering—and health-care costs—would rise dramatically if those drugs were as readily and legally available as alcohol and tobacco are now.

The costs of medical care, lost productivity and death stand in dramatic contrast to the crime costs, however. Those costs taken together totaled $14.6 billion for all illegal drugs, $80.7 billion for alcohol and $72 billion for tobacco. These figures show clearly that when drugs are legalized, they are used more widely—and the total costs of their use go up when compared to the costs of drugs still under prohibition. The costs of legal drugs are primarily costs related to medical care, lost productivity and death.

Table 1 also breaks out AIDS as a separate factor in the total costs of both legal and illegal drugs. But even when AIDS-related costs are added to the non-crime-related costs (medical care, lost productivity and death) for all illicit drugs, the total is $20.9 billion; the equivalent totals are $82.8 billion for alcohol and $72 billion for tobacco.

TABLE 1: ECONOMIC COSTS OF ADDICTION IN THE UNITED STATES, 1990

	Illicit Drugs		Alcohol		Tobacco	
Total Cost (billions)	$66.9		$98.6		$72.0	
Medical Care (%)	3.2	(4.8)	10.5	(10.7)	20.2	(28.0)
Lost Productivity (%)	8.0	(11.9)	36.6	(37.1)	6.8	(9.0)
Death (%)	3.4	(5.1)	33.6	(34.1)	45.0	(63.0)
Crime (%)	46.0	(68.8)	15.8	(16.0)	0.0	(0.0)
AIDS (%)	6.3	(9.4)	2.1	(2.1)	0.0	(0.0)

Source: Institute for Health Policy, Brandeis University. Substance Abuse: The Nation's Number One Health Problem — Key Indicators for Policy. Prepared for the Robert Wood Johnson Foundation, Princeton, NJ, 1993.

TABLE 2: AMERICAN DRUG USE IN THE PRIOR 30 DAYS (in millions)

	1985	1993	Decline from 1985 to 1993
Drugs Legal for Adults			
Alcohol	113	103	9%
Cigarettes	60	50	17%
The Most Widely Used Drugs That Are Illegal for All			
Marijuana	18	9	50%
Cocaine	6	1.3	78%

Some advocates of the legalization of now-illegal drugs claim that those drugs do not produce health costs on the scale of those produced by alcohol and tobacco. but the data show that illicit drugs produce higher levels of health and productivity costs *per user* than do legal drugs.

The United States has about 103 million current users of alcohol, 50 million current users of tobacco and 12 million current users of illicit drugs. The health-related costs per user per year, exclusive of crime costs, are $798 for users of alcohol, $1,440 for users of tobacco—and $1,742 for users of illicit drugs.

Under prohibition, the costs to society of illegal drugs are lower, overall, than the costs of legal drugs; and the costs of illicit drugs show up primarily in police and corrections budgets. Prohibition is currently reducing the total costs generated by drugs such as marijuana, cocaine and heroin. But human suffering—and health-care costs—would rise dramatically if those drugs were as readily and legally available as alcohol and tobacco are now.

THE DUTCH EXAMPLE

Those who support legalization widely praise the Dutch for permitting the purchase of marijuana for use by those over age 15. But the Dutch saw a 250 percent increase in adolescent marijuana use between 1984 and 1992. During the same period, American youth reduced their marijuana use by two thirds. Furthermore, between 1991 and 1993 the Dutch saw a 30 percent increase in registered marijuana addicts.

Those who support prohibition do not help their case by denying the magnitude of these costs. The question to ask is this: Are the high costs of prohibition justified in terms of reduced harm and an improved quality of life for most citizens? The evidence is clear; the answer is yes.

The evidence from the Netherlands suggests that if the United States were to legalize currently illicit drugs, the number of users would likely increase from the present 12 million to something like the 50 million who use tobacco or even the 103 million who use alcohol. The current prohibition in the United States works reasonably well in reducing both the amount and the costs of addictive drug use. Legalization would result both in the increased use of no-longer-illegal drugs and in more harm, which would be expressed in greater social costs.

WIDER USE EQUALS WIDER HARM

Those who would reform drug laws who also support harm-reduction objectives should focus their efforts on alcohol and tobacco—the two drugs responsible for the major part of the drug-caused harm now taking place in the United States and throughout the world. Those two substances are not causing the most harm because they are more dangerous—or more attractive—than marijuana, cocaine or heroin. Alcohol and tobacco are, in fact, less attractive to many experienced drug users; and they are much less dangerous than marijuana, cocaine and heroin. Alcohol and tobacco produce more harm than all of the illegal drugs combined—even when you include the costs of prohibition—simply because alcohol and tobacco are so much more widely used. Furthermore, alcohol and tobacco are more widely used by children because their use is legal for adults.

If all drugs were declared completely legal, many people would still choose not to use them, just as many adults choose not to use alcohol and tobacco today. And even under the most severe prohibition, some people still choose to use prohibited drugs. The question, however, is this: Would legalization, when compared to prohibition, increase both the number of drug users and the social harm produced by the use of these substances? The answer is yes.

THE COSTS OF PROHIBITION

Those who support legalization correctly point out that prohibition is an expensive strategy. Making the consumption of marijuana, cocaine, heroin and other drugs illegal costs society large sums of money for everything from police and prisons to the incentives that prohibition-inflated drug prices provide to illicit drug traffickers. There are costs, too, in the loss of privacy: Drug tests are widely used in the criminal-justice system, the workplace and elsewhere.

Those who support prohibition do not help their case by denying the magnitude of these costs. The question to ask is this: Are the high costs of prohibition justified in terms of reduced harm and an improved quality of life for most citizens? The evidence is clear; the answer is yes. Prohibition is worth its high costs.

THE VIEWS OF DRUG-TREATMENT PROFESSIONALS

One curious aspect of the legalization controversy is that people who are involved in drug treatment almost all oppose legalization. One would think that if they were operating in their own self interest, these people would welcome legalization; after all, it would substantially increase the need for the treatment of addiction. However, drug-treatment professionals generally oppose drug legalization because their dedication to the welfare of drug users is more powerful than their dedication to their own narrow economic interests.

Talk, too, to drug abusers in treatment or to those who have successfully developed solid, personal recovery programs. Few of them support legalization; they know that such an approach would make life harder for them and for all other recovering former users.

LIFE AFTER LEGALIZATION: A PROJECTION

Since many thoughtful people have proposed the legalization of drugs as a solution to the war we are waging against the financial, social, medical and political ravages of drug abuse, I would like to share my own projection of the results of such a decision. Here is my fantasy of life after drug legalization:

Let's say some community or nation were to give it a try, putting heroin, cocaine, LSD and the whole modern menu of addicting drugs on sale in local markets. The results of the experiment would not be long in coming, and they wouldn't be hard to predict.

First the good news: As a result of drug legalization, crime costs for prisons, courts and police would fall. Tax revenues would rise, and the illegal market for the newly legal drugs would be reduced.

Then the bad news: Health and productivity costs would increase dramatically, and the net costs to society would rise substantially. Worse, the human costs from drug use would rise over time as more people who tried the drugs used them and became addicted. And the highest costs of legalization would be paid by those most vulnerable to addiction: the young and the disadvantaged.

If any community in the world would be so foolish as to try the outright legalization of marijuana, cocaine, heroin and LSD, we might have less discussion of this thoroughly unworkable and dangerous—but endlessly seductive—idea.

But this fantasy of drug legalization is not merely speculative. The scenario has already been played out in the real world. In 1987 the Swiss opened a drug bazaar, called "Needle Park," for a few hundred addicts. By 1992, 20,000 addicts had swarmed to Switzerland, and that nation's heroin death rate had become Europe's highest. That same year, in the face of public outrage, the Swiss police closed Needle Park.

THE BETTER WAY

It has often been said that democracy—although a messy, expensive and flawed system of government—is better than any of the alternatives. The prohibition of currently illegal drugs is also a messy, expensive and flawed system; but, like democracy, it is better than the alternatives. This is not to say that drug-prohibition strategies cannot be improved; they almost certainly can be. But abundant evidence gathered from many societies over many years has shown that, in general, the prohibition of drugs such as marijuana, cocaine and heroin is a reasonable and generally effective way to deal with a difficult human problem.

The Golden Triangle's new king

FANG AND YANGON

FEW tourists bother to stop in Fang. An unremarkable collection of houses, shops and brothels, the Thai town boasts none of the exotic resorts that dot the rest of the border with Myanmar. Yet, though many towns trade on the glamour of being within the drugs area known as the Golden Triangle, Fang is undeniably authentic. It is generally believed to be one of the main entrepots for the shipment of heroin from Myanmar into Thailand and then on to the rest of the world.

The police in Fang insist that the nearest road into Myanmar is over 100 kilometres (65 miles) away. In fact, there are many small roads around Fang, some of them dirt tracks, a few paved, which go through the mountains to the border. Western officials say that among the drugs that cross the border along these byways are shipments of heroin from laboratories just inside Myanmar.

Any effort to attack the heroin trade at its source must deal with Myanmar, which is now reckoned to provide 60% of the world's heroin. According to the American State Department, Myanmar produced over 215 tonnes of heroin in 1993, compared with the 69 tonnes that came from Afghanistan, the next-largest producer. American officials say production inside Myanmar has increased by over 50% since the current military junta took power in 1988. The consequences are now visible in the streets of the West. In 1987 under 20% of the heroin seized in the United States came from the Golden Triangle. Today it is over 70%.

But a rare victory may be about to be won in the war on drugs. Khun Sa, a heroin warlord who commands a small army in Myanmar's Shan state, is in trouble. Myanmar's army is attacking his strongholds and several of his laboratories are believed to have closed. The Thais have tightened controls at border crossings near Mae Hong Son, south-west of Fang, through

which Khun Sa got most of his supplies. Meanwhile, ten men alleged to be close aides of the warlord have been arrested in Thailand and face extradition to America.

There is a snag. Khun Sa may not be as important as he is said to be. A western official says, "He's certainly the best-known player in the opium trade, but he's no longer the biggest." That dubious honour now falls to the Wa tribe, whose territory is largely to the north and east of Khun Sa's. The United Wa State Army, which numbers between 20,000 and 30,000 men, is headed by Chao Nyi Lai, a former communist. The bulk of the Wa army is based along the border between Myanmar and China. But the tribe's main link to the international heroin trade is provided by two brothers, the Weis, who are believed to be based in Myanmar along the Thai border, just opposite Fang. It seems that, as yet, they have little trouble getting drugs out through Thailand.

Like Khun Sa's Shan people, the Wa have long harboured separatist ambitions. But, unlike the Shan, the Wa signed a peace treaty with Myanmar's ruling junta in 1989. As Khun Sa has come under pressure, so the Wa army has moved in on his trade and territory. Sounds of the two armies fighting occasionally drift across the Thai border.

Myanmar's junta has used its operations against Khun Sa to gain favour abroad. But so long as the Wa and other tribes continue to harvest opium, the governments of the West are unlikely to be impressed. Observers of the drugs trade are divided over whether Myanmar's leaders profit personally from the traffic in heroin. Opium is most heavily cultivated in areas of Myanmar that are not under government control. But the most rapid expansion of production since 1988 has been in parts of the country that the government does control.

Most of the independent drug barons operating in Myanmar, Khun Sa excepted, have cordial relations with the junta. Western officials have been irritated by the sight of drug suspects playing golf in Yangon with Myanmar's generals. "We call them traffickers and they call them leaders of ethnic minorities," says a diplomat.

The expansion of heroin production in Myanmar since 1988 places the Americans, in particular, in a dilemma. After Myanmar's army killed or imprisoned thousands of democracy supporters in 1988, America suspended co-operation with Myanmar. Members of America's Drug Enforcement Agency make a link between the end of joint efforts at opium eradication and the subsequent leap in heroin production. Thomas Constantine, the head of the DEA, says that some co-operation with the government of Myanmar is now necessary.

But the State Department is reluctant to let Myanmar use drugs as a means of easing the country's isolation. And some Americans argue that the chief cause of increased heroin production since 1988 has not been the isolation of Myanmar but the junta's decision to make peace with rebel ethnic groups such as the Wa. Maintaining the fragile peace with ethnic rebels means allowing them to grow poppies. Myanmar's generals may not be willing to trade their hard-won peace treaties for a diplomatic breakthrough with America.

Prevention and Treatment

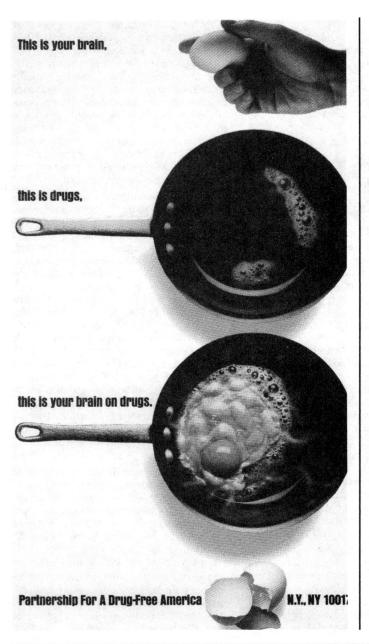

This is your brain,

this is drugs,

this is your brain on drugs.

Partnership For A Drug-Free America   N.Y., NY 1001...

Two thousand years ago an ancient Chinese warrior stated, "Winning without fighting is best." With respect to drug abuse, winning without fighting may not be possible. It may be that the best weapon in preventing drug abuse is drugs—the public's perception of a drug's safety is a leading influence on the use and abuse of certain drugs. Unfortunately, the process of learning is a slow one, and its benefits are reflected unevenly by different segments within the population. Alcohol and tobacco use and abuse are examples of slow progress and paradox. On the other hand, crack cocaine usage appeared to galvanize more quickly our concern about cocaine abuse, precipitating further declines in cocaine use over the past decade. There are no magic bullets for preventing drug abuse and treating drug-dependent persons. As the late John Kaplan of Stanford University stated some years ago, "Drug addicts can be cured but we're not very good at it."

Drug prevention and treatment philosophies subscribe to a multitude of modalities. Everything seems to work a little, and nothing seems to work completely. The following articles illustrate the diversity of methods utilized in prevention and treatment programs. Also illustrated is the struggle in which prevention and treatment programs compete for local, state, and federal resources.

Prevention A primary strategy of drug abuse prevention programs is to prevent and/or delay initial drug use. A secondary strategy is to discourage use by persons minimally involved with drugs. Both strategies include: (1) educating users and potential users; (2) teaching adolescents how to resist peer pressure; (3) addressing problems associated with drug abuse such as teen pregnancy, failure in school, and problems with the law; and (4) creating community support and involvement for prevention activities. Prevention programs also typically address alcohol and nicotine use by children.

Prevention programs are administered through a variety of mechanisms. Schools are an important delivery apparatus, as are local law enforcement agencies. Over 10,000 police officers are involved in the Drug Abuse Resistance Education Program (D.A.R.E.) provided to over 5 million students each year. Other prevention programs are community-based and sponsored by civic organizations, church groups, and private corporations. All programs pursue funding through public grants and private endowments. Federal grants to local, state, and private programs are critical components to program solvency.

Are prevention programs effective? Unfortunately, there has been little research into the impacts of general prevention programs on drug use. The multifaceted nature of prevention programs makes them difficult to assess categorically. It appears, however, that the most effective are school programs that emphasize the development of skills to resist social and peer influences.

Treatment Like prevention programs, drug treatment programs enlist a variety of methods to treat persons dependent upon legal and illegal drugs. There is no single-pronged approach to treatment for drug abuse, therefore treatment modality may differ radically from one user to the next. The user's background, physical and mental health, personal motivation, and support structure all have serious implications for treatment type. Lumping together the diverse needs of chemically dependent persons for purposes of applying a generic treatment process provides confounding results at best. A female crack addict 20 years of age may require a greatly different treatment process than the alcohol/heroin addict who is 35 years of age—the latter being the historical profile for which treatment programs were developed initially. In addition, most persons needing and seeking treatment have problems with more than one drug—polydrug use. Studies have also shown that 54 percent of drug abusers and 37 percent of alcohol abusers have, in addition to their drug problem, at least one serious mental illness. Identifying a user's drug and associated mental health problem is referred to as dual diagnosis. The implications of such a diagnosis are serious, as it is estimated that there are 30 to 40 million chemically dependent persons in this country. The popularity of cocaine and methamphetamine use is felt to have increased the percentage of dually diagnosed persons because of the potential of these drugs to alter neurochemical balance negatively, pushing already troubled persons into the realm of mental illness.

Although treatment programs differ in methods, most provide a combination of key services. These include drug counseling, drug education, pharmacological therapy, psychotherapy, relapse prevention, and assistance with support structures. Treatment programs may be outpatient oriented or residential in nature. Residential programs require patients to live at the facility for a prescribed period of time. These residential programs, often described as therapeutic communities (TCs), emphasize the development of social, vocational, and educational skills.

Providing effective, affordable drug treatment is a critical component in the fight against drug abuse. The number of available treatment programs is a continual political controversy with respect to federal and state drug budget expenditures. The current trend is toward increasing the availability of treatment programs. The best evidence suggests that although effective treatment is critical in the fight against drug abuse, it cannot effectively treat away America's drug problem. For every person in treatment, there exist an untold number who simply do not want it, and an untold number who are in denial and feel they do not need it. Drug treatment has positive effects on users, but it is not a panacea for curing addiction.

Looking Ahead: Challenge Questions

How effective are drug education and prevention programs? Are they too generic? How are they assessed and evaluated?

Where does the responsibility lie for drug education and prevention programs—the family, the schools, the police, or the federal government? Who is willing and unwilling to get involved?

How effective is drug treatment? Would providing free, publicly sponsored drug programs be one way to greatly reduce America's drug problem? Why or why not?

What must treatment programs and treatment philosophy consider when providing services to a diverse population of clients?

If an addicted friend or loved one asked your advice on finding treatment, how would you respond? What are your options?

IS DRUG ABUSE TREATMENT EFFECTIVE?

WHAT WE KNOW. WHAT WE DON'T. WHAT THIS MEANS FOR THE NATION'S DRUG STRATEGY.

Robert Apsler

Robert Apsler is an assistant professor of psychology in the Department of Psychiatry at the Harvard Medical School and president of Social Science Research and Evaluation, Inc. He has written on the cost-effectiveness of drug abuse treatment and is a contributor to When Drug Addicts Have Children: Reorienting Society's Response *(Child Welfare League/AEI Press, April 1994).*

In early February, the Clinton administration spelled out its national antidrug strategy. Much of the debate over the new program will turn on how much federal support should be made available for treating drug addicts. The administration plans to spend $355 million in new grants for the states to use to treat hard-core drug users, while cutting funds for interdiction. Many years of massive federal investment in interdiction—including involvement of the U.S. military—have failed to reduce the availability of low-cost street drugs. And the policy momentum is now toward shifting federal funds from supply reduction to demand reduction, a move that would benefit treatment and prevention programs. Also, news stories about the administration's deliberations often report on drug treatment programs with long waits for new admissions. What is implied if not stated is that the size of the country's drug abusing

> **Missing from the news stories and analyses is any frank discussion of the underlying assumption that drug abuse treatment is effective. We do not know that drug abuse treatment is effective.**

population, estimated by the Institute of Medicine to be 5.5 million people, would be significantly reduced if more money were spent for drug abuse treatment.

But missing from the news stories and analyses of proposed antidrug strategies is any frank discussion of the underlying assumption that drug abuse treatment is effective. This assumption is based largely on reports from clinicians and recovered drug addicts. It is encouraged by a growing drug treatment industry and accepted by a public that wishes for a solution to the drug problem. The premise may be accurate, but it is not yet supported by hard evidence. We do not know that drug abuse treatment is effective. Clinicians' reports in other areas have not always been reliable. For example, many medical procedures developed through clinical experience alone have been abandoned when researchers showed, through carefully controlled comparisons, that placebos or other alternatives matched their effectiveness.

With a few exceptions, drug abuse treatment has not been subjected to rigorous tests for effectiveness. Good research doesn't exist for a number of reasons. Researchers are hampered by fundamental conceptual issues. Even defining basic ideas is difficult. There are significant practical obstacles that make conducting research difficult as well, and little federal support for drug treatment research has been available for over a decade.

From *The American Enterprise* magazine, March/April 1994, pp. 46-53. © 1994 by the American Enterprise Institute. Reprinted by permission.

What Is "Drug Abuse Treatment"?

One of the conceptual and practical problems of research is the simple fact that no one process or combination of procedures comprises "drug abuse treatment." Nor do the various types of drug programs have much in common beyond the shared objective of reducing drug abuse.

There are four major types of drug treatment. *Residential therapeutic communities* are highly structured residential settings for drug addicts and typically employ a mixture of psychological and behavioral therapies. Duration of treatment varies widely among these programs. *Inpatient/outpatient chemical dependency treatment* begins with a three- to six-week residential stay in a clinic or hospital that uses the Alcoholics Anonymous philosophy. These clients are then encouraged to attend self-help groups for the rest of their lives. A third type, *outpatient methadone maintenance programs,* involves supervised addiction to methadone hydrochloride as a substitute for addiction to other narcotics, such as heroin. Programs may include counseling and other social services for clients. The fourth category, *outpatient nonmethadone treatment,* joins many different types of programs whose main similarity is that they tend not to treat individuals who are dependent on opiates such as heroin, morphine, and codeine.

This four-group classification is crude because the programs within each category differ markedly from each other. For example, methadone maintenance programs differ in the size of the methadone dose, the number and type of additional services provided, the frequency of urine testing, the strictness of program regulation enforcement, and whether clients are permitted to take their methadone dose home. Some programs focus on illicit drug use and criminal activity, while others target the overall functioning of clients. Some demand abstinence from all illicit drugs; others help clients gain control over their drug use. They differ in whether they concentrate on a particular drug and, if they do, on which drug. Some programs rely heavily on professional practitioners; others employ nonprofessionals, often ex-addicts, as counselors. Programs also differ in the clients they serve: those in the private sector cater mainly to employed drug abusers, whose care is covered by health insurance. The public sector programs serve large numbers of indigent clients.

The differences within each of the four major categories of drug programs are so great that information about the effectiveness

> Most experts reluctantly acknowledge that almost no drug abusers actually *want* treatment. The news reports implying that thousands of needy addicts would enter treatment and soon be on their way to recovery if the country were willing to spend more money and increase the number of drug programs are inaccurate.

of one program in a particular category tells us little about the effectiveness of other programs in the same category. In fact, some differences among programs within a classification group may prove to be more important than the differences among the four groups of programs. For example, new evidence shows that the sheer quantity of treatment provided to clients is crucial to a program's effectiveness. Thus, the amount of counseling and auxiliary services provided by a program may be a more important defining characteristic with respect to efficacy than the types of drug abuse it treats, its treatment philosophy, or whether it operates through a residential or outpatient setting.

What Is "Effective" Treatment?

Just as there is no simple answer to what comprises drug abuse treatment, neither is there an agreed-upon definition of what constitutes *effective* drug abuse treatment. Definitions clash in two important ways. First, strongly held views divide the treatment community on whether abstinence from illicit drug use is necessary. One position holds that successful treatment is synonymous with total abstinence from illicit drugs. The other position holds that treatment is successful if it ends clients' *dependence* on drugs. Continued, moderate drug use is accepted for those clients able to gain control over their drug use and prevent it from interfering with their daily functioning.

Definitions of effectiveness also differ in the number of behaviors they measure. The most common view of effectiveness judges treatment by its ability to reduce the two behaviors most responsible for society's strong reaction against drug abuse: illicit drug use and criminal activity. Others argue that a broader definition of effectiveness is necessary to describe treatment accurately. Advocates of the broader definition believe that treatment should not be considered effective if it can only demonstrate reductions in drug use and illegal activity, since these changes are likely to dissipate rapidly unless clients undergo additional changes. Returning clients who have completed treatment to their previous drug using environment, it is argued, subjects them to the same social and economic forces that contributed to their drug use. According to this view, sustained changes occur only when clients are willing and able to survive and prosper in new environments. To do so, clients must first develop the necessary employment, social, and other skills. Broad definitions of effectiveness usually include: (1) drug abuse, (2) illegal activities, (3) employment, (4) length of stay in treatment, (5) social functioning, (6) intrapersonal functioning, and (7) physical health and longevity.

Motivation and Crisis

Without having resolved even basic definitions about drug abuse treatment, the administration is nevertheless proceeding on the assumption that more money for treatment will mean more help. Doing so ignores the fact that we don't know very much in this area and also ignores the little we do know. We don't know much about client differences, for instance. But we do know that a drug addict's motivation for seeking treatment is crucial. Most clinicians believe that successful treatment is impossible if a client does not want help. Addicts must admit the existence of a serious problem and sincerely want to do something about it. Only then will they accept the assistance of clinicians. However, most experts in the drug abuse field reluctantly acknowledge that almost no drug abusers actually *want* treatment. The news reports implying that thousands of needy addicts would enter treatment and soon be on their way to recovery if the country were willing to spend more money and increase the number of drug programs are inaccurate. While waiting lists exist for some programs, others have trouble attracting addicts.

Furthermore, most drug abusers enter treatment when faced with a crisis, such as threats by a judge, employer, or spouse, or a combination of the three. As a result, the drug abuser's objective may be limited to overcoming the current problem. When the crisis has abated, patients often admit they do not intend all drug use to stop. A national survey of admissions to public drug programs from 1979 to 1981 found that pressure from the criminal justice system was the strongest motivation for seeking treatment. Thus, the existence of long waiting lists may tell us more about judges' efforts to find alternatives to incarceration in overcrowded jails than about the actual intentions of drug abusers or the effectiveness of treatment programs.

The assumption that drug addicts enter treatment at a crisis point has another important ramification for interpreting research on the effectiveness of treatment programs. Studies of treatment effectiveness typically measure clients at least twice: when they enter a program and when they complete treatment. If the first measurement occurs during a time of crisis, it will reflect clients' negative circumstances by showing high levels of drug use, criminal be-

> Some drug abusers, including heroin addicts, end drug use largely on their own. Until we know the recovery rates for untreated drug abusers, it is impossible to claim that treatment is more effective than the absence of treatment.

havior, unemployment, and so on. The second measure of clients, taken at the conclusion of treatment, will likely occur after the precipitating crisis has passed or at least lessened. Consequently, a comparison of the measurements taken at the beginning and end of treatment will show significant improvement for many clients. Is this improvement evidence of effective treatment? Or does it merely reflect the natural cycle of a passing crisis? The main problem is that the research designs used in nearly all drug treatment research cannot separate the effects of treatment from other factors such as these.

Research Problems

Questions about drug treatment effectiveness must be answered the same way as similar questions about treatments for the common cold, AIDS, or other ailments, that is, by obtaining evidence that compares the outcomes of treated and untreated individuals. While this may seem obvious, most drug treatment research has neither compared the necessary groups of drug users nor employed the types of research designs capable of producing strong conclusions. In addition, serious measurement and attrition problems weaken the conclusions of most studies of drug treatment effectiveness.

Research Design. Comparisons between drug users who receive treatment and others who do not are almost nonexistent. Researchers study only treated drug users. Yet the observed behavior of drug users who do not enter drug programs reinforces the need for researchers to include untreated addicts in their studies. We have known for years, for instance, that some drug abusers, including heroin addicts, end drug use largely on their own. Researchers have also observed large reductions in drug use among drug abusers waiting for, but not yet receiving, treatment for cocaine abuse.

The phenomenon of people ending their use of highly addictive *legal* substances on their own is well documented. For example, there is mounting evidence that smokers quit on their own at about the same rate as those attending smoking treatment programs. Estimates of remission from alcoholism and alcohol problems without formal treatment range from 45 to 70 percent. No comparable estimate is available for the number of drug users who quit on their own. Until we know the recovery rates for untreated drug abusers, it is impossible to claim that treatment is more effective than the absence of treatment.

Furthermore, the research designs and methods employed in most drug treatment research are so seriously flawed that the results can be considered no more than suggestive. Many investigations study a single group of treated clients and attempt to draw conclusions without a comparison group. Other investigations compare different groups of clients receiving different treatments. In nearly all such cases, the types of clients differ from group to group. Consequently, it is impossible to distinguish between effects caused by treatment differences and effects caused by client differences.

Measuring the Outcomes of Treatment. One major need in drug treatment research is for an objective, reliable, and inexpensive method for measuring treatment outcomes. Presently most treatment researchers rely entirely on clients' own reports of past and current behavior. Much of the behavior that clients are asked about is illegal, occurred while they were intoxicated, and may have taken place months, and even years, earlier. As one would expect, clients underreport their drug use and other illegal activities. Yet the drug treatment field continues to rely heavily on these dubious reports because there are no suitable alternatives. Chemical tests, such as urine and hair testing, are important adjuncts for validating clients' reports. But at best these tests confirm use or abstinence; they do not indicate anything about quantity or intervals of use. So they are crude measures that cannot easily track patterns of drug use over long periods after a client leaves a treatment program.

Many treatment studies measure clients at the beginning and end of treatment because it is so difficult and expensive to keep track of them after they have completed a program. Some studies do attempt to assess the impact of treatment six months, a year, or even longer after completion. But investigators can seldom locate more than 70 percent of clients, if that. Clients who cannot be contacted are often deceased, in prison, unemployed, and/or homeless. Leaving them out of the studies may skew the findings, making the conclusions appear more positive than is warranted.

Length of Treatment. The length of drug abuse treatment is a complex and confusing element in the overall picture of treatment effectiveness. To begin with, simply keeping clients in treatment is a major challenge for many drug programs. Most clients are forced into treatment. And many leave shortly thereafter. Therefore, merely remaining in treatment has become a widely accepted measure of treatment effectiveness. While it makes sense that clients can only benefit from treatment if they

remain in a program, there is the risk of confusing happenstance for cause and effect.

Addicts who truly want to change their lifestyles are likely to make many changes. Such changes include entering and remaining in a treatment program, reducing drug use, holding a steady job, eschewing illegal activities, and so on. Other individuals not willing to change their lifestyles are more likely to drop out of treatment after being forced into a drug program. They continue using drugs, do not hold steady jobs, engage in illegal activities, and so on. Thus, to prove that drug programs are effective, researchers must show that (1) drug programs help addicts commit to changing their lifestyles, and/or that (2) the resulting improvement among treated clients is greater than the improvement expected anyway from individuals who have already chosen to change their lifestyles.

Another challenge is determining the length of an optimum stay in a drug treatment program. Most private chemical dependency residential programs used to run for 28 days, though cost-reduction pressures have shortened this time. Outpatient nonmethadone treatment averages roughly six months of once-or-twice-a-week counseling sessions. Some therapeutic communities provide treatment for a year or more, while methadone maintenance programs may involve lifetime participation for clients. How much treatment is enough? Some research shows that methadone clients remain in treatment for an unnecessarily long time. This may mean that programs with waiting lists should consider ending treatment for long-term clients to make room for new ones. The impact of treatment may be much greater on someone receiving treatment for the first time than on an individual who has been on methadone for years.

The complex treatment histories of many drug addicts increase the difficulty of judging treatment effectiveness. Over the course of their addiction careers, typical drug addicts enter several different treatment programs. They may enter the same programs on different occasions for different lengths of time. At any point during this involved treatment history, addicts may find themselves participating in a study of treatment effectiveness. However, that study is likely to examine only the most recent treatment episode without taking into account previous treatment stays. Perhaps even small amounts of treatment accumulate over time until they influence an individual. Some drug addicts may try different forms of treatment until they find a type of treatment or a particular counselor that helps them.

However, existing treatment research cannot disentangle the effects of multiple treatment episodes in different types of drug programs that last for varying amounts of time.

What We Know About Treatment Programs

Because of research problems, very little is known about the effectiveness of three out of the four categories of drug abuse treatment identified earlier in this article—*residential therapeutic communities, inpatient/outpatient chemical dependency treatment,* and *outpatient nonmethadone maintenance programs.* Surveys of *residential therapeutic communities* have produced promising results, but important questions remain unanswered. Two longitudinal studies of many drug treatment programs reported reductions in drug use and criminal activity among therapeutic community clients who remained in treatment for at least several months. But therapeutic communities are highly selective in at least two ways. First, they appeal only to clients willing to enter a long-term residential setting. Second, most addicts who enter therapeutic communities quickly drop out. Thus, therapeutic communities may influence the drug addiction of only a small and select group of individuals. Furthermore, there is almost no research about the factors that affect success and failure in therapeutic communities.

As for the other two, almost nothing reliable has been produced on *inpatient/outpatient chemical dependency treatment,* though it has become the dominant approach of privately financed inpatient programs. Nor are there reliable findings on *outpatient/nonmethadone treatment.*

The strongest evidence that drug abuse treatment can be effective comes from randomized clinical trials of the remaining category of treatment programs, *methadone maintenance treatment* programs. Randomized clinical trials are powerful studies that randomly assign a pool of subjects to different conditions, such as different types of treatment; researchers are able to conclude that if some groups of subjects improve more than others, the improvement is probably due to the treatment condition, not to preexisting differences among the individuals. The first of three rigorous trials of methadone treatment, a U.S. study conducted in the late 1960s, randomly assigned highly motivated criminal addicts to either a methadone program or a waiting-list group that received no treatment. All 16 addicts on the waiting list quickly became readdicted to heroin, as did 4 addicts in

> The strongest evidence that drug abuse treatment can be effective comes from randomized clinical trials of methadone maintenance treatment programs.

the treatment group who refused treatment. Eighteen of the 20 untreated individuals who became readdicted returned to prison within 7 to 10 months. Only 3 of the 12 addicts who received treatment returned to prison during this period, and their heroin use decreased.

A test in 1984 of a methadone maintenance program in Sweden provides further evidence of treatment effectiveness, though the stringent client selection criteria make it difficult to generalize the findings. Heroin addicts became eligible for this study only after (1) a history of long-term compulsive abuse, and (2) repeated failures to stop, despite documented serious attempts to do so. Thirty-four addicts meeting these eligibility requirements were randomly assigned to either treatment or no-treatment. Two years later, 12 of the 17 drug addicts assigned to treatment had abandoned drug use and started work or studies. The remaining 5 still had drug problems, and 2 had been expelled from the program. Conversely, only 1 of the 17 addicts in the no-treatment group became drug free; 2 were in prison, 2 were dead, and the rest were still abusing heroin.

A very recent randomized clinical trial in the United States compared three levels of methadone treatment: (1) methadone alone without other services, (2) methadone plus counseling, and (3) methadone plus counseling and on-site medical/psychiatric, employment, and family therapy. The results showed that methadone alone was, at most, helpful to only a few clients. The results for clients who received methadone plus counseling were better, and clients who received additional professional services improved most of all. In sum, these three studies demonstrate that methadone treatment has the potential to reduce illicit narcotics use and criminal behavior among narcotics addicts.

To what extent do these findings apply to methadone maintenance programs in general? We do not know, and we must remain skeptical about the level of effectiveness of most methadone programs; their results could be quite different. For example, two of the three studies described above restricted their research to clients who were highly motivated to end their addiction. But methadone programs in this country typically treat individuals who are forced into treatment, many of whom exhibit little desire to change their addict lifestyles. The third study did not restrict the research to highly motivated clients. However, the study took place in a well-funded, stable, hospital-based, university-affiliated setting. Most methadone programs operate on small budgets that severely restrict their ability to provide services and hire qualified staff.

Therefore they differ in important ways from the study program.

To learn about the impact of less extraordinary methadone programs, a U.S. General Accounting Office study examined the efficacy of 15 methadone programs in a five-state survey. The survey found that (1) the current use of heroin and other opiates ranged from 2 to 47 percent of clients enrolled in the clinics, (2) many clients had serious alcohol problems, (3) clients received few comprehensive services despite high rates of unemployment, and (4) clinics did not know if clients used the services to which they were referred. Other research has shown that many methadone programs administer doses of methadone smaller than those known to be effective. In sum, typical methadone programs differ significantly from the methadone programs evaluated in the randomized clinical trials discussed above, and they may be less effective.

Conclusions

Drug abuse treatment features prominently in discussions of how the Clinton administration should respond to the country's concern about drug abuse. Yet little hard evidence documents the effectiveness of treatment. Almost nothing is known about (1) the effectiveness of three of the four major treatment modalities, (2) the relative effectiveness of different versions of each major treatment modality, and (3) the prognosis for different types of drug abusers. Instead of answering questions, drug treatment research raises troublesome issues for policymakers. How

can treatment work when clinicians claim that success depends on clients wanting help, and we know that most clients are forced into treatment? What happens to drug abusers who never seek treatment?

What can be said with some certainty is that (1) methadone maintenance programs can help clients who are highly motivated to end their drug abuse, and (2) a model program that provides counseling along with methadone has been able to help less well-motivated clients. But there is little good news here since most drug addicts do not want to end their drug use, and typical methadone maintenance programs may not possess the resources to duplicate the impact of the model program.

The absence of convincing evidence about the effectiveness of drug abuse treatment results from the lack of rigorous evaluations. Only a handful of randomized clinical trials have been conducted to date. More need to be done, and valid and comprehensive measures of treatment effectiveness need to be employed in these studies in order to end the reliance of treatment researchers on clients' self-reports of sensitive behaviors. Treatment research also needs more post-treatment follow-ups to show that treatment effects persist once clients leave their programs.

Finally, researchers must learn what happens to untreated drug abusers. Past and current research focuses almost exclusively on drug abusers who enter treatment. This research does not make comparisons between treated and untreated drug abusers and cannot answer the most fundamental question of all: is treatment more cost-effective than no treatment?

Back From The
DRINK

**Jill Neimark,
Claire Conway,
and Peter Doskoch**

Each year it kills 40,000 Americans. It can damage and destroy every organ in the body, scarring and pocking the liver until it looks like a lump of drying lava, laying waste to the heart, pancreas, arteries, throat, and stomach, snuffing out receptors in the brain. Every year alcoholism costs our country over $80 billion, is implicated in 30 percent of suicides and 46 percent of teen suicides, and is a factor in one of four hospital admissions. No wonder it has long been decried as not far removed from original sin.

Yet like the music of Greek sirens, alcohol has also been the hymn song of poets, monks, philosophers, and soldiers. It is a ritual substance in most religions, intimately linked to God and altered consciousness. It is the supreme seductress: "For not even the gates of heaven, opening wide to receive me," wrote author Malcolm Lowry of a bar in Mexico, "could fill me with such celestial complicated and hopeless joy as the iron screen that rolls up with a crash. All mystery, all hope, all disappointment, yes, all disaster, is here." Or, as Rabelais put it: "I drink for the thirst to come. I drink eternally. . . . The soul can't live in the dry."

What other substance has so mesmerized and polarized us as alcohol? It has a long and illustrious role in our culture, from social lubricant to lethal intoxicant. There are those who contend that culture itself owes its existence to alcohol—that the first primitive, agricultural societies sprang up around the farming and ferment of hops. Even now, as this issue goes to press, there is convening a worldwide conference on wine where health experts from Harvard and the World Health Organization advocate a glass or two of wine daily, citing wine's healthful antioxidants and significant potential to reduce heart disease. Yet the same organization has a formal policy calling for an astounding 25 percent reduction in alcohol consumption by the year 2000. Sound confusing? Not surprising. Alcohol is one of the most potent pharmacologic agents around, one whose effects seem as protean as human nature itself.

For that reason, perhaps, it has taken the maturation of neuroscience and psychology to give us a realistic glimpse into alcohol use and abuse—and the picture is no longer black or white. Researchers are now beginning to ferret out the caus-

"His [Dionysus'] blood, the blood of the grape, lightens the burden of our mortal misery. When, after their daily toils, men drink their fill, sleep comes to them, bringing relief from all their troubles. There is no other cure for sorrow."
Euripides

"Boys should abstain from all use of wine until their eighteenth year, for it is wrong to add fire to fire."
Plato

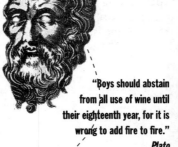

"A man hath no better thing under the sun, than to eat, and to drink, and to be merry."
Ecclesiastes 8:15

The new approach to alcoholism puts practicality before ideology. What works? Keeping motivation high, for starters. And it's not even necessary to admit you are an alcoholic to curb drinking.

es of alcohol addiction, of liquor's fiery path across the cells of the brain, its social underpinnings and cultural power—as well as new, innovative, and flexible treatments for this condition. "There's tremendous excitement, a watershed feeling, as if something is just beginning to happen," notes Henry Kranzler, M.D., a psychiatrist at the University of Connecticut who has pioneered new pharmacologic approaches to alcoholism. "This field now is at the same place that the treatment of depression was 30 or 40 years ago. We're really beginning to understand this condition, to develop promising medications and psychosocial interventions."

THE SHIFTS ARE PROFOUND. Perhaps most important, according to Dennis Donovan, M.D., a psychiatrist and director of the Alcohol and Drug Abuse Institute at the University of Washington, is the willingness to look at the goal of treatment for alcoholism as far more than abstinence or the lack of it. "Abstinence is no longer the gold standard, it's simply one standard."

There is a growing understanding among mental health experts that alcohol abuse occurs on a continuum and must be treated thusly. According to Steven Liljegren, Ph.D., clinical director of Child and Adolescent Services at Brookside Hospital in Nashua, New Hampshire, traditional alcohol treatment programs work for less than half of drinkers. An unprecedented multisite study called Project MATCH, involving over 80 therapists, is now underway to match patient characteristics with different kinds of therapy. Researchers are discovering that, while some former alcoholics require unequivocal abstinence, others can drink in moderation.

As the field moves away from an absolutist, all-or-nothing view, the definition of treatment success, too, is widening. Some of the new findings sweeping the field include:

• Alcohol is not, as was long believed, simply a chemical sledgehammer. It seems to act specifically on neurotransmitters and receptors, primarily GABA, the prime inhibitory neurotransmitter in the brain, and one that accounts for much of alcohol's effects. This discovery

may lead to new medications for helping drinkers overcome the condition.

• Most alcoholics do not have preexisting psychiatric conditions. However, about 20 percent are suffering from psychiatric disorders that they may be attempting to medicate with alcohol, and which are beginning to be treated with the latest psychotropic drugs.

• Social support—whether from friends, family, therapists, or self-help groups—is crucial to recovery. In fact, peer and family support may be the "missing link" that allows some alcoholics to quit on their own, without any formal treatment, according to Donovan. Social support can be provided by contact with recovering people, access to self-help groups, and a family that helps the drinker to readjust to life without substances. Social support does not mean that the family should keep on protecting the alcoholic when he or she is in trouble; it means creating enthusiasm in both the drinker and the family that a life without alcohol is possible.

• In the arena of alcoholism, motivation to quit reigns supreme. The latest research shows that brief, motivational-

TIPS FOR QUITTERS

Alcoholics can quit or control their drinking—in fact they do it all the time. The real issue is, how to sustain recovery? Relapse is the bugaboo of alcoholism treatment. Whether the goal is total abstinence or controlled, moderate alcohol consumption, there are effective ways to minimize the dangers of a relapse.

✓ Avoiding situations like parties or bars, where you might feel pressured to drink, minimizes the need for self-discipline. "If you need to be strong, you haven't been smart," says one expert.

✓ Rehearse in advance what you will do or say when you are confronted with a high-risk situation. You'll be better equipped to resist.

✓ Keep in mind that for most alcoholics, the urge to drink lessens over time. The first 90 days are the hardest.

✓ Motivation for abstinence is bound to waver. Renew that motivation by frequently reminding yourself why you quit in the first place.

✓ Realize that relapses will occur. Don't use a minor slip-up as an excuse to resume heavy drinking. Don't get fixated on recording consecutive days of abstinence. A relapse does not wipe out all that you've accomplished.

✓ Join a self-help group. AA is but one, Rational Recovery another. Recognize that they don't work for everyone, but since they're free, there's no risk in trying one.

8. PREVENTION AND TREATMENT

"Drunkeness is nothing but voluntary madness."
Seneca

"In vino veritas." (In wine there is truth.)
Pliny the Elder

"Total abstinence is easier to me than perfect moderation."
St. Augustine

"There are more old drunkards than old physicians."
Rabelais

"The innkeeper loves the drunkard, but not for a son-in-law."
Jewish proverb

"It provokes the desire, but it takes away the performance. Therefore, much drink may be said to be an equivocator with lechery."
William Shakespeare

ly based interventions, where counselors work with patients for one to four sessions—to both establish and to reinforce reasons for quitting—can be as effective as far more intensive therapy.

• The motivation to quit drinking varies considerably among alcoholics. For one, losing job and family isn't enough; for another, an embarrassing moment at a corporate party may change a man's life. It's always subjective.

• One of the key genetic factors in alcoholism is an ability to metabolize liquor too well, because of the presence of the liver enzyme alcohol dehydrogenase. Indeed, a common trait among alcoholics is the early ability to "drink others under the table."

• Twenty percent of all alcoholics can and do quit successfully on their own. Reseachers are just beginning to explore what is "special" about them and how to apply it to all alcoholics.

• In sum, no matter where and how an alcoholic recovers, this powerfully complex condition imposes three requirements for recovery: high, sustained motivation for quitting; readjustment to—and building—a life without liquor that includes family and peer support; and relapse prevention based on specific, well-rehearsed strategies of "cue" avoidance. These factors are being incorporated into treatment programs around the country.

As the tectonic plates of alcohol treatment shift, with new, flexible views sending

CAN YOU PICK HIM OUT OF A LINEUP?

Most alcoholics, explains Mark Schuckit, are not out on the street; they are individuals as unique and at the same time ordinary as you and me. That's one more reason not to apply a uniform treatment. "Alcoholics have jobs and close relationships, rarely (if ever) develop severe problems with the law, and many go unrecognized as alcoholics by their physicians. While most areas of these people's lives will eventually be impaired by their substance use, it is amazing how resilient people are." Other myths about the alcohol abuser:

• Drunks stay drunk. Actually, says Schuckit, most people drink more heavily on weekends, and start out each day alcohol-free.

• Drinkers can't quit. The truth is, substance abusers have little or no trouble quitting, and often do. Temporary drying out is easy and common. The problem is that sooner or later they begin drinking again.

• Alcoholics can't control their drinking. Actually, most alcohol abusers can and do control their drinking—for a short time, and often after a period of abstinence.

• Alcoholics have a preexisting psychiatric disorder, such as anxiety or depression, which they are attempting to medicate with alcohol. The truth: Only about 20 percent of alcoholics suffer from a psychiatric disorder. And though many claim they drink to combat depression or sleeplessness, those problems are often caused by drinking and disappear when drinking stops.

• Alcoholism is genetically determined. In fact, only about 20 percent of sons of alcoholics become alcoholics themselves; the number of women is even less. And though the risk of alcoholism is higher for identical than fraternal twins, most children of alcoholics do not become heavy drinkers themselves. As Schuckit emphasizes, "Predisposition does not mean predestination."

• Alcoholics drink because their friends do. Although it's true that we drink more often when our peers drink, the fact is that once a person begins to drink heavily, light-drinking or nondrinking friends are likely to fall away, leaving a peer group that consists mostly of other alcoholics.

• Once an addict, always an addict: therefore alcoholics should not take any psychotropic drugs, even prescribed medications. A growing body of research indicates that for some alcoholics, pharmacotherapy can provide a specifically targeted therapy that helps maintain recovery and abstinence. The AA model is traditionally distrustful of any medication.

a shudder through the mental health field, the person who may finally benefit is the alcoholic. New insights into alcoholism are yielding exciting treatment approaches, creative uses of medication, and innovative psychological interventions.

No one can ascertain exactly when man discovered that carbohydrates could be fermented into alcohol, although we know that in 6000 B.C., beer was made from barley in ancient Sumeria. What is clear is that societies have long venerated and feared alcohol. Ancient Egypt and Mesopotamia allowed liquor into temple rites but regulated its general use; the Greeks linked their entire intellectual flowering to grape and olive growing; medieval monks brewed beer.

In the U.S., in turn, alcohol has a history marked by ambivalence that has shaped treatment so powerfully that a singular model has prevailed for nearly a century.

During colonial days, alcohol consumption was extremely prevalent—and there was no concept of the "alcoholic." The dawn of the 19th century brought with it a temperance movement that, according to Harry Levine, Ph.D., professor of sociology at Queens College in New York City, viewed alcohol as an addictive substance as dangerous as today's heroin or crack. Abstinence was the only solution.

Prohibition flowered directly out of the rich soils of the temperance movement, and yet it only set the stage for a very dismal failure: Consumption of hard liquor (which was easier to smuggle) rose, while overall drinking fell. A typical "temperance" culture, the U.S. gave birth to Alcoholics Anonymous, which has flourished in other temperance cultures, such as England, Canada, and Scandinavia. Notes Levine, "AA is really a religious movement that has tremendous continuity with the 19th century temperance movement. And AA's understanding of alcoholism is the central understanding of addiction in American culture overall."

Alcohol consumption, especially hard liquor, has seen a steady decline to a mere 74 percent of its mid-1970s record high. Still, 13 million Americans are alcoholics. As researchers increasingly realize, a society's attitudes about alcohol strongly impact how individuals handle drinking. In Mediterranean, nontemperance cultures, wine is as common as bread, and individ-

MYTHOLOGY OR METHODOLOGY?

Bill Wilson, the founder of Alcoholics Anonymous, based his ground-breaking 12-step program on what worked for him. Half a century later there are 2 million AA members worldwide, half of them in this country, and many clinicians prescribe attendance. There's no doubt that AA has helped or even saved the lives of many. Yet the fundamental tenets of the AA-style self-help movement will always remain unverified—simply because the program is anonymous and cannot be formally studied.

According to Emil J. Chiauzzi, Ph.D., and Steven Liljegren, Ph.D., there is no rigorous scientific evidence to support some widespread AA teachings. Some of the disputed myths include:

• The most essential step in treatment is admitting alcoholism. Acceptance of the label "alcoholic" is considered half the battle in traditional treatment. "Hi, my name is John and I'm an alcoholic," is the typical opener at AA meetings. Yet researchers find that some individuals feel demoralized and depressed by labeling themselves the victims of an incurable, lifelong disease.

• Addicts cannot quit on their own. In fact, say Chiauzzi and Liljegren, 95-percent of smokers stop without the help of peers or professionals, even though addicted people themselves consider nicotine more addicting than alcohol. Although only about 20 percent of alcoholics recover solo, many may not be tapping their ability to do so.

• AA is crucial for maintaining abstinence. The number of alcoholics far outnumbers AA members (13 million versus 1 million), indicating that AA is not for everyone. Any increased propensity for AA members to stay on the wagon may reflect the fact that alcoholics who are already committed to recovery are also more likely to join AA.

• Recovering patients must avoid cues associated with drinking. Researchers find that systematically exposing the patient to long-standing cues can dramatically reduce the relapse danger those cues pose. Using slides, videotapes, and other paraphernalia, researchers found decreased reactivity among those addicted to heroin, cocaine, and alcohol. Cue exposure and coping skills may offer alcoholics a helpful tool in recovery.

uals drink every day without becoming "problem" drinkers. The per capita rate of alcohol consumption is high; cirrhosis is common; but behavioral problems from alcohol are rare, and society does not lay the blame for its ills at alcohol's door.

In sharp and astonishing contrast, a temperance culture is highly ambivalent about "demon" alcohol, which is seen as a

'In temperance cultures, people drink to get drunk. They tend to drink in short bursts of explosive, binge drinking.'

significant cause of our society's problems. In America, for instance, addiction is considered a root cause of violence. "In temperance cultures, people drink to get drunk. They tend to drink in short bursts of explosive, binge drinking. Wine cultures rarely get fall-down drunk," says Levine.

Levine cites the typical European view: "Papa comes in with liver disease, and the doctor calls in the family and says, 'Look, he's got to make life-style changes, stop drinking for a while, eat less fatty food, exercise, and minimize stress, and the whole family needs to work together to help him because these changes are hard.' Apparently this works. Tell these European practitioners that what they really need to do is send their patient to 90 meetings in 90 days and turn themselves over to a higher power and they'll say, 'I've got somebody with health and dietary problems and you've got a religious solution?'"

In a temperance culture where alcoholism is widely—if incorrectly—regarded as a disease, the cure until now has been relentless abstinence. Levine calls this model a "useful fiction" that works for some, but by no means all, alcoholics.

For any person, the first step in reducing alcohol intake is to understand alcohol itself. Advances in neuroscience have given us new insight into the actual impact of alcohol on the body—and the mind.

8. PREVENTION AND TREATMENT

FROM AN $800 BOTTLE OF DE LA Romanee-Conti, vintage 1978, to the crudest, rudest moonshine, alcohol impairs far more than our judgment and coordination. While we absorb the active ingredient of many psychoactive drugs in minuscule quantities—an ant can carry a few hits of LSD comfortably on its back—a drinker literally floods the body with alcohol. "Alcohol is problematic in part because it's so impotent," points out John Morgan, M.D., pharmacologist at City University Medical School in New York. "Other mood-altering substances are active in the bloodstream at literally thousands of magnitudes below what is required for alcohol."

As a result, alcohol—particularly in alcoholics, who can tolerate large amounts of liquor—exerts its toxic effect on virtually every organ system in the body, says Anthony Verga, M.D., medical director of Long Island's Seafield Center. The repercussions range from W.C. Fields's perpetually red nose to a torqued and failing liver common in alcoholics.

The liver, in fact, is the body's main line of defense against intoxication. But the fight is hardly fair. The organ's supply of alcohol dehydrogenase—the enzyme that helps break alcohol down into harmless water and carbon dioxide—can only handle about one drink's worth of alcohol an hour. Worse, the process produces acetaldehyde, a highly toxic chemical that attacks nearby tissues. The result is a variety of disorders. One of the gravest, cirrhosis, kills 26,000 Americans each year. But the liver is by no means the only casualty of alcoholism:

• After a few years of heavy drinking, some alcoholics develop pancreatitis, a painful inflammation of the pancreas.
• The heart wastes away, a condition called alcoholic cardiomyopathy.
• Drinking impairs blood flow. Heavy drinking can increase risk of stroke.
• A pregnant woman who drinks heavily can give birth to a baby with Fetal Alcohol syndrome (FAS), one of the leading causes of mental retardation. FAS occurs in up to 29 out of every 1,000 live births among known alcoholic mothers. Babies suffer lifelong neurological, anatomical, and behavioral problems. Some of them never learn to speak. Recent research indicates the casualty rate may be higher than once thought: Even babies appearing normal in infancy often grow up to manifest FAS disabilities.

• Alcohol takes its greatest toll on the brain. A small percentage of alcoholics may, after years, develop such severe brain damage that they remain permanently confused or become psychotic, suffering from auditory hallucinations. At least 45 percent of alcoholics entering treatment display some difficulty with problem solving, abstract thinking, psychomotor performance, and difficult memory tasks. About one in 10 suffers severe disorders like dementia.

Why can't a drunk brain think? Is there any way to correct the misfiring that chronic alcohol use induces? Alcohol appears to stimulate GABA in the brain: "What GABA does is slow down the firing of the cell on which the receptor is located," says Kranzler. This neuronal inhibition may contribute to the telltale signs of intoxication, from slurred speech to nodding off in mid-sentence. And, while Valium and barbiturates are distinctly different drugs than alcohol, they also target the GABA(A) receptor, suggesting a kinship.

> 'Traditional treatment says it's heresy to expose the drinker to cues, it will just increase his craving. In fact the opposite seems true.'

Alcohol cuts a far wider swath than GABA; it alters other receptors in the human brain:
• Drinking inhibits two of the three receptors for glutamate, the primary brain fuel and GABA's chemical opposite.
• Alcohol increases levels of a chemical messenger known as cyclic AMP, crucial for the healthy functioning of brain cells. To compensate, the brain reduces cyclic AMP levels, and over the long term, cells require alcohol to achieve normal levels.
• Levels of dopamine and serotonin, which contribute to behavioral reinforcement, also rise with alcohol consumption. Their increase may explain how alcohol tightens its grip on a drinker's habit.
• Alcohol increases levels of the brain's natural opiates, endorphins and enkephalins. This may be the key to the eternal, if politically incorrect, question: Why is drinking so much fun?

"One of the disadvantages of wine is that it makes a man mistake words for thoughts."
Samuel Johnson

"Bacchus has drowned more men than Neptune."
Giuseppe Garibaldi

"Bring in the bottled lightning, a clean tumbler, and a corkscrew."
Charles Dickens

"Malt does more than Milton can To justify God's ways to man."
A. E. Housman

"First you take a drink, then the drink takes a drink, then the drink takes you."
F. Scott Fitzgerald

"I'd rather have a bottle in front of me than a frontal lobotomy."
Tom Waits

Alcohol addiction is real, and withdrawal from alcohol can require a period of unpleasant detoxification. During that period, a former drinker can suffer acute anxiety, irritability, insomnia, increased blood pressure and body temperature, and severe, though temporary, confusion. Acute symptoms may fade after a week, but subtler symptoms of unease and insomnia may persist for months, making it difficult to remain alcohol-free.

Until recently, it has been an axiom of alcoholism treatment that withdrawal requires a (usually) month-long intensive inpatient treatment regimen, and then often a modified regimen where former drinkers live in halfway houses for up to six months. During the intensive phase, the alcoholic can detoxify from the drug while immersed in 24-hour support with other recovering alcoholics and counselors (often former alcoholics themselves). Group therapy is a feature of these programs, designed to break through the alcoholics' wall of denial and help set them on the straight and narrow path to a substance-free life. These programs can cost $16,000 or more per month.

The good news is that the very physiological nature of alcohol's seductive hold can lead us to new treatments for the condition. Pharmacologists are investigating drugs that may aid in nearly every aspect of alcohol abuse, reducing the craving of newly detoxified drinkers and even alleviating cognitive impairment.

NALTREXONE, FOR EXAMPLE—A DRUG originally developed to combat heroin addiction—may prevent binges when alcoholics relapse. Naltrexone blocks the opiates that the brain releases when someone drinks, so that an imbiber literally gets no kick from champagne. The drug may be most useful in the months after detoxification, when alcohol craving is strongest. Joseph R. Volpicelli, M.D., a University of Pennsylvania psychiatrist, and his colleagues found that only 23 percent of naltrexone patients relapsed within 12 weeks of treatment, versus 54 percent on placebo.

Volpicelli thinks that naltrexone may prove far more valuable than disulfiram, a 40-year-old drug well known as Antabuse. Disulfiram interferes with alcohol metabolism, so that takers suffer nausea, cramps, headaches, and vomiting when they drink. In practice, though, the drinker

stops taking it, because the physiological effects often build to such a crescendo—including violent heartbeats and hot flushes—that impending death is feared.

Buspirone (BuSpar), an antianxiety agent, may help alcoholics by minimizing the effects of withdrawal. Many doctors traditionally give benzodiazepine drugs, such as Valium, to dampen withdrawal symptoms—but those drugs can be addictive and may further blunt the memory of heavy drinkers. Buspirone may be a safer alternative. Other drugs that have shown promise include cipramine, which helps alcoholics who are also suffering from major depression, and deisipramine, another antidepressant that seems to reduce drinking.

The new view of alcoholism is of a complex condition arising from the intricate and unpredictable interplay of social, biological, and psychological factors. "Alcoholism is not a disorder caused uniquely by genes," explains Mark Schuckit, M.D., of the Veteran's Administration Medical Center in La Jolla, California. "Some persons become alcoholic solely through environmental exposure; others have biological and psychological predispositions. There are many different paths to alcoholism. Once a person drinks regularly, however, the body's reaction to and tolerance of alcohol changes, so that the person needs more alcohol. Patients need to be educated about the many factors that contribute to the disorder, so they can understand that the situation is not hopeless."

Studies show that the type of therapy an alcoholic receives isn't as important as the fact that he or she gets some treatment.

"There are very few harmful or useless treatment programs for substance use disorders," says Schuckit. "If you are highly motivated, then you are likely to do well in almost any program you choose."

The programs most alcoholics choose are based on the Minnesota Model, which views alcoholism as an incurable disease. It involves group counseling to confront a "denying" drunk, education about alcohol's consequences, and confessional self-help organizations like the AA.

There are already cracks in the Minnesota Model's clinical monopoly. Although the personal experiences of thousands of alcoholics attest to the model's value, its failure rate—about 50 percent—reveals the futility of assembly-line treatment. Indeed, aversion therapy, stress-

management, and family therapy are proving effective for many alcoholics.

Take the fact that an alcoholic's memory may be impaired—leading to treatment problems that have little to do with the so-called ubiquitous "denial" syndrome. "Ten years ago, if an alcoholic didn't seem to be catching on to treatment, it was assumed that he or she was 'in denial', " says Tim Sheehan, R.N., Ph.D., of Minnesota's Hazelden Foundation, arguably the archetypal inpatient treatment center. "Now we're recognizing that there may be lingering cognitive deficits." During treatment, these patients are exposed to fewer concepts, which are reinforced often.

THREE NEW APPROACHES—ALL OF them "heretical" by the traditional abstinence model—eschew ideology and spiritual baggage in favor of simple pragmatism. Some alcoholics do quite well with them. They are:

• Harm reduction, which recognizes that moderate drinking is preferable to lost weekends. Any decrease in alcohol intake is grounds for a (alcohol-free) toast.

• Brief intervention. In as little as half an hour, an intervention attempts to show the subject how drinking may be impairing everything from his liver to his livelihood; helps him rate himself on a series of questions about his life and drinking; and then places him on a continuum with his drinking peers so that he has a sense of the nature of his problem. In addition, brief sessions help the person focus on motivations for reducing drinking. Brief intervention, lasting four sessions at most, can be as effective as more intensive treatments for many individuals, says Donovan.

• Cue exposure, or systematically exposing and desensitizing the alcoholic to cues that might trigger drinking. According to Liljegren, "traditional treatment says it's heresy to expose the drinker, it will just increase his craving. In fact, the opposite seems true; the data suggest cue exposure is the very thing we should be doing."

By exposing the drinker to cues for drinking that might normally stimulate intense craving, and by refusing to reinforce those cues with the "pleasure" of drink, alcoholics become less responsive to those cues over time. The drinkers' sense of self-confidence and efficacy rise, proving that they can restrain from drinking in the presence of cues. And it provides the opportunity for drinkers to learn how to cope with their problem in the outside world.

8. PREVENTION AND TREATMENT

Typical drinking cues, notes Liljegren, include money, payday, peers, parties, bars and other drinking settings, and emotions—particularly anger, sadness, and fear. "I had a young woman here," recalls Liljegren, "who was very upset about her ex-boyfriend, who himself was a drinker. I asked her mother to bring in a picture of him. When she saw the picture she was very upset." Liljegren and the patient were able to explore the patient's feelings until she was confident that she would not drink when she actually bumped into the young man out in the world.

One of the biggest shifts in alcohol treatment is from inpatient to outpatient therapy. "Research has found that less costly outpatient programs may be as effective as inpatient programs," points out Donovan. Outpatient treatment allows patients whose prognosis is more favorable to adjust to life without booze in a real-world environment. And it's a lot cheaper.

In contrast, alcoholics with preexisting medical or psychiatric illnesses—and whose insurance company or bank account can cover bills—should consider inpatient treatment. So should those who have failed outpatient therapy, or whose family environment is chaotic.

It's during the months and years that follow initial treatment, says Schuckit, that the real work of recovery takes place. "Counselors work with the patient and family.

Giving up alcoholism is a loss of a way of life—and the alcoholic needs to grieve. Magical thinking needs to be corrected; many patients and families have the idea that all problems will fade as they become sober. Families need a way to deal with the spouse anger that inevitably comes out as the patient becomes sober, and to maintain enthusiasm.

"Contact with recovering people is important, as is access to self-help. The former drinker needs to set up plans about what to do with free time that used to be spent drinking. A whole life needs to be rebuilt without alcohol. Relapse prevention is important. A former alcoholic needs to identify the triggers to drink and rehearse strategies to help him handle those triggers. Perpetual alertness is required."

Ironically, the months following intensive treatment can put more strain on a family than years of chronic alcohol abuse. About 25 percent of marriages break up within a year of one partner's joining AA, says Barbara McCrady, Ph.D., clinical director of the Rutgers Center for Alcohol Studies. She cites three reasons:

• Traditional AA protocol calls for meetings—lots of them. "Spouses often say, 'First I lost him to alcohol, now I've lost him to AA,'" says McCrady. The alcoholic's reliance on fellow program members, rather than family, can foster considerable resentment.

• Some families have for years blamed all of their difficulties on the alcoholic's

addiction. Only when the drinker is no longer drinking do they realize that long-established alcohol problems do not just vanish overnight.

• Families that remain intact despite a member's drinking have worked out their own ways to remain a family unit. "They've reallocated responsibilities, roles, and chores, and the family functions pretty well," McCrady says. "Now there's this person who is sober and wants to reestablish a position in the family." But the family may be hesitant if the alcoholic has tried—and failed—to stay sober in the past.

Perhaps one of the most interesting new paths of research is the study of alcoholics who quit on their own. "We are beginning to explore in depth the characteristics of these people—the ones who can just walk away from their addiction in the absence of any formal treatment," explains Donovan. Perhaps they simply have in greater measure the same hope and courage of the ordinary alcoholic, who frequently quits for a day or a week or a month, and then returns to the bottle. As researchers are beginning to realize, if they can emphasize the innate capacity present in most drinkers to improve, a great deal may be gained. A shift in viewpoint can help lift the burden of an all-or-nothing view where "one drink, one drunk" means that a glass of champagne on one's wedding day is an unequivocal failure.

'Harm Reduction' Approach May Be Middle Ground

Paul Cotton

MEDICINE has been given a back seat in this country's so-called war on drugs.

Dealing with drug addiction was once primarily the purview of physicians. But since the initiation of prohibition in the early part of this century, and especially since the "war on drugs" was declared in the 1970s, drug use, abuse, and addiction have been treated primarily as crimes and only secondarily as a public health problem. Critics say this makes the public health problem worse.

Medicine as Cornerstone

Medicine, however, is the cornerstone of an alternative approach to drug policy referred to as "harm reduction." This approach emphasizes comprehensive and compassionate treatment for addiction, with physicians providing medical therapy and not viewing abstinence as the only worthy outcome.

International comparison studies suggest that the success of medical treatment for heroin addiction is related to the quality of the treating staff, especially the involvement of physicians, says John C. Ball, PhD, a visiting scientist at the National Institute on Drug Abuse (NIDA) Addiction Research Center. Yet physicians make up only a small percentage of the staff in most addiction treatment programs in the United States, which may in part explain why they are perceived by many here to be ineffective, says Ball.

Harm reduction also includes efforts, such as clean needle exchange programs, to minimize the adverse effects of drug abuse that often continue at diminished levels during treatment. Fears that needle exchange programs would increase drug abuse have not been borne out in scientific studies.

The harm reduction emphasis on caring over incarceration in some cases includes decriminalization or unofficial tolerance of illicit drug use, particularly of the "soft" drug marijuana, which is said to be less dangerous than "hard" drugs, like heroin and cocaine, and some say is even less dangerous than the legal drugs alcohol and tobacco.

While critics say any letup in law enforcement will lead to massive increases in the number of addicts, proponents of harm reduction say that this has not been the case in the Netherlands, where possession of up to 30 g of marijuana is tolerated, with no apparent increase in use, although reliable statistics are hard to come by.

Harm reduction is being implemented to differing degrees in parts of Europe and Australia and is advocated in the United States by a small but growing number of medical and political leaders. There were 11 physicians among 107 people who signed a full-page advertisement in the *New York Times* issue of February 27, 1994, which criticized current drug policies for failing to "deal with the excess crime, violence, and disease caused by drug prohibition."

The ad, placed by the Drug Policy Foundation, Washington, DC, says that "full legalization is not the only alternative. Many options are available, including decriminalizing users only, permitting doctors to prescribe some drugs to addicts to undercut the black market, borrowing elements of the European public health model, or shifting the allocation of anti-drug resources to focus mainly on treatment and prevention."

Call for Federal Commission

More than 100 physicians, including 15 members of the California Academy of Family Physicians board of directors, have signed a resolution by the National Coalition for Drug Policy calling for establishment of a federal commission to rewrite drug laws to "recognize drug use and abuse as the medical and social problems that they are."

The Clinton administration is leaning slightly in the harm reduction direction. Its drug policy budget proposal reduces interdiction funding by $95 million and adds $355 million in new funding for "hard-core" heroin- and cocaine-user therapy. "Effective therapy is the key to breaking the cycle of hard-core addictive drug use," says White House drug czar Lee Brown. He says 20% of cocaine users consume 80% of the cocaine sold. These hard-core users cause a "disproportionate share of violent crime and drive the demand for drugs." Targeting treatment at them is "a good investment for America," says Brown.

The $355-million increase is, however, enough to cover treatment for only about 140 000 addicts per year. The total amount for drug therapy will still be well under half what is needed. Currently, only an estimated 115 000 of the 600 000 heroin addicts in the United States are getting treatment.

Decriminalization is not on the official agenda either, a point underscored by the harsh reaction to the remark by Surgeon General Joycelyn Elders, MD, that legalization should be studied.

NIDA does have a Medications Development Division screening potential anticocaine agents in hopes of replicating the effective yet ever-controversial treatment of heroin addiction with methadone. Several products are in the pipeline, but none are in clinical trials yet.

In fact, antiaddiction drug development is nearly regulated to death by prohibition paranoia, especially the policies of the Drug Enforcement Administration. A report on NIDA's drug development program by the Institute of Medicine (IOM) notes that pharmaceutical firms have little interest in the field because of all the red tape, official suspicion, and the uncertain market created by these regulations, as well as by a perceived lack of interest among physicians in treating addiction.

This and a lack of federal leadership have resulted in what the IOM report calls an "inadequate science base on addiction." Prevention of compulsive drug use is the key problem, yet knowledge about the pathophysiology of abstinence, withdrawal, craving, and relapse "is still rudimentary. . . . Unless basic research is supported at an appropriate funding level, it will be difficult to make the necessary progress," says the IOM report, adding that the fiscal year 1994 appropriation of $36 million for NIDA's drug development program "has fallen far short" of what is needed.

The underfunding may stem in part from widespread fear of drugs, the myth that drug abuse is more a moral than a biological phenomenon, and that treating addiction with drugs merely replaces one addiction with another.

The public needs to understand that "addiction is not just a scourge but a disease," says NIDA Director Alan Leshner, PhD. "If we are going to have any significant inroads, we need to recognize that addiction is a brain disease, that it is treatable, and that treatment is complex."

There is theoretically great promise for developing antiaddiction medications. There are natural neural receptors and endogenous counterparts produced in humans for the commonly used illegal drugs. And while each drug acts on different receptors, "all seem to funnel through one common reward pathway in the brain," says Solomon Snyder, MD, director of neuroscience at The Johns Hopkins University School of Medicine, Baltimore, Md. This common anatomical pathway lies in neural circuitry leading from lower brain regions to the nucleus accumbens in the forebrain. It seems to play a role in normal satisfaction-seeking behaviors involving food and sex but gets exaggerated in addiction, says Snyder.

That exaggeration seems to be responsible for drug-seeking behavior and the propensity for craving and relapse that marks addiction. Once drug use turns into an addiction, "apparently there are some long-term changes there, like memory, which causes you to go back" to the drug, says Snyder. This mechanism may explain the seemingly involuntary nature of addiction. "Drug-seeking behavior does not occur because addicts are evil. It is because of biology, a disease," says Snyder.

While the causes of drug abuse, dependency, and addiction remain unclear, scientific evidence supports the view of addiction as a chronic disease, says Leshner. Addicts have a disability and therefore are "entitled to treatment," the same as patients with any other disease, he says.

However, that is not now the case. Those who treat addicts complain about a double standard that holds therapy for this chronic disease to be useless unless it results in a complete cure. They note that no one says insulin therapy is ineffective because it does not cure diabetes, no one expects heart disease patients to be weaned from medicines after 6 months, nor does anyone advocate withdrawal of treatment for such diseases if the patient binges on Big Macs.

But such unrealistic restrictions are put on methadone treatment for heroin addiction and on other addiction therapies. "Addiction is the single most stigmatized public health problem in this country," says Leshner. "It is viewed as being a terrible failure of will and moral weakness by a majority of people." The resulting restrictions on care represent a "fundamental misunderstanding" of the disease, the needs of the individual patient, and the efficacy of treatment, he says.

"There is no inherent reason why pharmacologic therapy cannot play as important a role in the treatment of drug addiction as other medicinal agents do in the treatment of heart disease, diabetes, and a host of other illnesses," says the IOM report. As with other chronic diseases, the fact that pharmacotherapy for addiction "might not treat root causes of the illness or offer a permanent cure does not detract from its value in improving both quality of life and mortality."

Treatment Is Not Temporary

"Some patients will benefit from ongoing therapy, perhaps for the rest of their lives, as is the case with insulin," says Mark W. Parrino, MPA, president of the American Methadone Treatment Association, New York, NY. "If the patient continues to benefit from continued use of medication, that is precisely what should be given. Nowhere else do we say to patients using medication that they need to curtail it at some particular point even though the patient continues to benefit from its use."

Methadone clinics in the United States vary widely in quality. However, daily methadone maintenance therapy for heroin addiction has been shown repeatedly to reduce the amount of opiate abuse by 80% or more and to similarly reduce the criminal activity necessary for most addicts to afford drugs. Rates of human immunodeficiency virus seroconversion are lower; in one NIDA study, only 3.5% of addicts in therapy seroconverted vs 22% of addicts not in treatment. Overall health and nutritional status improve markedly, and use of primary health care and emergency departments is reduced. Therapy is even easier since the approval of methadyl acetate (levo-alpha-acetylmethadol or LAAM), an agent similar to methadone that needs to be administered only three times per week.

While methadone is no magic bullet, proponents say it is a critical component of a comprehensive approach to intervention and sustained recovery in tandem with medical treatment, psychotherapy, psychosocial rehabilitation, and an array of appropriate social and economic support.

Also clearly documented, says Leshner, is the fact that 82% of addicts will relapse to pretreatment levels of heroin use within 1 year of discontinuing methadone maintenance therapy.

Still, many methadone programs try to wean patients from therapy in an attempt to make them "drug free." Data from Australia that was presented at the National Methadone Conference in Washington, DC, this spring document how such an approach, although well intentioned, is in fact counterproductive.

Outcomes have been followed up since 1986 at two clinics in working-class western suburbs of Sydney. One attempts to promote abstinence, continually lowering daily doses with the goal of getting patients permanently off all drugs. If patients continue to inject opioids during treatment, their methadone dose is reduced or cut off. The other clinic makes no attempt to decrease dosage and increases it if patients continue injecting opioids.

"Paradoxically, patients seem to be doing worse" in the abstinence-oriented program, says John R. M. Caplehorn, MD, University of Sydney Department of Public Health. These patients were twice as likely to continue using heroin while in treatment as those on indefinite maintenance. Comparison of dispensing records and urine test results shows that "as you start to reduce the methadone, the heroin use comes up. All the difference between the two clinics can be accounted for by methadone dose," he says.

More importantly, patients on indefinite maintenance were 70% less likely to die from drug use, and most of the difference in death rates was from accidental overdoses in patients who were supposed to have become drug free once they left treatment, says Caplehorn. There was also a lower rate of suicide with indefinite therapy.

Few other forms of preventive medicine are as effective, notes Caplehorn. "Taking aspirin every morning to prevent heart attacks is not nearly as effective. Asthma medication does not reduce the death rate as much as this."

Caplehorn says he had advocated low doses and weaning patients off methadone before seeing these results. He now concludes that the abstinence-oriented approach "needlessly" weakens methadone efficacy and is in fact "unethical."

Leshner says that while the treatment cost of properly used methadone is $3000 per year per addict, it can prevent $40 000 to $50 000 in crime and $35 000 in jail costs. "The impacts are astronomical. When we come out with a treatment equal to the quality of methadone for cocaine, it will have a phenomenal impact," says Leshner.

There are several candidate agents vying to become a methadonelike treatment for cocaine addiction. The goal is a long-acting agent that comes on slowly without inducing intense euphoria, says Bertha K. Madras, PhD, associate professor of psychobiology at Harvard Medical School. Her research at the New England Primate Center, Southborough, Mass, has demonstrated with positron emission tomography that one such agent, indatraline, remains latched onto cocaine receptors for more than 24 hours.

Cocaine Conundrum

But "whether a compound like this would produce tolerance or increase abuse liability is unknown because none of these compounds has been tested in humans," says Madras.

Although concerned about the danger of replacing a highly addictive drug like cocaine with another drug that also has potential to be highly addictive, she says that "if you look very carefully at the whole field, what have been successful are drug substitutes, compounds that behave similarly to the abused drug: methadone and LAAM for heroin and the nicotine patch for cigarette smoking," says Madras.

Still, cocaine addiction is different. Abusers tend to binge rather than maintain a steady blood level of the drug, as they do with heroin and nicotine. "People tend to get very high on cocaine and then crash. They're not going to be satisfied with just getting a dose regularly and leaving it at that," says Marc Galanter, MD, director of the Division of Alcohol and Drug Abuse at New York (NY) University School of Medicine and a board member of the American Society of Addiction Medicine.

The pharmacology is not so simple, either. While it is known that cocaine acts by inhibiting dopamine reuptake, the IOM report notes that other neurotransmitter and endogenous opiate peptide interactions are also likely to be important, making the development of medication "difficult because no single target site is immediately apparent." It is not clear whether the best strategy is to target the pleasure-seeking aspect of cocaine use or the dysphoria and distressful consequences of abstinence, says the report, concluding that "in fact, an optimal strategy might require the use of several drugs that have different mechanisms of action."

A monoclonal antibody vaccine that is in development cleaves cocaine, rendering it inactive. The IOM report notes that this has the advantage of leaving the essential dopamine system intact and functional and says it is something that NIDA's drug development program should "pursue aggressively."

For now, only the tricyclic antidepressant desipramine has been demonstrated to decrease the amount of cocaine use when studied in outpatients, says the IOM report. "But no medication is available to clinicians that will consistently reduce the return to cocaine use." Galanter says that caring for addicts in intensive, drug-free inpatient facilities appears to be the "appropriate" therapy for cocaine addiction, although they are expensive and limited in number.

Ambivalence on Marijuana

Medicine seems to be at a loss when confronted with marijuana, the most widely used illegal drug. It is unclear what level of marijuana use warrants therapy, says Galanter.

"Obviously, there are casual marijuana users who apparently do not suffer any serious ill effects." Even for daily users with functional deficits, "it is complicated as to how they might be treated, and most don't come in for treatment," says Galanter.

The natural receptor for marijuana and the previously unknown endogenous neurotransmitter that binds to it were recently identified. However, there apparently are no agonists or antagonists being developed as potential therapies. Some say there is no need for such therapies because marijuana is not, by most assessments, physically addictive. "There is no need to develop a drug to combat marijuana addiction if it's not addictive," says Snyder. He says he doubts that there is any role for medical therapy against marijuana abuse.

Galanter says network therapy, in which family and friends cooperate with clinicians in cajoling patients to quit, is probably the best therapy for marijuana dependency.

Network therapy works well for many substance-abusing patients, who are often afflicted with a "sense of despairing and being alone," says Galanter. Patients do better with treatment provided "in a context where there is a positive attitude, no recrimination," and support available when craving or relapse occur.

The traditional approach, "where patients talk about what's bothering them and the therapist tries to help understand and put things into perspective, does not really address the problem of relapse or prepare them for how to deal with it effectively," which is why so many patients do so poorly, he says.

Self-medication?

Discerning when drug abuse is in fact an attempt to self-medicate for other disorders may also improve treatment efficacy. Some studies suggest that more than two thirds of patients with drug disorders also have a mental disorder, and that almost a third of those with a mental disorder also have a drug problem.

NIDA recently funded a study of the possibility that some cocaine abusers suffer from attention deficit disorder. They may be self-medicating with cocaine "in the same way we give ritalin to kids. If we do a better job of figuring out these subgroups, we may be able to come up with appropriate treatment," says Herbert D. Kleber, MD, medical director of the Center on Addiction and Substance Abuse at Columbia University, New York, NY.

Individualized care for addicts may improve nonpharmacologic treatment, as well. Preliminary data from a patient-matching study in which therapy was tailored to individual alcohol addicts on the basis of extensive, 8-hour assessments show that patients on average are keeping two thirds of their appointments, a retention rate that is "incredible for alcoholism," says Richard K. Fuller, MD, director of clinical and prevention research at the National Institute on Alcohol Abuse and Alcoholism.

Snyder says the clearest example of self-medication is abuse of alcohol for depression. "Alcoholic families tend to be loaded with depression," he notes. And he speculates that the fact that people take cocaine for stimulation "indicates that life isn't adequately stimulating for them to start with, so they are at least a little bit depressed" as well.

In fact, the core of harm reduction may be in getting physicians and the rest of society to acknowledge that much drug abuse may represent attempts by addicts and abusers to self-medicate for addiction or other disorders that, for whatever reason, they themselves or the health care system are not otherwise treating.

"We have a group of people employed to control the flow of drugs in society called doctors," says Caplehorn. In Australia, the New South Wales government allows individual general practice physicians to become accredited to prescribe methadone.

Raymond Seidler, MD, a general practitioner in Waterloo, New South Wales, says he has heroin addicts "interspersed with my normal medical practice. It is no more difficult than treating a patient with diabetes. In fact, in my experience, methadone patients are more compliant than the average diabetic."

The Cost
of Living Clean

**When the answer is treatment, these are the
questions: What works, and what doesn't?
How much does it cost, and can we afford it?**

Norman Atkins

THEY APPEARED FROM the smoke and the shadows of the city. There had been no newspaper advertisements, not a single poster on a train platform or a public-service announcement on local TV. Yet when a new methadone program opened in Pittsburgh last year, heroin addicts kept filing in. Michael Dennis, who studies drug treatment there for the Research Triangle Institute, was stunned when he witnessed this response. It convinced him of the need for more programs. "Increase the supply of treatment," he says, "and you will increase the demand."

Mathea Falco, president of Drug Strategies, a nonprofit public-policy organization, estimates that there are 6 million Americans with serious drug problems, among whom perhaps 2 million are chronic, "hard-core" addicts. Roughly one-quarter of the addicts are hooked on heroin and three-quarters on cocaine; many are also alcoholic. For most, private rehab centers are prohibitively expensive, and locating an empty bed in a publicly funded facility requires a notoriously long wait.

Despite countless campaign promises of "treatment on demand," President Clinton's new anti-drug budget was scarcely a seismic shift. The budget calls for 74,000 new treatment slots, and the crime bill could add 66,000 more, but that's still a far cry from treatment on demand. Experts reckon that as few as one out of four of those who need treatment will be able to get it.

---

*Methadone is a legalized
synthetic opiate that blocks
heroin cravings, causes no
harmful side effects, and
produces no high.*

For those few the question is, what kind? What type of treatment works best for different people, and what are the most cost-effective models for the American taxpayers? Unfortunately, in the world of drug rehabilitation, there is no hard science to point the way to guaranteed cures. Programs can last from a few weeks to a few years. Some are led by saints, others by hucksters. Some cost upward of $25,000 a patient; others, like Narcotics Anonymous, cost nothing.

Therapeutic Communities (TCs) are highly structured, one- to two-year residential treatment programs, the largest of which is Phoenix House, which has roughly 15 percent of the nation's 12,000 beds. Phoenix House embodies a military-style, in-your-face, group-encounter approach. New residents scrub toilets and climb an elaborate hierarchy of work responsibilities. Facial hair and sex are *verboten;* using the phone is a privilege to be earned. Rule breakers wear signs around their necks advertising the error of their ways. Naturally, there is a high turnover in the first 60 days. While most of Phoenix House's long-term residents admit that they found it oppressive and weird at first, they now claim it was just what they needed to become drug free.

TCs tend to be best suited for hard-core addicts, or what UCLA researcher Douglas Anglin calls the "dysfunctionally dependent." Phoenix House costs about $15,000 per resident per year; some other programs run between $10,000 and $25,000, much of which comes from government support or charitable dollars. Phoenix House president Mitchell Rosenthal says the nation could plausibly expand TC capacity to 100,000 beds in the next four years, and he calls for converting abandoned military bases into TCs. Meanwhile, Mathea Falco argues that for an additional 10 percent investment on top of the $30,000 to $40,000 it costs to incarcerate a drug addict for a year, a prison-based TC can knock down ghastly recidivism rates.

For heroin injectors, methadone maintenance has been the treatment of choice since it was first introduced three decades ago. Methadone is a legalized synthetic opiate that blocks heroin cravings, causes no harmful side effects and produces no high. A small portion of the approximately 125,000 currently enrolled in methadone programs will use the drug as a bridge to abstinence; many others maintain a crime-free life while on methadone. Some critics worry that the treatment method simply replaces an illegal addiction with a legal one. Others point out that methadone can't neutralize cocaine, which many recovering heroin abusers still snort or smoke. Methadone is occasionally sold on the street when extra doses are dispensed to recovering addicts. It's expected that a new long-acting methadone approved by the Food and Drug Administration last year will put an end to this practice.

Chemical dependency programs offer short-term residential treatment.

The best methadone programs offer counseling and other rehabilitative services, and studies indicate that the rate of

crime commission drops 65 percent for those who stay in the program at least one year; after three years, there is an 85 percent decrease. Says Falco: "For heroin addicts who have truly tried over and over again to kick the habit, methadone may be the only course. It is often a very effective way of stabilizing their lives."

Chemical dependency (CD) programs offer short-term residential treatment, usually a monthlong stay, often starting with a period of detoxification. Ideally, the stay is followed by a year of after care, meaning anything from placement in a halfway house to attendance at self-help groups. Based on AA's 12-step model of personal change, CD programs specialize in treating alcoholics and are less effective, studies show, at helping drug addicts. But at Hazelden, in Center City, Minn., the nation's oldest and best regarded CD program, nearly half the residents abuse some combination of drugs and alcohol. "We think it's dependency and not the drug of choice that is the issue," says Jerry Spicer, Hazelden's president. At an average of $9,300 per month, Hazelden might be appropriate for residents whose private insurance will cover it or whose families can afford it. Since CD programs are generally not publicly financed, however, hard-core addicts (the vast majority of those seeking treatment are poor and uninsured) have to turn elsewhere.

In the 1980s, hospital-based CD programs were notorious for over-treating anyone with dirty urine as a way to suck up a seemingly endless supply of insurance coverage. Since then, with the insurance industry singing the mantra of managed care, half of the nation's CD programs have dried up, and there are only an estimated 9,000 beds in the country today. Says Dean Gerstein of the National Opinion Research Center, one of the nation's leading experts on treatment effectiveness: "The trend seems to be that the only good patient is an outpatient."

There are roughly 660,000 outpatients in day-treatment programs, ranging from a come-when-you-like drop-in center and weekly pep talks from a social worker to daily acupuncture sessions. (Chinese acupuncture techniques are reported to be able to suppress cocaine cravings.) The Matrix Institute, in Los Angeles, runs a highly structured program that meets four to six hours per week. Matrix claims that this is a "practical" option for working, functioning cocaine addicts who don't have either the time or the need for more intensive treatment. Such programs

generally are not well-suited to poverty-stricken hard-core addicts. "Brief interventions for the dysfunctionally dependent and lifetime poor," says Douglas Anglin, "is like pissing upwind."

When tied to mandates from a "drug court," however, day programs may be more promising. That's certainly what Jeffrey Tauber discovered when he suited up as an Oakland, Calif., municipal judge in drug court in 1986. "I kept seeing the same people going in and out of the system like

---

Treatment is a cost-effective strategy for reducing the more than $225 billion substance abuse costs in the United States.

---

a revolving door," he says, "and their drug problems certainly weren't being treated." So three and a half years ago, Tauber created a program that speedily steers almost everyone who appears in his court to drug treatment. Whereas people lingered in jail for two to three months after arrest, now Tauber disposes of their cases within two days. He gives them two years' probation and a contract that lays out rewards and sanctions and requires them to meet weekly with their probation officer, submit to random urine testing and enter an outpatient treatment program. "It's more important that they are in contact with the court system three or four days a week than what the treatment is," says Tauber.

Not only has the felony-recidivism rate among Tauber's probationers been cut in half, but Oakland earned $1 million last year renting its empty jail cells to neighboring counties. Drug courts in Portland, Ore., and Miami are experiencing similar success. "First-time nonviolent drug offenders should be steered to treatment before prison," says Falco. "It has nothing to do with being soft or tough on drug crime but with putting our resources into more effective alternatives."

Gerstein cautions against expecting scientific proof of some perfect rehabilitative method. Based on his extensive social-science research, however, he estimates that roughly half of those patients entering CD, outpatient or methadone programs will stick with their treatment regimen and one-half to three-quarters of those will recover from their addictions and stabilize their lives; one-quarter of TC residents will gut out the long-term treatment, and of those who do, 80 percent will continue to be drug-free on their own. But Gerstein and others also stress that many recovered addicts will relapse, sometimes many times through the years.

It is this notion that prompts Anglin to advocate a coordinated safety net of rehabilitative services that will catch addicts each time they slip and match them with treatment methods best suited to their needs at that time. Even with modest success rates, Anglin and others are convinced that treatment is a cost-effective strategy for reducing the more than $225 billion that substance abuse costs the United States each year. For those who doubt that addicts will avail themselves of new treatment programs, the lesson that Michael Dennis derives from the Pittsburgh methadone program is very simple: If you build it, they will come.

NORMAN ATKINS *interviewed Marian Wright Edelman in RS 645/646.*

New Drug Approval Approach Boosts

Fight Against Heroin Addiction

Dixie Farley

Dixie Farley is a staff writer for FDA Consumer.

A new approach to bringing drugs to market won high marks last year when the Food and Drug Administration approved levo-alpha-acetyl-methadol (Orlaam, also known as LAAM) in record time. LAAM is only the second synthetic narcotic medication approved to treat heroin and other opioid addiction through outpatient narcotic maintenance treatment programs. The other medication is methadone, approved almost 25 years ago.

Chronic and relapsing, heroin addiction controls its victims. It wastes lives and addicts newborns along with their mothers. It spreads infection with HIV, the virus that causes AIDS, and other infectious diseases through the sharing of dirty needles. It is connected with violent crime and casts a heavy economic burden upon society.

More than 586,000 Americans use heroin at least weekly, the Office of National Drug Control Policy reports.

LAAM was approved July 20, 1993, only 18 days after FDA received the new drug application.

The "new approach" that made this speedy approval possible involved cooperation among FDA drug review and compliance staffs, a new division of the National Institutes of Health's National Institute on Drug Abuse (NIDA), the Drug Enforcement Administration, and industry—in this case, Biometric Research Institute Inc., of Arlington, Va.

The cooperative clinical tests underpin-

ning the approval took just 18 months from protocol development to patient enrollment, completion of the first phase of the study, and report to the agency.

NIDA's Medications Development Division (MDD) was established in 1990 to encourage development of anti-addiction medications. Although LAAM had been studied for many years, it was sitting on a "back burner" at NIDA.

About the same time MDD was created, FDA set up its Pilot Drug Evaluation Staff to streamline drug approval. The agency assigned review of anti-addiction medications to the new staff, and hired experts in drug abuse issues, including senior scientist Michael Klein, Ph.D.

"In 1990, we advised NIDA," Klein says, "to reassemble the data on LAAM submitted in the 1980s in two rejected new drug applications, and give them back to us as an investigational new drug application. The IND gave us a way to get involved in development from step 1, and make recommendations for the eventual submission of the NDA."

Klein and others reviewed the IND and parceled out certain older studies for review by FDA's Drug Abuse Advisory Committee.

"We also wanted studies of the new population of patients," Klein says. "Many people abusing heroin today also use other drugs, such as crack cocaine, which wasn't around in the early 1980s."

MDD conferred with FDA to develop

directions for using LAAM. Researchers were to follow the directions, spot problems, and try to correct them. To eliminate bias, FDA specified using only clinics that had never studied LAAM.

MDD contracted for the FDA-guided trials with 26 Department of Veterans Affairs (VA) medical centers and university clinics. According to MDD health scientist administrator Paul Coulis, Ph.D., "We worked with FDA all along, sharing our findings as they developed."

Klein says, "We got a very nice picture of the adequacy of the labeling and potential problems today, which we could couple with the old studies, some of which did show efficacy."

Maintenance Medications, Close Up

Methadone and LAAM are oral narcotics that work in the body much like morphine does. When taken for short periods by non-addicts, they kill pain, sedate the central nervous system, and relax smooth muscle tissues.

Both medications can themselves produce dependence. But when taken as part of a maintenance treatment program, they do not cause euphoria. They in fact block the "highs" of other opioid narcotics, such as heroin, and suppress the symptoms of withdrawal. These symptoms include increased blood pressure and temperature, rapid heartbeat, "goose-flesh" (piloerection), runny nose (rhinorrhea), watery eyes (lacrimation), tremors, insom-

Methadone and LAAM can produce dependence, but they do not cause euphoria when taken as part of a maintenance treatment program.

nia, vomiting, abdominal cramps, restlessness, weakness, headache, hot or cold flashes, and drug craving. Withdrawal from methadone or LAAM causes similar symptoms, but starts more slowly, is less severe, and continues for a longer time.

LAAM's advantage is that it works for 48 to 72 hours after a dose is taken, compared to 24 hours for methadone. With fewer required visits, patients have the chance to lead a more normal existence and clinics have the option to treat more patients.

Methadone must be given every day, and take-home doses are permitted in selected cases.

LAAM is not approved for daily treatment because daily use of the usual doses will lead to serious overdose. Evaluated only as an in-clinic medication, LAAM is not allowed in take-home doses. In extreme situations, however, certain LAAM patients may be temporarily switched to methadone for a take-home dose when they know in advance they can't come to the clinic for a scheduled LAAM dose. Also, in-clinic dosing reduces the likelihood of patients' diverting the medication to street sales.

Methadone and LAAM can interact adversely with tranquilizers, tricyclic antidepressants, alcohol, and other drugs. They can worsen low blood pressure and asthma. They can cause breathing difficulty and impaired circulation. Less serious methadone side effects include dizziness, vomiting, and sweating; LAAM can cause flu-like symptoms, diarrhea, and muscle aches.

Maintenance Works

"If your goal is to reduce drug abuse," says Nicholas Reuter, a consumer safety officer in FDA's Office of Health Affairs, "a properly administered maintenance program appears to be the most effective treatment." Reuter is executive secretary of the federal interagency review board that coordinates regulation of the programs. Last year, the board reviewed U.S. and international research on methadone—which has been studied extensively—fol-

lowing media reports that questioned the safety of methadone treatment.

According to MDD's Coulis, effectiveness of maintenance treatment can be measured by these outcomes: reduced heroin use, staying in treatment, and perceptions by both patient and doctor of improved well-being.

Reuter adds that patients receiving maintenance treatment have a death rate 10 times lower than untreated addicts and an incidence of needle-sharing of 14 percent, compared to 47 percent before treatment. In a recent Swiss study of people with HIV infection, he says, 24 percent of maintenance program cases progressed to AIDS, compared to 41 percent of untreated heroin abusers.

"Retention in treatment is crucial," Reuter says. "In a direct line with the time patients spend in treatment, their general health and social productivity improve, and their drug abuse and criminal activities diminish." He says some studies show that patients stay in maintenance programs at a rate two-and-a-half times that of patients in self-help residential programs, and five times that of patients in drug-free outpatient programs. Of those who stop treatment, more than 80 percent relapse within a year.

"While maintenance treatment can't guarantee relapse prevention even during treatment," Reuter says, "it is consistent with medical management of chronic diseases such as diabetes, heart disease, and arthritis."

Suspicion

Despite more than two decades of documented success of maintenance therapy, the idea of treating addiction with addictive medications is often viewed by the public with suspicion.

One source of this uneasiness is a misunderstanding of heroin addiction, says Robert Lubran, chief of the Quality Assurance and Evaluation Branch, Division of State Programs, in the Substance Abuse and Mental Health Services Administration's (SAMHSA) Center for Substance Abuse Treatment.

"Many people," Lubran says, "don't realize that heroin addicts must fight their addiction all their lives. Others equate patients in maintenance programs with street addicts. In fact, the patients are at some level of recovery, which benefits society as well as the patient."

Another source of suspicion is the ineffectiveness of some programs, which Lubran attributes to poor medical or clinical practices, such as inappropriate medication dosing to control withdrawal, failure to properly screen and assess patients' needs for counseling and support services, and lack of qualified counseling staff. "Research indicates that a few patients may do all right with minimum services," he says. "Most do not."

Strong Medicines, Strong Rules

Narcotic maintenance treatment is regulated by FDA, the Drug Enforcement Administration, and state authorities. FDA approves only programs previously approved at the state level and registered with DEA. Currently approved are 791 maintenance programs and 282 hospital programs (see map), serving some 115,000 patients. Of these programs, 46 are approved to use LAAM. Maintenance medications are unique in drug regulation, and this type of regulation is unique in medical practice, says FDA Associate Commissioner for Health Affairs Stuart Nightingale, M.D., who chairs the programs' interagency review board.

"For no other class of drugs do we write and enforce rules that directly affect how they're used in treatment," Nightingale says. "With these medications, we specify rules for clinical practice, such as requiring physicians to prepare and sign a treatment plan for each patient and document all changes in dosing regimens."

Because of the implications for medical practice and other broad societal concerns, Nightingale says, "the interagency committee has been critical to the success of the federal coordination." The committee includes representatives from FDA, NIDA, SAMHSA, DEA, VA, the Office of the Secretary of Health and Human Ser-

Iɴ ᴇxᴛʀᴇᴍᴇ sɪᴛᴜᴀᴛɪoɴs, ᴄᴇʀᴛᴀɪɴ LAAM ᴘᴀᴛɪᴇɴᴛs ᴍᴀʏ ʙᴇ ᴛᴇᴍᴘoʀᴀʀɪʟʏ sᴡɪᴛᴄʜᴇᴅ ᴛo ᴍᴇᴛʜᴀᴅoɴᴇ ꜰoʀ ᴀ ᴛᴀᴋᴇ-ʜoᴍᴇ ᴅosᴇ.

Comprehensive Programs

Each patient attending a comprehensive narcotic maintenance treatment program receives:

Counseling, including
HIV counseling

Individualized treatment plan

Medical services

Vocational rehabilitation

vices, the Office of the Assistant Secretary for Health, and the Office of National Drug Control Policy.

Treatment clinics must register with DEA and meet security rules because methadone and LAAM are controlled substances (drugs regulated by the Federal Controlled Substances Acts). DEA requires additional registration by the physicians who treat narcotic addiction with narcotics.

In light of the addictive potential and potential for overdose, both FDA and state authorities require safety measures and medication control rules in programs using methadone or LAAM. The Department of Health and Human Services, FDA's parent agency, must by law provide treatment standards for narcotics used to treat narcotic dependence. These are minimum standards, currently in the form of

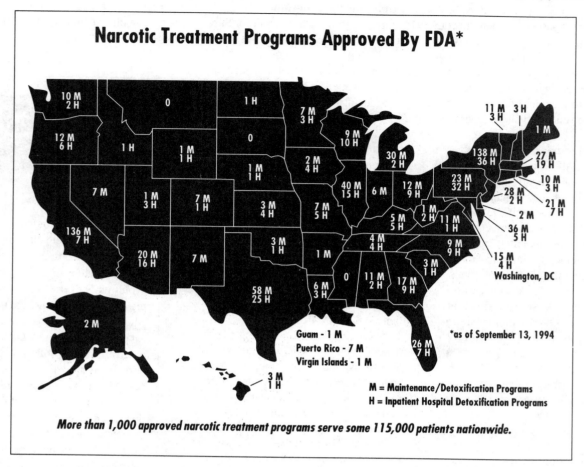

Narcotic Treatment Programs Approved By FDA*

Washington, DC

Guam - 1 M
Puerto Rico - 7 M
Virgin Islands - 1 M

*as of September 13, 1994

M = Maintenance/Detoxification Programs
H = Inpatient Hospital Detoxification Programs

More than 1,000 approved narcotic treatment programs serve some 115,000 patients nationwide.

regulations. Individual states can, and some do, develop stricter rules.

Under FDA rules, programs may admit only current addicts with at least a one-year history of addiction, although previously addicted pregnant women at risk of returning to addiction may also be admitted. Methadone maintenance, but not LAAM, is approved for patients under 18 who have twice failed detoxification or other drug-free treatment. A parent, guardian, or other designated responsible adult must sign the consent form.

Enrollment is voluntary. Patients must report to the same program, except in an emergency.

Among other agency requirements, comprehensive programs must provide:
• medical services, counseling, vocational rehabilitation, and treatment plans
• tuberculosis skin testing during the initial medical evaluation
• HIV counseling
• information to women about drug risks to the fetus
• pregnancy tests for women of childbearing potential before admission to LAAM maintenance, and monthly tests thereafter
• individualized dosage to control withdrawal symptoms without causing sedation or other effects of intoxication, with the lowest effective doses for pregnant women
• regular physician review of dosage levels

• observed dosing at the clinic (With methadone, visits are six days a week to start but, with successful treatment, may be reduced with use of take-home doses. With LAAM, visits are every other day to start but eventually may be every third day.)
• complete patient records, which physicians must sign and date to document dosage changes and reasons for reducing visits
• frequent random urine tests for drugs of abuse—including an initial screening test for prospective patients.

Publicly funded treatment accounts for the vast majority of patients in treatment, says FDA's Nightingale. These programs may be free or have sliding scale fees. The cost of private programs varies.

In addition, FDA and SAMHSA in 1993 issued interim narcotic maintenance program standards for heroin addicts who can't get into a nearby comprehensive program within two weeks. The ADAMHA Reorganization Act of 1992 required the standards to reduce the AIDS threat posed by injection of illegal drugs—the major source of new AIDS infection in the gen-

"In a direct line with the time patients spend in treatment, their general health and social productivity improve, and their drug abuse and criminal activities diminish." —Nicholas Reuter, FDA

eral population, according to NIDA. States would guarantee patients' transfer to comprehensive treatment no later than 120 days. Although no clinics have applied to enroll patients in interim programs, any programs adopted would be restricted to public, nonprofit clinics with federal- and state-approved comprehensive programs.

Managing Compliance Problems

FDA field staff inspect programs every two or three years, reporting problems to the agency's regulatory management branch. Follow-up visits are on a case-by-case basis. "If there are serious violations and we send a warning letter," says compliance officer Gerald Hajarian, "three to six months after the program responds with its correction plan, the district inspects again to make sure the violations no longer exist." (The facility must submit its correction plan to FDA within 15 days of receiving the warning letter.)

DEA inspects programs on a routine cycle—or more frequently if a program has a history of violations or pending allegations of impropriety. DEA requires that programs follow all security and record-keeping regulations. Violations may result in actions such as an Investigative Warning or Letter of Admonition for less serious violations, or an Administrative Hearing, Order to Show Cause, or civil or criminal actions for serious violations.

States inspect also.

There is continuing concern about some patients selling their take-home methadone doses on the street. In July 1990, FDA, DEA and NIDA warned program sponsors and medical directors that federal and state investigations confirmed increasing diversion of take-home medications, pointing out that diversion was one reason FDA requires frequent urine tests. (A negative test would indicate the patient hadn't taken the take-home medication.) They warned that, if necessary, they would revoke DEA registration or FDA approval.

Indeed, FDA and DEA in 1991 allowed two New York programs to stay open only after they presented evidence showing how they intended to remedy their problems. FDA, DEA, and Texas authorities in 1992 did close two Texas programs, with a third one closing voluntarily. Last February, FDA closed a New Mexico program.

Improving the Programs

Included among the Center for Substance Abuse Treatment's series of Treatment Improvement Protocols (or "TIPS") are several that cover narcotic maintenance treatment. These are developed by non-federal treatment experts.

"We take the scientific research and expertise of leading clinicians," the center's Lubran says, "and translate that into practical guidance that can help states, maintenance programs, and others improve the quality of services."

Several TIPS—some of which are still under development—provide recommendations about the most effective maintenance treatment practices for such groups as pregnant women and infants exposed to methadone, methadone patients who abuse stimulants (especially cocaine), and patients on LAAM treatment.

Technical assistance, training, and financial support to states and communities are also available. For example, when the state of Texas asked for assistance after media criticism of maintenance programs in the state, the center arranged for state and program representatives, treatment experts, and FDA and DEA officials to meet in Texas. The conferees identified system-wide problems and solutions and recommended improvement activities.

The center helped the state of Arkansas open its first program last December in Little Rock, which Lubran says reached three-fourths of the target population within three months. "We enabled them to gain invaluable exposure to quality treatment programs around the country to see how they work, and provided guidance with their state regulations," he says.

Another project educates judges and court administrators on how the programs can serve as alternative sentencing for people convicted of crimes related to heroin use or other drug abuse.

Incentives

As an incentive to firms to develop anti-addiction medications, FDA permits this class of drugs fast-track review and eligibility for orphan drug status, which confers tax credits and research grants. Orphan drugs receive seven years of marketing exclusivity. LAAM is a designated orphan drug.

MDD encourages development of

maintenance medications by assisting firms with research. MDD deputy director

CHANGES ON THE WAY?

In 1992, the Public Health Service a[s] the Institute of Medicine to study feder regulations on methadone maintenance treatment. According to Richard Rettig Ph.D., the study director, "We examine evolution of the rules, their role in prov ing the best treatment, and the role of complementary approaches, such as cli cal practice guidelines and formal quali control systems." IOM will publish a re port on the study late this year.

IOM already released a report this ye on development of anti-addiction medi tions such as methadone and LAAM. R ommendations included making the Tre ment IND route and parallel track mechanism available for anti-addiction medications, and assigning priority to t development of anti-addiction medicati through an executive order issued by th president. (The "parallel track" policy allows wider availability of promising i vestigational drugs—currently, only fo certain patients with AIDS or other HI related conditions—through protocols without control groups, which are con ducted parallel to controlled clinical tri necessary to establish safety and effecti ness.)

In the report, IOM identified reasons why firms are reluctant to develop anti- addiction medications. These included problems related to the limited scientifi knowledge about addiction, lack of fed leadership, and an uncertain market env ronment with issues such as pricing co cerns, liability, and limited and uncertai insurance coverage. Suggestions to res these and other issues are slated for a la report.

—D.F.

PATIENTS MUST REPORT TO THE SAME PROGRAM, EXCEPT IN AN EMERGENCY.

Frank Vocci, Ph.D., says his division is analyzing data from a study in 736 patients evaluating the safety and effectiveness of an oral sublingual (administered under the tongue) form of buprenorphine (Buprenex) in blocking heroin's euphoria. The drug is approved as an injectable narcotic analgesic.

A buprenorphine-naloxone formulation also is being developed. Although oral buprenorphine may block heroin's effects, the injected form can produce euphoria.

However, injected naloxone (Narcan), approved to treat overdose, blocks the euphoria, inducing withdrawal.

"The idea," Vocci says, "is if the drug is taken as prescribed, the naloxone won't kick in. But if patients abuse it by injecting it, the naloxone effect will predominate."

In another study, MDD tested a sustained-release naltrexone formulation that blocked heroin euphoria up to 30 days. Dosage in future trials will be based on the results of this study, Vocci says. Naltrexone (Trexan) is approved for use

with maintenance medication, but not as a maintenance medication itself.

These efforts, along with the new approach that brought LAAM to market, offer hope for more safe and effective maintenance medications, possibly to treat other addictions as well.

While there is no cure for heroin addiction, there is hope for recovery through narcotic maintenance treatment programs. Using legal oral synthetic narcotics, maintenance programs wean addicts off heroin, the first step to stable, productive lives.

FOR MORE INFORMATION

The Center for Substance Abuse Treatment National Drug Hotline
(1-800) 662-HELP

The National Clearinghouse for Alcohol and Drug Information
P.O. Box 2345
Rockville, MD 20847-2345
(1-800) 729-6686
TDD: (1-800) 487-4889

American Methadone Treatment Association, Inc.
253-255 Third Ave.
New York, NY 10010

Alcohol, Drug Addiction Recovery Rate Can Be Doubled With Program of Nutritional Support

Alcoholics' Allergic Response Compounds Problem: Antioxidant Vitamins, Minerals, Amino Acids, "Good" Fats Are Essential

Joseph D. Beasley, M.D.

Joseph D. Beasley, M.D. is a practicing physician who is board-certified as a specialist in addictive diseases and a Fellow of the American College of Clinical Nutrition. He is the Director of Comprehensive Medical Care in Amityville, New York, a clinic which takes a comprehensive body-mind-spirit approach to the diagnosis, treatment and prevention of disease.

Drug and alcohol additions are diseases that affect the body as much as the mind. Decades of research have shown that alcoholism, in particular, is genetically influenced. The children of persons suffering from alcoholism are at a 400 percent greater risk of developing alcoholism even if they are not raised in the same home. The closer you are genetically to a person with alcoholism, the more at risk you are of developing the disease yourself. Although research on drug addiction is relatively new, there is evidence that susceptibility to these addictions, like alcoholism, may also be genetically influenced.

People with a genetic predisposition to alcoholism have a unique predisposition to alcoholism have a unique biochemical response to alcohol. Their bodies become dependent on alcohol in order to function. When deprived, desperate cravings and physical symptoms plague the addicted persons, driving them to drink more in order to feel well again. Unless the body is healed, the mind and spirit can never attain their full promise in recovery.

Alcohol and drugs have a poisonous effect on every cell of the body, but particularly the liver, the body's main detoxification and nutrient-processing plant. As a result, the body loses its ability to detoxify poisons and utilize nutrients. Also disrupted is the normal chemical balance of the brain, depleting the supply of crucial chemicals and also suppressing the sections of the brain that control appetite, sexual behavior and sleep. Many of the organs that control immune function are also damaged, decreasing the body's ability to fight off infection and recover from illness, thereby making the alcohol/drug-addict far more susceptible to a wide range of diseases. Alcoholic persons have an unusually high degree of allergic or sensitivity responses, both to classic allergens, such as pollen, and to various foods. The toxic effects of alcohol and drugs makes themselves known in the body even in small quantities.

HOW NUTRITION CAN HELP

Years of research led noted nutrition researcher Roger Williams to believe that alcoholism and alcohol craving are linked to poor nutrition and that improving nutrition could vitally influence recovery. Since then, I and several other researchers have made use of William's theory to improve the treatment outcomes of drug- and alcohol-addicted patients. Before the use of nutritional therapy in the treatment of alcoholism, the recovery rate was never much above 35 percent of so in any of the numerous studies.

The addition of nutritional therapy in treating alcoholism has dramatically changed the picture. R. M. Guenther's study (*International Journal of Biosocial Research* 4:1983) showed that the recovery rate more than doubled (38% vs. 81%) when nutritional therapy was added. In her book *Alcoholism: The Biochemical Connection* (Villard Books), Joan M. Larson, Ph.D. describes the 81 percent recovery rate she has had when using biobehavioral treatment.

My own research has also shown impressive results. In a prospective study of 111 alcoholics (reported in the *Journal of Substance Abuse Treatment* 8:1991), 65 percent of whom already had significant liver damage and 40 percent of whom were also drug-users, I and my colleagues showed that including nutritional therapy in the treatment resulted in a recovery rate of 60.4 percent. Our treatment program included a healthy wholefoods diet, nutritional supplementation and education as well as exercise.

HOW ADDICTIONS AFFECT NUTRITION

Addiction affects nutrition by reducing overall food intake; poisoning the organs which absorb, process and utilize nutrients; and depleting nutritional reserves as a result of drug- or alcohol-induced vomiting, diarrhea and excessive urination.

As if this isn't bad enough, alcohol and drugs put such a tremendous strain on the body that it actually needs nutrients in order to process them. When the body can't get these nutrients from food, it has to draw on its nutritional reserves (vitamins and minerals) so that a good portion of the body's reserves is depleted.

Without the proper nutritional fuel, the body has difficulty carrying out its most basic functions. The brain is particularly sensitive to such deprivation, which is one of the reasons so many addicted persons are diagnosed as schizophrenic, depressed, neurotic and anxious. Alcoholism and drug addiction can mimic any mental illness and the utmost care must be taken not to wrongly label such a patient with a permanent psychiatric diagnosis.

Alcoholic patients cannot simply stop drinking all at once. Simultaneous nutritional supplementation is essential. "Cold turkey" withdrawal can be disastrous and sometimes it can be fatal. As part of a balanced total recovery program—one that encompasses the physical, psychological, social and spiritual aspects of addiction—nutritional supplements can make the recovery process much safer, faster and more effective. They may meet the often-neglected needs of the body in the recovery process.

An appropriate multivitamin multimineral supplement to be taken three times a day after meals would include the antioxidant vitamins (beta-carotene and vitamins C and E); the B vitamin complex; minerals such as calcium, magnesium, chromium and selenium; L-glutamine (to reduce cravings); and substantial amounts of the essential fatty acids (fish oils, flaxseed oil and black currant seed oil). I have put together an optimal nutritional supplement called the Physician's Recovery Formula (call 1-800-787-0230 for further

---

Alcohol Facts

• There are 18 million alcoholics in this country.

• Almost 1 in 5 Americans (18¢) lives with an alcoholic while growing up.

• Women metabolize alcohol less efficiently than men, leading to higher blood alcohol concentrations over a shorter period of time; they also wait longer than men before seeking help.

• A survey of 1986 deaths found that men who regularly drank 2 or more drinks a day were nearly twice as likely to die before age 65 than men who drank 12 or fewer drinks a year; their female counterparts were three times as likely to die before age 65.

• In 1989 the alcohol beverage industry spent $1.2 billion on advertising, more than that spent by the household equipment and electronic entertainment industries combined.

Statistics courtesy of NCADD

---

information), or one could easily find the components for a good recovery program in a health food store.

RECOMMENDED DIET

It is important for a recovering alcoholic to simply start eating again—three healthy meals a day with nutritious snacks midmorning, midafternoon and before bed can refuel the recovering body. One should choose fresh and complete foods, avoiding fast foods and snacks which have been so highly processed that few of the nutrients are left.

Alcoholism and drug addiction damage the liver, the body's detoxification center. It is therefore important to avoid chemicals (dyes, artificial flavorings, preservatives, etc) that will put any additional

stress on the already disordered organ. Fresh foods, in addition to being relatively free of chemicals, also have more of the nutrients intact. Select whole grain breads instead of white and eat only those prepared foods which have a minimum of additives and preservatives.

We recommend natural, unsaturated fats (olive oil, canola oil, safflower oil) that have been cold-pressed. A little butter is okay unless you are allergic to dairy products. Omega-3 oils are found in almost all fish oils and in vegetable oils like flaxseed and canola. They are especially important for recovery.

Avoid sugar and other highly processed carbohydrates such as bleached white flour (even if it's "enriched") and white rice. They contain few nutrients, and the body actually has to use stored nutrients in order to process them.

Proteins are important for recovery, since most alcoholics and drug addicts are highly protein deficient. Chicken and other poultry are good low-fat sources of protein, as are fish of all kinds. Brown rice, unenriched whole-grain breads and various beans will also provide needed proteins.

In addition to eating well and taking these supplements, it is important to help the body's heart and muscles revive by getting into some sort of exercise routine. Walk a few blocks. Go swimming. Take a ride on a bike. Increase the amount of exercise as your endurance improves. If you're over 40, or if you have a history of any heart problem, it is important to consult your physician and to have a stress test.

It is also wise to clean up your immediate environment and get rid of anything that could prompt some sort of allergic or immune reaction. The damage caused by addiction makes many recovering individuals far more sensitive to the effect of environmental and dietary allergens. If possible, have a respiratory and food allergy work-up to determine what, if anything, you are sensitive to.

Support groups and psychotherapy are also an essential part of a balanced recovery program which addresses the physical, psychological, social and spiritual aspects of addiction.

D.A.R.E. Bedeviled

A new study questions the effectiveness of the country's most popular drug-prevention program

Sylvester Monroe

Atlanta

The initials are plastered on bumper stickers and school bulletin boards from California to the Carolinas: DARE. The acronym stands for Drug Abuse Resistance Education, a $750 million-a-year drug-prevention program that is the most popular in the nation. But is it the most successful?

In the past three years, a number of parents' groups have organized against the program, protesting what they call the pseudo psychology at its core. Says Gay Peterson of Colorado, the founder of the fledgling national group Parents Against DARE: "Our schools are giving away more and more time to social-engineering programs that have not been sufficiently researched." Says Richard Evans of Northampton, Massachusetts: "DARE is awash in the touchy-feely stuff of the '70s. It's tricky and the kind of thing parents need to take a closer look at." Last week the critics of DARE received new ammunition by way of the biggest backer of DARE—the Department of Justice.

A three-year, $300,000 study has concluded that the effect of DARE's core curriculum—conducted by specially trained local police officers in 17 weekly, 45-to-60 min. sessions for fifth- and sixth-grade students—is statistically insignificant in preventing drug use among that group. Resources might be better spent on longer-term, more interactive programs. The study was conducted by the Research Triangle Institute in Durham, North Carolina, and commissioned by the National Institute of Justice, the research arm of the Department of Justice.

The Justice Department has refused to accept the report's key findings. Defenders of DARE question R.T.I.'s analysis of data, saying fifth- and sixth-graders rarely use drugs and were therefore the wrong sample to study. "It was too strong a statement," says William DeJong, a lecturer at the Harvard School of Public Health, who evaluated DARE in 1985. "It was a provocative conclusion not warranted by the study." R.T.I., however, stands by its conclusions, adding that it looked at fifth- and sixth-graders exactly because that has been DARE's target group. Said R.T.I. researcher Susan Ennett: "Unless there's some sort of booster session that reinforces the original curriculum, the effects of most drug-use-prevention programs decay rather than increase with time." Ray, 18, who came through the DARE program in Los Angeles, is a good case in point. He smokes pot. "Mostly everyone I know who was in DARE back with me are doing the same thing I'm doing and more," he says. "Everybody I know gets high. I don't think it worked. Not for me."

But if not DARE, what? Before DARE, says David Seibles, a 10-year veteran with the Gwinnett County police department in Georgia, "it used to be that you'd come in once a year and say, 'Don't do drugs,' and by the time you'd get to the front door, the kids had forgotten everything you said." Says Debbie Allred, principal of Cedar Hill Elementary School in Gwinnett County: "If we didn't have DARE, we'd miss it tremendously. It would be a great loss."

—With reporting by Lisa H. Towle/ Durham

Glossary

This glossary of drug terms is included to provide you with a convenient and ready reference as you encounter general terms in your study of drugs and drug and alcohol abuse that are unfamiliar, technical, or require a review. It is not intended to be comprehensive, but, taken together with many definitions included in the articles themselves, it should prove to be useful.

Absorption: The passage of chemical compounds, such as drugs or nutrients, into the bloodstream through the skin, intestinal lining, or other bodily membranes.

Abstinence: The total avoidance of a specific substance, such as alcohol, tobacco, and/or drugs.

Acetylcholine: A cholinergic transmitter that forms salts used to lower blood pressure and increases peristalsis; thought to be involved in the inhibition of behavior.

Acetylsalicylic acid (aspirin): A generic over-the-counter analgesic drug (painkiller).

Acupuncture: A traditional Chinese health-care technique for treating illness or administering anesthesia by inserting needles into specific points of the body in order to stimulate the production of natural endorphins.

Addiction: Use of a substance in a chronic, compulsive, or uncontrollable way.

Adrenergic system: The group of transmitters, including epinephrine, norepinephrine, and dopamine, that activates the sympathetic nervous system.

Alcohol abuse: *See* Alcoholism

Alcoholics Anonymous (AA): A voluntary organization founded in 1935, consisting of individuals seeking help for a drinking problem. The AA program is based on total abstinence, achieved by following a 12-step process.

Alcoholism: Any use of alcoholic beverages that causes damage to the individual or to society. *See also* Disease Model.

Amotivational syndrome: Apathy and loss of motivation that is believed to occur in long-term marijuana users.

Amphetamine psychosis: A psychotic disorder characterized by loss of contact with reality and hallucinations brought on by the stopping or cutting back of doses of amphetamines by an amphetamine-dependent person.

Amphetamines: A class of drugs, similar in some ways to the body's own adrenaline (epinephrine), that act as stimulants to the central nervous system.

Anabolic steroids: Synthetic derivatives of the male hormone testosterone.

Analgesics: Drugs that relieve pain.

Anesthetic: A medication that produces an artificial loss of sensation in order to relieve pain.

Angel dust: Phencyclidine, a synthetic depressant drug.

Anorectic: A drug that decreases appetite.

Antianxiety tranquilizers: Tranquilizers, like Valium and Librium, used to relieve anxiety and tension, sometimes called minor tranquilizers.

Anticholinergics: Drugs that block the transmission of impulses in the parasympathetic nerves.

Antidepressants: A group of medications that relieves or prevents psychological depression by increasing the activity of the neurotransmitter norepinephrine in the brain. *See also* Depression.

Antihistamines: Drugs that relieve allergy or cold symptoms by blocking the effects of histamine production.

Atropine: An alkaloid derivative of the belladonna and related plants that blocks responses to parasympathetic stimulation.

Axon: The core of the nerve fiber that conducts impulses away from the nerve cell to the neurons and other tissue.

Barbiturates: Drugs used for sedation and to relieve tension and anxiety.

Benzodiazepine: A minor tranquilizer; the best-known brand name for benzodiazepine is Valium.

Bipolar disorder: A mental illness characterized by intense mood swings of extreme elation and severe depression. Also known as manic depression.

Blood level: The concentration of alcohol in the blood, usually expressed in percent by weight.

Brain stem: The region of the brain that links the cerebrum to the spinal cord.

Caffeine: An alkaloid found in coffee, tea, and kola nuts, that acts as a stimulant.

Cannabis: *See* Marijuana.

Central nervous system (CNS): The brain and spinal cord.

China White: A synthetic reproduction of fentanyl, a widely used anesthetic and depressant. China White is very similar to heroin in its duration, blockage of pain, and euphoric effect.

Chlorpromazine: An antianxiety tranquilizer, manufactured under the name of Thorazine, used for treating severe psychoses. Also used as an antagonist to LSD panic reactions.

Choline: A transmitter, part of the cholinergic system.

Cocaine: A white, crystalline narcotic alkaloid derived from the coca plant and used as a surface anesthetic and a stimulant.

Codeine: A narcotic alkaloid found in opium, most often used as an analgesic or cough suppressant.

Coke: Slang term for cocaine.

Cold turkey: Slang expression for abrupt and complete withdrawal from drugs or alcohol without medication.

Contraindications: A condition that makes it inadvisable or hazardous to use a particular drug or medicine.

Controlled substances: All psychoactive substances covered by laws regulating their sale and possession.

Controlled Substances Act of 1970: Federal act that classifies controlled substances into five categories and regulates their use. Schedule I drugs are those most strictly controlled; they include heroin, marijuana, LSD, and other drugs believed to have high abuse potential. Schedule II drugs are also strictly controlled but have some medicinal uses; these drugs include morphine, methadone, and amphetamines. Schedule III, IV, and V substances include drugs that have increasingly less abuse potential; over-the-counter medicines not subject to any refill regulations fall into Schedule V.

Crack: A drug made by mixing cocaine, baking soda, other chemicals, and water, heating the mixture, and letting it solidify into "rocks" that are smoked.

Crisis intervention: The process of diagnosing a drug crisis situation and acting immediately to arrest the condition.

Decriminalization: The legal process by which the possession of a certain drug would become a civil penalty instead of a criminal penalty. *See also* Legalization.

Deliriants: Substances, like some inhalants, that produce delirium.

Delirium: State of temporary mental confusion and diminished consciousness, characterized by anxiety, hallucinations, and delusions.

Delta-9 tetrahydrocannabinol (THC): A psychoactive derivative of the cannabis plant.

Dependence: A state in which one cannot readily give up or stop the use of a drug; there are two types of dependence—physical and psychological.

269

Dependence, physical: The physical need of the body for a particular substance such that abstinence from the substance leads to physical withdrawal symptoms. *See also* Addiction; Withdrawal Syndrome.

Dependence, psychological: A psychological or emotional reliance on a particular substance; a strong and continued craving.

Depressants: Also known as sedative-hypnotics, depressants produce a state of behavioral depression while also depressing chemical transmission between nerve cells in the brain. Effects of depressants include drowsiness, some behavioral excitation, and loss of inhibition. Alcohol, barbiturates, and antianxiety drugs are depressants.

Depression: A mental state characterized by extreme sadness or dejection far out of proportion to the reality of the situation over which the sufferer is depressed. Depression can be a neurosis or psychosis, depending on its severity or duration.

Designer drug: Any drug that is designed to match a client's desired effect and manufactured by chemists in illicit laboratories. Ecstasy and China White are examples of designer drugs.

Detoxification: Removal of a poisonous substance, such as a drug or alcohol, from the body.

Disease model: A theory of alcoholism, endorsed by AA, in which the alcoholism is seen as a disease rather than a psychological or social problem.

DMT: Dimethyltryptamine, a psychedelic drug.

DNA: Deoxyribonucleic acid, the carrier of chromosomes in the cell.

Dopamine: A neurotransmitter that helps control and coordinate movement.

Downers: A slang term for drugs that act to depress the central nervous system.

Drug: Any substance that alters the structure or function of a living organism.

Drug abuse: The taking of a drug in a manner that causes bodily or mental harm.

Drug misuse: Use of a drug for any purpose other than that for which it is medically prescribed.

Drug paraphernalia: Materials, like hypodermic syringes, that are used for the preparation or administration of illicit drugs.

DWI: Driving while intoxicated.

Dysphoria: Emotional state characterized by anxiety, depression, and restlessness, as opposed to euphoria.

Ecstasy: A derivative of nutmeg or sassafras, causing euphoria and sometimes hallucinations; also known as XTC, Adam, or MDMA.

Employee assistance program (EAP): A program offered as a workplace benefit by an employer, providing counselling and referral services to employees with personal problems, including substance abuse.

Endorphins: Any group of hormones released by the brain that have painkilling and tranquilizing abilities.

Epinephrine: An adrenal hormone that acts as a transmitter and stimulates autonomic nerve action.

Ethical drugs: Drugs dispensed by prescription only.

Euphoria: Exaggerated sense of happiness or well-being.

Experimental drug use: According to the U.S. National Commission on Marijuana and Drug Abuse, the short-term non-patterned trial of one or more drugs, either concurrently or consecutively, with variable intensity but maximum frequency of ten times per drug.

Fetal alcohol syndrome (FAS): A pattern of birth defects, cardiac abnormalities, and developmental retardation seen in babies of alcoholic mothers.

Flashbacks: Spontaneous and involuntary recurrences of psychedelic drug effects after the initial drug experience.

Food and Drug Administration (FDA): Agency of the U.S. Department of Health and Human Services that administers federal laws regarding the purity of food, the safety and effectiveness of drugs, and the safety of cosmetics.

Freebase: A prepared form of cocaine that can be smoked.

Generic drugs: Prescription drugs manufactured to match the chemical composition of brand name drugs after their copyrights have expired.

Habituation: Chronic or continuous use of a drug, with an attachment less severe than addiction.

Hallucination: A sensory perception without external stimuli.

Hallucinogenic drugs: Drugs that cause hallucinations. Also known as psychedelic drugs.

Harrison Narcotics Act: Federal act passed in 1914 that controlled the sale and possession of prescription drugs, heroin, opium, and cocaine.

Hashish: The dried resin of the marijuana plant; often smoked in water pipes.

Herb: Commonly, any one of various aromatic plants used for medical or other purposes.

Heroin: An opiate derivative of morphine.

High: Intoxicated by a drug or alcohol; the state of being high.

Ibuprofen: An over-the-counter pain reliever that is an alternative to aspirin and acetaminophen; the active ingredient in Motrin, Advil, and Nuprin.

Illicit drug: An illegal drug; any drug or substance whose distribution to the general public is prohibited by the federal Controlled Substances Act of 1970.

Illy: Marijuana and mint leaves soaked in a deadly combination of embalming fluid and PCP.

Inhalants: Substances that emit fumes or gases that are inhaled and have the effect of psychoactive drugs. Also known as deliriants.

Interferon: A group of protein factors produced by certain cells in response to the presence of viruses.

Interleukin 2: A group of protein factors that acts as a messenger between white blood cells (leukocytes) involved in immune responses.

Intoxication: Medically, the state of being poisoned. Usually refers to the state of being drunk, falling between drunkenness and a mild high.

Intravenous (IV) drug users: Drug users who use hypodermic needles as a means of administering drugs; among the drugs normally administered in this manner is heroin, which may be injected either directly into a vein ("mainlining") or just under the surface of the skin ("skin popping").

Legalization: The movement to have the sale or possession of certain illicit drugs made legal.

Limbic system: A set of structures in the brain that influences motivation and emotional behavior.

LSD: Lysergic acid diethlamide-25, a hallucinogen.

Maintenance treatment: Treatment of drug dependence by a small dosage of the drug or another drug, such as methadone that will prevent withdrawal symptoms.

Marijuana: A preparation of the leaves and flowering tops of the cannabis plant, the smoke of which is inhaled for its euphoric effects. Also spelled: marihuana.

MDMA: *See* Ecstasy.

Medical model: A theory of drug abuse or addiction in which the addiction is seen as a medical, rather than a social, problem.

Mescaline: A hallucinogenic alkaloid drug, either derived from the peyote plant or made synthetically.

Methadone: A synthetic opiate sometimes used to treat heroin or morphine addiction. *See also* Maintenance treatment.

Methamphetamines: Stimulant drugs derived from and more potent than amphetamines. Also known as speed.

Methaqualone: A nonbarbiturate sedative/hypnotic drug, used to bring on feelings of muscular relaxation, contentment, and passivity. Also known as quaaludes.

Methylphenidate: Also known as Ritalin, its most popular brand name, methylphenidate is a stimulant used in treating hyperkinetic children (children who are hyperactive but have no academic difficulties).

Morphine: An organic compound extracted from opium; a light anesthetic or sedative.

Multimodality programs: Programs for the treatment of drug abuse or alcoholism involving several simultaneous treatment methods.

Narcotic: A drug that has both a sedative and a pain-relieving effect. Opiate drugs are narcotics.

Narcotics Anonymous (NA): An organization modeled after Alcoholics Anonymous to assist recovering drug dependents.

Neuroleptic: Any major, or antipsychotic, tranquilizer.

Neuron: The basic element responsible for the reception, transmission, and processing of sensory, motor, and other information of physiological or psychological importance to the individual.

Neurotransmitters: The chemicals that transmit messages from one neuron to another.

Nicotine: The main active ingredient of tobacco, extremely toxic and causing irritation of lung tissue, constriction of blood vessels, increased blood pressure and heart rate, and, in general, central nervous system stimulation.

Norepinephrine: Hormone found in the sympathetic nerve endings that acts as an adrenergic transmitter and is a vasoconstrictor.

Opiate narcotics: A major subclass of drugs that act as pain relievers as well as central nervous system depressants; includes opium, morphine, codeine, and methadone.

Opiates: The class of drugs that include opium, codeine, morphine, heroin, methadone, and other drugs derived from or chemically similar to opium; opiates are primarily used for pain relief.

Opium: A bitter brown narcotic drug that comes from the dried juice of the opium poppy, and from which such narcotics as heroin and morphine are derived.

Opoids: The group of synthetic drugs, including Demerol and Darvon, that resemble the opiates in action and effect.

Overmedication: The prescription and use of more medication than necessary to treat a specific illness or condition.

Over-the-counter drugs: Drugs legally sold without a prescription.

Parasympathetic Nervous System: The part of the autonomic nervous system that inhibits or opposes the actions of the sympathetic nerves.

Parasympathomimetics: Drugs that produce effects similar to those of the parasympathetic nervous system.

Parkinson's disease: A progressive disease of the nervous system characterized by muscular tremor, slowing of movement, partial facial paralysis, and general weakness.

Peyote: A drug derived from either the peyote or the mescal cactus, possessing hallucinogenic properties.

Phencyclidine (PCP): A synthetic depressant drug used as a veterinary anesthetic and illegally as a hallucinogen.

Phenylpropanolamine (PPA): A medication used to prevent or relieve nasal and upper respiratory congestion. PPA is also used as an appetite suppressant.

Phobias: Persistent, intense fears of specific persons, objects, or situations, accompanied by a wish to flee or avoid the fear-provoking stimulus.

Physical dependence: A form of dependence in which the body's physical need for a particular substance is such that stopping use leads to physical withdrawal symptoms.

Placebo: An inactive substance used as a control in an experiment.

Polyabuse: Abuse of various drugs simultaneously.

Pot: Slang term for marijuana.

Potency: Term used to compare the relative strength of two or more drugs used to produce a given effect.

Potentiate: To augment a depressant's effect by taking a combination of two or more depressants.

Prescription drugs: Drugs dispensed only by a physician's prescription.

Primary prevention: Efforts designed to prevent a person from starting to use drugs.

Proprietary drugs: Patent medicines.

Psilocybin: A naturally occurring psychedelic agent derived from the *Psilocybe Mexicana* mushroom.

Psychedelic drug: A drug that causes hallucinations; a hallucinogen.

Psychoactive: Affecting the mind or behavior.

Psychological dependence: A form of dependence in which the user's attachment to the emotional or psychological effects of a drug is such that he or she finds it difficult or impossible to stop use voluntarily; may or may not be accompanied by physical dependence.

Psychopharmacology: The study of the effects of drugs on mood, sensation, or consciousness, or other psychological or behavioral functions.

Psychosis: Severe mental disorder, characterized by withdrawal from reality and deterioration of normal intellectual and social functioning.

Psychosomatic: Describing a variety of physical reactions that are assumed to be closely related to psychological phenomena.

Psychotherapeutic drugs: Drugs that are used as medicines to alleviate psychological disorders.

Psychotomimetics: Drugs that produce psychosis-like effects.

Recidivism: Return to former behavior.

Recombinant DNA: DNA prepared in the laboratory by the transfer or exchange of individual genes from one organism to another.

Recreational drug use: Drug use that takes place in social settings among friends who want to share a pleasant experience; characterized by less frequency and intensity than addictive drug use. Also called social-recreational drug use.

Rehabilitation: Restoration of a person's ability to function normally.

Reinforcement: A stimulus that increases the probability that a desired response will occur.

Reticular activating system: A cluster of cell groups located in the upper part of the brain stem that controls the flow of information from the sensory organs to the cerebral cortex.

Reyes Syndrome: An often fatal childhood disorder whose cause is unknown, but has been associated with the use of aspirin as a treatment for chicken pox.

Rush: Slang term for an immediate feeling of physical well-being and euphoria after the administration of a drug.

Schedules: Categories of drugs as defined in the Controlled Substance Act of 1970.

Scopolamine: Poisonous alkaloid found in the roots of various plants, used as a truth serum or with morphine as a sedative.

Secondary prevention: Early treatment of drug abuse to prevent it from becoming more severe.

Sedative: A drug that depresses the central nervous system. Also known as sedative-hypnotics, sedatives include barbiturates, antianxiety drugs, and alcohol.

Sedative/hypnotics: A more technical term for depressants, drugs that are used for general anesthesia, induction of sleep, relief from anxiety, and recreational disinhibition (alcohol).

Serotonin: A neurotransmitter that is produced in the brain stem and is involved in sleep and sensory experiences.

Set: The combination of physical, mental, and emotional characteristics of an individual at the time a drug is administered.

Setting: The external environment of an individual at the time a drug is administered.

Side effects: Secondary effects, usually undesirable, of a drug or therapy.

Snuff: A preparation of pulverized tobacco that is inhaled into the nostrils.

Sobriety: The quality of being free from alcohol intoxication.

Social-recreational drug use: *See* Recreational drug use.

Socioeconomic: Both social and economic.

Somatic nervous system: That part of the nervous system that deals with the senses and voluntary muscles.

Speed: Slang term for methamphetamine, a central nervous system stimulant.

Stereospecificity: The matching of both electrical and chemical characteristics of the transmitter and receptor site so that binding can take place.

Stimulants: Chemical compounds that elevate mood, induce euphoria, increase alertness, reduce fatigue, and, in high doses, produce irritability, anxiety, and a pattern of psychotic behavior. Stimulants include amphetamines, nicotine, caffeine, and cocaine.

STP: Early slang term for phencyclidine.

Subcutaneous: Beneath the skin.

Substance abuse: Refers to overeating, cigarette smoking, alcohol abuse, or drug abuse.

Sympathetic nervous system: The part of the nervous system that carries neural signals that stimulate the body and prepare it for action.

Sympathomimetic: Any drug that produces effects like those resulting from stimulation of the sympathetic nervous system.

Synapse: The space, or gap, between two neurons.

Synesthesia: The blending of the senses so that two or more are perceived in combination in reaction to one stimulus.

Tars: The dark, oily, viscid substances created by burning tobacco, known to contain carcinogenic agents.

Temperance: The practice of moderation, especially with regard to alcohol consumption. The Temperance Movement was a popular movement in the nineteenth and twentieth centuries to restrict or prohibit the use of alcoholic beverages.

Tertiary prevention: Treatment to prevent the permanent disability or death of a drug abuser.

THC: Tetrahydrocannabinol, a psychoactive derivative of the cannabis plant.

Therapeutic community: Setting in which persons with similar problems meet and provide mutual support to help overcome those problems.

Titration: The ability to determine desired drug dosage.

Tolerance: The capacity to absorb a drug continuously or in large doses with no adverse effect.

Trance: Dazed or hypnotic state.

Tranquilizers: Drugs that depress the central nervous system, thus relieving anxiety and tension and sometimes relaxing the muscles, divided into the major tranquilizers, or antipsychotics, and minor tranquilizers, or antianxiety tranquilizers.

Treatment: Drug treatment programs can be drug-free or maintenance, residential or ambulatory, medical or nonmedical, voluntary or involuntary, or some combination of these.

Uncontrolled substance: Any chemical or drug whose distribution to the general public is unrestricted by governmental regulations (controls) other than those rules that apply to any similar consumer item.

Uppers: Slang term for amphetamines, and, sometimes, cocaine.

Valium: A brand name for benzodiazepine, a minor tranquilizer.

Withdrawal symptoms: The (usually unpleasant) set of physical symptoms experienced by the user as a result of stopping use of a drug upon which he or she has become dependent; these may include anxiety, insomnia, perspiration, hot flashes, nausea, dehydration, tremors, weakness, dizziness, convulsions, or psychotic behavior.

SOURCE
Drugs, Society, and Behavior (Wellness), 1992. Dushkin Publishing Group/Brown & Benchmark Publishers, Guilford, CT 06437. (1995–1996)

Credits/ Acknowledgments

Cover design by Charles Vitelli

1. Living with Drugs
Facing overview—American Cancer Society photo.

2. Understanding How Drugs Work—Use, Dependence, and Addiction
Facing overview—United Nations photo by John Isaac.

3. The Major Drugs of Use and Abuse
Facing overview—Photo by Pamela Carley.

4. Other Trends and Patterns in Drug Use
Facing overview—United Nations photo by John Robaton.

5. Drugs and Crime
Facing overview—United Nations photo by P. S. Sudhakaran.

6. Measuring the Social Costs of Drugs
Facing overview—AP/Wide World photo.

7. Creating and Sustaining Effective Drug Control Policy
Facing overview—United Nations photo.

8. Prevention and Treatment
Facing overview—Partnership for a Drug-Free America photo.

PHOTOCOPY THIS PAGE!!!*

ANNUAL EDITIONS ARTICLE REVIEW FORM

■ NAME: _____ DATE: _____

■ TITLE AND NUMBER OF ARTICLE: _____

■ BRIEFLY STATE THE MAIN IDEA OF THIS ARTICLE: _____

_____

■ LIST THREE IMPORTANT FACTS THAT THE AUTHOR USES TO SUPPORT THE MAIN IDEA:

_____

_____

_____

_____

_____

_____

■ WHAT INFORMATION OR IDEAS DISCUSSED IN THIS ARTICLE ARE ALSO DISCUSSED IN YOUR TEXTBOOK OR OTHER READING YOU HAVE DONE? LIST THE TEXTBOOK CHAPTERS AND PAGE NUMBERS:

_____

_____

_____

_____

_____

_____

■ LIST ANY EXAMPLES OF BIAS OR FAULTY REASONING THAT YOU FOUND IN THE ARTICLE:

_____

_____

_____

_____

■ LIST ANY NEW TERMS/CONCEPTS THAT WERE DISCUSSED IN THE ARTICLE AND WRITE A SHORT DEFINITION:

_____

_____

_____

_____

*Your instructor may require you to use this Annual Editions Article Review Form in any number of ways: for articles that are assigned, for extra credit, as a tool to assist in developing assigned papers, or simply for your own reference. Even if it is not required, we encourage you to photocopy and use this page; you'll find that reflecting on the articles will greatly enhance the information from your text.

ANNUAL EDITIONS: DRUGS, SOCIETY, AND BEHAVIOR 96/97
Article Rating Form

Here is an opportunity for you to have direct input into the next revision of this volume. We would like you to rate each of the 60 articles listed below, using the following scale:

1. **Excellent: should definitely be retained**
2. **Above average: should probably be retained**
3. **Below average: should probably be deleted**
4. **Poor: should definitely be deleted**

Your ratings will play a vital part in the next revision. So please mail this prepaid form to us just as soon as you complete it.
Thanks for your help!

Annual Editions revisions depend on two major opinion sources: one is our Advisory Board, listed in the front of this volume, which works with us in scanning the thousands of articles published in the public press each year; the other is you—the person actually using the book. Please help us and the users of the next edition by completing the prepaid article rating form on this page and returning it to us. Thank you.

Rating	Article	Rating	Article
	1. Opium, Cocaine, and Marijuana in American History		30. Colombia's Drugs Business: The Wages of Prohibition
	2. Alcohol in America		31. Drugs, Alcohol, and Violence: Joined at the Hip
	3. Worldwide Drug Scourge: The Expanding Trade in Illicit Drugs		32. Homicide in New York City: Cocaine Use and Firearms
	4. The Global Tobacco Epidemic		33. Why Good Cops Go Bad
	5. Global Reach: The Threat of International Drug Trafficking		34. Dealing with Demons of a New Generation
	6. What Are Some of the Historic Milestones in Early U.S. Drug Control Efforts?		35. A Society of Suspects: The War on Drugs and Civil Liberties
	7. Is Nicotine Addictive? It Depends on Whose Criteria You Use		36. Alcohol and Kids: It's Time for Candor
	8. Addictive Drugs: The Cigarette Experience		37. Should Cigarettes Be Outlawed?
	9. Brain by Design		38. A Most Complex Problem
	10. A Prescription for Trouble: When Medications Don't Mix		39. Pushing Drugs to Doctors
	11. Hooked/Not Hooked: Why Isn't Everyone an Addict?		40. It's Drugs, Alcohol and Tobacco, Stupid!
	12. Back from the Edge		41. Crackpot Ideas
	13. Selling Pot: The Pitfalls of Marijuana Reform		42. Crack Investigation
	14. Alcohol in Perspective		43. Drug Sentencing Frenzy
	15. Kicking Butts		44. Marijuana and the Law
	16. Heroin, Be the Death of Me		45. Why Drugs Keep Flowing: Too Little Emphasis on Treating Heavy Users
	17. The Kiss of Meth		46. The Drug War and Clinton's Policy Shift
	18. Wired in California		47. Toward a Policy on Drugs
	19. Overview of Key Findings		48. Military's Counterdrug Policy Restructured
	20. Pot Surges Back, It's Like a Whole New World		49. For Addicts, Alternatives to Prison
	21. Are America's College Students Majoring in Booze?		50. Teenage Smoking: Fact and Fiction
	22. The New View from On High		51. Alcohol and Other Drugs—Toward a More Rational and Consistent Policy
	23. Choose Your Poison		52. Will Legalizing Drugs Benefit Public Health?
	24. One Pill Makes You Larger, and One Pill Makes You Small . . .		53. The Golden Triangle's New King
	25. Mail-Order Muscles		54. Is Drug Abuse Treatment Effective?
	26. And Still the Drugs Sit There		55. Back from the Drink
	27. Killer Cowboys: The Violent Saga of the City's Deadliest Drug Gang		56. 'Harm Reduction' Approach May Be Middle Ground
	28. The Cocaine Money Market		57. The Cost of Living Clean
	29. Reducing Crime through Street-Level Drug Enforcement		58. New Drug Approval Approach Boosts Fight against Heroin Addiction
			59. Alcohol, Drug Addiction Recovery Rate Can Be Doubled with Program of Nutritional Support
			60. D.A.R.E. Bedeviled

(Continued on next page)

ABOUT YOU

Name _____ Date _____
Are you a teacher? ❑ Or student? ❑
Your School Name _____
Department _____
Address _____
City _____ State _____ Zip _____
School Telephone # _____

YOUR COMMENTS ARE IMPORTANT TO US!

Please fill in the following information:

For which course did you use this book? _____
Did you use a text with this Annual Edition? ❑ yes ❑ no
The title of the text? _____
What are your general reactions to the Annual Editions concept?

Have you read any particular articles recently that you think should be included in the next edition?

Are there any articles you feel should be replaced in the next edition? Why?

Are there other areas that you feel would utilize an Annual Edition?

May we contact you for editorial input?

May we quote you from above?

ANNUAL EDITIONS: DRUGS, SOCIETY, AND BEHAVIOR 96/97

BUSINESS REPLY MAIL

First Class   Permit No. 84   Guilford, CT

Postage will be paid by addressee

Dushkin Publishing Group/
Brown & Benchmark Publishers
Sluice Dock
Guilford, Connecticut 06437